Errata

Editor's Note: The current volume is a revised edition of an earlier volume published by the American Association for the Advancement of Science in 1998 with the title, *An Evolving Dialogue: Scientific, Historical, Philosophical and Theological Perspectives on Evolution.* The primary difference between this volume and that one is the last section. In the previous volume the last section was on "Evolution and Morality" and included the following articles: Theodosius Dobzhansky, "Ethics and Values in Biological and Cultural Evolution" from *Zygon,* vol. 8, no. 3-4 (Sept.-Dec. 1973): 261-281; Francisco J. Ayala, "The Difference of Being Human" from *Biology, Ethics and the Origins of Life,* Holmes Rolston III, ed. (Boston: Jones and Bartlett Publishers, 1994), 117-135; Michael Ruse, "Evolutionary Ethics: A Phoenix Arisen" from *Zygon,* vol. 21, no. 1 (March 1986): 95-112; Solomon Katz, "Biocultural Evolution and the Is/Ought Relationship" from *Zygon,* vol. 15, no. 2 (June 1980): 155-68; and, Colin Grant, "The Odds Against Altruism: The Sociobiological Agenda" from *Perspectives on Science & Christian Faith,* vol. 45, no. 2 (June 1993): 96-110.

Correction: Page 52, Note 3

3.   If there are two alleles, *A* and *a*, at a gene locus, three genotypes are possible, *AA, Aa,* and *aa.* If the frequencies of the two alleles are *p* and *q*, respectively, the equilibrium frequencies of the three genotypes are given by $(p + q)^2 = p^2 + 2pq + q^2$, for *AA, Aa,* and *aa*, respectively. The genotype equilibrium frequencies for any number of alleles are derived in the same way.

An Evolving Dialogue:

Theological and Scientific Perspectives on Evolution

An Evolving Dialogue:

√₁8₁

Theological
and
Scientific
Perspectives
on
Evolution

James B. Miller
editor

Trinity Press International

Harrisburg, Pennsylvania

Copyright © 2001 American Association for the Advancement of Science

Trinity Press International, P.O. Box 1321, Harrisburg, PA 17105

Trinity Press International is a division of the Morehouse Group.

Cover design: Corey Kent

Library of Congress Cataloging-in-Publication Data

An evolving dialogue : scientific, historical, philosophical, and theological
perspectives on evolution / edited by James Miller.
p.   cm.
Includes bibliographical references and index.
ISBN 1-56338-349-7 (alk. paper)
Evolution (Biology) 2. Creationism. 3. Evolution (Biology)—Religious
aspects—Christianity. I. Miller, James (James Bradley), 1942-

QH367 .E87 2001
576.8—dc21   00-054513

Printed in the United States of America

01 02 03 04 05 06   10 9 8 7 6 5 4 3 2 1

CONTENTS

Evolution and Design   437

Acknowledgments

A volume of this scope is not the product of a single person. The editor is especially grateful for the encouragement of Audrey Chapman who originally conceived of this project, to Michelle Thiemann who assisted in the location and acquisition of many of the articles contained herein and to Aaron Goldenberg who assisted in the acquisition of permissions to reprint. The contribution of the John Templeton Foundation to the development of science and religion courses has helped create a need for this volume. More directly the Foundation's support of the Program of Dialogue Between Science and Religion of the American Association for the Advancement of Science has substantively contributed to the production of this text. Finally, the editor wishes to express his deep gratitude to Francisco J. Ayala whose advice and encouragement in the development of this book have been invaluable.

The editor also acknowledges the cooperation of the following whose permission have made this collection possible:

"Biological Evolution: An Introduction" is a reprint, with some omissions and other slight modifications, from "The Evolution of Life: An Overview," in: R.J. Russell, W.R. Stoeger, and F.J. Ayala (eds.), *Evolutionary and Molecular Biology: Scientific Perspectives on Divine Action* (Berkeley and Rome: Center for Theology and the Natural Sciences and the Vatican Observatory, 1998). Printed here with permission.

"The Mechanism of Evolution" was originally published in *The Problems of Evolution*, Mark Ridley. (Oxford: Oxford University Press, 1985), pp. 26-42.

"Darwinism in an Age of Molecular Revolution" was originally published in *Evolution and the Molecular Revolution*, eds. Charles R. Marshall and J. William Schopf (Boston: Jones and Bartlett Publishers, 1996), pp. 1-30. Reprinted with permission.

"Speciation" was originally published in *Social Networks*, No. 11 (1989) pp. 257-272. Reprinted with permission.

"Levels of Selection: An Alternative to Individualism in Biology and Human Sciences" was originally published in *Nature*, vol. 366 (18 November 1993), pp. 223-227. Reprinted with permission.

"Why is Life So Complicated?" was originally published as Chapter 4 in *Origins of Life*, Freeman J. Dyson (Cambridge: Cambridge University Press, 1985), pp. 60-79. Reprinted with permission.

"The Evolution of Life on Earth" was originally published in *Scientific American*, vol. 271 (October 1994), pp. 84-91. Reprinted with permission.

"Punctuated Equilibrium Comes of Age" was originally published in *Nature*, vol. 366 (18 November 1993), pp. 223-227. Reprinted with permission.

"The Evolution of Darwinism" was originally published in *Scientific American*, July 1985, pp. 72-82. Reprinted with permission.

"What is a Species, and What is Not?" was originally published in *Philosophy of Science*, vol. 63 (June 1996), pp. 262-277. Reprinted with permission.

"Chance and Necessity: Adaptation and Novelty in Evolution" is a slightly modified reprint of F.J. Ayala, "Adaptation and Novelty: Teleological Explanations in Evolutionary Biology," *History and Philosophy of the Life Sciences*, vol. 20 (2), 1998. Reprinted with permission.

"A Critical-Historical Perspective on the Argument about Evolution and Creation" was originally published in *Evolution and Creation: A European Perspective*, Svend Anderson and Arthur Peacocke, eds. (Aarhus, Denmark: Aarhus University Press, 1987), pp. 12-26. Reprinted with permission.

"The Creationists" was originally published in *God and Nature: Historical Essays on the Encounter between Christianity* (Berkeley: University of California Press, 1986), pp. 391-423. Reprinted with permission.

"Nonoverlapping Magisteria" was originally published in *Natural History*, 3/97, pp. 16ff. Reprinted with permission.

"What Science Can and Cannot Offer to a Religious Narrative" was originally published in *Zygon*, vol. 29, no. 3 (September 1994), pp. 321-30. Reprinted with permission.

"Does Evolution Rule Out God's Existence?" is a revision of Chapter 2 in *Science and Religion: From Conflict to Conversation*, John F. Haught (New York: Paulist Press, 1996), pp. 47-71. Reprinted with permission.

"Does God Play Dice? Divine Providence and Chance" was originally published in *Theological Studies*, vol. 56 (1996), pp. 3-18. Reprinted here with permission.

"Welcoming the 'Disguised Friend': A Positive Theological Appraisal of Biological Evolution" was originally published in *Evolution and Molecular Biology: Scientific Perspectives on Divine Action* , Robert John Russell, William R. Stoeger and Francisco J. Ayala, eds. (Vatican City State: Vatican Observatory Publications and Berkeley: The Center for Theology and the Natural Sciences, 1998). Printed here with permission.

"The Evolution of the Created Co-Creator" was originally published in *Cosmos as Creation*, ed. Ted Peters (Nashville: Abingdon, 1989), pp. 211-233. Reprinted with permission.

"Agape and Human Nature: Contributions from Neo-Darwinism" was originally published in *Social Science Information*, vol. 31, no. 3 (1992), 509-529. Reprinted with permission.

"The Intelligent Design Movement" originally appeared in *Cosmic Pursuit*, Spring 1998. Reprinted with Permission

"Evidence for Intelligent Design from Biochemistry" is from a speech delivered at Discovery Institute's "God and Culture Conference" (August 10, 1996). Reprinted with permission.

"Life's Grand Design" was originally published in *Technology Review* (February/March 1994) Volume 97(2):24-32. Reprinted with permission.

"Intelligent Design as a Theory of Information" is from a paper presented at the "Naturalism, Theism and the Scientific Enterprise: An Interdisciplinary Conference" at the University of Texas, February 20, 1997. Reprinted with permission.

"How Not to Detect Design" was originally published in *Philosophy of Science*, 1999, 66: 472-488. Reprinted with permission.

"A Few Suggestions for the Proponents of Intelligent Design" was originally published in *Perspectives in Science and Christian Faith*, 47.3: (9/1995). Reprinted with permission.

Introduction: Setting the Contexts
JAMES B. MILLER

In October of 1996 in the popular press and on the World Wide Web there was a flurry of attention given to an address by Pope John Paul II to the Pontifical Academy of Sciences. In his remarks he observed that

> Today, almost half a century after the publication of the Encyclical [*Humani generis*], fresh knowledge has led to the recognition that evolution is more than a hypothesis. It is indeed remarkable that this theory has been progressively accepted by researchers, following a series of discoveries in various fields of knowledge. The convergence, neither sought nor fabricated, of the results of work that was conducted independently is in itself a significant argument in favor of this theory.[1]

While this was certainly one of the most affirmative of the few statements made by a 20th century Pontiff on evolutionary theory, it did not reflect any basic change of perspective within the Roman Catholic Church. For the Catholic educational institutions, from parochial elementary and secondary schools through Church-related colleges and universities, evolutionary biology has long been a staple of the science curriculum. But, if this is so, why did the Pope's statement garner such public attention?

One reason may be that the legacy of the Galileo affair makes any positive statement on science by the Roman Catholic hierarchy a newsworthy event. However, it is more likely that it was the contrast between this positive statement and the common sense that science and religion are in conflict over evolution that stimulated such attention in the news media. This assumption of conflict provides one of the historical contexts within which this current volume is offered.

Historical Contexts

The public perception that science and religion are in conflict is more associated with religious reactions to Darwin's Theory of Evolution than with the 16th and 17th century controversies surrounding Copernicus's *On the Revolutions of the Celestial Orbs.* Today, there is virtually no debate about teaching that the earth revolves around the sun. On the other hand, there are local school boards in the United States in which the teaching of evolutionary biology is a controversial matter.

There are historical reasons why evolutionary theory is seen as *a*, if not, *the* primary source of conflict between science and religion. There have been a number of public events that have become paradigmatic for this perception. These include: the debate between Thomas Henry Huxley (sometimes called "Darwin's bulldog") and Bishop Samuel Wilberforce at the 1860 meeting of the British Association for the Advancement of Science; the trial and conviction of John Thomas Scopes in Dayton, Tennessee, in 1925 for teaching evolution and, in that trial, the confrontation of William Jennings Bryan for the prosecution and Clarence Darrow for the defense; and the 1982 federal court case, McLean vs. the Arkansas Board of Education (sometimes referred to as "Scopes II"), that declared that the teaching of "scientific creationism" in public schools is a violation of the constitutional First Amendment separation of church and state.[2] More recently the intelligent design movement has justified itself, in part, as a counterattack against ontological naturalism and materialism that it views as necessary presuppositions of Darwinian evolutionary theory. As these events have shaped the public perception of the relationship between science and religion, generally, and evolutionary biology and religion, in particular, they have also obscured what has been a more constructive interaction between developments in evolutionary biology and religious thought. This positive engagement has seldom achieved the same level of public awareness.[3]

Philosophical Contexts

The perception that science and religion are in conflict arises both from historical fact and from a philosophical judgment. It is a fact that there have been historical occasions in which some forms of science and some forms of religion have been in conflict. However, it is a philosophical judgment that conflict is **the** characteristic relationship between science and religion.[4]

An alternative view is that science and religion are most appropriately understood as separate ways of approaching the world; each with different objects of interest, different methods, and different languages. When understood in this dualistic manner, science and religion cannot properly conflict. Conflicts are seen to arise only when there is an improper effort to force science and religion together. This is perhaps the prevalent perspective held personally by many members of both the scientific and the religious communities.

There is yet at least a third viewpoint about the relationship of science and religion. It sees the relationship as a constructive but asymmetrical one. Recent studies in the history of science and religion in Western culture indicate that this interactive relationship is a very complex one.[5] However, there does seem to be scholarly consensus that certain ideas about nature, transmitted in the Western religious traditions, provided an intellectual medium within which empirical science could emerge and flourish. Another way to say this is that the Western religious traditions provided a framework of meaning in which a particular form of inquiry about nature was meaningful. Thus, contemporary science can maintain an intellectual autonomy in its pursuit of understanding nature while, nevertheless, resting within philosophical presuppositions historically rooted in Western religious thought.

At the same time a religious perspective always assumes some understanding of the history and structure of nature. It is an understanding of nature that has been prevalent in the culture. This understanding is then given a religious interpretation.[6] Thus, the account of what the world **is** has a constructive influence on the interpretation of what the world **means**. To the extent that scientific inquiry within a culture changes the understanding of what the world is like, such change has a substantive relevance for any system of religious thought within that culture.

This present volume generally reflects this third position in that the scientific sections are presented as the autonomous findings or theoretical proposals of contemporary evolutionary biology. The theological sections, on the other hand, indicate ways in which these scientific findings or theories may be constructively engaged in religious reflection.

Scientific Context

Evolution is one of the prevalent paradigms within contemporary science generally. From cosmology to molecular biology scientific investigations into the structure of the world are intimately related to inquiries about the developmental history of the world. Certainly, there is no scientific field in which this is more the case than in biology. The centrality of an evolutionary perspective in biology is reflected in the often quoted declaration by Theodosius Dobzhansky that "Nothing in biology makes sense except in the light of evolution."[7] Therefore, if contemporary religious reflection is going to take account of contemporary biology at all, it is, of necessity, going to be evolutionary biology.

But evolutionary theory in biology is not an unchanging dogma. As the articles in the scientific sections of this volume will attest, evolutionary theory itself continues to develop, to evolve as advances in scientific methodology lead to new insights into the mechanisms of the evolutionary process and the events of evolutionary history.

Though Darwin's basic insight into the mechanisms of biological evolution is the historical cornerstone, contemporary evolutionary theory is much richer and more complex. Contributions from paleontology, molecular biology and biochemistry, genetics and a host of other disciplines, which were not available to Darwin, continue to refine, deepen and expand evolutionary theory. The scientific articles in this volume illustrate that evolutionary theory is a living theoretical tradition in science.

Practical Context

Finally, there is a practical context in which this volume appears. Over the last half of the past century, the renewed scholarly interest in the science and religion relationship has resulted in an increasing number of courses on this subject in colleges, universities and professional theological schools. In the past several years there has been a virtual explosion of such courses.

A chief characteristic of these courses is their interdisciplinary orientation. Even when taught by single faculty, they ordinarily draw insights from the sciences, history, philosophy, and religious studies. Yet, while the body of scholarship in the science and religion field has grown very rapidly in recent decades, single texts that incorporate distinct contributions from several disciplines are rare. It is the intent of the present volume to meet this practical pedagogical need.

Purpose and Structure

The purpose, then, of this volume is to provide a multidisciplinary educational resource for college, university and theological seminary educational settings, that will contribute to a constructive understanding of the dialogue between science and religion on the topic of biological evolution. The articles collected herein provide a basic introduction to contemporary evolutionary biology, provide historical and philosophical perspectives on the relationship between evolutionary biology and religious thought, and consider the intelligent design movement from scientific, philosophical and religious perspectives. Each section begins with a brief introduction that provides the reader with a guide to the articles contained there. The volume concludes with a brief bibliography on evolutionary science, history, philosophy, theology and ethics.

Notes

1. The official translation was published in *L'Osservatore Romano, "Weekly Edition in English,"* October 30, 1996.

2. For an assessment of the Huxley/Wilberforce encounter see J. R. Lucas, "Wilberforce and Huxley: A Legendary Encounter," *The Historical Journal,* vol. 22, no. 2 (1979), pp. 313-330. For a recent historical analysis of the Scopes trial and its aftermath see Edward J. Larson, *Summer for the Gods: The Scopes Trial and America's Continuing Debate over Science and Religion* (New York: Basic Books, 1997). The federal court decision in McLean vs. the Arkansas Board of Education can be found in *Science,* vol. 215, no. 4535 (February 19, 1982), pp. 934-943.

3. Even when events demonstrate a positive form of engagement between science and religion, they are often presented in the public media in such a way as to fall victim to the conflict perspective. For example, the headline in the *Chicago Tribune* (November 15, 1997) for a front page story reporting on an evolution and religion conference which exemplified such positive dialogue read, "Roll over, Darwin, those theologians at it again." The sub-headline continued this sense by stating, "It's science vs. religion, but today's battle of theories is far less heated." Even taking into account that headlines are not written by the reporters, these are descriptively very far from either the sense of the story that followed or the conference on which the story was based. They do, however, illustrate the "conflict" perspective so pervasive in the culture.

4. There are a number of proposals for how science and religion are related. Ian Barbour, *Religion and Science: Historical and Contemporary Issues* (San Francisco: HarperCollins, 1997) and John Haught, *Science and Religion: From Conflict to Conversation* (Mahwah, NJ: Paulist Press, 1998) offer four-fold typologies of the science and religion relationship. In the issue of *Zygon,* vol. 31, no. 2 (June 1996), Philip Hefner offers "six trajectories of the religion/science interface" (pp. 310-315) and Ted Peters describes "eight ways of relating science and theology" (pp. 325-331).

5. For example, see Lindburg, David C. and Ronald Numbers, ed., *God and Nature* (Berkeley: University of California Press, 1986).

6. This is one of the reasons that there is such a remarkable similarity between the order of the appearance of the world reflected in the Biblical Priestly account of creation (Gen. 1:1-2:4a) and in the Babylonian creation account in the *Enuma Elish*, though their theological interpretations of creation are very different.

7. "Nothing in Biology Makes Sense Except in the Light of Evolution," *American Biology Teacher*, 35: 125-129.

The Theory of Evolution

As the opening article in this section notes, the idea of evolution neither began nor ended with Darwin. Nevertheless, Darwin's insight into the structure of the evolutionary process in biology laid the foundation for what has developed into the "modern synthetic theory of evolution." The articles in this section provide an introduction to that theory beginning with Francisco Ayala's overview of the historical development and elements of the modern theory. This article sets the stage for the more detailed presentations which follow.

Mark Ridley's article discusses "The Mechanism of Evolution," focusing on natural selection as the means by which complex organs or organisms can evolve so as to be well adapted to their place in the body or within a larger environment. In particular he uses the evolution of the eye, of flight, and of the eukaryotic cell to illustrate this process.

In the 1930s the integration of genetics with the Darwinian theory established the modern synthetic theory. With the discovery of the structure of DNA by James Watson and Francis Crick in 1953 evolutionary theory was again deepened and its explanatory power expanded. Charles Marshall's article on "Darwinism in an Age of Molecular Revolution" illustrates the contributions made by molecular biology to the understanding of the evolutionary process.

Darwin's own revolutionary volume was titled *On the Origin of Species*. One of the central tasks of evolutionary theory is to explain how "descent with modification" can lead to the diverse forms of life that have inhabited the Earth. Douglas Futuyma's article on "Speciation" discusses the definition of species and the causes and rates of speciation.

The section concludes with an article by David Sloan Wilson on "Levels of Selection" which illustrates how natural selection may be understood to operate at the group as well as the individual organism level. The article also illustrates the potential significance of evolutionary theory beyond biology proper and into the social sciences.

2

Biological Evoution: An Introduction
FRANCISCO J. AYALA

Prelude

The great Russian-American geneticist and evolutionist Theodosius Dobzhansky wrote in 1973 that "Nothing in biology makes sense except in the light of evolution." The evolution of organisms, i.e., their common descent with modification from simple ancestors that lived many million years ago, is at the core of genetics, biochemistry, neurobiology, physiology, ecology, and other biological disciplines, and makes sense of the emergence of new infectious diseases and other matters of public health. The evolution of organisms is universally accepted by biological scientists, while the mechanisms of evolution are still actively investigated and are the subject of debate among scientists.

The 19th-century English naturalist, Charles Darwin, argued that organisms come about by evolution, and he provided a scientific explanation, essentially correct but incomplete, of how evolution occurs and why it is that organisms have features (such as wings, eyes, and kidneys) clearly structured to serve specific functions. Natural selection was the fundamental concept in his explanation. Genetics, a science born in the 20th century, revealed in detail how natural selection works and led to the development of the modern theory of evolution. Since the 1960s a related scientific discipline, molecular biology, has advanced enormously knowledge of biological evolution and has made it possible to investigate detailed problems that seemed completely out of reach a few years earlier—for example, how similar the genes of humans, chimpanzees, and gorillas are (they differ in about 1 or 2 percent of the units that make up the genes).

The diversity of living species is staggering. More than two million existing species of plants and animals have been named and described: many more remain to be discovered, at least ten million according to most estimates.

What is impressive is not just the numbers but also the incredible heterogeneity in size, shape, and ways of life: from lowly bacteria, less than one thousandth of a millimeter in diameter, to the stately sequoias of California, rising 300 feet (100 meters) above the ground and weighing several thousand tons; from microorganisms living in the hot springs of Yellowstone National Park at temperatures near the boiling point of water, some like *Pyrolobus fumarii* able to grow at more than 100° C (212° F), to fungi and algae thriving on the ice masses of Antarctica and in saline pools at -23° C (-73° F); from the strange worm-like creatures discovered in dark ocean depths at thousands of feet below the surface to spiders and larkspur plants existing on Mt. Everest more than 19,868 feet above sea level.

These variations on life are the outcome of the evolutionary process. All organisms are related by descent from common ancestors. Humans and other mammals are descended from shrew-like creatures that lived more than 150 million years ago; mammals, birds, reptiles, amphibians, and fishes share as ancestors small worm-like creatures that lived in the world's oceans 600 million years ago; plants and animals are derived from bacteria-like microorganisms that originated more than three billion years ago. Because of biological evolution, lineages of organisms change through time; diversity arises because lineages that descend from common ancestors diverge through the generations as they become adapted to different ways of life.

I intend to present in this article a brief summary of some central tenets of the theory of biological evolution. The process by which planets, stars, galaxies, and the universe form and change over time are a type of "evolution," but in a different sense. In both instances there is change over time but the processes are quite different. I will not discuss the evolution of the universe. The evolution of the hominids, the lineage that leads to our own species, will be very briefly outlined at the end.

Contrary to popular opinion, neither the term nor the idea of biological evolution began with Charles Darwin and his foremost work *On the Origin of Species by Means of Natural Selection* (1859). The *Oxford English Dictionary* (1933) tells us that the word *evolution*, to unfold or open out, derives from the Latin *evolvere*, which applied to the "unrolling of a book." It first appeared in the English language in 1647 in a nonbiological connection, and it became widely used in English for all sorts of progressions from simpler beginnings. Evolution was first used as a biological term in 1670 to describe the changes observed in the maturation of insects. However, it was not until the 1873 edition of *The Origin of Species* that Darwin first applied the term. He had earlier used the expression "descent with modification," which is still a good brief definition of biological evolution.

A distinction must be drawn at the outset between the questions (1) *whether* and (2) *how* biological evolution happened. The first refers to the finding, now supported by an overwhelming body of evidence, that descent with modification has occurred during some 3.5 billion years of earth's history. The second refers to the theory explaining how those changes came about. The mechanisms accounting for these changes are still undergoing investigation; the currently favored theory is an extensively modified version of Darwinian natural selection.

Early Ideas About Evolution

Explanations for the origin of the world, man, and other creatures are found in all human cultures. Traditional Judaism, Christianity and Islam explain the origin of living beings and their adaptations to their environments (wings, gills, hands, flowers) as the handiwork of an Omniscient God. The philosophers of ancient Greece had their own creation myths. Anaximander proposed that animals could be transformed from one kind into another, and Empedocles speculated that they could be made up of various combinations of preexisting parts. Closer to modern evolutionary ideas were the proposals of early Church Fathers like Gregory of Nazianzus and Augustine, who maintained that not all species of plants and animals were created as such by God; rather some had developed in historical times from other of God's creations. Their motivation was not biological but religious. Some species must have come into existence only after the Noachian Flood because it would have been impossible to hold representatives of all species in a single vessel such as Noah's Ark.

Christian theologians of the Middle Ages did not directly explore the notion that organisms may change by natural processes, but the matter was, usually incidentally, considered as a possibility by many, including Albertus Magnus and his student Thomas Aquinas. Aquinas concluded, after detailed discussion, that the development of living creatures like maggots and flies from nonliving matter like decaying meat was not incompatible with Christian faith or philosophy. But he left it to scientists to decide whether this actually happened in fact.

In the 18th century, Pierre-Louis Moreau de Maupertuis proposed the spontaneous generation and extinction of organisms as part of his theory of origins, but he advanced no theory about the possible transformation of one species into another through knowable, natural causes. One of the greatest naturalists of the time, Georges-Louis Leclerc (Buffon) explicitly considered— and rejected—the possible descent of several distinct kinds of organisms from a common ancestor. However, he made the claim that organisms arise from organic molecules by spontaneous generation, so that there could be as many kinds of animals and plants as there are viable combinations of organic molecules.

Erasmus Darwin, grandfather of Charles Darwin, offered in his *Zoonomia or the Laws of Organic Life* some evolutionary speculations, but they were not systematically developed and had no real influence on subsequent theories. The Swedish botanist Carolus Linnaeus devised the hierarchical system of plant and animal classification that is still in use in a modernized form. Although he insisted on the fixity of species, his classification system eventually contributed much to the acceptance of the concept of common descent.

The great French naturalist Jean-Baptiste Lamarck held the view that living organisms represent a progression, with humans as the highest form. In his *Philosophical Zoology*, published in 1809, the year in which Charles Darwin was born, he proposed the first broad theory of evolution. Organisms evolve through eons of time from lower to higher forms, a process still going on and always culminating in man.   As organisms become adapted to their environments through their habits, modifications occur. Use of an organ or structure reinforces it; disuse leads to obliteration. The characteristics acquired by use and disuse, according to this theory, would be inherited. This assumption, later called the inheritance of acquired characteristics, was thoroughly disproved in the 20th century. The notion that the same organisms repeatedly evolve in a fixed sequence of transition has also been disproved.

Darwin's Theory

Charles Darwin is appropriately considered the founder of the modern theory of evolution. The son and grandson of physicians, he enrolled as a medical student at the University of Edinburgh. After two years, however, he left to study at Cambridge University and prepare to become a clergyman. He was not an exceptional student, but he was deeply interested in natural history. On December 27, 1831, a few months after his graduation from Cambridge, he sailed as a naturalist aboard the HMS *Beagle* on a round-the-world trip that lasted until October 1836. Darwin was often able to disembark for extended trips ashore to collect natural specimens.

In Argentina he studied fossil bones from large extinct mammals. In the Galápagos Islands he observed numerous species of finches. These are among the events credited with stimulating Darwin's interest in how different species arise and become extinct. In 1859 he published *The Origin of Species*, a treatise providing extensive evidence for the evolution of organisms and proposing natural selection as the key process determining its course. He published many other books as well, notably *The Descent of Man and Selection in Relation to Sex* (1871), which provides an evolutionary account of human origins.

The origin of the Earth's living things, with their marvelous contrivances for adaptation, were generally attributed to the design of an Omniscient God. In the nineteenth century, Christian theologians had argued that the presence of design, so evident in living beings, demonstrates the existence of a Supreme Creator. The British theologian William Paley in his *Natural Theology* (1802) used natural history, physiology, and other contemporary knowledge to elaborate this argument from design. If a person should find a watch, even in an uninhabited desert, Paley contended, the intricate design and harmony of its many parts would force him to conclude that it had been created by a skilled watchmaker. How much more intricate and perfect in design is the human eye, Paley went on, with its transparent lens, its retina placed at the precise distance for forming a distinct image, and its large nerve transmitting signals to the brain.

Natural selection was proposed by Darwin primarily to account for the adaptive organizations of living beings: it is a process that promotes or maintains adaptation and, thus, gives the appearance of purpose or design. Evolutionary change through time and evolutionary diversification (multiplication of species) are not directly promoted by natural selection, but they often ensue as by-products of natural selection as it fosters adaptation to different environments. Darwin's theory of natural selection is summarized in *The Origin of Species* as follows:

> As many more individuals are produced than can possibly survive, there must in every case be a struggle for existence, either one individual with another of the same species, or with the individuals of distinct species, or with the physical conditions of life ... Can it, then, be thought improbable, seeing that variations useful to man have undoubtedly occurred, that other variations useful in some way to each being in the great and complex battle of life, should sometimes occur in the course of thousands of generations? If such do occur, can we doubt (remembering that many more individuals are born than can possibly survive) that individuals having any advantage, however slight, over others, would have the best chance of surviving and of procreating their kind? On the other hand, we may feel sure that any variation in the least degree injurious would be rigidly destroyed. This preservation of favorable variations and the rejection of injurious variations, I call Natural Selection.

The publication of *The Origin of Species* produced considerable public excitement. Scientists, politicians, clergymen, and notables of all kinds read and discussed the book, defending or deriding Darwin's ideas. The most visible actor in the controversies immediately following publication was T.H. Huxley, knows as "Darwin's bulldog," who defended the theory of evolution with articulate and sometimes mordant words on public occasions as well as in numerous writings. Serious scientific controversies also arose, first in Britain and then on the Continent and in the United States.

One occasional participant in the discussion was the naturalist Alfred Russel Wallace, who had independently discovered natural selection and had sent a short manuscript to Darwin from the Malay archipelago. A contemporary of Darwin with considerable influence during the latter part of the 19th and early 20th centuries was Herbert Spencer. He was a philosopher rather than a biologist, but he became an energetic proponent of evolutionary ideas, popularized a number of slogans, like "survival of the fittest" (which was taken up by Darwin in later editions of the *Origin*), and engaged in social and metaphysical speculations. His ideas considerably damaged proper understanding and acceptance of the theory of evolution by natural selection. Most pernicious was Spencer's crude extension of the notion of "struggle for existence" to human economic and social life that became known as social Darwinism.

The most serious difficulty facing Darwin's evolutionary theory was the lack of an adequate theory of inheritance that would account for the preservation through the generations of the variations on which natural selection was supposed to act. Current theories of "blending inheritance" proposed that the characteristics of parents became averaged in the offspring. As Darwin became aware, "blending inheritance" could not account for the conservation of variations, because halving the differences among variant offspring would rapidly reduce the original variation to the average of the preexisting characteristics.

Mendelian genetics provided the missing link in Darwin's argument. About the time *The Origin of Species* was published, the Augustinian monk Gregor Mendel was performing a long series of experiments with peas in the garden of his monastery in Brünn (now Brno, Czech Republic). These experiments and the analysis of their results are an example of masterly scientific method. Mendel's theory accounts for biological inheritance through particulate factors (genes) inherited one from each parent, which do not mix or blend but segregate in the formation of the sex cells, or gametes. Mendel's discoveries, however, remained unknown to Darwin and, indeed, did not become generally known until 1900, when they were simultaneously rediscovered by a number of scientists on the Continent.

Darwinism, in the latter part of the 19th century, faced an alternative evolutionary theory known as neo-Lamarckism. This hypothesis shared with

Lamarck's the importance of use and disuse in the development and obliteration of organs, and it added the notion that the environment acts directly on organic structures, which would explain their adaptation to their environments and ways of life. Adherents of this theory discarded natural selection as an explanation for adaptation to the environment. Prominent among the defenders of natural selection was the German biologist August Weismann, who in the 1880s published his germ-plasm theory. He distinguished two components in the make- up of an organism: the soma, which comprises most body parts and organs, and the germplasm, which contains the cells that give rise to the gametes and hence to progeny. The radical separation between germ and soma prompted Weismann to assert that inheritance of acquired characteristics was impossible, and it opened the way for his championship of natural selection as the only major process that would account for biological evolution. The formulation of the evolutionary theory championed by Weismann and his followers toward the end of the nineteenth century became known as "neo-Darwinism."

The Modern Theory of Evolution

The rediscovery in 1900 of Mendel's theory of heredity ushered in an emphasis on the role of heredity in evolution. Hugo de Vries in the Netherlands proposed a new theory of evolution known as mutationism, which essentially did away with natural selection as a major evolutionary process. According to de Vries (joined by other geneticists such as William Bateson in England), there are two kinds of variation that take place in organisms. One is the "ordinary" variability observed among individuals of a species, which is of no lasting consequence in evolution because, according to de Vries, it could not "lead to a transgression of the species border even under conditions of the most stringent and continued selection." The other consists of the changes brought about by mutations, spontaneous alterations of genes that yield large modifications of the organism and gave rise to new species. Mutationism was opposed by many naturalists, and in particular by the so-called biometricians, led by Karl Pearson, who defended Darwinian natural selection as the major cause of evolution through the cumulative effects of small, continuous, individual variations.

Arguments between mutationists (also referred to at the time as Mendelians) and biometricians approached a resolution in the 1920s and '30s through the theoretical work of geneticists. They used mathematical arguments to show, first, that continuous variation (in such characteristics as size, number of eggs laid, and the like) could be explained by Mendel's laws; and second, that natural selection acting cumulatively on small variations could yield major evolutionary changes in form and function. Distinguished members of this group of theoretical geneticists were R.A. Fisher and J.B.S. Haldane in Britain and Sewall Wright in the United States. Their work provided a theoretical framework for the integration of genetics into Darwin's theory of natural selection. Yet their work had a limited impact on contemporary biologists because it was almost exclusively theoretical, formulated in mathematical language and with little empirical corroboration. A major breakthrough came in 1937 with the publication of *Genetics and the Origin of Species* by Theodosius Dobzhansky, a Russian-born American naturalist and experimental geneticist.

Dobzhansky advanced a reasonably comprehensive account of the evolutionary process in genetic terms, laced with experimental evidence supporting the theoretical argument. *Genetics and the Origin of Species* may be considered the most important landmark in the formulation of what came to be known as the synthetic theory of evolution, effectively combining Darwinian natural selection and Mendelian genetics. It had an enormous impact on naturalists and experimental biologists, who rapidly embraced the new understanding of the evolutionary process as one of genetic change in populations. Interest in evolutionary studies was greatly stimulated, and contributions to the theory soon began to follow, extending the synthesis of genetics and natural selection to a variety of biological fields. Other writers who importantly contributed to the formulation of the synthetic theory were the zoologists Ernst Mayr and Sir Julian Huxley, the paleontologist George G. Simpson, and the botanist George Ledyard Stebbins. By 1950 acceptance of Darwin's theory of evolution by natural selection was universal among biologists, and the synthetic theory had become widely adopted.

Since 1950, the most important line of investigation has been the application of molecular biology to evolutionary studies. In 1953 James Watson and Francis Crick discovered the structure of DNA (deoxyribonucleic acid), the hereditary material contained in the chromosomes of every cell's nucleus. The genetic information is contained within the sequence of components (nucleotides) that make up the long chainlike DNA molecules, very much in the same manner as semantic information is contained in the sequence of letters in an English text. This information determines the sequence of amino acids in the proteins, including the enzymes that carry out the organism's life processes. Comparisons of the amino acid sequences of proteins in different species provides quantitatively precise measures of species divergence, a considerable improvement over the typically qualitative evaluations obtained by comparative anatomy and other evolutionary subdisciplines.

In 1968 the Japanese geneticist Motoo Kimura proposed the neutrality theory of molecular evolution, which assumes that at the level of DNA and protein sequence many changes are adaptively neutral and have little or no effect on the molecule's function. If the neutrality theory is correct, there should be a "molecular clock" of evolution; that is, the degree of divergence between species in amino acid or nucleotide sequence would provide a reliable estimate of the time since their divergence. This would make possible a reconstruction of evolutionary history that would reveal the order of branching of different lineages, such as those leading to humans, chimpanzees, and orangutans, as well as the time in the past when the lineages split from one another. During the 1970s and '80s it gradually became clear that the molecular clock is not exact; nevertheless, it has become a reliable source of evidence for reconstructing a history of evolution. In the 1990s, the techniques of DNA cloning and sequencing have provided new and more powerful means of investigating evolution at the molecular level.

Important discoveries in the earth sciences and ecology during the second half of the 20th century have also greatly contributed to advance our understanding of the theory of evolution. The science of plate tectonics has shown that the configuration and position of the continents and oceans are dynamic, rather than static, features of the Earth. Oceans grow and shrink, while continents break into fragments or coalesce into larger masses. The continents move across the Earth's surface at rates of a few centimeters a year, and over millions of years of geological history this profoundly alters the face of the Earth, causing major climatic changes along the way. These previously unsuspected massive modifications of the planet's environments have of necessity been reflected in the evolutionary history of life. Biogeography, the evolutionary study of plant and animal distribution, has been revolutionized by the knowledge, for example, that Africa and South America were part of a single landmass some 200 million years ago and that the Indian subcontinent was not connected with Asia until recent geologic times. The study of the interactions of organisms with their environments, known as the discipline of ecology, has evolved from descriptive studies ("natural history") into a vigorous biological discipline with a strong mathematical component, both in the development of theoretical models and in the collection and analysis of quantitative data. Another active field of research in evolutionary biology is evolutionary ethology, the study of animal behavior. Sociobiology, the evolutionary study of social behavior, is perhaps the most active and most controversial (because of its extension to human societies) subfield of ethology.

The Impact of Evolutionary Theory

Three different, though related, issues have been the main subjects of evolutionary investigations: (1) the fact of evolution—that is, that organisms are related by common descent with modification; (2) evolutionary history—that is, the details of when lineages split from one another and of the changes that occurred in each lineage; and (3) the mechanisms or processes by which evolutionary change occurs.

The fact of evolution is the most fundamental issue and the one established with utmost certainty.   Darwin gathered much evidence in its support, but the evidence has accumulated continuously ever since, derived from all biological disciplines.   As Pope John Paul II noted in an address to the Pontifical Academy of Sciences on 22 October 1996, "It is indeed remarkable that this theory [of evolution] has been progressively accepted by researchers, Following a series of discoveries in various fields of knowledge.   The convergence, neither sought nor fabricated, of the results of work that was conducted independently is in itself a significant argument in favor of this theory." Indeed, the evolutionary origin of organisms is today a scientific conclusion established with the kind of certainty attributable to such scientific concepts as the roundness of the Earth, the motions of the planets, and the molecular composition of matter.   This degree of certainty beyond reasonable doubt is what is implied when biologists say that evolution is a "fact"; the evolutionary origin of organisms is accepted by virtually every biologist.

The second and third issues go much beyond the general affirmation that organisms evolve.   The theory of evolution seeks to ascertain the evolutionary relationships between particular organisms and the events of evolutionary history, as well as to explain how and why evolution takes place.   These are matters of active scientific investigation.   Many conclusions are well established; for example, that the chimpanzee and gorilla are more closely related to humans than is any of those three species to the baboon or other monkeys; or that natural selection explains the adaptive configuration of such features as the human eye and the wings of birds.   Some other matters are less certain, others are conjectural, and still others—such as precisely when life originated on earth and the characteristics of the first living things—remain largely unresolved.

The theory of evolution has been seen by some people as incompatible with religious beliefs, particularly those of Christianity.[1] The first chapters of the book of Genesis describe God's creation of the world, the plants, the animals, and man.   A literal interpretation of Genesis seems incompatible with the gradual evolution of humans and other organisms by natural processes. Independently of the biblical narrative, the belief in the immortality of the soul and in man as "created in the image of God" have appeared to some as contrary to the evolutionary origin of man from non-human animals.[2]

Religiously motivated attacks started during Darwin's lifetime. In 1874 Charles Hodge, an American Protestant theologian, perceived Darwin's theory as "the most thoroughly naturalistic that can be imagined and far more atheistic than that of his predecessor Lamarck." He argued that the design of the human eye evinces that "it has been planned by the Creator, like the design of a watch evinces a watchmaker." He concluded that "the denial of design in nature is actually the denial of God." But, other Protestant theologians saw a solution to the difficulty in the idea that God operates through intermediate causes. The origin and motion of the planets could be explained by the law of gravity and other natural processes without denying God's creation and providence. Similarly, evolution could be seen as the natural process through which God brought living beings into existence and developed them according to his plan. Thus, A.H. Strong, the president of Rochester (NY) Theological Seminary, wrote in his *Systematic Theology* (1885): "We grant the principle of evolution, but we regard it as only the method of divine intelligence." The brutish ancestry of man was not incompatible with the excelling status as a creature in the image of God.

More recently, Biblical Fundamentalists, who make up a minority of Christians, have periodically gained considerable public and political influence in the United States. During the decade of the 1920s, more than 20 state legislatures were influenced by them to debate antievolution laws, and four states—Arkansas, Mississippi, Oklahoma, and Tennessee—prohibited the teaching of evolution in their public schools. But, in 1968 the Supreme Court of the United States declared unconstitutional any law banning the teaching of evolution in public schools.

Arguments for and against Darwin's theory have come from Roman Catholic theologians as well. Gradually, well into the 20th century, evolution by natural selection came to be accepted by the majority of Christian writers. Pope Pius XII in his encyclical *Humani Generis* (1950; "Of the Human Race") acknowledged that biological evolution was compatible with the Christian faith, although he argued that God's intervention was necessary for the creation of the human soul. In 1981 Pope John Paul II stated in an address to the Pontifical Academy of Sciences:

> The Bible itself speaks to us of the origin of the universe and its make-up, not in order to provide us with a scientific treatise but in order to state the correct relationships of man with God and with the universe. Sacred scripture wishes simply to declare that the world was created by God, and in order to teach this truth it expresses itself in the terms of the cosmology in use at the time of the writer ... Any other teaching about the origin and make-up of the universe is alien to the

intentions of the Bible, which does not wish to teach how the heavens were made but how one goes to heaven.

The Pope's point was that it would be a blunder to mistake the Bible for an elementary book of astronomy, geology, and biology. John Paul II returned in 1996 to the same topic. In the address to the Pontifical Academy of Sciences cited earlier, he stated that "the theory of evolution is more than a hypothesis."

The Evidence for Common Descent with Modification

Evidence for relationship among organisms by common descent with modification has been obtained by paleontology, comparative anatomy, biogeography, embryology, biochemistry, molecular genetics, and other biological disciplines. The idea first emerged from observations of systematic changes in the succession of fossil remains found in a sequence of layered rocks. Such layers are now known to have a cumulative thickness of many scores of kilometers and to represent at least 3.5 billion years of geological time. The general sequence of fossils from bottom upward in layered rocks had been recognized before Darwin perceived that the observed progression of biological forms strongly implied common descent. The farther back into the past one looked, the less the fossils resembled recent forms, the more the various lineages merged, and the broader the implications of a common ancestry appeared.

Paleontology, however, was still a rudimentary science in Darwin's time, and large parts of the geological succession of stratified rocks were unknown or inadequately studied. Darwin, therefore, worried about the rarity of truly intermediate forms. Anti-evolutionists have then and now seized on this as a weakness in evolutionary theory. Although gaps in the paleontological record remain even now, many have been filled by the researches of paleontologists since Darwin's time. Hundreds of thousands of fossil organisms found in well-dated rock sequences represent a succession of forms through time and manifest many evolutionary transitions. Microbial life of the simplest type (i.e., prokaryotes, which are cells whose nuclear matter is not bounded by a nuclear membrane) was already in existence more than 3 billion years ago. The oldest evidence suggesting the existence of more complex organisms (i.e., eukaryotic cells with a true nucleus) has been discovered in fossils that had been sealed in flinty rocks approximately 1.4 billion years old. More advanced forms like true algae, fungi, higher plants, and animals have been found only in younger geological strata. The following list presents the order in which progressively complex forms of life appeared:

Life Form	Millions of Years Since First Known Appearance (Approximate)
Microbial (prokaryotic cells)	3,500
Complex (eukaryotic cells)	1,400
First multicellular animals	670
Shell-bearing animals	540
Vertebrates (simple fishes)	490
Amphibians	350
Reptiles	310
Mammals	200
Nonhuman primates	60
Earliest apes	25
Australopithecine ancestors	5
Homo sapiens (modern humans)	0. 15 (150,000 years)

The sequence of observed forms and the fact that all except the first are constructed from the same basic cellular type strongly imply that all these major categories of life (including plants, algae, and fungi) have a common ancestry in the first eukaryotic cell. Moreover, there have been so many discoveries of intermediate forms between fish and amphibians, between amphibians and reptiles, between reptiles and mammals, and even along the primate line of descent from apes to humans that it is often difficult to identify categorically along the line when the transition occurs from one to another particular genus or from one to another particular species. Nearly all fossils can be regarded as intermediates in some sense; they are life forms that come between ancestral forms that preceded them and those that followed.

The fossil record thus provides compelling evidence of systematic change through time of descent with modification. From this consistent body of evidence it can be predicted that no reversals will be found in future paleontological studies. That is, amphibians will not appear before fishes nor mammals before reptiles, and no complex life will occur in the geological record before the oldest eukaryotic cells. That prediction has been upheld by the evidence that has accumulated thus far: no reversals have been found.

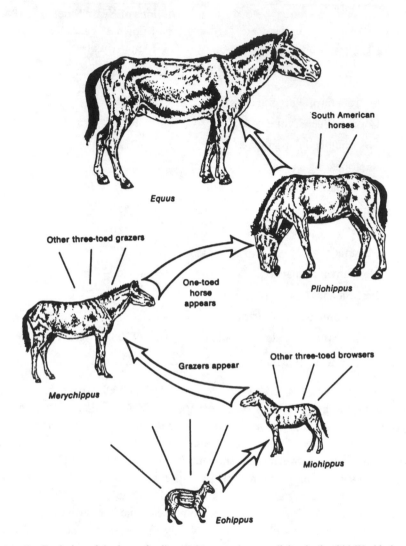

Figure 1: Evolution of the horse family. *Eohippus*, a browser living in the Old World about 50 million years ago, evolved into several forms. One of these (*Miohippus*) was a three-toed browser that evolved into several other browsers as well as into one form (*Merychippus*) that became a grazer. *Merychippus* was still three-toed and evolved into other three-toed grazers as well as into a one-toed horse (*Pliohippus*), which eventually gave rise to the modern horse (*Equus*) as well as to the South American horses.

Although some creationists have claimed that the entire geological record, with its orderly succession of fossils, is the product of a single universal flood that lasted a little longer than a year and covered the highest mountains to a depth of some 7 meters a few thousand years ago, there is clear evidence in the form of intertidal and terrestrial deposits that at no recorded time in the past has the entire planet been under water.   Moreover, a universal flood of sufficient magnitude to deposit the existing strata, which together are many scores of kilometers thick, would require a volume of water far greater than has ever existed on and in the earth, at least since the formation of the first known solid crust about 4 billion years ago.   The belief that all this sediment with its fossils was deposited in an orderly sequence in a year's time defies all geological observations and physical principles concerning sedimentation rates and possible quantities of suspended solid matter.   There were periods of unusually high rainfall and extensive flooding of inhabited areas has occurred, but there is no scientific support for the hypothesis of a universal mountain-topping flood.

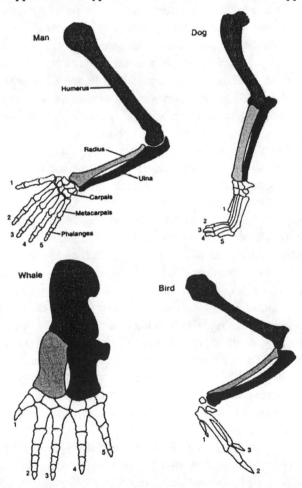

Figure 2: Bone composition of the forelimb of four vertebrates.

Inferences about common descent derived from paleontology have been reinforced by comparative anatomy. The skeletons of humans, dogs, whales, and bats are strikingly similar, despite the different ways of life led by these animals and the diversity of environments in which they have flourished. The correspondence, bone by bone, can be observed in every part of the body, including the limbs: yet a person writes, a dog runs, a whale swims, and a bat flies with structures built of the same bones. Scientists calls such structures homologous and have concurred that they are best explained by common descent. Comparative anatomists investigate such homologies, not only in bone structure but also in other parts of the body as well, working out relationships from degrees of similarity. Their conclusions provide important inferences about the details of evolutionary history that can be tested by comparisons with the sequence of ancestral forms in the paleontological record.

The mammalian ear and jaw offer an example in which paleontology and comparative anatomy combine to show common ancestry through transitional stages. The lower jaws of mammals contain only one bone, whereas those of reptiles have several. The other bones in the reptile jaw are homologous with bones now found in the mammalian ear. What function could these bones have had during intermediate stages? Paleontologists have now discovered intermediate forms of mammal-like reptiles (Therapsida) with a double jaw joint—one composed of the bones that persist in mammalian jaws, the other consisting of bones that eventually became the hammer and anvil of the mammalian ear. Similar examples are numerous.

Biogeography also has contributed evidence for common descent. The diversity of life is stupendous. Approximately 250 thousand species of living plants, 100 thousand species of fungi, and 1.5 million species of animals and microorganisms have been described and named, each occupying its own peculiar ecological setting or niche, and the census is far from complete. Some species, such as human beings and our companion the dog, can live under a wide range of environmental conditions. Others are amazingly specialized. One species of the fungus *Laboulbenia* grows exclusively on the rear portion of the covering wings of a single species of beetle (*Aphaenops cronei*) found only in some caves of southern France. The larvae of the fly *Drosophila carcinophila* can develop only in specialized grooves beneath the flaps of the third pair of oral appendages of the land crab *Gecarcinus ruricola* which is found only on certain Caribbean islands.

How can we make intelligible the colossal diversity of living beings and the existence of such extraordinary, seemingly whimsical creatures as *Laboulbenia*, *Drosophila carcinophila*, and others? Why are island groups like the Galápagos inhabited by forms similar to those on the nearest mainland but belonging to different species? Why is the indigenous life so different on different continents? Creationists contend that the curious facts of biogeography result from the occurrence of special creation events. A scientific hypothesis proposes that biological diversity results from an evolutionary process whereby the descendants of local or migrant predecessors became adapted to their diverse environments. A testable corollary of this hypothesis is that present forms and local fossils should show homologous attributes indicating how one is derived from the other. Also, there should be evidence that forms without an established local ancestry had migrated into the locality. Wherever such tests have been carried out, these conditions have been confirmed. A good example is provided by the mammalian populations of North and South America, where strikingly different endemic forms evolved in isolation until the emergence of the isthmus of Panama approximately 3 million years ago. Thereafter, the armadillo, porcupine, and opossum (mammals of South American origin) were able to migrate to North America along with many other species of plants and animals, while the placental mountain lion and other North American species made their way across the isthmus to the south.

The evidence that Darwin found for the influence of geographical distribution on the evolution of organisms has become stronger with advancing knowledge. For example, approximately two thousand species of flies belonging to the genus *Drosophila* are now found throughout the world. About one-quarter of them live only in Hawaii. More than a thousand species of snails and other land mollusks are also only found in Hawaii. The natural explanation for the occurrence of such great diversity among closely similar forms is that the differences resulted from adaptive colonization of isolated environments by animals with a common ancestry. The Hawaiian islands are far from, and were never attached to any mainland or other islands, and they have had few colonizers. Organisms that reached these islands found many unoccupied ecological niches where they could then undergo separate evolutionary diversifications. No mammals other than one bat species lived on the Hawaiian islands when the first human settlers arrived; very many other kinds of plants and animals were also absent. The scientific explanation is that these kinds of organisms never reached the islands because of their great geographic isolation, while those that reached there multiplied in kind, because of the absence of related organisms that would compete for resources.

The vagaries of biogeography cannot be attributed to environmental peculiarities alone. The Hawaiian islands are no better than other Pacific islands for the survival of *Drosophila*, nor are they less hospitable than other parts of the world for many organisms not indigenous to them. For example, pigs and goats have multiplied in Hawaii after their introduction by humans. The general observation is that all sorts of organisms are absent from places well suited to their occupancy. The animals and plants vary from continent to continent and from island to island in a distribution pattern consistent with colonization and evolutionary change, rather than being simply responsive to the conditions of place.

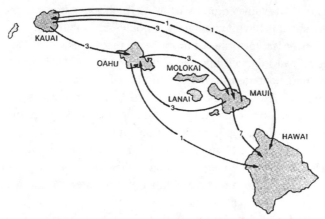

Figure 3: Minimum number of colonizations postulated to account for the evolution of the picture-winged *Drosophila* species of Hawaii. The arrows indicate the direction of migration; the numbers in each arrow indicate the minimum number of separate colonizations in the direction indicated.

Embryology, the study of biological development from the time of conception, is another source of independent evidence for common descent. Barnacles, for instance, are sedentary crustaceans with little apparent similarity to such other crustaceans as lobsters, shrimps, or copepods. Yet barnacles pass through a free-swimming larval stage, in which they look unmistakably like other crustacean larvae. The similarity of larval stages supports the conclusion that all crustaceans have homologous parts and a common ancestry. Human and other mammalian embryos pass through a stage during which they have unmistakable but useless grooves similar to gill slits found in fishes—evidence that they and the other vertebrates shared remote ancestors that respired with the aid of gills.

Finally, the substantiation of common descent that emerges from all the foregoing lines of evidence is being validated and reinforced by the discoveries of modern biochemistry and molecular biology, a biological discipline that has emerged in the mid-20th century. This new discipline has unveiled the nature of hereditary material and the workings of organisms at the level of enzymes and other molecules. Molecular biology provides very detailed and convincing evidence for biological evolution.

The Evidence from Molecular Biology

The hereditary material, DNA, and the enzymes that govern all life processes hold information about an organism's ancestry. This information has made it possible to reconstruct evolutionary events that were previously unknown and to confirm and adjust the view of events that already were known. The precision with which events of evolution can be reconstructed is one reason the evidence from molecular biology is so compelling. Another reason is that molecular evolution has shown all living organisms, from bacteria to humans, to be related by descent from common ancestors.

The molecular components of organisms exhibit a remarkable uniformity in the nature of the components as well as in the ways in which they are assembled and used. In all bacteria, plants, animals, and humans, the DNA is made up of the same four component nucleotides, although many other nucleotides exist, and all of the various proteins are synthesized from different combinations and sequences of the same 20 amino acids, although several hundred other amino acids do exist. The genetic "code" by which the information contained in the nuclear DNA is passed on to proteins is everywhere the same. Similar metabolic pathways are used by the most diverse organisms to produce energy and to make up the cell components.

This unity reveals the genetic continuity and common ancestry of all organisms. There is no other rational way to account for their molecular uniformity when numerous alternative structures are equally likely. The genetic code may serve as an example. Each particular sequence of three nucleotides in the nuclear DNA acts as a pattern, or code, for the production of exactly the same amino acid in all organisms. This is no more necessary than it is for a language to use a particular combination of letters to represent a particular reality. If it is found that many different combinations of letters, such as "planet," "tree," "woman," are used with identical meanings in a number of different books, one can be sure that the languages used in those books are of common origin.

Genes and proteins are long molecules that contain information in the sequence of their components in much the same way as sentences of the English language contain information in the sequence of their letters and words. The sequences that make up the genes are passed on from parents to offspring, identical except for occasional changes introduced by mutations. To illustrate, assume that two books are being compared; both books are 200 pages long and contain the same number of chapters. Closer examination reveals that the two books are identical page for page and word for word, except that an occasional word—say one in 100—is different. The two books cannot have been written independently; either one has been copied from the other or both have been copied, directly or indirectly, from the same original book. Similarly, if each nucleotide is represented by one letter, the complete sequence of nucleotides in the DNA of a higher organism would require several hundred books of hundreds of pages, with several thousand letters on each page. When the "pages" (or sequence of nucleotides) in these "books" (organisms) are examined one by one, the correspondence in the "letters" (nucleotides) gives unmistakable evidence of common origin.

Two arguments attest to evolution. Using the alphabet analogy, the first argument says that languages that use the same dictionary—the same genetic code and the same 20 amino acids—cannot be of independent origin. The second argument, concerning similarity in the sequence of nucleotides in the DNA or the sequence of amino acids in the proteins, says that books with very similar texts cannot be of independent origin.

The evidence of evolution revealed by molecular biology goes one step further. The degree of similarity in the sequence of nucleotides or of amino acids can be precisely quantified. For example, cytochrome c (a protein molecule) of humans and chimpanzees consists of the same 104 amino acids in exactly the same order; but differs from that of rhesus monkeys by one amino acid, that of horses by 11 additional amino acids, and that of tuna by 21 additional amino acids. The degree of similarity reflects the recency of common ancestry. Thus, the inferences from comparative anatomy and other disciplines concerning evolutionary history can be tested in molecular studies of DNA and proteins by examining their sequences of nucleotides and amino acids.

The authority of this kind of test is overwhelming; each of the thousands of genes and thousands of proteins contained in an organism provides an independent test of that organism's evolutionary history. Not all possible tests have been performed, but many hundreds have been done, and not one has given evidence contrary to evolution. There is probably no other notion in any field of science that has been as extensively tested and as thoroughly corroborated as the evolutionary origin of living organisms. There is no reason to doubt the evolutionary theory of the origin of organisms any more than to doubt the heliocentric theory of the rotations of the planets around the sun.

The Genetic Basis of Evolution

The central argument of Darwin's theory of evolution starts from the existence of hereditary variation. Experience with animal and plant breeding demonstrates that variations can be developed that are "useful to man." So, reasoned Darwin, variations must occur in nature that are favorable or useful in some way to the organism itself in the struggle for existence. Favorable variations are ones that increase chances for survival and procreation. Those advantageous variations are preserved and multiplied from generation to generation at the expense of less advantageous ones. This is the process known as natural selection. The outcome of the process is an organism that is well adapted to its environment, and evolution often occurs as a consequence.

Biological evolution is the process of change and diversification of living things over time, and it affects all aspects of their lives—morphology, physiology, behavior, and ecology. Underlying these changes are changes in the hereditary materials. Hence, in genetic terms, evolution consists of changes in the organism's hereditary makeup.

Natural selection, then, can be defined as the differential reproduction of alternative hereditary variants, determined by the fact that some variants increase the likelihood that the organisms having them will survive and reproduce more successfully than will organisms carrying alternative variants. Selection may be due to differences in survival, in fertility, in rate of development, in mating success, or in any other aspect of the life cycle. All of these differences can be incorporated under the term "differential reproduction" because all result in natural selection to the extent that they affect the number of progeny an organism leaves.

Darwin explained that competition for limited resources results in the survival of the most effective competitors. But natural selection may occur not only as a result of competition but also as an affect of some aspect of the physical environment, such as inclement weather. Moreover, natural selection would occur even if all the members of a population died at the same age, if some of them produced more offspring than others. Natural selection is quantified by a measure called Darwinian fitness, or relative fitness. Fitness in this sense is the relative probability that a hereditary characteristic will be reproduced, that is, the degree of fitness is a measure of the reproductive efficiency of the characteristic.

Evolution can be seen as a two-step process. First, hereditary variation takes place; second, selection occurs of those genetic variants that will be passed on most effectively to the following generations. Hereditary variation also entails two mechanisms: the spontaneous mutation of one variant to another, and the sexual process that recombines those variants to form a multitude of variations.

The "gene pool" of a species is the sum total of all of the genes and combinations of genes that occur in all organisms of the same species. The necessity of hereditary variation for evolutionary change to occur can be understood in terms of the gene pool. Assume, for instance, that at the gene locus that codes for the human *MN* blood groups, there is no variation; only the *M* form exists in all individuals. Evolution of the *MN* blood groups cannot take place in such a population, since the allelic frequencies have no opportunity to change from generation to generation. On the other hand, in populations in which both forms *M* and *N* are present, evolutionary change is possible.

The more genetic variation that exists in a population, the greater the opportunity for evolution to occur. As the number of genes that are variable increases and as the number of forms of each gene becomes greater, the likelihood that some forms will change in frequency at the expense of their alternates grows. The British geneticist R.A. Fisher mathematically demonstrated a direct correlation between the amount of genetic variation in a population and the rate of evolutionary change by natural selection. This demonstration is embodied in his fundamental theorem of natural selection: "The rate of increase in fitness of any organism at any time is equal to its genetic variance in fitness at that time." This theorem has been confirmed experimentally. Because a population's potential for evolving is determined by its genetic variation, evolutionists are interested in discovering the extent of such variation in natural populations. Techniques for determining genetic variation have been used to investigate numerous species of plants and animals. Typically, insects and other invertebrates are more varied genetically than mammals and other vertebrates; and plants bred by outcrossing exhibit more variation than those bred by self-pollination. But the amount of genetic variation is in any case astounding. Consider as an example humans, whose level of variation is about the same as that of other mammals. At the level of proteins, the human heterozygosity (the measure of genetic variation) value is stated as $H = 0.067$, which means that an individual is heterozygous (has two different gene forms) at 6.7 percent of his genes. It is not known how many gene loci there are in humans, but estimates range from 30,000 to 100,000. Assuming the lower estimate, a person would be heterozygous at 30,000 x 0.067 = 2,010 genes. This implies a typical human individual has the potential to produce $2^{2,010}$, or approximately 10^{605} (1 with 605 zeros following), different kinds of sex cells (eggs or sperm). But that number is much larger than the estimated number of atoms in the universe, 10^{76}, which is trivial by comparison. This calculation becomes yet more dramatic if it is made at the level of the DNA. Among the three billion nucleotides (the letters in the DNA) that we inherit from each one of our parents, more than one per thousand (that is, more than three million) are different between the paternal and maternal. By random recombination they have the potential to produce more $10^{750,000}$ (1 with 750,000 zeros following) different sex cells; and the set that can be produced by each person is different from the set of every other person.

The same can be said of all organisms that reproduce sexually; every individual represents a unique genetic configuration that will never be repeated again. This enormous reservoir of genetic variation in natural populations provides virtually unlimited opportunities for evolutionary change in response to the environmental constraints and the needs of the organisms, beyond the new variations that arise every generation by the process of mutation, which I shall now discuss.

The Origin of Genetic Variation

All living things have evolved from primitive living forms that lived about 3,500,000,000 years ago. At present there are more than two million known species, which are widely diverse in size, shape, and ways of life, as well as in the DNA sequences that contain their genetic information. What has produced the pervasive genetic variation within natural populations and the genetic differences among species?

Heredity is not a perfectly conservative process; otherwise, evolution could not have taken place. The information encoded in the nucleotide sequence of DNA is, as a rule, faithfully reproduced during replication, so that each replication results in two DNA molecules that are identical to each other and to the parent molecule. But, occasionally "mistakes," or mutations, occur in the DNA molecule during replication, so that daughter cells differ from the parent cells in at least one of the letters in the DNA sequence. A mutation first appears on a single cell of an organism, but it is passed on to all cells descended from the first. Mutations can be classified into two categories: gene, or point, mutations, which affect only a few letters (nucleotides) within a gene; and chromosomal mutations which either change the number of chromosomes or change the number or arrangement of genes on a chromosome. Chromosomes are the elongated structures that store the DNA of each cell.

Gene mutations can occur spontaneously; that is, without being intentionally caused by humans. They can also be artificially induced by ultraviolet light, X rays, and other high-frequency radiations, as well as by exposure to certain mutagenic chemicals, such as mustard gas. The consequences of gene mutations may range from negligible to lethal. Some have a small or undetectable effect on the organism's ability to survive and reproduce, because no essential biological functions are altered. But when the active site of an enzyme or some other essential function is affected, the impact may be severe.

Newly arisen mutations are more likely to be harmful than beneficial to their carriers, because mutations are random events with respect to adaptation;

that is, their occurrence is independent of any possible consequences. Harmful mutations are eliminated or kept in check by natural selection. Occasionally, however, a new mutation may increase the organism's adaptation. The probability of such an event's happening is greater when organisms colonize a new territory or when environmental changes confront a population with new challenges. In these cases, the established adaptation of a population is less than optimal, and there is greater opportunity for new mutations to be better adaptive. This is so because the consequences of mutations depend on the environment. Increased melanin pigmentation may be advantageous to inhabitants of tropical Africa, where dark skin protects them from the Sun's ultraviolet radiation; but it is not beneficial in Scandinavia, where the intensity of sunlight is low and light skin facilitates the synthesis of vitamin D.

Mutation rates are low, but new mutants appear continuously in nature, because there are many individuals in every species and many genes in every individual. The process of mutation provides each generation with many new genetic variations. More important yet is the storage of variation, arisen by past mutations, that is present in each organism, as calculated earlier for humans. Thus, it is not surprising to see that when new environmental challenges arise, species are able to adapt to them. More than 200 insect and rodent species, for example, have developed resistance to the pesticide DDT in different parts of the world where spraying has been intense. Although the insects had never before encountered this synthetic compound, they adapted to it rapidly by means of mutations that allowed them to survive in its presence. Similarly, many species of moths and butterflies in industrialized regions have shown an increase in the frequency of individuals with dark wings in response to environmental pollution, an adaptation known as industrial melanism. The examples can be multiplied at will.

Dynamics of Genetic Change

The genetic variation present in natural populations of organisms is sorted out in new ways in each generation by the process of sexual reproduction. But heredity by itself does not change gene frequencies. This principle is formally stated by the Hardy-Weinberg law, an algebraic equation that describes the genetic equilibrium in a population.[3]

The Hardy-Weinberg law assumes that gene frequencies remain constant from generation to generation—that there is no gene mutation or natural selection and that populations are very large.

But these assumptions are not correct; indeed, if they were, evolution cold not occur. Why, then, is the Hardy-Weinberg law significant if its assumptions do not hold true in nature? The answer is that the Hardy-Weinberg law plays in evolutionary studies a role similar to that of Newton's first law of motion in mechanics. Newton's first law says that a body not acted upon by a net external force remains at rest or maintains a constant velocity. In fact, there are always external forces acting upon physical objects (gravity, for example), but the first law provides the starting point for the application of other laws. Similarly, organisms are subject to mutation, selection, and other processes that change gene frequencies, and the effects of these processes are calculated by using the Hardy-Weinberg law as the starting point. There are four processes of gene frequency change: mutation, migration, drift, and natural selection.

The allelic variations that make evolution possible are generated by the process of mutation; but new mutations change gene frequencies very slowly, since mutation rates are low. Moreover, gene mutations are reversible. Changes in gene frequencies due to mutation occur, therefore, very slowly. In any case, allelic frequencies usually are not in mutational equilibrium, because some alleles are favored over others by natural selection. The equilibrium frequencies are then decided by the interaction between mutation and selection, with selection usually having the greater consequence.

I have already discussed the process of mutation. Migration, or gene flow, takes place when individuals migrate from one population to another and interbreed with its members. The genetic make-up of populations changes locally whenever different populations intermingle. In general, the greater the difference in allele frequencies between the resident and the migrant individuals, and the larger the number of migrants, the greater effect the migrants have in changing the genetic constitution of the resident population.

Moreover, gene frequencies can change from one generation to another by a process of pure chance known as genetic drift. This occurs because populations are finite in numbers, and thus the frequency of a gene may change in the following generation by accidents of sampling, just as it is possible to get more or less than 50 "heads" in 100 throws of a coin simply by chance. The magnitude of the gene frequency changes due to genetic drift is inversely related to the size of the population; the larger the number of reproducing individuals, the smaller the effects of genetic drift. The effects of genetic drift in changing gene frequencies from one generation to the next are quite small in most natural populations, which generally consist of thousands of reproducing individuals. The effects over many generations are more important. Genetic drift can have important evolutionary consequences when a new population becomes established by only a few individuals, as in the colonization of islands and lakes. This is one reason why species in neighboring islands, such as those in the

Hawaiian archipelago, are often more heterogeneous than species in comparable continental areas adjacent to one another.

The Process of Natural Selection

The phrase "natural selection" was used by Darwin to refer to any reproductive bias favoring some hereditary variants over others. He proposed that natural selection promotes the adaptation of organisms to the environments in which they live because the organisms carrying such useful variants would leave more descendants than those lacking them. The modern concept of natural selection derives directly from Darwin's but is defined precisely in mathematical terms as a statistical bias favoring some genetic variants over their alternates (the measure to quantify natural selection is called "fitness"). Hereditary variants, favorable or not to the organisms, arise by mutation. Unfavorable ones are eventually eliminated by natural selection; their carriers leave no descendants or leave fewer than those carrying alternative variants. Favorable mutations accumulate over the generations. The process continues indefinitely because the environments that organisms live in are forever changing. Environments change physically—in their climate, physical configuration, and so on—but also biologically, because the predators, parasites, and competitors with which an organism interacts are themselves evolving.

If mutation, migration, and drift were the only processes of evolutionary change, the organization of living things would gradually disintegrate, because they are random processes with respect to adaptation. Those three processes change gene frequencies without regard for the consequences that such changes may have in the ability of the organisms to survive and reproduce. The effects of such processes alone would be analogous to those of a mechanic who changed parts in a motorcar engine at random, with no regard for the role of the parts in the engine. Natural selection keeps the disorganizing effects of mutation and other processes in check because it multiplies beneficial mutations and eliminates harmful ones. But natural selection accounts not only for the preservation and improvement of the organization of living beings but also for their diversity. In different localities or in different circumstances, natural selection favors different traits, precisely those that make the organisms well adapted to their particular circumstances and ways of life.

The effects of natural selection can be studied by measuring the ensuing changes in gene frequencies; but they can also be explored by examining changes on the observable characteristics, or phenotypes, of individuals in a population. Distribution scales of phenotypic traits such as height, weight, number of progeny, or longevity typically show greater numbers of individuals with intermediate values and fewer and fewer toward the extremes (the so-called normal distribution).

When individuals with intermediate phenotypes are favored and extreme phenotypes are selected against, the selection is said to be stabilizing. The range and distribution of phenotypes then remains approximately the same from one generation to another. Stabilizing selection is very common. The individuals that survive and reproduce more successfully are those that have intermediate phenotypic values. Mortality among newborn infants, for example, is highest when they are either very small or very large; infants of intermediate size have a greater chance of surviving.

But the distribution of phenotypes in a population sometimes changes systematically in a particular direction. The physical and biological aspects of the environment are continuously changing, and over long periods of time the changes may be substantial. The climate and even the configuration of the land or waters vary incessantly. Changes also take place in the biotic conditions; that is, in the other organisms present, whether predators, prey, parasites, or competitors. Genetic changes occur as a consequence, because the genotypic fitnesses may be shifted so that different sets of variants are favored. The opportunity for directional selection also arises when organisms colonize new environments where the conditions are different from those of their original habitat. The process of directional selection often takes place in spurts. The replacement of one genetic constitution for another changes the genotypic fitnesses of genes for other traits, which in turn stimulates additional changes, and so on in a cascade of consequences.

The nearly universal success of artificial selection and the rapid response of natural populations to new environmental challenges are evidence that existing variation provides the necessary materials for directional selection as Darwin already explained. More generally, human actions have been an important stimulus to this type of selection. Mankind transforms the environments of many organisms, which rapidly respond to the new environmental challenges through directional selection. Well-known instances are the many cases of insect resistance to pesticides, synthetic substances not present in the natural environment. Whenever a new insecticide is first applied to control a pest, the results are encouraging because a small amount of the insecticide is sufficient to bring the pest organism under control. As time passes, however, the amount required to achieve a certain level of control must be increased again and again until finally it becomes ineffective or economically impractical. This occurs because organisms become resistant to the pesticide through directional selection. The resistance of the housefly, *Musca domestica*, to DDT was first reported in 1947. Resistance to one or more pesticides has now been recorded in more than 100 species of insects.

Sustained directional selection leads to major changes in morphology and ways of life over geologic time. Evolutionary changes that persist in a more or less continuous fashion over long periods of time are known as evolutionary trends. Directional evolutionary changes increased the cranial capacity of the human lineage from the small brain of *Australopithecus*, human ancestors of four million years ago, which was somewhat less than one pound, to a brain three and a half times as large in modern humans, *Homo sapiens*. The evolution of the horse family from more than 50 million years ago to modern times is another of the many well-studied examples of directional selection.

Sometimes, two or more divergent traits in an environment may be favored simultaneously, which is called diversifying selection. No natural environment is homogeneous; rather, the environment of any plant or animal population is a mosaic consisting of more or less dissimilar subenvironments. There is heterogeneity with respect to climate, food resources, and living space. Also, the heterogeneity may be temporal, with change occurring over time, as well as spatial, with dissimilarity found in different areas. Species cope with environmental heterogeneity in diverse ways. One strategy is the selection of a generalist genotype that is well adapted to all of the subenvironments encountered by the species. Another strategy is genetic polymorphism, the selection of a diversified gene pool that yields different genetic make-ups, each adapted to a specific subenvironment.

One important factor in reproduction is mutual attraction between the sexes. The males and females of many animal species are fairly similar in size and shape except for the sexual organs and secondary sexual characteristics such as the breasts of female mammals. There are, however, species in which the sexes exhibit striking dimorphism. Particularly in birds and mammals, the males are often larger and stronger, more brightly colored, or endowed with conspicuous adornments. But bright colors make animals more visible to predators; for example, the long plumage of male peacocks and birds of paradise and the enormous antlers of aged male deer are cumbersome loads in the best of cases. Darwin knew that natural selection could not be expected to favor the evolution of disadvantageous traits, and he was able to offer a solution to this problem. He proposed that such traits arise by "sexual selection," which "depends not on a struggle for existence in relation to other organic beings or to external conditions, but on a struggle between the individuals of one sex, generally the males, for the possession of the other sex." Thus, the colored plumage of the males in some bird species makes them more attractive to their females, which more than compensates for their increased visibility to potential predators. Sexual selection is a topic of intensive research at present.

The apparent altruistic behavior of many animals is, like some manifestations of sexual selection, a trait that at first seems incompatible with the theory of natural selection. Altruism is a form of behavior that benefits other individuals at the expense of the one that performs the action; the fitness of the altruist is diminished by its behavior, whereas individuals that act selfishly benefit from it at no cost to themselves. Accordingly, it might be expected that natural selection would foster the development of selfish behavior and eliminate altruism. This conclusion is not so compelling when it is noticed that the beneficiaries of altruistic behavior are usually relatives. They all carry the same genes, including the genes that promote altruistic behavior. Altruism may evolve by kin selection, which is simply a type of natural selection in which relatives are taken into consideration when evaluating an individual's fitness.

Kin selection is explained as follows. Natural selection favors genes that increase the reproductive success of their carriers, but it is not necessary that all individuals with a given genetic make-up have higher reproductive success. It suffices that carriers of the genotype reproduce more successfully on the average than those possessing alternative genotypes. A parent shares half of its genes with each progeny, so a gene that promotes parental altruism is favored by selection if the behavior's cost to the parent is less than half of its average benefits to the progeny. Such a gene will be more likely to increase in frequency through the generations than an alternative gene that does not promote parental care. The parent spends some energy caring for the progeny because it increases the reproductive success of the parent's genes. But kin selection extends beyond the relationship between parents and their offspring. It facilitates the development of altruistic behavior when the energy invested, or the risk incurred, by an individual is compensated in excess by the benefits ensuing to relatives.

In many species of primates (as well as in other animals), altruism also occurs among unrelated individuals when the behavior is reciprocal and the altruist's costs are smaller than the benefits to the recipient. This reciprocal altruism is found, for example, in the mutual grooming of chimpanzees as they clean each other of lice and other pests. Another example appears in flocks of birds that post sentinels to warn of danger. A crow sitting in a tree watching for predators, while the rest of the flock forages, incurs a small loss by not feeding, but this is well compensated by the protection it receives when it itself forages and others of the flock stand guard.

The Origin of Species

Darwin sought to explain the splendid diversity of the living world: thousands of organisms of the most diverse kinds, from lowly worms to spectacular birds of paradise, from yeasts and molds to oaks and orchids. His *Origin of Species* is a sustained argument showing that the diversity of organisms and their characteristics can be explained as the result of natural processes. As Darwin noted, different species may come about as the result of gradual adaptation to environments that are continuously changing in time and differ from place to place. Natural selection favors different characteristics in different situations.

In everyday experience we identify different kinds of organisms by their appearance. Everyone knows that people belong to the human species and are different from cats and dogs, which in turn are different from each other. There are differences among people, as well as among cats and dogs; but individuals of the same species are considerably more similar among themselves than they are to individuals of other species. But there is more to it than that; a bulldog, a terrier, and a golden retriever are very different in appearance, but they are all dogs because they can interbreed. People can also interbreed with one another, and so can cats, but people cannot interbreed with dogs or cats, nor these with each other. It is, then, clear that although species are usually identified by appearance, there is something basic, of great biological significance, behind similarity of appearance; namely, that individuals of a species are able to interbreed with one another but not with members of other species. This is expressed in the following definition: Species are groups of interbreeding natural populations that are reproductively isolated from other such groups.

The ability to interbreed is of great evolutionary importance, because it determines that species are independent evolutionary units. Genetic changes originate in single individuals; they can spread by natural selection to all members of the species but not to individuals of other species. Thus, individuals of a species share a common gene pool that is not shared by individuals of other species, because they are reproductively isolated.

Although the criterion for deciding whether individuals belong to the same species is clear, there may be ambiguity in practice for two reasons. One is lack of knowledge; it may not be known for certain whether individuals living in different sites below to the same species, because it is not known whether they can naturally interbreed. The other reason for ambiguity is rooted in the nature of evolution as a gradual process. Two geographically separate populations that at one time were members of the same species later may have diverged into two different species. Since the process is gradual there is not a particular point at which it is possible to say that the two populations have become two different species. It is an interesting curiosity that some anti-evolutionists have referred to the existence of species intermediates as evidence against evolution; quite the contrary, such intermediates are precisely expected.

A similar kind of ambiguity arises with respect to organisms living at different times. There is no way to test whether or not today's humans could interbreed with those who lived thousands of years ago. It seems reasonable that living people, or living cats, would be able to interbreed with people, or cats, exactly like those that lived a few generations earlier. But what about the ancestors removed by one thousand or one million generations? The ancestors of modern humans that lived 500 thousand years ago (about 20 thousand generations) are classified in the species *Homo erectus*, whereas present-day humans are classified in a different species, *Homo sapiens*, because those ancestors were quite different from us in appearance and thus it seems reasonable to conclude that interbreeding could not have occurred with modern-like humans. But there is not an exact time at which *Homo erectus* became *Homo sapiens*. It would not be appropriate to classify remote human ancestors and modern humans in the same species just because the changes from one generation to the next are small. It is useful to distinguish between the two groups by means of different species names, just as it is useful to give different names to childhood, adolescence and adulthood, even though there is not one moment when an individual passes from one to the other. Biologists distinguish species in organisms that lived at different times by means of a commonsense rule. If two organisms differ from each other about as much as two living individuals belonging to two different species differ, they will be classified in separate species and given different names.

Bacteria and blue-green algae do not reproduce sexually, but by fission. Organisms that lack sexual reproduction are classified into different species according to criteria such as external and morphology, chemical and physiological properties, and genetic constitution. The definition of species given above applies only to organisms able to interbreed.

Since species are groups of populations reproductively isolated form one another, asking about the origin of species is equivalent to asking how reproductive isolation arises between populations. Two theories have been advanced to answer this question. One theory considers isolation as an accidental by-product of genetic divergence. Populations that become genetically less and less alike (as a consequence, for example, of adaptation to different environments) may eventually be unable to interbreed because their gene pools are disharmonious. The other theory regards isolation as a product of natural selection. Whenever hybrid individuals are less fit than non-hybrids, natural selection will directly promote the development of RIMs. This occurs because genetic variants interfering with hybridization have greater fitness than those favoring hybridization, given that the latter are often present in poorly fit hybrids. Scientists have shown that these two theories of the origin of reproductive isolation are not mutually exclusive.

Adaptive Radiation

This is a form of speciation particularly apparent when colonizers reach geographically remote areas, such as islands, where they find few or no competitors and have an opportunity to diverge as they become adapted to the new environment. Sometimes a multiplicity of new environments becomes available to the colonizers, giving rise to several different lineages and species. This process of rapid divergence of multiple species from a single ancestral lineage is called adaptive radiation.

Examples of speciation by adaptive radiation in archipelagos removed from the mainland have already been mentioned. The Galápagos Islands are about 600 miles off the west coast of South America. When Darwin arrived there in 1835, he discovered many species not found anywhere else in the world—for example, 14 species of finch (known as Darwin's finches). These passerine birds have adapted to a diversity of habitats and diets, some feeding mostly on plants, others exclusively on insects. The various shapes of their bills are clearly adapted to probing, grasping, biting, or crushing—the diverse ways in which these different Galápagos species obtain their food. The explanation for such diversity (which is not found in finches from the continental mainland) is that the ancestor of Galápagos finches arrived in the islands before other kinds of birds and encountered an abundance of unoccupied ecological opportunities. The finches underwent adaptive radiation, evolving a variety of species with ways of life capable of exploiting niches that in continental faunas are exploited by different kinds of birds.

Striking examples of adaptive radiation occur in the Hawaiian Islands. The archipelago consists of several volcanic islands, ranging from less than one million to more than ten million years in age, far away from any continent or other large islands. An astounding number of plant and animal species of certain kinds exist in the islands while many other kinds are lacking. Among the species that have evolved in the islands, there are about two dozen (about one-third of them now extinct) of honeycreepers, birds of the family *Drepanididae*, all derived from a single immigrant form. In fact, all but one of Hawaii's 71 native bird species are endemic—that is, they have evolved there and are found nowhere else. More than 90 percent of the native species of the hundreds of flowering plants, land mollusks, and insects in Hawaii are also endemic, as are two-thirds of the 168 species of ferns. About one-third of the world's total number of known species of *Drosophila* flies (more than 500) are native Hawaiian species. The species of *Drosophila* in Hawaii have diverged by adaptive radiation from one or a few colonizers, which encountered an assortment of ecological opportunities that in other lands are occupied by different groups of flies or insects.

Quantum Speciation

Rapid modes of speciation are known by a variety of names, such as "quantum," "rapid," and "saltational" speciation, all suggesting the short time involved. An important form of quantum speciation is polyploidy, which occurs by the multiplication of entire sets of chromosomes. A typical (diploid) organism carries in the nucleus of each cell two sets of chromosomes, one inherited from each parent; a polyploid organism has several sets of chromosomes. Many cultivated plants are polyploid: bananas have three sets of chromosomes, potatoes have four, bread wheat has six, some strawberries have eight. All major groups of plants have natural polyploid species, but they are most common among flowering plants (angiosperms) of which about 47 percent are polyploids.

In animals, polyploidy is relatively rare because it disrupts the balance between chromosomes involved in the determination of sex. But polyploid species are found in hermaphroditic animals (individuals having both male and female organs), which include snails and earthworms, as well as in forms with parthenogenetic females (which produce viable progeny without fertilization), such as some beetles, sow bugs, goldfish, and salamanders.

Reconstruction of Evolutionary History

It is possible to look at two sides of evolution: one, called "anagenesis," refers to changes that occur within a lineage; the other, called "cladogenesis," refers to the split of a lineage into two or more separate lineages. Anagenetic evolution has, over the last four million years more than tripled the size of the human brain; in the lineage of the horse, it has reduced the number of toes from four to one. Cladogenetic evolution has produced the extraordinary diversity of the living world, with more than two million species of animals, plants, fungi, and microorganisms.

The evolution of all living organisms, or of a subset of them, can be represented as a tree, with branches that divide into two or more as time progresses. Such "trees" are called phylogenies. Their branches represent evolving lineages, some of which eventually die out while others persist down to the present time. Evolutionists are interested in the history of life and hence in the topology, or configuration, of evolution's trees. They also want to know the anagenetic changes along lineages and the timing of important events.

Tree relationships are ascertained by means of several complementary sources of evidence. First, there is the fossil record, which provides definitive evidence of relationships among some groups of organisms, but is far from complete and often seriously deficient. Second, there is comparative anatomy, the comparative study of living forms; and the related disciplines of comparative embryology, cytology, ethology, biogeography, and others. In recent years the comparative study of informational macromolecules—proteins and nucleic acids—has become a powerful tool for the study of evolution's history. We saw earlier how the results from these disciplines demonstrate that evolution has occurred.   Advanced methods have now been developed to reconstruct evolution's history.

These methods make it possible to identify when the correspondence of features in different organisms is due to inheritance from a common ancestor, which is called "homology." The forelimbs of humans, whales, dogs, and bats are homologous. The skeletons of these limbs are all constructed of bones arranged according to the same pattern because they derive from an ancestor with similarly arranged forelimbs (see Figure 2). Correspondence of features due to similarity of function but not related to common descent is termed "analogy." The wings of birds and of flies are analogous. Their wings are not modified versions of a structure present in a common ancestor but rather have developed independently as adaptations to a common function, flying.

Homology can be recognized not only between different organisms but also between repetitive structures of the same organism. This has been called serial homology. There is serial homology, for example, between the arms and legs of humans, among the seven cervical vertebrae of mammals, and among the branches or leaves of a tree. The jointed appendages of arthropods are elaborate examples of serial homology. Crayfish have 19 pairs of appendages, all built according to the same basic pattern but serving diverse functions—sensing, chewing, food handling, walking, mating, egg carrying, and swimming. Serial homologies are not useful in reconstructing the phylogenetic relationships of organisms, but they are an important dimension of the evolutionary process.

Relationships in some sense akin to those between serial homologs exist at the molecular level between genes and proteins derived from ancestral gene duplications. The genes coding for the various hemoglobin chains are an example (see Figure 4 on following page). About 500 million years ago a chromosome segment carrying the gene coding for hemoglobin became

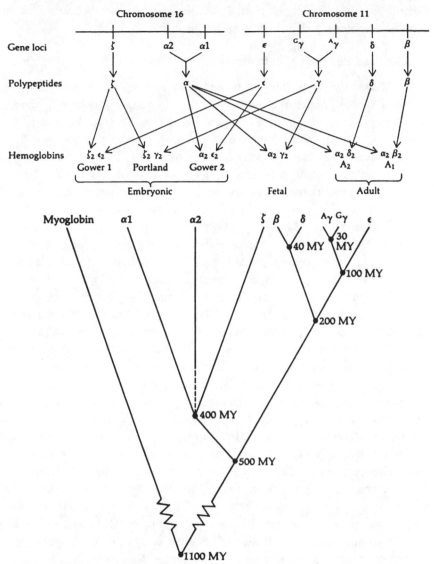

Figure 4: Position of several genes for hemoglobin in the human chromosomes 11 and 16. These genes have arisen by duplication over millions of years and are active at different ages of the individual and serve slightly different functions.

duplicated, so that the genes in the different segments thereafter evolved in somewhat different ways, one eventually giving rise to the modern gene coding for alpha hemoglobin, the other for beta hemoglobin. The beta hemoglobin gene became duplicated again about 200 million years ago, giving rise to the gamma (fetal) hemoglobin. The alpha, beta, and gamma hemoglobin genes are homologous; similarities in their DNA sequences occur because they are modified descendants of a single ancestral sequence.

Gradual and Punctuational Evolution

Morphological evolution is by and large a gradual process, as shown by the fossil record. Major evolutionary changes are usually due to a building up over the ages of relatively small changes. But the fossil record is discontinuous. Fossil strata are separated by sharp boundaries; accumulation of fossils within a geologic deposit (stratum) is fairly constant over time, but the transition from one stratum to another may involve gaps of tens of thousands of years. Different species, characterized by small but discontinuous morphological changes, typically appear at the boundaries between strata, whereas the fossils within a stratum exhibit little morphological variation. That is not to say that the transition from one stratum to another always involves sudden changes in morphology; on the contrary, fossil forms often persist virtually unchanged through several geologic strata, each representing millions of years.

Paleontologists attributed the apparent morphological discontinuities of the fossil record to the discontinuity of the sediments; that is, to the substantial time gaps encompassed in the boundaries between strata. The assumption is that, if the fossil deposits were more continuous, they would show a more gradual transition of form. Even so, morphological evolution would not always keep progressing gradually, because some forms, at least, remain unchanged for extremely long times. Examples are the lineages known as "living fossils": the lamp shell *Lingula*, a genus of brachiopod that appears to have remained essentially unchanged since the Ordovician Period, some 450 million years ago; or the tuatara (*Sphenodon punctatus*), a reptile that has shown little morphological evolution for nearly 200 million years since the early Mesozoic.

According to some paleontologists, however, the frequent discontinuities of the fossil record are not artifacts created by gaps in the record, but rather reflect the true nature of morphological evolution, which happens in sudden bursts associated with the formation of new species. The lack of morphological evolution, or stasis, of lineages such as *Lingula* and *Sphenodon* is in turn due to lack of speciation within those lineages. The proposition that morphological evolution is jerky, with most morphological change occurring during the brief speciation events and virtually no change during the subsequent existence of the species, is known as the "punctuated equilibrium" model of morphological evolution.

The question whether morphological evolution in the fossil record is predominantly punctuational or gradual is a subject of active investigation and debate. The imperfection of the record makes it unlikely that the issue will be settled in the foreseeable future. Intensive study of a favorable and abundant set of fossils may be expected to substantiate punctuated or gradual evolution in particular cases. But the argument is not about whether only one or the other pattern ever occurs; it is about their relative frequency. Some paleontologists argue that morphological evolution is in most cases gradual and only rarely jerky, whereas others think the opposite is true. Much of the problem is that gradualness or jerkiness is in the eye of the beholder.

Consider the evolution of rib strength (the ratio of rib height to rib width) within a lineage of fossil brachipods of the genus Eocelia. An abundant sample of fossils from the Silurian Period in Wales has been analyzed, with the results shown in Figure 5 (on the following page). One possible interpretation of the data is that rib strength changed little or not at all from 415 to 413 million years ago; rapid change ensued for the next one million years, with virtual absence of change from 412 to 407 million years ago; another short burst of change occurred around 406 million years ago, followed by a final period of stasis (absence of morphological change). On the other hand, the record shown in the figure may be interpreted as not particularly punctuated but rather as a gradual process, with the rate of change somewhat greater at particular times.

DNA and Protein Evolution

The advances of molecular biology have made possible the comparative study of proteins and the nucleic acid DNA, which is the repository of hereditary (evolutionary and developmental) information. The relationship of proteins to the DNA is so immediate that they closely reflect the hereditary information. This reflection is not perfect, because the genetic code is redundant and, consequently, some differences in the DNA do not yield differences in the proteins. Moreover, it is not complete, because a large fraction of the DNA (about 90 percent in many organisms) does not code for proteins. Nevertheless, proteins are so closely related to the information contained in the DNA that they, as well as the nucleic acids, are called informational macromolecules.

Nucleic acids and proteins are linear molecules made up of sequences of units—nucleotides in the case of nucleic acids, amino acids in the case of proteins—which retain considerable amounts of evolutionary information. Comparing two macromolecules establishes the number of their units that are different. Because evolution usually occurs by changing one unit at a time, the number of differences is an indication of the recency of common ancestry. Changes in evolutionary rates may create difficulties, but macromolecular studies have two notable advantages over comparative anatomy and other

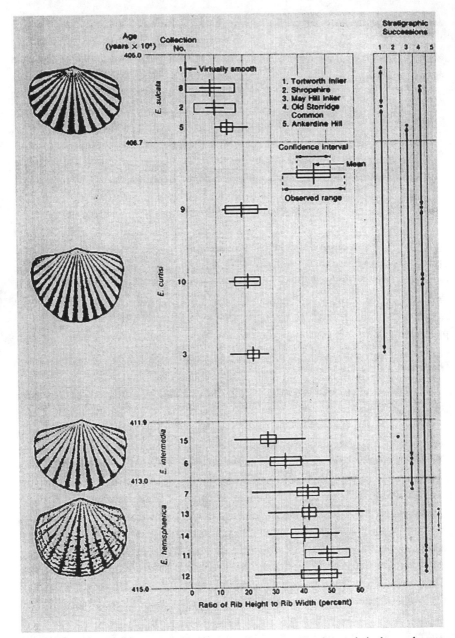

Figure 5: Evolution of rib strength in the brachiopod *Eocoelia*. The time scale in the graph ranges from about 405 to 415 million years ago; rib strength is indicated on the horizontal scale. It remained rather constant until near 413 million years ago, when it changed rapidly for a while, and then continued to change more gradually until 405 million years ago. Rate of change in this character can easily be expressed as change in the ratio of rib height to rib width per million years.

classical disciplines. One is that the information is more readily quantifiable. The number of units that are different is precisely established when the sequence of units is known for a given macromolecule in different organisms. The other advantage is that comparisons can be made even between very different sorts of organisms. There is very little that comparative anatomy can say when organisms as diverse as yeasts, pine trees, and human beings are compared; but there are homologous DNA and protein molecules that can be compared in all three.

Informational macromolecules provide information not only about the topology of evolutionary history (that is, the configuration of evolutionary trees), but also about the amount of genetic change that has occurred in any given branch. It might seem at first that determining the number of changes in a branch would be impossible for proteins and nucleic acids, because it would require comparison of molecules from organisms that lived in the past with those from living organisms. But this determination can actually be made using elaborate methods developed by scientists who investigate the evolution of DNA and proteins.

The Molecular Clock of Evolution.

One conspicuous attribute of molecular evolution is that differences between homologous molecules can readily be quantified and expressed as, for example, proportions of nucleotides or amino acids that have changed. Rates of evolutionary change can, therefore, be more precisely established with respect to DNA or proteins than with respect to morphological traits. Studies of molecular evolution rates have led to the proposition that macromolecules evolve as fairly accurate clocks. The first observations came in the 1960s when it was noted that the numbers of amino-acid differences between homologous proteins of any two given species seemed to be nearly proportional to the time of their divergence from a common ancestor.

If the rate of evolution of a protein or gene were approximately the same in the evolutionary lineages leading to different species, proteins and DNA sequences would provide a molecular clock of evolution. The sequences could then be used not only to reconstruct the evolutionary tree (that is the configuration of the branches), but also the time when the various branching events occurred. Consider, for example, the tree shown in Figure 6 (on the following page). If the substitution of nucleotides in the gene coding for cytochrome c occurred at a constant rate through time, one could determine the time elapsed along any branch of the tree simply by examining the number of nucleotide substitutions along that branch. One would need only to calibrate the clock by reference to an outside source, such as the fossil record, that would give us the actual geologic time elapsed in at least one specific lineage.

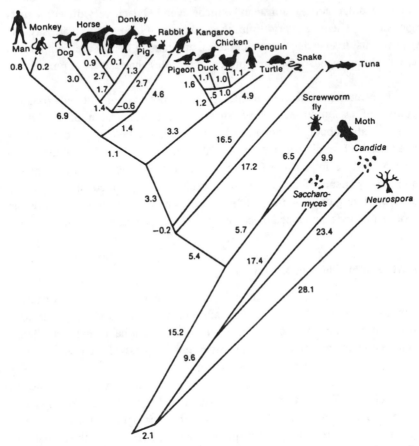

Figure 6: Evolutionary tree of 20 species derived from the composition of the protein cytochrome c. The numbers are estimates of the changes in this protein that have occurred during evolution. The tree agrees well with the pattern of phylogenetic relationships worked out by classical techniques of comparative morphology and from the fossil record. This tree, first published in 1967, is one of the earliest examples of the reconstruction of evolution's history by molecular evolution.

The molecular evolutionary clock is not a metronomic clock, like a watch or other timepiece that measures time exactly, but a stochastic clock like radioactive decay. In a stochastic clock, the probability of a certain amount of change is constant, although some variation occurs in the actual amount of change. Over fairly long periods of time, a stochastic clock is quite accurate. The enormous potential of the molecular evolutionary clock lies in the fact that each gene or protein is a separate clock. Each clock "ticks" at a different rate—

the rate of evolution characteristic of a particular gene or protein, but each of the thousands and thousands of genes or proteins provides an independent measure of the same evolutionary events (see Figure 7).

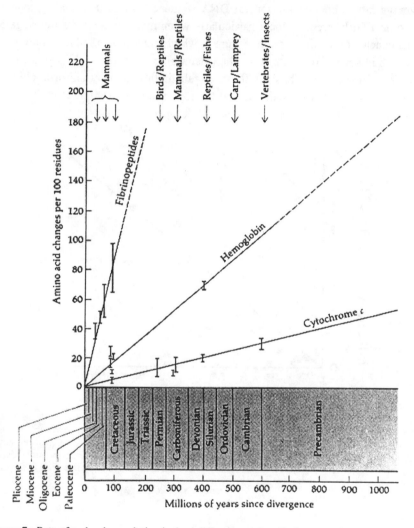

Figure 7: Rate of molecular evolution in three different proteins. Each gene and protein evolves at a distinct rate. Several can be used in combination in order to elucidate with precision a particular question.

Evolutionists have found that the amount of variation observed in the evolution of DNA and proteins is greater than is expected from a stochastic clock; in other words, the clock is inaccurate. The discrepancies in evolutionary rates along different lineages are not excessively large, however. It turns out that it is possible to time phylogenetic events with as much accuracy as may be desired; but more genes or proteins (about two to four times as many) must be examined than would be required if the clock were stochastically accurate. The average rates obtained for several DNA sequences or proteins taken together become a fairly precise clock, particularly when many species are investigated. This conclusion is illustrated in Figure 8, which plots the cumulative number of changes in seven proteins against the paleontological dates of divergence of 17 species of mammals. The overall rate of substitution is fairly uniform, although some primates (shown by the dots at the lower left of the figure) evolved at a slower rate than the average for the rest of the species.

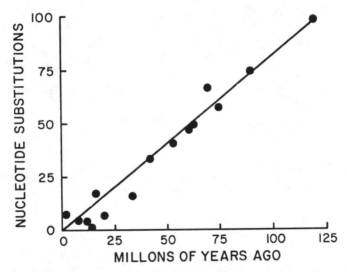

Figure 8: Cumulative change ("nucleotide substitutions") for seven proteins in 17 species of mammals. The solid line has been drawn from the origin to the outermost point, and corresponds to the average rate of evolution for all species. The fit between the observed number of nucleotide substitutions and the solid line is fairly good in general. However, in the primates (points below the diagonal at lower left) protein evolution seems to have occurred at a slower rate than in the other mammals.

Human Evolution

Many fossils representing recent ancestors of our species have been discovered, particularly in the last two decades. A very brief summary of what is known goes as follows. Our closest biological relatives are the great apes and, among them, the chimpanzees, who are more related to us than they are to the gorillas, and much more than to the orangutans. The hominid lineage diverged from the chimpanzee lineage 5-7 million years ago (Mya) and it evolved exclusively in the African continent until the emergence of *Homo erectus*, somewhat before 1.8 Mya. The first known hominid, *Ardipithecus ramidus*, lived 4.4 Mya, but it is not certain that it was bipedal or in the direct line of descent to modern humans, *Homo sapiens*. The recently described *Australopithecus anamensis*, dated 3.9-4.2 Mya, was bipedal and has been placed in the line of descent to *Australopithecus afarensis, Homo habilis, H. erectus*, and *H. sapiens*. Other hominids, not in the direct line of descent to modern humans, are *Australopithecus africanus, Paranthropus aethiopicus, P. boisei*, and *P. robustus*, who lived in Africa at various times between 3 and 1 Mya, a period when three or four hominid species lived contemporaneously in the African continent.

Shortly after its emergence in tropical or subtropical eastern Africa, H. erectus spread to other continents. Fossil remains of *H. erectus* are known from Africa, Indonesia (Java), China, the Middle East, and Europe. *H. erectus* fossils from Java have been dated 1.81+0.04 and 1.66+0.04 Mya, and from Georgia between 1.6 and 1.8 Mya. Anatomically distinctive *H. erectus* fossils have been found in Spain, deposited before 780 thousand years ago, the oldest in southern Europe.

The transition from *H. erectus* to *H. sapiens* occurred around 400 thousand years ago, although this date is not well determined owing to uncertainty as to whether some fossils are erectus or "archaic" forms of sapiens. *H. erectus* persisted for some time in Asia, until 250 thousand years ago in China and perhaps until 100 thousand years ago in Java, and thus was coetaneous with early members of its descendant species, *H. sapiens*. Fossil remains of Neanderthal hominids (*Homo neanderthalensis*) appeared in Europe around 200 thousand years ago and persisted until thirty or forty thousand years ago. The Neanderthals had, like *H. sapiens*, large brains. Until recently, they were thought to be ancestral to anatomically modern humans, but now we know that modern humans appeared at least 100 thousand years ago, much before the disappearance of the Neanderthals. Moreover, in caves in the Middle East, fossils of modern humans have been found dated 120-100 thousand years ago, as well as Neanderthals dated at 60 and 70 thousand years ago, followed again by modern humans dated at 40 thousand years ago. It is unclear whether the two forms repeatedly replaced one another by migration from other regions, or whether they coexisted in some areas. Recent genetic evidence indicates that interbreeding between *sapiens* and *neanderthalensis* never occurred.

There is considerable controversy about the origin of modern humans. Some anthropologists argue that the transition from *H. erectus* to archaic *H. sapiens* and later to anatomically modern humans occurred consonantly in various parts of the Old World. Proponents of this "multiregional model" emphasize fossil evidence showing regional continuity in the transition from *H. erectus* to archaic and then modern *H. sapiens*. In order to account for the transition from one to another species (something which cannot happen independently in several places), they postulate that genetic exchange occurred from time to time between populations, so that the species evolved as a single gene pool, even though geographic differentiation occurred and persisted, just as geographically differentiated populations exist in other animal species, as well as in living humans. This explanation depends on the occurrence of persistent migrations and interbreeding between populations from different continents, of which no direct evidence exists. Moreover, it is difficult to reconcile the multiregional model with the contemporary existence of different species or forms in different regions, such as the persistence of H. erectus in China and Java for more than one hundred thousand years after the emergence of *H. sapiens*. Other scientists argue instead that modern humans first arose in Africa or in the Middle East somewhat prior to 100 thousand years ago and from there spread throughout the world, replacing elsewhere the preexisting populations of *H. erectus* or archaic *H. sapiens*. The African (or Middle East) origin of modern humans is supported by a wealth of recent genetic evidence and is, therefore, favored by many evolutionists.

Notes

1.   An excellent collection of essays on the conflict between Christianity and science is David C. Lindberg and Ronald N. Numbers, eds., *God and Nature: Historical Essays on the Encounter between Christianity and Science* (Berkeley and Los Angeles: University of California Press, 1986), pp. xi-516.

2.   The perception of conflict is far from universal. Pope John Paul II has been cited earlier. On the matter of the immortality of the soul and, more generally, the uniqueness of humans as created "in the image of God," see Warren S. Brown, Nancey Murphy, and H. Newton Malony, eds., *Portraits of Human Nature* (Minneapolis: Fortress Press, 1998).

3.   The perception of conflict is far from universal. Pope John Paul II has been cited earlier. On the matter of the immortality of the soul and, more generally, the uniqueness of humans as created "in the image of God," see Warren S. Brown, Nancey Murphy, and H. Newton Malony, eds., Portraits of Human Nature (Minneapolis: Fortress Press, 1998).

3

The Mechanism of Evolution

MARK RIDLEY

We have discussed so far two requirements of a valid theory of evolution: it must explain why evolution takes place and it must fit the facts of heredity. There is one further requirement. The theory must explain why organisms are well designed for life. The traits of organisms encoded by Mendelian genes are not just any old traits, and the changes of evolution are not any old changes. The traits of organisms are well designed; they are (as we say) adaptations.

An example may make the meaning of adaptation clear. The appearance of many animals makes them difficult to detect; they are camouflaged. Coloration, structure, and behaviour may all contribute. The coloration of many moths, for instance, resembles the tree bark on which they rest; the structure of leaf insects resembles a leaf. Behavioural adaptation is also necessary, for a camouflaged animal must be able to recognize and imitate the bit of the environment to which it is adapted. A leaf insect must settle on the branch of a tree—it would not be camouflaged on the trunk—and, like a leaf, it should sway gently in the breeze.

Camouflage is an adaptation. It makes the camouflaged animal less likely to be eaten by a predator. The camouflaged animal would survive better than a similar, but uncamouflaged, animal. Adaptation means good design for life. To understand how any particular property of an organism is adapted, it is necessary to think how it enhances its bearer's chances of survival and reproduction. For camouflage this is quite easy. Camouflage makes it more difficult for predators to see the camouflaged prey, which is therefore eaten less. That is the argument that allows us to call camouflage an adaptation; without it we could not say how camouflage was adaptive, or even whether it was an adaptation at all.

The problem of the mechanism of evolution is to find a theory that can explain evolution, that can explain adaptation, and that fits the facts of heredity. Only one theory is known that passes all three tests: the theory of natural selection. It is the work of this chapter to explain natural selection and to show that it can indeed account for all of the facts of evolution and adaptation. The absence of an alternative, together with the fact that no known properties of organisms are inconsistent with natural selection, means that this problem of evolution, like the previous two, is effectively solved. Not everyone, however, would agree.

To explain natural selection, we can stay with the case of camouflage. It supplies one of the classic pieces of work on natural selection, that of H. B. D. Kettlewell on industrial melanism in the peppered moth *Biston betulania* in Great Britain. This moth has two types, a dark melanic type and a lighter peppered type. The difference is controlled by Mendelian genes, although not by a single gene, as was the case for tall and short pea plants. The facts, considerably simplified, are these. Before the Industrial Revolution the peppered type was much the commoner of the two. Then in the early and mid-nineteenth century, in industrial areas, the melanic type increased in frequency to become the more abundant of the two; in non-industrial areas the peppered type remained the commoner. As industrial activity decreased in some areas during the twentieth century, the peppered type became common again.

Such are the facts. Now for the explanation. The soot discharged by great factories kills the lichen that grow on tree trunks, leaving the tree trunks bare and dark. The peppered type is camouflaged on a lichen-covered trunk, but not on a bare lichen-less trunk; the melanic type is camouflaged on the bare lichen-less trunks, but stands out on the lichen-covered, normal trunks. The moths are eaten by birds, which hunt for their prey visually. That is enough to explain the facts. During the Industrial Revolution, the background on which the moths settle changed colour. It changed from a light peppered colour to black. Where the peppered type had previously been camouflaged, it now became conspicuous: it was more easily seen by birds, and was eaten more. Where the melanic type was previously conspicuous, it now became camouflaged, and was eaten less. The change in the relative frequencies of the two types was caused by bird predation against a changing background.

Kettlewell checked his interpretation by experiment. He placed melanic and peppered types on tree trunks in industrial and in non-industrial areas; from a hide, he measured the rate at which the two kinds were taken by birds. The results fitted the theory. The birds behaved as it demanded. The melanic type was taken more in the non-industrial area, the peppered type in the industrial area.

The true causes of the change in the frequencies of peppered and melanic types of *Biston betularia* are known to be more complex than that simple summary. But the summary will serve to illustrate natural selection. The type that survived better, in one area, increased in frequency: there was an evolutionary change, towards the better-adapted type, in the moth population.

We have seen natural selection in an example. Let us now consider it in the abstract. What are the factors needed in order for evolution to result? The first is that the difference between types must be heritable. Evolution would be impossible otherwise. If the difference were not heritable, the offspring of the two types would both contain the same frequencies of melanic and peppered types; and then even if the melanic type survived better, and left more offspring, evolution would not take place towards the melanic type. Differential survival, although it cannot by itself produce evolution, is another requirement. In order for the melanic type to increase in frequency it had to survive better. But differential survival only matters because it usually results in differential reproduction. The melanic type actually increased in frequency in industrial areas because (being more likely to survive to reproduce) it contributed relatively more offspring to the next generation than did the peppered types.

Natural selection can also, in theory, work on differential reproduction without differential survival. If the two types survived equally well, but one laid more eggs on average than the other, then there would be an evolutionary increase in the frequency of the more fecund type even though the chance of survival of the two was the same.

We have now defined the abstract conditions for evolution by natural selection. The different types must be genetically different and they must reproduce at different rates; there must then automatically be an evolutionary increase in the frequency of the type that reproduces more. It is inevitable. If the premises are met, the conclusion must follow.

It is one thing to show that natural selection works in the case of camouflage. It is another to extend the principle to all the other traits of organisms. But Darwin provided a general argument. It is his famous Malthusian argument. Organisms produce more offspring than can survive: most of them die before maturity. The result is a perpetual struggle for existence. Any heritable improvement in any trait will therefore increase in frequency in the population. Natural selection is constantly at work on all the properties of an organism. Camouflage is not an exception.

Now that we have seen what natural selection is, we can ask whether it meets the three requirements to explain evolution, explain adaptation, and fit the facts of heredity. The example showed that it can, but let us consider how. It explains adaptation almost automatically. Forms that are better designed for life in their environments will tend to leave more offspring. By natural selection, they will come to predominate over less well designed forms.

The explanation is so automatic that some critics have suspected it is merely verbal. They have sniffed a tautology. Indeed, Darwin's argument has been accompanied, almost throughout its history, by the criticism that it is circular. The Bishop of Carlisle (I think) stated it first in 1890, but it has become especially popular recently. Natural selection is often summarized as 'the survival of the fittest'. (The phrase is Herbert Spencer's, not Darwin's. Darwin never liked it, although not because it made his argument sound circular.) The criticism is this. Survival just means staying alive; but what about 'the fittest'? That too, in the end, only seems to mean those that survive. 'The survival of the fittest' can then be translated as the survival of those that survive, which is clearly a tautology. As Sir Karl Popper has remarked, 'there is hardly any possibility of testing a theory as feeble as this'.

If the criticism is valid, Darwin's theory would be in peril. The interest of natural selection is that it purports to explain the traits of organisms. But if it is circular it cannot be explanatory. Circular arguments do not explain anything. If the only criterion of an adaptation is survival, natural selection means adaptation rather than explains it. The Darwinian theory therefore must possess a criterion of an adaptation independent of whether natural selection favours the trait. Fittest must mean more than just survival.

Let us reconsider the camouflage of *Biston betularia*, to see whether adaptation in this case means anything more than mere survival. If the theory of natural selection were circular it would merely say that the type that survived better increased in frequency in evolution. But is that all it says? No, it is not. The important part has been omitted: it is so obvious in this case that it might be overlooked by a hasty critic. The missing part is the explanation of why one type survives better: camouflage. Camouflage matters because peppered moths are killed by visually hunting birds. On a lichen-less trunk, the melanic type is less easy to see than the peppered type. The melanic type does increase in frequency where it survives best: but the explanation of this fact is that the melanic type is better camouflaged, and less subject to avian predation, in polluted woods.

The arguments concerning camouflage and predation provide the criterion of adaptation. They are independent of survival. They are also testable. We can test, by observation, whether melanic moths are better camouflaged in polluted areas. Human vision may differ from bird vision, but we can test for that too and (if necessary) make allowance. Measurements of which trait survives best in an environment are not the criterion of adaptation: the criterion comes from an argument of design, which must explain how the trait is designed for life in its natural environment, and whose assumptions have been tested as thoroughly as possible. The best-designed form should (if the argument is correct) also survive best. But the measurement of survival rates is a laborious task, rarely performed in practice. More often the biologist remains content with the argument of design. That argument alone provides the criterion, independent of survival, of the 'fittest' in that phrase 'the survival of the fittest'. The theory of natural selection that the Bishop of Carlisle and Sir Karl Popper thought tautologous was an incomplete version of the theory. When its original parts are restored, the circular argument becomes a scientific theory.

So natural selection passes the first test: it explains adaptation. But what about evolution? It succeeds here too, for it will cause evolution when the environment changes. The evolution of the moth population was driven by a change in the colour of its background environment. In this case the relevant environmental variable is fairly obvious. But the 'environment' will often be a more subtle property than background colour. It may be any property of the inanimate world in which the organism lives, or of the living forms that it competes with, of its own or other species. A predator is a part of the environment of its prey: a change in a predator that makes it better at finding prey will be experienced, by the prey species, as a change in the environment. The change may cause the evolution of some new counter-adaptation to foil the predator, or (failing that) it may drive the prey species extinct. A change in the courtship demands of a female will be experienced, by the male of the species, as an environmental change, which demands the evolution of new courting behaviour.

Finally, natural selection fits the Mendelian facts. We have seen that, within heredity, there is no directing process that could cause evolution. There is the potential for random drift, but not for directed change. This is exactly what natural selection requires. Natural selection itself acts as a directing process, which drives evolution towards adapted states. From heredity, it requires no more than raw material. Mendelism provides that. Raw material comes from recombination, mutation, and the inheritance of pre-existing genetic variants. Mendelian genes are particulate—they do not blend—which conserves the variation while natural selection operates on it.

So far we have considered only evolution on the small scale: changes in the relative frequencies of two pre-existing types, the peppered and melanic types, within one moth species. But natural selection can also produce a population of well-adapted moths from a new mutation. If the melanic type did not already exist in the industrial area, it might have arisen as a new mutation and exactly the same process could have carried it up to become predominant type in the population. In order for the well-adapted type to be naturally selected it does have to appear to begin with by a chance mutation, but that is not very unlikely. Mutations will be appearing all the time, in all directions, some darker, some lighter, some with different patterns of peppering.

Mutation itself, it is important to realize, is not responsible for producing the population of adapted moths. Mutations are random, but adaptations are non-random states of nature.   Mutation therefore cannot alone explain adaptation. Natural selection is needed, to select out those minority of mutants that happen to be adapted to the prevailing local environment. The selection, not the mutational, process produces adaptation. Chance is only needed to produce the random variation that selection works from.   Darwinism emphatically is not a theory of evolution by chance. Unfortunately, some of its critics have supposed that it is. Starting with the distinguished astronomer Sir John Herschel, who after reading the Origin dismissed it as 'the law of higgledy piggledy', they have pointed out that Darwin's theory cannot possibly be right, because life is a highly non-random state of nature. The argument is correct, but misdirected: evolution cannot indeed be explained by chance, but natural selection does not try to do so.

Natural selection has passed all three tests. Its main alternatives are all theories of directed variation. The inheritance of acquired characters is the best known of them. How do these theories fare in our three tests? They can all explain evolution, but (as we saw in the previous chapter) they all fail on the facts of heredity. They could be rejected for that reason alone. But facts, in science, are often short-lived.   Although no one has yet succeeded in demonstrating the inheritance of acquired characters (and not for want of trying, sometimes too hard) perhaps someone one day will succeed. It is therefore interesting to see whether the theory of the inheritance of acquired characters can survive the third test: can it, in principle, explain adaptation?

Richard Dawkins has asked this question. He has answered it too, in the negative. How does the inheritance of acquired characters explain adaptation? It is undoubtedly adaptive for a blacksmith to grow bigger muscles. If all the population followed the blacksmith's calling, they would presumably all grow bigger muscles. If that acquired adaptation were then inherited, the population would soon come to contain more muscular men, whose muscularity was adaptive. The inheritance of acquired characters does thus appear to explain adaptation. But when it is examined more closely, the appearance turns out to be deceptive. In truth, the theory takes the whole problem of adaptation for granted. That the blacksmith should make an adaptive response, growing larger muscles when larger muscles are needed, has been assumed; it has not been proved. But it needs proof. Why should a blacksmith's muscles grow larger when exercised? They might just as well grow smaller, because they are being used up. *In fact* they grow larger, but the fact itself is what needs to be explained. The extra growth is an adaptation, which the theory must explain, not merely take for granted.

To explain the adaptive response of the blacksmith's arm, the theory of the inheritance of acquired characters would have to fall back on some other theory that actually did explain adaptation. Natural selection is the only known theory that does. To grow bigger muscles when they are needed is an adaptive response. If that trait enabled the blacksmith's ancestors to reproduce more than competitors who lacked it, then it would have been favoured by natural selection. Even if acquired characters were inherited, therefore (which they are not), the true explanation of adaptation would have to come from the theory of natural selection. Without it the inheritance of acquired characters fails the third test.

All theories of 'directed' variation must suffer from the same defect. They all lack an explanation of how the directed variations manage to be adapted to the environment in which they must live. They must either fall back on natural selection to explain adaptation, or fail to explain it. In the former case, directed variation can be no more than an additional factor, and not an alternative, to natural selection; in the latter case, it must be rejected because it cannot explain the most striking feature of life, that living things are designed for living.

The same general kind of argument, although in a more specific form, has been turned against natural selection. Natural selection could undoubtedly have produced some kinds of adaptations, such as camouflage, but could it have produced them all? It has been argued that it could not. The particular kind of adaptation that (it has been said) natural selection in principle cannot produce may be exemplified by that highly complex structure, the eye. The eye is not only complex, but 'co-adapted' in the sense that the different parts making up the whole are closely adapted to each other. The shape of the lens, for instance, is adapted to the size of the eye. It is difficult to imagine how one part could be changed without appropriate changes in all the other parts that it co-operates with. Natural selection, however, can only change one part at a time, for the following reason. The chance of a single advantageous mutation is low enough; but the chance of simultaneous advantageous mutations, in the different parts of a complex organ, must be lower still. If the chance of one correct mutation is (say) less than one in a million, then the chance of ten correct ones would be impossibly small. For ten changes the chance will be one in 10^{-60}, which is far too low a probability for the event ever to have taken place. Natural selection can only work on mutations that actually have arisen, and advantageous mutations are only likely to arise one at a time. This being so, if there are complex organs that could only have arisen by exact changes in many different parts at the same time then they probably could not have evolved by natural selection. The critic of natural selection will claim that such organs exist; the Darwinian will reply that they do not. We have now defined the problem of co-adaptation.

The Darwinian theory has three solutions. The first, which we shall consider for the eye, is to argue that the co-adapted organ actually could have evolved in small stages, gradually improving at its constant function; let us call this piecemeal evolution. The second, which we shall consider for the evolution of flight, is to argue that the organ evolved in small stages, but that it changed its function during evolution. Feathers, for example, might initially have served in thermo-regulation, and only later have come to be used in flight. The third solution is symbiosis. In this case, the parts of a complex organ evolve separately, in different species, and are only put together later, when many of the parts have been separately perfected. In all three cases the Darwinian denies (as he must) that the complex co-adaptation arose in a single chance event.

I should have liked to use the origin of life as an example of piecemeal evolution. The origin of life is (next to the eye) the most commonly alleged instance of co-adaptation. The case against natural selection runs something like this. Even the simplest self-sufficient self-reproducing organisms, such as the simplest bacteria, contain many interacting parts. There is not only a complex hereditary molecule of DNA; there are also many (perhaps a minimum of 50) different proteins, a membrane, and other structures. They are all essential for the bacterium to live: if you took away any of them, it would die without reproducing. Natural selection could not then have built up bacteria from simpler forms of life. Without natural selection, all that the Darwinian is left with to explain the origin of the bacterium is chance. But the chance that molecules, combined at random, would form something as well designed as a bacterium is impossibly small.

For the pure nihilist, this is all very well. But for anyone who wants to understand the origin of life, it is something of a paradox. Natural selection is the only theory that we have to explain evolution; an explanation, if it is going to come from anywhere, will come from natural selection. If it really were true that no living thing could be simpler than a bacterium, then we really should have a problem. But no one has ever proved that simpler life forms could not exist. The Darwinian would try to explain the origin of life through a series of intermediate stages between a pre-biotic chemical stage and the bacterium. Such intermediate stages can be imagined. But merely imagining them does not serve any very useful purpose. What are required are chemical experiments on the possible life forms that could have arisen from a pre-biotic chemistry. Such experiments have been, and are being, conducted in great numbers; but still so little is known about the origin of life that it cannot support an instructive discussion of co-adaptation. The discussion would be excessively speculative. The origin of life is a case in which ignorance cuts both ways. If a Darwinian cannot prove that life did evolve from pre-biotic chemicals by natural selection, nor can a critic prove that it did not.

So for our example of the gradual, piecemeal evolution of a complex organ, let us return to the eye. Actually, the intermediate stages in the evolution of the eye are not known for sure; but some plausible intermediates do at least exist. They enable a relatively concrete discussion. It has often been declared by critics of Darwinism that so complex, so co-adapted an organ as the eye could not have been built in small stages by natural selection; to be advantageous it would have to exist as a whole; part of an eye would be useless. But when it is considered in detail it starts to appear more possible. Darwin gave two reasons for thinking that the eye evolved in small stages: that we can both imagine functional simple eyes, and that we can find them in living species.

The simplest kind of eye is a bowl-shaped invagination on the surface of the animal, with pigmented light-sensitive cells around the bowl. Leeches and flatworms possess this kind of eye. They cannot see much with it, but it does indicate the general direction of light and can sense the presence of any object that is so large or close that it blocks the outside opening of the bowl. It is easy to imagine that natural selection could favour such an eye. It is also easy to imagine how it could arise by a single chance mutation: the mutation only has to produce a light-sensitive pigment.

In the next stage, the bowl becomes larger and the hole (that opens to the outside) smaller. It is an improvement, because it makes the eye able to discriminate smaller objects. It increases the eye's resolution. This kind of pin-hole camera eye is rather rare in nature, but the mollusk *Nautilus* has one. The resolution of the eye increases as the pin-hole gets smaller, but there is the disadvantage that it lets in less light. The obvious next stage is to evolve a lens.

The simplest kind of lens is only a small change from the lensless pin-hole camera of *Nautilus*. A jelly, that fills the eye, extending from the transparent opening to the light-sensitive retina, can act as a lens. It is a simple and optically poor lens; it cannot form an image, but does allow the opening to the outside to be larger than in the pin-hole camera eye. It could therefore be advantageous: natural selection could favour it. Some types of worm, such as *Nerels*, have a jelly-filled eye. The next stage is to improve the material of the lens and to decrease its size. There can then be a gap between lens and retina, which will make room for an image to form.

We have now reached, by small steps, the best-engineered eyes in nature, those of the cephalopods and vertebrates. A few more improvements are needed to reach that final stage—special techniques to correct for close-up vision and refined optical aberrations—but we need not go into them. Enough has been said to show how even a complex, co-adapted organ could have evolved, by natural selection, in many small stages, without the need for an impossible coincidence of random mutations.

In the evolution of the eye, if the story above is correct, the function of the evolving organ remained constant: it was always an adaptation for seeing. In the evolution of other complex organs there may have been a change in function. The evolution of flight may provide an example. The case against natural selection would here run like this. If feathers were an adaptation for flight, they could not have evolved by natural selection until the bird could already fly. But in order for a bird to fly it needs a fairly well formed wing. The wing must be powerful and of the correct aerodynamic shape. Any stage intermediate in strength or design between a flightless and a flying form could not support flight, and could not be favoured. Natural selection, then, could not have driven evolution from a scaly, flightless to a feathered, flying form.

Or could it? The problem of strength is not difficult. Wings could not support powered flight without many other structural adaptations, but a feebler apparatus could support passive flight. An early stage of a wing might, for instance, have eased falls from trees. At the next stage the wings might be substantial enough to enable a longer period of gliding. Thus wings could have increased in strength, under natural selection, from weak beginnings to their modern powerful form. That is the same principle as we used for the eye. Feathers, however, illustrate a different principle. Feathers are adapted for flight, but that is not their only function. By trapping a layer of air next to the body surface, they also assist in thermo-regulation. Feathers may have evolved first to help small warm-bodied proto-birds retain their body heat. Only later did they assist in flight. Their function then changed, or at least became more complex.

While feathers have adapted for flight, they have kept their original function of thermo-regulation. A more extreme change would be for an organ, after a change of function, to lose its original function, in what A. G. Cairns-Smith has called an evolutionary takeover. The elephant's trunk, in the interpretation of D. M. S. Watson, may be an example. In ancestors of the modern elephant, which are known from fossils, the lower jawbone was extended far forwards, and used to scoop and excavate food from the ground. The upper lip would have extended forwards to meet the lower jaw; it would also have been mobile, to move food back into the mouth. The upper lip then became sufficiently manoeuvrable to pick up and put food into the mouth without the support of the long lower jaw. The lower jaw was then lost, and the extended upper lip was left by itself as a trunk. It had evolved outwards to meet an ever extending lower jaw; but when that jaw was lost, the trunk had taken over for itself the whole function of feeding. The initial and intermediate stages can no longer be seen among modern forms, but they can be (after some interpretation) in the fossil record, Without that fossil evidence, which happens to be particularly good for elephants, the initial evolution of the elephant's trunk might have been difficult to explain.

The third Darwinian answer to the problem of complexity is evolution by symbiosis. Let us take as an example the evolution of the eukaryotic cell. In nature, there are two main kinds of cell. Simple organisms such as bacteria are of the cellular type called prokaryotic; more complex organisms, including all plants and animals, are built of eukaryotic cells. The most important difference between eukaryotic and prokaryotic cells is that eukaryotic cells have a nucleus. The nucleus is a separate compartment containing, within a membrane, the eukaryotic genetic material. The prokaryotic cell has no separate nucleus and the genetic material floats freely within the cell. There are other differences too. Most eukaryotic cells possess organelles called mitochondria; mitochondria are the cell's boiler houses, which supply the cell with energy. Within plant cells there are organelles called chloroplasts, which are the site of photosynthesis.

Prokaryotes evolved before eukaryotes. The earliest prokaryotic fossils are from almost the earliest rocks on the Earth, about 3,500 million years old. It is not known when eukaryotes first evolved. The earliest uncontroversial eukaryotic fossils are only about 700 million years old. All we can say is that the eukaryotic cell probably evolved from the prokaryotic cell between 3,500 and 700 million years ago. Now, eukaryotes are much more complex than prokaryotes. If evolution must proceed in small stages, where are the intermediates between prokaryotes and eukaryotes? Nowhere to be seen.

There are two main theories of how the eukaryotic cell might have evolved from the prokaryotic. One is the theory of internal differentiation, according to which the complexities of the eukaryotic cell evolved from the less complex parts of their prokaryotic ancestors; all the evolutionary stages would then have been internal changes inside the prokaryotic cell. If it is correct, there must have been a smooth series of evolutionary stages, like in the evolution of the eye, between the prokaryotes and eukaryotes, but which are not now preserved either in fossils or modern forms. The nucleus probably did evolve internally within a prokaryote. But for the mitochondria and chloroplasts there is another theory.

Mitochondria and chloroplasts may have originally been independent bacteria-like organisms. They may at some stage have entered other prokaryotic cells. Just why they did is a separate question, but perhaps the pre-mitochondria were just engulfed as food, or joined for some temporary purpose. However that may be, the partnership might then have lasted longer and longer, until it became permanent. The partnership (which is called a symbiosis) was advantageous to both the mitochondria, which are provided with food, and the host cell, which gains energy. Conversely, the chloroplast provides food, manufactured in photosynthesis, to the cell in which it lives, and obtains raw materials. After millions of years of evolutionary dependence on their host cells, mitochondria and chloroplasts have given up their means of independence. They retain only a few curious vestiges (if the symbiosis theory is correct) of their former lives.

The vestiges (if that is what they are) of former independence retained by mitochondria and chloroplasts are the main evidence that they originated as symbiotic partners of the cells they now inhabit. For instance, chloroplasts and mitochondria both possess some genetic material; and both look rather like modified bacteria. Moreover, the molecules made by their genes are more similar to their equivalents in free-living bacteria than to their equivalents made by the eukaryotic cell they occupy. Why should mitochondria make bacteria-like molecules if they were not once independent bacteria themselves?

The symbiotic theory of the origins of the mitochondria and chloroplast is not universally accepted. But we only need it to illustrate a principle. When a symbiotic innovation takes place during evolution, there can be a great increase in the complexity of life. This is true of symbiosis in general. In the case of the eukaryotic cell, the increase in complexity would be particularly large and of immense evolutionary importance. But if the symbiotic theory of eukaryotic origins is false, the principle still stands. There are many other examples of symbiosis: no biologists doubt that some symbiotic events have taken place in evolution. At the origin of each new symbiotic association, a new level of complexity would be created in a single event, without contradicting the theory of natural selection. The new level of complexity is created only by recombining previously existing complex organization, which in turn must have been built up in small stages.

Natural selection can therefore account for the evolution of the eye, of flight, and of the eukaryotic cell. All three organs at first appear impossible to build up in a series of small but advantageous stages. But in fact they probably were. I chose them as difficult tests for the theory of natural selection. If it can explain these, it can probably explain other cases as well. There are no known organs that natural selection definitely cannot explain.

In all these cases, including symbiosis, complex organs have been built up in small stages. Now that the principle is established we can use it more aggressively. Let us just watch it in action against the theory of macro-mutations. A macro-mutation is a very large mutation, one that produces a whole new organ, such as a liver or a heart, in a single mutational event. According to the Darwinian theory, macro-mutations are unimportant in evolution. The reason is that all the right changes needed to make a complex organ like a liver could not possibly all spontaneously arise at the same time. Mutational changes arise by chance changes in pre-existing parts; all the changes needed to make a liver would therefore have to arise by chance. That is not possible. The only way that an unlikely state of nature such as a liver could have evolved from chance changes, is for the changes to be spread out over a long time. Then each change, provided that it is small, will have sufficient opportunity to arise by chance. That a light-sensitive pigment might arise in a cell by chance is not improbable. That a whole eye could so arise is impossible. That is why Darwinism excludes macro-mutations. Complex adaptations must have evolved by the natural selection of a large number of small mutations over a long period of time.

4

Darwinism in an Age of Molecular Revolution

CHARLES R. MARSHALL

INTRODUCTION

This chapter introduces Darwin's theory, or more correctly theories (Mayr, 1991), of evolution and discusses the types of contributions the molecular revolution has made to our understanding of evolution. In so doing, the chapter also provides an introduction to the rest of the book.

The core of Darwin's theories of evolution is remarkably simple. The first part of the chapter summarizes this core and some of its more important ramifications. The chapter also provides a brief review of how Darwin's theories are now viewed, 135 years after the publication of his book, *On the Origin of Species.*

The molecular revolution has been a genuine revolution, changing the face of almost every subdiscipline of biological science. It has been so pervasive that a comprehensive survey of the molecular revolution is not possible, nor desirable, in a book such as this. Instead, this chapter emphasizes the more recent aspects of the molecular revolution that have been among the most important in deepening our understanding of the evolution of life.

DARWIN'S EVOLUTION

In 1859, Charles Darwin published *On the Origin of Species.* Arguing against the idea that each species was created independently, Darwin outlined a compelling case for the origin of new species from previously existing species. Darwin's monograph is unusual for a revolutionary book, in that it is easily understood by those without specialized training, and because of the simplicity of its central tenets. In fact, the core of his argument is encapsulated in the book's Introduction [emphasis added]:

> As many more individuals of each species are born than can possibly survive; and as, consequently, there is a frequently recurring struggle for existence, it follows that any being, if it vary however slightly in any manner profitable to itself, under the complex and sometimes varying conditions of life, will have a better chance of surviving, and thus be **naturally selected**. From the strong principle of inheritance, any selected variety will tend to propagate its new and modified form. (Darwin, 1859)

Alfred Russel Wallace (1823-1913), a naturalist studying plants and animals in the Malay Archipelago at about the time Darwin was writing *On the Origin of Species*, independently arrived at the same conclusion. Note that the driving force of the evolutionary process is the struggle for survival, and that this struggle is driven by the fecundity of nature—it is this feature, the propensity of nature to overreproduce, that provides a basic condition necessary for the operation of Darwin's and Wallace's natural selection. Darwin felt that his theories could satisfactorily explain adaptation and its maintenance, as well as the origin of organic diversity.

Darwin's logical argument, or syllogism, can be recast in a number of different ways. Box 1.1 provides one version. The term phenotype refers to the observable characteristics of an organism, including its morphological, biochemical, and behavioral traits. The phenotype is the result both of genetic information (the genotype) and of the interaction of the organism with the environment.

Box 1.1 Darwin's Syllogism

Condition 1:	*If there is a*	Struggle for Existence, *and*
Condition 2:	*If the*	Phenotype Variable, *and*
Condition 3:	*If*	Existence Depends (at least in part) on the Phenotype, *and*
Condition 4:	*If*	Phenotypic Attributes are (at least in part) Heritable,
	Then	There will be Descent with Modification *that is,*
		Transformation of Species over Time

The syllogism is straightforward. However, in Darwin's day it was not clear whether, or to what degree, the conditions of his logical argument were satisfied in nature. Much of *On the Origin of Species* is devoted to discussing the extent to which each of the conditions listed actually does exist in the natural world. There is perhaps one other condition that should be added to the syllogism: Local environments must vary over time to some degree. The term "environment" in this context has a very wide meaning, including not only physical conditions such as rainfall, temperature, seasonality, and so forth, but ecologic (for example, animal-animal, animal-plant) interactions as well. It should be noted that to a large degree organisms define and create their own environments; they are not just objects passively affected by environmental influences (Lewontin, 1983).

Darwin felt that what he termed natural selection was the most important cause of modification. Perhaps the most cited example of the operation of this natural selection is the explanation he offered for the origin of the long neck in the giraffe. Assuming that there is variation in neck length, and that this variation is, at least in part, heritable, Darwin argued that under the circumstances of low rainfall and drought, giraffes with slightly longer necks would have access to food not reached by others and, thus, the likelihood of survival of such long-necked individuals would be enhanced. It is important to note that the selective pressure for longer necks need not be applied continuously, or indeed even often—all that is required are occasional droughts to effect an increase in neck length over many generations. To establish that there is indeed a struggle for survival during drought, Darwin gave the example of the demise of the Niata cattle of South America during drought. Unlike horses and common cattle, Niata cattle cannot feed on twigs of trees, reeds, and so forth, and will starve during drought if not fed by their owners.

Darwin's interpretation of the evolution of the giraffe's neck also became a focus of criticism. For example, the English biologist George Jackson St. Mivart (1827-1900) argued that if a long neck were so good for a giraffe, why is such a neck not also beneficial to all other beasts that feed on vegetation? Darwin replied that selection for increased neck length operates only on the tallest animals; for example, a sheep with a slightly longer neck gains no advantage if its world is populated with cows and horses that are much taller than itself: "The competition of browsing on higher branches of the acacias and other trees must be between giraffe and giraffe, not with other ungulate animals" (Darwin, 1859, p. 193).

A more telling criticism highlights the lack of knowledge of the material basis of heredity at that time. In 1867, Fleeming Jenkin pointed out that any favorable mutation would soon become unimportant, swamped out by more normal organisms as the single mutant individual bred with other members of the population. This criticism would be valid if the hereditary material were infinitely divisible—for example, if it were like a droplet of wine diluted in a glass of water. Darwin certainly took Jenkin's criticism seriously because his model of inheritance was a blending one. However, with the rediscovery of

Mendel and the development of population genetics by Wright, Fisher, and Haldane this issue was resolved. We now know that the hereditary material is not infinitely divisible or dilutable; instead, it is particulate in nature (made up of what are called genes). The introduction of a new trait into a population is more analogous to the addition of a red marble to a bag of blue marbles.

The Principle of Frustration

If natural selection purges relatively less fit characteristics from a population of organisms, how do we explain the maintenance of apparently deleterious traits in some populations, such as the maintenance of the gene for sickle cell anemia in some populations of humans? In humans suffering from sickle cell anemia, the hemoglobin molecules attach to each other when oxygen levels are low, causing the red blood cells to become contorted in a banana- or sickle-shaped fashion. These deformed erythrocytes may become trapped in the capillaries, causing pain and inflammation. They may also become permanently sickled, and these cells tend to have a shorter than average lifetime-patients thus afflicted will become anemic and they often die.

In each human cell there are two copies of each chromosome (one derived from the mother, the other from the father), and there are therefore two copies of each gene (that portion of the chromosome that contains the coded information to make a protein or RNA product). There is usually more than one version, or allele, of each gene. Sickle cell anemia is caused by a particular allele of hemoglobin called hemoglobin S. Individuals who have the hemoglobin S allele on both chromosomes (that is, who are homozygous for the hemoglobin S allele) often die as children (although in some environmentally benign locales, particularly those having advanced medical facilities, homozygous carriers may survive into adulthood). Yet despite its obviously deleterious effects, the allele is quite prevalent in some human populations, notably those in equatorial Africa.

So, if Darwin was right, why isn't the allele eliminated by natural selection? The reason is that although there is indeed strong natural selection against hemoglobin S homozygotes, individuals having only one copy of the hemoglobin S gene (referred to as heterozygotes) have an increased resistance to another potentially lethal disease, namely, malaria. Thus, in equatorial Africa, as well as in other places where malaria-carrying mosquitoes abound, having the hemoglobin S allele is both an advantage, if heterozygous, and a disadvantage, if homozygous (Allison, 1956). In contrast, in regions that lack malaria, the allele responsible for sickle cell anemia has been, as expected, purged from human populations.

The story of sickle cell anemia demonstrates a most important feature of the evolutionary process—the Principle of Frustration. All organisms live in, and help create, a complex environment, and they all have complex needs. Optimization to meet one need may not be optimal for another. For most organisms, most of the time, there are likely to be many selective forces operating simultaneously. The Principle of Frustration states that the best compromise solution to the inevitably conflicting demands of each of the organism's requirements is unlikely to be optimal for any single function. In fact, this principle may explain why there are so many different types of organisms. With the operation of conflicting selective forces, there are often many solutions that are more or less equally good in meeting the myriad of conflicting demands.

Niklas (1994), using a computer simulation of terrestrial plant morphology, has provided an elegant example of how the Principle of Frustration can lead to multiple successful solutions. Starting from a morphology similar to that of the earliest known land plants, he considered the morphologies that would be most favored if there were selection for one of three different functions. First, reproductive success was examined, in which the ability to produce many branches (and therefore many seeds) as high off the ground as possible (so that the seeds can disperse easily) was favored. Second, the ability to harvest tight was examined, which favors the production of many nonoverlapping horizontal branches. And third, he examined the mechanical stability of these computer-generated plants, a character that, because of branch weight, favors morphologies having a limited number of branches, especially long horizontal ones. In each case, the resulting morphologies were certainly plantlike, but there were relatively few optimal solutions and none of the resulting trees looks especially like familiar trees such as maples or oaks. Niklas then ran a simulation in which all three constraints were optimized simultaneously. This resulted in a dramatic increase in the range of optimal solutions, though none was optimal for any single function. Significantly, many of them look quite treelike. It would appear, at least from this simulation, that the range of tree shapes with which we are familiar is the consequence of the simultaneous selection for several partially conflicting needs.

The Theory of Evolution is Not like Physical Law

Darwin's contribution to our understanding of the world of nature is justifiably ranked alongside the works of Newton and Einstein (indeed, Darwin is buried alongside Newton in London's Westminster Abbey). However, as a cornerstone theory, the theory of evolution is different from the theoretical contributions of either Newton or Einstein. One of the remarkable features of the laws of physics is that the relationships encapsulated in equations, such as e = mc2, are thought to hold virtually everywhere in the universe, both in space and time; gravitation and electromagnetic fields are properties of the universe that cannot easily be avoided. Given a set of initial conditions (e.g., a forming solar system of some specified mass, angular momentum, and so forth), and the appropriate laws (e.g., the Law of Conservation of Angular Momentum), the future development of that system can be predicted with some degree of certainty. In this sense, time is subordinate to physical law.

However, the theory of evolution does not state that evolution must occur; it is simply a list of conditions that, if met, will result in descent with modification. It does not preclude the occurrence of other processes that might be responsible for descent with modification. More important, the direction of evolution cannot be predicted in the same way that the future of (some) physical or chemical systems can be predicted. One of the most significant aspects of the evolutionary theory is that it implies that the development of life is historically contingent, that is, that what happens in the future depends very much on what is happening in the present and has happened in the past (Gould, 1989; Mayr, 1988).

For example, during the Triassic Period of geologic time, some 230 million years ago, the first turtles appeared. These are easily recognized because they possessed fully developed shells. However, no known Triassic turtle could retract its neck into its shell. By the Cretaceous Period, beginning about 100 million years later, two evolutionary lineages, each having a completely different neck-retraction mechanism, had become firmly established. In one of these, the neck was bent vertically (the so-called cryptodires, having a type of neck retraction that today is found only in turtles of the northern hemisphere); in the other, the neck was bent sideways (the pleurodires, found now only in the southern hemisphere).

With the appearance of a well-developed shell it is perhaps understandable (at least in retrospect) that neck retraction developed. First, because having a shell impeded mobility, it would be advantageous to be able to retract the head to escape pressure from predators. Second, the shell would offer a safe place into which the head could retract. However, once the ancestral stocks that were unable to retract their necks became extinct, developing a third neck-retraction mechanism would have been difficult. First, because neck-retraction mechanisms were already in place, there would not have been intense selection pressure to develop a new method of neck retraction, and second, it is difficult to envision how one of the known mechanisms of neck retraction could have been transformed into another. The evolution of the turtle shell opened opportunity for the evolution of neck-retraction mechanisms, and the disappearance of the ancestral forms that were unable to retract their necks evidently closed that evolutionary window.

Significance of Darwin

The idea that there has been descent with modification was not new with Darwin. This idea had already been gaining acceptance in the first half of the nineteenth century through the works of the great French naturalists such as Jean Baptiste Lamarck, Geoffroy Saint-Hilaire, and several others whose work Darwin reviews at the beginning of *On the Origin of Species*.

What was unique about Darwin's and Wallace's view of the process of evolution was that it was the first to provide a clear mechanism for the origin of species and their descent with modification. One of their most significant breakthroughs was their clear separation of the source of variation from the needs or requirements of the individual organisms. There is no divine or organismic "vote" on the variants produced; that is, variation is not directed by some outside agency, and the organism does not actively "try" to change or evolve. Mayr (1991) captured this key point in his characterization of evolution as a two-step process, as shown in Box 1.2.

Box 1.2   Evolution Is a Two-Step Process.

Step 1:	Variation
Step 2:	Selection

The first five chapters of On the Origin of Species concern the existence and nature of variation, and the causes and character of natural selection. In discussions of variation, two significant points must be borne in mind (Box 1.3). It is quite a mouthful to say that "variation is random in the sense that the variants produced by nature do not anticipate the needs of the organism," so this is often abbreviated by stating simply that "variation is random." However, this abbreviation has been a source of misunderstanding. When read at face value, it would seem to suggest that any type of variant can be, and is, produced by nature. But this is not the case.

Box 1.3   Variation.

1. Random:	In the sense that the variants produced do not anticipate the "needs" of the organism
2. Darwin:	"We are profoundly ignorant of the cause of each slight variation ..." (Darwin, 1859, p. 171)

A delightful example of the limits on variation is Wayne's (1986) study of variation in domestic animals. There are a great many types of domestic dogs, ranging from great danes to pugs, but there is much less diversity among domestic cats. It could be argued that this difference has been brought about by humans, who have placed higher value on having many more types of dogs than cats, and this could well be the case. But there may be a much more profound reason for dogs showing more variation than cats. During its development, the relative proportions of a dog's skull change dramatically. Young dogs have broad and short skulls in comparison with those of adult dogs. In cats, however, the proportions of the face and head remain essentially constant during their growth to adulthood. This simple observation suggests that if there are large differences between the morphologies (the shape and form) of juveniles and adults in a species, a relatively greater range of varieties can be generated. This rule also holds for horses, the skulls of which show relatively little change of shape during growth and of which there are relatively few domestic varieties. On the other hand, pigs show dramatic face changes during their development and there are hundreds of different breeds. Wayne's analysis suggests that certain types of cat and horse skull morphologies are essentially impossible, not because they would be disadvantageous, but because the development of cats and horses proceeds in such a way that a whole suite of shapes simply cannot be readily generated. Clearly, the range of variation that can be produced by nature is not random with respect to the range of shapes and forms that can be imagined by humans!

The second significant point is that, in Darwin's day, the nature of heredity, let alone the source of heritable variation, was entirely unknown. In *On the Origin of Species*, Darwin's efforts were centered on demonstrating the existence of variation and describing the extents and types of variations that are present in organisms. Of course, the notion that there are variants is not surprising—after all, each of us looks different from everybody else. We still have much to learn about the nature of variation, and as was true in the nineteenth century, so during the twentieth century much more emphasis has been placed on understanding the selection stage of the two-step evolutionary process summarized in Box 1.2.

Perhaps the most controversial aspect of Darwin's theory was the idea that the direction of evolution is determined by natural selection—that it is not guided or directed by some transcendent force. Given the importance of this point, and Darwin's ignorance of the nature and cause of variation, he placed much more emphasis on the second step of the two-step process: Natural selection. His emphasis on natural selection had the unfortunate consequence of leading many to equate evolution with selection itself. However, these two should not be equated; as discussed below there can be selection without evolution, and evolution without selection. But first we need clear definitions of evolution and natural selection (Box 1.4):

Box 1.4   Definitions.

Evolution:	Descent with Modification
Natural Selection:	Preferential survival of individuals having profitable (advantageous) variations

The definition of Natural selection given in Box 1.4 requires some comment. Natural selection can be said to have operated if the survival of an organism depended, at least in part, on the presence of some profitable characteristic or trait not found in other members of the same species. It is important to recognize that, as used here, the word "profitable" is not meant to invoke notions of exploitation or selfishness. Rather, it is a value-free term in that it pertains to any characteristic that improves the chance of an organism producing offspring for the next generation. Profitable (advantageous) characteristics can in fact be selfish (the ability to wrestle away limited resources from others, for example), but they can also be innocuous (the ability to successfully ward off predators), or may even be cooperative (the ability to form groups in order to gain protection or to gather food).

Natural Selection without Evolution

Imagine a situation in which every generation had a few percent of all offspring born with some sort of deformation of their limbs. Presumably, these malformed individuals would be selected against, because they would be unable to move (to escape predators, for example) as easily as other members of the population. Here natural selection operates, but there is no evolution; that is, there is no descent with modification. In any situation in which the average phenotype (the normal characteristics of the species) is most suited to the environment, natural selection will favor the existing average phenotype at the expense of other unusual phenotypes that differ from the average. This type of selection is termed **stabilizing selection**. We encountered stabilizing selection earlier in this chapter. In the case of sickle cell anemia, discussed above, the intermediate phenotype (produced by the heterozygous genotype) was of selective advantage in malaria-infested regions; humans homozygous for the sickle cell anemia allele are selected against, as are those who lack the allele altogether. Selection without evolution is commonplace in the natural world.

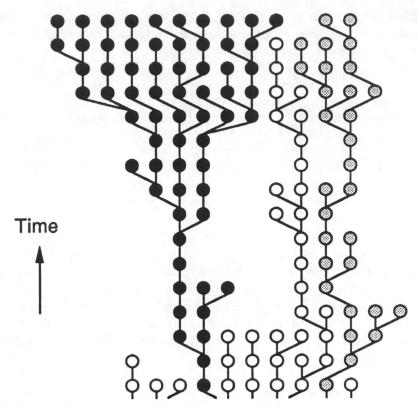

Figure 1.1: Evolution without natural selection. The lineage represented by black circles is more successful than that of the white lineage or the stippled lineage. However, this success is not from selection for some intrinsically superior characteristic but, in this random simulation (see text), from chance alone.

EVOLUTION WITHOUT SELECTION

Figure 1.1 shows, in schematic form, a population tree, showing the relationship between parents in a population and their offspring. At the beginning of the sequence (shown at the bottom of the figure) there are 10 individuals, each able to reproduce asexually (that is, to divide and produce up to two offspring, each an exact copy of the parent). In each generation (represented by each row of circles), the organisms either become extinct (that is, they fail to reproduce); they reproduce themselves (one offspring survives); or they double in number (two offspring survive). After sixteen generations (shown at the top of the figure), there has been descent with modification in the population. Offspring have survived from only two of the original ten lineages, and members of the lineage represented by the black circles have increased in number to dominate the group. Moreover, there appears to have been an interesting "evolutionary dynamic"—early extinction of some lineages, followed by an especially successful evolutionary rebound by the black progeny. It would be tempting to conclude that the original black individual (at the bottom of the figure) had some sort of selective advantage over organisms of the other lineages—certainly, a pattern like that shown in Figure 1.1 could be the consequence of a selective process.

Surprisingly, however, the pattern shown in Figure 1.1 was generated by a purely random process. To make Figure 1.1, I first drew the ten circles of the first generation. I then pulled two pennies from my pocket and, to determine the fate of each individual in the next generation, I tossed the two coins. If two tails came up, the lineage became extinct. One head and one tail, a single offspring survived (the individual reproduced itself). Two heads, both offspring survived. I then repeated this procedure for each surviving individual in each successive generation. There was evolution (descent with modification), but because this was an entirely random process, there was no selection.

Does evolution without selection occur in nature? By the middle of the twentieth century, the answer to this question for the phenotype was no, or at least, only rarely. Evolution without selection was widely regarded as implausible. Reasoning that if this were true for the phenotype, it must also apply to the genotype, the Alexander Agassiz Professor of Vertebrate Paleontology at Harvard University, George Gaylord Simpson, declared that completely neutral genes or alleles—that is, genes or alleles that confer no selective advantage or disadvantage whatever—must be very rare, if they exist at all (Simpson, 1964). Most felt that the molecular makeup of an organism was likely to be so important to the survival of each individual that all portions of all molecules must be under selective constraint, including those molecules that make up genes. However, this could hardly have been further from the truth. Starting with Kimura (1968), and followed by a seminal paper by King and Jukes (1969), it has been established that neutral alleles predominate in genomes. In Chapter 2, Jukes explores the contribution that our understanding of the genetic basis of heredity has made to deciphering the importance of selection in genotypic evolution.

Provocatively, King and Jukes entitled their paper "Non-Darwinian Evolution," and in their very first sentence they asserted that "Darwinism is so well established that it is difficult to think of evolution except in terms of selection for desirable characteristics and advantageous genes."

Here is reflected the prevailing spirit of the time, the view that Darwinian evolution and natural selection were one and the same, that one could not occur without the other. However, Darwin, in the last sentence of his introduction to

On the Origin of Species, states [emphasis added]: "Furthermore, I am convinced that Natural Selection has been the most important, **but not the exclusive**, means of modification."

Thus, Darwin explicitly recognized that evolution can occur without selection (though he did not have neutral alleles in mind when writing this statement!). In fact, molecular evolution is not non-Darwinian, although evolution without selection is probably much more common at the genotypic than at the phenotypic level. Darwin's syllogism, his central logical argument, and its pervasive implications, have not been affected by the new insights provided by the molecular revolution (Brunk, 1991).

Explaining Today's Biosphere—Beyond the Darwinian Syllogism?

Among large vertebrates in today's terrestrial ecosystems, mammals are dominant. Why is this so? Why not an abundance of large reptiles, such as crocodiles, lizards, or even dinosaurs? Of course, if one were transported back to the Mesozoic Era (some 65 million to 250 million years ago) there would be no large mammals; dinosaurs were dominant at that time. Why the difference between then and now? A conventional explanation might be that mammals "out-competed" the dinosaurs, that mammals were somehow "better" than their reptilian relatives. This seems reasonable because the last dinosaurs are found in rocks 65 million years old (marking the end of the Cretaceous Period), and mammals first became abundant shortly after the dinosaur became extinct.

However, there is another possible explanation: Luck! It seems certain that Earth was blasted by a very large meteorite at essentially the same time as dinosaurs (and a great number of other groups) disappeared, at the end of the Cretaceous Period. The meteorite is thought to have been massive, having a diameter of approximately 10 km; its impact with the Earth would have ejected enough material into the atmosphere to cause drastic short-term changes in both the global climate and the chemistry of the world's oceans. The impact may have been the primary cause of the worldwide "mass extinction" that occurred at the end of the Cretaceous Period (Alvarez, 1983). Recently, the site of the impact was identified in Yucatan, Mexico-the huge Chlcxulub crater, 180 km or more across (Sharpton et al., 1993).

It may be difficult to imagine that a meteorite impact could have truly global consequences. However, a back-of-the-envelope calculation shows that a large meteorite could have dramatic effects. As a standard for comparison, the Mt. St. Helens volcano ejected about 1 km^3 of material into the atmosphere when it exploded in 1980. Mt. Pinatubo, in the Philippines, was even more explosive, spewing out some 7 km^3 of rocky dust into the atmosphere when it erupted in 1991; it affected the world's climate for many months afterwards (for details, see the AGU Special Paper on Volcanism and Climate Change listed in the references for this chapter). It is estimated that the Cretaceous Period meteorite ejected as much as 22,000 km^3 of material into the atmosphere, certainly enough to affect the entire globe. The July 1994 bombardment of Jupiter by the fragments of the comet Shoemaker-Levy 9 should dispel any lingering doubts that collisions with large extraterrestrial objects can, and do, happen.

What are the ecological consequences of rapid climatic change? The fossil record, both at the end of the Cretaceous Period and at the end of the relatively recent last Ice Age (10,000 to 12,000 years ago), suggests that species with large body sizes are especially prone to becoming extinct during environmental crises. At the end of the Ice Age in North America, among other large animals, mammoths, giant ground sloths, camels, horses, lions, and saber-toothed cats all became extinct (possibly exterminated by humans). In fact, virtually all animals weighing more than about 50 kilograms (110 pounds) became extinct. Smaller beasts, such as coyotes, badgers, and raccoons faired much better and persist to the present. So also at the end of the Cretaceous Period all large species seem to have become extinct (Alvarez et al., 1980), whereas, for smaller species, some did and some did not.

Why large species seem to be more "extinction-prone" than small species at times of crisis is not known, but it is worth noting that at the end of the Cretaceous Period there were virtually no small dinosaurs, whereas all mammals at that time were small. Perhaps the main reason the dinosaurs became extinct is that there were simply no species with small body sizes present that might have survived. This idea, of course, is rather speculative. However, if it is correct, it has important implications for understanding the long-term history of biodiversity on Earth. In particular, it suggests that the reason why mammals are dominant now may be that the previously dominant vertebrates, the dinosaurs, were removed from the scene by the catastrophic impact, freeing up space that the mammals could then exploit. If so, mammals are not to be viewed as selectively superior to dinosaurs-they were simply lucky! Moreover, this hypothesis fits with the fact that mammals and dinosaurs coexisted for 160 million years before the end of the Cretaceous Period, with mammals remaining small and inconspicuous throughout this enormously long period.

Thus, while variation followed by selection (the operation of Darwin's syllogism) is most likely responsible for the appearance of new morphological traits, such as those features that make mammals different from dinosaurs, both the processes of Darwinian evolution and the occurrence of chance events appear to play a role in determining which groups survive over geologically long periods (tens to hundreds of millions of years) (Raup, 199 1). Factors in addition to those included in Darwin's syllogism (Box 1. 1) may also be important in determining the range of biodiversity of the modem world, or of that at any other time in Earth's history.

The effects on the biota of long-term geologic change should not be underestimated. For example, for the first 99% of their history, the small North American predators of the present day, such as the coyote and bobcat, coexisted with much larger predators, such as giant lions and saber-toothed cats. It is only in the last 10,000 to 12,000 years that these smaller predators have had North America to themselves, unhampered by competition with larger carnivores. Thus, many of the behavioral and morphological characteristics of these small currently living predators may be in part the product of nearly 2 million years of earlier competition with now extinct megacarnivores, a factor that must be taken into account in deciphering their evolutionary history. Without an appreciation of how radically, and how recently (in geologic time), the ecology of North America has changed, serious errors can be made in identifying the selective pressures that have shaped the characteristics of animals such as coyotes and bobcats (Van Valkenburgh and Hertel, 1993).

THE MOLECULAR REVOLUTION: RECOGNIZING SPECIES

We now turn to some of the major contributions molecular studies have made to our understanding of the history of life. Darwin discusses at some length the difficulties in distinguishing between populations that belong to different species and those that are simply different varieties of a single species. This difficulty is not surprising; gradations between varieties and species in a world with descent with modification are likely to be seen. In Darwin's time, as today, there is no universally agreed upon, comprehensive definition of a species. Nevertheless, for sexually reproducing organisms, one of the most widely accepted definitions is the Biological Species Concept proposed by Mayr (1942):

> Species are groups of actually or potentially interbreeding natural populations, which are reproductively isolated from other such groups.

Although applicable to many forms of life, this definition is not all-inclusive. For example, it obviously cannot be applied to organisms that reproduce asexually (most microbes and many protozoans and single-celled algae, for example), nor can it be applied directly to fossil species. In addition, and although it is a definition that works in theory, it is often not possible to know whether members of geographically isolated populations can actually mate. Other definitions of species have been proposed (summarized by Coyne, 1994), but none is any freer from difficulties.

Finding a comprehensive definition of species is complicated by other problems as well. For example, seven subspecies of the salamander *Ensatina eschscholtzii* (found in Washington, Oregon, and California) are recognized primarily by their coloration. In California, the salamanders primarily inhabit the foothills that surround the Central Valley. One subspecies (*Ensatina eschscholtzii eschscholtzii* [*eschscholtzii* for short]; an unblotched form), is thought to have migrated down the coast, and is found in coastal southern California; another subspecies (*klauberi*, a blotched form) is thought to have migrated from the Sierra Nevada to the mountains of southern California. In most cases, adjacent subspecies show evidence of interbreeding: The blotched subspecies in mountainous southern California (*klauberi*) can interbreed with the subspecies occurring in the southern Sierran foothills to the north (*croceator*), and *croceator* can interbreed with the more northern California subspecies (*platensis*); *platensis* can interbreed with the central Californian coastal subspecies (*oregonensis* and *xanthoptica*), and these subspecies, in turn, can interbreed with the unblotched subspecies of coastal southern California (*eschscholtzii*).   Because all these subspecies can interbreed, by Mayr's definition, they all fit into a single biological species.

The blotched (*klauberi*) and unblotched (*eschscholtzii*) subspecies that occupy southern California are in contact. Surprisingly, however, *klauberi* and *eschscholtzii* are unable to interbreed. By Mayr's definition, they should be assigned to different species.   If one starts with the southwestern-most subspecies (*klauberi*) and goes counterclockwise around the Central Valley there appears to be one species of *Ensatina eschscholtzii*, but if one proceeds around the ring in the opposite direction, there appear to be two species. *Ensatina eschscholtzii* is a famous example of a so-called ring species, and it highlights some of the practical difficulties in recognizing and defining species. However, because there are sometimes fuzzy lines between species and varieties (subspecies), does not mean that the concept of a species should be abandoned; there are no sharp boundaries between the colors in a rainbow, but color is nevertheless an important tool when negotiating traffic signals! Weiner (1994) provides an excellent review of the evidence that natural selection and speciation are real processes.

Ring species are relatively uncommon, but the same basic problem of distinguishing between varieties, subspecies, and species often plagues species recognition. Morphologically, it is difficult to distinguish between varieties and species. Molecules have provided an additional way of addressing the question of when a species is truly a species.

Mitochondrial DNA and Intraspecific Relationships

Virtually all cells of plants and animals contain energy-producing organelles known as mitochondria. Each mitochondrion contains its own circular piece of gene-containing DNA (mtDNA). Mitochondria are usually inherited from the mother. Over time, mutations (changes in, the genes) occur, and all the descendants of the mother that first received the mutation inherit the mutant gene. (As discussed above, most of these changes are thought to be neutral, giving no advantage or disadvantage in the struggle for survival.) Thus, mutated mitochondria are like family names (except that they are inherited from the mother, rather than the father) and can be used to trace familial genealogical relationships. During the course of evolution, populations that are not in close contact tend to develop different mtDNA sequences. This property can be used to help distinguish populations of true, noninterbreeding species from those of interbreeding subspecies and varieties. In the case discussed earlier of the amphibian ring species, *Ensatina eschscholtzii*, mitochondrial DNA studies have confirmed that it is indeed a ring species (Moritz et al., 1992).

Conservation Biology and the Case of the Dusky Seaside Sparrow

The dusky seaside sparrow was first described in 1872 and was largely confined to Brevard County on the central Atlantic coast of Florida. In the early 1960s, flooding for mosquito control and conversion of woodlands into pasture caused a significant drop in population numbers of this sparrow and, by 1966, it was listed as an endangered species. By 1980, only six birds, all male, remained. Five of these were crossed with females obtained from a population of closely related sparrows inhabiting the western coast of Florida on the Gulf of Mexico. The last purebred dusky seaside sparrow died on June 16, 1987. Considerable effort had been spent trying to save the species, or to preserve at least some of its genetic diversity, by crossing the last survivors with the Gulf Coast sparrows. However, genetic analysis revealed that this effort may have been misspent.

When the mitochondria of the dusky seaside sparrow were compared with other sparrows from both the Gulf and Atlantic Coasts, two startling patterns were discovered (Avise and Nelson, 1989). First, dusky seaside sparrow mitochondria were remarkably similar to those of all other Atlantic Coast species. Second, their genetic makeup differed greatly from the mitochondria in populations from the Gulf of Mexico, including those in sparrows from western Florida. Thus, it appears that the dusky seaside sparrow was not different from the other Atlantic species at all. Moreover, if its genetic diversity were to be preserved, the few remaining male birds should have been crossed with females from other conspecific Atlantic coast populations, not with those from populations from Florida's Gulf Coast. Loss of genetic diversity is certainly an important problem, but at a time when many bona fide species are threatened with extinction, mainly because of the activities of humans, it is crucial that the limited conservation resources available be concentrated on the most pressing cases. Molecular studies are playing an increasingly major role in conservation biology.

How Do Sea Turtles Find Their Nesting Grounds?

For most of their lives sea turtles live thousands of miles from their nesting grounds. An intriguing problem has been how they determine where to nest. Do females return to nest on the beach of their birth (a behavior known as natal homing), or do they follow experienced females to some other beach that the experienced females happen to select (social facilitation)? It has been impossible to trace the life of individual turtles from birth until they begin nesting because infant mortality is high, it takes many years for turtles to mature, and it has proven difficult to devise a tag that can be attached to juveniles that will survive until their adulthood.

However, this problem can be addressed by tracing female lineages through their mitochondrial DNAs. If natal homing is the primary mechanism of nesting site selection, members of the same lineage should return to the same site through the generations; there should be distinct types of mtDNA at each site, and they should differ from one beach to the next. If social facilitation is the primary mechanism of nest choice, various mtDNA types should be found across the range of nesting grounds, because females hatched on one beach may deposit eggs on many others.

Avise and his colleagues (Bowen et al., 1993) examined the mtDNA of loggerhead turtles in the northwestern Atlantic Ocean and the Mediterranean Sea. Of the five mtDNA "family names" found, there were two nesting localities in which only one of the five occurred; thus, evidently, nesting turtles return to the beach of their birth. However, there is some mixing of mtDNA types between beaches, so there is also apparently some degree of social facilitation, but this is relatively rare. These data have important conservation implications: If a nesting site is destroyed, females that hatched on that beach will not easily find their way to another beach to deposit eggs and that turtle population will most likely become extinct. Here, molecular data have not only answered an interesting biological question, but they have also suggested specific strategies that might be employed if the survival of the loggerhead turtle is valued.

THE MOLECULAR REVOLUTION: DETERMINING EVOLUTIONARY RELATIONSHIPS

Descent with modification (and the assumption that all living things share a common ancestor) implies that all species are related to each other. Hence, it should be possible to determine the genealogical relationships among species, that is, to reconstruct the Tree of Life. Traditionally, the differing degrees of morphological similarity among species were used to determine relative degrees of relatedness. Systematists (scientists concerned with the classification of species) search for shared evolutionary innovations (synapomorphies) as indicators of relationship. For example, in the late 1700s, the French comparative anatomist, Georges Cuvier (1769-1832), recognized that a very large and highly unusual fossil skull found in the Maastricht region of what is now the southernmost region of the Netherlands had affinities with lizards. The fossil belonged to a Cretaceous marine reptile known as a mosasaur, and was identified as being related to modem varanid lizards, a group that includes the largest of all living lizards, the Komodo Dragon of Indonesia, as well as the goannas, or monitors, of Australia and southeast Asia. One of the major criteria for Cuvier's identification was a joint in the mosasaur's lower jaw, known to be present only in living varanids and fossil mosasaurs. Thus, this jaw Joint is a synapomorphy, an evolutionary innovation shared by these two types of reptiles.

The use of morphological data to infer evolutionary relationships has generally been very successful with vertebrate organisms, in part because of the complexity of their skeletons and soft tissues, and in part also, perhaps because humans as vertebrates have an uncommon interest in vertebrate anatomy. However, for animals without backbones, the invertebrates, and even more so for minute single-celled organisms such as bacteria, there is less morphology to work with and evolutionary relationships have been less well understood. With these groups the use of molecules has been revolutionary for our understanding of relationships.

Just as with morphological data, so with molecular data, unique evolutionary innovations (molecular synapomorphies) can be sought as indicators of relatedness (Box 1.5). An advantage of using molecular sequence data for reconstructing evolutionary trees is that, potentially, there are millions of synapomorphies waiting to be discovered. One of the most important molecules studied for this purpose is a ubiquitous and highly conserved molecule—that is, a molecule that has changed little during evolution-known as the small subunit ribosomal RNA (rRNA). Figure 1.2 (on the following page)

Box 1.5   Use of DNA Sequences to Determine Evolutionary Relationships.

The DNA nucleotide sequence (A = adenine, T = thymine, C = cytosine, and G = guanine) for two small regions of the small subunit rRNA gene for two mammals, two birds, and a lobe-finned fish.†

Site Numbers:	920			980
Mammal (Human)	CCGCC	.. TTTCG	GAACT	GAGGC
Mammal (Mouse)	CCGCC	.. TTTCG	GAACT	GAGGC
Bird (Chicken)	CCGCC	.. TTTCG	GAAAC	GGGGC
Bird (American Robin)	CCGCC	.. TTTCG	GAAAC	GGGGC
Lobe-finned fish (Coelacanth)	TCGCT	.. TTTCG	GAACT	GGGGC

If the lobe-finned fish (Coelacanth) sequence is assumed the primitive sequence, the sequences support this evolutionary tree:

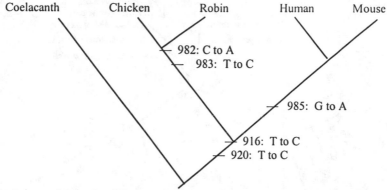

Each internal branch of the tree is supported by one or two unique evolutionary innovations (synapomorphies); for example, the human and mouse sequences both have A (adenine) at site 985, in contrast to all other species; this is a molecular synapomorphy uniting human and mouse to the exclusion of the other three species. The sequences in this example illustrate one of the ways DNA sequences can be used to reconstruct evolutionary relationships. The regions of the molecule were deliberately chosen to give consistent results; in reality, the analysis of DNA sequences is not so simple because there is usually conflicting information in any single data set. For example, at site 1068 (not shown here), the robin, human, and mouse share a G (guanine), while the chicken and coelacanth share an A. Based only on this site the robin would appear to be more closely related to the two mammals than it is to a chicken! One of the greatest challenges in the use of molecules to reconstruct evolutionary histories is to develop robust methods by which to deal with the conflicting information contained in molecular data sets.

†Hedges et al., 1990.

shows an evolutionary tree derived from the nucleotide sequences found in this molecule in a large number of different types of organisms. Several conclusions can be drawn from this tree: (1) Because RRNA occurs in all organisms except viruses, the degree of relatedness among every form of life can be determined by studies of this single type of molecule. Moreover, the universality of RRNA provides strong evidence that all life that exists today shared a common ancestor (of course, even stronger evidence comes from the fact that the genetic code is the same for all organisms). (2) the molecular differences within the animal and plant branches of the tree (stippled) are trivial in comparison with the molecular diversity exhibited by all life. (3) not only is there a great diversity within the bacteria, but they fall into one of two widely divergent groups, the Eubacteria, and the Archaebacteria.

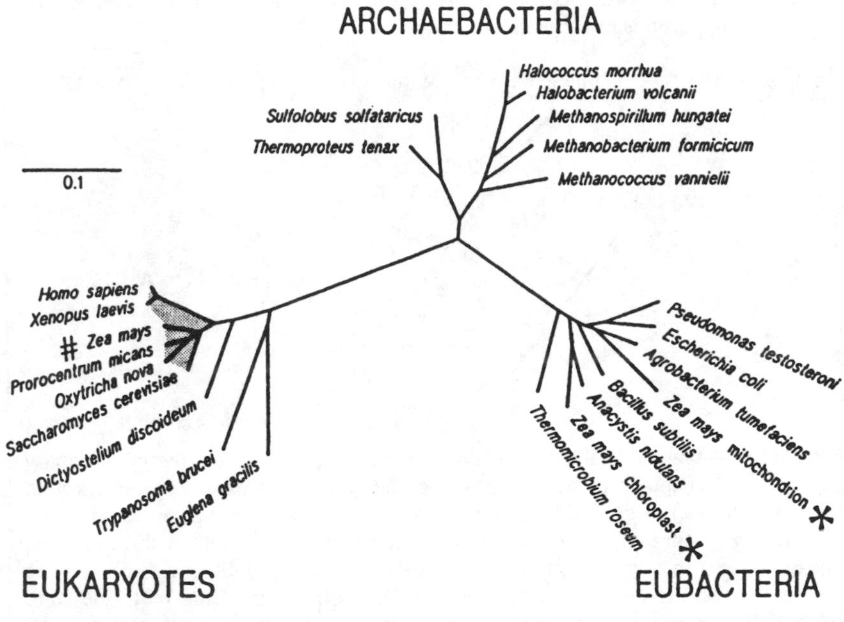

Figure 1.2: The universal Tree of Life. The relationships shown were derived from the analysis of nucleotide sequences of the small subunit ribosomal RNA molecule extracted from diverse types of organisms. Animals (represented by Homo sapiens and the frog Xenopus laevis), plants (corn Zea mays), and fungi (the yeast Saccaromyces cerevisiae) occupy just a small corner of the tree (stippled). Note that the mitochondrial and chloroplast sequences for corn (*) are not closely related to the sequence from the cell nucleus of corn (#), but are closely related to the Eubacteria. This provides powerful evidence that mitochondria and chloroplasts are evolutionary derivatives of bacteria that were engulfed by an ancestral eukaryotic cell. (Details of the relationships among the Archaebacteria may be incorrect (see Chapter 3 in Evolution and the Molecular Revolution).) The root of this Tree of Life (not shown) probably lies in the region between the Eubacteria and the Archaebacteria. Scale bar shows distances on the tree that correspond to a 10% difference in nucleotide sequence. (Modified from Olsen, 1989. Reprinted with permission.)

There is also another conclusion that can be drawn from the Tree of Life shown in Figure 1.2. Most animal cells contain two discrete sources of DNA:

Nuclear DNA, organized in the familiar chromosomes that make up most (>99.99%) of the cell's DNA, and mitochondria that contain their own DNA. Plant cells, in addition to nuclei and mitochondria, have a third source of DNA, chloroplasts, that house the machinery for photosynthesis. It has long been proposed that the ancestors of chloroplasts and mitochondria were once free-living bacteria, and that an early eukaryotic cell acquired these by engulfing them from their environment.

Alternative Approaches to Molecular Phylogenetics

Although nucleotide sequences of RNA and DNA are most commonly used to reconstruct evolutionary relationships, there is other information in the genome that can be used to infer phylogenies (evolutionary trees). In particular, the genome contains a record of rare genomic events that may have phylogenetic value.

Most genetic information is passed from one generation to the next through sexual or asexual reproduction. This standard form of inheritance is termed vertical descent. But, very occasionally, a piece of DNA is transmitted between different species. This type of rare genomic event is termed horizontal transfer. An example of horizontal transfer is the case of a 10-kilobase (kb) piece of DNA that belonged to a particular type of virus, called a retrovirus, that was transmitted from an ancestor of the baboon to an ancestor of many types of cats, including the black-footed cat, African wildcat, sand cat, domestic cat, European wildcat, and jungle cat (Benveniste, 1985). All these cats have multiple copies of this retroviral DNA in their cells. However, no other member of the cat family (felids) has the sequence—it is not present in the leopard cat, bobcat, lion, caracal, and many others. Just as the joint in the lower jaw of the mosasaur indicated its evolutionary relationships with the varanids, the presence of this retrovirus sequence indicates that the six species of cat that have copies of the 10-kb piece of DNA are more closely related to each other than to any other felid. The shared presence of the primate retroviral sequence in their genomes is an excellent molecular synapomorphy for this group of cats.

Apparently, about 5 to 10 million years ago in North Africa, an ancestor of the cats that now share the retroviral sequence somehow became infected with the retrovirus from a primate that was ancestral to both the baboon and the gelada. Even though all primates, including humans, have copies of the retrovirus in their genomes, the cats seem to have received it from an ancestor of the baboon and gelada because the cat sequences show the greatest similarity to the retroviral sequences present in these two primates. It is possible that the infection occurred after the cat devoured the primate. This piece of DNA from the primate managed to incorporate itself into the DNA of the sperm or egg cells of the cat, and from there it was inherited vertically by all individuals descended from that initial cat. Although such horizontal transfers are rare, other examples are also known (Benveniste, 1985). However, the use of rare genomic events like this to reconstruct evolutionary relationships is limited because they are rare, and therefore they cannot be searched for systematically. In Chapter 3, Runnegar explores the use of molecular data to unravel the early history of life, and in Chapter 4, Schopf discusses the origin and evolution of the fundamental biochemical pathways used by all life.

The Molecular Revolution: Explaining Morphological Transitions

A major area of current research is focused on the use of molecular data to reconstruct the Tree of Life, but what more can be learned once such a tree has been defined? One of the most interesting questions is how the various morphologies seen in extinct and extant organisms originated. As Gould (1980) pointed out in his essay on the panda's thumb, new structures generally do not originate *de novo* in evolution; they are usually modifications of previous structures.

One might be tempted to ask how did a chimpanzee become human? Or what were the steps taken to transform an arthropod into a dinosaur? These, however, are not good questions. Chimpanzees were not transformed into humans, nor arthropods into dinosaurs. The species are related, certainly, but one did not evolve into the other. The real questions are what was the most recent common ancestor of the organisms of interest, and how did each evolving lineage acquire its unique characteristics since the time of that shared ancestor?

In some cases, comparative morphology provides a fairly complete picture of the nature of morphological innovation. For instance, the transformation of three of the bones of the lower jaw of the ancestors of living reptiles and mammals into the bones of the middle ear of extant mammals is relatively well described on the basis of the fossil record and embryological studies (Romer and Parsons, 1986). However, the simpler the morphology of an organism, the harder it is to trace the origins of its novel structures. For example, one of the most striking evolutionary transformations among animals was the evolution of an amphioxus-like animal into a fish. Amphioxus lacks most of the structures found in the heads of all vertebrates; it does not have an organized brain, it lacks organized sensory structures such as eyes, and it has no skull. How did the vertebrate head, with its well-developed brain and sense organs originate from such humble beginnings? Is the vertebrate head a new feature, added to the anterior end of an amphioxus-like ancestor, or is the vertebrate head just a highly modified front end of an amphioxus-like animal? Proposal of the first of these ideas, the "new head" hypothesis (Gans and Northcutt, 1983; Northcutt and Gans, 1983; Gans, 1989), was prompted in part by the observation that the notochord, a stiff, phosphatic rod that functions to preserve body shape during locomotion in amphioxus, runs the entire length of the body in amphioxus, but extends only as far forward as the midbrain in the embryos of vertebrates. Although intriguing, this hypothesis is difficult to test.

In this case, our understanding of the genetic basis of development offers great potential. A series of genes, called homeobox genes, are crucial to development. Many of the homeobox genes found in the fruitfly, *Drosophila*, are also found in amphioxus and in vertebrates. (These genes are homologous, i.e., they share a common evolutionary derivation.) Remarkably, many of these homologous genes have been found to be expressed in the same part of the body in very different animals. For example, homologous homeobox genes in amphioxus and chicken are found to affect essentially the same positions along the head to tail (anteroposterior) axis of both organisms (Holland et al., 1992). This suggests the new head hypothesis is incorrect (Peterson, 1994). Similarly, genes expressed in the developing brains of *Drosophila* are also found in the developing brains of mice (Simeone et al., 1992), which suggests that similarities between vertebrate and arthropod heads are not merely a matter of coincidence, but remarkably are due to the same developmental mechanism. In short, both dinosaurs and arthropods, despite their dramatic differences, share essentially the same sort of developmental program for the head, one that was presumably present in their last common ancestor.

The studies by Holland et al. (1992) and Simeone et al. (1992) show that developmental biology offers great potential to help explain the origin of new structures; patterns of gene expression can be used to identify homologous regions of the body long after those regions have become so different in form and shape as to be otherwise unrecognizably related.

EVOLUTION AS THE CONTROL OF DEVELOPMENT BY ECOLOGY

The simple two-step view of the evolutionary process—variation followed by selection—does not do justice to the complexity of the process as it occurs in nature. However, there is a way to consider the two-step process to address some of the underlying complexity by invoking two central subdisciplines of biology: Developmental biology and ecology. Variation in the phenotype among members of a species' population is a result of development. Natural selection is a consequence of the interactions of organisms and their environments; thus, natural selection lies primarily in the domain of ecology. Hence, the two-step characterization of the Darwinian syllogism, variation followed by selection, can be re-expressed as the control of development by ecology (Van Valen, 1973, 1974).

This characterization is not quite satisfactory, in that ecology does not exactly control development. Rather, development produces forms and ecological interactions help determine which of these forms generated by developmental processes survives in the next generation. Nonetheless, this recasting of variation-followed-by-selection focuses attention on the interrelations between two central aspects of biology: development and ecology.

Pioneering developmental biologists, such as Ernst Heinrich Haeckel (1834-1919) and Karl Ernst von Baer (1792-1876), were major contributors to evolutionary biology in the late nineteenth and early twentieth centuries. In the last few decades molecular techniques have revitalized the study of development, yet developmental biology has made relatively little contribution to evolutionary studies during this time. The source and nature of variation have received only limited attention (Raff and Kaufman, 1983), perhaps because of the inherent difficulties in analyzing organismal development. In the future there should be a much greater contribution of developmental biology to our understanding of evolution. Some of the most exciting developments in the field are surveyed by De Robertis (Marshall and Schopf, 1995) and in Akam et al. (1994).

THE UNEXPECTED: DNA AS THE NOT-SO-STATIC-BLUEPRINT

DNA is commonly regarded as the "blueprint of life," and as such may be viewed as a passive archive of information, sequestered away from the normal dynamics of cellular processes, although it participates in cell division, gene expression, and the like. However, the organization of the DNA itself may be modified by cellular processes (e.g., as discussed above regarding the incorporation of the 10-kb retrovirus DNA from primates into the cat genome). Another interesting example is the case where manipulation of the DNA is needed to activate genes that are required for major morphological and biochemical changes in certain types of eubacterial cyanobacteria. Nitrogen is necessary for life; it is required for the synthesis of amino acids, the building blocks of proteins, and nucleotides, the building blocks of DNA and RNA. The most abundant source of nitrogen is atmospheric nitrogen, N_2. However, only a relatively few species of microorganisms can make use of (fix) N_2 directly. One of the most diverse groups of nitrogen-fixing organisms are the cyanobacteria.

Filamentous cyanobacteria consist of strings of cells that do not fix N_2 if other sources of nitrogen (such as ammonia or nitrate) are available. However, if starved of these alternate nitrogen sources, certain cyanobacteria develop specialized cells called heterocysts at regular intervals along the filament. Within each heterocyst, approximately 1000 heterocyst-specific gene products are synthesized that, among other things, build the machinery needed to fix nitrogen from the atmosphere (Haselkom, 1992). The thick wall of the heterocyst is important in keeping out oxygen, which inhibits nitrogen fixation.

Among the more important genes in nitrogen fixation are the *ni*trogen *fix*ation genes themselves, the *nif* genes. In vegetative (normal) cells of the cyanobacterium *Anabaena*, a crucial *nif* gene, *nifD*, and another gene, *fdxN*, are each split into two segments, separated by extremely large stretches of non-coding DNA (insertions). Functional proteins cannot be made from either of these two genes with the insertions present. However, as part of the process of heterocyst formation, the intervening pieces of DNA are cut out of the genome, reuniting the severed regions of each of the genes, and nitrogen fixation can proceed. Interestingly, the enzymes required to excise the insertions are coded for within the insertions themselves. Thus, in *Anabaena*, the DNA itself is modified as part of heterocyst formation.

Another example involves "mobile DNA," which has been implicated in human disease. In the human genome there is a sequence of approximately 300 nucleotides, called the "Alu sequence," of which more than 500,000 copies occur in each cell. It is unclear whether any of these copies serves any function. From time to time, new copies of Alu are produced and inserted into the genome. Recently, Goldberg et al. (1993) proposed that some patients with Huntington's disease—a fatal disease that appears in mid-life, causing personality and cognitive disturbances and involuntary movements—may be caused by the insertion of an Alu sequence into a sensitive region of the genome.

Our knowledge of the human genome and of its properties is far from complete. New discoveries will not only increase our understanding of the evolution of life, but may also offer new approaches and possibilities for control of disease. Simpson (Marshall and Schopf, 1995) reviews the progress that has been made in developing diagnoses for one of the most serious diseases in South and Central America, Chagas' disease. The tools being developed are centered around the very unusual and remarkable way that some proteins are encoded in the genome of the parasites that cause Chagas' disease. We will increasingly find surprises as we continue to probe the genomes of the natural world.

CONCLUSION

Darwin established beyond a reasonable doubt that natural processes are responsible for the origin and transformation of biological species through time. His central contribution was a syllogism, a logical construct, that provided a mechanism for the occurrence of descent with modification. The basic syllogism remains sound, though there have been elaborations and changes in emphasis as explanations for phenotypic evolution and genotypic evolution have been propounded. In Darwin's day, many basic properties of biological systems were a mystery. Although many still remain mysterious, the molecular revolution has enabled questions to be answered that were wholly unanswerable in Darwin's time, and has opened many new areas of evolutionary inquiry. The five chapters that follow provide a more comprehensive introduction to some of the central breakthroughs contributed by the molecular revolution to studies of the evolution of life.

References

Akam, M., Holland, P., Ingham, P., and Wray, G. 1994. *The Evolution of Developmental Mechanisms.* Development 1994 Supplement (Cambridge, U.K.: Company of Biologists).

Allison, A.C. 1956. "Sickle Cells and Evolution." *Scientific American* 195(2): 87-94.

Alvarez, L.W. 1983. "Experimental Evidence That an Asteroid Impact Led to the Extinction of Many Species 65 million Years Ago." *Proc. Natl. Acad. Sci. USA.* 80: 627-642.

Alvarez, L.W., Alvarez, W., Asaro, F., and Michel, H.V. 1980. "Extraterrestrial Cause for the Cretaceous-Tertiary Extinction." *Science* 208: 1095-1108.

American Geophysical Union Special Report on Volcanism and Climate Change. May, 1992 (Washington, D.C.: American Geophysical Union).

Avise, J.C., and Nelson, W.S. 1989. "Molecular Genetic Relationships of the Extinct Dusky Seaside Sparrow." *Science* 243: 646-648.

Benton, M.J. 1990. *Vertebrate Paleontology* (London: Unwin Hyman).

Benveniste, R. 1985. "The Contributions of Retroviruses to the Study of Mammalian Evolution." In: R. J. MacIntyre (ed.), *Molecular Evolutionary Genetics* (New York: Plenum), pp. 359-417.

Bowen, B., Avise, J.C., Richardson, J.1., Meylan, A.B., Margaritoulis, D., and Hopkins-Murphy, S.R. 1993. "Population Structure of Loggerhead

Turtles (Caretta caretta) in the Northwestern Atlantic Ocean and Mediterranean Sea." *Conserv. Biol.* 7: 834-844.

Brunk, C.F. 1991. "Darwin in an Age of Molecular Revolution." *Contention* 1: 131-150.

Brusca, R.C. and Brusca G.J. 1990. *Invertebrates* (Sunderland, MA: Sinauer).

Colbert, E.H. and Morales, M. 1991. *Evolution of the Vertebrates* (4th ed.) (New York: Wiley-Liss).

Coyne, J.A. 1994. "Ernst Mayr and the Origin of Species." *Evolution* 48: 19-30.

Darwin, C. 1859. *On the Origin of Species*. (1st ed.) (London: John Murray).

De Rijk, P., Neefs, J.-M., Van de Peer, Y., and De Wachter, R. 1992. "Compilation of Small Ribosomal Subunit RNA Sequences." *Nuc. Acid Res.* 20: 2075-2089.

Frolich, L.M. 1991. "Osteological Conservatism and Developmental Constraint in the Polymorphic "Ring Species" *Ensatina eschscholtzii* (*Amphibia: Plethodontidae*)." *Biol. J. Linn. Soc.* 43: 81-100.

Gans, C. 1989. "Stages in the Origins of Vertebrates: Analysis by the Means of Scenarios." *Biol. Rev. Camb. Phil. Soc.* 64: 221-268.

Gans, C., and Northcutt R.G. 1993. "Neural Crest and the Origin of Vertebrates: A New Head." *Science* 220: 268-274.

Goldberg, Y.P., Rommens, J.M., Andrew, S.E., Hutchinson, G.B., Lin, B., Theilmann, J., Graham, R., Glaves, M.L., Starr, E., McDonald, H., Nasir, J., Schappert, K., Kalchman, M.A., Clarke, L.A., and Hayden, M.R. 1993. "Identification of an Alu Retrotransposition Event in Close Proximity to a Strong Candidate Gene for Huntington's Disease." *Nature*, 362: 370-373.

Gould, S.J. 1980. *The Panda's Thumb* (New York: Norton).

Gould, S.J. 1989. *Wonderful Life* (New York: Norton).

Haselkom, R. 1992. "Developmentally Regulated Gene Rearrangements in Prokaryotes." *Annu. Rev. Genet.* 26: 113-130.

Hedges, S.B., Moberg, K.D., and Maxson, L.R. 1990. "Tetrapod phylogeny inferred from 18S and 28S ribosomal RNA sequences and a review of the evidence for amniote relationships." *Mol. Biol. Evol.* 7.- 607-633.

Holland, P.W.H., Holland, L.Z., Williams, N.A., and Holland, N.D. 1992. "An amphioxus homeobox gene: Sequence conservation, spatial expression during development and insights into vertebrate evolution." *Development* 116: 653-661.

Kimura, M. 1968. "Evolutionary rate at the molecular level." *Nature* 217: 624-626.

King, L.K., and Jukes, T.H. 1969. "Non-Darwinian evolution." *Science* 164: 788-798.

Lewontin, R.C. 1983. "The organism as the subject and object of evolution." *Scientia* 118: 65-82.

Mayr, E. 1942. *Systematics and the Origin of Species* (New York: Columbia Univ.).

Mayr, E. 1988. *Toward a New Philosophy of Biology* (Cambridge: Harvard Univ. Press).

Mayr, E. 1991. *One Long Argument* (Cambridge: Harvard Univ. Press).

Moritz, C., Schneider, C.J. and Wake, D.B. 1992. "Evolutionary relationships within the *Ensatina eschscholtzii* complex confirm the ring species interpretation." *Syst. Biol.* 41: 273-291.

Niklas, K.J. 1994. "Morphological evolution through complex domains of fitness." *Proc. Natl. Acad. Sci.* USA 91: 6772-6779.

Northcutt, R.G., and Gans, C. 1983. "The genesis of neural crest and epidermal placodes: A reinterpretation of vertebrate origins." *Quart. Rev. Biol.* 58: 1-28.

Olsen, G.J. 1987. "Earliest phylogenetic branchings: Comparing rRNA-based evolutionary trees inferred with various techniques." *Cold Spring Harbor Symp. Quant. Biol.* 52: 825-837.

Paul, G.S. 1989. *Predatory Dinosaurs of the World* (New York: Simon & Schuster).

Peterson, K.J. 1994. "The origin and early evolution of the Craniata." In D.R. Prothero and R.M. Schoch (eds.), *Major Features of Vertebrate Evolution. Short Courses in Paleontology* 7: 14-37.

Raff, R.A., and Kaufman, T.C. 1983. *Embryos, Genes and Evolution* (New York: Macmillan).

Raup, D.M. 1991. *Extinction: Bad Genes or Bad Luck?* (New York: Norton).

Ridley, M. 1993. *Evolution* (Boston: Blackwell Scientific).

Romer, A.S., and Parsons, T.S. 1986. *The Vertebrate Body* (6th ed.). (Philadelphia: Saunders).

Sharpton, V.L., Burke, K., Camargo-Zanoguera, A., Hall, S.A., Lee D.S., Marfn, L.E., SudrezReynoso, G., Quezada-Muneton, J.M., Spudis, P.D., and Urrutia-Fucugauchi, J. 1993. "Chicxulub multiring impact basin: Size and other characteristics derived from gravity analysis." *Science* 261: 1564--1567.

Simeone, A., Acampora, D., Gulisano, M., Stomaiuolo, A., and Boncinelli, E. 1992. "Nested expression domains of four homeobox genes in developing rostral brain." *Nature* 358: 687-690.

Simpson, G.G. 1964. "Organisms and molecules in evolution." *Science* 146: 1535-1538.

Van Valen, L. 1974. "A natural model for the origin of some higher taxa." *J. Herp.* 8: 109-121.

Van Valen, L. 1973. "Festschrift." *Science* 180: 488.

Van Valkenburgh, B., and Hertel, F. 1993. "Tough times at La Brea: Tooth breakage in large carnivores of the late Pleistocene." *Science.* 261: 456-459.

Wayne, R.K. 1986. "Cranial morphology of domestic and wild canids: The influence of development on morphological change." *Evolution* 40: 243-261.

Weiner, J. 1994. *The Beak of the Finch* (New York: Knopf).

FURTHER READING

Darwin and Darwinism

Darwin, C. 1859. *On the Origin of Species* (Facsimilie of I st ed.). Reprinted 1979 (Cambridge: Harvard Univ. Press).

Dawkins, R. 1987. *The Blind Watchmaker: Why the Evidence of Evolution Reveals a Universe Without Design* (New York: Norton).

Depew, D.J., and Weber, B.H. 1995. *Darwinism Evolving* (Cambridge: MIT Press).

Ghiselin, M.T. 1969. *The Triumph of the Darwinian Method* (Berkeley: Univ. California Press).

Mayr, E. 1991. *One Long Argument* (Cambridge: Harvard Univ. Press).

Weiner, J. 1994. *The Beak of the Finch* (New York: Knopf).

Textbooks on Evolution, Development and Evolution, and Molecular Biology

Futuyma, D.J. 1986. *Evolutionary Biology* (Sunderland, MA: Sinauer).

Raff, R.A., and Kaufman, T.C. 1983. *Embryos, Genes and Evolution* (New York: Macmillan).

Ridley, M. 1993. *Evolution* (Boston: Blackwell Scientific).

Skelton, P. 1993. *Evolution: A Biological and Paleontological Approach* (Reading, MA: AddisonWesley).

Watson, J.D., Hopkins, N.H., Roberts, J.W., Steitz, J.A., and Weiner, A.M. 1987. *Molecular Biology, of the Gene* (Menlo Park, CA: Benjamin/ Cummings).

5

Speciation

DOUGLAS FUTUYMA

Speciation is the evolutionary process by which two or more descendant species are formed from an immediately ancestral species. The definition of speciation hinges on the meaning of "species." Most evolutionary biologists use the "biological species concept, according to which a species is a population or group of populations that actually or potentially interbreed and is prevented by its biological properties from freely interbreeding with other such groups." The process of speciation therefore resides in the evolution of differences among populations that prevent interbreeding, i.e., the exchange of genes between them.

I. DIVERSITY AND SPECIATION

Perhaps 1.4 million living species have been named, but the total number of species alive today is certainly far greater—surely at least 10 to 15 million, and possibly as high as 30 million! Vast numbers of species of insects, mites, and nematodes await description, as well as many thousands that inhabit the deep sea and other almost unexplored habitats such as the interstices between sand grains, where a diverse fauna of tiny animals thrives. Living species, moreover, compose less than one percent of those that have existed in the past. All these species form a great "tree of life," or phylogeny, of organisms descended from a single common ancestor. This diversity has been generated by two related processes: anagenesis, the transformation of characteristics of each individual evolutionary lineage; and cladogenesis, the branching of ancestral lineages into two or more descendants. Each branch in phylogeny originated in the division of one species into two or more, which, it is generally agreed, were at first very similar, but which, embarking on different paths of change, anagenetically accumulated such differences that their descendants are classified as different genera, families, or still higher categories. Speciation is the fundamental cause of diversity.

Changes in the number of species in a clade (i.e., a group such as beetles that is descended from a single ancestor) depend on both the rate of speciation and the rate of extinction. Given an estimate of the age of a group from the first appearance of fossils, and an estimate of the number of species (N) at some time t million years later (such as the present), the average rate of increase (R) in species number per preexisting species can be estimated from the expression $N = N_0 \exp (Rt)$, assuming that the initial number of species, N_0, is 1. These rates of increase, R, vary greatly. According to S. M. Stanley, they are lower in bivalves, for example $(R = 0.06)$, than in bovid ruminants $(R = 0.15)$, murid rodents $(R = 0.35)$, and colubrid snakes $(R$ perhaps as high as 0.56 per million years). The net rate of increase, R, is the speciation rate (S) per species less the extinction rate (E), which can sometimes be estimated from the fossil record. Stanley finds that in rapidly radiating clades, rates of speciation and extinction are correlated, and that S varies among groups; for instance, S is in the range of 0.43 to 0.93 new species per preexisting species of mammal, per million years, but only 0.09 to 0. 15 for bivalves.

II. Species

A. Concepts of Species and Speciation

The definition of "species" (Latin for "kind") has been and still is controversial for two centuries, partly because of real biological ambiguities and partly because it is used in two research traditions, taxonomy and evolutionary biology, with somewhat different histories, concepts, and aims. Pre-Darwinian taxonomists viewed species as "kinds" separately created. Holding an "essentialist" or "typological" philosophy inherited from Plato and Aristotle, according to which each "kind" has an immutable ideal "essence," they sought to ignore variation among individual organisms, and classified each individual based on its morphological conformity to the species' ideal "type."

Later taxonomists became aware of the considerable morphological variation within species, especially among specimens taken from different localities (geographic variation). A continuum of degree of difference from slight to great exists. In some instances very different-looking forms, such as striped and ringed snakes, were found in litters from the same mother and so were acknowledged as conspecific (the phenomenon of polymorphism). Early in this century, it was further found that morphologically indistinguishable forms of organisms such as mosquitoes, fruit flies, flycatchers, and *Paramecium* differed in ecological and behavioral features, chromosome structure, and often slightly in morphology if examined closely enough. Such "sibling species" indicated that morphological differences were not sufficient for distinguishing species. Confronted with evidence that forms do or do not interbreed, almost all taxonomists gave precedence to this criterion over the morphological degree of difference.

In the late 1930s and the 1940s, there emerged from such taxonomic and biological evidence and from the genetical theory of evolution being developed at that time, the concept that community versus discontinuity of reproduction is the defining concept of species. The evolutionary geneticists Theodosius Dobzansky and Hermann Muller, and especially the systematist Ernst Mayr, rather successfully promulgated the *biological species concept,* which Mayr defined in 1942 as: "species are groups of actually or potentially interbreeding populations, which are reproductively isolated from other such groups." "Reproductive isolation" need not mean hybrid sterility: many species can produce fertile offspring if forced to cross, yet do not interbreed in nature because of differences in behavior or other features (see later). The biological differences that confer reproductive isolation were termed "isolating mechanisms" by Dobzhansky.

The biological species concept (BSC) has been widely adopted by evolutionary biologists because it best describes patterns of variation in most organisms. Moreover, reproductive isolation plays a critical role in evolutionary theory. As long as populations are capable of free interbreeding, genetic differences between them either cannot develop to a substantial degree (if they actually interbreed freely) or once developed may be lost (if segregated populations meet and interbreed). Thus reproductive isolation confers on populations the ability to diverge genetically, following independent evolutionary trajectories, to any degree. Without speciation, there would be precious little diversity, and indeed little evolution.

Many biologists have objected to the BSC. Some objections arise from the two overlapping but distinct uses of "species" in contemporary biology. To most evolutionary biologists, the species is an *evolutionary concept,* as described earlier. But the species is also a *taxonomic category:* organisms with names such as *Escherichia coli, Homo sapiens,* and the red oak *Quercus rubra* are taxa in the category species, just as *Homo* and *Quercus* are taxa in the category "genus." Many "taxonomic species" do not fit the BSC. For example, predominantly asexual organisms such as *Escherichia coli* are taxonomic but not biological species, simply because the domain of the BSC is restricted to sexually reproducing organisms. Different stages in a single evolving lineage may be named by paleontologists as different taxonomic species ("chronospecies"), such as *H. sapiens* and its antecedent *Homo erectus*, but the domain of the BSC is restricted to fairly narrow intervals of time within which populations might exchange genes. Some systematists have proposed a "phylogenetic species concept," according to which, if a phylogenetic tree can be constructed for a set of populations, any population characterized by a new ("derived") evolutionary feature will be designated a species, whether it interbreeds with other populations or not. Defenders of the BSC maintain that when the biology of organisms places them within the domain of the BSC, it is a useful definition that should be adopted. Organisms that do not fall within its domain, such as asexual forms, have different evolutionary dynamics, require different criteria for designation of species (or perhaps should be described in other terms entirely), and do not vitiate the BSC within its proper domain.

Some opponents of the BSC identify the concept with Dobzhansky's term "isolating mechanism." They hold that "mechanism" implies an adaptive function favored by natural selection (e.g., the heart is a mechanism for circulating blood) and that there is little evidence that biological barriers to gene exchange have evolved in order to accomplish this effect (see later). These authors (e.g., H. Paterson) argue that species should be defined not by reproductive isolation, but instead by their sharing in a common "specific mate recognition system." Adherents to the BSC view this as merely the opposite side of the same coin, and object only to these authors' exclusion of hybrid sterility and inviability as possible (though not universal) criteria of species difference.

The principal real difficulty of the BSC is that the extent of gene exchange (or its converse, reproductive isolation) is not an all-or-none affair: populations with adjacent *(parapatric)* or coexisting *(sympatric)* geographic distributions may exhibit partial reproductive isolation in varying degree. Sympatric forms sometimes interbreed to some extent, yet retain their identity by and large, with most individuals readily classifiable.Sympatric hybridization appears to be more frequent among plants than animals (for example, the red oak *Quercus rubra* hybridizes with several closely related species). Parapatric forms often form a narrow "hybrid zone" where they meet, yet are fully distinctive shortly distant from the zone, implying that many genes from the one population (or "semispecies") are eliminated from the "gene pool" of the other. The fire-bellied and yellow-bellied toads *(Bombina bombina* and *B. variegate),* each distributed broadly in Europe, hybridize in a region only about 20 km wide. Such cases, in which it's rather arbitrary whether one species or two be recognized, are expected if, and indeed demonstrate that, the genetic divergence that causes speciation is a gradual process. They do not invalidate the BSC where it *does* apply (which is to say, for the majority of sympatric species). It simply must be acknowledged that not all populations fit into discrete definitional categories.

B.   Definition versus Diagnosis of Species

A practical, although not a conceptual, drawback of the BSC is that *allopatric* populations, those that occupy separate geographic areas, can be shown to be different species only by placing samples together and finding that they fail to mate or that the hybrids are inviable or sterile. Such experiments are more feasible with some organisms (e.g., *Drosophila* or rapidly growing plants) than with others. To determine whether a sample of specimens from the same place consists of one or more than one species does not, however, require breeding experiments. Although reproductive discontinuity *defines* species, they may be recognized by the consequences of reproductive isolation, namely discontinuities in genetically based characteristics of any kind. A single discrete difference, such as stripes versus rings in the California king snake *(Lampropeltis getulus)*, may be a single-gene polymorphism in a single species; but if several such characters, whether of morphology, behavior, or other features, segregate the sample into two or more discrete groups, they show reproductive isolation. This is a consequence of simple principles of population genetics. If the frequencies of two alleles at a locus (A, A') are p and q (where $p + q = 1$), the proportion of heterozygotes should be $2pq$ under random mating. A strong deficiency of heterozygotes, or of intermediate phenotypes if neither allele is dominant, is evidence of some reproductive discontinuity. Moreover, recombination causes alleles at two or more variable loci (A and B) to become uncorrelated in a single randomly mating population; thus if a strong association is found between A and B and between A' and B', these combinations ($AABB$ and $A'A'B'B'$) are likely to mark distinct species. Thus if loci A and B affect different characters, a sample of two species will form two "character clusters"; if they affect the same (polygenic) character such as bristle number in flies, the character may show a bimodal distribution. Most sympatric species have been named by taxonomists on the basis of discrete sets of phenotypic differences that betoken genetic discontinuity and are indeed good species.

III. Characteristics of Species

A. Barriers to Gene Flow

Species status depends on biological differences that potentially or actually impede gene flow between populations. These barriers ("isolating mechanisms") fall roughly into prezygotic and postzygotic categories (Table 1).

TABLE 1
Biological Barriers to Gene Exchange

I.   Prezygotic barriers (preventing union of gamete nuclei)

   1.   Potential mates do not meet (isolation by habitat or by season, time of day of mating).

   2.   Potential mates meet but do not mate.

      a.   Animals: ethological (= behavioral or "sexual" isolation).

      b.   Plants: transfer of pollen reduced by different pollinators or flower form.

   3.   Mating occurs (or is attempted) but gametes do not unite.

      a.   Animals: insemination prevented by mechanical or structural barriers (when fertilization is internal), or chemical (e.g., cell surface) incompatibility between gametes.

      b.   Plants: physiological (chemical) incompatibility between pollen and pistil, or between gamete cells.

II.   Postzygotic barriers (reduction in fitness of hybrid zygotes)

   1.   Egg is fertilized but zygote mortality is high (inviability, due to developmental incomparability, ecological selection, or both).

   2.   Viable adult hybrids have reduced fertility (sterility, of one or both sexes).

      a.   Incompatibility among genes, or between gene combinations and maternal cytoplasm, prevents development of viable gametes.

      b.   Proportion of viable gametes reduced by aneuploidy (unbalanced chromosome complement) resulting from failure of chromosomes to pair or from structural rearrangements yielding unbalanced gene complements.

      c.   Offspring of hybrids have reduced viability.

Prezygotic barriers, those that reduce the likelihood of the union of gametes, include ecological differences, such as mating on different host plants in the case of many host-specific insects; temporal differences, such as different flowering seasons in many groups of plants; gametic incompatibility, such as the failure of eggs and sperm, cast into water by many marine invertebrates, to "recognize" each other; and ethological ("sexual") isolation, especially important in animals. Differences in mating signal and response are exemplified by the mating calls of frogs and crickets, the sexual pheromones (chemical signals) of many insects and mammals, and courtship behaviors and associated visual and/or vocal signals in many birds, fishes, and flies. These are the chief barriers to interbreeding in nature, and many such species (e.g., of ducks) can be hybridized, producing fertile offspring, in the zoo or laboratory. In flowering plants, the analogue of ethological isolation is attraction of different pollinating animals or differences in flower form that ensure deposition of pollen on conspecific stigmas instead of on those of other species.

Postzygotic barriers, arising from incompatible genetic programs for development, include the inviability or infertility (sterility) of F_1 or backcross hybrids; both inviability and infertility can vary in degree from slight to complete. A conspicuous feature of postzygotic barriers has been termed "Haldane's rule:" if there is a sexual difference in hybrids in the degree of inviability or infertility, this is more accentuated in the sex with only one X chromosome. Thus postzygotic isolation is typically more pronounced in male than in female hybrids (e.g., in flies and mammals), but the reverse holds in butterflies and birds, in which the female is XY and the male is XX.

B. Hybrid Zones

Hybrid zones, such as in *Bombina* toads, have been important in studies of speciation. The width of a hybrid zone is directly proportional to the average distance of dispersal of individuals of each species, or of hybrids, into the range of the other and is inversely proportional to the strength of selection against the hybrid gene combinations. Such selection may arise through differences in the ecological environment of the two populations, within which certain genes of the other species are disadvantageous, or it may arise because of the intrinsically lower fitness of hybrid gene combinations. For instance, heterozygosity for a certain locus or chromosome may lower viability or fertility, as when the populations are fixed (homozygous) for different inversions or other rearrangements of a chromosome, and the heterozygous F_1 hybrid suffers low fertility because of aneuploid segregation. This selection against the heterozygote prevents either chromosome from increasing in frequency when it is spread from one population to the other by interbreeding. Selection against hybrids may often arise from the inferior adaptive value of hybrid combinations of genes (an instance of *epistasis*); for example, *AA* and *AA'* may confer high fitness in combination with genotype *BB* at a second locus, and the combination *A'A'B'B'* may likewise have high fitness, whereas other gene combinations may reduce viability or fertility. In this instance, it is likely that the prevalent genotypes in the two populations will be *AABB* and *A'A'B'B'*, respectively.

The fitness of hybrid gene combinations in some instances depends on environmental factors. Thus it is not uncommon to find plant species (e.g., certain irises) that are reproductively isolated in natural environments in which each species is adapted to a different habitat, but which form "hybrid swarms" where habitats have been greatly disturbed, providing intermediate microhabitats within which backcross hybrids thrive.

If F_1 hybrids are capable of some reproduction, and so by backcrossing conduct genes from each semispecies into the other, an allele that reduces the fitness of backcross hybrids will attain only low frequency in the semispecies into which it is introduced, and there will be a steep *cline* of decreasing allele frequency away from the hybrid zone (Figure 1). This is also true at closely

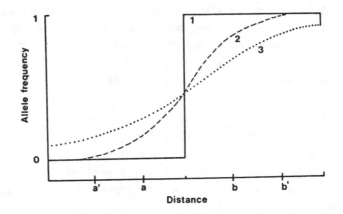

FIGURE I - Idealized allele frequency clines in hybrid zones. Curve 1 (solid): No gene exchange between parapatric populations due to complete pre- or postzygotic reproductive isolation. Curve 2 (dashed): A steep cline across interval a-b due to strong selection relative to gene flow. Curve 3 (dotted): A shallow cline across interval a'-b' due to weaker selection relative to gene flow. Curves such as 2 and 3 may be displayed by different loci in a single hybrid zone.

linked loci, but the cline will be less steep at loci that are more loosely linked to a selected locus because recombination in backcross progeny dissociates selected from nonselected alleles, so the latter flow more freely between the semispecies. The spatial profile of neutral alleles at a marker locus therefore suggests whether or not it is closely linked to a selected locus that contributes to reproductive isolation. By extension, steep clines at few versus many neutral marker loci, distributed throughout the genome, can tell whether reproductive isolation is caused by only a few genes or many. In the case of the *Bombina* hybrid zone, J. Szymura and N. Barton found that most electrophoretic markers are characteristic of one or the other species and decline rapidly in frequency past the narrow hybrid zone; they concluded that almost every marker locus is therefore rather closely linked to a selected locus and that the number of such loci is at least 55. Barton likewise concluded that at least 150 loci each slightly diminish hybrid fitness and contribute to reproductive isolation between "races" of the grasshopper *Podisma pedestris*.

C. The Genetic Basis of Species Differences

The genetic differences between two closely related species include those that contribute to pre- or postzygotic reproductive isolation (i.e., those that cause the populations to be different species) and those that do not. The latter may include selectively neutral differences, such as perhaps many allozymes, and selectively important differences such as those that underlie ecological differentiation, but which are not necessarily causal in speciation. For any class of genes, the overall degree of genetic difference between two populations that do not exchange genes (either because of allopatry or reproductive isolation) should increase over time because of genetic drift and/or natural selection. Even if selection maintains the same mean state of a *character* in both species, its underlying genetic basis is likely to turn over. (For example, the same mean for an additively inherited polygenic character can be produced by any of many gene combinations that may be selectively equivalent, so allele frequencies at the constituent loci can change by genetic drift.) The genetic basis of speciation is better sought among recently differentiated populations or species than among long-differentiated taxa that have acquired further differentiation subsequent to the speciation event.

An enormous literature on electrophoretic (allozyme) differences among populations and closely related species has shown that (a) the degree of differentiation constitutes a continuum, from slight differences among conspecific populations, to greater differentiation as we pass through "subspecies," semispecies, and full species; and (b) the level of difference between reproductively isolated species differs greatly from one comparison to another. Molecular investigations show almost no differences between species in certain groups, such as some African cichlid fishes that are nonetheless strongly differentiated in ecological habits, behavior, and color pattern. In these and other such groups, molecular and other evidence indicate that speciation has been both rapid and recent, and that reproductive isolation is conferred primarily by sexual and/or ecological isolation, with postzygotic inviability or infertility playing a small role, if any.

Investigation of the genetic basis of morphological or other phenotypic differences among species has been limited to cases in which at least some fertile hybrids can be obtained and backcrossed. An extensive classical literature, treating plants especially, showed that the individual morphological characters that distinguish species typically are inherited as polygenic traits, as is usually true also of character variation within species. In many cases, the character is inherited more or less additively, but strong epistatic effects are sometimes evident. Among the most striking of these is the observation, first made by the great geneticist A. H. Sturtevant, that a feature which is identical in two species may nevertheless have a very different genetic foundation: hybrids between *Drosophila melanogaster* and *D. simulans* have aberrant, highly variable patterns of dorsal bristles, even though the two species have identical, almost invariant patterns. This observation implies incompatible interactions between different sets of genes governing the development of the bristles (and of the nervous system, of which these structures are part). In the same vein, a gene encoding a black spot in one species of platyfish *(Poecilia)* causes melanotic tumors when crossed into another species, implying that the interaction with "alien" genes disrupts its normal developmental function. These and many like observations led Mayr, Dobzhansky, and others to conclude that speciation entails the evolution of different, *coadapted,* systems of interacting genes. According to this view, the evolution of a given genetic difference imposes selection for "modifiers"—alleles at other loci—which interact favorably with the primary gene to yield harmonious function. Instances such as the platyfish pigment gene show, further, that genes detected by their morphological effects can have pleiotropic effects on development and thus on hybrids' viability or fertility.

Hybrid infertility is sometimes attributable solely to chromosome differences that prevent proper meiotic pairing and segregation. In crosses between some plant species, such as between certain primroses and between radish *(Raphanus sativus)* and cabbage *(Brassica oleracea)* that have the same chromosome number, the diploid F_1 hybrid is almost entirely sterile and the chromosomes do not pair. Doubling the chromosomes of the F_1, however, results in a tetraploid hybrid with the same genetic constitution as the diploid, but in which each chromosome can pair with its identical partner. These hybrids are fully fertile, showing that the diploid's sterility is caused by structural chromosome differences instead of differences at individual genes. Each of the chromosome differences that commonly distinguish related species probably lowers hybrid fertility only slightly. Chromosome differentiation does not necessarily accompany speciation; some species of Hawaiian *Drosophila,* for example, have identical chromosome structure.

Postzygotic barriers such as sterility are often, and prezygotic barriers almost always, based on genic differences instead of gross chromosomal rearrangements. The genetic basis of such characters can be analyzed indirectly, as Barton did from clinal patterns of gene frequency, or more directly by backcrossing hybrids. Some such studies have used the methods of quantitative genetics, which provide very inexact estimates of the "effective number" of gene differences from data on the means and variances of a character in F_1, F_2, and backcross generations. For example, Hawaiian species of *Drosophila* have diversified greatly in male secondary sexual characteristics on the legs, head, and mouth parts. *Drosophila heteroneura* differs from its close relative *D. silvestris* in that the male's head is greatly expanded to either side. *Drosophila silvestris* itself is divided into two allopatric "races," one of which has only 1 or 2, and the other about 30, long bristles on the male's foreleg, used to brush the female during courtship. An analysis of backcross hybrids of the races of *D. silvestris* provided evidence that about 30% of the difference in bristle number is due to one or more X-linked genes and the remainder to genes on at least two of the five autosomes. The three "effective genes" are certainly an underestimate because the method cannot detect additional linked genes or genes with small effects. A similar analysis of the head shape difference between *D. silvestris* and *D. heteroneura* concluded that at least six to eight gene differences are involved.

The other method of genetic analysis, almost limited so far to certain species of *Drosophila,* takes advantage of mutant markers on most or all of the chromosomes (or even chromosome arms) and of the lack of recombination in males. This enables an investigator to identify, among the backcross progeny, individuals with different mixtures of chromosomes from each species. Differences in morphology, fertility, or viability among these classes enable one to determine which marked chromosome(s) contributes to the difference between species. These studies, in several species groups of *Drosophila,* have generally shown that for characters such as male and female fertility and male genitalic morphology, the number of gene differences is as great as the number that the method can detect (i.e., at least one gene difference per chromosome arm if each arm carries a mutant marker) (Figure 2).

These polygenic differences suggest, as does variation in the degree of reproductive isolation among populations in many taxa, that reproductive isolation evolves gradually, by the successive substitution of many allelic differences between species. However, studies of populations that have diverged more recently, such as *Drosophila pseudo-obscure* from the United

States versus Colombia, suggest that only a few gene differences may confer substantial intersterility. An interesting case is the European corn borer *(Ostrinia "nubilalis")*, which consists of two "pheromone races." A single gene difference determines whether the female moth releases one or another blend of sex pheromones, and another single gene difference determines the male's almost exclusive attraction to one or the other. Perhaps speciation is effected by fewer gene substitutions than previous evidence has suggested.

Most studies of the genetic basis of isolation indicate that the genes occupy consistent chromosomal sites, which together with other evidence indicates that (contrary to some speculations) transposable elements probably do

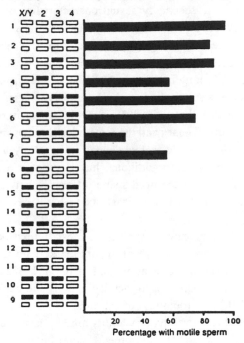

FIGURE 2 Male sterility in backcross hybrids with different mixtures of *Drosophila pseudoobscura* (white) and *D. persimilis (black)* chromosomes. The X chromosome has the greatest effect (compare genotypes 1-8 with 9-16), but each autosome (chromosomes 2, 3, and 4) also has an effect (e. g., genotypes 1 vs 2 and 7 vs 8).

not contribute to speciation. On the other hand, cytoplasmically inherited factors often cause inviability or infertility in insects, if combined with the nuclear genome of another species. These factors are usually endosymbiotic bacteria.

It should be stressed that the postzygotic isolation analyzed in many genetic studies may not be the effective barrier to gene flow among these species in nature, where prezygotic isolation is usual.

IV. MECHANISMS OF SPECIATION

A. Geography of Speciation

Speciation usually takes too long to observe directly. Hence our understanding of the mechanisms of speciation must rely less on experiments than on observations of patterns in nature, interpreted through theory. The applicability of one or another theoretical model, however, depends on data, which together with models help us to evaluate the likelihood of alternative explanations in any given case.

For example, population genetic models show that absent strong selection, a barrier to free interbreeding is necessary if strong interlocus associations, such as those among the several or many loci that contribute to a pre- or postzygotic isolating "mechanism," are to develop. Such a barrier could in principle be provided by a distributional gap between two initially genetically similar populations, by selection counteracting gene flow among neighboring populations, or by a genetic polymorphism that creates *assortative mating* or some other interruption to gene exchange within a population. These possibilities constitute the *allopatric, parapatric,* and *sympatric* models of speciation.

Allopatric speciation is unquestionably a major, if not the major, mode of speciation. From a theoretical point of view, the forces of genetic drift and natural selection will inevitably engender genetic differences among separated populations that confer reproductive isolation, given long enough time. The empirical evidence includes: (1) Conspecific populations vary in genetic composition, to a greater or lesser degree, in every kind of feature, including those that confer reproductive isolation. (2) The proliferation of closely related species is frequently correlated with the abundance of topographical or habitat barriers to gene flow. A species is often separated from its closest relative by such a barrier, as in fishes on either side of the Isthmus of Panama. Particularly strong evidence is afforded by island archipelagoes, in which each island is typically inhabited by more species than are single isolated islands; for example, Cocos Island, distant from the Galápagos archipelago, has only one species of Darwin's finch, whereas most of the Galápagos Islands harbor several. This pattern is attributed to speciation by isolation on different islands, followed by recolonization and sympatry. (3) Genetic differentiation among populations is most pronounced in organisms with a low capacity for dispersal and gene flow, such as land snails and wingless grasshoppers.

Hybrid zones between populations (such as *Bombina*) that are differentiated at many loci are thought often to represent *secondary contact* between formerly allopatric populations that, subsequent to differentiation, have expanded their range.

A continuum among two extreme patterns of allopatric speciation has been posited by Mayr and other authors. One extreme is the so-called "dumbbell" or vicariance model, in which a widely distributed species is sundered into two widely distributed entities by the emergence of a topographic barrier such as a mountain range or body of water. The two entities then diverge. At the other extreme, a population differentiates in a restricted locality after colonization from the main body of the species. The latter mode (peripatric speciation) has been considered by Mayr and others to be more frequent, based on observations that strongly differentiated populations and distinct species commonly have very limited distributions peripheral to the more widely distributed but more uniform "Parent" species. Speciation by "vicariance" appears often to be slower than in localized populations, but few if any studies have demonstrated the effect on the speciation rate of population size per se by controlling for levels of gene flow and time since isolation (both difficult to determine).

The incidence of parapatric and sympatric speciation is highly controversial. Parapatric speciation might happen if sufficiently strong selection for different genes in different habitats were to counteract gene flow, engendering genetic differences sufficient to confer reproductive isolation. Among the few documented examples is divergence of grass populations adapted to soils impregnated with toxic metals from mine wastes; these have diverged not only in metal tolerance, but also in flowering time and the rate of self-fertilization, both of which confer partial reproductive isolation from populations on nearby normal soils. However, most hybrid zones between parapatric semispecies seem to have been formed by secondary contact rather than differentiation *in situ* and appear not to evolve the prezygotic reproductive barriers that characterize fully formed species.

Speciation by polyploidy is universally accepted as a mechanism of sympatric speciation because a polyploid plant is instantly postzygotically isolated from the parent diploid. Sympatric speciation by genic divergence is far more controversial, and population genetic theory implies that it is unlikely. A common model envisions that in, say, an insect that feeds on two plant species, each homozygote *(AA, aa)* is best adapted to a different plant, with the heterozygote *(Aa)* less well adapted. Selection might then favor associative mating *(AA* with *AA, aa* with *aa),* yielding adapted progeny. If mate preference depends on another locus *(B, b),* however, the rarer of these alleles can increase in frequency (forming two partially reproductively isolated subpopulations) only if an association (linkage disequilibrium) develops between alleles at the two loci (i.e., if the *AB* and *ab* combinations are more prevalent than *Ab* and *aB).* This can happen only if recombination is counteracted by strong selection on the *A* locus, and is facilitated if the basis for associative mating is attraction to and mating on the different plants.

One case which may illustrate the first step toward sympatric speciation is the true fruit fly *Rhagoletis pomonella,* in which samples from apple and hawthorn trees differ genetically in the time of emergence, which is correlated with the fruiting phenology of their hosts. In few other instances, however, is there evidence of strong selection of different genotypes on different plants, so the requirements for sympatric speciation may seldom be met.

B. Causes of Speciation

The causes of speciation are the area of greatest ignorance and controversy. The central questions are whether the genetic differences that confer reproductive isolation are caused by genetic drift (chance), natural selection, or some combination of the two; and if selection is primary, what its agents may be. The critical point is that speciation is the formation of gene complexes, differing typically at two or more loci, that are incompatible in heterozygous condition. If the heterozygote *Aa* has lower fitness than genotypes *AA* and *aa,* either allele is reduced in frequency by natural selection if it is rare. The problem then is to explain how two populations, both initially *AA* (or *aa),* can diverge so that the alternative allele is fixed in one of them. Divergence at many such loci (or chromosome rearrangements) poses the same problem. In an "adaptive landscape" that represents the mean fitness of genotypes in a population as a function of gene frequencies at one or more loci (Figure 3), two species may be considered to occupy distinct peaks, with the low-fitness valley between them representing a population of hybrids. As long as the landscape (dictated by the fitnesses of the various genotypes under a certain constellation of environmental selective factors) is fixed, changes in gene frequency that move a population downslope are opposed by natural selection. An increase in the frequency of a rare allele, deleterious in a heterozygous condition, would be such a prohibited change. The problem then is how a population shifts from one adaptive peak to another.

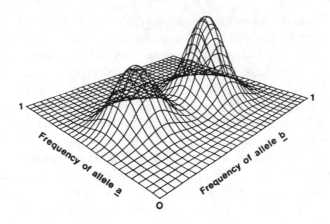

FIGURE 3 An "adaptive landscape" with two fitness peaks. The height of each point on the surface is the mean fitness of individuals in a hypothetical population with a specified gene frequency at each of two loci, specified by the horizontal axes. Gene frequencies change by natural selection so that a population evolves only up slope toward a peak.

There are two theoretical solutions (Figure 4).   One is for the allele frequencies to change rapidly in opposition to natural selection so that the genetic composition "leaps" across an adaptive valley to the slope of another peak. This might be accomplished by genetic drift, which in a sufficiently small population can counteract natural selection. Natural selection, which increases mean fitness, would then move the population up hill to a new, adaptive, genetic constitution (Fig. 4B). This is the "peak shift" model. An analogue to this was proposed by Mayr in 1954, who, seeking to explain the apparently rapid divergence of small peripheral populations, postulated that a population founded by a few colonists would by chance carry aberrant gene frequencies at certain loci. Because of epistatic interactions, gene frequency changes at other loci (modifiers) would occur under the guidance of natural selection, so that the initially random changes at some loci would set in motion the evolution of a new system of coadapted genes.   Mayr's "founder effect speciation" or "peripatric speciation" is therefore a mixed model of random genetic drift and natural selection. The other theoretical solution for getting populations onto different adaptive peaks is to change the landscape: in populations in different localities with different environments, different genotypes are favored by natural selection, i.e., they evolve on different adaptive landscapes (Fig. 4A). Because of its relative simplicity, this "adaptive divergence" model is favored by many population geneticists, who consider founder effect speciation unlikely.

Under either model, the impact of genetic changes on reproductive isolation must be viewed as an *incidental* (pleiotropic) effect instead of having evolved to serve the specific function of reproductive isolation. This is evident from the observation that allopatric populations, not faced with the "threat" of

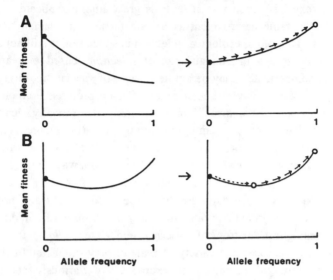

FIGURE 4 Two models of evolution of a population (circle) to a new genetic equilibrium on a one-locus adaptive landscape. (A) Adaptive shift. A changed environment alters relative fitnesses, and the population evolves solely by natural selection. (B) Peak shift. Genetic drift moves the population (broken arrow) to the slope of a second peak, and natural selection (solid arrows) then moves it up slope. The ecological environment has not changed.

hybridizing, diverge in both pre- and postzygotic characters. The possibility exists that the reproductive isolation acquired in allopatry may be reinforced by natural selection if the populations expand and meet.

What is the evidence that the genetic changes responsible for speciation are caused by natural selection? Surprisingly, there is precious little. Genes conferring copper tolerance in a mine-associated population of monkeyflower *(Mimulusguttatus)* are lethal in hybrids with nontolerant populations; in the ground finches *(Geospiza)* of the Galápagos Islands, differences in beak size, an adaptation to feeding on different kinds of seeds, are also the signals for mate choice and sexual isolation. Although related species usually differ in many adaptive characteristics related to their different ecology, it is not known if, in general, these genetic differences are pleiotropically responsible for reproductive isolation. If sympatric speciation by adaptation to different resources were common, such instances of speciation would be driven by natural selection; but it is not known if this is the case. In several experiments with *Drosophila,* divergent selection among or within laboratory populations (for characteristics such as bristle number, food preference, and temperature tolerance) has brought about incipient sexual isolation; but in one such experiment, sexual isolation was at least as great among replicate populations subjected to the same environment as among those that adapted to different environments. The role of ecological selection in speciation is still not known.

In many groups of animals, *sexual selection,* based on variation in success at obtaining mates, may be a potent agent of speciation. Given genetic variation in a male display character and in female preference among variant male phenotypes, a "runaway" process may theoretically lead to an extraordinary elaboration of seemingly arbitrary features. Moreover, random differences among populations in the frequencies of alleles for various such features and female responses may initiate rapid runaway divergence. The consequence will be prezygotic, sexual isolation. The effects of sexual selection are conspicuous in many groups that have speciated rapidly and prolifically, such as cichlid fishes in the African Rift valley lakes, birds of paradise in New Guinea, hummingbirds in tropical America, and *Drosophila* in the Hawaiian islands. In all these cases, the variety of male display organs and behaviors is extraordinary; birds of paradise, for example, are variously adorned with elaborate modifications of the feathers of the tail, back, breast, and head. A comparable runaway process of coevolving signals and responses between plants and pollinators may be responsible for the high speciation rate in orchids, in which astonishing modifications of the flowers promote pollination by different insects.

Although at least some degree of reproductive isolation evolves while populations are allopatric, Dobzhansky postulated that it would become accentuated when incipient species meet, for selection should favor individuals which, by avoiding hybridization, produce fitter offspring. Dobzhansky therefore viewed barriers to gene exchange as "mechanisms" selected, at least in part, for isolation. (This hypothesis can apply only to prezygotic barriers since alleles that increase sterility cannot increase in frequency by natural selection for reproductive isolation.) Population genetic models show that this hypothesis is less plausible than it sounds; as in models of sympatric speciation, it requires tight linkage between genes that lower hybrid fitness and those responsible for assortative mating, which if loosely linked will become dissociated by backcrossing. Moreover, gene flow from neighboring populations can counteract selection within a narrow hybrid zone, and selection for modifiers that improve the fitness of hybrids could eliminate the raison d'être for discrimination in mating.

The hypothesis of reinforcement predicts that sexual isolation, or differences in associated display characters, should be more pronounced between sympatric populations of two species than between allopatric populations of these species, which are not subject to selection for assortative mating. Although numerous such comparisons have been made, in only a few cases has the expected pattern (termed reproductive *character displacement*) been found. One such instance is provided by a pair of species of Australian tree frogs, in which males from sympatric populations differ more in the mating call than do allopatric populations. Many investigators have experimentally measured sexual and postzygotic isolation among various populations and species of *Drosophila*. Using the level of allozyme differentiation as a measure of time since divergence, J. Coyne and H. A. Orr found, in a compilation of this literature, that among allopatric taxa, both sexual and postzygotic isolation increase gradually over time at similar rates; but among sympatric taxa, sexual isolation increases faster than the level of hybrid sterility or inviability (Figure 5). This is, to date, the best evidence that selection to avoid hybridization may

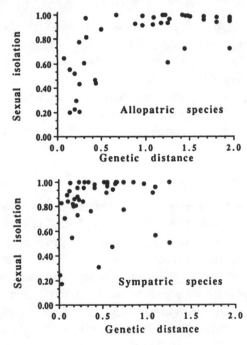

FIGURE 5 Genetic distance versus degree of sexual isolation between pairs of allopatric (top) and sympatric (bottom) *Drosophila* species. Genetic distance, a measure of divergence in allozyme frequencies, is correlated with time since isolation. At low genetic distance (e.g., 0.2), a higher level of sexual isolation is displayed by more sympatric than allopatric pairs, suggesting reinforcement in sympatry.

generally enhance reproductive isolation. The paucity of such evidence, incidentally, argues against the prevalence of parapatric speciation.

The greatest contemporary controversy about causes of speciation concerns peak shift models, in which genetic drift in an initially small population initiates a shift to a new genetic composition. This concept arose from evidence of the prevalence of epistatically coadapted gene pools, implying that gene frequency changes at some loci might constitute selection for change at still other loci, and from the apparently rapid divergence of small, localized populations, e.g., of *Hawaiian Drosophila* and various Pacific island birds. These observations, however, do not constitute *evidence* for peak shifts because new coadapted genomes can evolve solely by natural selection (e.g., in a changed environment) and because small populations typically occupy small ranges, which, being ecologically more homogeneous than wider regions, should differ more in species composition and other environmental agents of selection.

Experiments will probably be necessary to elucidate the role of peak shifts in the evolution of reproductive isolation. For example, E. Bryant and L. Meffert subjected large experimental populations of houseflies *(Musca domestics)* to repeated "bottlenecks" of small size. The bottlenecked populations diverged in elements of male courtship behavior and exhibited some slight sexual isolation both among each other and with reference to a large control population. More research will be needed, however, before the controversy about peak shifts reaches resolution.

C. Ecology of Speciation

Ecology plays a threefold role in speciation: it affects the opportunity for spatial isolation, selection for genetic divergence, and the fate of newly formed species. The opportunity for spatial isolation of populations depends on dispersal and on how exacting the organism's ecological requirements are. Species with high rates of long-distance dispersal, such as the coconut, red mangrove, and many aquatic birds, are typically widely distributed and show little propensity for speciation compared to organisms that disperse little. Highly specialized species are often distributed as isolated populations in widely scattered suitable habitats; for example, this may be one explanation for the great numbers of closely related species in many groups of host-specialized herbivorous insects.

It has been noted that the role of ecological agents of natural selection in the evolution of reproductive isolation is little understood. Ecology, finally, is important in the fate of newly formed species. The principle that excessively similar competing species cannot indefinitely coexist (the competitive exclusion principle) undoubtedly governs many interactions. Allopatrically formed species that expand their range will not overlap, according to this principle, unless they differ sufficiently in resource use (or, in general, that the species' densities not be limited as if they constituted a single population). Surely many newly formed species must be too similar to coexist; this is doubtless reflected by the parapatric distributions of many close relatives (e.g., of birds in New Guinea) that do not interpenetrate each other's range. In at least some instances, such as among the ground finches of the Galápagos, species respond to competition by evolving differences in resource use (ecological character displacement) and can then stably coexist. Such ecological diversification is typical of many of the most prolifically speciating groups, such as African lake cichlids, among which closely related species occupy an extraordinary variety of specialized niches.

V. CONSEQUENCES OF SPECIATION

A. Rates of Speciation

The phrase "speciation rate" can mean either the rate at which species grow in number by speciation alone or the rate at which populations acquire reproductive isolation, i.e., become different species. The first is limited by the second. For instance, Stanley estimates the mean speciation rate (S) for several bivalve families to be 0. 09 to 0.15 per million years, where S is the per capita rate of increase in species number, less the extinction rate estimated from the fossil record. The time required for the number of species to double by speciation alone is then (ln 2)/S, or 7.7 to 4.6 million years. The average value for several groups of mammals is 1.6 to 0.75 million years. These are very approximate estimates of the mean time between successive speciation events in a clade; the actual time required for each such event (evolution of reproduction isolation) could be less. But if it required a minimum of, say 3 million years for each speciation event to transpire, the number of mammal species presumably could not have increased as rapidly as it seems, in fact, to have done.

The time required for speciation to transpire has been estimated, for recently originated species, from geological data on the age of barriers or of habitats, and from levels of genetic divergence (especially allozyme data) which are also calibrated by geological data. Instances of very rapid speciation include the African lake cichlids: 170 species, apparently from a single ancestor, have evolved in Lake Victoria, which is 0.50-0.75 million years old; and five species have arisen in a small satellite lake that is only 4000 years old. During the Pliocene, more than 30 endemic genera of limnocardiid snails diversified from a single ancestor in less than 3 million years in the present region of the Caspian sea. The island of Hawaii, 800,000 to 1 million years old, has endemic species of *Drosophila* derived from ancestors on the older islands. Among *Drosophila* species generally, reproductive isolation is reached, on average, at levels of genetic difference (calculated from allozyme data) thought to correspond to 1. 5 to 3.5 million years of separation, although some pairs of species have arisen in less than 1 million years. Instantaneous speciation by polyploidy is of course the most rapid of all. A new species of cordgrass *(Spartina anglica)* has arisen by allopolyploidy within this century.

Factors conducive to rapid speciation are likely to include: (a) low vagility, fostering genetic divergence of spatially segregated populations; (b) strong sexual selection, perhaps especially in forms with complex precopulatory behavior; (c) ecological opportunity for divergence in different "niches," which may enhance selection for genetic change, ecological isolation, and persistence of newly formed species; and (d) perhaps features of the genetic system, such as strong epistasis, that facilitate peak shifts.

B. Macroevolutionary Consequences of Speciation

Among the important consequences of speciation for evolutionary history writ large, the most self evident was that it is the source of diversity. An individual species can, by genetic polymorphism and alternative developmental pathways, fill an appreciable diversity of niches, but the range of intraspecific variation is far more limited than the variation among species.

Another effect of speciation is that while ancestral characters are transformed in some lineages, they may be retained in others. Thus living club mosses, silverfish, and lungfishes retain features that would have been erased among plants, insects, and vertebrates by anagenetic evolution had speciation not occurred. The persistence of "primitive" character states enables us to trace phylogenies and sometimes to infer the course of evolution of characteristics, even in the absence of a fossil record.

The most controversial issue is the extent to which anagenetic evolution may depend on or be facilitated by speciation. In 1972, N. Eldredge and S. J. Gould proposed *punctuated equilibrium* as both a description of a pattern they claimed is common in the fossil record and as a hypothesis about the evolutionary process. The pattern is one of *stasis*–a lineage often displays no substantial change for several millions of years—*punctuated* by rapid shifts in one or more morphological features (such as the number of rows of eye lenses in trilobites). The explanatory hypothesis (as distinct from observed pattern) of punctuated equilibrium is that a lineage is prevented from evolving, by internal genetic constraints, except when a localized population undergoes a peak shift in genetic constitution, during which both morphology and reproductive isolation evolve. This hypothesis applies to the fossil record Mayr's theory of founder effect (peripatric) speciation; indeed, Mayr had foreshadowed the punctuated equilibrium hypothesis in 1954.

Both Eldredge and Gould and also S. Stanley concluded that if departures from the ancestral morphology require speciation (splitting), then long-term evolutionary trends (anagenesis) may be attributable not to simple evolution within a single unbranching lineage, but to differences in rates of speciation and extinction among species in a clade.   For example, several lineages of gastropods display an evolutionary trend away from the planktonic juvenile state, apparently because of a greater speciation rate in forms with more sedentary juveniles.   Stanley termed this "species selection," a higher-level analogue of natural selection among individual organisms.

The hypothesis of punctuated equilibrium predicts that morphological shifts should be accompanied by speciation (splitting). Although several such instances have been described by paleontologists, other cases merely show the rapid (i.e., on the order of 10,000 to 100,000 years) evolution of certain features in nondividing lineages. Mere changes in the evolutionary rate are explicable as simple effects of natural selection in an altered environment. Paleontologists are strongly divided on the prevalence of the pattern that Eldredge and Gould claimed, and population geneticists are almost universally opposed to the hypothesis that genetic constraints prevent evolution except in association with speciation.   They cite as counterevidence the abundance of genetic variation within populations, the many examples of rapid adaptation observed in natural and experimental populations, and the prevalence of geographic variation within species, much of which has demonstrably originated very recently.

An alternative explanation of the paleontological patterns has been suggested by D. Futuyma, who pointed out that although spatially segregated populations may diverge greatly in morphology and ecological roles, the divergent characters of a local population will ultimately be lost by interbreeding with more widely distributed phenotypes because populations move about the landscape in response to climatic and other environmental changes, and so ultimately will have the opportunity to interbreed (Figure 6). If a divergent local

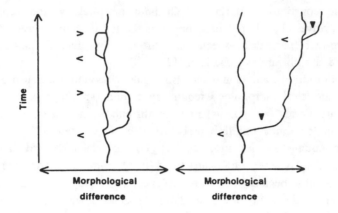

FIGURE 6 The possible role of speciation in anagenesis. (Left) A large, morphologically stable species buds off (<) allopatric isolates, which diverge but then lose their divergent character by subsequent interbreeding (>) with the parent species. (Right) An allopatrically formed (<) isolate retains its divergent features if it evolves reproductive isolation (▼) and can subsequently generate still more divergent allopatric (<) populations that repeat the process.

population has achieved reproductive isolation, however, it can retain its distinctive ecology and morphology even when sympatric with the parent form; its divergence from the ancestral state, instead of being lost by recombination, can persist long enough both to be registered in the fossil record and to be modified still further in the same manner. Thus speciation may facilitate anagenesis not by freeing populations from the bonds of internal constraints, but by acting, like a mountaineer's pitons, to preserve successive steps in evolution away from the ancestral condition.

C. Species, Speciation, and Environmental Biology

The existence of reproductive isolation among populations, i.e., the existence of species, has many practical consequences for human affairs and for conservation. For example, the potential for gene flow among populations of a widespread species (i.e., the lack of reproductive isolation) has consequences in epidemiology. A gene for insecticide resistance in the mosquito *Culex pipiens* in Africa, Asia, and North America is identical at the molecular level, evidence that it originated as a single mutation that has been spread worldwide by gene flow.

Recognizing that an apparently single species actually consists of sibling species with different ecological characteristics can be exceedingly important. Some of the mosquito species formerly included under *"Anopheles maculipennis"* carry malaria whereas others do not. In agricultural ecology, it is critical to recognize sibling species of insects with different host plant associations, and of parasitic insects that may be used for biological control of pests, but which differ in the hosts they attack.

The loss of biological diversity, because of habitat destruction, pollution, and other onslaughts originating in the growth of human populations, is one of the great contemporary tragedies. Human activity is probably responsible for the extinction of about 20% of bird species, and about 11% of the surviving species are endangered. Many of the extraordinary cichlid species of Lake Victoria have been extinguished by a predatory fish introduced for sport. Even by conservative estimates, the current rate of extinction is probably 1000 times the average throughout evolutionary history. Each such species is a unique gene pool, a unique book in the world library of genetic diversity. Some of these gene pools can be useful as agents of pest control, as sources of food or medicine, or as banks of useful genes that modern genetic technology could use for improving domesticated plants and animals. But utility is the less important reason for conservation. The astonishing diversity, the exquisite adaptations, and the profound intricacy and beauty of species are justification enough to save them, as we would a national gallery of art. Each extinction is an irreversible impoverishment, and the rate of speciation is far too slow to replenish it.

GLOSSARY

Allozyme   One of several forms of an enzyme, encoded by different alleles; usually distinguished by electrophoretic mobility.

Allopatric   Allopatric, parapatric, and sympatric populations occupy separate, adjacent, and the same geographic areas, respectively.   Allopatric populations need only be distant enough for gene flow between them to be slight.

Aneuploid   A cell or organism with an unbalanced chromosome complement, i.e., an excess or deficiency of one or more chromosomes.

Assortative mating   Nonrandom mating among like phenotypes.

Cline   A gradual change in an allele frequency or in the mean of a character over a geographic transect.

Epistasis   A synergistic effect of genes at two or more loci, whereby their joint effect differs from the sum of their individual effects.

Fitness   Average contribution of one allele or genotype to the population in succeeding generations compared with that of other alleles or genotypes.

Linkage disequilibrium   Association of alleles at two or more loci, at a different frequency than predicted from the individual allele frequencies: an excess or deficiency of certain gene combinations.

Pleiotropy   Multiple phenotypic effects of a gene.

Polymorphism   Existence within a population of two or more genotypes for a locus or trait, the rarest exceeding some arbitrarily low frequency (e.g., 1%).

Polyploid   A cell or organism with more than two sets of chromosomes.

Sexual selection   Variation in fitness, usually among males, due to differences in the number of matings achieved as a consequence of competition among males or of female "choice" among male phenotypes.

Sibling species   Species that are difficult or impossible to distinguish by morphological features.

Bibliography

Atchley, W. R., and Woodruff, D. S., eds. (1981). *Evolution and Speciation: Essays in Honor of M. J. D. White*. Cambridge: Cambridge Univ. Press.

Coyne, J. A. (1992). "Genetics and speciation." *Nature* 355, 511-515.

Futuyma, D. J. (1986). *Evolutionary Biology*, 2nd Ed.   Sunderland, MA: Sinauer.

Futuyma, D. J. (1987). "On the role of species in anagenesis." *Am. Nat.* 130, 465-473.

Harrison, R. G. (1990). "Hybrid zones: Windows on evolutionary processes." In *Oxford Surveys in Evolutionary Biology* (D. J. Futuyma and J. Antonovics, eds.), Vol. 7, pp. 69-128. New York: Oxford Univ. Press.

Mayr, E. (1970). *Populations, Species, and Evolution*. Cambridge, MA: Belknap Press.

Otte, D., and Endler, J. A., (eds.) (1989). *Speciation and Its Consequences*. Sunderland, MA: Sinauer.

Stanley, S. M. (1979). *Macroevolution: Pattern and Process*. San Francisco: Freeman.

Templeton, A. R. (1981). "Mechanisms of speciation: A population genetic approach." *Annu. Rev. Ecol. Syst.* 12, 23-48.

6

Levels of Selection

DAVID SLOAN WILSON

Biology and many branches of the human sciences are dominated by an individualistic tradition that treats groups and communities as collections of organisms without themselves having the properties implicit in the word organism. In biology, the individualistic tradition achieves generality only by defining self-interest as "anything that evolves by natural selection." A more meaningful definition of self-interest shows that natural selection operates on a hierarchy of units from genetic elements to multi-species communities, and that a unit becomes organismic to the degree that natural selection operates at the level of that unit. In this paper I review levels-of-selection theory in biology and sketch a parallel argument for the human sciences.

1. Introduction

The related concepts of adaptation, function, intention and purpose are central to both biology and the human sciences. Natural selection endows species with the functional design required to survive and reproduce in their environments. Humans organize their behavior to achieve various proximate goals in their everyday lives.

Biology and the human sciences also share a controversy over the units that can be said to have the properties of adaptation, function, intention and purpose. Almost everyone would grant these properties to individuals, but some biologists also speak of social groups and multi-species communities as if they were single purposeful organisms. Similarly, some psychologists, anthropologists and sociologists speak of culture and society as superorganisms in which individuals are mere cells.

In recent decades the hierarchical view of functional organization has fallen on hard times. Larger entities are regarded as mere collections of organisms, without themselves having the properties of organisms. In biology the reductionistic trend has proceeded so far that even individuals are sometimes treated as upper units of the hierarchy, mere collections of "selfish" genes (Dawkins 1976, 1982). The human sciences are more heterogeneous, but many of its branches appear to be dominated by the individualistic view.

Despite its widespread acceptance, the case for individualism as a general prediction that emerges from evolutionary theory, or as a general principle to explain human behavior, actually is very frail. In this paper I will describe why functional organization in nature is necessarily hierarchical and then will attempt to sketch a parallel argument for the human sciences.

2. The evolution of altruism

In biology, the debate over units of adaptation has centered on the evolution of seemingly altruistic behaviors that benefit others at the expense of the self. Consider a population of N individuals. Two types exist, A and S, in proportions p and $(1 - p)$ respectively. Each A-type expresses a behavior toward a single recipient, chosen at random from the population. As a result, the recipient has an additional number b of offspring while the altruist has c fewer offspring. The average number of offspring, W, can then be calculated for each type.

$$W_A = X - c + b\,(Np - 1)\,/\,(N - 1), \qquad W_S = X + bNp\,/\,(N - 1) \qquad (1)$$

X is the number of offspring in the absence of altruistic behaviors, and is the same for both types. In addition to the cost of being an altruist, each A-type can serve as a recipient to the $(Np - 1)$ other altruists who are distributing their benefits among $(N - 1)$ individuals in the group. Selfish S-types have no cost of altruism and can serve as recipients to all Np altruists in the group. S-types have more offspring than A-types whenever $W_S > W_A$, which reduces to the inequality

$$b\,/\,(N - 1) > -\,c \qquad (2)$$

This inequality always holds, because b, c and N are positive numbers and N is greater than 1. Thus, selfish types always have more offspring than altruistic types. To the degree that the behaviors are heritable, selfish types will be found at a greater frequency in the next generation.

A numerical example is shown in Table 1, in which $N = 100$, $p = 0.5$, $X = 10$, $b = 5$ and $c = 1$. Thus, the altruist bestows an additional 5 offspring on the recipient at a cost of 1 offspring to itself. The average altruist has 11.47 offspring, while the average selfish type has 12.53 offspring. Assume that the types reproduce asexually, such that the offspring exactly resemble the parents.

The proportion of altruists among the progeny is then $p' = 0.478$, a decline from the parental value of p = 0.5. Since populations cannot grow to infinity, we also assume that mortality occurs equally among the A- and S-types, returning the

Table 1

Evolution in a single population. The altruistic type declines from a frequency of $p = 0.5$ before selection to a frequency of $p' = 0.478$ after selection.

$N = 100, p = 0.5, X = 10, b = 5, c = 1$

$W_A = X - c + b(Np - 1) / (N - 1) = 10 - 1 + 49(5)/99 = 11.47$

$W_S = X + bNp /(N - 1) = 10 + 50(5)/99 = 12.53$

$N' = N(pW_A + (1 - p) W_S) = 100(0.5(11.47) + 0.5(12.53)) = 1200$

$p' = NpW_A / N' = 100(0.5)(11.47)/1200 = 0.478$

---

population to a density of $N = 100$. At this point we expect approximately 52 selfish and 48 altruistic types. If this procedure is iterated many times, representing natural selection acting over many generations, the A-types continue to decline in frequency and ultimately become extinct.

This is the paradox that makes altruism such a fascinating subject for evolutionary biologists. As humans we would like to think that altruism can evolve, as biologists we see animal behaviors that appear altruistic in nature, yet almost by definition it appears that natural selection will act against them. This is the sense in which evolution appears to be an inherently selfish theory.

The paradox, however, can be resolved by a simple alteration of the model. Table 2 [on the next page] differs from Table 1 in only two respects; (a) we now have two groups instead of one; and (b) the groups have different proportions of altruistic and selfish types. Looking at each group separately, we reach the same conclusion as for Table 1; selfish types have more offspring than altruistic types. Adding the individuals from both groups together, however, we get the opposite answer; altruistic types have more offspring than selfish types.[1]

What has happened to produce this interesting (and for many people counterintuitive) result? First, there must be more than one group; there must be a *population of groups*. Second, the groups cannot all have the same proportion of altruistic types, for then the results would not differ from a single group. The

Table 2
Evolution in two groups that differ in the proportion of the altruistic type. Values for X, b, c and the functions for W_A and W_S are provided in Table 1. The altruistic type declines in frequency within each group (compare p_1' with p_1, and p_2' with p_2) but increases in frequency when both groups are considered together (compare P' with P). This is because group 2, with the most altruists, is more productive than group 1 (compare N_2' with N_2')

Group 1	Group 2
$N_1 = 100, P_2 = 0.2$	$N_2 = 100, P_2 = 0.8$
$W_A = 10 - 1 + 19(5)/99 = 9.96$	$W_A = 10 - 1 + 79(5)/99 = 12.99$
$W_S = 10 + 20(5)/99 = 11.01$	$W_S = 10 + 80(5)/99 = 14.04$
$N'_1 = 1080$	$N'_2 = 1320$
$P'_1 = 0.184$	$p'_2 = 0.787$

Global population
$N = 200, P = 0.5$
$N' = N'_1 + N'_2 = 2400$
$P' = (N'_1 p'_1 + N_2' p_2') - (N'_1 + N'_2) = 0.516$

groups must vary in the proportion of altruistic types. Third, there must be a direct relationship between the proportion of altruists and the total number of offspring produced by the group; groups of altruists must be more fit than groups without altruists. These are the necessary conditions for the evolution of altruism in the elaborated model. To be sufficient, the differential fitness of groups—the force favoring the altruists—must be great enough to counter the differential fitness of individuals within groups—the force favoring the selfish types.

Readers familiar with evolutionary theory immediately will recognize a similarity between the above conditions and Darwin's original theory of natural selection, which requires a *population of individuals*, that *vary* in their genetic composition, with some variants *more fit* than others. Thus, natural selection can operate simultaneously at more than one level. Individual selection promotes the fitness of individuals relative to others in the same group. Group selection promotes the fitness of groups, relative to other groups in the global population. These levels of selection are not always in conflict. A single behavior can benefit both the individual performing it and others in the group. Altruistic behaviors by definition are costly to self and beneficial to others, however, and so are favored by group selection and disfavored by individual selection.

This simple numerical example shows that the process of natural selection does not inevitably evolve selfish behaviors. A notion of *group-*

interest must be added to the notion of *self-interest*, to the extent that group selection is important in nature.

3. Valid individualism and cheap individualism

Let us now consider the individualistic claim that "virtually all adaptations evolve by individual selection." If by individual selection we mean within-group selection, we are saying that A-types virtually never evolve in nature, that we should observe only S-types.   This is a meaningful statement because it identifies a set of traits that conceivably could evolve, but doesn't, because between-group selection is invariably weak compared to within-group selection. Let us call this *valid individualism*.

There is, however, another way to calculate fitness in the two-group model that leads to another definition of individual selection.   Instead of separately considering evolution within groups and the differential fitness of groups, we can directly average the fitness of A- and S-types across all groups. Thus, the 2 A-types in group one have 9.96 offspring and the 8 A-types in group two have 12.99 offspring, for an average fitness of 0.2(9.96) + 0.8(12.99) = 12.38. The 8 S-types in group one have 11.01 offspring and the 2 S-types in group two have 14.04 offspring, for an average fitness of 0.8(11.01) + 0.2(14.04) = 11.62. The average A-type individual is more fit than the average S-type individual, which is merely another way of saying that it evolves.

Let us now return to the individualistic claim that "virtually all adaptations evolve by individual selection." If by individual selection we mean the fitness of individuals averaged across all groups, we have said nothing at all. Since this definition includes both within- and between-group selection, it makes "individual selection" synonymous with "whatever evolves," including either S-types or A-types. It does not identify any set of traits that conceivably could evolve but doesn't. Let us therefore call it *cheap individualism*.

Cheap individualism is so meaningless that no one would explicitly endorse it. Even the most ardent individualists, such as G.C. Williams (1966, 1985), R. Dawkins (1976, 1982) and J. Maynard Smith (1987), believe that there is something outside individual selection called group selection that in principle can evolve altruistic traits. Nevertheless, the history of individual selection from 1960 to the present has been a slow slide from valid individualism to cheap individualism. Before documenting this claim it is necessary to review three reasons why the slide could occur unnoticed.

First, group-structured population models such as the one described above can be applied to an enormous range of biological phenomena. The single groups can be isolated demes that persist for many generations, groups of parasites interacting within single hosts, clusters of caterpillars interacting on a single leaf, or coalitions of baboons that behaviorally segregate within a larger troop. The groups can be communities whose members are separate species, social units whose members are conspecifics, or even single organisms whose "members" are genes or cell lineages (Crow 1979; Cosmides and Tooby 1981; Buss 1987). Historically, however, the first group selection models focused on a particular conception of isolated demes that persist for many generations. Thus, it has been possible for biologists studying other kinds of groups to assume that they are not invoking group selection, when in fact their models are miniature versions of traditional group selection models.

Second, many biologists today regard group selection as a heretical concept that was discarded twenty years ago and consider their own work to be entirely within the grand tradition of "individual selection." Gould (1982: xv) remembers "the hooting dismissal of Wynne-Edwards and group selection in any form during the late 1960's and most of the 1970's," and even today graduate students tell me how difficult it is for them to think about group selection in a positive light after being taught in their courses that it "just doesn't happen." The vast majority of authors who claim that such-and-such evolves by individual selection don't even include an explicit model of group selection to serve as a possible alternative. Individual selection truly has become the modern synonym for "everything that evolves in my model," and group selection is mentioned only as a bogey man in the introduction or the conclusion of the paper.

Third, averaging the fitness of individual types across groups is a useful, intuitively reasonable procedure that correctly predicts the outcome of natural selection. Biologists commonly average the fitness of types across a range of physical environments, and it seems reasonable to average across social environments in the same way. I emphasize that there is nothing wrong with this procedure—it merely cannot be used to define individual selection because it leaves nothing outside of it.

Now I must document my claim that individualism in biology achieves generality only by averaging the fitness of individuals across groups.

4. Three examples of cheap individualism in biology

4. 1. The evolution of avirulence in parasites and diseases

Disease organisms provide an excellent real-world example of a group-structured population similar to the model outlined above. Each infected host comprises an isolated group of disease organisms, that compete with other groups to infect new hosts. Natural selection within single hosts is expected to favor strains with high growth rates. Excessively high growth rates tend to kill the host, however, driving the entire group of disease organisms extinct (assuming that transmission requires the host to be alive). Avirulent strains therefore can be envisioned as "altruists" that increase the survival of entire groups, but which nevertheless decline in frequency within every group containing more virulent strains. Lewontin (1970) was the first to recognize that avirulence evolves by between-group selection, and the process has been well documented in a myxoma virus that was introduced into Australia to control the European rabbit (Fenner and Ratcliffe 1965).   Nevertheless, consider the following account in the first edition of Futuyma's (1979: 455) textbook *Evolutionary Biology*:

> In many interactions the exploiter cannot evolve to be avirulent; it profits a fox nothing to spare the hare. But if the fitness of an individual parasite or its offspring is lowered by the death of its host, avirulence is advantageous.   The myxoma virus, introduced into Australia to control European rabbits, at first caused immense mortality. But within a few years mortality levels were lower, both because the rabbits had evolved resistance and because the virus had evolved to be less lethal.... Because the virus is transmitted by mosquitoes that feed only on living rabbits, *virulent virus genotypes are less likely to spread than benign genotypes* [italics mine]. Avirulence evolves not to assure a stable future supply of hosts, but to benefit individual parasites.

Thus, by the simple procedure of comparing the fitness of virulent and avirulent types across all hosts (see italicized portion of text), rather than within single hosts, the evolution of avirulence can be made to appear an individualistic process. Futuyma, incidentally, is sympathetic to the concept of group selection and properly attributes avirulence to between-group selection in the second edition of his textbook (1986: 496-497). This example of cheap individualism therefore is inadvertent, and shows how easily selection at multiple levels can be represented as occurring entirely at the lowest level.

4.2. Inclusive fitness theory

Within the individualistic tradition in biology, natural selection is widely thought to maximize a property called inclusive fitness, which is the sum of an individual's effects on the fitness of others multiplied by the probability that the others will share the genes causing the behavior. As Hamilton (1963: 354-355) originally put it:

> Despite the principle of "survival of the fittest" the ultimate criterion which determines whether G [an altruistic allele] will spread is not whether the behavior is to the benefit of the behavior but whether it is to the benefit of the gene G; and this will be the case if the average net result of the behavior is to add to the gene-pool a handful of genes containing G in higher concentration than does the gene-pool itself. With altruism this will happen only if the affected individual is a relative of the altruist, therefore having an increased chance of carrying the gene, and if the advantage conferred is large enough compared to the personal disadvantage to offset the regression, or "dilution", of the altruist's genotype in the relative in question.

In this formulation, individuals evolve to maximize the fitness of "their genes" relative to other genes in the population, regardless of whether "their genes" are located in children, siblings, cousins, parents, and so on. Aid-giving towards relatives therefore ceases to appear altruistic, and becomes part of an individual's "selfish" strategy to maximize its inclusive fitness. Even sterility and death can be inclusive fitness maximizing if the positive effects on relatives is sufficiently great.

Let us pursue this idea by considering an Aa female who mates with an aa male and produces a clutch of ten offspring, five of whom are Aa and the other five aa. The dominant allele A codes for an altruistic behavior that is expressed only towards siblings. The sibling group therefore is equally divided between altruists and non-altruists, and the fitness of the two genotypes from equation (1) is

$$W_{Aa} = X - c + b\,(4/9), \; W_{aa} = X + b\,(5/9).$$

The selfish aa genotype is inevitably most fit, which merely reiterates the general conclusion obtained in section 2 for evolution in all single groups. The fact that the group in this case consists of full siblings is irrelevant to the conclusion. To see how altruism expressed towards siblings evolves, we must consider a large number of family groups, initiated by all combinations of parental genotypes -AA × AA, AA × Aa, Aa × Aa, AA × aa, Aa × aa, aa × aa. Within-group selection favors the selfish a-allele in all groups containing both altruistic and selfish genotypes. The fitness of entire sibling groups, however, is directly proportional to the frequency of altruistic A-alleles in the group. Thus, Hamilton's conclusions cannot be reached without combining within-group selection and between-group selection into a single measure of "inclusive fitness."

The idea that aid-giving toward relatives is a form of "true" altruism that requires between-group selection has been reached by many authors (reviewed in Wilson 1983). Nevertheless, evolutionists within the individualistic tradition continue to use inclusive fitness theory as their guiding light to explain the evolution of "apparently" altruistic behaviors, "without invoking group selection." This is cheap individualism.

4.3. Diploid population genetics and evolutionary game theory

My final example involves a comparison between two seemingly different bodies of theory in evolutionary biology. Diploid population genetics models begin with a population of gametic types (A, a) which combine into pairs to form diploid genotypes (AA, Aa, aa). Selection usually is assumed to occur in the diploid stage, after which the genotypes dissociate back into gametes and the process is reiterated. The most common way for selection to occur in these models is for some genotypes to survive and reproduce better than others, the standard process of between-individual selection. In addition, however, it is possible for some alleles to survive and reproduce better than others *within single individuals*. For example, the rules of meiosis usually cause the two chromosome sets to be equally represented in the gametes. Some alleles manage to break the rules of meiosis, however, biasing their own transmission into the sperm and eggs of heterozygotes. The differential fitness of alleles within heterozygotes is termed meiotic drive, and can cause the evolution of genes that have neutral or even deleterious effects on the fitness of individuals (Crow 1979; Cosmides and Tooby 1981). In short, diploid population genetics models are explicitly hierarchical by recognizing the existence of both between- and within-individual selection.

Evolutionary game theory (also called ESS theory for "evolutionarily stable strategy") begins with a population of individual types (A, a) that combine into groups of size N for purposes of interaction. Selection occurs during the grouped stage, after which the groups dissociate back into individuals and the process is reiterated. Usually $N = 2$, which yields three types of groups (AA, Aa, aa). ESS theory was borrowed directly from economic game theory (Maynard Smith and Price 1973; Maynard Smith 1982) but the two are not identical. In particular, economic game theory assumes that the players are rational actors trying to maximize their (absolute) payoff, while ESS theory assumes that natural selection will favor the strategy that delivers the highest payoff relative to other competing strategies in the population.

It should be obvious that the population structure of genes combining into individuals in a diploid model is identical to the population structure of individuals combining into groups of $N = 2$ in an ESS model. Similarly, natural selection in an ESS model can happen in two ways: groups can outperform other groups or individuals can outperform other individuals within groups. In the familiar hawk-dove model, for example, dove-dove groups (in which resources are equitably shared) are more fit than hawk-hawk groups (in which resources are contested), while hawks are more fit than doves within hawk-dove groups. To be consistent with population genetics models we should say that hawks are favored by within-group selection and doves by between-group selection. ESS theorists, however, average the fitness of individual types across groups and call everything that evolves the product of "individual selection." The term between-group selection is never used, and Maynard Smith actually borrowed game theory from economics as an alternative to group selection (Maynard Smith and Price 1973; Maynard Smith 1982). As Dawkins (1980: 360) puts it:

> There is a common misconception that cooperation within a group at a given level of organization must come about through selection between groups.... ESS theory provides a more parsimonious alternative.

This one passage provides all the elements of cheap individualism: the fitness of individuals is averaged across groups, everything that evolves is called the product of individual selection, and something else is called group selection, which is outside the model and completely unspecified, except to say that it needn't be invoked.

These three examples show that, despite its widespread acceptance, individualism in biology is on very thin ice. Self-interest defined as "whatever evolves" is meaningless, and yet when self-interest is defined more meaningfully as "within-group selection" it cannot claim to explain everything that evolves in nature. We must therefore accept a hierarchical view of evolution in which the properties of functional organization implicit in the word "organism" need not be restricted to individuals. The differential fitness of genetic elements within individuals ushers us into a bizarre world in which the genetic elements are the purposeful organisms and individuals are mere collections of quarreling genes, the way we usually think of groups. The differential fitness of individuals within groups ushers us into a familiar world in which groups are mere collections of purposeful individuals. The differential fitness of groups ushers us into another bizarre world (for individualists) in which the groups are the organisms whose properties are caused by individuals acting in a coordinated fashion, the way we usually think of genes and the organs they code for. See Wilson and Sober (1989) for a more detailed review of levels-of-selection theory in biology.

5. A parallel argument for the human sciences

If human behavior is measured against the dual standard of effects on self and effects on others, it appears to show the full range of potential. Individuals have sacrificed their lives for the benefit of others, and they have sacrificed the lives of others for their own trivial gain. Viewed at the society level, some human groups are so well coordinated that they invite comparison to single organisms, while others show all the disorganization of a bar-room brawl.

Humans also are frequently embedded in a complex network of interactions in which single expressions of a behavior affect the actor and a relatively small number of associates. Put another way, human populations are subdivided into clusters of associates similar to the local populations of the evolutionary models outlined above. It seems possible that a theory of human behavior in social networks could be developed that parallels levels-of-selection theory in biology, leading to a similar hierarchical view of functional organization in human affairs.

As with any theory of human behavior, the first step is to specify the rules that cause people to choose among alternative behaviors, which serve as the analog of natural selection in an evolutionary model. Following Axelrod and others (Axelrod and Hamilton 1981; Brown et al. 1982; Pollock 1988), assume that humans adopt behaviors that maximize a given utility, relative to competing behaviors in the population.[2] The utility might be pleasure (to a psychologist), annual income (to an economist) or genetic fitness (to a sociobiologist). The details of the utility are relatively unimportant because the hallmark of a hierarchical model is not the nature of the utility, but the way it is partitioned into within- and between-group components. Consider, for example, a behavior that decreases the utility of self and increases the utility of others. If others include the entire population, then the utility of those expressing the behavior will be lower than those that don't and the behavior will be rejected precisely as it is selected against in the one-group evolutionary model. Now assume that the human population is subdivided into a mosaic of associates in which the expression of behavior is non-random; some groups of associates behave primarily one way, other groups the other way. The utility of the behaviors now depends on the frame of comparison. The behavior fares poorly in all groups in which the alternative behavior is expressed, but may still deliver the highest utility when averaged across all groups, exactly as in the multi-group evolutionary model. Adoption of the behavior therefore depends on two factors, the effect on self and others and the interaction structure within which the behavior is embedded.

Theories of behavior in the human sciences frequently consider both factors but combine them into an overarching definition of self-interest as "utility-maximizing behavior"—i.e., all behaviors adopted by rational humans! This is cheap individualism that achieves generality only by definitional fiat. Levels-of-selection theory keeps the factors separate, defining behaviors as self-interested when they increase relative utility within single groups, and group-interested when they increase the average utility of groups, relative to other groups.   This provides a framework in which rational (utility-maximizing) humans need not be self-interested by definition.

As for the situation in biology, many human behaviors that are categorized as selfish by cheap individualism emerge as "groupish" in a levels-of-selection model.   The concept of morality, for example, involves rules of conduct that promote the common good. This implies a category of immoral behaviors—frequently termed "selfish" in everyday language—that benefit individuals at the expense of the common good.   Since moral behaviors are vulnerable to exploitation, they succeed only if they can be segregated from the expression of immoral behaviors.   This is nicely illustrated by the following passage from a seventeenth century Hutterite document (English translation in Ehrenpreis 1978: 67):

> The bond of love is kept pure and intact by the correction of the Holy Spirit. People who are burdened with vices that spread and corrupt can have no part in it. This harmonious fellowship excludes any who are not part of the unanimous spirit.... If a man hardens himself in rebellion, the extreme step of separation is unavoidable. Otherwise the whole community would be dragged into his sin and become party to it.... The Apostle Paul therefore says, "Drive out the wicked person from among you."

The maintenance of behaviorally pure groups allowed the Hutterites to practice such extreme altruism that their communities are best regarded as the human equivalent of a bee colony (a metaphor that they themselves used to describe themselves).   More generally, human societies everywhere possess mechanisms for segregating behaviors, allowing less extreme forms of morally acceptable behavior to be successful.   The distinction between moral and immoral behavior, and the mechanisms whereby both can be advantageous, correspond nicely to "groupish" and "selfish" behaviors in a levels-of-selection model. In contrast, cheap individualism is placed in the awkward situation of defining both moral and immoral behavior as brands of self-interest.

Many authors have expressed the idea that higher entities such as biological communities and human societies can be organisms in their own right. Unfortunately, the idea usually is stated as a poetic metaphor or as an axiom that is not subject to disproof. Levels-of-selection theory shows that single-species groups and multi-species communities can become functionally organized by the exact same process of between-unit selection that causes the groups of genes known as individuals to become functionally organized. For the first time, the hierarchical view in biology now enjoys a solid mechanistic foundation. Perhaps this foundation also will be useful within the human sciences to show how people sometimes coalesce into society-level organisms.

Notes

1. Adding the contents of both groups is justified biologically only if the occupants of the groups physically mix during a dispersal stage or compete for the colonization of new groups. See Wilson (1977, 1980, 1983) for a more detailed discussion of the nature of groups in levels-of-selection models.
2. Both cheap individualism and levels-of-selection models define their terms on the basis of utilities, which do not translate easily into psychological definitions of altruism and selfishness based on internal motivation. In outlining his economic theory of human behavior, Becker (1976:7) states that it doesn't matter how people actually feel or think about what they do as long as the end result of their behavior is utility maximizing. In the same way, behaviors categorized as group-interested in a levels-of-selection model do not imply that the actor is internally motivated to help others. This does not mean that psychological definitions of altruism are irrelevant, but only that their relationships with definitions based on utility are complex. I hope to explore the complexities in a future paper.

References

Axelrod, R. and W.D. Hamilton (1981) "The evolution of cooperation." *Science* 211: 1390-1396.

Becker, G.S. (1976) *The Economic Approach to Human Behavior*. Chicago: Chicago, University Press.

Brown, J. S., M. J. Sanderson and R. E. Michod (1982) "Evolution of social behavior by reciprocation." *Journal of Theoretical Biology* 99: 319-339.

Buss, L.W. (1987) *The Evolution of Individuality*. Princeton: Princeton University Press.

Cosmides, L. M. and J. Tooby (1981) "Cytoplasmic inheritance and intragenomic conflict". *Journal of Theoretical Biology* 89: 83-129.

Crow, J.F. (1979) "Genes that violate Mendel's rules." *Scientific American* 240: 104-113.

Dawkins, R. (1976) *The Selfish Gene*. Oxford: Oxford University Press.

_____. (1980) "Good strategy or evolutionary stable strategy?" In G. W. Barlow and J. Silverberg (eds.), *Sociobiology: Beyond Nature/Nurture?* pp. 331-367. Boulder, CO: Westview Press.

_____. (1982) *The Extended Phenotype.* Oxford: Oxford University Press.

Ehrenprels, A.   (1978) *Brotherly Community: The Highest Command of Love.* Rifton, NY: Plough Publishing Co.

Fenner, F. and F.N. Ratcliffe (1965) *Myxomatosis.* London: Cambridge University Press.

Futuyma, D.J.   (1979) *Evolutionary Biology.* Sunderland, MA: Sinauer Press.

_____. (1986) *Evolutionary Biology* (2d ed.). Sunderland, MA: Sinauer Press.

Gould, S.J.   (1982)   *The Uses of Heresy: An Introduction to Richard Goldschmidt's The Material Basis of Evolution,* pp. xiii-xlii. New Haven, CT: Yale University Press.

Hamilton, W. D.   (1963) "The evolution of altruistic behavior." *American Naturalist* 97: 354-356.

Lewontin, R.C.   (1970) "The units of selection." *Annual Review of Ecology and Systematics* 1: 1-18.

Maynard Smith, J.   (1982) *Evolution and the Theory of Games.*   Cambridge, UK: Cambridge, University Press.

_____. (1987) "How to model evolution." In J. Dupre (ed.), *The Latest on the Best: Essays on Evolution and Optimality,* pp. 117-131. Cambridge, MA: MIT press.

Maynard Smith, J. and G.R. Price (1973) "The logic of animal conflict." *Nature* 246: 15-18.

Pollock, G. B.   (1988) "Population structure, spite, and the iterated prisoner's dilemma." *American Journal of Physical Anthropology* 77: 459-469.

Williams, G.C.   (1966) *Adaptation and Natural Selection.*   Princeton: Princeton University Press.

_____.   (1985) "A defense of reductionism in evolutionary biology." In R. Dawkins and M. Ridley (eds.), *Oxford Surveys in Evolutionary Biology,* Vol. 2, pp. 1-27. Oxford: Oxford University Press.

Wilson, D.S. (1977) "Structured demes and the evolution of group-advantageous traits." *American Naturalist,* 111: 157-185.

_____. (1980) *The Natural Selection of Populations and Communities.* Menlo Park, CA: Benjamin-Cummings.

_____. (1983) "The group selection controversy: history and current status." *Annual Review of Ecology and Systematics* 14: 159-187.

Wilson, D.S. and E. Sober (198)9 "Reviving the superorganism." *Journal of Theoretical Biology,* 136: 337-356.

The History of Life

Scientists from a variety of disciplines contribute to the task of writing Life's biography. Zoologists, molecular biologists, geneticists, paleontologists, and physical anthropologists all provide insights into the history of life.

This section begins with the question of the beginning of life. Freeman Dyson proposes a theory concerning the first emergence of life that focuses on metabolic rather than replicative processes. He also explores the implications of such a theory for other branches of science.

In science there can be agreement on the broad outlines of a theory, while there are disagreements about the details. Such is the case with evolutionary theory. There is no scientific debate about whether life evolved. There is, however, a great deal of discussion about how to account for the observed historical pathway of life. The next three articles illustrate this discussion.

Stephen Jay Gould offers one telling of "The Evolution of Life on Earth." In particular he proposes that natural selection by itself is insufficient to account for the history of life, particularly with respect to the rate of evolution. In the next article along with Niles Eldredge, Gould elaborates on their proposal that the pace of evolution is not slow and steady. Rather they propose that there are long periods of species stability punctuated by relatively short bursts of speciation, a process they call "punctuated equilibrium." G. Ledyard Stebbins and Francisco Ayala critically place Gould's and Eldredge's proposal within the larger theoretical history of Darwinism. They show how evolutionary theory itself is evolving, so that there is both theoretical continuity and innovation.

The final article in this section provides an account of the evolutionary rise of humanity. In "Human Origins: An Overview" Ian Tattersall sketches the long trail which has led to modern humans. An important point he makes is that modern humans (*Homo sapiens*) are only one small branch, the sole surviving twig, on the large evolutionary bush of the family *Hominidae*.

7

Why is Life So Complicated?

FREEMAN J. DYSON

It is now time to sum up what we may have learned from the first three chapters of *Origins of Life*. Chapter 1 describes the historical development of ideas leading up to the question that I consider to be fundamental to all investigation of the origin of life: Is the origin of life the same thing as the origin of replication? I give some reasons why I am inclined to answer no to this question, to give a tentative preference to the hypothesis that metabolism and replication had separate origins. Chapter 2 gives a sketchy account of some of the classic experiments and some of the classic theories concerning the origin of life. I observe that the experiments since the time of Max Delbrück have been spectacularly successful in elucidating the structure and function of the apparatus of replication and much less successful in giving us a deep understanding of metabolism. The one-sided success of the experiments has resulted in a corresponding bias of theories. The most popular theories of the origin of life are the theories of Manfred Eigen, which concentrate almost exclusively on replication as the phenomenon to be explained. Chapter 3 describes my own attempt to build a model of the origin of life with a bias opposite to Eigen's, assuming as a working hypothesis that primitive life consisted of purely, metabolic machinery without replication.

This last chapter is concerned with the open questions raised by the model and with more general questions concerning possible experimental approaches to the origin of metabolism. But all these questions are subsidiary to another question: Why is life so complicated? This is perhaps not a well-posed scientific question. It might be interpreted as merely the lament of an elderly scientist recalling the lost simplicity of youth. Or it might be interpreted as an ineffectual protest against the intractability of the human condition in the modern world. But I mean the question to refer specifically to cellular structure. The essential characteristic of living cells is homeostasis, the ability to maintain a steady and more-or-less constant chemical balance in a changing environment. Homeostasis is the machinery of chemical controls and feed-back cycles which make sure that each molecular species in a cell is produced in the right proportion, not too much and not too little. Without homeostasis, there can be no ordered metabolism and no quasi-stationary equilibrium deserving the name of life. The question "Why is life so complicated?" means in this context "Given that a population of molecules is able to maintain itself in homeostatic equilibrium at a steady level of metabolism, how many different molecular species must the population contain?"

The biological evidence gives a rather definite answer to the question how many kinds of molecule are needed to make a homeostatic system, at least so long as we are talking about homeostatic systems of the modern type. There is a large number of different varieties of bacteria and most of them contain a few thousand molecular species if one judges the number by the few million base-pairs in their DNA. It seems that under modern conditions homeostatic systems work efficiently with a few thousand components and work less efficiently with fewer. If a bacterium could dispense with half of its molecular components and still metabolize efficiently, there would be a great selective advantage in doing so. From the fact that bacteria have generally refused to shrink below a certain level of complexity we may deduce that this level is in some sense an irreducible minimum.

If modern cells require a few thousand types of molecule for stable homeostasis, what does this tell us about primitive cells? Strictly speaking, it tells us nothing. Without the modern apparatus of genes and repressors the ancient mechanisms of homeostasis must have been very different. The ancient mechanisms might have been either simpler or more complicated. Still it is a reasonable hypothesis that the ancient mechanisms were simpler. There remains the question "How simple could they have been?" This question must be answered before we can build credible theories of the origin of life. It can be answered only by experiment.

In the toy model that I discuss in Chapter 3 of *Origins of Life*, I deduced from the arithmetic of the model that the population of a cell making the transition from disorder to order should have been between 2,000 and 20,000 monomers combined into a few hundred species of polymers. I claim that this number, a few hundred, was reasonable for the number of species of polymer molecule required for a primitive homeostatic system. That claim is, of course, based on nothing but guesswork. We know that a few thousand species of molecule are sufficient for a modern cell. It seems unlikely that anything resembling biochemical homeostasis could be maintained with a few tens of species. And so we guess quite arbitrarily, guided only by our familiarity with the decimal system of counting, that a few hundred kinds of molecule is the right number for the origin of homeostasis. Whether a few hundred molecular species are either necessary or sufficient for homeostasis we do not know.

It is of interest in this connection to see how an experimental approach was successfully applied to answer the corresponding question concerning the origin of replication. What is the smallest molecular population that is able to constitute a self-replicating system? This question was answered by two classic experiments, one done by Sol Spiegelman (Spiegelman, 1967), the other by Manfred Eigen and his colleagues (Eigen et al., ig8i). I describe Eigen's experiment in Chapter 2 of *Origins of Life*. Spiegelman's experiment began with a living Q_B virus, a creature able to survive and ensure its own replication in nature by means of the information coded in a single RNA molecule composed of 4500 nucleotides. The virus is normally replicated inside a host cell using a replicase enzyme which the viral RNA causes the host's ribosomes to manufacture. The viral RNA also causes the host to manufacture a coat protein and various other components that are required for the complete viral life-cycle. Now, Spiegelman proceeded to debauch the virus by stripping off its protein coat and providing it with replicase enzyme in a test-tube so that it could replicate without going to the trouble of invading a cell and completing its normal parasitic life-cycle. The test-tube also contained an ample provision of free nucleotide monomers, with a continuous-flow arrangement to keep the virus from exhausting the supply. The results were spectacular. The viral RNA continued for a while to be replicated accurately with the help of the replicase enzyme. But soon a mutant RNA appeared, having lost some of the genes that were no longer required for its survival. The mutant, having fewer than 4500 nucleotides, was replicated more quickly than the original virus and soon displaced it in the Darwinian struggle for existence. Then another still shorter mutant appeared to displace the first, and so it went on. The virus no longer needed to carry the genes for replicase and coat protein in order to survive. On the contrary, it could only survive by getting rid of all superfluous baggage. The requirement for survival was to be as simple and as small as possible. The virus finally degenerated into a little piece of RNA with only 220 nucleotides containing the recognition site for the replicase enzyme and not much else. The final state of the virus was called by geneticists the "Spiegelman monster." It provides a good object-lesson demonstrating what happens to you when life is made too easy. The little monsters would continue for ever to replicate at high speed in the artificial environment of Spiegelman's test-tube but could never hope to survive anywhere else.

The experiment of Manfred Eigen was the opposite of Spiegelman's experiment. Both experiments used a test-tube containing replicase enzyme and free nucleotides. Spiegelman put into this soup a living virus, Eigen put in nothing. Spiegelman was studying the evolution of replication from the top down, Eigen from the bottom up. Eigen's experiment produced a self-generated population of RNA molecules replicating with the help of the replicase enzyme, just like the Spiegelman monsters. The Eigen replicator and the Spiegelman monster were not identical but they were first cousins. Eigen's replicators, after they had evolved to a steady state, contained about 120 nucleotides each, compared with the 220 in a Spiegelman monster. The difference between 120 and 220 nucleotides is a small gap between a molecule which grew from nothing and a molecule which was once alive.

The experiments of Spiegelman and Eigen together give a clear answer to the question: What is the minimum population-size required for a replicating system? The answer is, a single RNA molecule with one or two hundred nucleotides. This answer shows in a nutshell how simple the phenomenon of replication is compared with the phenomenon of homeostasis. I am conjecturing that the minimum population-size required for homeostasis would be about a hundred times larger, namely, a few hundred molecules containing ten or twenty thousand monomer units. And more importantly, I am suggesting that the most promising road to an understanding of the origin of life would be to do experiments like the Spiegelman and Eigen experiments, but this time concerned with homeostasis rather than with replication.

How could such experiments be done? I am acutely aware that it is much easier to suggest experiments than to do them. What is required first of all is to find the working materials which make experiments possible, the equivalent for a homeostatic system of Spiegelman's Q_β virus and Eigen's nucleotide soup. The objective should be once again to work from both ends, from the top down and from the bottom up, and to find out where in the middle the two ends meet. From the top, we need to find a suitable creature, an enucleated cell which has lost its replicative apparatus but still preserves the functions of metabolism and homeostasis, and we need to keep it alive artificially while stripping it gradually of inessential molecular components. We may hope in. this way, with many trials and errors, to find out roughly the irreducible minimum degree of complication of a homeostatic apparatus. From the bottom, we need to experiment with synthetic populations of molecules confined in droplets in the style of Oparin, adding various combinations of catalysts and metabolites until a lasting homeostatic equilibrium is achieved. If we are lucky, we may find that the experiments from the top and those from the bottom show some degree of convergence. In so far as they converge, they will indicate a possible pathway which life might have followed in its original progress from chaos to homeostasis.

These suggestions for future experiments probably sound naive and simple-minded to experimenters whose daily lives are spent in constant battle against the recalcitrance of real cells and real chemicals. I do not know when experiments along the lines that I have suggested will become feasible. I suggest them with diffidence, being myself incapable of doing an experiment even in my own field of physics. Nevertheless, I make these suggestions with serious intent. If I did not believe that such experiments are potentially important, I would not have ventured to talk about the origin of life in the first place. If a theoretical physicist has anything of value to say about the fundamental problems of biology, it can only be through making suggestions for new types of experiment. Forty years ago, Erwin Schrödinger suggested to biologists that they should investigate experimentally the molecular structure of the gene. That suggestion turned out to be timely. I am now suggesting that biologists investigate experimentally the population structure of homeostatic systems of molecules. If I am lucky, this suggestion may also turn out to be timely.

Before leaving the subject of future experiments, I would like to add some remarks about computer simulations. In population biology the computer is a source of experimental data at least as important as field observation. Computer simulations of population dynamics are indispensable for the planning of field observations and for the interpretation of results. Computer simulations are not only quicker than field observations but also cheaper. Every serious programme of research in population biology includes computer simulations as a matter of course. Since I am advocating a programme of research in the population biology of molecules, computer simulations will be essential here too.

Ursula Niesert's computer simulations of the Eigen hypercycle model of the origin of life (Niesert et al., 1981) exposed several serious weaknesses of that model. As Niesert observed as a result of her simulations, the failures of the hypercycle model are mainly due to the fact that a single RNA molecule is supposed to be performing simultaneously three separate functions. The three functions are: replicating itself with the help of a replicator molecule to which it is specifically adapted, carrying a message to promote the synthesis of another molecule and acting as agent for the specific transfer of amino-acids. The computer models show that RNA molecules have a natural tendency to specialize. They prefer to perform a single function well rather than to perform three functions badly. This conclusion is not surprising. In the natural ecology of species, it is a general rule that most species survive by becoming specialists. Niesert's simulation showed that the same rule applies in the ecology of molecules in the hypercycle model. Her criticism of the model enables us to understand it better and perhaps to improve it. In the same way, computer simulations of models of the origin of homeostasis will show us what is wrong with the models and will help us to replace them with better ones. Like the hypercycle model, models of homeostasis are likely to be vulnerable to the three dangers which Niesert described in her paper "Origin of life between Scylla and Charybdis." I describe the three dangers in Chapter 2 of *Origins of Life*. As soon as realistic models of homeostatic populations become available, computer simulations will probably reveal a variety of additional catastrophes to which they are liable. Only when we have explored all the possible modes of breakdown of homeostasis will we have a right to say that we understand what homeostasis means. Computer simulations will be essential to the growth of such understanding. In our search for an answer to the question "Why is life so complicated?," biological and chemical experiments and computer simulations must always go hand in hand.

Other questions suggested by the toy model

I now return to the toy model of Chapter 3 of *Origins of Life* and examine some other questions which it raises. The questions are not specific to this particular model. They will arise for any model of the origin of life in which we have molecular populations achieving metabolism and homeostasis before they achieve replication. The questions refer not to the model itself but to the implications of the model for the subsequent course of biological evolution. I comment briefly on each question in turn. After another twenty years of progress in biological research we may perhaps know whether my tentative answers are correct.

Were the first living creatures composed of proteins or nucleic acids or a mixture of the two?

I have already stated my reasons for preferring proteins. I prefer proteins partly because my model works well with ten species of monomer and works badly with four species, partly because amino-acids fit better than nucleotides the requirements of pre-biotic chemistry, and partly because I am attracted by the Margulis vision of parasitism as a driving force of early evolution and I like to put nucleic acids into the role of primeval parasites. None of these reasons is scientifically compelling.

At what stage random genetic drift give way to natural selection?

The model has life originating by neutral evolution according to the ideas of Kimura (Kimura, 1970, 1983). A population crosses the saddle-point to the ordered state by random genetic drift. The model does not allow natural selection to operate because it does not allow the populations in cells to grow or to reproduce. So long as there is no birth and death of cells, there can be no natural selection. However, once a cell has reached the ordered state as defined in the model, it can go beyond the model and pass into a new phase of evolution by assimilating fresh monomers from its environment. A cell which increases its population N by assimilation will quickly become stabilized against reversion to the disordered state since the lifetime of the ordered state increases exponentially with N. It can then continue to grow until some physical disturbance causes it to divide. If it divides into two cells there is a good chance that both daughter populations contain a sufficient assortment of catalysts to remain n the ordered state. The processes of growth and division can continue until tile cells begin to exhaust the supply of nutrient monomers. When the monomers are in short supply, some cells will lose their substance and die. From that point on, evolution will be driven by natural selection.

As soon as natural selection begins to operate, there will be an enormous advantage accruing to any cell which acquires the knack of dividing itself spontaneously instead of waiting for some natural process such as wave motion or turbulent flow to break it apart. At first, spontaneous division might be an accidental consequence of a tendency of the cell surface to weaken as the cell expands in volume. At a later stage, the weakening of the surface and the subsequent spontaneous division would become organized and integrated into the metabolic cycle of the cell. Cells would then be competing with one another in a straightforward Darwinian Fashion, with the prize of survival going to those which had learned to grow and divide most rapidly and reliably. In this way the processes of natural selection could have been well established long before the cells had acquired anything resembling the modern machinery of cell division.

Does the contradict the Central Dogma of molecular biology,?

The Central Dogma says that genetic information is carried only by nucleic acids and not by proteins. The dogma is true for all contemporary organisms, with the possible exception of the parasites responsible for scrapie and kuru. Whether or not the scrapie parasite turns out to be a true exception to the dogma, my model implies that the dogma was untrue for the earliest forms of life. According to the model, the first cells passed genetic information to their offspring in the form of enzymes which were probably proteins. There is no logical reason why a population of enzymes mutually catalysing each other's synthesis should not serve as a carrier of genetic information.

The question "How much genetic information can be carried by a population of molecules without exact replication?" is intimately bound up with the question of the nature of homeostasis. Homeostasis is the preservation of the chemical architecture of a population in spite of variations in local conditions and in the numbers of molecules of various kinds. Genetic information is carried in the architecture and not in the individual components. But we do not know how to define architecture or how to quantify homeostasis. Lacking a deep understanding of homeostasis, we have no way of calculating how many items of genetic information the homeostatic machinery of a cell may be able to preserve. It seems to be true, both in the world of cellular chemistry and in the world of ecology, that homeostatic mechanisms have a general tendency to become complicated rather than simple. Homeostasis seems to work better with an elaborate web of interlocking cycles than with a small number of cycles working separately. Why this is so we do not know. We are back again with the question "Why is life so complicated?" But the prevalence of highly complex homeostatic systems, whether we understand the reasons for it or not, is a fact. This fact is evidence that large amounts of genetic information can in principle be expressed in the architecture of molecular populations without nucleic acid software and without apparatus for exact replication.

How did nucleic acids originate?

I remark earlier (Chapter 2 of *Origins of Life*) on the curious fact that nucleic acids are chemical cousins of the ATP molecule, which is the chief energy-carrier in the metabolism of modern cells. I like to use this fact to explain the origin of nucleic acids as a disease arising in some primitive cell from a surfeit of ATP. The Margulis picture of evolution converts the nucleic acids from their original status as indigestible by-products of ATP metabolism to disease agents, from disease agents to parasites, from parasites to symbionts and finally from symbionts to fully integrated organs of the cell.

How did the modern genetic apparatus evolve?

The modern genetic apparatus is enormously fine-tuned and must have evolved over a long period of time from simpler beginnings. Perhaps some clues to its earlier history will be found when the structure of the modern ribosome is explored and understood in detail. The following sequence of steps is a possible pathway to the modern genetic apparatus, beginning with a cell which has RNA established as a self-reproducing cellular parasite but not yet performing a genetic function for the cell. (a) Non-specific binding of RNA to free amino-acids, activating them for easier polymerization; (b) specific binding of RNA to catalytic sites to give them structural precision; (c) RNA bound to amino-acids becomes transfer RNA; (d) RNA bound to catalytic sites becomes ribosomal RNA; (e) catalytic sites evolve from special-purpose to general-purpose by using transfer RNA instead of amino-acids for recognition; (f) recognition unit splits off from ribosomal RNA and becomes messenger RNA; (g) ribosomal structure becomes unique as the genetic code takes over the function of recognition. This is only one of many possible pathways that might have led to the evolution of the genetic code. The essential point is that all such pathways appear to be long and tortuous. In my opinion, both the metabolic machinery of proteins and the parasitic self-replication of nucleic acids must have been in place before the evolution of the elaborate translation apparatus linking the two systems could begin.

How late was the latest common ancestor of all living species?

The universality of the genetic code suggests that the latest common ancestor of all living creatures already possessed a complete genetic apparatus of the modern type. The geological record tells us that cells existed very early, as long as I eons ago. It is generally assumed that the earliest cells which are preserved as microfossils already possessed a modern genetic apparatus, but this assumption is not based on concrete evidence. It is possible that the evolution of the modern genetic apparatus took eons to complete. The ancient microfossils may date from a time before there were genes and ribosomes. The pace of evolution may have accelerated after the genetic code was established, allowing the development from ancestral procaryote to eucaryotic cells and multicellular organisms to be completed in less time than it took to go from primitive cell to ancestral procaryote. It is therefore possible that the latest common ancestor came late in the history of life, perhaps as late as half-way from the beginning.

Does there exist a chemical realization of my model, for example a population of a few thousand amlino-acids forming an association of polypeptides which can catalyse each other's synthesis with 80 per cent accuracy? Can such an association of molecules be confined in a droplet and supplied with energy and raw materials in such a way as to maintain itself in a stable homeostatic equilibrium?

These are the crucial questions which only experiment can answer.

What will happen to my little toy model when the problem of the origin of life is finally solved?

This is the last question raised by the model and it is easily answered. The answer was given nearly two hundred years ago by my favourite poet, William Blake (A Vision of the Last Judgment, Rossetti MS, 1810):

> To be an Error and to be Cast out
> is a part of God's design.

Wider implications

At the end of his book *What is Life?* Schrödinger put a four-page epilogue with the title "On determinism and free will." He there states his personal philosophical viewpoint, his reconciliation between his objective understanding of the physical machinery of life and his subjective experience of free will. He writes with a clarity and economy of language which have rarely been equalled. I will not try to compete with Schrödinger in summing up in four pages the fruits of a lifetime of philosophical reflection. Instead I will use my last pages to discuss some of the wider implications of our thoughts about the origin of life, not for personal philosophy but for other areas of science. I use the word science here in a broad sense, including social as well as natural sciences. The sciences that I have particularly in mind are ecology, economics and cultural history. In all these areas we are confronting the same question that is at the root of the problem of understanding the origin of life: "Why is Life so Complicated?" It may be that each of these areas has something to learn from the others.

The concept of homeostasis can be transferred without difficulty from a molecular context to ecological, economic and cultural contexts. In each area we have the unexplained fact that complicated homeostatic mechanisms are more prevalent and seem to be more effective, than simple ones. This is most spectacularly true in the domain of ecology, where a typical stable community, for example a few acres of woodland or a few square feet of grassland, comprises thousands of diverse species with highly specialized and interdependent functions. But a similar phenomenon is visible in economic life and in cultural evolution. The open market economy and the culturally open society, notwithstanding all their failures and deficiencies, seem to possess a robustness which centrally planned economies and culturally closed societies lack. The homeostasis provided by unified five-year economic plans and by unified political control of culture does not lead to a greater stability of economics and cultures. On the contrary, the simple homeostatic mechanisms of central control have generally proved more brittle and less able to cope with historical shocks than the complex homeostatic mechanisms of the open market and the uncensored press.

But I did not come to Cambridge to give a political pep-talk in defense of free enterprise. My purpose in mentioning the analogies between cellular and social homeostasis was not to draw a political moral from biology but rather to draw a biological moral from ecology and social history. Fortunately, I can claim the highest scientific authority for drawing the moral in this direction. It is well known to historians of science that Charles Darwin was strongly influenced in his working-out of the theory of evolution by his readings of the political economists from Adam Smith to Malthus and McCullough. Darwin himself said of his theory: "This is the doctrine of Malthus applied to the whole animal and vegetable kingdom." What I am proposing is to apply in the same spirit the doctrines of modern ecology to the molecular processes within a primitive cell. In our present state of ignorance we have a choice between two contrasting images to represent our view of the possible structure of a creature newly emerged at the first threshold of life. One image is the hypercycle model of Eigen, that is to say a molecular structure tightly linked and centrally controlled, replicating itself with considerable precision and achieving homeostasis by strict adherence to a rigid pattern. The other image is the "tangled bank" of Darwin, an image which Darwin put at the end of his *Origin of Species* to make vivid his answer to the question "What is Life?"—an image of grasses and flowers and bees and butterflies growing in tangled profusion without any discernible pattern, achieving homeostasis by means of a web of interdependences too complicated for us to unravel. The tangled bank is the image that I have in mind when I try to imagine what a primeval cell would look like. I imagine a collection of molecular species that are tangled and interlocking like the plants and insects in Darwin's microcosm. This was the image which led me to think of error-tolerance as the primary requirement for a model of a molecular population taking its first faltering steps toward life. Error-tolerance is the hall-mark of natural ecological communities, of free market economies and of open societies. I believe it must have been a primary quality of life from the very beginning. But replication and error-tolerance are naturally antagonistic principles. That is why I like to exclude replication from the beginnings of life, to imagine the first cells as error-tolerant tangles of nonreplicating molecules, and to introduce replication as an alien parasitic intrusion at a later stage. Only after the alien intruder has been tamed is the reconciliation between replication and error-tolerance achieved in a higher synthesis, through the evolution of the genetic code and the modern apparatus of ribosomes and chromosomes.

The modern synthesis reconciles replication with error tolerance by establishing the division of labour between hardware and software, between the genetic apparatus and the gene. In the modern cell, the hardware of the genetic apparatus is rigidly controlled and error-intolerant. The hardware must be error-intolerant in order to maintain the accuracy of replication. But the error-tolerance which I like to believe was inherent in life from its earliest beginnings has not been lost. The burden of error-tolerance has merely been transferred to the software. In the modern cell, with the infrastructure of hardware firmly in place and subject to a strict regime of quality-control, the software is free to wander, to make mistakes and occasionally to be creative. The transfer of architectural design from hardware to software allowed the molecular architects to work with a freedom and creativity which their ancestors before the transfer could never have approached.

The analogies between the genetic evolution of biological species and the cultural evolution of human societies have been brilliantly explored by Richard Dawkins in his book *The Selfish Gene* (Dawkins, 1976). The book is mainly concerned with biological evolution. The cultural analogies are pursued only in the last chapter. Dawkins' main theme is the tyranny which the rigid demands of the replication apparatus have imposed upon all biological species throughout evolutionary history. Every species is the prisoner of its genes and is compelled to develop and to behave in such a way as to maximize their chances of survival. Only the genes are free to experiment with new patterns of behaviour. Individual organisms must do what their genes dictate. This tyranny of the genes has lasted for three thousand million years and has been precariously overthrown only in the last hundred thousand years by a single species, *Homo sapiens*. We have overthrown the tyranny by inventing symbolic language and culture. Our behaviour patterns are now to a great extent culturally rather than genetically determined. We can choose to keep a defective gene in circulation because our culture tells us not to let hemophiliac children die. We have stolen back from our genes the freedom to make choices and to make mistakes.

In his last chapter Dawkins describes a new tyrant which has arisen within human culture to take the place of the old. The new tyrant is the "meme," the cultural analogue of the gene. A meme is a behavioural pattern which replicates itself by cultural transfer from individual to individual instead of by biological inheritance. Examples of memes are religious beliefs, linguistic idioms, fashions in art and science, in food and clothes. Almost all the phenomena of evolutionary genetics and speciation have their analogues in cultural history, with the meme taking over the functions of the gene. The meme is a self-replicating unit of behaviour, like the gene. The meme and the gene are equally selfish. The history of human culture shows us to be as subject to the tyranny of our memes as other species are to the tyranny of genes. But Dawkins ends his discussion with a call for liberation. Our capacity for foresight gives us the power to transcend our memes just as our culture gave us the power to transcend our genes. We, he says, alone on earth, can rebel against the tyranny of the selfish replicators.

Dawkins' vision of the human situation as a Promethean struggle against the tyranny of the replicators contains important elements of truth. We are indeed rebels by nature, and his vision explains many aspects of our culture that would otherwise be mysterious. But his account leaves out half the story. He describes the history of life as the history of replication. Like Eigen, he believes that the beginning of life was a self-replicating molecule. Throughout his history, the replicators are in control. In the beginning, he says, was simplicity. The point of view that I am expounding in these lectures is precisely the opposite. In the beginning, I am saying, was complexity. The essence of life from the beginning was homeostasis based on a complicated web of molecular structures. Life by its very nature is resistant to simplification, whether on the level of single cells or ecological systems or human societies. Life could tolerate a precisely replicating molecular apparatus only by incorporating it into a translation system that allowed the complexity of the molecular web to be expressed in the form of software. After the transfer of complication from hardware to software, life continued to be a complicated interlocking web in which the replicators were only one component. The replicators were never as firmly in control as Dawkins imagined. In my version the history of life is counterpoint music, a two-part invention with two voices, the voice of the replicators attempting to impose their selfish purposes upon the whole network, and the voice of homeostasis tending to maximize diversity of structure and flexibility of function. The tyranny of the replicators was always mitigated by the more ancient cooperative structure of homeostasis that was inherent in every organism. The rule of the genes was like the government of the old Hapsburg Empire: "Despotismus gemildert mit Schlamperei," "Despotism tempered by sloppiness."

One of the most interesting developments in modern genetics is the discovery of 'junk DNA', a substantial component of our cellular inheritance which appears to have no biological function. Junk DNA is DNA which does us no good and no harm, merely taking a free ride in our cells and taking advantage of our efficient replicative apparatus. The prevalence of junk DNA is a striking example of the sloppiness which life has always embodied in one form or another. It is easy to find in human culture the analogue of junk DNA. Junk culture is replicated together with memes, just as junk DNA is replicated together with genes. Junk culture is the rubbish of civilization, television commercials and astrology and juke-boxes and political propaganda. Tolerance of junk is one of life's most essential characteristics. In every sphere of life, whether Cultural, economic, ecological or cellular, the systems which survive best are those which are not too fine-tuned to carry a large load of junk. And so, I believe, it must have been at the beginning. I would be surprised if the first living cell were not at least 25 per cent junk.

That is the end of my story, and it brings me back to the beginning. I have been trying to imagine a framework for the origin of life, guided by a personal philosophy which considers the primal characteristics of life to be homeostasis rather than replication, diversity rather than uniformity, the flexibility of the genome rather than the tyranny of the gene, the error-tolerance of the whole rather than the precision of the parts. The framework that I have found is an abstract mathematical model which is far too simple to be true. But the model incorporates in a crude fashion the qualitative features of life that I consider essential, looseness of structure and tolerance of errors. The model fits into an overall view of life and evolution that is more relaxed than the traditional view. The new and looser picture of evolution is strongly supported by recent experimental discoveries in the molecular biology of eucaryotic cells. Edward Wilson, who was also my illustrious predecessor as Tarner Lecturer in Cambridge (Wilson, 1982), describes the new picture of the eucaryotic genome as "a rainforest with many niches occupied by a whole range of elements, all parts of which are in a dynamic state of change." My philosophical bias leads me to believe that Wilson's picture describes not only the eucaryotic genome but the evolution of life all the way back to the beginning. I hold the creativity of quasi-random complicated structures to be a more important driving force of evolution than the Darwinian competition of replicating monads.   But philosophy is nothing but empty words if it is not capable of being tested by experiment. If my remarks have any value, it is only insofar as they suggest new experiments. I leave it now to the experimenters to see whether they can condense some solid facts out of this philosophical hot air.

References

Anderson, P. W. (1983). "Suggested model for prebiotic evolution: The use of chaos." *Proc. Nat. Acad. Sci.* USA 80, 3386-90.

Cairns-Smith, A. G. (1982). *Genetic Takeover and the Mineral Origin of Life.* New York: Cambridge University Press.

Dawkins, R. (1976). *The Selfish Gene.* New York: Oxford University Press.

Dyson, F. J. (1982). "A model for the origin of life." *J. Mol. Evol.* 18, 344-50.

Eigen, M., Gardiner, W., Schuster, P. & Winckler-Oswatitch, R. (1981). "The origin of genetic information," *Sci. Am.* 244, No. 4, 88-118

Kimura, M. (1970). "Stochastic processes in population genetics." In *Mathematical Topics in Population Genetics*, ed. K. I. Kojima, pp. 178-209. Berlin: Springer.

---------. (1983). *The Neutral Theory of Molecular Evolution.* New York: Cambridge University Press.

Margulis, L. (1970). *Origin of Eucaryotic Cells.* New Haven: Yale University Press

---------. (1970). *Symbiosis in Cell Evolution.* San Francisco: Freeman and Co.

Miller, S. M. & Orgel, L. E. (1974). *The Origin of Life on the Earth.* Englewood Cliffs, NJ: Prentice-Hall, Inc.

Niesert, U., Harnasch, D. & Bresch, C. (1981). "Origin of life between Scylla and Charybdis." *J. Mol. Evol.* 17, 348-53.

Oparin, A. I. (1957). *The Origin of Life on the Earth*, 3rd edn, translated by Ann Synge. Edinburgh: Oliver and Boyd.

Prusiner, S. B. (1982). "Novel proteinaceous infectious particles, cause scrapie." *Science* 216, 136-44.

Schrödinger, E. (1944). *What is Life? The Physical Aspect of the Living Cell.* Cambridge University Press.

Spiegelman, S. (1967). "An in vitro analysis of a replicating molecule." *American Scientist* 55, 3-68.

Terzaghi, E. A., Wilkins, A. S. & Penny, D. (1984). *Molecular Evolution: An Annotated Reader.* Boston: Jones and Bartlett.

Von Neumann, J. (1948). "The General and Logical Theory of Automata." Lecture given 1948. In *Cerebral Cerebral Mechanisms in Behavior—The Hixon Symposium*, ed. L. A. Jeffress, pp. 1-41. New York: John Wiley, 1951; and In *J. Von Neumann, Collected Works*, ed. A. H. Taub. Vol. 5, pp, 288-328. New York: MacMillan, 1961-63.

Wilson, E. 0. (1982). Remarks quoted by R. Lewin. *Science* 216, 1091-2.

8

The Evolution of Life on Earth

STEPHEN JAY GOULD

Some creators announce their inventions with grand éclat. God proclaimed, "Fiat lux," and then flooded his new universe with brightness. Others bring forth great discoveries in a modest guise, as did Charles Darwin in defining his new mechanism of evolutionary causality in 1859: "I have called this principle, by which each slight variation, if useful, is presented, by the term Natural Selection."

Natural selection is an immensely powerful yet beautifully simple theory that has held up remarkably well, under intense and unrelenting scrutiny and testing, for 135 years. In essence, natural selection locates the mechanism of evolutionary change in a "struggle" among organisms for reproductive success, leading to improved fit of populations to changing environments. (Struggle is often a metaphorical description and need not be viewed as overt combat, guns blazing. Tactics for reproductive success include a variety of nonmartial activities such as earlier and more frequent mating or better cooperation with partners in raising offspring.) Natural selection is therefore a principle of local adaptation, not of general advance or progress.

Yet powerful though the principle may be, natural selection is not the only cause of evolutionary change (and may, in many cases, be overshadowed by other forces). This point needs emphasis because the standard misapplication of evolutionary theory assumes that biological explanation may be equated with devising accounts, often speculative and conjectural in practice, about the adaptive value of any given feature in its original environment (human aggression as good for hunting, music and religion as good for tribal cohesion, for example). Darwin himself strongly emphasized the multifactorial nature of evolutionary change and warned against too exclusive a reliance on natural selection, by placing the following statement in a maximally conspicuous place at the very end of his introduction: "I am convinced that Natural Selection has been the most important, but not the exclusive, means of modification."

Natural selection is not fully sufficient to explain evolutionary change for two major reasons. First, many other causes are powerful, particularly at levels of biological organization both above and below the traditional Darwinian focus on organisms and their struggles for reproductive success. At the lowest level of substitution in individual base pairs of DNA, change is often effectively neutral and therefore random. At higher levels, involving entire species or faunas, punctuated equilibrium can produce evolutionary trends by selection of species based on their rates of origin and extirpation, whereas mass extinctions wipe out substantial parts of biotas for reasons unrelated to adaptive struggles of constituent species in "normal" times between such events.

Second, and the focus of this article, no matter how adequate our general theory of evolutionary change, we also yearn to document and understand the actual pathway of life's history. Theory, of course, is relevant to explaining the pathway (nothing about the pathway can be inconsistent with good theory, and theory can predict certain general aspects of life's geologic pattern). But the actual pathway is strongly *underdetermined* by our general theory of life's evolution. This point needs some belaboring as a central yet widely misunderstood aspect of the world's complexity. Webs and chains of historical events are so intricate, so imbued with random and chaotic elements, so unrepeatable in encompassing such a multitude of unique (and uniquely interacting) objects, that standard models of simple prediction and replication do not apply.

History can be explained, with satisfying rigor if evidence be adequate, after a sequence of events unfolds, but it cannot be predicted with any precision beforehand. Pierre-Simon Laplace, echoing the growing and confident determinism of the late 18th century, once said that he could specify all future states if he could know the position and motion of all particles in the cosmos at any moment, but the nature of universal complexity shatters this chimerical dream. History includes too much chaos, or extremely sensitive dependence on minute and unmeasurable differences in initial conditions, leading to massively, divergent outcomes based on tiny and unknowable disparities in starting points. And history includes too much contingency, or shaping of present results by long chains of unpredictable antecedent states, rather than immediate determination by timeless laws of nature.

Homo sapiens did not appear on the earth, just a geologic second ago, because evolutionary theory predicts such an outcome based on themes of progress and increasing neural complexity. Humans arose, rather, as a fortuitous and contingent outcome of thousands of linked events, any one of which could have occurred differently and sent history on an alternative pathway that would not have led to consciousness. To cite just four among a multitude: (1) If our inconspicuous and fragile lineage had not been among the few survivors of the initial radiation of multicellular animal life in the Cambrian explosion 530 million years ago, then no vertebrates would have inhabited the earth at all. (Only one member of our chordate phylum, the genus *Pikaia*, has been found among these earliest fossils. This small and simple swimming creature, showing its allegiance to us by possessing a notochord, or dorsal stiffening rod, is among the rarest fossils of the Burgess Shale, our best preserved Cambrian fauna.) (2) If a small and unpromising group of lobe-finned fishes had not evolved fin bones with a strong central axis capable of bearing weight on land, then vertebrates might never have become terrestrial. (3) If a large extraterrestrial body had not struck the earth 65 million years ago, then dinosaurs would still be dominant and mammals insignificant (the situation that had prevailed for 100 million years previously). (4) If a small lineage of primates had not evolved upright posture on the drying African savannas just two to four million years ago, then our ancestry might have ended in a line of apes that, like the chimpanzee and gorilla today, would have become ecologically marginal and probably doomed to extinction despite their remarkable behavioral complexity.

Therefore, to understand the events and generalities of life's pathway, we must go beyond principles of evolutionary theory to a paleontological examination of the contingent pattern of life's history on our planet—the single actualized version among millions of plausible alternatives that happened not to occur. Such a view of life's history is highly contrary both to conventional deterministic models of Western science and to the deepest social traditions and psychological hopes of Western culture for a history culminating in humans as life's highest expression and intended planetary steward.

Science can, and does, strive to grasp nature's factuality, but all science is socially embedded, and all scientists record prevailing "certainties," however hard they may be aiming for pure objectivity. Darwin himself, in the closing lines of *The Origin of Species*, expressed Victorian social preference more than nature's record in writing: "As natural selection works solely by and for the good of each being, all corporeal and mental endowments will tend to progress towards perfection."

Life's pathway certainly includes many features predictable from laws of nature, but these aspects are too broad and general to provide the "rightness" that we seek for validating evolution's particular results—roses, mushrooms, people and so forth. Organisms adapt to, and are constrained by, physical principles. It is, for example, scarcely surprising, given laws of gravity, that the largest vertebrates in the sea (whales) exceed the heaviest animals on land (elephants today, dinosaurs in the past), which, in turn, are far bulkier than the largest vertebrate that ever flew (extinct pterosaurs of the Mesozoic era).

Predictable ecological rules govern the structuring of communities by principles of energy flow and thermodynamics (more biomass in prey than in predators, for example). Evolutionary trends, once started, may have local predictability ("arms races," in which both predators and prey hone their defenses and weapons, for example—a pattern that Geerat J. Vermeij of the University of California at Davis has called "escalation" and documented in increasing strength of both crab claws and shells of their gastropod prey through time). But laws of nature do not tell us why we have crabs and snails at all, why insects rule the multicellular world and why vertebrates rather than persistent algal mats exist as the most complex forms of life on the earth.

Relative to the conventional view of life's history as an at least broadly predictable process of gradually advancing complexity through time, three features of the paleontological record stand out in opposition and shall therefore serve as organizing themes for the rest of this article: the constancy of modal complexity throughout life's history; the concentration of major events in short bursts interspersed with long periods of relative stability; and the role of external impositions, primarily mass extinctions, in disrupting patterns of "normal" times. These three features, combined with more general themes of chaos and contingency, require a new framework for conceptualizing and drawing life's history, and this article therefore closes with suggestions for a different iconography of evolution.

The primary paleontological fact about life's beginnings points to predictability for the onset and very little for the particular pathways thereafter. The earth is 4.6 billion years old, but the oldest rocks date to about 3.9 billion years because the earth's surface became molten early in its history, a result of bombardment by large amounts of cosmic debris during the solar system's coalescence, and of heat generated by radioactive decay of short-lived isotopes. These oldest rocks are too metamorphosed by subsequent heat and pressure to preserve fossils (though some scientists interpret the proportions of carbon isotopes in these rocks as signs of organic production). The oldest rocks sufficiently unaltered to retain cellular fossils—African and Australian sediments dated to 3.5 billion years old—do preserve prokaryotic cells (bacteria and cyanophytes) and stromatolites (mats of sediment trapped and bound by these cells in shallow marine waters). Thus, life on the earth evolved quickly and is as old as it could be. This fact alone seems to indicate an inevitability, or at least a predictability, for life's origin from the original chemical constituents of atmosphere and ocean.

No one can doubt that more complex creatures arose sequentially after this prokaryotic beginning—first eukaryotic cells, perhaps about two billion years ago, then multicellular animals about 600 million years ago, with a relay of highest complexity among animals passing from invertebrates, to marine vertebrates and, finally (if we wish, albeit parochially, to honor neural architecture as a primary criterion), to reptiles, mammals and humans. This is the conventional sequence represented in the old charts and texts as an "age of invertebrates," followed by an "age of fishes," "age of reptiles," "age of mammals," and "age of man" (to add the old gender bias to all the other prejudices implied by this sequence).

I do not deny the facts of the preceding paragraph but wish to argue that our conventional desire to view history as progressive, and to see humans as predictably dominant, has grossly distorted our interpretation of life's pathway by falsely placing in the center of things a relatively minor phenomenon that arises only as a side consequence of a physically constrained starting point. The most salient feature of life has been the stability of its bacterial mode from the beginning of the fossil record until today and, with little doubt, into all future time so long as the earth endures. This is truly the "age of bacteria" —as it was in the beginning, is now and ever shall be.

For reasons related to the chemistry of life's origin and the physics of self-organization the first living things arose at the lower limit of life's conceivable, preservable complexity. Call this lower limit the "left wall" for an architecture of complexity. Since so little space exists between the left wall and life's initial bacterial mode in the fossil record, only one direction for future increment exists—toward greater complexity at the right. Thus, every once in a while, a more complex creature evolves and extends the range of life's diversity in the only available direction. In technical terms, the distribution of complexity becomes more strongly right skewed through these occasional additions.

But the additions are rare and episodic. They do not even constitute an evolutionary series but form a motley sequence of distantly related taxa, usually depicted as eukaryotic cell, jellyfish, trilobite, nautiloid, eurypterid (a large relative of horseshoe crabs), fish, an amphibian such as *Eryops*, a dinosaur, a mammal and a human being. This sequence cannot be construed as the major thrust or trend of life's history. Think rather of an occasional creature tumbling into the empty right region of complexity's space. Throughout this entire time, the bacterial mode has grown in height and remained constant in position. Bacteria represent the great success story of life's pathway. They occupy a wider domain of environments and span a broader range of biochemistries than any other group. They are adaptable, indestructible and astoundingly diverse. We cannot even imagine how anthropogenic intervention might threaten their extinction, although we worry about our impact on nearly every other form of life. The number of *Escherichia coli* cells in the gut of each human being exceeds the number of humans that has ever lived on this planet.

One might grant that complexification for life as a whole represents a pseudotrend based on constraint at the left wall but still hold that evolution within particular groups differentially favors complexity when the founding lineage begins far enough from the left wall to permit movement in both directions. Empirical tests of this interesting hypothesis are just beginning (as concern for the subject mounts among paleontologists), and we do not yet have enough cases to advance a generality. But the first two studies—by Daniel W. McShea of the University of Michigan on mammalian vertebrae and by George F. Boyajian of the University of Pennsylvania on ammonite suture lines—show no evolutionary tendencies to favor increased complexity.

Moreover, when we consider that for each mode of life involving greater complexity, there probably exists an equally advantageous style based on greater simplicity of form (as often found in parasites, for example), then preferential evolution toward complexity seems unlikely a priori. Our impression that life evolves toward greater complexity is probably only a bias inspired by parochial focus on ourselves, and consequent overattention to complexifying creatures, while we ignore just as many lineages adapting equally well by becoming simpler in form. The morphologically degenerate parasite, safe within its host, has just as much prospect for evolutionary success as its gorgeously elaborate relative coping with the slings and arrows of outrageous fortune in a tough external world.

Even if complexity is only a drift away from a constraining left wall, we might view trends in this direction as more predictable and characteristic of life's pathway as a whole if increments of complexity accrued in a persistent and gradually accumulating manner through time. But nothing about life's history is more peculiar with respect to this common (and false) expectation than the actual pattern of extended stability and rapid episodic movement, as revealed by the fossil record.

Life remained almost exclusively unicellular for the first five sixths of its history—from the first recorded fossils at 3.5 billion years to the first well-documented multicellular animals less than 600 million years ago. (Some simple multicellular algae evolved more than a billion years ago, but these organisms belong to the plant kingdom and have no genealogical connection with animals.) This long period of unicellular life does include, to be sure, the vitally important transition from simple prokaryotic cells without organelles to eukaryotic cells with nuclei, mitochondria and other complexities of intracellular architecture—but no recorded attainment of multicellular animal organization for a full three billion years. If complexity is such a good thing, and multicellularity represents its initial phase in our usual view, then life certainly took its time in making this crucial step. Such delays speak strongly against general progress as the major theme of life's history, even if they can be plausibly explained by lack of sufficient atmospheric oxygen for most of Precambrian time or by failure of unicellular life to achieve some structural threshold acting as a prerequisite to multicellularity.

More curiously, all major stages in organizing animal life's multicellular architecture then occurred in a short period beginning less than 600 million years ago and ending by about 530 million years ago—and the steps within this sequence are also discontinuous and episodic, not gradually accumulative. The first fauna, called Ediacaran to honor the Australian locality of its initial discovery but now known from rocks on all continents, consists of highly flattened fronds, sheets and circlets composed of numerous slender segments quilted together. The nature of the Ediacaran fauna is now a subject of intense discussion. These creatures do not seem to be simple precursors of later forms. They may constitute a separate and faded experiment in animal life, or they may represent a full range of diploblastic (two-layered) organization, of which the modem phylum Cnidaria (corals, jellyfishes and their allies) remains as a small and much altered remnant.

In any case, they apparently died out well before the Cambrian biota evolved. The Cambrian then began with an assemblage of bits and pieces, frustratingly difficult to interpret, called the "small shelly fauna." The subsequent main pulse, starting about 530 million years ago, constitutes the famous Cambrian explosion, during which all but one modem phylum of animal life made a first appearance in the fossil record. (Geologists had previously allowed up to 40 million years for this event, but an elegant study, published in 1993, clearly restricts this period of phyletic flowering to a mere five million years.) The Bryozoa, a group of sessile and colonial marine organisms, do not arise until the beginning of the subsequent, Ordovician period, but this apparent delay may be an artifact of failure to discover Cambrian representatives.

Although interesting and portentous events have occurred since, from the flowering of dinosaurs to the origin of human consciousness, we do not exaggerate greatly in stating that the subsequent history of animal life amounts to little more than variations on anatomical themes established during the Cambrian explosion within five million years. Three billion years of unicellularity followed by five million years of intense creativity and then capped by more than 500 million years of variation on set anatomical themes can scarcely be read as a predictable, inexorable or continuous trend toward progress or increasing complexity.

We do not know why the Cambrian explosion could establish all major anatomical designs so quickly. An "external" explanation based on ecology seems attractive: the Cambrian explosion represents an initial filling of the "ecological barrel" of niches for multicellular organisms, and any experiment found a space. The barrel has never emptied since; even the great mass extinctions left a few species in each principal role, and their occupation of ecological space forecloses opportunity for fundamental novelties. But an "internal" explanation based on genetics and development also seems necessary as a complement: the earliest multicellular animals may have maintained a flexibility for genetic change and embryological transformation that became greatly reduced as organisms "locked in" to a set of stable and successful designs.

In any case, this initial period of both internal and external flexibility yielded a range of invertebrate anatomies that may have exceeded (in just a few million years of production) the full scope of animal form in all the earth's environments today (after more than 500 million years of additional time for further expansion). Scientists are divided on this question. Some claim that the anatomical range of this initial explosion exceeded that of modem life, as many early experiments died out and no new phyla have ever arisen. But scientists most strongly opposed to this view allow that Cambrian diversity at least equaled the modem range—so even the most cautious opinion holds that 500 million subsequent years of opportunity have not expanded the Cambrian range, achieved in just five million years. The Cambrian explosion was the most remarkable and puzzling event in the history of life.

Moreover, we do not know why most of the early experiments died, while a few survived to become our modern phyla. It is tempting to say that the victors won by virtue of greater anatomical complexity, better ecological fit or some other predictable feature of conventional Darwinian struggle. But no recognized traits unite the victors, and the radical alternative must be entertained that each early experiment received little more than the equivalent of a ticket in the largest lottery ever played out on our planet—and that each surviving lineage, including our own phylum of vertebrates, inhabits the earth today more by the luck of the draw than by any predictable struggle for existence. The history of multicellular animal life may be more a story of great reduction in initial possibilities, with stabilization of lucky survivors, than a conventional tale of steady ecological expansion and morphological progress in complexity.

Finally, this pattern of long stasis, with change concentrated in rapid episodes that establish new equilibria, may be quite general at several scales of time and magnitude, forming a kind of fractal pattern in self-similarity. According to the punctuated equilibrium model of speciation, trends within lineages occur by accumulated episodes of geologically instantaneous speciation, rather than by gradual change within continuous populations (like climbing a staircase rather than rolling a ball up an inclined plane).

Even if evolutionary theory implied a potential internal direction for life's pathway (although previous facts and arguments in this article cast doubt on such a claim), the occasional imposition of a rapid and substantial, perhaps even truly catastrophic, change in environment would have intervened to stymie the pattern.   These environmental changes trigger mass extinction of a high percentage of the earth's species and may so derail any internal direction and so reset the pathway that the net pattern of life's history looks more capricious and concentrated in episodes than steady and directional.   Mass extinctions have been recognized since the dawn of paleontology; the major divisions of the geologic time scale were established at boundaries marked by such events.   But until the revival of interest that began in the late 1970s, most paleontologists treated mass extinctions only as intensifications of ordinary events, leading (at most) to a speeding up of tendencies that pervaded normal times.   In this gradualistic theory of mass extinction, these events really took a few million years to unfold (with the appearance of suddenness interpreted as an artifact of an imperfect fossil record), and they only made the ordinary occur faster (more intense Darwinian competition in tough times, for example, leading to even more efficient replacement of less adapted by superior forms).

The reinterpretation of mass extinctions as central to life's pathway and radically different in effect began with the presentation of data by Luis and Walter Alvarez in 1979, indicating that the impact of a large extraterrestrial object (they suggested an asteroid seven to 10 kilometers in diameter) set off the last great extinction at the Cretaceous-Tertiary boundary 65 million years ago. Although the Alvarez hypothesis initially received very skeptical treatment from scientists (a proper approach to highly unconventional explanations), the case now seems virtually proved by discovery of the "smoking gun," a crater of appropriate size and age located off the Yucatan peninsula in Mexico.

This reawakening of interest also inspired paleontologists to tabulate the data of mass extinction more rigorously.   Work by David M. Raup, J. J. Sepkoski, Jr., and David Jablonski of the University of Chicago has established that multicellular animal life experienced five major (end of Ordovician, late Devonian, end of Permian, end of Triassic and end of Cretaceous) and many minor mass extinctions during its 530-million-year history.   We have no clear evidence that any but the last of these events was triggered by catastrophic impact, but such careful study leads to the general conclusion that mass extinctions were more frequent, more rapid, more extensive in magnitude and more different in effect than paleontologists had previously realized.   These four properties encompass the radical implications of mass extinction for understanding life's pathway as more contingent and chancy than predictable and directional.

Mass extinctions are not random in their impact on life. Some lineages succumb and others survive as sensible outcomes based on presence or absence of evolved features. But especially if the triggering cause of extinction be sudden and catastrophic, the reasons for life or death may be random with respect to the original value of key features when first evolved in Darwinian struggles of normal times. This "different rules" model of mass extinction imparts a quirky and unpredictable character to life's pathway based on the evident claim that lineages cannot anticipate future contingencies of such magnitude and different operation.

To cite two examples from the impact-triggered Cretaceous-Tertiary extinction 65 million years ago: First, an important study published in 1986 noted that diatoms survived the extinction far better than other single-celled plankton (primarily coccoliths and radiolaria). This study found that many diatoms had evolved a strategy of dormancy by encystment, perhaps to survive through seasonal periods of unfavorable conditions (months of darkness in polar species as otherwise fatal to these photosynthesizing cells; sporadic availability of silica needed to construct their skeletons). Other planktonic cells had not evolved any mechanisms for dormancy. If the terminal Cretaceous impact produced a dust cloud that blocked light for several months or longer (one popular idea for a "killing scenario" in the extinction), then diatoms may have survived as a fortuitous result of dormancy mechanisms evolved for the entirely different function of weathering seasonal droughts in ordinary times. Diatoms are not superior to radiolaria or other plankton that succumbed in far greater numbers; they were simply fortunate to possess a favorable feature, evolved for other reasons, that fostered passage through the impact and its sequelae.

Second, we all know that dinosaurs perished in the end Cretaceous event and that mammals therefore rule the vertebrate world today. Most people assume that mammals prevailed in these tough times for some reason of general superiority over dinosaurs. But such a conclusion seems most unlikely. Mammals and dinosaurs had coexisted for 100 million years, and mammals had remained rat-sized or smaller, making no evolutionary "move" to oust dinosaurs. No good argument for mammalian prevalence by general superiority has ever been advanced, and fortuity seems far more likely. As one plausible argument, mammals may have survived partly as a result of their small size (with much larger, and therefore extinction-resistant, populations as a consequence, and less ecological specialization with more places to hide, so to speak). Small size may not have been a positive mammalian adaptation at all, but more a sign of inability ever to penetrate the dominant domain of dinosaurs. Yet this "negative" feature of normal times may be the key reason for mammalian survival and a prerequisite to my writing and your reading this article today.

Sigmund Freud often remarked that great revolutions in the history of science have but one common, and ironic, feature: they knock human arrogance off one pedestal after another of our previous conviction about our own self-importance.   In Freud's three examples, Copernicus moved our home from center to periphery; Darwin then relegated us to "descent from an animal world"; and, finally (in one of the least modest statements of intellectual history), Freud himself discovered the unconscious and exploded the myth of a fully rational mind.

In this wise and crucial sense, the Darwinian revolution remains woefully incomplete because, even though thinking humanity accepts the fact of evolution, most of us are still unwilling to abandon the comforting view that evolution means (or at least embodies a central principle of) progress defined to render the appearance of something like human consciousness either virtually inevitable or at least predictable. The pedestal is not smashed until we abandon progress or complexification as a central principle and come to entertain the strong possibility that *H. sapiens* is but a tiny, late-arising tail on life's enormously arborescent bush—a small bud that would almost surely not appear a second time if we could replant the bush from seed and let it grow again.

Primates are visual animals, and the pictures we draw betray our deepest convictions and display our current conceptual limitations. Artists have always painted the history of fossil life as a sequence from invertebrates, to fishes, to early terrestrial amphibians and reptiles, to dinosaurs, to mammals and, finally, to humans. There are no exceptions; all sequences painted since the inception of this genre in the 1850s follow the convention.

Yet we never stop to recognize the almost absurd biases coded into this universal mode. No scene ever shows another invertebrate after fishes evolved, but invertebrates did not go away or stop evolving! After terrestrial reptiles emerge, no subsequent scene ever shows a fish (later oceanic tableaux depict only such returning reptiles as ichthyosaurs and plesiosaurs). But fishes did not stop evolving after one small lineage managed to invade the land. In fact, the major event in the evolution of fishes, the origin and rise to dominance of the teleosts, or modern bony fishes, occurred during the time of the dinosaurs and is therefore never shown at all in any of these sequences—even though teleosts include more than half of all species of vertebrates. Why should humans appear at the end of all sequences? Our order of Primates is ancient among mammals, and many other successful lineages arose later than we did.

We will not smash Freud's pedestal and complete Darwin's revolution until we find, grasp and accept another way of drawing life's history. J.B.S. Haldane proclaimed nature "queerer than we can suppose," but these limits may only be socially imposed conceptual locks rather than inherent restrictions of our neurology. New icons might break the locks. Trees—or rather copiously and luxuriantly branching bushes—rather than ladders and sequences hold the key to this conceptual transition.

We must learn to depict the full range of variation, not just our parochial perception of the tiny right tail of most complex creatures. We must recognize that this tree may have contained a maximal number of branches near the beginning of multicellular life and that subsequent history is for the most part a process of elimination and lucky survivorship of a few, rather than continuous flowering, progress and expansion of a growing multitude. We must understand that little twigs are contingent nubbins, not predictable goals of the massive bush beneath. We must remember the greatest of all Biblical statements about wisdom: "She is a tree of life to them that lay hold upon her; and happy is every one that retaineth her."

Further Reading

The Burgess Shale. Henry B. Whittington. Yale University Press, 1985.

Extinction: A Scientific American Book. Steven M. Stanley. W. H. Freeman and Company, 1987.

Wonderful Life: The Burgess Shale and the Nature of History. S. J. Gould. W. W. Norton, 1989.

The Book of Life. Edited by Stephen Jay Gould. W. W. Norton, 1993.

9

Punctuated Equilibrium Comes of Age

STEPHEN JAY GOULD and NILES ELDREDGE

Punctuated equilibrium has finally obtained an unambiguous and incontrovertible majority—that is, our theory is now 21 years old. We also, with parental pride (and, therefore, potential bias), believe that primary controversy has ceded to general comprehension and that punctuated equilibrium has been accepted by most of our colleagues (a more conventional form of majority) as a valuable addition to evolutionary theory.

Kellogg[1] began the best book written to celebrate Darwinism's fiftieth birthday by noting how often (and how continually) various critics had proclaimed the *Sterbelager* (death bed) of natural selection. Punctuated equilibrium[2] has also prospered from announcements of its death or triviality[3-5] and has been featured in much recent discussion.[6-8]

As a neonate in 1972, punctuated equilibrium entered the world in unusual guise. We claimed no new discovery, but only a novel interpretation for the oldest and most robust of palaeontological observations: the geologically instantaneous origination and subsequent stability (often for millions of years) of palaeontological 'morphospecies'. This observation had long been ascribed, by Darwin and others, to the notorious imperfection of the fossil record, and was therefore read in a negative light—as missing information about evolution (defined in standard palaeontological textbooks of the time[9] as continuous anagenetic transformation of populations, or phyletic gradualism).

In a strictly logical sense, this negative explanation worked and preserved gradualism, then falsely equated with evolution itself, amidst an astonishing lack of evidence for this putative main signal of Darwinism. But think of the practical or heuristic dilemma for working palaeontologists: if evolution meant gradualism, and imperfection precluded the observation of such steady change, then scientists could not access the very phenomenon that both motivated their interest and built life's history. As young, committed and ambitious parents, we therefore proposed punctuated equilibrium, hoping to validate our profession's primary data as signal rather than void. We realized that a standard biological account, Mayr's[10] peripatric theory of speciation in small populations peripherally isolated from a parental stock, would yield stasis and punctuation when properly scaled into the vastness of geological time—for small populations speciating away from a central mass in tens or hundreds of thousands of years, will translate in almost every geological circumstance as a punctuation on a bedding plane, not gradual change up a hill of sediment, whereas stasis should characterize the long and recoverable history of successful central populations.

Punctuated equilibrium then grew during its childhood and adolescence, in ways both unruly and orderly. Unruly accidents of history included the misunderstandings of colleagues (who, for example, failed to grasp the key claim about geological scaling, misread geological abruptness as true suddenness, and then interpreted punctuated equilibrium as a saltational theory), and the purposeful misuses of creationist foes as this political issue heated up in the United States during the late 1970s (although we took pride in joining with so many colleagues for a successful fight against this philistine scourge, as one of us testified in the Arkansas 'monkey' trial in 1981[11] and the other wrote a book on creationist distortions[12]).

But orderly extensions, implicit in the undeveloped logic of our original argument, fuelled the useful growth of punctuated equilibrium to fruitful adulthood. (We now realize how poorly we initially grasped the implications of our original argument; we thank our colleagues, especially S. M. Stanley[13] and E.S. Vrba[14], for developing several extensions). We originally focused on tempo, but more important theoretical arguments flowed from implications concerning evolution's mode[15-17] —particularly the causes surrounding our two major claims for equilibrium, or stasis of established species, and the need to reformulate macroevolution, notably the key phenomenon of trends, as an accumulation of discrete speciation events treated as entities rather than undefinable segments of continua—a subject encompassed by debate about species selection[13] or species sorting.[18]

Punctuated equilibrium and macroevolution

Stasis and Its meaning. We opened our original paper with a section on what philosopher N.R. Hanson called "the cloven hoofprint of theory,"[19] or the structuring of all supposedly objective observation by expectations of prevailing general views. Stasis, as palpable and observable in virtually all cases (whereas rapid punctuations are usually, but not always, elusive), becomes the major empirical ground for studying punctuated equilibrium. Putting together the philosophical insight of ineluctable theoretical bias, with the empirical theme of the tractability of stasis, we devised a motto: "stasis is data." For no bias can be more constricting than invisibility—and stasis, inevitably read as absence of evolution, had always been treated as a non-subject. How odd, though, to define the most common of all palaeontological phenomena as beyond interest or notice! Yet palaeontologists who never wrote papers on the absence of change in lineages before punctuated equilibrium granted the subject some theoretical space. And, even worse, as palaeontologists didn't discuss stasis, most evolutionary biologists assumed continual change as a norm, and didn't even know that stability dominates the fossil record. Mayr has written: "Of all the claims made in the punctuationalist theory of Eldredge and Gould, the one that encountered the greatest opposition was that of 'pronounced stasis as the usual fate of most species', after having completed the phase of origination ... I agree with Gould that the frequency of stasis in fossil species revealed by the recent analysis was unexpected by most evolutionary biologists." [20]

As the most important change in research practice provoked by punctuated equilibrium, stasis has now exited from its closet of non-definition to become a subject of quantitative investigation in all major fossil groups—from microfossils[21,22] (27,000 measured specimens from 400 closely spaced samples spanning 8 million years in the latter study), to molluscs,[23-27] to mammals.[28-30] Although punctuated equilibrium deals directly only with stability of species through time, the higher-level analogue of non-trending in larger clades has also graduated from an undefined non-subject to a phenomenon worth documenting.[31] Moreover, because species often maintain stability through such intense climatic change as glacial cycling,[32] stasis must be viewed as an active phenomenon, not a passive response to unaltered environments. Many leading evolutionary theorists, while not accepting our preference for viewing stasis in the context of habitat tracking[17] or developmental constraint,[33,34] have been persuaded by punctuated equilibrium that maintenance of stability within species must be considered as a major evolutionary problem.

Macroevolution as a problem in species sorting. If punctuated equilibrium has provoked a shift in paradigms for macroevolutionary theory (see ref. 35 for a defence of this view), the main insight for revision holds that all substantial evolutionary change must be reconceived as higher-level sorting based on differential success of certain kinds of stable species, rather than as progressive transformation within lineages (see Eldredge[36] on taxic versus transformational views of evolution; Simpson,[37] however, in the canonical palaeontological statement of the generation before punctuated equilibrium, had attributed 90% of macroevolution to the transformational mode, and only 10% to speciation)....

Darwin's theory of natural selection locates the causality of evolutionary change at one domain on one level: natural selection operating by struggle among individual organisms for reproductive success. Given Darwin's crucial reliance upon Lyellian uniformity for extrapolating this mode of change to encompass all magnitudes through all times, the interposition of a level for sorting among stable species breaks this causal reduction and truly, in Stanley's felicitous term,[38] "decouples" macro- from microevolution. Decoupling is not a claim for the falseness or irrelevancy of microevolutionary mechanisms, especially natural selection, but a recognition that Darwinian extrapolation cannot fully explain large-scale change in the history of life.

The main point may be summarized as follows. Most macroevolution must be rendered by asking what kinds of species within a clade did better than others (speciated more frequently, survived longer), or what biases in direction of speciation prevailed among species within a clade. Such questions enjoin a very different programme of research from the traditional 'how did natural selection within a lineage build substantial adaptation during long stretches of time?' The new questions require a direct study of species and their differential success; older queries focused downward upon processes within populations and their extrapolation through time. Darwin's location of causality in organisms must be superseded by a hierarchical model of selection, with simultaneous and important action at genic, organismal and taxic levels.[39,40] Williams,[34] who so stoutly defended classical Darwinism against older, invalid, and very different forms of group selection,[41] now acknowledges the importance of such clade selection in macroevolution. Punctuated equilibrium has been used as a central concept in the development of hierarchy theory in evolutionary biology.

Implications. Any theory with a claim to novelty in broad perspective must enlighten old problems and suggest extensions. The speciational view of macroevolution, which does not strictly require punctuated equilibrium, but which was nurtured and has thrived in its context, requires a reformulation of nearly all macroevolutionary questions. For example, so-called living fossils, once treated as lineages rendered static by optimal adaptation, unusually stable environment, or lack of genetic variation, should be reconceptualized as members of groups with unusually low speciation rates, and therefore little opportunity to accumulate change.[42] (We have no evidence that the species of 'living fossil' groups are particularly old. For example, the western Atlantic horseshoe crab, *Litnulus polyphemus*—the 'type example' of the phenomenon

—has no fossil record at all, whereas the genus can only be traced to the Miocene.)

Going further, the entire tradition of expressing evolutionary change in darwin units (where 1 darwin equals character change by a factor of e in 1 million years)[43] makes no sense in a speciational context. (If a lineage goes from species A to D in 10 million years through three episodes of rapid change with intervening stasis, a cited rate of so many millidarwins becomes a meaningless average.) We learn as a received truth of evolution for example, that human brain size increased at an extraordinary (many say unprecedented) rate during later stages of our lineage. But this entrenched belief may be a chimaera born of an error in averaging rates over both punctuations and subsequent periods of stasis. Homo sapiens is a young species, perhaps no more than 200,000 years old. If most of our increment accrued quickly at our origin, but we then express this entirety from our origin to the present time as a darwin rate, we calculate a high value because our subsequent time of stasis has been so short. But if the same speciation event, with the same increment in the same time, had occurred two million years ago (with subsequent stasis), the darwin rate for the identical event would be much lower.

Cope's rule, the tendency for phyletic increase in body size had generally been attributed to selective value of large size within anagenetic lineages, but is probably better interpreted[44,45] as greater propensity for speciation in smaller species, for whom increasing size is the only 'open' pathway (see Martin[46] on the negative correlation of generic species richness and body size). Raup and Sepkoski[47] proposed a conventional explanation for decreasing rate of background extinction through geological time: generally better adaptation of later species. But Valentine[48] and Gilinsky (personal communication) offer an interesting speciational alternative: if extinction intensities were constant through time, groups with equally high speciation and extinction rates would fare just as well as groups with equally lower rates. But extinction intensities vary greatly, and the geological record features episodes of high dying, during which extinction-prone groups are more likely to disappear, leaving extinction-resistant groups as life's legacy. Valentine concludes that "these clade-characteristic rates are of course not adaptations *per se*, but effects flowing from clade properties that were established probably during the early radiations that founded the clades."

The most exciting direct extensions of punctuated equilibrium now involve the study of correlated punctuational events across taxa, and the ecological and environmental sources of such cohesion. Eminently testable are Vrba's[49] "turnover-pulse hypothesis" of evolution concentrated in punctuational bursts at times of worldwide climatic pulsing, one of which, about 2.5 million years ago, may have stimulated the origin of the genus *Homo*; and Brett's[50] hypothesis of "coordinated stasis" for the structuring of major palaeontological faunas. What might be the ecological source of such striking coherence across disparate taxa through such long times?[51]

The empirics of punctuated equilibrium

Like all major theories in the sciences of natural history, including natural selection itself, punctuated equilibrium is a claim about relative frequency, not exclusivity.[52] Phyletic gradualism has been well documented, again across all taxa from microfossils[53] to mammals.[54,55] Punctuated equilibrium surely exists in abundance, but validation of the general hypothesis requires a relative frequency sufficiently high to impart the predominant motif and signal to life's history. The issue remains unsettled, but we consider (in our biased way) that four classes of evidence establish a strong putative case for punctuated equilibrium in this general sense.

Individual cases. Examples of stasis alone (cited earlier) and simple abrupt replacement, although conforming to expectations of punctuated equilibrium, are not direct evidence for our mechanism: for stasis might just be a lull in anagenetic gradualism (though pervasive stasis for long periods in all species of a fauna (a common finding) would require special pleading from gradualists), and replacement might represent rapid transformation without branching, or migration of a distant (phyletic or geographic) relative rather than evolution in situ. A good test of punctuated equilibrium requires (in addition to the obvious need for documented rapidity in an interval known to be sufficiently short) both a phyletic hypothesis to assert sistergroup relationship of the taxa involved, and survival of putative ancestors to affirm an event of true branching rather than rapid phyletic transformation.

Given these stringent requirements, and in the light of such an imperfect fossil record, we are delighted that so many cases have been well documented, particularly in the crucial requirement of ancestral survival after punctuated branching.[32,56-61] Williamson's discovery[62] of multiple molluscan speciation events in isolated African lakes, with return of ancestral lineages upon reconnection with parental water bodies, has been most widely discussed[63] and disputed[64] (although all accept the punctuational pattern). Cheetham's elegant and meticulously documented[65,66] story of evolution in the bryozoan *Metrarabdotos* from Tertiary strata of the Caribbean is particularly gratifying ... in the number of purely punctuational events, the full coverage of the lineage, and the unusual completeness of documentation, especially as Cheetham began his study expecting to reconfirm a gradualistic interpretation (writing to

McKinney: "The chronocline I thought was represented ... is perhaps the most conspicuous casualty of the restudy, which shows that the supposed cline members largely overlap each other in time. Eldredge and Gould were certainly right about the danger of stringing a series of chronologically isolated populations together with a gradualist's expectations.")

On the subject of punctuational corrections for received gradualistic wisdom, Prothero and Shubin[67] have shown that the most 'firmly' gradualistic part of the horse lineage (the general, and false, exemplar of gradualism in its totality), the Oligocene transition from *Mesohippus* to *Miohippus*, conforms to punctuated equilibrium, with stasis in all species of both lines, transition by rapid branching rather than phyletic transformation, and stratigraphic overlap of both genera (one set of beds in Wyoming has yielded three species of *Mesohippus* and two of *Miohippus*, all contemporaries). Prothero and Shubin conclude: "This is contrary to the widely-held myth about horse species as gradualistically-varying parts of a continuum, with no real distinctions between species. Throughout the history of horses, the species are well-marked and static over millions of years. At high resolution, the gradualistic picture of horse evolution becomes a complex bush of overlapping, closely related species."

Relative frequencies. Elegant cases don't make punctuated equilibrium any more than a swallow makes a summer, but there are a growing number of reports documenting an overwhelming relative frequency (often an exclusivity) for punctuated equilibrium in entire groups or faunas. Consider the lifetime testimonies of taxonomic experts on microfossils,[69] on brachiopods[70,71] and on beetles.[72] Fortey[73] has concluded for trilobites and graptolites "that the gradualistic mode does occur especially in pelagic or planktic forms, but accounts for 10% or less of observations of phyletic change, and is relatively slow."

Other studies access all available lineages in entire faunas and assert the dominance of punctuated equilibrium. Stanley and Yang[26] found no gradualism at all in the classic Tertiary molluscan sequences of the Gulf and Atlantic Coasts. With the exception of *Gryphaea*, Hallam[23] detected no phyletic change in shape (but only for body size) in any Jurassic bivalve in Europe. Kelley[24,25] documented the prevalence of punctuation for molluscs in the famous Maryland Miocene sequence, and Vrba[74] has done the same for African bovids. Even compilations from the literature, so strongly biased by previous traditions for ignoring stasis as non-data and only documenting putative gradualism, grant a majority to punctuated equilibrium, as in Barnovsky's[75] compendium for Quaternary mammals, with punctuated equilibrium "supported twice as often as phyletic gradualism ... the majority of species considered exhibit most of their morphological change near a speciation event, and most species seem to be discrete entities." When controlled studies are done by one team in the field, punctuated equilibrium almost always seems to predominate.   Prothero[76] "examined all the mammals with a reasonably complete record from the Eocene-Oligocene beds of the Big Badlands of South Dakota and related areas in Wyoming and Nebraska.... With one exception (gradual dwarfing in the oreodont *Miniochoerus*), we found that all of the Badlands mammals were static through millions of years, or speciated abruptly (if they changed at all)."

Inductive patterns. Even more general inductive patterns should be explored as criteria. Stanley[38,77] has proposed a series of tests, all carried out to punctuated equilibrium's advantage.   Others suggest that certain environments and ecologies should be conducive to one preferred mode along the continuum of possibilities. Johnson[78,79] suggests that punctuated equilibrium should dominate in the benthic environments that yield most of our fossil record, while gradualism might prevail in pelagic realms. Sheldon[80] proposes the counter-intuitive but not unreasonable idea that punctuated equilibrium may prevail in unstable environments, gradualism in stable regimes.

Tests from living organisms. Distinct evolutionary modes yield disparate patterns as results; punctuated equilibrium might therefore be tested by studying the morphological and taxonomic distributions of organisms, including living faunas. (Several of Stanley's tests38 use modem organisms, and other criteria from fossils should be explored—especially the biometric discordance or orthogonality, favourable to punctuated equilibrium and actually found where investigated[25, 81] of within and between species trends.)

Cladistic patterns should provide a good proving ground.   Avise[82] performed an interesting and much quoted test, favourable to gradualism, by comparing genetic and morphological differences in two fish clades of apparently equal age and markedly different speciation frequencies.   But as Mayden[83] argued this test was wrong in its particular case, and non-optimal as a general procedure; a better method would compare cladistic sister groups, guaranteed by this status to be equal in age.   Mindel *et al.*[84,85] have now performed such a test on the reptilian genus *Sceloporus* and on allozymic data in general, and have validated punctuated equilibrium's key claim for positive correlation of evolutionary distance and speciation frequency.   Lemen and Freeman's[86] interesting proposal for additional cladistic tests cannot be sustained because they must assume that unbranched arms of their cladograms truly feature no speciation events along their routes, whereas numerous transient and extinct species must populate most of these pathways. Wagner[87] has developed a way of estimating rapidly branching speciation versus gradual speciation or transformation from cladograms, and his initial results favour predominant rapid-branching in Palaeozoic gastropods.

Difficulties and prospects

Many semantic and terminological muddles that once impeded resolution of this debate have been clarified. Opponents now accept that punctuated equilibrium was never meant as a saltational theory, and that stasis does not signify rock-hard immobility, but fluctuation of little or no accumulated consequence, and temporal spread within the range of geographic variability among contemporary populations—by Stanley's proper criterion, so strikingly validated in his classic study.[26] We trust that everyone now grasps the centrality of relative frequency as a key criterion (and will allow, we may hope, that enough evidence has now accumulated to make a case, if not fully prove the point).

Evolutionary biologists have also raised a number of theoretical issues from their domain of microevolution. Some, like the frequency of sibling speciation, seem to us either irrelevant or untroublesome as a bias against, rather than for, our view (as we then underestimate the amount of true speciation from palaeontologically defined morphospecies, and such an underestimate works against punctuated equilibrium). Others, like the potential lack of correspondence between biospecies and palaeontological morphospecies, might be worrisome, but available studies, done to assess the problem in the light of punctuated equilibrium, affirm the identity of palaeontological taxa with true biospecies (see Jackson and Cheetham[88] on bryozoan species, and Michaux[27] on palaeontological stasis in gastropod morphospecies that persist as good genetic biospecies).

But continuing unhappiness, justified this time, focuses upon claims that speciation causes significant morphological change, for no validation of such a position has emerged (while the frequency and efficacy of our original supporting notion, Mayr's "genetic revolution" in peripheral isolates, has been questioned). Moreover, reasonable arguments for potential change throughout the history of lineages have been advanced,[6,34] although the empirics of stasis throws the efficacy of such processes into doubt. The pattern of punctuated equilibrium exists (at predominant relative frequency, we would argue) and is robust. *Eppur non si muove*; but why then? For the association of morphological change with speciation remains as a major pattern in the fossil record.

We believe that the solution to this dilemma may be provided in a brilliant but neglected suggestion of Futuyma.[89] He holds that morphological change may accumulate anywhere along the geological trajectory of a species. But unless that change be "locked up" by acquisition of reproductive isolation (that is, speciation), it cannot persist or accumulate and must be washed out during the complexity of interdigitation through time among varying populations of a species. Thus, species are not special because their origin permits a unique moment for instigating change, but because they provide the only mechanism for protecting change. Futuyma writes: "In the absence of reproductive isolation, differentiation is broken down by recombination. Given reproductive isolation, however, a species can retain its distinctive complex of characters as its spatial distribution changes along with that of its habitat or niche.... Although speciation does not accelerate evolution within populations, it provides morphological changes with enough permanence to be registered in the fossil record. Thus, it is plausible to expect many evolutionary changes in the fossil record to be associated with speciation." By an extension of the same argument, sequences of speciation are then required for trends: "Each step has had a more than ephemeral existence only because reproductive isolation prevented the slippage consequent on interbreeding with other populations ... Speciation may facilitate anagenesis by retaining, stepwise, the advances made in any one direction." Futuyma's simple yet profound insight may help to heal the remaining rifts and integrate punctuated equilibrium into an evolutionary theory hierarchically enriched in its light.[17,18]

In summarizing the impact of recent theories upon human concepts of nature's order, we cannot yet know whether we have witnessed a mighty gain in insight about the natural world (against anthropocentric hopes and biases that always hold us down), or just another transient blip in the history of correspondence between misperceptions of nature and prevailing social realities of war and uncertainty. Nonetheless, contemporary science has massively substituted notions of indeterminacy, historical contingency, chaos and punctuation for previous convictions about gradual, progressive, predictable determinism. These transitions have occurred in field after field; Kuhn's[90] celebrated notion of scientific revolutions is, for example, a punctuational theory for the history of scientific ideas. Punctuated equilibrium, in this light, is only palaeontology's contribution to a *Zeitgeist*, and *Zeitgeists*, as (literally) transient ghosts of time, should never be trusted. Thus, in developing punctuated equilibrium, we have either been toadies and panderers to fashion, and therefore destined for history's ashheap, or we had a spark of insight about nature's constitution. Only the punctuational and unpredictable future can tell.

Notes

1. Kellogg, V. L. *Darwinism Today* (Bell. London, 1907).

2. Eldredge, N. & Gould, S. J. in *Models in Paleobiology*, Schopf, T.J.M. 82-115 (Freeman, Cooper, San Francisco, 1972).

3. Dawkins, R. *The Blind Watchmaker* (Norton, New York, 1986).

4. Levinton, J. *Genetics, Paleontology and Macroevolution* (Cambridge Univ. Press, New York, 1988).

5. Hoffman, A. *Arguments on Evolution* (Oxford Univ. Press, New York, 1989).

6. Ridley, M. *Evolution* (Blackwell Scientific, Boston, 1993).

7. Erwin, D. *Speciation in the Fossil Record* 138-140 (Geol. Soc. Am. Ann. Meeting, Abstr.. Boulder, Colorado, 1992).

8. Mayr, E., Boulding, K. E. & Masters, R. D. in *The Dynamics of Evolution: The Punctuated Equilibrium Debate in the Natural and Social Sciences* (eds Somit, A. & Peterson, S. A.) (Cornell Univ. Press. Ithaca, NY, 1992).

9. Moore, R. C., Lalicker. C. G. & Fischer, A. G. *Invertebrate Fossils* (McGraw-Hill, New York, 1952).

10. Mayr, E. *Animal Species and Evolution* (Harvard Univ. Press, Cambridge, MA, 1963).

11. Gould, S. J. *Hen's Teeth and Horse's Toes* (Norton, New York. 1983).

12. Eldredge, N. *The Monkey Business. A Scientist Looks at Creationism* (Pocket Books, New York. 1982).

13. Stanley, S. M. *Proc. Natn. Acad. Sci.* U.SA. 72, 646-650 (1975).

14. Vrba, E. S. S. *Afr. J. Sci.* 76, 61-84 (1980).

15. Gould. S. J. & Eldredge, N. *Paleobiology* 3, 115-151 (1977).

16. Gould. S. J. in *Perspectives on Evolution* (ad. Milkman, R.) 83,-104 (Sinauer, Sunderland, MA. 1982).

17. Eldredge, N. *Macroevolutionary Dynamics* (McGraw-Hill, New York, 1989).

18. Vrba, E. & Gould, S. J. *Paleobiology* 12, 217-228 (1986).

19. Hanson, N. R. *Perception and Discovery* (Freeman, Cooper. San Francisco, 1969).

20. Mayr. E. in *The Dynamics of Evolution* (eds Somit, A. & Peterson, S. A.) 21-53 (Cornell Univ. Press, Ithaca, NY, 1992).

21. Sorhannus, U. *Hist. Biol.* 31, 241-247 (1990).

22. Thomas, E. *Lltrecht Micropat. Bull.* 23, 1-167 (1980).

23. Hallam, A. *Paleobiology* 4, 16-25 (1978).

24. Kelley, P. H. *J. Paleontol.* 57, 581-598 (1983).

25. Kelley, P. H. *J. Paleontol.* 52, 1235-1250 (1984).

26. Stanley, S. M. & Yang, X. *Paleobiology* 13, 113-139 (1987).

27. Michaux, B. *Biol. J. Linn.* Soc. 33, 239-255 (1989).

28. West, R. M. *Paleobiology* 5, 252-260 (1979).

29. Schankler, D. M. *Nature* 293, 135-138 (1981).

30. Lich, D. K. *Paleobiology* 16, 384-395 (1990).

31. Budd, A. F. & Coates. A. G. *Paleobiology* 18, 425-446 (1992).

32. Cronin, T. M. *Science* 227, 60-63 (1985).

33. Maynard Smith, J. *A. Rev. Genet.* 17, 11-25 (1984).

34. Williams. G. C. *Natural Selection: Domains, Levels and Challenges* (Oxford Univ. Press, New York, 1992).

35. Ruse, M. in *The Dynamics of Evolution* (eds Somit, A. & Peterson, S. A.) 139-168 (Cornell Univ. Press. Ithaca, NY, 1992).

36. Eldredge, N. *Bull. Carnegie Mus. Nat. Hist.* 13, 7-19 (1979).

37. Simpson, G. G. *The Major Features of Evolution* (Columbia Univ. Press, New York, 1953).

38. Stanley, S. M. *Marcroevolution* (Freeman, San Francisco, 1979).

39. Lloyd. E. A. *The Structure and Confirmation of Evolutionary Theory* (Greenwood, New York, 1988).

40. Brandon, R. N. *Adaptation and Environment* (Princeton Univ. Press, Princeton, NJ, 1990).

41. Williams. G. C. *Adaptation and Natural Selection* (Princeton Univ. Press, Princeton. NJ, 1966).

42. Eldredge, N. & Stanley, S. M. *Living Fossils* (Springer, New York, 1984).

43. Haldane, J. B. S.,*Evolution* 3, 51-56 (1949).

44. Stanley, S. M. *Evolution* 27, 1-26 (1973).

45. Gould, S. J. *J. Paleont.* 62, 319-329 (1988).

46. Martin, R. A. *Hist. Biol.* 6, 73-90 (1992).

47. Raup, D. M. & Sepkoski, J. J. Jr. *Science* 215, 1501-1503 (1982).

48. Valentine, J. W. in *Molds, Molecules and Metazoa* (eds Grant, P. R. & Horn, H. S.) 17-32 (Princeton Univ. Press, Princeton, NJ. 1992).

49. Vrba, E. S. *Suid-Afrikaanse Tydskvif Wetens* 81, 229-236 (1985).

50. Brett, C. E. *Coordinated Stasis and Evolutionary Ecology of Silurian-Devonian Marine Biotas in the Appalachian Basin* 139 (Geol. Soc. Am. Ann. Meeting, Abstr., Boulder, Colorado, 1992).

51. Morris, P. J., Ivany, L & Schopf, K. M. *Paleoecological Stasis in Evolutionary Theory* 313 (Geol. Soc. Am. Ann. Meeting, Boulder, Colorado, 1992).

52. Gould, S. *J. Am. Sci.* 74, 60-69 (1986).

53. MacLeod, N. *Paleobiology* 17, 167-188 (199).

54. Gingerich, P. D. *Am. J. Sci.* 276, 1-28 (1976).

55. Chaline. J. & Laurin, B. *Paleobiology* 12, 203-216 (1986).

56. Bergstrom, J. & Levi-Setti. R. *Geol. Palaeontol.* 12, 1-40 (1978).

57. Smith, A. B. & Paul, C. R. C. *Sp. Pap. Palaeont.* 33, 29-37 (1985).

58. Flynn, L. J. *Contr. Geol. Univ. Wyoming* 3, 273-285 (1986).

59. Finney, S. C. *Geol. Sac. Sp. Pub.* 20, 103-113 (1986).

60. Wei, K. Y. & Kennett, J. P. *Paleobiology* 14, 345-363 (1988).

61. Nehm, R. H. & Geary, D. H. *Paleontol. Soc. Sp. Pub.* 6, 222 (1992).

62. Williamson, P. G. *Nature* 293, 437-443 (1981).

63. Williamson, P. G. *Biol. J. Linn. Soc.* 26, 307-324 (1985).

64. Fryer, G., Greenwood, P. H. & Peake, J. F. *Biol. J. Linn. Soc.* 20, 195-205 (1983).

65. Cheatham, A. H. *Pateobiology* 12, 190-202 (1986).

66. Cheetham, A. H. *Paleobiology* 13, 286-296 (1987).

67. Prothero, D. R. & Shubin, N. in *The Evolution of Perissodactyls* (eds Prothero, D. R. & Schoch, R. M.) 142-175 (Oxford Univ. Press. Oxford. 1989).

68. Simpson, G. G. *Horses* (Oxford Univ. Press, Oxford, 1951).

69. MacG!Ilavry, H. J. *Bildragen tot de Dierkunde* 38, 69-74 (1968).

70. Agar, D. V. *Proc. Geologists' Ass.* 87, 131-160 (1976).

71. Agar, D. V. *Palaeontology* 26, 555-565 (1983).

72. Coope, G. R. A. *Rev. Ecol. Syst.* 10, 247-267 (1979).

73. Fortey, R. A. *Sp. Pap. Palaeontol.* 33, 17-28 (1985).

74. Vrba, E. S. in *Living Fossils* (eds Eldredge, N. & Stanley, S. M.) 62-79 (Springer. New York. 1984).

75. Barnovsky, A. D. *Curr. Mammal.* 1, 109-147 (1987).

76. Prothero, D. R. *Skeptic* 1, 38-47 (1992).

77. Stanley, S. M. *Paleobiology* 4, 26-40 (1978).

78. Johnson, J. G. *Pateontol.* 49, 646-661 (1975).

79. Johnson, J. G. *Pateontol.* 56, 1329-1331 (1982).

80. Sheldon, P. R. *Nature* 345, 772 (1990).

81. Shapiro, E. A. *Natural Selection in a Miocene Pectinid: A Test of the Punctuated Equilibria Model* 490 (Geol. Soc. Am. Ann. Meeting, Abstr., Boulder. Colorado, 1978).

82. Avise, J. C. *Proc. Natn. Acad. Sci.* U.SA. 74, 5083-5087 (1977).

83. Mayden, R. L *Syst. Zool.* 35, 591-602 (1986).

84. Mindell, D. P., Sites. J. R. Jr & Graur. D. *Cladistics* 5, 49-61 (1989).

85. Mindell, D. P., Sites, J. W. Jr. & Graur, O. *J. Evol. Biol.* 3, 125-131 (1990).

86. Lemen, C. A. & Freeman, P. W. *Evolution* 43, 1538-1554 (1989).

87. Wagner, P. J. *Cladograms as Tests of Speciation Patterns* 139 (Geol. Soc. Am. Ann. Meeting, Abstr., Boulder, Colorado, 1992).

88. Jackson, S. B. C. & Cheatham, A. H. *Science* 248, 579-583 (1990).

89. Futuyma, D. J. *Am. Nat.* 130, 465-473 (1987).

90. Kuhn, T. S. *The Structure of Scientific Revolutions* (Univ. Chicago Press, Chicago, 1962).

10

The Evolution of Darwinism
G. LEDYARD STEBBINS AND FRANCISCO J. AYALA

When biologists refer to the theories of evolution nowadays, they are usually thinking not of Charles Darwin's original statement of the theory but of a modified and expanded version of Darwinism that took shape in the 1930s and 1940s. First known as the Neo-Darwinian theory and later as the synthetic theory, it affirmed the fundamental tenets of Darwinism. It held that evolution proceeds through the natural selection of heritable differences arising at random in each generation. Differences that render their carriers better adapted to the environment are multiplied and those that are harmful are eliminated. Like Darwinism, the synthetic theory stressed that evolution through natural selection is opportunistic, in that variations arise by chance and are selected in accordance with the demands of the environment, and that it takes place steadily.

To this Darwinian foundation the architects of the synthetic theory, who included the geneticist Theodosius Dobzhansky, the biogeographer and systematist Ernst Mayr, the paleontologist George Gaylord Simpson, the biologist Julian Huxley and one of us (Stebbins), added new elements. The science of genetics made it possible to identify the determinants of the traits on which natural selection acts as genes: heritable units of information governing structure, development and function. Variant traits were held to result from mutations, or lasting alterations that arise at random in individual genes. From population biology came a second new feature of the synthetic theory: an emphasis on the importance of population structure and distribution in the development of new species. The synthetic theory also incorporated the biological concept of species, which leans more heavily on reproductive isolation (an inability to interbreed) than on visible differences in Distinguishing species. Although some biologists initially resisted the synthetic theory for four decades most evolutionists have considered it the best explanation of evolutionary processes, and it has taken a central place in biology.

In the 1970s and 1980s new developments confronted the synthetic theory. An explosion of investigation into the structure of DNA, the carrier of genetic information, has enabled biologists to study the mechanisms of evolution at the molecular level. The new work has thereby amplified the synthetic theory much as the discovery of genes amplified Darwinism.

The molecular studies have also led to two direct challenges to the synthetic theory. One is a proposal that a kind of molecular determinism, rather than pure chance, impels the development of variations in DNA. The other is a contrasting claim, known as the neutral theory, that chance governs not only the initial appearance of genetic variations but also their subsequent establishment in a population. A different kind of challenge, based on new interpretations of the fossil record, has emerged from paleontology. Known as punctuated equilibrium, it holds that evolution proceeds not at a steady pace but irregularly, in fits and starts.

At the outset it must be said that unlike attacks by creationists and other nonscientists—none of these challenges denies that evolutionary chance occurs, that current species have descended from common ancestors or that Darwinian natural selection plays an important part in the process. The disputes are conflicts of degree and emphasis within a shared evolutionary outlook. We believe, moreover, that with modifications both to the traditional views and to the competing theories most of the challenges can be accommodated within the encompassing vision of the synthetic theory.

Molecular Evolution

The most dramatic changes in thinking about evolution stem from new knowledge about genetic processes at a molecular level, and yet many of the implications of that knowledge for evolutionary theory remain obscure. The molecular pathways that lead from genes to visible characteristics are long, complex and as yet largely unexplored. Until the relation of genes to development is better understood at a molecular level the full impact of molecular biology on evolutionary theory cannot be assessed.

Certain consequences of the recent findings are already evident, however. They have shown genetic variation to be far more complex than was thought, involving changes in the number and configuration of genes as well as, mutations in individual genes. Mutations and structural channels are now known to affect not only genes but also sequences of DNA that cannot be called genes because they do not code for proteins. Even as the new molecular biology has complicated the traditional picture of genetic variation, it can also be said to have buttressed the synthetic theory by supplying mechanisms underlying many processes the theory invokes. The meaning of evolution at a Molecular level is beginning to come clear. It is now possible, for example, to give incipient answers to the question: How do new genes arise?

The importance of the development of new genes (and not simply the modification of old ones) in the process of evolution is reflected in the relation between the amount of genetic material and the complexity of organisms. The genome, or total genetic complement, of a virus amounts to between 1,300 and 20,000 nucleotide pairs (np). (Nucleotides are the subunits of DNA which are strung together in pairs to form the two strands of the double helix.) The genome of bacteria includes, on the average, about four million np. Among eukaryotes (organisms with distinct cell nuclei) fungi have between and 20 million np per cell, most animals and plants have several billion np per cell.

The relation between the amount of DNA and the complexity of the organism or its developmental pattern is not precise. A few groups of higher plants, salamanders and some primitive fishes have 1010 np per cell, much more than most mammals. The largest amounts of DNA, some 1012 np per cell, are found in eukaryotes that are relatively simple in structure and development, such as certain species of amoeba and the *Psilopsida*, primitive relatives of the ferns. Such species can have thousands of copies of some genes as well as long stretches of DNA that do not code for proteins and are not considered to be genes at all.

Indeed, segments of DNA with no known function have been found in surprising numbers. In the human genome a sequence called *Alu* that is about 300 np long is present in some 300,000 copies, corresponding to 3 percent of the total human DNA; another short segment of about 100 np recurs nearly a million times in the mouse genome. The discovery of these seemingly meaningless repetitions led to the speculation that some molecular evolution is deterministic, proceeding in a particular direction that is independent of chance and natural selection. Such sequences are held to have multiplied not through a series of random events but because a kind of "molecular drive" impelled each sequence to reproduce itself within the genome. Mathematical models have indicated, however, that traditional concepts of evolution suffice to explain the proliferation of such segments.

In spite of the exceptions we have noted and in spite of the fraction of total DNA made up of meaningless sequences, the amount of genetic information carried in each cell does in general increase steadily from bacteria to molds to higher plants and animals. A typical gene consists of a thousand or more nucleotides arrayed in an order as crucial as the sequence of letters in a sentence. A random sequence of a thousand letters is not likely to make sense;

they must be organized in order to convey information. How have meaningful sequences of DNA accumulated in the course of evolution?

One way in which an organism's complement of genes can increase abruptly is through polyploidy: a doubling of the number of chromosomes from one generation to the next, producing offspring that usually are reproductively isolated from the parent generation and in effect constitute a new species [see "Cataclysmic Evolution," by G. Ledyard Stebbins, Jr.; *Scientific American*, April, 1951]. Some organisms with very large amounts of DNA, such as *Psilopsida*, are polyploid. Indeed, about 47 percent of all flowering plants are polyploid, including cultivated plants such as the potato, the strawberry and wheat. Nevertheless, many complex plants and animals are not polyploid, and polyploidy does not explain the origin of genes. It is simply a mechanism by means of which existing genes are multiplied.

New Genes

A process that does create entirely new genes is the tandem multiplication, over evolutionary history, of a short sequence of nucleotides. A tandem multiplication is the repetition of a sequence in adjacent sites along a chromosome. The multiplication can occur as matching chromosomes pair during the process of meiosis, the cell divisions that give rise to gametes, or sex cells. As the chromosomes line up they sometimes exchange segments; if the chromosomes have paired out of alignment, the exchange can yield one chromosome in which a particular sequence is repeated. Because it is carried by a sex cell, the repetition will be preserved in the genome of the next generation.

In some cases, such as the $\alpha2(I)$ collagen gene in the chicken, the origin of a gene through tandem multiplication is evident in its structure. Collagen is the main structural protein of bone, cartilage, connective tissue and skin in vertebrates. In chickens the $\alpha2(I)$ gene consists of more than 50 exons, which are discrete sequences of DNA that code for proteins and are separated by noncoding intervening sequences, or introns; the gene has a total length of about 38,000 np. The exons consist of a repeated sequence nine nucleotides long. The repetitions differ somewhat in their component nucleotides, but their common origin can be recognized because the triplet of amino acids for which each sequence codes invariably begins with the amino acid glycine; proline often occupies either or both of the two subsequent positions in the triplet.

From the gene's structure its evolutionary history can be reconstructed. A series of tandem repetitions of the ancestral 9-np sequence yielded an exon 54 np long. Next the basic exon was multiplied about 50 times. The repetitions have yielded some exons with nucleotide numbers other than 54, but they are always a multiple of nine. Because of the recurrence of the 9-np sequence within each exon, misaligned paring of chromosomes during meiosis sometimes left corresponding exons overlapping by some multiple of nine. Changed nucleotide numbers resulted when the chromosomes exchanged segments.

Susumu Ohno of the City of Hope Medical Center and his collaborators have traced a similar origin for some of the genes coding for immunoglobulins, or antibody molecules, in mice. Immunoglobulins are proteins consisting of two large ("heavy") and two smaller ("light") polypeptide chains. In each heavy and light chain a region whose nucleotide sequence is nearly invariant is joined to an extremely variable region; possible combinations of the variable regions yield the enormous diversity of antibodies that serve to protect mammals from foreign substances.

Ohno and his colleagues have found that the genes, each about 600 np long, coding for the variable region of the immunoglobin heavy chain evolved from an ancestral gene that in turn was the result of 12 tandem repetitions of a primordial sequence of 48 np. Further analysis showed that the 48-np building block represents an association of three segments, 14, 21 and 15 np long. Although they have been modified by point mutations over the course of evolutionary history, the three segments retain enough similarities to suggest that they represent a tandem triplication of an even smaller building block.

The gene encoding the constant region of an immunoglobulin heavy chain in mice evinces a different evolutionary history, one that may also be common. The heavy chain's constant region includes three protein domains with distinct functions. One domain interacts with cell surfaces, another activates complement (a group of proteins that destroy foreign cells) and a third forms the attachment point for the light chain. In addition the heavy chain has a fourth segment, a hinge region that separates two portions of the molecule. Each of the four exons in the gene codes for one of the four components of the chain, suggesting each represents a small primordial gene that once coded for a separate polypeptide with a function ancestral to that of the modern protein component.

Gene Duplication

In such cases diverse genes have united to form a single gene. In other instances a single complex gene has given rise to a number of separate genes through duplication. Like the tandem multiplication of a short DNA sequence, the process probably occurs as matching chromosomes exchange segments in the course of meiosis. The original gene and the duplicate may retain the same function; alternatively, one of the genes may preserve the original function while the other evolves a different, albeit related, function. Even before recombinant-DNA techniques were introduced the origin of related genes through the duplication in toto of an ancestral gene was well known; the amino acid sequences of groups of related proteins gave incontrovertible evidence of the common ancestry of the genes coding for them. The globin genes, which code for the four polypeptides that make up human hemoglobin molecules, are an example of a group of genes for which such an origin is apparent.

The globin genes have maintained varying degrees of similarity since the duplication events that gave rise to them. In another evolutionary pattern, a duplicated gene may diverge freely from the original gene because it is superfluous and therefore not subject to the constraints of natural selection. Examples came to light when the length of DNA containing the globin genes was sequenced. Known as pseudogenes, they are sequences homologous to functional genes, from which they arose through duplication, but they contain mutations that prevent them from making a functional polypeptide. The mutations were able to accumulate unhindered by selective pressures because the organism retained a duplicate gene capable of performing the original function. Pseudogenes are now thought to be common in vertebrates and perhaps in other organisms as well.

When new genes arise through duplication, the original and the duplicate gene are usually transmitted together to the descendants of the organism in which the duplication occurred. An apparent twist in the process has been discovered, however, another of the seemingly limitless ways in which evolution proceeds at the genetic level. Occasionally the original gene is found in one species and the duplicate in a totally unrelated organism. The phenomenon is called horizontal DNA transfer, because the DNA is passed from one species to another coexisting species rather than vertically, from parents to their descendants within a single species.

The genetic material of certain sea urchins gives evidence of the process. Among different species of sea urchins the genes encoding proteins of the family known as histones differ in their precise nucleotide sequence by an amount roughly proportional to the time since the species separated in the course of evolution. In the species *Psammechinus miliaris*, however, the genes coding for two histones, *H3* and *H4*, seem to have diverged much more slowly from corresponding genes in related species than the other histone genes have.

A possible explanation is that unknown selective constraints reduce the rate of evolution of the *H3* and *H4* genes in *Psammechinus* to a fraction of their rate in other species. An alternative hypothesis is that a cluster of genes coding for *H3* and *H4* was transferred to *Psammechinus* from another species, *Strongylocentrotus drobachensis*, less than a million years ago; the original and the duplicate gene cluster have evolved since then at the usual rate. Because the last common ancestor of the two urchin species lived some 65 million years ago, the historic genes not affected by gene transfer have diverged much further.

The actual mechanisms of horizontal gene transfer are not known. Perhaps the agents are the small circular bits of DNA known as plasmids, which can carry genetic material from one cell to another. Whatever its mechanism, horizontal gene transfer cannot be common. The genes of an organism are coadapted: new or altered genes are favored by natural selection not only because of the function they perform in isolation but also because they complement other genes. Genes are like the players in an orchestra: however virtuosic they may be as soloists, they must also play the same piece or the effect will be cacophony. The coadaptation of the genome reduces the incorporation of functional foreign genes, if it occurs at all, to the realm of rare evolutionary events.

Variation

Molecular biology has yielded insights into not only genetic change over time but also the precondition for such evolution: genetic variation. Evolutionists have shown that among populations in identical or similar environments, the rate of evolution is proportional to the amount of genetic variation within each population [see "The Mechanisms of Evolution," by Francisco J. Ayala; *Scientific American*, September, 1978]. The techniques of molecular biology allow the genetic variation within a population to be gauged much more readily than was possible when the synthetic theory was formulated.

Significant measures of the genetic variation within populations became available in the late 1960s. Gel electrophoresis (in which proteins are embedded in a gel and their mobility in an electric field is compared) and other simple techniques made it possible to determine how many forms of a protein exist in a given species, and in what frequencies. The variation can be expressed as the degree of heterozygosity: the proportion of gene loci in an average individual where the two members of a pair of genes, one gene from each parent, encode different proteins. In the several hundred species studied by electrophoresis and other methods the proportion of heterozygous loci detected ranges from 5 to 20 percent.

The amount of variation implied by such studies turns out to be much larger than expected. One reason is that as the various alleles (the distinct forms of a variable gene) are assorted into gametes in the course of meiosis, an individual heterozygous at a loci can give rise to 2^n different kinds of gametes. If an organism with 10,000 gene pairs is heterozygous for 10 percent of them, it could produce $2^{1,000}$ different gametes, a number much larger than the number of atoms in the universe.

Moreover, the amount of genetic variation in a population is usually larger than the results of electrophoresis suggest. Because the technique relies on the differential mobility of proteins in an electric field, differences in the amino acid sequence of a protein that do not change its net electric charge may not be detected. Furthermore, not all nucleotide differences in the DNA sequence result in different protein sequences. The reasons are that different triplets of nucleotides can code for the same amino acid and that some nucleotide sequences do not code for amino acids at all.

One way to detect some of the genetic variation thus hidden from ordinary electrophoresis is to digest each polypeptide chain of a protein into its component peptides (sequences of a few amino acids) and then compare the individual peptides by means of electrophoresis or chromatography. Differences in electric charge and other properties that were concealed when the peptides were incorporated in the longer polypeptide chain are thereby revealed. One of us (Ayala) applied the technique to two enzymes, alcohol dehydrogenase and superoxide dismutase, from the fruit fly *Drosophila*. In both cases about one in 10 polypeptides that had appeared to be identical when they were tested by electrophoresis turned out to be different in amino acid sequence when they were digested into peptides.

The most direct way to determine genetic variability is to obtain the nucleotide sequence of the same gene in different individuals of a species. This has been done for only a few genes. In 1980 two human genes coding for the same hemoglobin protein were sequenced in the laboratory of Oliver Smithies at the University of Wisconsin at Madison. Although the genes encoded the same product, they differed in their nucleotide sequences by 8 percent if only actual substitutions of one nucleotide for another were counted and by 2.4 percent if nucleotides present in one gene but not in the other were also included. Other genes that have been sequenced, from human beings, mice and fruit flies, have shown comparable degrees of variation. Such results suggest that at the level of the DNA sequence, organisms may be heterozygous at almost all gene loci.

The Neutral Theory

The extensive variation such studies have revealed is one of the bases of the neutral theory, the second of the challenges to the synthetic theory that have emerged from molecular biology. Its chief exponent is Motoo Kimura of the National Institute of Genetics in Japan [see "The Neutral Theory of Molecular Evolution," by Motoo Kimura; *Scientific American*, November, 1979].

Neutralists contend that if most genetic differences are under the control of natural selection (as the synthetic theory implies), the observed degree of variation should be low because adaptively beneficial differences should spread through the population and harmful ones should be eliminated. The finding of considerable variation suggests to neutralists that most of the genetic differences neither foster nor hinder an organism's survival and that their persistence or elimination within a population is a matter of chance.

Yet the magnitude of the variation also makes it possible to reconcile the assertion that most differences among alleles are adaptively neutral with the synthetic view, which affirms the importance of Darwinian natural selection. There is so much variation within each generation that even if the majority is neutral, the differences that do have an adaptive effect would supply abundant raw material for the creative force of natural selection.

The question, then, is not which is correct, neutrality, or Darwinian natural selection. It is instead how much of the genetic variation persists through chance and how much persists because it confers an adaptive advantage. For example, a mutation of the third nucleotide in a codon (the triplet of nucleotides coding for a particular amino acid) often produces a new codon that is synonymous in translation: both the original and the altered triplet code for the same amino acid. Such "silent" mutations, which do not affect the protein encoded by the gene, might indeed be adaptively neutral, and their frequencies in populations may be due largely to chance. On the other hand, the frequency of the mutation causing the single amino acid difference between the hemoglobin of sickle-cell anemia and normal hemoglobin is clearly under the control of natural selection. When an individual has two copies of the sickle-cell allele, the mutation is fatal, but heterozygosity (possession of one mutant and one normal allele) allows the carrier to be reasonably healthy and confers an adaptive advantage: resistance to malaria.

The Molecular Clock

The neutral theory is based not only on the amount of variation prevailing within a given generation but also on discoveries about the rate of genetic chance across generations. Studies relating evolutionary history to the number of molecular differences in DNA sequences or proteins common to several species suggest that a given gene or protein can be regarded as a molecular clock. Its rate of evolution is fairly constant over long periods and it evolves at much the same rate in different species.

This apparent constancy, the neutralists argue, is incompatible with the notion that molecular change reflects the activity of natural selection. They maintain that the synthetic theory implies variable rates of molecular evolution because selective pressures should vary in intensity over time and from species to species. The chance incorporation of variations into the gene pool of a species is a better way to account for the molecular clock, say the neutralists, because the process would take place at a more or less constant rate.

The synthetic theory does not, however, require the rate of molecular evolution to be as irregular as the critics assume. As long as the function of a gene or a protein is the same in different evolutionary lineages it is not surprising that over millions of years it would appear to evolve at the same rate, since the functional constraints to which it is subject will be much the same. Histone proteins evolve very slowly because they act as a structural support for DNA, and extensive amino acid changes would impair their function; fibrinopeptides, substances involved in blood clotting, evolve much faster because they are not subject to such tight constraints and because the clotting process is often modified in response to environmental changes. The constraints on the evolution of most molecules are intermediate between these two extremes.

The constancy over time of rates of molecular evolution can also be reconciled with the synthetic theory. The number of nucleotide or amino acid substitutions may indeed be greater during a given interval as a result of natural selection, when an evolutionary lineage is becoming adapted to a new environment that requires simultaneous changes in many functions. Chance itself can result in abrupt increases in the rate of genetic change. When a species passes through a population bottleneck in which the number of individuals is drastically reduced, virtually neutral variations present in the genes of the survivors may become dominant in the genetic makeup of the population as a whole.

If the fundamental function of a gene or a protein does not change in the course of evolution however, there is no reason to expect that fluctuations in the rate at which it evolves will be frequent or extended. The enormous lengths of time over which rates of molecular evolution are calculated cause the fluctuations that do occur to average out, yielding the apparent constancy of evolutionary rates. John Gillespie of the University of California at Davis has constructed mathematical models showing the existence of a molecular clock is compatible with the assumption that molecular evolution is driven by natural selection.

Punctuated Equilibrium

A different kind of question about evolutionary rate is central to the conflict between the synthetic theory and the theory of punctuated equilibrium, advanced by Niles Eldredge of the American Museum of Natural History and Stephen Jay Gould of Harvard University. In this case the argument centers on morphological evolution, in which visible characteristics are changed rather than on evolution at the molecular level, and in this dispute the positions are reversed. Whereas the neutralists contend that the rate of molecular evolution is too regular for the synthetic theory to hold, the punctualists argue from fossil evidence that the rate of morphological evolution is less regular than the synthetic theory requires.

Eldredge and Gould reject the explanation Simpson and others had offered for the rarity or absence in the fossil record of specimens that are intermediate in morphology between successive fossil forms: that the record is incomplete. Instead they take the record at face value and maintain that the abrupt appearance of new fossil species reflects their development in bursts of evolution after which the species may have changed little over millions of years. In their view the notion of gradualism must be replaced by a picture in which spurts of change alternate with long periods of stasis.

The dispute with the punctualists loses some of its focus when one recognizes that it is partly an artifact of a radical difference in time scales: the time scale of the paleontologists who propose the theory of punctuated equilibrium and that of the geneticists who were instrumental in formulating the synthetic theory. Since successive layers in geologic strata may have been laid down tens of thousands of years apart, morphological changes that developed over thousands of generations may make an abrupt appearance in the fossil record. In contrast, geneticists refer to changes that require 200 generations or more as gradual, since they exceed the time span of all experiments except those on microorganisms. In speaking on the one hand of sudden change and on the other of gradual evolution, the punctualists and the gradualists are in many cases talking about the same thing.

The apparent episodes of abrupt change in the fossil record, then, do not necessarily weigh against the synthetic theory and its emphasis on gradual processes. Can the same be said for the long periods of stasis the punctualists point to, in which the visible characteristics of a species change either little or not at all? Taking a closer look at the fossil record, many paleontologists outside the punctualist camp agree that the stability of visible characteristics over millions of years is much greater than the architects of the mid-century synthetic theory thought at the time. Some of the apparent constancy in the record, however, may reflect a phenomenon known as mosaic evolution, first described by the British evolutionist Sir Gavin de Beer.

The term refers to the fact that different parts of an organism do not change at a uniform rate in the course of evolution. Just as genes and proteins do not evolve in lockstep, so the visible characteristics they govern do not evolve at the same rate either. A fossil that lies halfway along a temporal sequence from one organism to the next is not intermediate between the two with respect to every trait. Instead the creature can be compared to a mosaic, resembling the ancestral organism in some characteristics but the descendant in others. *Archeopteryx*, the fossil species intermediate between the reptiles and the birds, has a skeleton considered to be full reptilian, but its feathers are birdlike, even to the differentiation between fluffy feathers on the body and longer, stiffer wing feathers. The australopithecines (creatures of two to four million years ago that, are ancestral or very nearly ancestral to human beings) resemble humans in that their hipbones are shaped for walking erect, but their cranial capacity is more simian than human.

Some of the stasis apparent in the fossil record may be a product of this evolutionary pattern. When the evolution of a single salient trait is followed in the fossil record, long periods of little change may be evident. While one trait is becalmed by evolution, however, other characteristics that may not be recorded in the fossils can continue to evolve. The punctualist argument may be more convincing with respect to single traits than it is with respect, to entire organisms.

Morphology and Speciation

A long with a distinctive claim about the rate of evolution the theory of punctuated equilibrium also makes a specific argument about the mode of evolution. Eldredge and Gould believe anagenesis (changes in morphology along a lineage) and cladogenesis (the splitting of a single species into two species). They maintain that there is a brief burst of morphological change precisely when a small population diverges from an original species and forms a new species; little change then ensues until the species either goes extinct or gives rise to new ones. The opposing view which the punctualists associate with the synthetic theory is that gradual morphological change occurs within a species, dividing it into races and subspecies, long before new species can be said to have formed.

Actually evolutionary change follows; both patterns, and many others. Numerous studies have shown that morphological change and the development of reproductive isolation (the condition that defines new species) are genetically distinct phenomena: they can occur either together or separately. Arne Müntzing of the University of Lund showed many years ago that the genes coding for morphological differences among species of flowering plants are not linked with those that interfere with the fertility of hybrids and thereby keep species reproductively distinct. He crossed two species of hemp nettle. The resulting hybrids were partially fertile, enabling Müntzing to produce a second-generation of hybrids.

Some of the second-generation hybrids were intermediate between the parent species, suggesting they had inherited genes governing morphology from both species. In these intermediate species, however, the genes that maintain reproductive isolation appeared not to have been inherited with the genes for morphology, because a few of these second-generation hybrids were completely fertile. Other hybrids, which were not intermediate morphologically but instead resembled one of the parent species, were sterile. Since Müntzing's work similar results have been obtained in other plants.

Morphological differentiation and the reproductive isolation that distinguishes species develop independently in animals as well. In the continental U.S. many sibling species of *Drosophila* are morphologically alike but are reproductively isolated. In the Hawaiian archipelago, where several hundred species of *Drosophila* have arisen, the pattern is quite different. There are conspicuous morphological differences between species that are little differentiated genetically and even between geographically separated, interfertile populations of the same species. Many groups of mammals also exhibit this disjunction between morphological evolution and chromosomal differentiation or other modes of reproductive isolation.

These and numerous other examples indicate that the conditions leading to innovative morphological adaptations and those that favor speciation need not occur together. Morphological change proceeds in response to environmental challenges, such as exposure to new predators or the opening of a new habitat, whereas the splitting of a population into new species occurs as a consequence of population structure: patchy distribution in spatially restricted habitats, for example.

Both kinds of circumstance do often occur at once or in close succession thereby bringing about the linkage of speciation with morphological change that is central to the theory of punctuated equilibrium. The fossil snails Gould studied from Pleistocene (Ice Age) strata in Bermuda may fit the pattern. They seem to define a branching phylogeny in which each branch represents a new species as well as a recognizable change, although not a profound one, in shell morphology. One must recognize the possibility of circular reasoning, however.   A new species is identified each time morphological change is apparent along a sequence of fossils.   Hence speciation and morphological evolution are necessarily associated. Actually speciation may have taken place, unrecorded in the fossils, between the recognizable changes, and some of the visible differentiation may define populations that were interfertile and so do not qualify as separate species.

Species Selection

In keeping with their contention that evolution within a species is largely irrelevant to evolutionary trends, the punctualists have embraced a concept known as species selection. Species selection expands the province of natural selection (which is ordinarily held to act on individuals or, more precisely, on genes) to include entire species. The concept assumes that a species with a certain attribute will be more likely to persist and give rise to new species than one lacking the attribute. In a given group of organisms, for example, species with large individuals might be more likely to "bud off " new species, or less likely to become extinct, than species with small individuals. Over evolutionary time the average size of the organisms within the group of species would increase. The increase would result not from evolution toward a larger size within any given lineage but from an increase in the number of species that have large individuals.

There is a fundamental difference, however, between the comparative fates of species and the spread of genes and gene combinations within populations. Since the alleles of a gene contain alternative bits of information, only one of which can be present at a chromosomal locus, an increase in the number of individuals carrying one allele of a gene necessarily entails a reduction in the frequency of the other alleles. Alleles can therefore be said to compete, through their adaptive effects on their carriers, for prevalence in the gene pool of a population.

For species the situation is different. Related species do not usually compete directly. Morphologically similar sibling species of *Drosophila*, for example, exist side by side, exploiting the environment in slightly different ways. The origin and spread of a species does not necessarily cause other species in the same lineage to decline or become extinct. When a species does become extinct, it is usually not because of competition with related species but because its gene pool fails to become adapted to a changing environment. Environmental challenges may include competition with other species, to be sure, but those species are often entirely unrelated to the one that becomes extinct.   Insofar as it implies a parallel to the natural selection of genes, then, the notion of species selection is of dubious worth.

It is true, as Simpson recognized some 40 years ago, that evolutionary trends in morphology are the result not only of genetic evolution within species but also of the differential survival and multiplication of species. The former process is the fundamental one, however. The fate of species depends on the ability of the individuals making up the species to cope with the environment, and such ability can only result from the natural selection of genes.

A New Synthesis

How has the mid-century synthesis weathered recent developments in research and theory?   The new molecular biology, by showing that the evolutionary process at the level of DNA is far more complex than had been thoughts, casts doubt on some old certainties. It has also, however, provided the beginnings of answers to a fundamental matter the architects of the synthetic theory could not address: how genetic information accumulates over evolutionary history. Neutralists and selectionists, strange bedfellows at first glance, can both retain their basic postulates within the harmony of a more comprehensive theory, one that allows chance a greater role in genetic change. Some of the tenets of punctuated equilibrium can be refuted; others are compatible with a modified synthetic theory that encompasses the notions of species stasis and mosaic evolution.

Whatever new consensus emerges from ongoing research and controversy, it is not likely to require rejection of the basic tenets of Darwinism and the mid-century theory. The synthetic theory of the 21st century will differ considerably from the one developed a few decades ago, but the process by which it emerges will be one of evolution rather than upheaval.

11

Human Evolution: An Overview

IAN TATTERSALL

Over the last century or so, paleoanthropologists have toyed with many different notions of what it was that first set hominids on the road to humanity. Today we have large brains, small faces and dentitions, dextrous hands which we use to make tools, and a habitual upright posture and striding gait; and each of these has at one time or another been touted as the key "adaptation" that led ultimately to all the others. I use quotes around "adaptation," by the way, because the concept of adaptation has been widely abused by paleoanthropologists in the service of the notion that our biological history has been one of a slow, steady progress from primitiveness to perfection. Not only is this gradualist scenario of human evolution plainly wrong, as our fossil record shows, but it is equally erroneous to think of evolution as being somehow "driven" by adaptation. Any new characteristic has to arise within a population before it can serve an adaptive function, and it is only after a novelty has appeared that it can be favored (or not) by natural selection. More importantly, natural selection is itself a here-and-now process that depends on fickle and ever-shifting environmental conditions. The evolutionary history of any lineage, not least our own, is thus subject to a healthy dose of chance, something that it is useful to bear in mind as we survey the major events that have marked the human evolutionary story. I belabor this at the very start of this article because there is something inherently and distortingly linear about looking backwards at our prehistory, as I shall necessarily be doing. Picking out the major events in the lineage that led ultimately to *Homo sapiens* tends inevitably to obscure the fact that the history of the family Hominidae has been one of frequent speciation and evolutionary experimentation, a process that over a vast span of time gave rise to a vast branching bush of related forms. In pondering our history as human beings we should never forget that we are simply the sole surviving twig on this ramifying bush, rather than the products of a slow, steady and singleminded process of perfection.

The Earliest Hominids

There is some question as to the identity of the first known specifically human precursors. In 1994 researchers described various 4.4 million year-old (4.4 myr-old) fragments from Aramis, in Ethiopia, as representing the early hominid genus and species *Ardipithecus ramidus*. The key character to which they pointed was a forwardly-shifted foramen magnum (the hole through which the spinal cord exits the bottom of the skull), which in their view implied that the head was held erect, in turn suggesting that this creature had walked bipedally. If true this was highly significant, since the fossil record had by that time amply confirmed that postural uprightness was the crucial behavioral/ anatomical shift that got our lineage started. Other characteristics, such as the dentition, are, however, more arguable, and it is only with fossils from Kenya, dated in the 4.2-3.9 myr range, and assigned to the species *Australopithecus anamensis*, that we are securely in the hominid camp. Not only do leg bones of this form show unmistakable indications of uprightness, but the jaws and teeth of *A. anamensis* are quite similar to those of the later species *Australopithecus afarensis,* known from sites in Ethiopia and Tanzania dated between 3.8 and 3.0 million years ago (mya).

The best known representative of *A. afarensis* is "Lucy," a partial skeleton of a young adult who died about 3.2 mya. Lucy shows signs throughout the preserved portions of her body of postural uprightness; but uprightness of a kind not familiar today. These early hominids walked erect, but at the same time preserved features that would have been very useful in the trees. These included narrow shoulders, relatively short hindlimbs, and longish feet that were better capable of grasping than ours are. That these small-bodied hominids (females stood only about 3 ½ feet tall, the considerably larger males about a foot taller) were capable of a striding gait on the ground is indisputable, as the famous 3.5 myr-old footprint trails found at Laetoli, in Tanzania, show; but at the same time they would have had considerable facility in the trees, which would have provided them with both food and shelter. A recently discovered foot and ankle from the South African site of Sterkfontein, perhaps as much as 3 ½ myr old, shows that although the ankle was relatively like ours, the long foot had a somewhat divergent big toe, with powerful grasping potential.

The environment in which these early bipeds lived matches these anatomical characteristics quite well. For a long time it had been thought that human bipedlaism evolved in an open-country context, as a worldwide drying trend (particularly well documented in Africa, on which continent early hominids are exclusively known until about 2 mya) replaced forests by grasslands, evicting some groups of hominids (members of the group to which humans and apes both belong) from their arboreal habitat and precipitating them onto the expanding savannas. Now, however, it seems that early hominids are often associated with quite densely wooded environments, where they may have mainly exploited the forest fringes but were nonetheless at home both in the more thickly forested and the more open areas of their ranges. The reasons for their adoption of bipedalism are debated. It is still unclear whether moving on two legs was more energetically efficient than moving on four, and it has been pointed out that apes tend to move bipedally in the trees much more frequently than has been assumed. One intriguing possibility is that moving out of the shade of the trees exposed early hominids to much more intense solar radiation than they had been accustomed to, and that by standing upright they managed to minimize the amount of solar energy they absorbed. Keeping the brain cool is critical for any animal; and, lacking any specialized mechanisms for this, our hominoid ancestors may have benefited from the whole-body cooling promoted by upright posture. This posture also permits efficient cooling by the evaporation of sweat, which may be associated with the hairlessness that has very likely been characteristic of humans ever since.

Whatever the case, the have-your-cake-and-eat-it locomotor adaptation of early hominids was clearly successful. For this body form remained essentially stable for at least a couple of million years, even as hominid species diversified, came, and went. Over a 3-2 million year (myr) period, for example, there is evidence of more than one "gracile" (lightly-built) species of australopith at sites in South Africa; and in a slightly later period fossils are found there of a "robust" australopith group, characterized by enormous grinding dentitions, whose origins can be traced to before about 2 ½ myr in East Africa, where the robust record persists to not much more than 1 mya. None of these early hominids had brains much bigger than those of today's apes, and there is no evidence that any of them made tools; there is, indeed, little to suggest that their cognitive capacities were vastly improved relative to those of modern apes, which is one reason why some paleoanthropologists have characterized this initial radiation of hominids as "bipedal chimpanzees."

The Origins of the genus *Homo*

When and how our own genus *Homo* emerged is also a subject of some debate. Fragmentary fossils from sites in Ethiopia and Malawi dated to about

2 ½ mya suggest that by this time a dental pattern significantly different from those of the australopiths had emerged, and in the period around 2 mya a very motley assemblage of fossils from eastern and southern Africa has been assigned to the species *Homo habilis*. Initially named from specimens about 1.8 myr old found at Tanzania's Olduvai Gorge, this species was placed in *Homo* principally because of its presumed association with crude stone artifacts found at the Gorge, and has since been augmented with fossils found in Kenya's East Turkana region and elsewhere. These include specimens with australopith-sized brains, and some with somewhat larger ones, notably the famous ER-1470 cranium from East Turkana. Associated postcranial elements are also hard to interpret, with some isolated leg bones from Turkana looking somewhat advanced while, for instance, the fragmentary partial skeleton OH 62 from Olduvai has been described as even more primitive in its proportions than Lucy. Clearly we have a mixture of species here, and sorting the mess out is a major task for the future.

What is clear, however, is that hominids of some kind began making stone tools by possibly as much as 2 ½ mya. These were not necessarily, of course, the first human tools of any kind—after all, chimpanzees make tools of perishable substances such as twigs—but they are the first of which tangible evidence is preserved in the archaeological record, and there is plenty of evidence that these crude but sharp flakes, chipped off small nodules of fine-grained rock, were used in activities such as butchering the carcasses of dead animals. This doesn't mean, however, that these animals were hunted; more likely, they were scavenged natural deaths or carnivore kills: resources that may have been particularly plentiful in the zone of intergradation between forest or woodland and savanna. Nonetheless, the mere existence of stone tools, however crude, marks a cognitive leap away from anything of which the great apes are capable. Figuring out how to hit one stone with another at the precise angle necessary to detach a sharp flake is a feat beyond the capacity of any ape, even one that has been intensively coached; and there is good evidence that these tools were not just ad hoc responses to immediate needs, but that planning and forethought (generally lacking in ape hunting behaviors) were involved. For example, suitable stones were carried distances of a couple of miles or more from their nearest natural sources, and were then worked when the occasion demanded, as shown by the fact that archaeologists have been able to reconstruct entire cobbles from fragments found at butchery sites.

A couple of decades ago much was made of the notion that many early sites at which, for example, an unexpectedly high proportion of ungulate limb bones were found, might have been "home bases," to which animal parts were habitually transported for sharing among the group—which in turn carried overtones of a complex social lifestyle and elaborate inter-individual communication. It has since been realized, however, that such interpretations, depending as they do on the idea that if these creatures weren't apes they must have been primitive forms of ourselves, lean excessively toward viewing these early hominids in our own image. More recent archaeological interpretations have been considerably more circumspect.

Early Humans of Modern Body Form

If the degree of physical modernity of the earliest toolmakers is equivocal, there is no doubt about a new group of early humans whose remains are first known from the Turkana region in the period following about 1.8 mya. This is largely due to the discovery of the "Turkana Boy" in West Turkana in the mid-1980s.   The Boy consists of an astonishingly well-preserved skull and postcranial skeleton of an adolescent who died at the age of nine (though developmentally he is more advanced than modern nine-year-olds), some 1.6 mya. He is generally associated with slightly older adult specimens from East Turkana, which include a fairly complete cranium (ER 3733) and braincase (ER 3883), and are increasingly assigned to the species *Homo ergaster*, although some prefer to regard them as "early African *Homo erectus.*" Here is a form with a much more modern-looking skull and dentition than any australopith, and a brain well over half the size of our own (australopiths run about a third). The skull of *Homo ergaster* is nonetheless significantly less modern-looking than its body skeleton, as judged from the Boy.   Early hominids were rather small-bodied, but here we have an individual who was five feet three inches tall when he died, but would have stood a full six feet tall had he survived to adulthood. What's more, his body proportions were those typical of people who live today in hot, arid environments such as the one in which he lived—these early humans were clearly at home out on the savanna, far from forests—with long, slender arms, legs and torso. There were differences from us, of course, but in essence here is an individual of modern body form.

Culturally, however, little had changed, at least at the start. The earliest *Homo ergaster* continued to make stone tools similar to those that had been made hundreds of thousands of years earlier. This may seem a little surprising, but a moment's thought will show that it's really what we should expect. There's no reason– or need –to expect technological innovation with the arrival of a new species, because there's really only one place where such innovations can occur, and that's within a species.   Nonetheless, true technological innovation was not long to await. A hundred thousand years or so after the Boy lived, we begin to find a radically new kind of stone tool in the archaeological record. This is the "Acheulean" handaxe and related implements. Unlike the early "Oldowan" tools, that were produced simply to obtain an attribute such as a sharp cutting edge, handaxes were large–six to eight inches long and more– and consciously shaped on both sides to a standard symmetrical form. These were general-purpose tools that were used for a variety of purposes such as cutting, scraping and hacking, and their utility is attested to by the fact that they lingered in the archaeological record for well over a million years. How this new tool type reflected larger changes in lifestyle is not clear, but it is nonetheless evident that it embodies evidence of a significant cognitive advance.

It is in the period following about 2 mya that we first begin to find evidence for humans outside Africa. Very early dates for human presence in Asia (in the range of 1.8-1.5 myr) are individually debated, but collectively suggest that humans exited Africa for the first time hard on the heels of their acquisition of modern body form and the striding gait that came with it. Humans are walking machines, not fast but with incredible endurance, and they wasted no time in capitalizing on this ability. A very early departure from Africa also has the advantage of explaining why eastern Asian *Homo erectus* (physically not too dissimilar from *Homo ergaster,* as far as we can tell) never acquired Acheulean technology: its emigrant ancestors left the continent of their birth before its invention.

The Ice Ages and the Earliest Europeans

The emergence of *Homo ergaster* also more or less coincided with a period of unsettled climates and geography known as the "Ice Ages." For the last 1.8 myr or so, major cycles of cooling and warming have occurred worldwide with a frequency of about 100 thousand years (100 kyr). In cold times, the polar and montane ice caps expanded, "locking up" water, reducing sea levels, extending shorelines, and uniting continental islands with the mainland; in warmer periods the ice caps contracted, sea levels rose, and islands were once again cut off. Many fluctuations occurred within the major cycles, and the net result was to produce extremely propitious conditions for evolutionary innovation, by environmental change and even more importantly by the fragmentation of populations and the formation of isolates in which new features could most easily become fixed.

It was in this context that the first human populations invaded Europe, which from this point on will assume an ever larger role in the human story if only because the record is incomparably better from this part of the Old World than from elsewhere. The earliest European human fossils known, just under 800 kyr old, come from the site of the Gran Dolina in the Atapuerca Hills of

Spain, and consist of various fragments that have been very recently allocated to the new species *Homo antecessor*.   It is unclear whether these specimens represent the precursors of later Europeans or whether they are the result of an initial, and ultimately unsuccessful, invasion of the region.   The describers of the new species believe that it represents the common ancestor of two lineages that led to *Homo sapiens* on the one hand, and, on the other, via a form known as *Homo heidelbergensis* to the Neanderthals, *Homo neanderthalensis.*   I should probably note at this point that not all authorities agree on the existence of so many human species over the past 1 myr or so, and that some, indeed, would view all these forms (plus *Homo ergaster* and *Homo erectus*) as varieties of our own species *Homo sapiens.*   Such views are, however, unsustainable in light of what we know about interspecies variability in other speciose primate genera, and about the evolutionary process itself.

Homo erectus lingered on in eastern Asia into quite recent times while, in Africa, *Homo ergaster* gave rise at some point over about 600 thousand years ago (kya) to the species *Homo heidelbergensis*, representatives of which are also later on found in Europe.   With *Homo heidelbergensis* we are approaching a more familiar skull form, with brain sizes up quite close to the modern average—although, in contrast to *Homo sapiens*, in which a small facial skeleton is tucked beneath the front of a high, rounded cranial vault with a sharply rising forehead, these forms had relatively long and low braincases with forwardly positioned faces surmounted by distinct brow ridges.   The archaeological record of *Homo hedelbergensis* is best in Europe, where several sites bear witness to the lifeways of these early humans, and to several significant innovations.   Although handaxes eventually reached Europe, the earlier stone tool assemblages wielded by *Homo heidelbergensis* there tend to be pretty unsophisticated; greater interest attaches, for example, to the fact that the 400 kyr-old site of Terra Amata in southern France (which unfortunately lacks human fossils) has yielded the earliest traces of constructed shelters, in the form of saplings embedded in the ground in an oval arrangement, and bent inwards to come together over the center of the hut.   Inside these structures animal bone refuse was haphazardly scattered around, although in one such hut there is a shallow, scooped-out hearth containing burned cobbles.   Although there are traces of fire preserved at African sites as much as 1.5 myr old, Terra Amata provides us with the earliest substantial evidence of the domestication of fire, surely one of the most significant events in the history of human technology.

At the entrance to the cave of Arago, of similar age but a couple of hundred miles to the west, fossils of *Homo heidelbergensis* have been found in a succession of "living floors" characterized by an abundance of stone tools and animal bones.   It is still debated whether or not these bones or those found at

Terra Amata testify to the hunting skills of *Homo heidelbergensis*—they might, after all, have been scavenged or accumulated by natural forces—but the recent discovery of miraculously preserved wooden throwing spears at a 400 kyr-old German site seems to tip the balance in favor of some active hunting, at least. What's more, the nature of sites such as Terra Amata and Arago offer the first plausible intimations of the "home base" of which recent studies have deprived earlier toolmakers. If this is correct, we are able to glimpse here the first glimmerings of some of those behavioral attributes we associate with our own kind. Yet, once more, specifics are elusive. Even the evidence of fire from Terra Amata is hard to interpret, since the control of fire in hearths only became a regular feature of the archaeological record subsequent to about 150 kya. Particularly since the advantages of domesticating fire seem so evident, it's hard to know what to make of isolated instances such as this.

The Neanderthals and their Successors

Without any question, the best known of our extinct relatives is the species *Homo neanderthalensis*, known widely from sites in Europe and western Asia dated to between about 200 and 30 kya. These distinctive humans had brains that were as large as our own, but that were housed in a long, low skull with a narrow and protruding face. They also differed from us in various minor features of the postcranial skeleton, which is generally said to be highly robust, but is in some respects less so than is often claimed. The ultimate origins of the Neanderthals are unclear, although several European fossils in the range of 300 - 200 kya are said to show features that anticipate them. These include some exquisitely preserved crania from the "Pit of the Bones" in Spain's Atapuerca Hills, a slightly crushed cranium from Steinheim in Germany, and fossils from Reilingen, also in Germany, and Swanscombe, in England. Fuller analysis may show, however, that the Neanderthals are but one component of an endemic radiation of hominids in Europe, rather than the culmination of a single lineage of which these other fossils were earlier members. There is a growing consensus that the Neanderthals (and other subsequent humans) were ultimately derived from *Homo heidelbergensis*. However, certain features of the latter, such as an extreme development of the sinuses of the skull, may cast some doubt on this.

At some time before we have definitive evidence of *Homo neanderthalensis* (dating is vague) we find another significant technological innovation in the archaeological record. This involved preparing a nucleus of rock in such a way that a single blow would detach a flake which might serve as a finished tool or which could be modified for a number of purposes. In some cases a succession of blows would detach a series of flakes, each of which could be used in this way. This technique had the prime advantage of producing a single continuous cutting edge all around the periphery of the tool, rather than a succession of surfaces at various angles; and it also provided greater economy of raw materials. Whoever invented this technique, however, it was taken to its highest pitch of perfection by the Neanderthals, whose "Mousterian" stoneworking tradition produced a wide variety of finely-made tools, although attempts to categorize them have been confounded by the fact that many forms seem to result from a process of reduction, as blunted old tools were reworked to renew their edges. There was perhaps more regional variety than has generally been recognized, but Mousterian tools remained essentially uniform over the long tenure of the Neanderthals, and throughout the vast area of the world they inhabited. Nonetheless, the fact that Neanderthal toolmakers made a variety of different tools to patterns that they held in their minds bespeaks a degree of cognitive refinement relative to anything that went before.

Probably the major reason why the Neanderthals are so much better known biologically than earlier humans is that, at least occasionally, they buried their dead—a factor that favors preservation and contributes to the relatively large number of quasi-complete skeletons that have been found. More profoundly, however, this practice speaks to us as an intensely human type of behavior, although the motives of Neanderthals were not necessarily those which inspire humans to indulge in similar practices today. For, significantly, we have little evidence in a fairly abundant Neanderthal record of any other activities which we might regard as symbolic. This stands in dramatic contrast to the record left behind by the modern humans who entered Europe about 40 kya and had entirely eliminated the Neanderthals from the region—how exactly is unclear, although it was certainly not by genetic absorption, as has often been claimed—by a little under 30 kya. Not only did these *Homo sapiens* bury their dead with a variety of rich grave goods, but they left behind evidence of abundant symbolic activities of other kinds. Starting well over 30 kya we find notations on plaques of bone and stone; bone flutes with complex sound capabilities; elaborate symbolic systems on cave walls; and, in media ranging from engraving to bas-relief to monochrome drawings to sculpture and polychrome paintings, some of the finest art that has ever been created. What's more, it is clear that such activities were not oddities, but were integral parts of these people's daily lives and belief systems. These people were us.

In the technological realm, the contrasts between *Homo neanderthalensis* and *Homo sapiens* were equally stark. While Neanderthals worked virtually exclusively in stone, the moderns showed mastery of diverse materials including bone and antler, even producing tiny-eyed needles from these materials by 26 kya, and thereby announcing the advent of tailored clothing. At the same time, stoneworking was refined with numerous long "blades" that were adaptable to multiple specific functions; and traditions of producing such tools diversified rapidly in different regions. Uses of fire became more complex; indeed, in one area of central Europe fire was used to heat kilns in which clay images were baked. The animal bones found at early modern human sites became more varied, coming to include fish and birds, for instance, and bearing witness to varied and sophisticated hunting techniques. The list of such contrasts could go on and on; but the essential point is that Neanderthals and moderns were creatures of a different order—in other words, the Neanderthals did not simply do what we do but not as well. Their approach to the world and life, like those of their predecessors, was radically different from ours. And, though the Neanderthals' way was successful for longer than *Homo sapiens* has been on the Earth, it eventually lost out to this new force on the landscape.

The Origin of Modern Humans

Where did these extraordinary new creatures come from? I've noted that these people, identical physically to ourselves, first entered Europe, fully fledged, some 40 kya. But anatomically "modern" humans have been around much longer than that. There are hints in Africa of anatomically modern *Homo sapiens* as much as 120 kya, or perhaps even a little more; but all of these remains are fragmentary or poorly dated, or both. Still, the notion of an African origin for our species is supported by studies of genetic diversity, and more controversially, by mtDNA dating. What's more, the Levant, on the fringes of Africa and faunally part of the same province, has yielded good fossil evidence for anatomically modern humans in the period around 100 kya, notably at the Israeli site of Jebel Qafzeh. The problem is, though, that anatomically modern humans somehow shared the Levant with Neanderthals from at least that time up to about 40 kya. Throughout this long period, these two kinds of humans also shared virtually identical technologies—and, as far as we can tell, lifestyles—although a recent study suggests that Neanderthals and moderns may have had different approaches to exploiting the landscape.

What was going on? One suggestion is that the Neanderthals were "cold-adapted," and moved into the Levant from areas to the north in cooler periods, while the moderns retreated to the balmier climes of Africa. The reverse would have happened in warmer times. This maybe so, but it does not explain the virtually identical toolkits of the two forms. Clearly, humans can be modern in two distinct senses: anatomical and behavioral. (There is no big surprise here; remember that I have already remarked that innovations of all kinds necessarily arise *within* species). Anatomical modernity almost certainly had its origins in Africa, though we don't yet understand the details of this because the record is poor there. Behavioral modernity also may have arisen in Africa, though at a later time; for although the African record lacks the extravagance of symbol that we see in Europe, we have very early hints there of bone and blade tools, flint mining, and long-distance transport of materials: all things that are associated at a later date in Europe with art, music, notation and all those other aspects of life that make it so easy to identify with the early Europeans as people like ourselves. Whatever the case, it is clear that *Homo sapiens* must have originated in a specific place—for all species do—and it was most likely born with a behavioral potential that was only later fully realized (again, nothing surprising; the history of life abounds with examples of capacities born in one context, and only later exploited in another).

What lies at the root of behavioral modernity?   The complex and often unfathomable behaviors of people today are without a doubt a reflection of our capacity for symbolic thought, something the Neanderthals probably did not possess.   And virtually synonymous with symbolic thought is language.   For language is not simply a matter of stringing words together, but is rather a complex symbolic system in itself, which not only allows us to express associations we make in our minds but also allows certain kinds of association to be made. Those early Europeans who eliminated the Neanderthals certainly possessed language; while the Neanderthals, even though they may well have had a fairly complex system of inter-individual communication, almost equally certainly did not. Studies of the cranial base, which forms the roof of the vocal tract, show that the ability to form the sounds associated with modern speech was beginning to develop in *Homo ergaster*, and that it was probably fully formed in *Homo heidelbergensis*.

The latent ability to produce speech thus goes back a long way, and we must hence conclude that the critical and much more recent leap to modernity was made in the brain, capitalizing on a pre-existing vocal potential. In which case, there was either a major biological change among humans subsequent to their acquisition of the skeletal modernity that we can detect in the fossil record —implausible on a variety of grounds—or, the concealed potential for symbolic reasoning was born along with skeletal modernity, lying fallow for many millennia until it was kicked into action by some cultural stimulus, most plausibly the invention of language. This innovation was then able to spread rapidly by cultural contact among populations all having the latent ability to acquire it: a much more convincing scenario than the only alternative, which involves the wholesale replacement of populations Old World-wide in a relatively short period of time.

It is particularly frustrating that the event of events—the birth of our own unique species—is obscured by the apparent poverty of the available record. But actually this is a matter of perspective. If we knew as much about the remote process of the adoption of bipedalism by our earliest ancestors, or about the origin of the genus *Homo* as we do about the much more recent origin of *Homo sapiens,* we would doubtless discern a much more complex situation than we are able to at present, and would feel an equal measure of frustration. The history of our lineage has been a long and complex one, and increasing knowledge will only serve to emphasize this complexity. For every problem that is solved, several more will emerge as our fossil and archaeological records enlarge. And perhaps that is how it should be.

References

This brief essay is not referenced in the text, but fuller discussion of matters both raised and neglected here will be found in the following recent books:

Eldredge, Niles 1995 *Reinventing Darwin: The Great Debate at the High Table of Evolutionary Theory.* New York: John Wiley.

Johanson, Donald and Blake Edgar 1996 *From Lucy to Language.* New York: Simon and Schuster.

Potts, Rick 1996 *Humanity's Descent: The Consequences of Ecological Instability.* New York: William Morrow.

Schick, Kathy D. and Nicholas Toth 1993 *Making Silent Stones Speak: Human Evolution and the Dawn of Technology.* New York: Simon and Schuster.

Stanley, Steven M. 1996. *Children of the Ice Age: How A Global Catastrophe Allowed Humans to Evolve.* New York: Harmony Books.

Stringer, Christopher and Robin McKie 1996 *African Exodus: The Origins of Modern Humanity.* New York: Henry Holt.

Tattersall, Ian 1995 *The Fossil Trail: How We Know What We Think We Know About Human Evolution.* New York: Oxford University Press.

Tattersall, Ian 1995 *The Last Neanderthal: The Rise, Success and Mysterious Extinction of Our Nearest Human Relatives.* New York: Macmillan.

Tattersall, Ian 1998 *Becoming Human: Evolution and Human Uniqueness.* New York: Harcourt Brace.

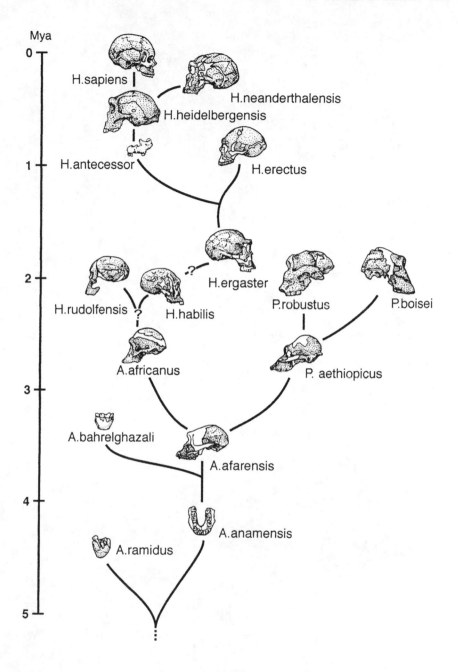

One possible "family tree" of hominid species.

Historical and Philosophical Perspectives

Scientists rely upon certain assumptions and definitions in order to practice their disciplines. These presuppositions are not themselves scientific discoveries nor simple observations of nature; they are intellectual constructs. An example of this is the definition of the term: "species." Ernst Mayr's article opens this section with a discussion of the philosophical issues which surround this primary biological concept.

The findings which are the outcome of scientific inquiry often raise questions that require philosophical clarification. Prior to Darwin, the order of the biological world, the integrity of the parts of the body, and the fit of species in their environment were taken to be evidence of a divine creative purpose in nature. Darwin's theory provided an alternative explanation for such order without necessary reference to an external divine source. Does evolutionary theory remove purposefulness from nature? How is the occurrence of novelty in the biological world to be understood? Francisco Ayala's article discusses these philosophical issues and offers a clarification of the idea of "teleology in biology."

When Darwin's theory first appeared, some critics judged that it was in conflict with a religious interpretation of nature. The view that there is an inevitable conflict between science and religion, especially over evolution, persists to this day. However, John Durant's "critical-historical" assessment of arguments about evolution and religion demonstrates that the issues are far less obvious than the conflict view allows. The following article, by Ronald Numbers, provides an historical sketch of the "creationists." While indicating the variety of views which can fall under that label, he particularly chronicles the development of strict or young-earth creationists as a social and political movement in this century.

The section concludes with a reflection by Stephen Jay Gould on the statement about evolution by Pope John Paul II noted in the introduction of this volume and elsewhere. Gould proposes that science and religion cannot conflict because each has its own proper domain of "teaching" authority.

12

What is a Species, and What is Not?

ERNST MAYR

I analyze a number of widespread misconceptions concerning species. The species category, defined by a concept, denotes the rank of a species taxon in the Linnaean hierarchy. Biological species reproduce isolated from each other, which protects the integrity of their genotypes. Degree of morphological difference is not an appropriate species definition. Unequal rates of evolution of different characteristics and lack of information on the mating potential of isolated populations are the major difficulties in the demarcation of species taxa.

1. What is a Species, and What is Not?

As someone who has published books and papers on the biological species for more than 50 years, and who has revised and studied in detail more than 500 species of birds and many species of other groups of organisms, the reading of some recent papers on species has been a rather troubling experience for me. There is only one term that fits some of these authors: armchair taxonomists. Since many authors have never personally analyzed any species populations or studied species in nature, they lack any feeling for what species actually are. Darwin already knew this when, in September 1845, he wrote to Joseph Hooker: "How painfully true is your remark that no one has hardly the right to examine the question of species who has not minutely described many" (Darwin 1987, 253). These authors make a number of mistakes that have been pointed out again and again in the recent literature. Admittedly, the relevant literature is quite scattered, and some of it is perhaps rather inaccessible to a non-taxonomist. Yet, because the species concept is an important concept in the philosophy of science, every effort should be made to clarify it. It occurred to me that instead of criticizing certain recently published papers individually, it would be more constructive and helpful if I would attempt here to present, from the perspective of a practicing systematist, a concise overview of the philosophically important aspects of the problem of the "species." There is nothing of the sort in the literature.

The species is the principal unit of evolution and it is impossible to write about evolution, and indeed about almost any aspect of the philosophy of biology, without having a sound understanding of the meaning of biological species. A study of the history of the species problem helps to dispel some of the misconceptions (Mayr 1957, Grant 1994).

2. Species of Organisms Are Concrete Phenomena of Nature.

Some recent authors have dealt with the concept of species as if it were merely an arbitrary, man-made concept, like the concepts of reduction, demarcation, cause, derivation, prediction, progress, each of which may have almost as many definitions as there are authors who have written about them. However, the concept biological species is not like such concepts. The term "species" refers to a concrete phenomenon of nature and this fact severely constrains the number and kinds of possible definitions. The word "species" is, like the words "planet" or "moon," a technical term for a concrete phenomenon. One cannot propose a new definition of a planet as "a satellite of a sun that has its own satellite," because this would exclude Venus, and some other planets without moons. A definition of any class of objects must be applicable to any member of this class and exclude reference to attributes not characteristic of this class. This is why any definition of the term "species" must be based on careful study of the phenomenon of nature to which this term is applied. Alas, this necessity is not appreciated by all too many of those who have recently discussed the species problem after a mere analysis of the literature.

The conclusion that there are concrete describable objects in nature which deserve to be called "species" is not unanimously accepted. There has been a widespread view that species are only arbitrary artifacts of the human mind, as some nominalists, in particular, have claimed. Their arguments were criticized by Mayr (1949a, 371).

3. Why Are There Species of Organisms?

Why is the total genetic variability of nature organized in the form of discrete packages, called species? Why are there species in nature? What is their significance? The Darwinian always asks "why?" questions because he knows that everything in living nature is the product of evolution and must have had some selective significance in order to have evolved.[1] He therefore asks: What selection forces in nature favor the origin and maintenance of species?

The answer to this question becomes evident when one makes a certain thought experiment.

"It is quite possible to think of a world in which species do not exist but are replaced by a single reproductive community of individuals, each one different from every other one, and each one capable of reproducing with those other individuals that are most similar to it. Each individual would then be the center of a concentric series of circles of genetically more and more unlike individuals. What would be the consequence of the continuous uninterrupted gene flow through such a large system? In each generation certain individuals would have a selective advantage because they have a gene complex that is specially adapted to a particular ecological situation. However, most of these favorable combinations would be broken up by pairing with individuals with a gene complex adapted to a slightly different environment. In such a system there is no defense against the destruction of superior gene combinations except the abandonment of sexual reproduction. It is obvious that any system that prevents such unrestricted outcrossing is superior"[2] (Mayr 1949b, 282). The biological species is such a system.

The biological meaning of species is thus quite apparent: "The segregation of the total genetic variability of nature into discrete packages, so called species, which are separated from each other by reproductive barriers, prevents the production of too great a number of disharmonious incompatible gene combinations. This is the basic biological meaning of species and this is the reason why there are discontinuities between sympatric species. We do know that genotypes are extremely complex epigenetic systems. There are severe limits to the amount of genetic variability that can be accommodated in a single gene pool without producing too many incompatible gene combinations" (Mayr 1969, 316). The validity of this argument is substantiated by the fact that hybrids between species, particularly in animals, are almost always of inferior viability and more extreme hybrids are usually even sterile. "Almost always" means that there are species interpreted to be the result of hybridization, particularly among plants, but except for the special case of allopolyploidy, such cases are rare.

Among the attributes members of a species share, the only ones that are of crucial significance for the species definition are those which serve the biological purpose of the species, that is, the protection of a harmonious gene pool. These attributes were named by Dobzhansky (1935) *isolating mechanisms*. It is immaterial whether or not the term isolating mechanism was well chosen, nor is it important whether one places the stress on the prevention of interbreeding with non-conspecific individuals or the facilitation ("recognition") of breeding with conspecific individuals. The concept I have just developed is articulated in the so-called biological species definition: *"Species are groups of interbreeding natural populations that are reproductively isolated from other such groups."* The isolating mechanisms by which reproductive isolation is effected are properties of individuals. Geographic isolation therefore does not qualify as an isolating mechanism.

Reproductive Isolation. The biological species definition includes the statement that the populations of one species are "reproductively isolated" from the populations of all other species. Typologically conceived, this would mean that no individual of species A would ever hybridize with any individual of species B. Botanists soon pointed out that this did not correctly describe many situations in nature. They discovered case after case of occasional (sometimes even rather frequent) hybridization between seemingly "good" sympatric species. Anderson (1949) went so far as to claim that this was the normal situation with closely related sympatric species and that through such "introgressive hybridization," as he called it, either species would be enriched by genes from other species. Other authors minimized the frequency of such hybridization and considered parallel variation in sympatric species as the residues of ancestral polymorphisms. Recent molecular analysis has, however, confirmed the frequency of clandestine introgression. However, if the two species continue their essential integrity, they will be treated as species, in spite of the slight inefficiency of their isolating mechanisms.

There is at least one case among oaks (*Quercus*) and one among birches (*Betula*) where such introgression has apparently been going on for millions of years without leading to a fusion of the parental species. Similar cases apparently occur also in animals. After the destruction of much of the southern periphery of the habitat of the gray wolf, the area was invaded by coyotes and, owing to the fertility of the hybrids, the crossing of male wolves with female coyotes led to an introgression of alien genes into both wolf and coyote populations. The same was shown by Templeton and associates (1989, 12) for the sympatric Hawaiian species *Drosophila silvestris* and *D. heteroneura*. The fact that the mitochondria are inherited only through the females greatly facilitates the discovery of such cases of hybridization.

It is thus well established that a leakage of genes occurs among many good "reproductively isolated" species. This induced me to revise the definition of isolating mechanisms to "biological properties of individuals which prevent the interbreeding [fusion] of populations" (1970, 56).   Thus, isolating mechanisms do not always prevent the occasional interbreeding of non-conspecific individuals, but they nevertheless prevent the complete fusion of such species populations. Clandestine hybridization is apparently far more common among plants than among higher animals.

Among the invalid objections to the Biological Species Concept (BSC) is the claim that it would work only if the acquisition of the isolating mechanisms was a teleological process (Paterson 1985). However, Darwin already knew that reproductive isolation between species is not acquired by teleological ad hoc selection but simply as a byproduct of the process of divergence. H. J. Muller and E. Mayr have further emphasized this point in their writings and Mayr in particular has demonstrated that indeed behavioral isolating mechanisms can be acquired through a change of function of factors favoring sexual selection. Paterson's arguments do not in the least weaken the validity of the BSC (Mayr 1988b, Coyne et al. 1987). The contingent nature of the acquisition of isolating mechanisms is documented by their great diversity. It would seem to be merely a matter of chance what kind of device is made use of by a given incipient species to protect itself against outcrossing. It includes not only purely genetic mechanisms such as sterility factors, but the use of ecological and life history factors and (in animals) a number of behavioral devices.

The evolutionist always stresses the genetic uniqueness of every individual of a sexually reproducing population. However, the members of any species also have in common many species-specific properties. This includes, in particular, the isolating mechanisms but also many adaptations, for instance, for niche utilization, as well as certain contingent, species-specific properties. If one knew the genetic basis of all the species-specific characteristics, one might be able to give a genetic characterization of a species taxon.

The BSC is based on the recognition of properties of populations. It depends on the fact of non-interbreeding with other populations. For this reason the concept is not applicable to organisms which do not form sexual populations. The supporters of the BSC therefore agree with their critics that the BSC does not apply to asexual (uniparental) organisms. Their genotype does not require any protection because it is not threatened by destruction through outcrossing. There are a number of suggestions on how species taxa in asexual organisms can be delimited and defined, but this is outside the present discussion. However, I find that any endeavor to propose a species definition that is equally applicable to both sexually reproducing and asexual populations misses the basic characteristics of the biological species definition (the protection of harmonious gene pools).

It is important to emphasize that in the study of biological species one deals with biological populations. Some non-biologists, including some philosophers, seem to have difficulties appreciating how different biological populations are from classes of inanimate objects (Kitcher 1989, 189-194).

Only a small fraction of any biological population reproduces, because not every individual in a population survives up to the reproductive age and reproduces successfully. This is true on the average for only two of the total number of offspring of a prenatal pair in a sexually reproducing species. For example, a mentally retarded individual may have no opportunity to reproduce but he is still a member of his population. In most marine organisms, with their high number of larvae, successful survival and reproduction is to a large extent a matter of chance, but most of the zygotes have, at the moment of their formation, an equal probability of success. Kitcher describes six situations which to him seem to cause difficulty for the concept of population as presented by me. I believe that his objections can be answered, although it would take me too far afield to do so here. The simplest solution in most cases is to say that whatever is the product of the same gene pool belongs to the same population, together with any new immigrants.

4. The Two Meanings of the Term Species.

What the scientist actually encounters in nature are populations of organisms. There is a considerable range in the size of populations, ranging from the local deme to the species taxon. The local deme is the community of potentially interbreeding individuals at a locality (see also Mayr 1963, 136), and the species taxon has been referred to by Dobzhansky as the "largest Mendelian population." The task of the biologist is to assign these populations to species. This requires two operations: (1) to develop a concept of what a species is resulting in the definition of the species category in the Linnaean hierarchy, and (2) to apply this concept when combining populations into species taxa.

A number of recent writers on the species problem have failed to appreciate that the word "species" is applied to these two quite different entities in nature, species taxa and the concept of the category species. As a result, their so-called species definition is nothing but a recipe for the demarcation of species taxa. This is, for instance, true for most of the recent so-called phylogenetic species definitions. It is also largely true for Templeton's (1989, 1994) cohesion species concept. A paper often quoted as a decisive refutation of the BSC (Sokal and Crovello 1970) is perhaps an extreme example of the confusion resulting from the failure to discriminate between species as category (concept) and as taxon.

(1) The species taxon. The word taxon refers to a concrete zoological or botanical object consisting of a classifiable population (or group of populations) of organisms. The house sparrow (*Passer domesticus*) and the potato (*Solanum tubersum*) are species taxa. Species taxa are

particulars, "individuals," biopopulations. Being particulars, they can be described and delimited against other species taxa.

(2) The species category. Here the word "species" indicates the rank in the Linnaean hierarchy. The species category is the class that contains all taxa of species rank. It articulates the concept of the biological species and is defined by the species definition. The principal use of the species definition is to facilitate a decision on the ranking of species level populations, that is, to answer the question about an isolated population: "Is it a full species or a subspecies?" The answer to this question has to be based on inference (the criteria on the basis of which such a decision is made are listed in the technical taxonomical literature, e.g., in Mayr and Ashlock 1991, 100-105). A complication is produced by the fact that in the Linnaean hierarchy asexual "species" are also ranked in the species category, even though they do not represent the BSC.

The literature traditionally has referred to the "species problem." However, it is now quite clear that there are two different sets of species problems, one being the problem of how to define the species (what species concept to adopt), and the other being how to apply this concept in the demarcation of species taxa. It is necessary to discuss these two sets of problems separately. Let me begin with a discussion of the meaning and history of the term "biological species."

5. Typological Species Versus Biological Species.

The Biological Species Concept developed in the second half of the 19th century. Up to that time, from Plato and Aristotle until Linnaeus and early 19th century authors, one simply recognized "species," eide (Plato), or kinds (Mill). Since neither the taxonomists nor the philosophers made a strict distinction between inanimate things and biological species, the species definitions they gave were rather variable and not very specific. The word "species" conveyed *the idea of a class of objects, members of which shared certain defining properties.* Its definition distinguished a species from all others. Such a class is constant, it does not change in time. All deviations from the definition of the class are merely "accidents," that is, imperfect manifestations of the essence (eidos). Mill in 1843 introduced the word 'kind' for species (and John Venn introduced "natural kind" in 1866) and philosophers have since used the term natural kind occasionally for species (as defined above), particularly after B. Russell and Quine had adopted it. However, if one reads a history of the term "natural kind" (Hacking 1991) one has the impression that no two authors understood quite the same thing by this term, nor did they clearly discriminate between a term for classes of inanimate objects and biological populations of organisms. There is some discussion among philosophers whether there are several types of natural kinds. But I will refrain from entering that discussion. The traditional species concept going back to Plato's eidos is often referred to as the typological species concept.

The current use of the term species for inanimate objects like nuclear species or species of minerals reflects this classical concept. Up to the 19th century this was the most practical species concept also in biology. The naturalists were busy making an inventory of species in nature and the method they used for the discrimination of species was the identification procedure of downward classification (Mayr 1982, 1992a). Species were recognized by their differences—they were kinds, they were types. This concept was usually referred to as the morphological or typological species concept.

Even though this was virtually the universal concept of species, there were a number of prophetic spirits who, in their writings, foreshadowed a different species concept, later designated as the *Biological Species Concept*. The first among these was perhaps Buffon (Sloan 1987), but a careful search through the natural history literature would probably yield quite a few similar statements. Darwin unquestionably had adopted a biological species concept in the 1830s in his *Transmutation Notebook*, even though later he largely gave it up (Kotller 1978, Mayr 1992b). Throughout the 19th century, quite a few authors proposed a species definition that was an approach to the BSC (Mayr 1957).

Late in the 19th century and in the first quarter of the 20th century, taxonomists like K. Jordan, E. Poulton, L. Plate, and E. Stresemann were among those who most clearly articulated the biological species concept, as will be shown below.

As long as taking the inventory of kinds of organisms was the primary concern of the students of species, the typological species concept was a reasonably satisfactory concept. But when species were studied more carefully, all sorts of properties were discovered that did not fit with a species concept that was strictly based on morphology. This was particularly true for behavioral and ecological properties. Most damaging was the discovery of the unreliability of morphological characteristics for the recognition of biological species.

Morphological difference had traditionally been the decisive criterion of species. Population A (e.g., continental North American savanna sparrows) was determined to be a different species from population B (e.g., savanna sparrows from Sable Island, Nova Scotia), if it was deemed to be sufficiently different from it by morphological characteristics. This definition was very useful in various clerical operations of the taxonomist such as in the cataloguing of species taxa and their arrangement in keys and in collections. However, for two reasons it was inadequate, if not misleading, for a study of species in nature. The first one is that, as is now realized, there are many good biological species that do not differ at all morphologically or only very slightly. Such cryptic species have been designated *sibling species*. They occur at lesser or greater frequency in almost all groups of organisms (Mayr 1948). They are apparently particularly common among protozoans. Sonneborn (1975) eventually recognized 14 sibling species under what he had originally considered a single species, *Paramecium aurelia*. Many sibling species are genetically as different from each other as morphologically highly distinct species. A second reason why a morphological species concept proved unsatisfactory is that there are often numerous different morphological types within a biological species, either due to individual genetic variation or due to different life history categories (males, females, immatures) that are morphologically far more different from each other than are the corresponding morphological types in different species.

The morphological difference between two species fails to shed any light on the true biological significance of species, the Darwinian "why?" question. So-called "morphological species definitions" are in principle merely operational instructions for the demarcation of species taxa. The realization of these deficiencies of the typological species concept led, in due time, to its almost complete replacement among zoologists by the BSC.

Many of the authors who profess to adhere to the morphological species concept do not seem to realize that unconsciously they base their decisions ultimately on the reproductive community principle of the BSC. They combine drastically different phenotypes into a single species because they have observed that they were produced by the same gene pool. This was already done by Linnaeus when he synonymized the names he had given to the female mallard and the immature goshawk.

6. Insufficient or Erroneous Species Criteria.

6.1 Characterized by its Evolutionary Potential. Some 50 years ago the fact that species are not constant, but the product of evolution and still potentially continuing to evolve, was included by several authors in the species definition. For instance, in 1945 A.E. Emerson defined the biological species as follows: "A species is an evolved or evolving genetically distinctive, reproductively isolated, natural population." Indeed, nothing distinguishes a biological species better from a natural kind than its capacity to evolve. Yet, this is not a sufficient criterion. Everything else in living nature also has the capacity to evolve. Every population, every structure and organ is the product of evolution and continues to evolve, genera and higher taxa evolve, and so do faunas and floras. Most of all, the capacity for evolving is not the crucial biological criterion of a species, which is the protection of its gene pool.   It is for this reason that I and most adherents of the BSC omit "evolving" from the species definition.   Those authors who still emphasize the evolutionary aspect of the species have never made it clear what the real significance of species is.

The paleontologist Simpson attempted to make evolution the basis of a species concept: "An evolutionary species is a lineage (an ancestral-descendant sequence of populations) evolving separately from others and with its own unitary evolutionary role and tendencies" (1961, 153). He replaced the clear-cut criterion (reproductive isolation) of the BSC with such undefined vague terms as "maintains its identity" (does this include geographical barriers?), "evolutionary tendencies" (what are they and how can they be determined?), and "historical fate."   What population in nature can ever be classified by its "historical fate" when this is entirely in the future?

Furthermore, as I pointed out previously (Mayr 1988a. 323--324), this concept encounters three additional major difficulties: (1) it is applicable only to monotypic species and every geographical isolate would, by implication, have to be treated as a different species; (2) there are no empirical criteria by which either evolutionary tendency or historical fate can be observed in a given fossil sample (Simpson 1961, 154 160); and (3) the definition does not help in the lower or upper demarcation of chronospecies, even though the main reason why the evolutionary species concept was apparently introduced, was in order to deal with the time dimension, which is not considered in the non-dimensional BSC. Indeed, Simpson's definition is essentially an operational recipe for the demarcation of fossil species.

6.2 Other Unsatisfactory Species Concepts.   The so-called phylogenetic species concept (Wheeler, 1996) is actually nothing more than the revival of a purely morphological species concept (Mayr 1996).   The so-called ecological species concept, based on the niche occupation of a species, is for two reasons not workable.   In almost all more widespread species there are local populations which differ in their niche occupation.   An ecological species definition would require that these populations be called different species even though, on the basis of all other criteria, it is obvious that they are not.   More fatal for the ecological species concept are the trophic species of cichlids (A. Meyer 1990) that differentiate within a single set of offspring from the same parents.   Finally, there are the numerous cases (but none exhaustively analyzed) where two sympatric species seem to occupy the same niche, in conflict with Gause's rule. All this evidence shows not only how many difficulties an ecological species concept faces but also how unable it is to answer the Darwinian "why?" question for the existence of species.

Perhaps Templeton's (1989, 1994) cohesion species concept should be mentioned here. It attempts to combine the best components of several other species concepts but fails to escape the resulting conflicts. It emphasizes the presence of gene flow, but fails to distinguish between the internal (isolating mechanisms) and external (geographic isolation) barriers to gene flow; it stresses cohesion through gene flow, but claims also to be "applicable to taxa reproducing asexually," which have no gene flow. It attempts to characterize an evolutionary lineage, but does not indicate how to delimit such an open-ended lineage at either end; and he does not state how to deal with the geographic variation of demographic-ecological attributes in widespread polytypic species. I do not see any advantages of this concept over the BSC.

6.3 Two Origins of Species. Normally one calls a population a species when it has acquired isolating mechanisms, protecting its gene pool against its parental or a sister species. In other words, such a species is the product of the process of multiplication of species. However, the paleontologist also encounters cases where a phyletic lineage changes over time to such a degree that sooner or later it is considered to be a different species. The occurrence of the origin of such phyletic species is usually ignored when non-paleontologists speak of speciation. Phyletic evolution does not produce an additional entity, it merely modifies an existing one. Nevertheless, the changes are sometimes sufficiently pronounced so that the paleontologist gives a new species name to the modified phyletic lineage. Gingerich (1979), in particular, has called attention to the relative infrequency of such cases. Such new species differ usually only in size and proportions, but not in the acquisition of any notable innovations. Such phyletic speciation must be mentioned because it is what a paleontologist usually seems to have in mind when he speaks of speciation. It is for such species that Simpson proposed the evolutionary species definition. It has been impossible so far to discover any criteria by which a phyletic species can be demarcated against ancestral and descendent "species." It is for this reason that Hennig (1966) rejects the recognition of new species without branching.

In his discussion of the origin of species, Hennig (1966) only considers the case of a phyletic lineage splitting by dichopatric speciation into two daughter species. He considers both daughter species as new species. He ignores the more frequent case where by budding from a phyletic lineage a new daughter species originates through peripatric speciation. By his definition, Hennig is forced to call the phyletic lineage after the budding point a new species, even though it has not changed at all. Hennig's species definition also results in difficulties when a phyletic lineage gradually changes into a new species, even though there has been no splitting of the lineage nor any budding. Hennig is forced to ignore such phyletic speciation no matter how conclusive the indirect (morphological) evidence for the origin of a new species may be. On the whole, whenever a biologist speaks of species, he has in mind the product of the process of multiplication of species, not the product of phyletic evolution.

6.4 Multidimensional Species Taxa.   Species taxa ordinarily have an extension in space (geography) and in time. They are composed of local or temporally circumscribed populations that differ slightly from each other.   Such populations, when they are considered to be conspecific, are combined into a *polytypic species.* The major species problem in species level taxonomy is to decide which local populations to combine into polytypic species.   Since this decision is based on inference, it is always somewhat uncertain.   The paleontologist encounters in the time dimension the same problem which the student of the geographic variation of species encounters in the spatial dimension.   During the period when the typological species concept was dominant, almost any isolated population that differed by a morphological character was called a different species. Since the rise of the BSC, the question is always asked whether or not such a population would interbreed with other populations differing in space or time if they would meet in nature.

The widespread use of polytypic species has several advantages for information conveyance as pointed out by Mayr and Ashlock (1991, 41). Conspecific populations that differ from each other morphologically are called subspecies. If such subspecies are part of a series of contiguous populations, they are a purely taxonomic device. However, they are incipient species if such subspecies are geographically isolated.   They may in due time acquire the needed isolating mechanisms to function as well-separated species. Owing to the gradualness of the process of speciation, every incipient species at one time in its cycle goes through the subspecies stage.

7. A Major Criticism of the Biological Species Concept.

The biological species concept is least vulnerable to criticism in the non-dimensional situation, as I have emphasized in numerous previous papers. When two populations (in reproductive condition) meet at the same place at the same time, they either interbreed because they are conspecific or they do not do so because they are different reproductive communities (different species).   In that case, their isolating mechanisms keep them apart.

A geographically isolated population also has the isolating mechanisms of the species to which it belongs, but they are, so to speak, invisible, since they do not need to be activated. In some of my earlier species definitions I said of isolated populations that they might be "potentially" reproductively isolated. If in the future any contact with a different species population was going to be established, the isolating mechanism would at once spring into action, thereby documenting their existence.

Speciation, as Darwin has shown, is normally a gradual populational phenomenon. Sudden, saltational speciation as in the case of allopolyploidy, seems to be virtually absent in most groups of sexually reproducing organisms. Owing to the gradualness of the speciation process, one should find in nature populations that are on the way to becoming separate species, but have not yet quite completed the process. Such "semi-species" are indeed found. They are documented, for instance, by the so-called zones of secondary hybridization. Here two incipient species, usually expanding from a Pleistocene refuge, hybridize along a more or less long contact line, but the hybrid zone stays narrow, often less than 100 km wide, even though this contact zone may have existed for 5-10,000 years. Both of the two semi-species discriminate against introgressing genes of the other semi-species, as documented by the lowered fertility of hybrid pairs. Hybridization is too indiscriminate in the contact zone to permit a selection for isolating mechanisms, as Darwin already remarked. The effects of continuing hybridization completely override the counterselection against inferior hybrids and introgressing genes so that it does not come to any parapatric speciation. Isolating mechanisms, however, can be further improved after speciation between overlapping species has been completed (Bullin 1989; Lion and Price 1994)

During a period of geographic isolation the presence of species-specific isolating mechanisms can only be inferred. Curiously, there are large numbers of taxonomists who seem to be unaware of how frequent the need is for inference making in scientific theorizing. The most helpful inference on the species status of isolated populations is greater morphological difference as compared to other populations that are seemingly conspecific. To be able to use degree of morphological difference in order to infer species status, one must have a "yard stick," that determines which of the isolated populations already have reached species status and which others have not. Constructing such a yard stick requires a thorough knowledge of related species and subspecies and is a rather technical procedure. It is described in Mayr and Ashlock (1991, 100-105.)

What must be emphasized, because this is so often misunderstood, is that this procedure is not a falling back on a morphological species concept, but simply uses the degree of morphological difference as an indication of the underlying degree of reproductive isolation. This procedure is very much the same as that described so perceptively by G.G. Simpson (1961) for identical twins: an individual is an identical twin not because he is so similar to another individual, but rather, he is so similar to it because he is its identical (monozygotic) twin. Analogously, an individual belongs to species X not because it has the same species-specific characteristics as other individuals of species X, but it has these species-specific characteristics because, like other conspecifics, it is part of the species.

Curiously, Mahner (1994) has reversed the roles of the concept of reproductive community and species-specific characteristics. For a Darwinian to determine the significance of a biological process one always starts with the Darwinian "why?" question. As far as the species is concerned, the answer clearly is protection of the gene pool through establishment of a reproductive community. The next question is "how?" And here the answer is isolating mechanisms and other species-specific attributes. These are indicators of species status, but do not constitute the basic meaning of species. I have pointed this out as the reason why isolation is the primary and recognition (the answer to the how question) the secondary aspect of the species (Mayr 1988b). When I used morphological inferences (Mayr 1992a) to determine which nominal species of plants in the township of Concord (Massachusetts) were good biological species, I did not shift to a morphological species concept, as Whittemore (1993) seemed to think.

8. The Ontology of the Species Taxon.

A considerable clarification of the status of species taxa was achieved when it was realized by some taxonomists that species taxa are not classes but particulars or "individuals" or biopopulations, or whatever other term you may want to use to characterize this difference. Much of the argument on this issue seems to be semantic, and this is not the place to deal once more with that problem. The belief that species are concrete particulars was recently rediscovered by Ghiselin and Hull, but it has actually been the view of many—if not most—naturalists for more than one hundred years, as I have shown (Mayr 1988a). As early as 1866, Haeckel said "Die Art ist ein Individuum." For a detailed discussion of this conclusion, see papers by Ghiselin (1971-1972), Hull (1975), and Mayr (1987, 1988a).

One could also say that organisms that belong to sexually reproducing species have two sets of characteristics: First, those that serve as isolating mechanisms and are jointly responsible for the fact that this population of individuals constitutes a biological species, and, second, all other properties of the species. Organisms which belong to two related species usually share a large number of characteristics but this does not make them conspecific. The important thing is that they differ by a certain limited number of attributes, their *isolating mechanisms*, which prevent them from interbreeding and thus prevent the destruction of the integrity of their gene pool. To repeat, certain individuals are part of a certain species not because they have certain characteristics in common but they share these characteristics because they belong to a single reproductive community, a biological species. And this is the reason why we must rely on the biological meaning of species in articulating the BSC.

9. Difficulties in Delimiting Species Taxa.

There are a number of evolutionary processes that make the delimitation of species taxa from each other and the determination of their rank often very difficult. The most important is so-called mosaic evolution. This means that certain characteristics may evolve much more readily than others. This results in a discord between the message provided by various characteristics. In particular, reproductive isolation and morphological difference often do not evolve in parallel with each other. This is why sibling species exist; they are reproductively isolated but morphologically indistinguishable. There is no simple recipe by which the problem posed by mosaic evolution can be solved. The decision has to be made in each case on the basis of the totality of information as well as the usefulness of the proposed classification.

What is often the basic problem is an insufficiency of needed information. This is why the decision about the status of isolated populations has to be based on inference, it is not given directly by the available data. This is as true for populations that are geographically isolated as for stages in the evolution of a single phyletic lineage.

The basic message which emerges from this account of the numerous difficulties of the species problem is that the definition of the biological species must be based on its biological significance, which is the maintenance of the integrity of well balanced, harmonious gene pools. The actual demarcation of species taxa uses morphological, geographical, ecological, behavioral, and molecular information to infer the rank of isolated populations.

Notes

1. I am not aware of a single major feature of living nature of which this claim could be refuted.

2. By "superior" I meant would be rewarded by leaving a greater number of viable descendants.

References

Anderson, E. (1949). *Introgressive hybridization.* New York: Wiley.

Bullin, R. (1989). "Reinforcement of premating isolation," in Otte and Endler (eds.). *Speciation and its Consequences.* Sunderland, MA: Sinauer, pp. 158-179.

Coyne, J. A., H. A. Orr and D. J. Futuyma. (1988), "Do We Need a New Definition of Species?," *Systematic Zoology 37:* 190-200.

Darwin. C. [1987], *The Correspondence of Darwin.* F. Burkhardt and S. Smith (eds.), Vol. 3 (1844-1846). Cambridge: Cambridge University Press.

Dobzhansky, Th. (1935), "A Critique of' the Species Concept in Biology," *Philosophy of Science* 2,: 344-355.

Emerson, A.E. (1945), "Taxonomic Categories and Population Genetics," *Ent. News.* 56.

Ghiselin, M.T. (1971-1972), "The Individual in the Darwinian Revolution," *New Lit. Hist.* 3:123.

Gingerich, P.D. (1979), "The Stratophenetic Approach to Phylogeny Reconstruction in Vertebrate Paleontology," in J. Cracraft and N. Eldredge (eds.) *Phylogenetic Analysis and Paleontology.* New York: Columbia University Press. pp. 42-77.

Grant, V. (1994). "Evolution of the Species Concept," *Biol. Zentbl.* 113: 401-415.

Hacking, I. (1991). "A tradition of natural kinds," *Philos. Studies* 61:109-126.

Hennig, W. (1966). *Phylogenetic Systematics.* Urbana: University of Illinois Press.

Hull, D.L. (1975). "Are species really individuals?," *Systematic Zoology* 25:174-191.

Kitcher, P. (1989). "Some Puzzles about Species," in M. Ruse (ed.) *What the Philosophy of Biology Is.* Dordrecht: Kluwer Acad. Pub.

Kottler, M. (1978). "Charles Darwin's Biological Species Concept and Theory or Geographic Speciation: the Transmutation Notebooks." *Ann. Sci.* 35:275-297.

Lion, L.W., and Price, T. D. (1994), "Speciation by Reinforcement of Premating Isolation," *Evolution* 48: 1451-1459.

Mahner. M. (1994). "Phanomenalistische Erblast in der Biologie," *Biol Zentbl.* 113: 435-448.

Mayr. E. (1948) "The Bearing of the New Systematics on Genetical Problems: the Nature of Species," *Adv. Genet.* 2: 205-237.

_____. (1949a) "The species concept: semantics versus semantics," *Evolution,* 3:371-372.

_____. (1949b) "Speciation and systematics," in G.L. Jepsen, G.G. Simpson, and E. Mayr (eds.) *Genetics, Paleontology, and Evolution.* Princeton: Princeton University Press. pp. 281-298.

_____. (1957). "Species concepts and definitions," in E. Mayr (ed.), *The Species Problem,* Amer. Assoc. Adv. Sci., Publ. No. 50

_____. (1969). *Principles of Systematic Zoology.* New York: McGraw-Hill, p. 316.

_____. (1970), *Populations, Species, and Evolution.* Cambridge, MA: Harvard University Press.

_____. (1982), *The Growth of Biological Thought: Diversity, Evolution, and Inheritance.* Cambridge, MA and London: The Belknap Press of Harvard University Press.

_____. (1987), "The Ontological Status of Species: Scientific Progress and Philosophical Terminology," *Biology and Philosophy.* 2: 145-166.

_____. (1988a.), *Toward a New Philosophy of Biology: Observations of an Evolutionist.* Cambridge, MA: Harvard University Press.

_____. (1988b.), "The Why and How of Species," *Biology and Philosophy* 3: 431-441.

_____. (1992a.), "A Local Flora and the Biological Species Concept," *American Journal of Botany* 79: 222-238.

_____. (1992b.), "The principle of divergence," *Journal of the History of Biology* 25: 343-359.

_____. (1996), (in press), "The Biological Species Concept," in Q. D. Wheeler (ed.), *The Phylogenetic Species.* Ithica: Cornell University Press.

Mayr, E. and Ashlock, P. (1991), *Principles of Systematic Zoology.* Revised ed. New York: McGraw-Hill.

Meyer, A. (1990), "Ecological and Evolutionary Aspects of the Trophic Polymorphism in *Cichlasoma citrinellum* (Pieces: Cichlidae)," *Biol. J. Linn. Soc* 39: 279-299.

Paterson, H. E. H. (1985), "The Recognition Concept of Species," in E. S. Vrba (ed.) *Species and Speciation,* pp. 21-29. Pretoria: Transvaal Museum Monograph No. 4.

Simpson, G. G. (1961), *Principles of Animal Taxonomy.* New York: Columbia University Press.

Sloan, P. (1987), "Buffon's Species concept. From Logical Unviersals to Historical Individuals: Buffon's Idea of Biological Species," in J. Roger and F. L. Fischer (eds.) *Historie du Concept d'Espece dans les Sciences de la Vie.* Paris: Fondation Singer-Polignac, pp. 101-140.

Sokal, R. R. and Crovello, T. J. (1970), "The Biological Species Concept: a Critical Evaluation," *American Naturalist* 104:127-153.

Sonneborn, T. M. (1975), "The *Paramecium aurelia* complex of fourteen sibling species," *Transactions of the American Microscopical Society* 94: 155-178.

Templeton, A. R. (1980), "The Theory of Speciation via the Founder Principle," *Genetics* 94:1011-38

_____. (1989), "The Meaning of Species and Speciation: A Genetic Perspective," in Otte and Endler (eds.), *Speciation and its Consequences.* Sunderland, MA: Sinauer, pp. 3-27.

_____. (1994), "The Role of Molecular Genetics in Speciation Studies," in B. Schierwater et. al. (ed.) *Molecular Ecology and Evolution.* Basel: Birkhauser, pp. 455-477.

Wheeler, Q. D. (1996), *The Phylogenetic Species.* Ithaca: Cornell University Press.

Whittemore, A. T. (1993), "Species Concepts: A Reply to Ernst Mayr," *Taxon* 42:573-583.

13

Chance and Necessity: Adaptation and Novelty in Evolution

FRANCISCO J. AYALA

Introduction

Knives, birds' wings, and mountain slopes are used for certain purposes: cutting, flying, and climbing. A bird's wings have in common with knives that they have been "designed" for the purpose they serve, which purpose accounts for their existence, whereas mountain slopes have come about by geological processes independently of their uses for climbing. A bird's wings differ from a knife in that they have not been designed or produced by any conscious agent; rather, the wings like the slopes are outcomes of natural processes without any intentional causation.

Darwin discovered that the functional design of living beings can be explained as the result of a natural process, natural selection, without a need to resort to a Creator or other external agent. The origin and adaptations of organisms in their profusion and wondrous variations were thus brought into the realm of science, by explaining them as the result of natural laws manifested in natural processes. The presence of design in living organisms is a distinctive consequence of natural selection in the unending sequence of interactions between organisms and their environments.

Natural selection has been compared to a sieve which retains the rarely arising useful genes and lets go the more frequently arising harmful mutants. Natural selection acts in that way, but it is much more than a purely negative process, for it is able to generate novelty by increasing the probability of otherwise extremely improbable genetic combinations. Natural selection is thus creative in a way. It does not "create" the entities upon which it operates, but it produces adaptive genetic combinations which would not have existed otherwise owing to the enormous improbability of their coming about by chance. Natural selection generates novelty in the form of accumulated hereditary information that is expressed in organisms and their functional attributes.

Evolutionary biologists use teleological language and teleological explanations. I propose that this use is appropriate, because teleological explanations are hypotheses that can be subject to empirical testing. The distinctiveness of teleological hypotheses is that they account for the existence of a feature in terms of the function it serves; for example, wings have evolved and persist because flying is beneficial to birds by increasing their chances of surviving and reproducing. Features of organisms that are explained with teleological hypotheses include structures, such as wings; processes, such as development from egg to adult; and behaviors, such as nest building. A proximate explanation of these features is the function they serve; an ultimate explanation that they all share is their contribution to the reproductive fitness of the organisms. I distinguish several kinds of teleological explanations, such as natural and artificial, or bounded and unbounded, some of which but not others apply to biological explanations.

Darwin's Devolution

The steering wheel of a car has been designed for turning; the human eye has been designed for seeing. Most of us would be willing to accept these two statements, but would probably balk if somebody claimed that a mountain has been designed for climbing. We might note that mountain slopes are there whether or not there is anybody to climb them, but steering wheels would never have been produced if it were not for the purpose they serve. Mountain slopes and steering wheels have in common that they are used for certain purposes, but differ because steering wheels, but not mountain slopes, have been specially created for the purpose they serve. This is what we mean when we say that steering wheels are "designed" for turning: the reason why steering wheels exist at all and exhibit certain features is that they have been designed for turning the car. This is not so with mountain slopes. But what about eyes? I will expound in the pages that follow the proposition that human eyes share something in common with steering wheels and something with mountain slopes. Human eyes like steering wheels have been "designed," because were it not for the function of seeing they serve, eyes would have never come to be; and the features exhibited by eyes specifically came to be in order to serve for seeing. But eyes share in common with mountain slopes that both came about by natural processes, the eyes by natural selection, the mountain slopes by geological movements and erosion. Steering wheels, on the contrary, are designed and produced by human engineers. The issue at hand is, then, how to account for design, as in the design of the eye, without a designer. This conundrum was solved by Charles Darwin.[1]

In *The Origin of Species* Darwin accumulated an impressive number of observations supporting the evolutionary origin of living organisms. Moreover, and most importantly, he advanced a causal explanation of evolutionary change—the theory of natural selection, which provides a natural account of the design of organisms, or as we say in biology, their adaptation. Darwin accepted that organisms are adapted to live in their environments, and that their parts are adapted to the specific functions they serve. Penguins are adapted to live in the cold, the wings of birds are made to fly, and the eye is made to see. Darwin accepted the facts of adaptation, but advanced a scientific hypothesis to account for the facts. It may count as Darwin's greatest accomplishment that he brought the design aspects of nature into the realm of science. The wonderful designs of myriad plants and animals could now be explained as the result of natural laws manifested in natural processes, without recourse to an external Designer or Creator.

Before Darwin, the obvious adaptations of organisms and their organs were commonly attributed to the design of an omniscient Creator. In the nineteenth century the English theologian William Paley in his *Natural Theology* (1802) elaborated the argument-from-design as forceful demonstration of the existence of the Creator. The functional design of the human eye, argued Paley, provides conclusive evidence of an all-wise Creator. It would be absurd to suppose, he wrote, that the human eye by mere chance "should have consisted, first, of a series of transparent lenses ... secondly of a black cloth or canvas spread out behind these lenses so as to receive the image formed by pencils of light transmitted through them, and placed at the precise geometrical distance at which, and at which alone, a distinct image could be formed ... thirdly of a large nerve communicating between this membrane and the brain." Similarly, the Bridgewater Treatises, published between 1833 and 1840, were written by eminent scientists and philosophers to set forth "the Power, Wisdom, and Goodness of God as manifested in the Creation." The complex functional organization of the human hand was, for example, cited as incontrovertible evidence that the hand had been designed by the same omniscient Power that had created the world.

The strength of the argument-from-design to demonstrate the role of the Creator is easily set forth. Wherever there is function or design we look for its author. A steering wheel is made for turning, a knife is made for cutting, and a clock is made to tell time; their functional designs have been contrived by an engineer, a blacksmith, and a watchmaker. The exquisite design of Leonardo da Vinci's *Mona Lisa* proclaims that it was created by a gifted artist following a preconceived purpose. Organisms and their structures, organs, and behaviors are also precisely designed to serve certain functions. The functional design of organisms and their features would therefore seem to argue for the existence of a designer.

Natural Selection and Adaptation

The central argument of the theory of natural selection is summarized by Darwin in *The Origin of Species* as follows:

> As more individuals are produced than can possibly survive, there must in every case be a struggle for existence, either one individual with another of the same species, or with the individuals of distinct species, or with the physical conditions of life. ... Can it, then, be thought improbable, seeing that variations useful to man have undoubtedly occurred, that other variations useful in some way to each being in the great and complex battle of life, should sometimes occur in the course of thousands of generations? If such do occur, can we doubt (remembering that more individuals are bom than can possibly survive) that individuals having any advantage, however slight, over others, would have the best chance of surviving and of procreating their kind? On the other hand, we may feel sure that any variation in the least degree injurious would be rigidly destroyed. This preservation of favorable variation and the rejection of injurious variations, I call Natural Selection.[2]

Darwin's argument addresses the problem of explaining the adaptive features of organisms. Darwin argues that adaptive variations ("variations useful in some way to each being") occasionally appear, and that these are likely to increase the reproductive chances of their carriers. Over the generations favorable variations will be preserved, injurious ones will be eliminated. In one place, Darwin avers: "I can see no limit to the amount of change, to the beauty and infinite complexity of the coadaptations between all organic beings, one with another and with their physical conditions of life, which may be effected in the long course of time by nature's power of selection."[3] Natural selection was proposed by Darwin primarily to account for the adaptive organization, or "design," of living beings; it is a process that promotes or maintains adaptation. Evolutionary change through time and evolutionary diversification (multiplication of species) are not directly promoted by natural selection, but they often ensue as by-products of natural selection fostering adaptation to diverse and ever changing environments.

Darwin formulated natural selection primarily as differential survival. The modern understanding of the principle of natural selection is formulated in genetic and statistical terms as differential reproduction. Natural selection implies that some genes and genetic combinations are transmitted to the following generations on the average more frequently than their alternates. Such genetic units will become more common in every subsequent generation and their alternates less common. Natural selection is simply a statistical bias in the relative rate of reproduction of alternative genetic units. But the reproductive bias, argued Darwin, will likely favor the variants that are useful to the organisms, precisely because it is this usefulness that increases the reproductive chances of their carriers. Gazelles that run swifter will better escape their predators and so gazelles come to have swift legs.

Evolutionary Novelty

Some strains of the colon bacterium, *Escherichia coli*, in order to be able to reproduce in a culture medium, require that a certain substance, the amino acid histidine, be provided in the medium. When a few such bacteria are added to a cubic centimeter of liquid culture medium, they multiply rapidly and produce between two and three billion bacteria in a few hours. Spontaneous mutations to streptomycin resistance occur in normal (i.e., sensitive) bacteria at rates of the order of one in one hundred million (1×10^{-8}) cells. In our bacterial culture we expect between twenty and thirty bacteria to be resistant to streptomycin due to spontaneous mutation. If a proper concentration of the antibiotic is added to the culture, only the resistant cells survive. The twenty or thirty surviving bacteria will start reproducing, however, and allowing a few hours for the necessary number of cell divisions, several billion bacteria are produced, all resistant to streptomycin. Among cells requiring histidine as a growth factor, spontaneous mutants able to reproduce in the absence of histidine arise at rates of about four in one hundred million (4×10^{-8}) bacteria. The streptomycin resistant cells may now be transferred to a culture with streptomycin but with no histidine. Most of them will not be able to reproduce, but about a hundred will start reproducing until the available medium is saturated.

Natural selection has produced in two steps bacterial cells resistant to streptomycin and not requiring histidine for growth. The probability of the two mutational events happening in the same bacterium is of about four in ten million billion ($1 \times 10^{-8} \times 4 \times 10^{-8} = 4 \times 10^{-16}$) cells. An event of such low probability is unlikely to occur even in a large laboratory culture of bacterial cells. With natural selection cells having both properties are the common result.[4]

As illustrated by the bacterial example, natural selection produces combinations of genes that would otherwise be highly improbable because natural selection proceeds stepwise. The vertebrate eye did not appear suddenly in all its present perfection. Its formation requires the appropriate integration of many genetic units, and thus the eye could not have resulted from random processes alone. The ancestors of today's vertebrates had for more than half a billion years some kind of organs sensitive to light. Perception of light, and later vision, were important for these organisms' survival and reproductive success. Sunlight is, and as been for millions of years, a pervasive feature of the environments in which many animals live.[5] Accordingly, natural selection has favored genes and gene combinations promoting the functional efficiency of the eye. Such genetic units gradually accumulated, eventually leading to the highly complex and efficient vertebrate eye.[6] Natural selection can account for the rise and spread of genetic constitutions, and therefore of types of organisms, that would never have existed under the uncontrolled action of random mutation. In this sense, natural selection is a creative process, although it does not create the raw materials—the genes—upon which it acts.

Natural selection has no foresight, nor does it operate according to some preconceived plan. Rather it is a purely natural process resulting from the interacting properties of physicochemical and biological entities. Natural selection is simply a consequence of the differential multiplication of living beings. It has some appearance of purposefulness because it is conditioned by the environment: which organisms reproduce more effectively depends on what variations they possess that are useful in the environment where the organisms live. But natural selection does not anticipate the environments of the future; drastic environmental changes may be insuperable to organisms that were previously thriving.

Natural selection does not strive to produce predetermined kinds of organisms, but only organisms that are adapted to their present environments. Which characteristics are selected depends on which variations happen to be present at a given time in a given place. This in turn depends on the random process of mutation, as well as on the previous history of the organisms (i.e., on the genetic make-up they have as a consequence of their previous evolution). Natural selection is an "opportunistic" process. The variables determining in what direction it will go are the environment, the preexisting constitution of the organisms, and the randomly arising mutations.

Determinism and Contingency

Adaptation to a given environment may occur in a variety of different ways. An example may be taken from the adaptations of plant life to desert climate. The fundamental adaptation is to the condition of dryness, which involves the danger of desiccation. During a major part of the year, sometimes for several years in succession, there is no rain. Plants have accomplished the urgent necessity of saving water in different ways. Cacti have transformed their leaves into spines, having made their stems into barrels containing a reserve of water; photosynthesis is performed in the surface of the stem instead of in the leaves. Other plants have no leaves during the dry season, but after it rains they burst into leaves and flowers and produce seeds. Ephemeral plants germinate from seeds, grow, flower, and produce seeds—all within the space of the few weeks while rainwater is available; the rest of the year the seeds lie quiescent in the soil.[7]

The opportunistic character of natural selection is also well-evidenced by the phenomenon of adaptive radiation. The evolution of *Drosophila* flies in Hawaii is a relatively recent adaptive radiation. There are about 1,500 *Drosophila* species in the world. Approximately 500 of them have evolved in the Hawaiian archipelago, although this has a small area, about one twenty-fifth the size of California. Moreover, the morphological, ecological, and behavioral diversity of Hawaiian *Drosophila* exceeds that of *Drosophila* in the rest of the world.

Why should have such "explosive" evolution have occurred in Hawaii? The overabundance of *Drosophila* flies there contrasts with the absence of many other insects. The ancestors of Hawaiian *Drosophila* reached the archipelago before other groups of insects did, and thus they found a multitude of unexploited opportunities for making a living. They responded by a rapid adaptive radiation; although they are all probably derived from a single colonizing species, they adapted to the diversity of opportunities available in diverse places or at different times by developing appropriate adaptations, which range broadly from one to another species.

The process of natural selection can explain the adaptive organization of organisms; as well as their diversity and evolution as a consequence of their adaptation to the multifarious and ever changing conditions of life. The fossil record shows that life has evolved in a haphazard fashion. The radiations, expansions, relays of one form by another, occasional but irregular trends, and the ever present extinctions, are best explained by natural selection of organisms subject to the vagaries of genetic mutation and environmental challenge.

Natural selection accounts for the design of organisms, as expounded earlier, because adaptive variations tend to increase the probability of survival and reproduction of their carriers at the expense of maladaptive, or less adaptive, variations. The arguments of Paley and other natural theologians against the incredible improbability of chance accounts of the origin of organisms are well taken as far as they go. But neither these scholars, nor any other authors before Darwin, were able to discern that there is a natural process (namely, natural selection) that is not random but rather is oriented and able to generate order or "create." The traits that organisms acquire in their evolutionary histories are not fortuitous but determined by their functional utility to the organisms.

Chance is, nevertheless, an integral part of the evolutionary process. The mutations that yield the hereditary variations available to natural selection arise at random, independently of whether they are beneficial or harmful to their carriers. This random process (as well as others that come to play in the great theatre of life) is counteracted by natural selection, which preserves what is useful and eliminates the harmful. Without mutation, evolution could not happen because there would be no variations that could be differentially conveyed from one to another generation. Without natural selection, the mutation process would yield disorganization and extinction because most mutations are disadvantageous. Mutation and selection have jointly driven the marvelous process that starting from microscopic organisms has spurted orchids, birds, and humans.

The theory of evolution manifests chance and necessity jointly intertwined in the stuff of life; randomness and determinism interlocked in a natural process that has brought forth the most complex, diverse, and beautiful entities in the universe: the organisms that populate the earth, including humans who think and love, endowed with free will and creative powers, and able to analyze the process of evolution itself that brought them into existence. This was Darwin's fundamental discovery, that there is a natural process that is creative, though not conscious.

Teleological Explanations

As I have written elsewhere,[8] the biological literature abounds in statements such as the following (*emphasis* added): "Any biological mechanism produces at least one effect that can properly be called its *goal*: vision for the eye or reproduction and dispersal for the apple ... Thus I would say that reproduction and dispersal are the *goals*, or *functions* or *purposes* of apples and that the apple is a means or mechanism by which such goals are realized by apple trees."[9] "Generation by generation, step by step, the *designs* of all the diverse organisms alive today—from redwoods and manta rays to humans and yeast—were permuted out of the original, very simple, single-celled ancestor through an immensely long sequence of successive modifications."[10] "[T]he design of eyes reflects the properties of light, objects, and surfaces; the design of milk reflects the dietary requirements of infants the design of claws reflects things such as the properties of prey animals, the strength of predator limbs, and the task of capture and dismemberment."[11] "Fig wasps don't transport pollen for food. They deliberately take it on board, using special pollen-carrying pockets, *for the sole purpose* of fertilizing figs (which benefits the wasps only in a more indirect way)."[12] "Our mouth, throat, and larynx ... were originally '*designed*' for swallowing food and breathing. They were modified so that we could produce sounds that were easy to understand."[13] These statements refer in one way or other to the functional organization of organisms and their constituent parts that comes about by natural selection, as Darwin saw it. Nobel Laureate Peter Medawar and Jeanne Medawar have written that "It is folly or ignorance to deny that the purpose of nests is to protect the relatively helpless young of birds and mammals ... The purpose of teeth ... is mastication; of eyes to see, and of ears to hear."[14]

No similar statements are found in the writings of physical scientists. The configuration of sodium chloride depends on the structure of sodium and chlorine, but no chemist is likely to write that sodium chloride has been *designed* for certain purposes, such as tasting salty. The earth's continents move, but geologists do not claim that this is for the **purpose** of facilitating vicariate evolution. The motion of the earth around the sun results from the laws of gravity, but astrophysicists do not state that this happens in order to produce the seasons.

Biologists need to account for the functional features of organisms, their "design," in terms of the goals or purposes they serve, which is accomplished by means of teleological hypotheses or teleological explanations. Physical scientists do not face similar demands. A dictionary definition of "teleology" is "the use of design, purpose, or utility as an explanation of any natural phenomenon" (*Merriam Webster's Collegiate Dictionary, Tenth Edition* 1994). The same dictionary defines "teleological" as "exhibiting or relating to design or purpose esp. in nature." *The Oxford Dictionary* includes virtually identical definitions: "teleological," "dealing with design or purpose, esp. in natural phenomena"; "teleology," "such design as exhibited in natural objects or phenomena."

An object or a behavior can be said to be teleological, or telic, when it gives evidence of design or appears to be directed towards certain ends, goals, or purposes.[15] For example, the behavior of human beings is often teleological. A person who buys an airplane ticket, reads a book, or cultivates the earth is trying to achieve a certain goal: getting to a given city, acquiring knowledge, or getting food. Objects and machines made by people also are usually teleological: a knife is made for cutting, a clock is made for telling time, a thermostat is made to regulate temperature. In a similar fashion, I have argued, features of organisms have come to be because they serve certain purposes or functions, and in this sense they can be said to be teleological: a bird's wings are for flying, eyes are for seeing, kidneys are constituted for regulating the composition of the blood. The features of organisms that may be said to be teleological are those that can be identified as adaptations, whether they are structures like a wing or a hand, organs like a kidney, or behaviors like the courtship displays of a peacock. Adaptations are features of organisms that have come about by natural selection because they increase the reproductive success of their carriers.

Inanimate objects and processes (other than those created by humans) are not teleological because they are not directed toward specific ends, they do not exist to serve certain purposes. The configuration of sodium chloride depends on the structure of sodium and chlorine, but it makes no sense to say that that structure is made up so as to serve a certain end. Similarly, the slopes of a mountain are the result of certain geological processes and weather erosion, but did not come about so as to serve a certain end, such as skiing. The motion of the earth around the sun results from the laws of gravity, but it does not exist in order to satisfy certain ends or goals, such as producing the seasons.

We may use sodium chloride as food, a mountain for skiing, and take advantage of the seasons, but the use that we make of these objects or phenomena is not the reason why they came into existence or why they have certain configurations. On the other hand, a knife and a car exist and have particular configurations precisely in order to serve the ends of cutting and transportation. Similarly, the wings of birds came about precisely because they permitted flying, which was reproductively advantageous. The mating display of peacocks came about because it increased the chances of mating and thus of leaving progeny.

The previous observations point out the essential characteristics of teleological phenomena, i.e., phenomena whose existence and configuration can be explained teleologically. I now propose the following definition. "Teleological explanations account for the existence of a certain features in a system by demonstrating the feature's contribution to a specific property or state of the system, in such a way that this contribution *is the reason why the feature or behavior exists at all.*" Teleological explanations require that the feature or behavior being explained contribute to the existence or maintenance of a certain state or property of the system. But, the essential component of my definition is that teleological explanations apply only to features or behaviors that could not have come about were it not for the particular end or purpose they serve. The end, goal, or purpose served is, therefore, the explanatory reason for the existence of the feature or behavior and its distinctive characteristics. A teleological hypothesis purports to identify the function or purpose that accounts for the evolution of a particular feature.

The configuration of a molecule of sodium chloride contributes to its property of tasting salty and therefore to its use as food, not vice versa; the potential use of sodium chloride as food is not the reason why it has a particular molecular configuration. The motion of the earth around the sun is the reason why seasons exist; the existence of the seasons is not the reason why the earth moves about the sun. On the other hand, the sharpness of a knife can be explained teleologically because the knife has been created precisely to serve the purpose of cutting. Automobiles exist and have particular configurations because they serve for transportation, and thus can be explained teleologically. (Not all features of a car contribute to the purpose of efficient transportation— some features are added for aesthetic or other reason. But as long as a feature is added because it exhibits certain properties—like appeal to the aesthetic preferences of potential customer—it may be explained teleologically. Nevertheless, there may be features in a car, a knife, or any other human-made object that need not be explained teleologically. That knives have handles is to be explained teleologically, but the fact that a particular handle is made of pine rather than oak might simply be due to the availability of material. Similarly, not all features of organisms have teleological explanations.[16]

Many features and behaviors of organisms meet the requirements of teleological explanations. The human hand, the bird's wings, the structure and behavior of kidneys, the mating displays of peacocks are examples already given. In general, as pointed out above, those features and behaviors that are considered adaptations are explained teleologically. This is simply because adaptations are features that come about by natural selection. As I have indicated above, an account of natural selection says that among alternative genetic variants that arise by mutation or recombination, the ones that become propagated in a species are those that contribute more to the reproductive success of their carriers. The effects on reproductive success are mediated by some function or property. Wings and hands acquired their present configuration through long-term accumulation of genetic variants adaptive to their carriers.

How natural selection yields adaptive features may now be reiterated with a simple human example where the adaptation arises as a consequence of a single gene mutation, such as the presence of normal hemoglobin rather than hemoglobin S in most people.   One amino acid substitution in the beta hemoglobin chain results in hemoglobin molecules less efficient for oxygen transport. The general occurrence in human populations of normal rather than S hemoglobins is explained teleologically by the contribution of hemoglobin to effective oxygen transport and thus to reproductive success. A second simple and well known non-human example concerns the difference between peppered-gray moths and melanic moths. The replacement of gray moths by melanics in polluted regions is explained teleologically by the fact that in such regions melanism decreases the probability that a moth be eaten by a bird.   The predominance of peppered forms in non-polluted regions is similarly explained.[17]

But it must also be reiterated that not all features of organisms need to be explained teleologically, since not all come about as a direct result of natural selection. Some features may become established by random genetic drift, by chance association with adaptive traits, by physical constraint, by historical contingency, or in general by processes other than natural selection. Proponents of the neutrality theory of protein evolution, for example, argue that many alternative protein variants are adaptively equivalent to one another.   Most evolutionists would admit that at least in certain sites the selective differences between alternative nucleotides in DNA or of amino acids in proteins must be virtually nil, particularly when population size is very small.   The presence of one nucleotide or amino acid rather than another adaptively equivalent to the first, would not then be explained teleologically, but as a consequence of chance and historical contingency.

Teleological Features and Behaviors in Organisms

I will now identify three categories of biological phenomena where teleological explanations are pertinent, although the distinction between the categories need not always be clearly defined, and it is also possible to subdivide them or reformulate them in a different and more prolific array. These three classes of teleological phenomena are established according to the mode of relationship between the structure or process and the property or end-state that accounts for its presence. Other classifications of teleological phenomena are possible according to other principles of distinction, including some that are suggested below.

(1) A behavior such that the end-state or goal is consciously anticipated by the agent. This is purposeful activity, which if it is understood in a strict sense occurs probably only in humans. With a lesser degree of intentionality, behaviors initiated in order to reach a goal also occur in other animals. I am

acting teleologically when I buy an airplane ticket to fly to Mexico City. A cheetah hunting a gazelle gives at least the appearance of purposeful behavior. We may notice that according to those who believe in "special" creation, the existence of organisms and their adaptations is the result of the consciously intended activity of a Creator seeking to create specifically each kind. Biologists recognize purposeful activity in the living world, at least in humans; but the existence of the living world, including humans, need not be explained as the result of purposeful behavior.[18]

(2) Self-regulating of teleonomic systems, when there exists a mechanism that enables the system to reach or to maintain a specific property in spite of environmental fluctuations. The regulation of body temperature in mammals is a teleological mechanism of this kind. In general, the homeostatic reactions of organisms belong to this category of teleological phenomena.

Two types of homeostasis are usually distinguished by biologists— physiological and developmental homeostasis, although intermediate and additional types do exist.[19] Physiological homeostatic reactions enable the organism to maintain a certain physiological steady state in spite of environmental shocks. The regulation of the composition of the blood by the kidneys, or the hypertrophy of muscle in case of strenuous use, are examples of this type of homeostasis.

Developmental homeostasis refers to the regulation of the different paths that an organism may follow in its progression from zygote to adult. The development of a chicken from an egg is a typical example of developmental homeostasis. The process can be influenced by the environment in various ways, but the characteristics of the adult individual, at least within a certain range, are largely predetermined in the fertilized egg.[20]

Self-regulating systems or servo-mechanisms built by humans belong in this second category of teleological phenomena. A simple servo-mechanism is a thermostat unit that maintains a specified room temperature by turning on and off the source of heat or cooling. Self-regulating mechanisms of this kind, living or human-made, are controlled by feed-back information. Robots programmed to perform certain functions are additional examples.

(3) Organs, limbs, and other features anatomically and physiologically constituted to perform a certain function. The human hand is made for grasping, and the eye for vision. Tools and certain types of human-made machines are teleological in this third sense. A watch, for instance, is made to tell time, and a faucet to draw water. The distinction between the (2) and (3) categories of teleological systems is sometimes blurred. Thus, the human eye is able to regulate itself within a certain range to the conditions of brightness and distance so as to perform its function more effectively.

Adaptation and Teleology

The adaptations of organisms—whether organs, homeostatic mechanisms, or patterns of behavior—are explained teleologically as a consequence of natural selection, because their existence is ultimately accounted for in terms of their contribution to the reproductive fitness of the species. A feature of an organism that increases its reproductive fitness will be selectively favored. Given enough generations it will extend to the whole species.

Patterns of behavior, such as the migratory habits of certain birds or the web-spinning of spiders, have developed because they favored the reproductive success of their possessors in the environments where the population lived. Similarly, natural selection can account for the existence of homeostatic mechanisms. Some living processes can be operative only within a certain range of conditions. If the environmental conditions oscillate frequently beyond the functional range of the process, natural selection will favor self-regulating mechanisms that maintain the system within the functional range. In humans, death results if the body temperature is allowed to rise or fall by more than a few degrees above or below normal. Body temperature is regulated by dissipating heat in warm environments through perspiration and dilation of the blood vessels in the skin. In cool weather the loss of heat is minimized, and additional heat is produced by increased activity and shivering. Finally, the adaptation of an organ or feature to its function is also explained teleologically by natural selection in that the existence of the organ or feature is accounted for in terms of the contribution it makes to the reproductive success of its carriers. The vertebrate eye arose because genetic mutations responsible for its development occurred, and were gradually combined in progressively more efficient patterns, the successive changes increasing the reproductive fitness of their possessors in the environments in which they lived.

Proximate and Ultimate Teleology of Natural Selection

There are in all organisms two levels of teleology that may be labeled *proximate* (or *particular*) and *ultimate* (or *generic*). There usually exists a specific and proximate end for every feature of an animal or plant. The existence of the feature is thus explained in terms of the function or property that it serves. This function or property can be said to be the particular or proximate end of the feature. Thus, seeing is a particular, specific, or proximate end served by an eye, and flying is a particular, specific, or proximate end served by a wing. There is also an ultimate goal to which all features contribute or have contributed in the past—reproductive success. The general or ultimate end to which all features and their functions contribute is increased reproductive efficiency. The presence of the functions themselves—and therefore of the features which serve them—is ultimately explained by their contribution to the reproductive fitness of the organisms in which they exist. It is in this sense that the ultimate source of teleological explanation in biology is the principle of natural selection.

It is because of the reasoning just advanced that I suggested in the past that natural selection can be said to be a teleological process in a causal sense, namely as a distinctive process, uniquely acting in the living world, which accounts for the adaptive features of organisms.[21] I could have said instead that natural selection is a *teleology-inducing* process, intending to convey the same idea. But this might also be misunderstood and it might be best to discard these designations. Natural selection is not an entity or an agent, and thus it is not a cause in the usual sense. Nor does natural selection result in predetermined or pre-conceived features or organisms, as I will further expound. To reiterate the point, natural selection is not an entity but a purely material or natural process governed by the laws of physics, chemistry, and other natural laws. If one would want to designate it as a "teleological process" would be exclusively to convey the meaning that natural selection results in the production and preservation of end-directed organs and behaviors, when the functions these serve contribute to the reproductive effectiveness of the organisms.

In any case, the process of natural selection is not at all teleological in a different sense. Natural selection is not in any way directing toward the production of specific kinds of organisms or toward organisms having certain specific properties. The over-all process of evolution cannot be said to be teleological in the sense of proceeding toward certain specified goals, preconceived or not. Natural selection is nothing else than the outcome of differential reproduction. The final result of natural selection for any species may be extinction, as shown by the fossil record, if the species fails to cope with environmental change.

I have argued that the presence of organs, processes, and patterns and behavior can be explained teleologically by exhibiting their contribution to the reproductive fitness of the organisms in which they occur. This does not imply that reproductive fitness is a consciously intended goal. Such intent must be denied except in the case of the voluntary behavior of humans. In teleological explanations the end-state or goal is not to be understood as the efficient cause of the object or process that it explains. The end-state is causally posterior, the outcome of a process, not its cause.

Natural versus Artificial Teleology; and Bounded versus Unbounded Teleology

I have already identified several kinds of biological phenomena that call for teleological accounts, and have pointed out that such accounts also apply to purposeful behavior and to human made objects. It will be helpful to characterize some differentiating features of these categories of teleological entities; particularly, the biological in general and the distinctively human.

Actions are *purposeful* when an end-state or goal is consciously intended by an agent. Thus, a person mowing a lawn is acting teleologically in the purposeful sense; a lion hunting deer and a bird building a nest manifest at least the appearance of purposeful behavior. A knife, a car, and a thermostat are objects or systems intended (and produced) by humans. Actions or objects resulting from purposeful behavior may be said to exhibit *artificial* (or external) teleology. Their teleological features have come about because they were consciously intended by some agent.

Systems with teleological features that are not due to the purposeful action of an agent but result from natural process may be said to exhibit *natural* (or *internal*) teleology. The wings of birds have a natural teleology; they serve an end, flying, but their configuration is not due to the conscious design of any agent. The development of an egg into a chicken is a teleological process also of the internal or natural kind, since it comes about as a natural process, both in terms of its proximate causation, the concatenation of events by which the egg ultimately develops into a chicken; and in its remote causation, the evolutionary process by which chicken and their developmental processes came to be.

We may distinguish two kinds of natural teleology: *determinate* (or *bounded* or *necessary*) and *contingent* (or *indeterminate* or *unbounded*). This distinction applies as well to purposeful objects and behaviors, but human actions are predominantly determinate, in the sense that they are consciously intended. Humans can of course walk randomly or act aimlessly and can produce objects, such as a die, that behave randomly, but for the most part these are nevertheless products of intentionality.

Determinate natural teleology exists when a specific end-state is reached in spite of environmental fluctuations. The development of an egg into a chicken, or of a human zygote into a human being, are examples of determinate natural teleological processes. The regulation of body temperature in a mammal is another example. In general, the homeostatic processes of organisms are instances of determinate natural teleology.

Indeterminate or unbounded teleology occurs when the end-state served is not specifically intended or predetermined, but rather is the result of a natural process selecting one among several available alternatives. For teleology to exist, the selection of one alternative over another must be deterministic and not purely stochastic. But what alternative happens to be selected may depend on environmental and/or historical circumstances and thus the specific end-state is not generally predictable. Indeterminate teleology results from a mixture of stochastic (at least from the point of view of the teleological system) and deterministic events.

Many features of organisms are teleological in the indeterminate sense. The evolution of birds' wings requires teleological explanation: the genetic constitutions responsible for their configuration came about because wings serve for flying and flying contributes to the reproductive success of birds. But there was nothing in the constitution of the remote ancestors of birds that would necessitate the appearance of wings in their descendants. Wings came about as the consequence of a long sequence of events, where at each stage the most advantageous alternative was selected among those that happened to be available; which alternatives were available at any one time depended at least in part on contingent events.

In spite of the role played by stochastic events in the phylogenetic history of birds, it would be mistaken to say that wings are not teleological features. As pointed out earlier, there are differences between the teleology of an organism's adaptations and the non-teleological potential uses of natural inanimate objects. A mountain may have features appropriate for skiing, but those features did not come about so as to provide skiing slopes. On the other hand, the wings of birds came about precisely because they serve for flying. One explanatory reason for the existence of wings and their configuration is the end they serve—flying—which in turn contributes to the reproductive success of birds. If wings did not serve an adaptive function they would have never come about, and would gradually disappear over the generations.

The indeterminate character of the outcome of natural selection over time is due to a variety of non-deterministic factors. The outcome of natural selection depends, first, on what alternative genetic variants happen to be available at any one time. This in turn depends on the stochastic processes of mutation and recombination, and also on the past history of any given population. (Which new genes may arise by mutation and which new genetic constitutions may arise by recombination depend on which genes happen to be present—which depends on previous history. The outcome of natural selection depends also on the conditions of the physical and biotic environment. Which alternatives among available genetic variants may be favored by selection depends on the particular set of environmental conditions to which a population is exposed. The historical process of evolution is contingent, but at each step there is a predominantly deterministic component, provided by the natural selection of favorable variants among those that happen to be present. Organisms are adapted to their environments and exhibit adaptive features owing to this deterministic component. The contingency of history and environment make long term evolution undetermined or unbounded. There can be little doubt that if the process of evolution on earth would start again from where it was three billion years ago, the evolved organisms would be conspicuously different from the ones that have come about in the first run of the process.

Teleology and Causality

Teleological explanations are fully compatible with causal explanations.[22] It is possible, at least in principle, to give a causal account of the various physical and chemical processes in the development of an egg into a chicken, or of the physicochemical, neural, and muscular interactions involved in the functioning of the eye. (I use the "in principle" clause to imply that any component of the process can be elucidated as a causal process if it is investigated in sufficient detail and in depth; but I know of no developmental process for which all the steps have been so investigated, with the possible exception of the flatworm *Caenorhabditis elegans*. The development of *Drosophila* fruitflies has also become known in much detail, but not yet completely.) It is also possible in principle to describe the causal processes by which one genetic variant becomes eventually established in a population. But these causal explanations do not make it unnecessary to advance teleological explanations where appropriate. Both teleological and causal explanations are called for in evolutionary biology.

According to Nagel, "a teleological explanation can always be transformed into a causal one." Consider a typical teleological statement in biology, "The function of gills in fishes is respiration." This statement is a telescoped argument the content of which can be unraveled approximately as follows: Fish respire; if fish have no gills, they do not respire; therefore fish have gills. According to Nagel, the difference between a teleological explanation and a non-teleological one is, then, one of emphasis rather than of asserted content. A teleological explanation directs our attention to "the *consequences* for a given system of a constituent part or process." The equivalent non-teleological formulation focuses attention on "some of the *conditions* ... under which the system persists in its characteristic organization and activities."[23]

Nagel's account, however, misses an essential feature of teleological explanations, which invalidates his claim that they are equivalent to (even if less cumbersome than) causal accounts. Although a teleological explanation can be reformulated in a non-teleological one, the teleological explanation connotes something more than the equivalent non-teleological one. In the first place, a teleological explanation implies that the system under consideration is directively organized. For that reason teleological explanations are appropriate in biology and in the domain of human creations but make no sense when used in the physical sciences to describe phenomena like the fall of a stone or the slopes of a mountain. Teleological explanations imply, while non-teleological ones do not, that there exists a distinctive, or specific means-to-end relationship in the systems under description the eye is for seeing, the egg develops into a chicken, the knife is used for cutting.

In addition to connoting that the system under consideration is directively organized, and most importantly, teleological explanations account for the existence of specific functions in a system and more generally for the existence of the directive organization itself. A teleological explanation accounts for the presence in an organism of a certain feature, say the gills, because it contributes to the performance or maintenance of a certain function, respiration in this example. The teleological explanation also connotes, in the case of organisms, that the function came about because it contributes to the reproductive fitness of the organism. In the non-teleological translation given above, the major premise states that "fish respire." Such formulation assumes the presence of a specified function, respiration, but it does not account for its existence. A teleological explanation implicitly (or explicitly) accounts for the presence of the function itself by connoting (or stating explicitly) that the function in question contributes to the reproductive fitness of the organism in which it exists and that *such is the reason why the function and feature came about in evolution.* The teleological explanation gives the reason why the system is directively organized. The apparent purposefulness of the ends-to-means relationship existing in organisms is a result of the process of natural selection which favors the development of any organization that increases the reproductive fitness of the organisms.

It follows that teleological explanations are not only acceptable in biology, but also indispensable as well as distinctive of the discipline. It further follows that for this reason alone (and I have alleged others) biology cannot be reduced to the physical sciences.[24]

Teleological Explanations as Testable Hypotheses

One question biologists ask about features of organisms is "What for?" That is, "What is the function or role of a particular structure or process?" The answer to this question must be formulated teleologically. A causal account of the operation of the eye is satisfactory as far as it goes, but it does not tell all that is relevant about the eye, namely that it is useful to the organism because it serves to see. Evolutionary biologists are interested in the question why one particular genetic alternative rather than others came to be established in a species. This question also calls for teleological explanations of the type: "Eyes came into existence because they serve to see, and seeing increases reproductive success of certain organisms in particular circumstances." In fact, eyes came about in several independent evolutionary lineages: cephalopods, arthropods, vertebrates.[25]

There are two questions that must be addressed by a teleological account of evolutionary events. First, there is the question of how a genetic variant contributes to reproductive success; a teleological account states that an existing genetic constitution (say, the gene coding for a normal hemoglobin beta chain) enhances reproductive fitness better than alternative constitutions. Then there is the question of how the specific genetic constitution of an organism enhances its reproductive success; a teleological explanation states that a certain genetic constitution serves a particular function (for example, the molecular composition of hemoglobin has a role in oxygen transport).

Both questions call for specific teleological hypotheses that can be empirically tested.[26]   It sometimes happens, however, that information is available on one or the other question but not for both. In population genetics the fitness effects of alternative genetic constitutions can often be measured, while the mediating adaptive function responsible for the fitness differences may be difficult to identify. We know, for example, that in the fruitfly *Drosophila pseudoobscura* different inversion polymorphisms are favored by natural selection at different times of the year but we are largely ignorant of the physiological processes involved.   In a historical account of evolutionary sequences the problem is occasionally reversed: the function served by an organ or structure may be easily identified, but it may be difficult to ascertain why the development of that feature enhanced reproductive success and thus was favored by natural selection. One example is the large human brain, which makes possible culture and other important human attributes. We may advance hypotheses about the reproductive advantages of increased brain size in the evolution of man, but these hypotheses are difficult to test empirically.

Teleological explanations in evolutionary biology have great heuristic value. They are also occasionally very facile, precisely because they may be difficult to test empirically. Every effort should be made to formulate teleological explanations in a fashion that makes them readily subject to empirical testing. When appropriate empirical tests cannot be formulated, evolutionary biologists should use teleological explanations only with the greatest restraint.[27]

It has been argued by some authors that the distinction between systems that are goal directed and those which are not is highly vague. The classification of certain systems as teleological is allegedly rather arbitrary. A chemical buffer, an elastic solid or a pendulum at rest are examples of physical systems that appear to be goal directed. I suggest using the criterion of utility to determine whether an entity is teleological or not. The criterion of utility can be applied to both natural and artificial teleological systems. Utility in an organism is defined in reference to the survival and reproduction of the organism itself. A feature of a system will be teleological in the sense of natural (internal) teleology if the feature has utility for the system in which it exists and if such utility explains the presence of the feature in the system. Operationally, then, a structure or process of an organism is teleological if it can be shown to contribute to the reproductive efficiency of the organism itself, and if such contribution accounts for the existence of the structure or process. Eyes, gills, and homeostatic developmental processes are features beneficial to the organisms in which they exist.

In artificial (external) teleology, utility is defined in reference to the creator of the object or system. Human-made tools and machines are teleological with external teleology if they have been designed to serve a specified purpose, which therefore explains their existence and properties. If the criterion of utility cannot be applied, a system is not teleological. Chemical buffers, elastic solids, and a pendulum at rest are not teleological systems.

The utility of features of organisms is with respect to the individual or the species in which they exist at any given time. It does not include usefulness to any other organisms. The elaborate plumage and display is a teleological feature of the peacock because it serves the peacock in its attempt to find a mate. The beautiful display is not teleologically directed toward pleasing our human aesthetic sense. That it pleases the human eye is accidental, because this does not contribute to the reproductive fitness of the peacock (except, of course, in the case of traits selected by humans, such as milk production by cows or dog breeds).

The criterion of utility introduces needed objectivity in the determination of which biological mechanisms are end-directed. Provincial human interests should be avoided when using teleological explanations, as Nagel has written. But he selects the wrong example when he observes that "the development of corn seeds into corn plants is sometimes said to be natural, while their transformation into the flesh of birds or men is asserted to be merely accidental.[28] The adaptations of corn seeds have developed to serve the function of corn reproduction, not to become a palatable food for birds or humans. The role of wild corn as human food is indeed accidental to the corn, and cannot be considered a biological function of corn seeds in the teleological sense."[29]

Some features of organisms are not useful by themselves. They have arisen as concomitant or incidental consequences of other features that are adaptive or useful. In some cases, features which are not adaptive in origin may become useful at a later time. For example, the sound produced by the beating of the heart has become adaptive for modern humans because it helps the physician to diagnose the condition of health of the patient. The origin of such features is not explained teleologically, although their preservation might be so explained in certain cases.

Features of organisms may be present because they were useful to the organisms in the past, although they are no longer adaptive. Vestigial organs, like the vermiform appendix of man, are features of this kind. If they are neutral to reproductive fitness, these features may remain in a species indefinitely. The origin of such organs and features, although not their preservation, is accounted for in teleological terms.

Objections, Responses, and Interpretations

Some evolutionists have rejected the teleological mode of explanation in evolutionary biology because they have failed to recognize the various meanings that the term "teleology" may have.[30] These biologists are correct in excluding certain forms of teleological explanations from biology, but they err when they claim that teleological explanations should be excluded altogether from evolutionary theory. In fact, they themselves often use teleological explanations in their works, but fail to recognize them as such, or prefer to call them by some other name, such as "teleonomic." Teleological explanations, as expounded above, are appropriate in evolutionary theory, and are recognized by evolutionary biologists and philosophers of science.[31] Some kinds of teleological explanations that are appropriate and some that are inappropriate with respect to various biological questions may be briefly specified.

According to Mayr[32] teleological explanations have been applied to two different sets of biological phenomena. "On the one hand is the production and perfection throughout the history of the animal and plant kingdoms of ever-new and ever-improved DNA programs of information. On the other hand is the testing of these programs and their decoding throughout the lifetime of each individual. There is a fundamental difference between end-directed behavioral activities or developmental processes of an individual or system which are controlled by a program and the steady improvement of the genetically coded programs. This genetic improvement is evolutionary adaptation controlled by natural selection." The "decoding" and "testing" of genetic programs of information are the issues considered, respectively, by developmental biology and functional biology. The historical and causal processes by which genetic programs of information come about are the concern of evolutionary biology. Grene uses the term "instrumental" for the teleology of organs that act in a functional way, such as the hand and the eye; "developmental" for the teleology of such processes as the maturation of a limb; and "historical" for the process (natural selection) producing teleologically organized systems.[33]

In the terminology that I have proposed, organs and features such as the eye and the hand have natural and determinate teleology. These organs serve determinate ends (seeing or grasping) but have come about by natural processes that did not involve the conscious design of any agent.   Physiological homeostatic reactions and embryological development are processes that also have determinate natural teleology. These processes lead to end-states (from egg to chicken) or maintain properties (body temperature in a mammal) that are on the whole determinate. Thus, Mayr's "decoding" of DNA programs of information and Grene's "instrumental" and "developmental" teleology, when applied to organisms, are cases of determinate natural teleology. Human tools (such as a knife), machines (such as a car), and servomechanisms (such as a thermostat) also have determinate teleology, but of the artificial kind, since they have been consciously designed.

Some authors exclude teleological explanations from evolutionary biology because they believe that teleology exists only when a specific goal is purposefully sought. This is not so. Terms other than "teleology" could be used for natural teleology, but this might in the end add more confusion than clarity. Philosophers as well as scientists use the term, "teleological" in the broader sense, to include explanations that account for the existence of an object in terms of the end-state or goal that they serve.

It is important, for historical reasons, to reiterate that the process of evolution by natural selection is not teleological in the purposeful sense. The natural theologians of the nineteenth century erroneously claimed that the directive organization of living beings evinces the existence of a Designer. The adaptations of organisms can be explained as results of natural processes without recourse to conscious intention.   There is purposeful activity in the world, at least in humans; but the existence of particular organisms, including humans, and their features need not be explained as a result of purposeful behavior.

Some scientists and philosophers who held that evolution is a natural process erred, nevertheless, in seeing evolution as a determinate, or bounded, process. Lamarck thought that evolutionary change necessarily proceeds along determined paths from simpler to more complex organisms.[34] Similarly, the evolutionary philosophies of Bergson, Teilhard de Chardin, and the theories of *nomogenesis, aristogenesis, orthogenesis,* and the like are erroneous because they all claim that evolutionary change necessarily proceeds along determined paths.[35] These theories mistakenly take embryological development as the model of evolutionary change, regarding the teleology of evolution as determinate. Although there are teleologically determinate processes in the living world, like embryological development and physiological homeostasis, the evolutionary origin of living beings is teleological only in the indeterminate sense. Natural selection does not in any way direct evolution toward any particular kind of organism or toward any particular properties.

Teleology and Teleonomy, Aristotle and Aquinas

I want to take up two more issues. The first is a semantic question, the second a historical one. Pittendrigh,[36] Simpson,[37] Mayr,[38] Williams,[39] and others, have proposed to use the term "teleonomic" to describe end-directed processes that do not imply that future events are active agents in their own realization, or that things or activities are conscious agents or the product of such agents. These authors argue that the term "teleology" has sometimes been used to explain the animal and plant kingdoms as the result of a preordained plan necessarily leading to the existing kinds of organisms. To avoid such connotation, the authors argue, the term teleonomy should be used to explain adaptation in nature as the result of natural selection.

Although the notion of teleology has been used, and it is still being used, in the alleged sense, it is also true that other authors, like Dobzhansky, Simpson, and Nagel[40] employ the term "teleology" without implying a preordained relationship of means to an end. Thus, it might originate more confusion than clarity to repudiate the notion of teleology on the grounds that it connotes an intentional relationship of means to an end. The point is that what is useful is to clarify the notion of teleology by explaining the various uses of the term. One may then explicitly express in which sense the term is used in a particular context.

As I have written elsewhere, should the term "teleology" eventually be discarded from the scientific vocabulary, or restricted in its meaning to preordained end-directed processes, I would welcome such event. But the substitution of a term by another does not necessarily clarify the issues at stake. It would still be necessary to explicate whatever term is used instead of teleology, whether teleonomy or any other.[41]

Pittendrigh has written that "It seems unfortunate that the term 'teleology' should be resurrected ... The biologists' long-standing confusion would be more fully removed if all end-directed systems were described by some other term, like 'teleonomic,' in order to emphasize that the recognition and description of end-directedness does not carry a commitment to Aristotelian teleology as an efficient causal principle."[42] The Aristotelian concept of teleology allegedly implies that future events are active agents in their own realization. According to other authors, Aristotelian teleology connotes that there exists an overall design in the world attributable to a Deity, or at least that nature exists only for and in relation to man, considered as the ultimate purpose of creation.[43]

Science, for Aristotle, is a knowledge of the "whys," the "reasons for" true statements. Of a thing we can ask four different kinds of questions: "What is it?", "Out of what is it made?", "By what agent?", "What for?" The four kinds of answers that can be elicited to these questions are Aristotle's four causes—formal, material, efficient, and final. Only the third type of answer is causal in the modern scientific sense. *Aition*, the Greek term that Cicero translated "cause" (*causa*, in Latin) means literally ground of explanation, i.e., what can be answered to a question. It does not necessarily mean causality in the sense of efficient agency.

According to Aristotle, to fully understand an object we need to find out, among other things, its end, what function does it serve or what results it produces. An egg can be understood fully only if we consider it as a possible chicken. The structures and organs of animals have functions, are organized towards certain ends. Living processes proceed towards certain goals. Final causes, for Aristotle, are principles of intelligibility; they are not in any sense active agents in their own realization. For Aristotle, ends "never do anything. Ends do not act or operate, they are never efficient causes."[44]

According to Aristotle there is no intelligent maker of the world. The ends of things are not consciously intended. Nature, man excepted, has no purposes. The teleology of nature is objective, and empirically observable. It does not require the inference of unobservable causes.[45] There is no God designer of nature. According to Aristotle, if there is a God, He cannot have purposes.[46]

Finally, for Aristotle, the teleology of nature is wholly "immanent." The end served by any structure or process is the good or survival of that kind of thing in which they exist. Animals, plants, or their parts do not exist for the benefit of any other thing but themselves. Aristotle makes it clear that nutritious as acorns may be for a squirrel, they do not exist to serve as a squirrel's meal. The natural end of an acorn is to become an oak tree. Anything else that may happen to the acorn is accidental and may not be explained teleologically. Aristotle's insight concerning this matter surpasses Nagel's.[47]

Aristotle's main concern was the study of organisms, and their processes and structures. He observed the facts of adaptation and explained them with considerable insight considering that he did not know about biological evolution. His error was not that he used teleological explanations in biology, but that he extended the concept of teleology to the nonliving world. In the Middle Ages, Aristotle was "Christianized," particularly in the works of the great theologian St. Thomas Aquinas (1225-1274). It was Aquinas, not Aristotle, who accounted for the teleology of organisms, and of nature in general, as the intended purpose of an Omniscient Creator.[48]

Notes

1.   Thomas H. Huxley, Darwin's younger contemporary, wrote that "perhaps the most remarkable service to the philosophy of Biology rendered by Mr. Darwin is the reconciliation of Teleology and Morphology, and the explanation of the facts of both which his views offer ... There is a wider Teleology, which is not touched by the doctrine of Evolution, but is actually based upon the fundamental proposition of Evolution." "The Genealogy of Animals." In: T.H. Huxley, *Critiques and Addresses*, New York: Appleton, 1873: 272.

2.   C. Darwin, *On the Origin of Species*, facsimile of the first edition, New York: Atheneum, 1967, ch. 3, p. 63; and ch. 4, pp. 80-81.

3.   Ibid., ch. 4, p. 109.

4.   The process described in this example is indeed natural selection, in contrast with the artificial selection when an animal breeder selects, for example, the cows that produce the most milk in order to breed the next generation. In the bacterial selection, human intervention is restricted to changing the environments in which the bacteria breed, rather than selecting the bacteria that breed best in each particular case. In nature, environments change endlessly from place to place and from one time to the next. This persistent environmental variation prompts evolution by natural selection, as variations favored in one environment become replaced by those favored in the next.

5.   "The sun provided not only the energy to drive the chemical cogwheels of life. It also offered the chance of a remote guidance technology. It pummelled every square millimetre of Earth's surface with a fusillade of photons: tiny

particles travelling in straight lines at the greatest speed the universe allows, crisscrossing and ricocheting through holes and cracks so that no nook escaped, every cranny was sought out. Because photons travel in straight lines and so fast, because they are absorbed by some materials more than others and reflected by some materials more than others, and because they have always been so numerous and so all-pervading, photons provided the opportunity for remote-sensing technologies of enormous accuracy and power. It was necessary only to detect photons and-more difficult-distinguish the directions from which they came. Would the opportunity be taken up? Three billion years later you know the answer, for you can see these words." R. Dawkins, *Climbing Mount Improbable*, New York: Norton, 1996.- 138-139.

6. Eyes have evolved in animals in at least forty different types. The human (vertebrate) eye is one type; others are the squid's, the snail's, and the fly's. R. Dawkins has discussed the evolution of eyes, authoritatively and with beautiful prose: *Climbing Mount Improbable*, pp. 13 8-197.

7. I cited earlier another example of the different ways in which organisms adapt to the same environmental features. Very diverse types of eyes have evolved in different kinds of animals, taking advantage of the ubiquitous presence of sunlight for finding food and shelter, escaping predators, directing daily or seasonal rhythms, and so on. The detailed steps in the evolution of several eye types can be found in R. Dawkins' *Climbing Mount Improbable*, cited above.

8. F.J. Ayala, "Teleological Explanations versus Teleology," *History and Philosophy of the Life Sciences*, XX (1998), XX-XX.

9. G. C. Williams. *Adaptation and Natural Selection*, Princeton, New Jersey: Princeton University Press, 1966: 8-9.

10. J. Tooby and L. Cosmides, "The Psychological Foundations of Culture." In: J. H. Barkow, L. Cosmides and J. Tooby (eds.), *The Adapted Mind*, New York.-Oxford University Press, 1992: 52.

11. Ibid: 68.

12. R. Dawkins, *Climbing Mount Improbable*, New York: Norton, 1996: 302.

13. P. Lieberman, *Eve Spoke: Human Language and Human Evolution*, New York: Norton, 1998: 20.

14. P.J. Medawar and J. S. Medawar, *Aristotle to Zoos*, Cambridge, Massachusetts: Harvard University Press, 1983: 256.

15. In the pages that follow and to the extent that I do not specify otherwise in a particular case, I shall use the terms "ends," "goals" and "purposes" as largely equivalent and/or complementary. Obviously, in this context, I do not mean by "end" simply the point of termination, as in "the end of the line" or "the end of a book," but rather something to be achieved as in the phrases "the means to an end," or "the end sought" or "the end served." "Purpose" and to a lesser extent "goal" often implies intention, or conscious pursuit. I do not intend this more restricted meaning, except when explicitly so stated or obvious from the context. I also consider "telic" and "teleological" to have largely overlapping meanings so that they can often be used interchangeably, but I will mostly limit myself to using the terms "teleological" and "teleology."

16. G.C. Williams has noted in *Adaptation and Natural Selection* that teleological, or adaptationist hypotheses are onerous and thus should be used with restraint. He has in mind, particularly, "group selection" accounts. The facile recourse or even abuse of teleological explanations (adaptational accounts, in their terminology) has been criticized by S.J. Gould and R.C. Lewontin, "The spandrels of San Marco and the Panglossian Paradigm'," *Proceedings of the Royal Society of London*, B205 (1979), 581-598.

17. I have selected the two particular examples in this paragraph because we know of environmental variations that shift their adaptive value. In regions of tropical Africa where malaria is rife and a major debilitating disease and cause of mortality, the incidence of S hemoglobin is high, because it protects against malarial infection. Starting in the mid-nineteenth century, the frequency of melanic moths rapidly increased in English regions heavily polluted by burning industrial coal. Since the mid-1960s, pollution controls have gradually eliminated the soot covering tree trunks, and the incidence of peppered-gray moths has concomitantly increased at the expense of the melanics.

18. A very common reason why biologists do not use the term "teleology" is that they believe it necessarily implies that function and design must be attributed to an external agent; i.e., that the design features of organisms have been created by God. I take up this matter below. It is in any case amusing to read statements of denial of teleology in articles and books pervaded with teleological language and teleological explanations. One is reminded that "a rose by any other name is still a rose." It has been informally attributed to one or another distinguished evolutionist the witticism: "Teleology is like a mistress. A man does not want to be seen in her company, but he cannot do without her."

19. For instance, the persistence of a genetic polymorphism in a population due to heterosis (advantage of individuals who inherit a different allele from each parent) may be considered a homeostatic mechanism acting at the population level. One example is the presence of the "normal" and the S forms of hemoglobin in human populations severely infected with malaria. The S form protects against malaria and the "normal" variant avoids falciform anemia.

20. Aristotle, Saint Augustine, and other ancient and medieval philosophers, took developmental homeostasis as the paradigm of all teleological mechanisms. According to Saint Augustine, God did not create directly all living species of organisms, but these were implicit in the primeval forms created by Him. The existing species arose by a natural "unfolding" of the potentialities implicit in the primeval forms or "seeds" created by God. These ancient or medieval views are not intended here, of course.

21. See F.J. Ayala, "Teleological Explanations in Evolutionary Biology," *Philosophy of Science*, 37 (1970), 1-15 and "Biology as an Autonomous Science," *American Scientist* 56 (1968), 207-221.

22. See E. Nagel, *The Structure of Science*, New York: Harcourt, Brace and World, 1961; E. Nagel, "Types of Causal Explanation in Science." In: D. Lemer (ed.), *Cause and Effect*, New York: Free Press, 1965: 11-32. See also F.J. Ayala, "Teleological Explanations in Evolutionary Biology," *Philosophy of Science*, 37 (1970), 1-15; and F.J. Ayala, "The Distinctness of Biology." In: F. Weinert (ed.), *Laws of Nature: Essays on the Philosophical, Scientific and Historical Dimensions*. Berlin: Walter de Gruyter, 1995: 268-285.

23. "The function of gills in fishes is respiration, that is the exchange of oxygen and carbon dioxide between the blood and the external water." A statement of this kind, according to Nagel, accounts for the presence of a certain feature *A* (gills) in every member of a class of systems *S* (fish) which possess a certain organization *C* (the characteristic anatomy and physiology of fishes). It does so by declaring that when *S* is placed in a certain environment *E* (water with dissolved oxygen) it will perform a function *F* (respiration) only if S (fish) has A (gills). The teleological statement, says Nagel, is a telescoped argument the content of which can be unraveled approximately as follows. When supplied with water containing dissolved oxygen, fish respire; if fish have no gills, they do not respire even if supplied with water containing dissolved oxygen; therefore fish have gills. More generally, a statement of the form "The function of *A* in a system *S* with organization *C* is to enable *S* in environment *E* to engage in process F" can be formulated more explicitly: "Every system *S* with organization *C* and in environment *E* engage in function *F*; if *S* with organization *C* and in environment E does not have A, then S cannot engage in *F*; hence, *S* must have *A*." According to Nagel, the difference between a teleological explanation and a non-teleological one is, thus, one of emphasis rather than of asserted content.

24. F.J. Ayala, "Philosophical Issues." In: Th. Dobzhansky, F.J. Ayala, G.L. Stebbins and J.W. Valentine, *Evolution*, San Francisco: Freeman, 1977: ch. 16, pp. 474-516; F.J. Ayala, "Biology as an Autonomous Science," *American Scientist* 56 (1968), 207-221.

25. See footnote 6, above.

26. This point has been belabored, for example, by J. Tooby and L. Cosmides, "The Psychological Foundations of Culture." In: J. H. Barkow, L. Cosmides and J. Tooby (eds.), *The Adapted Mind*, New York: Oxford University Press.

27. See footnote 16, above.

28. E. Nagel, *The Structure of Science*, New York: Harcourt, Brace and World, 1961: 424.

29. This point was clearly and repeatedly made by Darwin. For example "Natural selection will modify the structure of the young in relation to the parent, and of the parent in relation to the young. In social animals it will adapt the structure of each individual for the benefit of the community; if each in consequence profits by the selected change. What natural selection cannot do, is to modify the structure of one species, Without giving it any advantage, for the good of another species; and though statements to this effect may be found in works of natural history, I cannot find one case which will bear investigation." C. Darwin, *On the Origin of Species*, facsimile of the first edition, New York: Atheneum, 1967: ch. 4, pp. 86-87.

30. M.T. Ghiselin, *The Economy of Nature and the Evolution of Sex*. Berkeley: University of California Press, 1974. E. Mayr, "Cause and effect in Biology." In: D. Lemer (ed.), *Cause and Effect*, New York: Free Press, 1965: 33-50. E. Mayr, "Teleological and Teleonomic, a New Analysis." In: R.S. Cohen and M.W. Wartofsky (eds.), *Boston Studies in the Philosophy of Science*, XIVL. Boston: Reidel, 1974: 91-117. C. S. Pittendfigh, "Adaptation, Natural Selection, and Behavior." In: A. Roe and G. G. Simpson (eds.), *Behavior and Evolution*, New Haven, Connecticut: Yale University Press, 1958: 390-416. G.C. Williams, *Adaptation and Natural Selection*, Princeton, New Jersey: Princeton University Press, 1966.

31. M. Beckner, *The Biological Way of Thought*, New York: Columbia University Press, 1959. W. Christensen, "A Complex Systems Theory of Teleology," *Biology and Philosophy*, II (I 996), 301-320. H. Binswanger, *The Biological Basis of Theological Concepts*, Los Angeles, California: The Ayn Rand Institute Press. T. Dobzhansky, *Genetics of the Evolutionary Process*, New York: Columbia University Press, 1970. T.A. Goudge, *The Ascent of Life*, Toronto, Canada: University of Toronto Press, 1961. D. Hull, *Philosophy of Biological Science*. Englewood Cliffs, New Jersey: Prentice-Hall, 1974. E. Nagel, *The Structure of Science*, New York: Harcourt, Brace, and World, 1961. G. G. Simpson, *This View of Life*, New York: Harcourt, Brace, and World, 1964. W.C. Wimsatt, "Teleology and the Logical Structure of Function Statements," *Studies in the History and Philosophy of Science*, 3 (1972), 1-80.

32. E. Mayr, "Cause and Effect in Biology." In: D. Lemer (ed.), *Cause and Effect*, New York: Free Press, 1965: 33-50.

33. M. Grene, *The Understanding of Nature: Essays in the Philosophy of Biology*, Boston: Reidel, 1974.

34. J.B. Lamarck, *Zoological Philosophy* (1809), translated by H. Elliot, New York: Hafner (reprinted), 1963.

35. E. S. Berg, *Nomogenesis or Evolution Determined by Law* (1926), London, Boston: MIT Press (reissued), 1969. H. Bergson, *L'Évolution Créatrice* (1907). English translation, *Creative Evolution*, New York, 1911. H.F. Osborn, "Aristogenesis: the Creative Principle in the Origin of Species," *American Naturalist*, 68 (1934), 193-235. P. Teilhard de Chardin, *The Phenomenon of Man*, New York: Harper, 1959. *Webster's Third New International Dictionary*, 1966.

36. C. S. Pittendrigh, "Adaptation, Natural Selection, and Behavior." In: A. Roe and G. G. Simpson (eds.), *Behavior and Evolution*, New Haven, Connecticut: Yale University Press, 1958: 390-416.

37. G. G. Simpson, *This View of Life*. New York: Harcourt, Brace, and World, 1964.

38. E. Mayr, "Cause and effect in biology." In: D. Lemer (ed.), *Cause and Effect*, New York: Free Press, 1965: 33-50.

39. G.C. Williams, *Adaptation and Natural Selection*, Princeton, New Jersey: Princeton University Press, 1966.

40. See footnote 31, above.

41. F. J. Ayala, "Teleological Explanations in Evolutionary Biology," *Philosophy of Science*, 37 (1970),1-15.

42. C. S. Pittendrigh, "Adaptation, Natural Selection, and Behavior." In: A. Roe and G.G. Simpson (eds.), *Behavior and Evolution*, New Haven, Connecticut: Yale University Press, 195 8: 3 94.

43. See E. Mayr, 'Cause and Effect in Biology'. In: D. Lemer (ed.), *Cause and Effect*, New York: Free Press, 1965: 33-50; and G.G. Simpson, *This View of Life*, New York: Harcourt, Brace, and World, 1964.

44. J.H. Randall, *Aristotle*, New York: Columbia University Press, 1960: 128.

45. D. Ross, *Aristotle*, 5th edition, New York: Bames and Noble, 1949; see also J.H. Randall, footnote 44.

46. J.H. Randall, *Aristotle*, New York: Columbia University Press, 1960: 125.

47. See above, p. 254 about the teleology of corn seeds.

14

A Critical-Historical Perspective on the Argument about Evolution and Creation

JOHN R. DURANT

Creation versus Evolution?

Just a few weeks before the convening of the first European Conference on Science and Religion, the University of Oxford's undergraduate debating society, the Oxford Union, saw fit to consider the subject of evolution and religion. Representing religion on this occasion were A. E. Wilder-Smith, a pharmacologist and a consultant based in Geneva; and Edgar Andrews, a Professor of Materials Science in the University of London. These men are prominent spokesmen in the English-speaking world for what has come to be known as "scientific creationism"; and for more than two hours they defended the motion "That the doctrine of creation is more valid than the theory of evolution" against two prominent British evolutionary biologists, Dr. Richard Dawkins and Professor John Maynard Smith.

There is a great deal of historical irony in this event. For it was in the Oxford University Museum, and as long ago as 1860, that Charles Darwin's young supporter Thomas Henry Huxley clashed with Bishop Samuel Wilberforce over the very same question. On that occasion, less than a year after the publication of the *Origin of Species,* Huxley condemned the Bishop of Oxford for attempting to defeat Darwinism with nothing more than ignorant contempt. 126 years later, Oxford University's undergraduate body finally gave its verdict on the issue. After due consideration, it came down cautiously on Huxley's side: on 14 February 1986, the motion "That the doctrine of creation is more valid than the theory of evolution" was defeated by 198 votes to l5.

At first glance, we may be inclined to suppose that Huxley would have been pleased at this outcome.A master debater himself, he knew the importance of winning crucial public engagements of this kind. On reflection, however, we may wonder instead whether Huxley would not have been both amazed and disappointed at this second Oxford debate: amazed that religiously-motivated anti-evolutionary sentiment is still so strong that it can command the support of no less than 15 undergraduates at one of Europe's foremost universities; and disappointed that the scientific community still has to spend its time defending ground that was supposedly won for it more than a century ago.

Over the past 10-20 years, religiously-motivated anti-evolutionism has grown to the point where today it constitutes a significant threat to the teaching and practice of evolutionary biology in North America and, to a lesser extent, in Europe as well. For the first time since the early-nineteenth century, significant numbers of Protestant evangelicals are today attempting to develop a non-evolutionary view of origins, a so-called "creation science"; and in pursuit of this aim, they are writing articles, publishing textbooks, founding colleges, and entering into political battles with evolutionary biologists in the media, in local school boards and colleges, and even in the lawcourts (for reviews and analysis see Durant ed. 1985; Godfrey ed. 1983; Kitcher 1982; Montagu ed. 1984; Nelkin 1982).

The single crucial assumption which underlies the so-called creation science movement is that the theological doctrine of creation is fundamentally incompatible with the scientific theory of evolution. The scientific creationists believe that people must choose between creation and evolution; they believe that as the Oxford Union motion put it, the one must be "more valid" than the other. Professor Edgar Andrews, who was one of the Oxford speakers, is President of the British Biblical Creation Society, an organization with several hundred members whose purpose is "to demonstrate the importance of the Biblical teaching on Creation, and its incompatibility with the general theory of organic evolution" (*Biblical Creation* 2, 1980). Though rather different in emphasis, this society shares with the much larger and more explicitly fundamentalist American Creation Research Society the belief that evolution is inherently and profoundly anti-Christian. Indeed, leading American scientific creationists have equated evolution with atheism, materialism, and immorality at a personal level; as well as with anarchism, liberalism and communism at a political level (Morris ed. 1974). For them, Darwinism is not just wrong; it is of the devil.

Extravagant claims such as these are but one, albeit extreme, reflection of what is a long-standing and widespread sense of unease in the Christian community about evolutionary theory. Many even among those who accept that evolution is true do so rather reluctantly, almost as if by making this admission they were giving house-room to an unwelcome guest. Some theologians, for example, who are happy for the most part to take on trust the conclusions of theoretical science, stumble when they are confronted by the Darwinian theory of evolution by natural selection (see, for example, Montefiore 1985); and innumerable ordinary Christian folk, who take no particular interest in science, nonetheless feel obliged to "have a view" on this matter. Far beyond the circles of the scientific creationists, there is a conviction that evolution theory presents special problems or difficulties for Christian faith. Indeed, this is surely implied by the fact that "The Argument about Evolution and Creation" was chosen as the topic for the first European Conference on Science and Religion.

The Historical Perspective

Faced with this widespread religious unease about evolution, it can be helpful to look back to the past. History does not, of course, teach us any simple or straightforward lessons; and by itself, it cannot solve any of the great scientific or theological problems in which we may be interested. However, history can give us a better sense of perspective on these problems. In particular, it can help us to shake free from the particular prejudices of our day, both by suggesting new ways of thinking about our problems, and by revealing a wider range of possible solutions to these problems than may have been apparent at first sight.

In reviewing the history of discussions of evolution and creation, however, it is important to bear in mind that the past is another place in which things were often done differently. For example, from an historical point of view it is not possible to make a clear distinction between scientific and theological discussions of evolution. Throughout the first half of the nineteenth century, which is the period in which modern evolutionary theory first arose, much biology was deeply religious and much religion was profoundly biological. At that time science as a whole was far less insular and far less secular than it is today; and this means that in dealing with our subject we must inevitably move rather freely between science and theology.

Precisely because many early workers failed to make a clear distinction between science and theology, they often argued from the one to the other as if such arguments were free of all philosophical difficulty. Even Charles Darwin, that most cautious of nineteenth-century evolutionary biologists, occasionally drew theological conclusions from what were essentially scientific premises. It is a major theme of this chapter that we are to a large extent the unwitting victims of a persistent conflation or confusion between science and theology which has occurred throughout the history of debates about evolution and creation. If today we continue to be worried about the relationship between Darwinism and Christian belief, more often than not it is because we are faced either with science masquerading as theology or with theology masquerading as science. Only history can show us the full extent of the damage that is done by such pretence.

There have been many different ideas and speculations about organic origins; but in the modern period there has been only one really successful scientific theory of organic origins, and that is Charles Darwin's and Alfred Russel Wallace's theory of evolution by natural selection (Darwin and Wallace 1958; Darwin 1859). The great achievement of the Darwin-Wallace theory is to show how in principle new species may arise from ancestor species by a process of descent with modification. The theory is entirely typical of great discoveries in science in that it invokes some relatively familiar features of the living world (the principles of inheritance, genetic variation, and over-reproduction), but draws an entirely unexpected consequence from them: namely, natural selection, or the differential survival and reproduction of favourable over unfavourable variations in the struggle for existence.

Darwin's bold claim was that natural selection has been the principal (though not the sole) agent of organic evolution. This claim has always been controversial, of course; but it is impossible to dispute the fact that natural selection remains to this day the centre-piece of evolutionary biology. Undergirded by modern population genetics, and applied in countless detailed studies of the evolution of both physical and behavioural traits, natural selection is the only half-way adequate theory of evolution that has ever been proposed (Dawkins 1986). For this reason alone, it is to the history of Darwinism and its relations with religious belief that the bulk of this paper is devoted. As a first step in considering the impact of Darwinism on religious belief, however, it is necessary to begin with the earlier view of organic origins that it was intended to replace.

The Theory of Special Creation

Throughout the seventeenth and eighteenth centuries in Europe, the study of life was intimately intertwined with religious, and more particularly, with Christian beliefs about the inter-relationships between God, nature, human nature, and human society. In this period, there was fashioned a broad synthesis of natural history and religion which, albeit in many different forms, was every bit as powerful as the synthesis of Aristotelian cosmology and Christian theology in the medieval period. This synthesis is to be found in embryo in the work of the seventeenth-century English naturalist John Ray, in vigorous youth in the ideas of the eighteenth-century Swedish taxonomist Carolus Linnaeus, in subtle maturity in the writings of the French comparative anatomist Georges Cuvier and the German polymath Johann Wolfgang von Goethe, and in advanced and somewhat decrepit old age in the publications of the Swiss-American palaeontologist Louis Agassiz and the English comparative anatomist Richard Owen (for a competent historical review, see Bowler 1984).

The synthesis, which may be discerned in the work of all these and many more naturalists, represented the coming together of three great intellectual traditions. In order of age, these were: Greek philosophy, and particularly Plato's idealist doctrine of specific forms and Aristotle's teleological doctrine of final causes; Christian theology, and particularly the doctrine of divine creation; and classical natural history, and more particularly the establishment of a comprehensive natural classification of plants and animals. It will be useful to summarize the contributions of each of these traditions in turn, and then to present a brief description of the resulting synthesis.

From classical Greece the seventeenth and eighteenth centuries took two key notions, among many others. First, there was Plato's doctrine that true reality is not the mundane world of varied and varying sense experience, but rather the transcendent world of pure and immutable forms. On this view, the objects we see around us are the flickering and temporary images of ideal types to which they are at best only crude approximations—in Plato's famous allegory in the *Republic*, they are mere shadows cast by the eternal light on the walls of the cave. There have been many different versions of Platonic idealism, including specifically theological ones in which the pure forms are interpreted as ideas in the mind of God. In one version or another, however, Plato's doctrine of forms has been a recurrent theme in the history of Western philosophy and science.

The same is true of a second Greek idea which is attributable to Plato's pupil Aristotle. Aristotle was a good deal more interested than Plato had been in studying the real world, including the world of life; and in pursuing a combination of philosophical wisdom and empirical ("scientific") knowledge, he modified and added to his master's ideas in many ways. For example, Aristotle took over Plato's doctrine of form, but emphasized the immanence of form within the physical world. Moreover, he complemented Plato's interest in form with a concern for function. According to Aristotle, an essential part of explaining anything consisted in giving an account of the end or purpose for which that thing exists (its "final cause"); and, once again in myriad different ways, this teleological approach shaped centuries of scientific thought to come.

Here, then, in rude outline are two key Greek contributions to seventeenth and eighteenth century ideas about the living world. In contrast, the key Christian contribution was a doctrine concerned primarily not with the explanation of the forms and functions of particular things, but rather with the explanation of why there are any things at all. In the doctrine of creation, Christianity portrayed the universe as the dependent and strictly temporal handiwork of God. This doctrine of creation was quite distinct from (though it was often confused with) Greek notions of origins; for where the one envisaged a free creation *ex nihilo* by a transcendent and omnipotent God, the other envisaged a constrained forming of pre-existent unformed matter by a demiurge. In one form or another, the Christian doctrine of creation has been a major influence on western thought, and more especially on western science.

The third and final ingredient of our synthesis is classical natural history, and particularly classical taxonomy. Taxonomy is the science of classification of living organisms. Aristotle himself had been interested in classification, and he had distinguished many different "natural kinds" of animals within a roughly linear series, the scale of nature or *scala naturae*. The notion of a linear "chain of being" was enormously influential in the 17th and 18th centuries (Lovejoy 1936), particularly as classification moved to centre stage in the study of natural history. The guiding principle in the work of most naturalists at this time was the attempt to construct a systematic and orderly arrangement of species or other natural kinds. Some adopted the principle of the scale of nature, while others went for hierarchical schemes involving nested sets of related groups. Either way, however, the search was on for general principles by which organic species could be classified on the basis of observed structural similarities and differences of form and function.

It is not difficult to see how the three traditions of Greek philosophy, Christian theology and classical natural history may be combined. By identifying the Platonic demiurge with the Christian creator, and giving this creator the task of fashioning out of unformed matter a formal array of exquisitely adapted species, it is possible to arrive at an idealistic synthesis according to which each species (or other chosen natural kind) of plant or animal is the embodiment of a transcendent idea in the mind of the creator, or, with a little more subtlety, perhaps, to arrive at a synthesis in which each species is seen as an individually tailored variation upon a far smaller set of transcendental themes. On this view, the living world is portrayed as a static array of diverse forms, each of which is primitively distinct from all others by virtue of its unique divine origin. For want of a better term, we may refer to this view as the "special creation theory" of organic origins.

It would be wrong to suggest that there was anything like complete agreement among those who supported this way of looking at the living world. For example, and most important of all, there was a persistent tension between the Platonic or idealist and the Aristotelian or teleological elements within the theory.Thus, in early nineteenth-century England two partially separate special-creationist traditions flourished alongside one another, the one concerned primarily with the idealist explanation of organic form in terms of transcendent "Archetypes," and the other concerned primarily with the teleological explanation of organic function in terms of divine design (Bowler 1977, 1984; Ospovat 1978, 1981). The idealist anatomist Richard Owen put his finger on the crucial difference between these two traditions by distinguishing between homologies (cases in which the same basic structure serves different functions) and analogies (cases in which quite different structures serve the same basic function; see Owen 1848). Owen insisted that adequate biological analysis required the investigation of both homologies and analogies; and this claim was part of a campaign to effect a compromise between the idealist and the teleological traditions of special creationism.

From our point of view, these details are of little concern. What really matters is the simple fact that for a very long period of time theoretical explanations of organic origins were dominated by a synthesis in which the Christian doctrine of creation was tied to a very particular set of philosophical and scientific beliefs about the natural world. As we have seen, the philosophical beliefs were overwhelmingly idealist and teleological; and they were used to support the scientific notion that species (or other natural kinds) are primitively distinct. As Owen himself put it in connection with the vertebrate skeleton (quoted in Aulie 1972):

> The Divine mind which planned the Archetype also foreknew all its modifications. The archetypal idea was manifested in the flesh, under diverse such manifestations, upon this planet, long prior to the existence of those animal species that actually exemplify it.

From Special Creation to Natural Selection

From as early as the 1830s, when he first began to think seriously about the problem of origins, Charles Darwin firmly rejected the idealist elements within the theory of special creation. However, he did not reject the teleological elements within it anything like so easily. In fact, Darwin was greatly influenced by the Anglican clergyman William Paley, the greatest exponent of teleological special creationism in the early nineteenth century. Paley, of course, had emphasized function at the expense of form, for he had virtually identified the doctrine of creation with the fact of the overwhelming adaptedness of living organisms.   In his *Natural Theology* (1802), Paley presented the innumerable contrivances of life as a cumulative argument from design for the existence of God. Paley's God was a craftsman, he was a superlative mechanic who had thrown together not merely cunningly contrived machines but machines so cunningly contrived that they were capable of reproducing themselves indefinitely without external assistance.

Darwin took this view extremely seriously. In fact, for several years he appears entirely to have accepted Paley's version of the argument from design. Throughout his life, Darwin never for an instant questioned Paley's assumption that what required explanation above all else was organic adaptation. For both men it was true that, as Darwin himself once put it, "the whole universe is full of adaptations;" but from about 1837 Darwin added to this conviction the non-Paleyan belief that these adaptations were "only direct consequences of still higher laws" (Gruber and Barrett 1974). Here again Darwin was following the lead of the special creationists, who had already offered innumerable transcendental laws as putative explanations of organic form and function. The only difference between Darwin and the special creationists was that Darwin would have nothing to do with the esoteric principles of transcendentalism, which he regarded as simply absurd. When he went in search of a "higher law" regulating the production of organic adaptations, what he sought was not a transcendental principle but rather a mundane process capable of simulating intelligent design.

Discovered by Darwin in 1838, the principle of natural selection represented the unexpected fulfillment of the promise of the theory of special creation. It was unexpected, of course, in the sense that it replaced the idea of species as individually crafted products of a Platonic demiurge with the radical idea of species as historical products of the differential survival and reproduction of favourable over unfavourable variant individuals in the struggle for existence; but it was the fulfillment of the promise of the theory of special creation, in the sense that it accounted for the observed pattern of organic form and function with the aid of but a single overarching theoretical principle.

The idea that Darwin's theory of evolution by natural selection represents the fulfillment of the special-creationist tradition is still not widely acknowledged. This is a little surprising, for Darwin himself made it abundantly clear in his own writings. The frontispiece of the first edition of the *Origin of Species*, for example, contained two quotations, one from Francis Bacon on the "two books of divine revelation," and the other from the Reverend William Whewell, an English natural theologian, who had observed that "with regard to the material world...we can perceive that events are brought about not by insulated interpositions of Divine power, exerted in each particular case, but by the establishment of general laws." Together, these passages gave notice to Darwin's readers that his book fell squarely within the conventions of natural theology; and Darwin further underlined this point towards the end of the *Origin* where he stated that, "To my mind, it accords better with what we know of the laws impressed upon matter by the Creator, that the production and extinction of the past inhabitants of the world should have been due to secondary causes, like those determining the birth and death of the individual" (Darwin 1859). Thus, Darwin explicitly invited his readers to see evolution by natural selection as the means adopted by the creator to populate the earth with a diversity of well-adapted species.

Of course, things were not really quite as simple as this. Until well after the publication of the *Origin,* Darwin continued to present his theory in the orthodox language of the doctrine of divine creation; and throughout his life he insisted that there was nothing either anti-religious or atheistic in his work. Privately, however, he was increasingly troubled and perplexed by these matters. For example in the course of a long and rather inconclusive correspondence about the theological implications of natural selection with his friend, the American botanist Asa Gray, he once wrote: "You say that you are in a haze; I am in thick mud; the orthodox would say in fetid, abominable mud; yet I cannot keep out of the question" (Darwin ed. 1887). To see exactly what the "fetid, abominable mud" was, and why he was stuck fast in it, we must review briefly Darwin's changing views on religion.

Darwin was a "quite orthodox" Christian at the time he traveled aboard the *H.M.S. Beagle* in the early 1830s. Indeed, he describes how he was "heartily laughed at by several of the officers...for quoting the bible as an unanswerable authority on some point of morality" (Barlow ed. 1958). In the late 1830s, however, Darwin gradually abandoned Christianity, first for what may be termed deism (the belief in an impersonal divine author of the universe), and then for a rather uneasy agnosticism. As he himself once put it, "In my most extreme fluctuations I have never been an atheist in the sense of denying the existence of God. I think that generally (and more and more as I grow older), but not always, that an Agnostic would be the more correct description of my state of mind" (Darwin ed. 1887).

In a recent study, the historian John Hedley Brooke has re-examined the causes of Darwin's changing religious views (Brooke 1985). Certainly, he suggests, there were scientific elements in Darwin's abandonment of religious belief: for example, he was greatly impressed by the universality of natural law as an objection to the possibility of miracles; and he appears to have found the arbitrariness, the contingency and the radical purposelessness of evolution by natural selection a real source of difficulty. Yet this was far from being the whole story. For Darwin's loss of faith was also bound up with that moral revolt against Christianity which historians have seen as such a significant part of the decline of orthodox belief in the Victorian period.

Thus in his autobiography, having described his orthodoxy at the time of the Beagle voyage, Darwin moved immediately into a discussion of the causes of his growing unbelief. Significantly, this discussion is not taken up principally with scientific matters. Instead, Darwin records that, "I had gradually come...to see that the Old Testament from its manifestly false history of the world...and from its attributing to God the feelings of a revengeful tyrant, was no more to be trusted than the sacred books of the Hindoos, or the beliefs of any barbarian" (Barlow ed. 1958). Darwin was struck as much by the moral and intellectual parochialism of Christianity as he was by its supposed conflict with the findings of science. He detested the doctrine of eternal damnation, and he found the problem of both animal and human suffering a major objection to religious belief —"I cannot see as plainly as others do, and as I should wish to do, evidence of design and beneficence on all sides of us," he wrote to Asa Gray, "There seems to me too much misery in the world." (Darwin ed. 1887). As Brooke notes, these factors point not so much to Darwin's science as to the resonance between his science and the wider culture as the source of his growing unbelief.

The Divorce of Science from Theology

This brief historical sketch of the emergence of Darwinism, and of Darwin's own views on religion, provides the context for a critical re-assessment of the relationship between evolution and creation. Such a re-assessment undermines all naive notions of any necessary conflict between the two ideas, and in this sense it radically undercuts the position of the so-called "scientific creationists." At the same time, however, it lends support to the idea that the Darwinian revolution did indeed have profound implications for the relationship between science and religious belief. That these implications are not necessarily the ones most commonly associated with the name of Charles Darwin today serves only to reinforce the importance of the historical perspective in contemporary debates about evolution and creation.

We have seen that the theory of evolution by natural selection fulfilled the promise of the special creationist tradition; but it also destroyed that tradition by undermining the particular alliance of philosophy, theology, and natural science upon which it rested. In a Darwinian universe, there was no place for Platonic idealism and no place for Aristotelian teleology; above all, there was no place for special creation. By showing convincingly how in principle new species might arise in nature, Darwin made redundant centuries of philosophizing and theologizing about organic origins. What is vitally important to notice, however, is that neither in aim nor in effect did he undermine the Christian doctrine of creation itself. Rather, by separating that doctrine from its two-centuries-long marriage of convenience with Greek philosophy and classical natural history, Darwin forced the radical re-examination of the relationship between theology and natural science.

Out of this process of re-examination there emerged in the late nineteenth-century a whole array of different "solutions" to the problem of the relationship between science and theology, evolution and creation. To the English biologist, Thomas Huxley, for example, Darwinism was a vindication of an agnostic and liberal scientific world-view that would free humankind altogether from the shackles of theology; to Ernst Haeckel, it was a proof of the truth of "Monism," a secular philosophy in which matter and mind were regarded as but two aspects of the same universal and progressively developing substance; and to Karl Marx, it was the basis in natural history for an atheistic, dialectical, and historically materialist view of human nature and society. Here, then, were a variety of anti-Christian reformulations of the relationship between science and theology in a Darwinian universe.

Yet before we jump to the conclusion that Darwinism was inherently anti-Christian, we shall do well to recall an equally wide range of pro-Christian reformulations of the science-theology relationship which were produced in response to Darwinism in the late nineteenth-century. Thus, to the close friend of Thomas Huxley, the Anglican clergyman, naturalist, and novelist Charles Kingsley, Darwinism entailed a "loftier" view of God's work in creation than that which had been contained in the older, creationist synthesis (Darwin ed. 1887); to the close friend of Darwin, the American Presbyterian Asa Gray, Darwinism afforded "higher and more comprehensive, and perhaps worthier, as well as more consistent, views of design in Nature than heretofore" (quoted in Moore 1979); and to the close friend of the Darwinian biologists E.B. Poulton and G.J. Romanes, the Oxford Anglo-Catholic Aubrey Moore, Darwinism was "infinitely more Christian than the theory of special creation" because it implied "the immanence of God in nature, and the omnipresence of his creative power" (Moore 1889).

Quite clearly, a very great variety of views of the evolution-creation relationship was on offer in the late-nineteenth century. To a very considerable extent, Darwinism appears to have become all things to all men (virtually without exception those involved were, of course, all men); and it was precisely this pluralism that was its greatest influence on debates about science and theology. For any theory of origins that is capable of sustaining an indefinitely large number of different philosophical and religious interpretations is profoundly secularizing in its effects. The greatest tangible result of the Darwinian revolution in the domain of science and theology was not the triumph of any single view within either domain but rather the growing realization that these were indeed two domains, and not (as the theory of special creation had implied) one.

A particularly stark illustration of the dawning of this new realization is provided by an intriguing Victorian institution known as the Metaphysical Society. Founded in 1869 by no less than 62 eminent scientists, theologians, and literary figures, this society met regularly for a period of around 11 years in order to try to find a new foundation for an integrated understanding of the interrelationships between God, nature, humankind, and society. It failed, of course; and this failure has been represented by the historian Robert Young as symptomatic of a profound fragmentation of intellectual culture that took place in the mid-Victorian period. According to William Gladstone, for example, there was a simple lesson to be learnt from the proceedings of the Metaphysical Society: "Let the scientific men stick to their science, and leave philosophy and religion to poets, philosophers, and theologians" (quoted in Young 1985).

The Myth and the Reality of Secular Science

Gladstone's view is the official myth by which we live today. Over the past century science in general and evolutionary biology in particular, have seen themselves as essentially secular endeavours, entirely divorced from the domains of poetry, philosophy, and theology. Officially, at least, contemporary evolutionary biology is precisely what Darwin himself intended it to be: an entirely naturalistic body of knowledge which makes no direct contact of any kind with matters theological. Individual scientists are generally regarded as being free to hold any personal views they like on matters of philosophy and religion; but as soon as they are tempted to claim scientific authority for these views, they are seen as stepping beyond the domain of evolutionary biology and into that larger field that Gladstone wished to leave to the poets, the philosophers, and the theologians.

This, then, is the official myth of twentieth century secular science. The unofficial reality, however, is somewhat different. For despite the Darwinian revolution, scientists and others have continued to try to construct coherent world-views embracing philosophy, theology, and evolutionary biology. Among the founders of the modern, so-called "synthetic" theory of evolution by natural selection, for example, Theodosius Dobzhansky, George Gaylord

Simpson, and Julian Huxley stand out as men who wished to integrate their science with larger views concerning the nature and significance of life in the universe. That both Dobzhansky and Huxley should have drawn inspiration from the theological writings of the Jesuit palaeontologist Teilhard de Chardin (1959) simply underlines the extent to which the official boundaries between science and theology have remained blurred in the post-Darwinian era (for further discussion of this issue, see Greene 1981).

Despite the complexity of the current scene, however, it remains true that we have come a long way from the days when philosophical, religious and scientific discussions of origins were dominated by the theory of special creation. Today, it is at least possible to distinguish between conventional Darwinian evolutionary biology and that larger evolutionary world-view constructing enterprise that is represented by men like Huxley and Teilhard. For the plain fact is that those who accept the essentially secular terms of Darwinism are free to select amongst a variety of alternative world-views according to their own particular philosophical or religious preferences. In exercising this freedom, of course, people are not making a scientific choice. For Darwinism as such rests upon no distinctive metaphysical or religious propositions; and it offers no distinctive support to any particular world-view, be it pro-Christian, anti-Christian or merely neutral. Rightly conceived, theological questions must be decided on theological grounds, and not upon the territory of the paleontologist or the population geneticist.

Conclusion

I have suggested that much of the argument about evolution and creation arises from the belief that, since these two things are opposed to one another, we must choose between them. This belief is simply false. The theory of evolution by natural selection is not atheistic but rather secular, and there is no necessity for it to be in conflict with, or indeed to make any sort of contact with, the theological doctrine of creation. Historical analysis, however, tells us why the idea that there is conflict between evolution and creation has persisted for so long. For just as in medieval times Christian theology was fused with classical cosmology, so in the 17th and 18th centuries Christian theology was fused with classical philosophy and classical natural history; and just as the Copernican astronomers found themselves confronting the Church, when really they should have been confronting only Aristotle and Ptolemy, so the Darwinists found themselves confronting the representatives of Christianity, when really they should have been confronting only Plato and Paley.

Of course, in one sense to confront Paley was to confront Christianity, since Paley was a representative of Christian natural theology; my point is that precisely that was the problem. For Paley and the special creationists attached the credibility of the Christian doctrine of creation to a particular set of philosophical and scientific beliefs about species with which it need never have been directly associated; and Christendom today is still paying the price for this historic association. The so-called scientific creationists of contemporary America portray themselves as defenders of time-honoured Christian orthodoxy. What they are really doing, however, is reviving the old 17th and 18th century theory of special creation, with all of its idealist and classical, as well as Christian, overtones. Thus, for example, in the creationist textbook *Biology, A Search for Order in Complexity* (Moore and Slusher 1970), we find an interpretation of vertebrate homologies that would have delighted Richard Owen:

> Creationists believe that when God created the vertebrates, He used a single blueprint for the body plan but varied the plan so that each "kind" would be perfectly equipped to take its place in the wonderful world He created for them.

In connection with this kind of thing, which abounds in creationist writings, those Christians who find themselves troubled by Darwinism may care to ask the following questions: where are the specifically Christian grounds for the notions of "blueprints" and "body plans"? and where are the specifically Christian grounds for supposing that special creation according to a small number of demiurgic archetypes was the divine method of creation? Unless and until they receive adequate replies to these questions, those Christians who are troubled by Darwinism are entitled to conclude that the so-called scientific creationists are not the defenders of time-honoured Christian or Biblical orthodoxy, after all, but rather the hopelessly stranded representatives of the outmoded scientific hypotheses of the past.

This, at any rate, was the view of the matter that was held by that most perceptive of commentators upon the Darwinian scene, the late-Victorian Oxford Anglo-Catholic Aubrey Moore. "The dead hand of an exploded scientific theory," Moore once wrote, "rests upon theology.... Christians in all good faith set to work to defend a view which has neither Biblical, nor patristic, nor mediaeval authority.... If the theory of 'special creation' existed in the Bible or in Christian antiquity," he went on, "we might bravely try and do battle for it. But it came to us some two centuries ago from the side of science, with the *imprimatur* of a Puritan poet [the reference is, of course, to Milton]." Thus, Moore concluded, "It is difficult...to see how the question [of evolution *versus* creation], except by a confusion, becomes a religious question at all" (Moore 1889). The confusion that Moore identified almost exactly a century ago is with us still; and it serves the true interests neither of science nor of religion.

References

Aulie, R.P. 1972. "The doctrine of special creation." *American Biology Teacher* 34: 191-200, 261-268.

Barlow, N., ed. 1958. *The Autobiography of Charles Darwin, 1809-1882.* London & Glasgow: Collins.

Bowler, P.J. 1977. "Darwinism and the argument from design: Suggestions for a reevaluation." *Journal of the History of Biology* 10: 29-43.

_____. 1984. *Evolution. The History of an Idea.* Berkeley: University of California Press.

Brooke, J.H. 1985. "The relations between Darwin's science and his religion." in *Darwinism and Divinity: Essays on Evolution and Religious Belief.* Oxford: Blackwell: 40-75.

Darwin, C.R. 1859 *On the Origin of Species by Means of Natural Selection.* London: Murray.

Darwin, C.R. and A.R. Wallace 1958. *Evolution by Natural Selection*, With a Foreword by Gavin de Beer. Cambridge: Cambridge University Press.

Darwin, F. ed. 1887. *The Life and Letters of Charles Darwin.* 3 vols. London: Murray.

Dawkins, R. 1986. *The Blind Watchmaker.* Harlow: Longman Burnt Mill.

Durant, J.R. ed. 1985. *Darwinism and Divinity: Essays on Evolution and Religious Belief.* Oxford: Blackwell.

Godfrey, L.R. 1983. *Scientists Confront Creationism.* New York: Norton.

Greene, J.C. 1981. *Science, Ideology and World View: Essays in the History of Evolutionary Ideas.* Berkeley: University of California Press.

Gruber, H.E. and Barrett, P.H. 1974. *Darwin on Man. A Psychological Study of Scientific Creativity...together with Darwin's Early and Unpublished Notebooks.* London: Wildwood House.

Kitcher, P. 1982. *Abusing Science. The Case Against Creationism.* Cambridge Mass.: MIT Press.

Lovejoy, A.O. 1936. *The Great Chain of Being: A Study in the History of an Idea.* Reprint 1960. New York: Harper.

Montagu, A., ed. 1984. *Science and Creationism.* Oxford: Oxford University Press.

Montefiore, H. 1985. *The Probability of God.* London: SCM Press.

Moore, A.L. 1889. *Science and the Faith: Essays on Apologetic Subjects*. London: Kegan, Paul, Trench, Trubner & Co.

Moore, J.N. and H.S. Slusher, eds. 1970. *Biology: A Search for Order in Complexity*. Grand Rapids, Michigan: Zondervan Publishing House.

Moore, J.R. 1979. *The Post-Darwinian Controversies*. Cambridge: Cambridge University Press.

Morris, H.M., ed. 1974. *Scientific Creationism*. San Diego: Creation-Life Publishers.

Nelkin, D. 1982. *The Creation Controversy: Science or Scripture in the Schools*. New York: Norton.

Ospovat, D. 1978. "Perfect adaptation and teleological explanation: approach to the problem of the history of life in the mid-nineteenth-century." *Studies in the History of Biology* 2: 33-56.

_____. 1981. *The Development of Darwin's Theory: Natural History, Natural Theology, and Natural Selection, 1838-1859*. Cambridge: Cambridge University Press.

Owen, R. 1848. *On the Archetypes and Homologies of the Vertebrate Skeleton*. New York: AMS Press.

Teilhard de Chardin, P. 1959. *The Phenomenon of Man*. Introduced by Julian Huxley. London: Collins.

Young, R.M. 1985. *Darwin's Metaphor: Nature's Place in Victorian Culture*. Cambridge: Cambridge University Press.

15

The Creationists

Ronald L. Numbers

Scarcely twenty years after the publication of Charles Darwin's *Origin of Species* in 1859, special creationists could name only two working naturalists in North America, John William Dawson (1820-99) of Montreal and Arnold Guyot (1806-84) of Princeton, who had not succumbed to some theory of organic evolution (Pfeifer 1974, 203; Gray 1963, 202-3). The situation in Great Britain looked equally bleak for creationists; and on both sides of the Atlantic, liberal churchmen were beginning to follow their scientific colleagues into the evolutionist camp.[1] By the closing years of the nineteenth century evolution was infiltrating even the ranks of the evangelicals, and, in the opinion of many observers, belief in special creation seemed destined to go the way of the dinosaur. However, contrary to the hopes of liberals and the fears of conservatives, creationism did not become extinct. The majority of late-nineteenth-century Americans remained true to a traditional reading of Genesis, and as late as 1982 a public-opinion poll revealed that 44 percent of Americans, nearly a fourth of whom were college graduates, continued to believe that "God created man pretty much in his present form at one time within the last 10,000 years" ("Poll" 1982, 22).[2]

Such surveys failed, however, to disclose the great diversity of opinion among those professing to be creationists. Risking oversimplification, we can divide creationists into two main camps: "strict creationists," who interpret the days of Genesis literally, and "progressive creationists," who construe the Mosaic days to be immense periods of time. Yet, even within these camps substantial differences exist. Among strict creationists, for example, some believe that God created all terrestrial life—past and present—less than ten thousand years ago, while others postulate one or more creations prior to the seven days of Genesis. Similarly, some progressive creationists believe in numerous creative acts, while others limit God's intervention to the creation of life and perhaps the human soul.   Since this last species of creationism is practically indistinguishable from theistic evolutionism, this essay focuses on the strict creationists and the more conservative of the progressive creationists, particularly on the small number who claimed scientific expertise.   Drawing on their writings, it traces the ideological development of creationism from the crusade to outlaw the teaching of evolution in the 1920s to the current battle for equal time.   During this period the leading apologists for special creation shifted from an openly biblical defense of their views to one based largely on science. At the same time they grew less tolerant of notions of an old earth and symbolic days of creation, common among creationists early in the century, and more doctrinaire in their insistence on a recent creation in six literal days and on a universal flood.

The Loyal Majority

The general acceptance of organic evolution by the intellectual elite of the late Victorian era has often obscured the fact that the majority of Americans remained loyal to the doctrine of special creation (Dillenberger & Welch 1954,227).   In addition to the masses who said nothing, there were many people who vocally rejected kinship with the apes and other, more reflective, persons who concurred with the Princeton theologian Charles Hodge (1797-1878) that Darwinism was atheism.   Among the most intransigent foes of organic evolution were the premillennialists, whose predictions of Christ's imminent return depended on a literal reading of the Scriptures (Whalen 1972, 219-29; Numbers 1975, 18-23).   Because of their conviction that one error in the Bible invalidated the entire book, they had little patience with scientists who, as described by the evangelist Dwight L. Moody (1837-99), "dug up old carcasses ... to make them testify against God" (McLoughlin 1959, 213).

Such an attitude did not, however, prevent many biblical literalists from agreeing with geologists that the earth was far older than six thousand years. They did so by identifying two separate creations in the first chapter of Genesis: the first, "in the beginning," perhaps millions of years ago, and the second, in six actual days, approximately four thousand years before the birth of Christ. According to this so-called gap theory, most fossils were relics of the first creation, destroyed by God prior to the Adamic restoration (Numbers 1977, 89-90; Ramm 1954, 195-98).   In 1909 the *Scofield Reference Bible*, the most authoritative biblical guide in fundamentalist circles, sanctioned this view. [3]

Scientists like Guyot and Dawson, the last of the reputable nineteenth-century creationists, went still further to accommodate science by interpreting the days of Genesis as ages and by correlating them with successive epochs in the natural history of the world (O'Brien 1971; Numbers 1977, 91-100). Although they believed in special creative acts, especially of the first humans, they tended to minimize the number of supernatural interventions and to maximize the operation of natural law. During the late nineteenth century their theory of progressive creation circulated widely in the colleges and seminaries of America.[4]

The early Darwinian debate focused largely on the implications of evolution for natural theology (Moore 1979); and so long as these discussions remained confined to scholarly circles, those who objected to evolution on biblical grounds saw little reason to participate. However, when the debate spilled over into the public arena during the 1880s and 1890s, creationists grew alarmed. "When these vague speculations, scattered to the four winds by the million-tongued press, are caught up by ignorant and untrained men," declared one premillennialist in 1889, "it is time for earnest Christian men to call a halt" (Hastings 1889).

The questionable scientific status of Darwinism undoubtedly encouraged such critics to speak up ("Evolutionism in the Pulpit" 1910-15; Bowler 1983). Although the overwhelming majority of scientists after 1880 accepted a long earth history and some form of organic evolution, many in the late nineteenth century were expressing serious reservations about the ability of Darwin's particular theory of natural selection to account for the origin of species. Their published criticisms of Darwinism led creationists mistakenly to conclude that scientists were in the midst of discarding evolution. The appearance of books with such titles as *The Collapse of Evolution* and *At the Death Bed of Darwinism* bolstered this belief and convinced anti-evolutionists that liberal Christians had capitulated to evolution too quickly. In view of this turn of events it seemed likely that those who had "abandoned the stronghold of faith out of sheer fright will soon be found scurrying back to the old and impregnable citadel, when they learn that "the enemy is in full retreat" (Young 1909, 41).

For the time being, however, those conservative Christians who would soon call themselves fundamentalists perceived a greater threat to orthodox faith than evolution—higher criticism, which treated the Bible more as an historical document than as God's inspired Word. Their relative apathy toward evolution is evident in *The Fundamentals*, a mass-produced series of twelve booklets published between 1910 and 1915 to revitalize and reform Christianity around the world. Although one contributor identified evolution as the principal cause of disbelief in the Scriptures and another traced the roots of higher criticism to Darwin, the collection as a whole lacked the strident anti-evolutionism that would characterize the fundamentalist movement of the 1920s (Mauro 1910-15; Reeve 1910-15).

This is particularly true of the writings of George Frederick Wright (1838-1921), a Congregational minister and amateur geologist of international repute (Wright 1916). At first glance his selection to represent the fundamentalist point of view seems anomalous. As a prominent Christian Darwinist in the 1870s he had argued that the intended purpose of Genesis was to protest polytheism, not teach science (Wright 1898). By the 1890s, however, he had come to espouse the progressive creationism of Guyot and Dawson, partly, it seems, in reaction to the claims of higher critics regarding the accuracy of the Pentateuch (Wright 1902). Because of his standing as a scientific authority and his conservative view of the Scriptures, the editors *of The Fundamentals* selected him to address the question of the relationship between evolution and the Christian faith.

In an essay misleadingly titled "The Passing of Evolution" Wright attempted to steer a middle course between the theistic evolution of his early days and the traditional views of some special creationists. On the one hand, he argued that the Bible itself taught evolution, "an orderly progress from lower to higher forms of matter and life." On the other hand, he limited evolution to the origin of species, pointing out that even Darwin had postulated the supernatural creation of several forms of plants and animals, endowed by the Creator with a "marvelous capacity for variation." Furthermore, he argued that, despite the physical similarity between human beings and the higher animals, the former "came into existence as the Bible represents, by the special creation of a single pair, from whom all the varieties of the race have sprung" (Wright 1910-15). [5]

Although Wright represented the left wing of fundamentalism, his moderate views on evolution contributed to the conciliatory tone that prevailed during the years leading up to World War I. Fundamentalists may not have liked evolution, but few, if any, at this time saw the necessity or desirability of launching a crusade to eradicate it from the schools and churches in America.

The Anti-Evolution Crusade

Early in 1922 William Jennings Bryan (1860-1925), Presbyterian layman and thrice-defeated Democratic candidate for the presidency of the United States, heard of an effort in Kentucky to ban the teaching of evolution in public schools. "The movement will sweep the country," he predicted hopefully, "and we will drive Darwinism from our schools" (Levine 1965, 277). His prophecy proved overly optimistic, but before the end of the decade more than twenty state legislatures did debate anti-evolution laws, and four—Oklahoma, Tennessee, Mississippi, and Arkansas—banned the teaching of evolution in public schools (Shipley 1927; 1930). At times the controversy became so tumultuous that it looked to some as though "America might go mad" (Nelson 1964, 319). Many persons shared responsibility for these events, but none more than Bryan. His entry into the fray had a catalytic effect (Szasz 1982, 107-16) and gave anti-evolutionists what they needed most: "a spokesman with a national reputation, immense prestige, and a loyal following" (Levine 1965, 272).

The development of Bryan's own attitude toward evolution closely paralleled that of the fundamentalist movement. Since early in the century he had occasionally alluded to the silliness of believing in monkey ancestors and to the ethical dangers of thinking that might makes right, but until the outbreak of World War I he saw little reason to quarrel with those who disagreed. The war, however, exposed the darkest side of human nature and shattered his illusions about the future of Christian society. Obviously something had gone awry, and Bryan soon traced the source of the trouble to the paralyzing influence of Darwinism on the human conscience. By substituting the law of the jungle for the teaching of Christ, it threatened the principles he valued most: democracy and Christianity. Two books in particular confirmed his suspicion. The first, Vernon Kellogg's *Headquarters Nights* in 1917, recounted firsthand conversations with German officers that revealed the role Darwin's biology had played in persuading the Germans to declare war. The second, Benjamin Kidd's *Science of Power* in 1918, purported to demonstrate the historical and philosophical links between Darwinism and German militarism (Levine 1965, 261-65).

About the time that Bryan discovered the Darwinian origins of the war, he also became aware, to his great distress, of unsettling effects the theory of evolution was having on America's own young people. From frequent visits to college campuses and from talks with parents, pastors, and Sunday school teachers, he heard about an epidemic of unbelief that was sweeping the country. Upon investigating the cause, his wife reported, "he became convinced that the teaching of Evolution as a fact instead of a theory caused the students to lose faith in the Bible, first, in the story of creation, and later in other doctrines, which underlie the Christian religion" (Williams 1936, 448). Again Bryan found confirming evidence in a recently published book, *Belief in God and Immortality*, authored in 1916 by the Bryn Mawr psychologist James H. Leuba, who demonstrated statistically that college attendance endangered traditional religious beliefs (Levine 1965, 266-67).

Armed with this information about the cause of the world's and the nation's moral decay, Bryan launched a nationwide crusade against the offending doctrine. In one of his most popular and influential lectures, "The Menace of Darwinism," he summed up his case against evolution, arguing that it was both un-Christian and unscientific. Darwinism, he declared, was nothing but "guesses strung together," and poor guesses at that. Borrowing from a turn-of-the-century tract, he illustrated how the evolutionist explained the origin of the eye:

> The evolutionist guesses that there was a time when eyes were unknown—that is a necessary part of the hypothesis ...a piece of pigment, or, as some say, a freckle appeared upon the skin of an animal that had no eyes. This piece of pigment or freckle converged the rays of the sun upon that spot and when the little animal felt the heat on that spot it turned the spot to the sun to get more heat. The increased heat irritated the skin—so the evolutionists guess, and a nerve came there and out of the nerve came the eye! (Bryan 1922, 94, 97-98).[6]

"Can you beat it?" he asked incredulously—and that it happened not once but twice? As for himself, he would take one verse in Genesis over all that Darwin wrote.

Throughout his political career Bryan had placed his faith in the common people, and he resented the attempt of a few thousand scientists "to establish an oligarchy over the forty million American Christians," to dictate what should be taught in the schools (Coletta 1969, 230). To a democrat like Bryan it seemed preposterous that this "scientific soviet" (Levine 1965, 289) would not only demand to teach its insidious philosophy but impudently insist that society pay its salaries. Confident that nine-tenths of the Christian citizens agreed with him, he decided to appeal directly to them, as he had done so successfully in fighting the liquor interests.[7] "Commit your case to the people," he advised creationists. "Forget, if need be, the highbrows both in the political and college world, and carry this cause to the people. They are the final and efficiently corrective power" ("Progress" 1929, 13).

Who were the people who joined Bryan's crusade? As recent studies have shown, they came from all walks of life and from every region of the country. They lived in New York, Chicago, and Los Angeles as well as in small towns and in the country. Few possessed advanced degrees, but many were not without education. Nevertheless, Bryan undeniably found his staunchest supporters and won his greatest victories in the conservative and still largely rural South, described hyperbolically by one fundamentalist journal as "the last stronghold of orthodoxy on the North American continent," a region where the "masses of the people in all denominations 'believe the Bible from lid to lid'" ("Fighting Evolution" 1925, 5).[8]

The strength of Bryan's following within the churches is perhaps more difficult to determine, because not all fundamentalists were creationists and many creationists refused to participate in the crusade against evolution. However, a 1929 survey of the theological beliefs of seven hundred Protestant ministers provides some valuable clues (Betts 1929, 26, 44). The question "Do you believe that the creation of the world occurred in the manner and time recorded in Genesis?" elicited the following positive responses:

Lutheran	89%
Baptist	63%
Evangelical	62%
Presbyterian	35%
Methodist	24%
Congregational	12%
Episcopalian	11%
Other	60%

Unfortunately, these statistics tell us nothing about the various ways respondents may have interpreted the phrase "in the manner and time recorded in Genesis," nor do they reveal anything about the level of political involvement in the campaign against evolution. Lutherans, for example, despite their overwhelming rejection of evolution, generally preferred education to legislation and tended to view legal action against evolution as "a dangerous mingling of church and state" (Rudnick 1966, 88-90; Szasz 1969, 279). Similarly, premillennialists, who saw the spread of evolution as one more sign of the world's impending end, sometimes lacked incentive to correct the evils around them (Sandeen 1971, 266-68). [9]

Baptists and Presbyterians, who dominated the fundamentalist movement, participated actively in the campaign against evolution. The Southern Baptist Convention, spiritual home of some of the most outspoken critics of evolution, lent encouragement to the creationist crusaders by voting unanimously in 1926 that "this Convention accepts Genesis as teaching that man was the special cremation of God, and rejects every theory, evolution or other, which teaches that man originated in, or came by way of, a lower animal ancestry" (Clark 1952, 154; Thompson 1975-76). The Presbyterian Church contributed Bryan and other leaders to the creationist cause but, as the above survey indicates, also harbored many evolutionists. In 1923 the General Assembly turned back an attempt by Bryan and his fundamentalist cohorts to cut off funds to any church school found teaching human evolution, approving instead a compromise measure that condemned only materialistic evolution (Loetscher 1954, 111). The other major Protestant bodies paid relatively little attention to the debate over evolution; and Catholics, though divided on the question of evolution, seldom favored restrictive legislation (Morrison 1953). [10]

Leadership of the anti-evolution movement came not from the organized churches of America but from individuals like Bryan and interdenominational organizations such as the World's Christian Fundamentals Association, a predominantly premillennialist body founded in 1919 by William Bell Riley (1861-1947), pastor of the First Baptist Church in Minneapolis.[11] Riley became active as an anti-evolutionist after discovering, to his apparent surprise, that evolutionists were teaching their views at the University of Minnesota. The early twentieth century witnessed an unprecedented expansion of public education; enrollment in public high schools nearly doubled between 1920 and 1930 (Bailey 1964, 72-73). Fundamentalists like Riley and Bryan wanted to make sure that students attending these institutions would not lose their faith. Thus they resolved to drive every evolutionist from the public school payroll. Those who lost their jobs as a result deserved little sympathy, for, as one rabble-rousing creationist put it, the German soldiers who killed Belgian and French children with poisoned candy were angels compared with the teachers and textbook writers who corrupted the souls of children and thereby sentenced them to eternal death (Martin 1923, 164-65).

The creationists, we should remember, did not always act without provocation. In many instances their opponents displayed equal intolerance and insensitivity. In fact, one contemporary observer blamed the creation-evolution controversy in part on the "intellectual flapperism" of irresponsible and poorly informed teachers who delighted in shocking naive students with unsupportable statements about evolution. It was understandable, wrote an Englishman, that American parents would resent sending their sons and daughters to public institutions that exposed them to "a multiple assault upon traditional faiths" (Beale 1936, 249-51).

Creationist Science and Scientists

In 1922 Riley outlined the reasons why fundamentalists opposed the teaching of evolution. "The first and most important reason for its elimination," he explained, "is the unquestioned fact that evolution is not a science; it is a hypothesis only, a speculation" ([Riley] 1922, 5). Bryan often made the same point, defining true science as "classified knowledge ... the explanation of facts" (Bryan 1922, 94). Although creationists had far more compelling reasons for rejecting evolution than its alleged unscientific status, their insistence on this point was not merely an obscurantist ploy. Rather it stemmed from their commitment to a once-respected tradition, associated with the English philosopher Sir Francis Bacon (1561-1626), that emphasized the factual, nontheoretical nature of science (Marsden 1977, 214-15). By identifying with the Baconian tradition, creationists could label evolution as false science, could claim equality with scientific authorities in comprehending facts, and could deny the charge of being anti-science. "It is not 'science' that orthodox Christians oppose," a fundamentalist editor insisted defensively. "No! no! a thousand times, No! They are opposed only to the theory of evolution, which has not yet been proved, and therefore is not to be called by the sacred name of *science*" (K[eyser] 1925, 413).

Because of their conviction that evolution was unscientific, creationists assured themselves that the world's best scientists agreed with them. They received an important boost at the beginning of their campaign from an address by the distinguished British biologist William Bateson (1861-1926) in 1921, in which he declared that scientists had not discovered "the actual mode and process of evolution" (Bateson 1922).[12] Although he warned creationists against misinterpreting his statement as a rejection of evolution, they paid no more attention to that caveat than they did to the numerous pro-evolution resolutions passed by scientific societies (Shipley 1927, 384).

Unfortunately for the creationists, they could claim few legitimate scientists of their own: a couple of self-made men of science, one or two physicians, and a handful of teachers who, as one evolutionist described them, were "trying to hold down, not a chair, but a whole settee, of 'Natural Science' in some little institution."[13] Of this group the most influential were Harry Rimmer (1890-1952) and George McCready Price (1870-1963).

Rimmer, Presbyterian minister and self-styled "research scientist," obtained his limited exposure to science during a term or two at San Francisco's Hahnemann Medical College, a small, homeopathic institution that required no more than a high school diploma for admission. As a medical student he picked up a vocabulary of "double-jointed, twelve cylinder, knee-action words" that later served to impress the uninitiated (Rimmer 1945, 14). After his brief stint in medical school he attended Whittier College and the Bible Institute of Los Angeles for a year each before entering full-time evangelistic work. About 1919 he settled in Los Angeles, where he set up a small laboratory at the rear of his house to conduct experiments in embryology and related sciences. Within a year or two he established the Research Science Bureau "to prove through findings in biology, paleontology, and anthropology that science and the literal Bible were not contradictory." The bureau staff—that is, Rimmer—apparently used income from the sale of memberships to finance anthropological field trips in the western United States, but Rimmer's dream of visiting Africa to prove the dissimilarity of gorillas and humans failed to materialize. By the late 1920s the bureau lay dormant, and Rimmer signed on with Riley's World's Christian Fundamentals Associations as a field secretary.[14]

Besides engaging in research, Rimmer delivered thousands of lectures, primarily to student groups, on the scientific accuracy of the Bible. Posing as a scientist, he attacked Darwinism and poked fun at the credulity of evolutionists. To attract attention, he repeatedly offered one hundred dollars to anyone who could discover a scientific error in the Scriptures; not surprisingly, the offer never cost him a dollar ("World Religious Digest" 1939, 215). He also, by his own reckoning, never lost a public debate. Following one encounter with an evolutionist in Philadelphia, he wrote home gleefully that "the debate was a simple walkover, a massacre-murder pure and simple. The eminent professor was simply scared stiff to advance any of the common arguments of the evolutionists, and he fizzled like a wet firecracker" (Edmondson 1969, 329-30, 333-34).

Price, a Seventh-day Adventist geologist, was less skilled at debating than Rimmer but more influential scientifically. As a young man Price attended an Adventist college in Michigan for two years and later completed a teacher training course at the provincial normal school in his native New Brunswick. The turn of the century found him serving as principal of a small high school in an isolated part of eastern Canada, where one of his few companions was a local physician. During their many conversations, the doctor almost converted his fundamentalist friend to evolution, but each time Price wavered, he was saved by prayer and by reading the works of the Seventh-day Adventist prophetess Ellen G. White (1827-1915), who claimed divine inspiration for her view that Noah's flood accounted for the fossil record on which evolutionists based their theory. As a result of these experiences, Price vowed to devote his life to promoting creationism of the strictest kind.[15]

By 1906 he was working as a handyman at an Adventist sanitarium in southern California. That year he published a slim volume entitled *Illogical Geology: The Weakest Point in the Evolution Theory*, in which he brashly offered one thousand dollars "to any one who will, in the face of the facts here presented, show me how to prove that one kind of fossil is older than another." (Like Rimmer, he never had to pay.) According to Price's argument, Darwinism rested "logically and historically on the succession of life idea as taught by geology" and "if this succession of life is not an actual scientific fact, then Darwinism ... is a most gigantic hoax" (Price 1906, 9).[16]

Although a few fundamentalists praised Price's polemic, David Starr Jordan (1851-1931), president of Stanford University and an authority on fossil fishes, warned him that he should not expect "any geologist to take [his work] seriously." Jordan conceded that the unknown author had written "a very clever book" but described it as:

a sort of lawyer's plea, based on scattering mistakes, omissions and exceptions against general truths that anybody familiar with the facts in a general way cannot possibly dispute. It would be just as easy and just as plausible and just as convincing if one should take the facts of European history and attempt to show that all the various events were simultaneous."[17]

As Jordan recognized, Price lacked any formal training or field experience in geology. He was, however, a voracious reader of geological literature, an armchair scientist who self-consciously minimized the importance of field experience.

During the next fifteen years Price occupied scientific settees in several Seventh-day Adventist schools and authored six more books attacking evolution, particularly its geological foundation. Although not unknown outside his own church before the early 1920s, he did not attract national attention until then. Shortly after Bryan declared war on evolution, Price published in *1923 The New Geology*, the most systematic and comprehensive of his many books. Uninhibited by false modesty, he presented his "great *law of conformable stratigraphic sequences* ... by all odds the most important law ever formulated with reference to the order in which the strata occur." This law stated that "*any kind of fossiliferous beds whatever, 'young' or 'old,' may be found occurring conformably on any other fossiliferous beds, 'older' or 'younger'*" (Price 1923, 637-38).[18] To Price, so-called deceptive conformities (where strata seem to be missing) and thrust faults (where the strata are apparently in the wrong order) proved that there was no natural order to the fossilbearing rocks, all of which he attributed to the Genesis flood.

A Yale geologist reviewing the book for *Science* accused Price of "harboring a geological nightmare" (Schuchert 1924). Despite such criticism from the scientific establishment—and the fact that his theory contradicted both the day-age and gap interpretations of Genesis—Price's reputation among fundamentalists rose dramatically. Rimmer, for example, hailed *The New Geology* as "a masterpiece of REAL science [that] explodes in a convincing manner some of the ancient fallacies of science 'falsely so called'" (Rimmer 1925, 28). By the mid-1920s Price's byline was appearing with increasing frequency in a broad spectrum of conservative religious periodicals, and the editor of *Science* could accurately describe him as "the principal scientific authority of the Fundamentalists" (*Science* 1926).

The Scopes Trial and Beyond

In the spring of 1925 John Thomas Scopes, a high school teacher in the small town of Dayton, Tennessee, confessed to having violated the state's recently passed law banning the teaching of human evolution in public schools. His subsequent trial focused international attention on the anti-evolution crusade and brought William Jennings Bryan to Dayton to assist the prosecution. In anticipation of arguing the scientific merits of evolution, Bryan sought out the best scientific minds in the creationist camp to serve as expert witnesses. The response to his inquiries could only have disappointed the aging crusader. Price, then teaching in England, sent his regrets—along with advice for Bryan to stay away from scientific topics (Numbers 1979, 24). Howard A. Kelly, a prominent Johns Hopkins physician who had contributed to *The Fundamentals*, confessed that, except for Adam and Eve, he believed in evolution. Louis T. More, a physicist who had just written a book in 1925 on *The Dogma of Evolution*, replied that he accepted evolution as a working hypothesis. Alfred W. McCann, author in 1922 of *God—or Gorilla*, took the opportunity to chide Bryan for supporting prohibition in the past and for now trying "to bottle-up the tendencies of men to think for themselves."[19]

At the trial itself things scarcely went better. When Bryan could name only Price and the deceased Wright as scientists for whom he had respect, the caustic Clarence Darrow (1857-1938), attorney for the defense, scoffed: "You mentioned Price because he is the only human being in the world so far as you know that signs his name as a geologist that believes like you do.... every scientist in this country knows [he] is a mountebank and a pretender and not a geologist at all." Eventually Bryan conceded that the world was indeed far more than six thousand years old and that the six days of creation had probably been longer than twenty-four hours each—concessions that may have harmonized with the progressive creationism of Wright but hardly with the strict creationism of Price (Numbers 1979, 24; Levine 1965, 349).

Though one could scarcely have guessed it from some of his public pronouncements, Bryan had long been a progressive creationist. In fact, his beliefs regarding evolution diverged considerably from those of his more conservative supporters. Shortly before his trial he had confided to Dr. Kelly that he, too, had no objection to "evolution before man but for the fact that a concession as to the truth of evolution up to man furnishes our opponents with an argument which they are quick to use, namely, if evolution accounts for all the species up to man, does it not raise a presumption in behalf of evolution to include man?" Until biologists could actually demonstrate the evolution of one species into another, he thought it best to keep them on the defensive.[20]

Bryan's admission at Dayton spotlighted a serious and long-standing problem among anti-evolutionists: their failure to agree on a theory of creation. Even the most visible leaders could not reach a consensus. Riley, for example, followed Guyot and Dawson (and Bryan) in viewing the days of Genesis as ages, believing that the testimony of geology necessitated this interpretation. Rimmer favored the gap theory, which involved two separate creations, in part because his scientific mind could not fathom how, given Riley's scheme, plants created on the third day could have survived thousands of years without sunshine, until the sun appeared on the fourth. According to the testimony of acquaintances, he also believed that the Bible taught a local rather than a universal flood (Culver 1955, 7). Price, who cared not a whit about the opinion of geologists, insisted on nothing less than a recent creation in six literal days and a worldwide deluge. He regarded the day-age theory as "the devil's counterfeit" and the gap theory as only slightly more acceptable (Price 1902, 125-27; 1954, 39). Rimmer and Riley, who preferred to minimize the differences among creationists, attempted the logically impossible, if ecumenically desirable, task of incorporating Price's "new geology" into their own schemes (Riley & Rimmer n.d.; Riley 1930, 45).

Although the court in Dayton found Scopes guilty as charged, creationists had little cause for rejoicing. The press had not treated them kindly, and the taxing ordeal no doubt contributed to Bryan's death a few days after the end of the trial. Nevertheless, the anti-evolutionists continued their crusade, winning victories in Mississippi in 1926 and in Arkansas two years later (Shipley 1930, 330-32). By the end of the decade, however, their legislative campaign had lost its steam. The presidential election of 1928, pitting a Protestant against a Catholic, offered fundamentalists a new cause, and the onset of the depression in 1929 further diverted their attention (Szasz 1981, 117-25).

Contrary to appearances, the creationists were simply changing tactics, not giving up. Instead of lobbying state legislatures, they shifted their attack to local communities, where they engaged in what one critic described as "the emasculation of textbooks, the 'purging' of libraries, and above all the continued hounding of teachers" (Shipley 1930, 330). Their new approach attracted less attention but paid off handsomely, as school boards, textbook publishers, and teachers in both urban and rural areas, North and South, bowed to their pressure. Darwinism virtually disappeared from high school texts, and for years many American teachers feared being identified as evolutionists (Beale 1936, 228-37; Gatewood 1969, 39; Grabiner & Miller 1974; Laba & Gross 1950).

Creationism Underground

During the heady days of the 1920s, when their activities made front-page headlines, creationists dreamed of converting the world; a decade later, forgotten and rejected by the establishment, they turned their energies inward and began creating an institutional base of their own. Deprived of the popular press and frustrated by their inability to publish their views in organs controlled by orthodox scientists, they determined to organize their own societies and edit their own journals (Carpenter 1980).[21] Their early efforts, however, encountered two problems: the absence of a critical mass of scientifically trained creationists and lack of internal agreement.

In 1935 Price, along with Dudley Joseph Whitney, a farm journalist, and L. Allen Higley, a Wheaton College science professor, formed a Religion and Science Association to create "a united front against the theory of evolution." Among those invited to participate in the association's first—and only— convention were representatives of the three major creationist parties, including Price himself, Rimmer, and one of Dawson's sons, who, like his father, advocated the day-age theory.[22] But as soon as the Price faction discovered that its associates had no intention of agreeing on a short earth history, it bolted the organization, leaving it a shambles.[23]

Shortly thereafter, in 1938, Price and some Seventh-day Adventist friends in the Los Angeles area, several of them physicians associated with the College of Medical Evangelists (now part of Loma Linda University), organized their own Deluge Geology Society and, between 1941 and 1945, published a *Bulletin of Deluge Geology and Related Science*. As described by Price, the group consisted of "a very eminent set of men.... In no other part of this round globe could anything like the number of scientifically educated believers in Creation and opponents of evolution be assembled, as here in Southern California" (Numbers 1979, 26). Perhaps the society's most notable achievement was its sponsorship in the early 1940s of a hush-hush project to study giant fossil footprints, believed to be human, discovered in rocks far older than the theory of evolution would allow. This find, the society announced excitedly, thus demolished that theory "at a single stroke" and promised to "*astound the scientific world!*" Yet despite such activity and the group's religious homogeneity, it, too, soon foundered—on "the same rock," complained a disappointed member, that wrecked the Religion and Science Association, that is "*pre-Genesis time for the earth.*" [24]

By this time creationists were also beginning to face a new problem: the presence within their own ranks of young university-trained scientists who wanted to bring evangelical Christianity more into line with mainstream science.

The encounter between the two generations often proved traumatic, as is illustrated by the case of Harold W. Clark (b. 1891). A former student of Price's, he had gone on to earn a master's degree in biology from the University of California and taken a position at a small Adventist college in northern California. By 1940 his training and field experience had convinced him that Price's *New Geology* was "entirely out of date and inadequate" as a text, especially in its rejection of the geological column. When Price learned of this, he angrily accused his former disciple of suffering from "the modern mental disease of university-itis" and of currying the favor of "tobacco-smoking, Sabbath-breaking, God-defying" evolutionists. Despite Clark's protests that he still believed in a literal six-day creation and universal flood, Price kept up his attack for the better part of a decade, at one point addressing a vitriolic pamphlet, *Theories of Satanic Origin*, to his erstwhile friend and fellow creationist (Numbers 1979, 25).

The inroads of secular scientific training also became apparent in the American Scientific Affiliation (ASA), created by evangelical scientists in 1941.[25] Although the society took no official stand on creation, strict creationists found the atmosphere congenial during the early years of the society. In the late 1940s, however, some of the more progressive members, led by J. Laurence Kulp, a young geochemist on the faculty of Columbia University, began criticizing Price and his followers for their allegedly unscientific effort to squeeze earth history into less than ten thousand years. Kulp, a Wheaton alumnus and member of the Plymouth Brethren, had acquired a doctorate in physical chemistry from Princeton University and gone on to complete all the requirements, except a dissertation, for a Ph.D. in geology. Although initially suspicious of the conclusions of geology regarding the history and antiquity of the earth, he had come to accept them. As one of the first evangelicals professionally trained in geology, he felt a responsibility to warn his colleagues in the ASA about Price's work, which, he believed, had "infiltrated the greater portion of fundamental Christianity in America primarily due to the absence of trained Christian geologists." In what was apparently the first systematic critique of the "new geology" Kulp concluded that the "major propositions of the theory are contraindicated by established physical and chemical laws" (Kulp 1950).[26] Conservatives within the ASA not unreasonably suspected that Kulp's exposure to "the orthodox geological viewpoint" had severely undermined his faith in a literal interpretation of the Bible ("Comment" 1950, 2).

Before long it became evident that a growing number of ASA members, like Kulp, were drifting from strict to progressive creationism and sometimes on to theistic evolutionism. The transition for many involved immense personal stress, as revealed in the autobiographical testimony of another Wheaton alumnus, J. Frank Cassel:

> First to be overcome was the onus of dealing with a "verboten" term and in a "nonexistent" area. Then, as each made an honest and objective consideration of the data, he was struck with the validity and undeniability of datum after datum. As he strove to incorporate each of these facts into his Biblico-scientific frame of reference, he found that—while the frame became more complete and satisfying—he began to question first the feasibility and then the desirability of an effort to refute the total evolutionary concept, and finally he became impressed by its impossibility on the basis of existing data. This has been a heart-rending, soul-searching experience for the committed Christian as he has seen what he had long considered the raison d'être of God's call for his life endeavor fade away and as he has struggled to release strongly held convictions as to the close limitations of Creationism.

Cassel went on to note that the struggle was "made no easier by the lack of approbation (much less acceptance) of some of his less well-informed colleagues, some of whom seem to question motives or even to imply heresy" (Cassel 1959, 26-27).[27]   Strict creationists, who suffered their own agonies, found it difficult not to conclude that their liberal colleagues were simply taking the easy way out. To both parties a split seemed inevitable.

Creationism Abroad

During the decades immediately following the crusade of the 1920s American anti-evolutionists were buoyed by reports of a creationist revival in Europe, especially in England, where creationism was thought to be all but dead. The Victoria Institute in London, a haven for English creationists in the nineteenth century, had by the 1920s become a stronghold of theistic evolution. When Price visited the institute in 1925 to receive its Langhorne-Orchard Prize for an essay on "Revelation and Evolution," several members protested his attempt to export the fundamentalist controversy to England. Even evangelicals refused to get caught up in the turmoil that engulfed the United States. As historian George Marsden has explained, English evangelicals, always a minority, had developed a stronger tradition of theological toleration than revivalist Americans, who until the twentieth century had never experienced minority status. Thus, while the displaced Americans fought to recover their lost position, English evangelicals adopted a nonmilitant live-and-let-live philosophy that stressed personal piety (Numbers 1975, 25; Marsden 1977; 1980, 222-26).

The sudden appearance of a small but vocal group of British creationists in the early 1930s caught nearly everyone by surprise. The central figure in this movement was Douglas Dewar (1875-1957), a Cambridge graduate and amateur ornithologist, who had served for decades as a lawyer in the Indian Civil Service. Originally an evolutionist, he had gradually become convinced of the necessity of adopting "a provisional hypothesis of special creation ... Supplemented by a theory of evolution." This allowed him to accept unlimited development within biological families. His published views, unlike those of most American creationists, betrayed little biblical influence (Dewar 1931, 158; Lunn 1947, 1, 154; *Evolution Protest* 1965). His greatest intellectual debt was not to Moses but to a French zoologist, Louis Vialleton (1859-1929), who had attracted considerable attention in the 1920s for suggesting a theory of discontinuous evolution, which anti-evolutionists eagerly—but erroneously—equated with special creation (Paul 1979, 99-100).

Soon after announcing his conversion to creationism in 1931, Dewar submitted a short paper on mammalian fossils to the Zoological Society of London, of which he was a member. The secretary of the society subsequently rejected the piece, noting that a competent referee thought Dewar's evidence "led to no valuable conclusion." Such treatment infuriated Dewar and convinced him that evolution had become "a scientific creed." Those who questioned scientific orthodoxy, he complained, "are deemed unfit to hold scientific offices; their articles are rejected by newspapers or journals; their contributions are refused by scientific societies, and publishers decline to publish their books except at the author's expense. Thus the independents are today pretty effectually muzzled" (Dewar 1932, 142). Because of such experiences Dewar and other British dissidents in 1932 organized the Evolution Protest Movement, which after two decades claimed a membership of two hundred ("EPM" 1972).

Henry M. Morris and the Revival of Creationism

In 1964 one historian predicted that "a renaissance of the [creationist] movement is most unlikely" (Halliburton 1964, 283). And so it seemed. But even as these words were penned, a major revival was underway, led by a Texas engineer, Henry M. Morris (b. 1918). Raised a nominal Southern Baptist, and as such a believer in creation, Morris as a youth had drifted unthinkingly into evolutionism and religious indifference. A thorough study of the Bible following graduation from college convinced him of its absolute truth and prompted him to reevaluate his belief in evolution. After an intense period of soul-searching he concluded that creation had taken place in six literal days, because the Bible clearly said so and "God doesn't lie." Corroborating evidence came from the book of nature. While sitting in his office at Rice Institute, where he was teaching civil engineering, he would study the butterflies and wasps that flew in through the window; being familiar with structural design, he calculated the improbability of such complex creatures developing by chance. Nature as well as the Bible seemed to argue for creation.[28]

For assistance in answering the claims of evolutionists, he found little creationist literature of value apart from the writings of Rimmer and Price. Although he rejected Price's peculiar theology, he took an immediate liking to the Adventist's flood geology and in 1946 incorporated it into a little book, *That You Might Believe*, the first book, so far as he knew, "published since the Scopes trial in which a scientist from a secular University advocated recent special creation and a worldwide flood" (Morris 1978, 10). In the late 1940s he joined the American Scientific Affiliation—just in time to protest Kulp's attack on Price's geology. Yet his words fell largely on deaf ears. In 1953 when he presented some of his own views on the flood to the ASA, one of the few compliments came from a young theologian, John C. Whitcomb, Jr., who belonged to the Grace Brethren. The two subsequently became friends and decided to collaborate on a major defense of the Noachian flood. By the time they finished their project, Morris had earned a Ph.D. in hydraulic engineering from the University of Minnesota and was chairing the civil engineering department at Virginia Polytechnic Institute; Whitcomb was teaching Old Testament studies at Grace Theological Seminary in Indiana.[29]

In 1961 they brought out *The Genesis Flood*, the most impressive contribution to strict creationism since the publication of Price's *New Geology* in 1923. In many respects their book appeared to be simply "a reissue of G. M. Price's views, brought up to date," as one reader described it. Beginning with a testimony to their belief in "the verbal inerrancy of Scripture," Whitcomb and Morris went on to argue for a recent creation of the entire universe, a Fall that triggered the second law of thermodynamics, and a worldwide flood that in one year laid down most of the geological strata. Given this history, they argued, "the last refuge of the case for evolution immediately vanishes away, and the record of the rocks becomes a tremendous witness ... to the holiness and justice and power of the living God of Creation!" (Whitcomb & Morris 1961, xx, 451).

Despite the book's lack of conceptual novelty, it provoked an intense debate among evangelicals. Progressive creationists denounced it as a travesty on geology that threatened to set back the cause of Christian science a generation, while strict creationists praised it for making biblical catastrophism intellectually respectable. Its appeal, suggested one critic, lay primarily in the fact that, unlike previous creationist works, it "looked *legitimate* as a scientific contribution," accompanied as it was by footnotes and other scholarly appurtenances. In responding to their detractors, Whitcomb and Morris repeatedly refused to be drawn into a scientific debate, arguing that "the real issue is not the correctness of the interpretation of various details of the geological data, but simply what God has revealed in His Word concerning these matters" (Morris & Whitcomb 1964, 60).[30]

Whatever its merits, *The Genesis Flood* unquestionably "brought about a stunning renaissance of flood geology" (Young 1977, 7), symbolized by the establishment in 1963 of the Creation Research Society. Shortly before the publication of his book Morris had sent the manuscript to Walter E. Lammerts (b. 1904), a Missouri Synod Lutheran with a doctorate in genetics from the University of California. As an undergraduate at Berkeley Lammerts had discovered Price's *New Geology*, and during the early 1940s, while teaching at UCLA, he had worked with Price in the Creation-Deluge Society. After the mid-1940s, however, his interest in creationism had flagged—until awakened by reading the Whitcomb and Morris manuscript. Disgusted by the ASA's flirtation with evolution, he organized in the early 1960s a correspondence network with Morris and eight other strict creationists, dubbed the "team of ten." In 1963 seven of the ten met with a few other like-minded scientists at the home of a team member in Midland, Michigan, to form the Creation Research Society (CRS) (Lammerts 1974).

The society began with a carefully selected eighteen-man "innercore steering committee," which included the original team of ten. The composition of this committee reflected, albeit imperfectly, the denominational, regional, and professional bases of the creationist revival. There were six Missouri Synod Lutherans, five Baptists, two Seventh-day Adventists, and one each from the Reformed Presbyterian Church, the Reformed Christian Church, the Church of the Brethren, and an independent Bible church. (Information about one member is not available.) Eleven lived in the Midwest, three in the South, and two in the Far West. The committee included six biologists but only one geologist, an independent consultant with a master's degree. Seven members taught in church-related colleges, five in state institutions; the others worked for industry or were self-employed.[31]

To avoid the creeping evolutionism that had infected the ASA and to ensure that the society remained loyal to the Price-Morris tradition, the CRS required members to sign a statement of belief accepting the inerrancy of the Bible, the special creation of "all basic types of living things," and a worldwide deluge (*Creation Research* 1964, [131]). It restricted membership to Christians only. (Although creationists liked to stress the scientific evidence for their position, one estimated that "only about five percent of evolutionists-turned-creationists did so on the basis of the overwhelming evidence for creation in the world of nature;" the remaining 95 percent became creationists because they believed in the Bible [Lang 1978, 2]).[32]   To legitimate its claim to being a scientific society, the CRS published a quarterly journal and limited full membership to persons possessing a graduate degree in a scientific discipline.

At the end of its first decade the society claimed 450 regular members, plus 1,600 sustaining members, who failed to meet the scientific qualifications. Eschewing politics, the CRS devoted itself almost exclusively to education and research, funded "at very little expense, and ... with no expenditure of public money" (Lammerts 1974, 63).   CRS-related projects included expeditions to search for Noah's ark, studies of fossil human footprints and pollen grains found out of the predicted evolutionary order, experiments on radiation-produced mutations in plants, and theoretical studies in physics demonstrating a recent origin of the earth (Gish 1975). A number of members collaborated in preparing a biology textbook based on creationist principles (Moore & Slusher 1970). In view of the previous history of creation science, it was an auspicious beginning.

While the CRS catered to the needs of scientists, a second, predominantly lay organization carried creationism to the masses. Created in 1964 in the wake of interest generated by *The Genesis Flood*, the Bible-Science Association came to be identified by many with one man: Walter Lang, an ambitious Missouri Synod pastor who self-consciously prized spiritual insight above scientific expertise.   As editor of the widely circulated *Bible-Science Newsletter* he vigorously promoted the Price-Morris line—and occasionally provided a platform for individuals on the fringes of the creationist movement, such as those who questioned the heliocentric theory and who believed that Albert Einstein's theory of relativity "was invented in order to circumvent the evidence that the earth is at rest." Needless to say, the pastor's broadmindedness greatly embarrassed creationists seeking scientific respectability, who feared that such bizarre behavior would tarnish the entire movement (Lang 1977a, 4-5; 1977b, 2-3; 1978b, 1-3; Wheeler 1976, 101-2).

Scientific Creationism

The creationists' revival of the 1960s attracted little public attention until late in the decade, when fundamentalists became aroused about the federally funded Biological Sciences Curriculum Study texts (Skoog 1979; "A Critique" 1966, 1), which featured evolution, and the California State Board of Education voted to require public school textbooks to include creation along with evolution.   This decision resulted in large part from the efforts of two southern California housewives, Nell Segraves and Jean Sumrall, associates of both the

Bible-Science Association and the CRS. In 1961 Segraves learned of the U.S. Supreme Court's ruling in the Madalyn Murray case protecting atheist students from required prayers in public schools. Murray's ability to shield her child from religious exposure suggested to Segraves that creationist parents like herself "were entitled to protect our children from the influence of beliefs that would be offensive to our religious beliefs." It was this line of argument that finally persuaded the Board of Education to grant creationists equal rights (Bates 1976, 58; "Fifteen Years" 1979, 2; Wade 1972; see also Moore 1974-, and Nelkin 1982).

Flushed with victory, Segraves and her son Kelly in 1970 joined an effort to organize a Creation-Science Research Center (CSRC), affiliated with Christian Heritage College in San Diego, to prepare creationist literature suitable for adoption in public schools. Associated with them in this enterprise was Morris, who resigned his position at Virginia Polytechnic Institute to help establish a center for creation research. Because of differences in personalities and objectives, the Segraveses in 1972 left the college, taking the CSRC with them; Morris thereupon set up a new research division at the college, the Institute for Creation Research (ICR), which, he announced with obvious relief, would be "controlled and operated by scientists" and would engage in research and education, not political action. During the 1970s Morris added five scientists to his staff and, funded largely by small gifts and royalties from institute publications, turned the ICR into the world's leading center for the propagation of strict creationism (Morris 1972).[33] Meanwhile, the CSRC continued campaigning for the legal recognition of special creation, often citing a direct relationship between the acceptance of evolution and the breakdown of law and order. Its own research, the CSRC announced, proved that evolution fostered "the moral decay of spiritual values which contribute to the destruction of mental health and ... [the prevalence of] divorce, abortion, and rampant venereal disease" (Segraves 1977, 17; "Fifteen Years" 1979, 2-3).

The 1970s witnessed a major shift in creationist tactics. Instead of trying to outlaw evolution, as they had done in the 1920s, anti-evolutionists now fought to give creation equal time. And instead of appealing to the authority of the Bible, as Morris and Whitcomb had done as recently as 1961, they consciously downplayed the Genesis story in favor of what they called "scientific creationism." Several factors no doubt contributed to this shift. One sociologist has suggested that creationists began stressing the scientific legitimacy of their enterprise because "their theological legitimation of reality was no longer sufficient for maintaining their world and passing on their world view to their children" (Bates 1976, 98). However, there were also practical considerations. In 1968 the U.S. Supreme Court declared the Arkansas anti-evolution law unconstitutional, giving creationists reason to suspect that legislation requiring the teaching of biblical creationism would meet a similar fate. They also feared that requiring the biblical account "would open the door to a wide variety of interpretations of Genesis" and produce demands for the inclusion of non-Christian versions of creation (Morris 1974a, 2; see also Larson 1984).

In view of such potential hazards, Morris recommended that creationists ask public schools to teach "only the scientific aspects of creationism" (Morris 1974a, 2), which in practice meant leaving out all references to the six days of Genesis and Noah's ark and focusing instead on evidence for a recent worldwide catastrophe and on arguments against evolution. Thus the product remained virtually the same; only the packaging changed. The 1974 ICR textbook *Scientific Creationism*, for example, came in two editions: one for public schools, containing no references to the Bible, and another for use in Christian schools that included a chapter on "Creation According to Scripture" (Morris 1974b).

In defending creation as a scientific alternative to evolution, creationists relied less on Francis Bacon and his conception of science and more on two new philosopher-heroes: Karl Popper and Thomas Kuhn. Popper required all scientific theories to be falsifiable; since evolution could not be falsified, reasoned the creationists, it was by definition not science. Kuhn described scientific progress in terms of competing models or paradigms rather than the accumulation of objective knowledge.[34] Thus creationists saw no reason why their flood-geology model should not be allowed to compete on an equal scientific basis with the evolution model. In selling this two-model approach to school boards, creationists were advised: "Sell more SCIENCE.... Who can object to teaching more science? What is controversial about that? ... do not use the word 'creationism.' Speak only of science. Explain that withholding scientific information contradicting evolution amounts to 'censorship' and smacks of getting into the province of religious dogma.... Use the 'censorship' label as one who is against censoring science. YOU are for science; anyone else who wants to censor scientific data is an old fogey and too doctrinaire to consider" (Leitch 1980, 2). This tactic proved extremely effective, at least initially. Two state legislatures, in Arkansas and Louisiana, and various school boards adopted the two-model approach, and an informal poll of school board members in 1980 showed that only 25 percent favored teaching nothing but evolution ("Finding" 1980, 52; Segraves 1977, 24). In 1982, however, a federal judge declared the Arkansas law, requiring a "balanced treatment" of creation and evolution, to be unconstitutional ("Creationism in Schools" 1982). Three years later a similar decision was reached regarding the Louisiana law.

Except for the battle to get scientific creationism into public schools, nothing brought more attention to the creationists than their public debates with prominent evolutionists, usually held on college campuses. During the 1970s the ICR staff alone participated in more than a hundred of these contests and, according to their own reckoning, never lost one. Although Morris preferred delivering straight lectures—and likened debates to the bloody confrontations between Christians and lions in ancient Rome—he recognized their value in carrying the creationist message to "more non-Christians and non-creationists than almost any other method" (Morris 1981, ni; 1974d, 2). Fortunately for him, an associate, Duane T. Gish, holder of a doctorate in biochemistry from the University of California, relished such confrontations. If the mild-mannered, professorial Morris was the Darwin of the creationist movement, then the bumptious Gish was its T. H. Huxley. He "hits the floor running" just like a bulldog, observed an admiring colleague; and "I go for the jugular vein," added Gish himself. Such enthusiasm helped draw crowds of up to five thousand.[35]

Early in 1981 the ICR announced the fulfillment of a recurring dream among creationists: a program offering graduate degrees in various creation-oriented sciences ("ICR Schedules" 1981). Besides hoping to fill an anticipated demand for teachers trained in scientific creationism, the ICR wished to provide an academic setting where creationist students would be free from discrimination. Over the years a number of creationists had reportedly been kicked out of secular universities because of their heterodox views, prompting leaders to warn graduate students to keep silent, "because if you don't, in almost 99 percent of the cases you will be asked to leave." To avoid anticipated harassment, several graduate students took to using pseudonyms when writing for creationist publications.[36]

Creationists also feared—with good reason—the possibility of defections while their students studied under evolutionists. Since the late 1950s the Seventh-day Adventist Church had invested hundreds of thousands of dollars to staff its Geoscience Research Institute with well-trained young scientists, only to discover that in several instances exposure to orthodox science had destroyed belief in strict creationism. To reduce the incidence of apostasy, the church established its own graduate programs at Loma Linda University, where Price had once taught (Numbers 1979, 27-28; Couperus 1980).

To All the World

It is still too early to assess the full impact of the creationist revival sparked by Whitcomb and Morris, but its influence, especially among evangelical Christians, seems to have been immense. Not least, it has elevated the strict creationism of Price and Morris to a position of apparent orthodoxy. It has also endowed creationism with a measure of scientific respectability unknown since the deaths of Guyot and Dawson. Yet it is impossible to determine how much of the creationists' success stemmed from converting evolutionists as opposed to mobilizing the already converted, and how much it owed to widespread disillusionment with established science. A sociological survey of church members in northern California in 1963 revealed that over a fourth of those polled—30 percent of Protestants and 28 percent of Catholics—were already opposed to evolution when the creationist revival began (Bainbridge & Stark 1980, 20). Broken down by denomination, it showed:

Liberal Protestants (Congregationalists, Methodists, Episcopalians, Disciples)	11%
Moderate Protestants (Presbyterians, American Lutherans, American Baptists)	29%
Church of God	57%
Missouri Synod Lutherans	64%
Southern Baptists	72%
Church of Christ	78%
Nazarenes	80%
Assemblies of God	91%
Seventh-day Adventists	94%

Thus the creationists launched their crusade having a large reservoir of potential support.

Has belief in creationism increased since the early 1960s? The scanty evidence available suggests that it has. A nationwide Gallup poll in 1982, cited at the beginning of this paper, showed that nearly as many Americans (44 percent) believed in a recent special creation as accepted theistic (38 percent) or nontheistic (9 percent) evolution ("Poll" 1982, 22). These figures, when compared with the roughly 30 percent of northern California church members who opposed evolution in 1963, suggest, in a grossly imprecise way, a substantial gain in the actual number of American creationists. Bits and pieces of additional evidence lend credence to this conclusion. For example, in 1935 only 36 percent of the students at Brigham Young University, a Mormon school, rejected human evolution; in 1973 the percentage had climbed to 81 (Christensen & Cannon 1978). Also, during the 1970s both the Missouri Synod Lutheran and Seventh-day Adventist churches, traditional bastions of strict creationism, took strong measures to reverse a trend toward greater toleration of progressive creationism ("Return to Conservatism" 1973, 1; Numbers 1979, 27-28). In at least these instances, strict creationism did seem to be gaining ground.

Unlike the anti-evolution crusade of the 1920s, which remained confined mainly to North America, the revival of the 1960s rapidly spread overseas as American creationists and their books circled the globe. Partly as a result of stimulation from America, including the publication of a British edition of *The Genesis Flood* in 1969, the lethargic Evolution Protest Movement in Great Britain was revitalized; and two new creationist organizations, the Newton Scientific Association and the Biblical Creation Society, sprang into existence (Barker 1979; [Clark] 1972-73; 1977; "British Scientists" 1973; "EPM" 1972).[37] On the Continent the Dutch assumed the lead in promoting creationism, encouraged by the translation of books on flood geology and by visits from ICR scientists (Ouweneel 1978). Similar developments occurred elsewhere in Europe, as well as in Australia, Asia, and South America. By 1980 Morris's books alone had been translated into Chinese, Czech, Dutch, French, German, Japanese, Korean, Portuguese, Russian, and Spanish. Strict creationism had become an international phenomenon.[38]

Notes

1. Michael Ruse (1979) argues that most British biologists were evolutionists by the mid-1860s, while David L. Hull, Peter D. Tessner, and Arthur M. Diamond (1978, 721) point out that more than a quarter of British scientists continued to reject the evolution of species as late as 1869. On the acceptance of evolution among religious leaders see, e.g., Frank Hugh Foster (1939, 38-58) and Owen Chadwick (1972, 23-24).

2. According to the poll, 9 percent of the respondents favored an evolutionary process in which God played no part, 38 percent believed God directed the evolutionary process, and 9 percent had no opinion.

3. On the influence of the Scofield Reference Bible see Ernest R. Sandeen (1971, 222).

4. On the popularity of the Guyot-Dawson view, also associated with the geologist James Dwight Dana, see William North Rice (1904, 101).

5. The Scottish theologian James Orr contributed an equally tolerant essay in *The Fundamentals* (Orr 1910-15).

6. "The Menace of Darwinism" appears in Bryan's book *In His Image* as chapter 4, "The Origin of Man." Bryan apparently borrowed his account of the evolution of the eye from Patterson (1902, 32-33).

7. Bryan gives the estimate of nine-tenths in a letter to W. A. McRae, 5 Apr. 1924 (Bryan Papers, box 29).

8. The best state histories of the anti-evolution crusade are Bailey (1950); Gatewood (1966); and Gray (1970). Szasz (1969, 351) stresses the urban dimension of the crusade.

9. For examples of prominent fundamentalists who stayed aloof from the anti-evolution controversy see Stonehouse (1954, 401-2) and Lewis (1963, 86-88).

10. Furness (1954) includes chapter-by-chapter surveys of seven denominations.

11. On Riley, see Riley (1938, 101-2) and Szasz (1980, 89-91). Marsden (1980, 167-70) stresses the interdenominational character of the anti-evolution crusade.

12. The creationists' use of Bateson provoked the evolutionist Henry Fairfield Osborn into repudiating the British scientist (Osborn 1926, 29).

13. Heber D. Curtis to W. J. Bryan, 22 May 1923 (Bryan Papers, box 37). Two physicians, Arthur I. Brown of Vancouver and Howard A. Kelly of Johns Hopkins, achieved prominence in the fundamentalist movement, but Kelly leaned toward theistic evolution.

14. See Edmondson (1969, 276-336); Cole (1931, 264-65); B[oyer] (1939, 6-7); and "Two Great Field Secretaries" (1926, 17).

15. This and the following paragraphs on Price closely follow the account in Numbers (1979, 22-24).

16. Price's first anti-evolution book was published four years earlier (Price 1902).

17. David Star Jordan to G. M. Price, 5 May 1911 (Price Papers).

18. The discovery of Price's law was first announced in Price (1913, 119).

19. Howard A. Kelly to W. J. Bryan, 15 June 1925; Louis T. More to W. J. Bryan, 7 July 1925; and Alfred W. McCann to W. J. Bryan, 30 June 1925 (Bryan Papers, box 47).

20. W. J. Bryan to Howard A. Kelly, 22 June 1925 (Bryan Papers, box47). In a letter to the editor of The Forum, Bryan (1923) asserted that he had never taught that the world was made in six literal days. I am indebted to Paul M. Waggoner for bringing this document to my attention.

21. For a typical statement of creationist frustration see Price (1935). The title for this section comes from Morris (1974, 13).

22. See "Announcement of the Religion and Science Association" (Price Papers); "The Religion and Science Association" (1936, 159-60); "Meeting of the Religion and Science Association" (1936, 209); Clark (1977, 168).

23. On the attitude of the Price faction see Harold W. Clark to G. M. Price, 12 Sept. 1937 (Price Papers).

24. Ben F. Allen to the Board of Directors of the Creation-Deluge Society, 12 Aug. 1945 (courtesy of Molleurus Couperus). Regarding the fossil footprints, see the Newsletters of the Creation-Deluge Society for 19 Aug. 1944 and 17 Feb. 1945.

25. On the early years of the American Scientific Affiliation see Everest (1951).

26. Kulp (1949, 20) mentions his initial skepticism of geology.

27. For a fuller discussion see Numbers (1984).

28. Interviews with Henry M. Morris, 26 Oct. 1980 and 6 Jan. 1981. See also the autobiographical material in Morris (1984).

29. Interviews with Morris.

30. The statement regarding the appearance of the book comes from Walter Hearn, quoted in Bates (1976, 52). See also Roberts (1964); Van de Fliert (1969); and Lammerts (1964). Among the Missouri Synod Lutherans, John W. Klotz (1955) may have had an even greater influence than Morris and Whitcomb.

31. Names, academic fields, and institutional affiliations are given in Creation Research Society Quarterly (1964, [13]); for additional information I am indebted to Duane T. Gish, John N. Moore, Henry M. Morris, Harold Slusher, and William J. Tinkle.

32. Other creationists have disputed the 5 percent estimate.

33. Information also obtained from the interview with Morris, 6 Jan. 1981.

34. On Popper's influence see, e.g., Roth (1977). In a letter to the editor of *New Scientist*, Popper (1980) affirmed that the evolution of life on earth was testable and, therefore, scientific. On Kuhn's influence see, e.g., Roth (1975); Brand (1974); and Wheeler (1975, 192-210).

35. The reference to Gish comes from an interview with Harold Slusher and Duane T. Gish, 6 Jan. 1981.

36. Evidence for alleged discrimination and the use of pseudonyms comes from: "Grand Canyon Presents Problems for Long Ages" (1980); interview with Ervil D. Clark, 9 Jan. 1981; interview with Steven A. Austin, 6 Jan. 1981; and interview with Duane T. Gish, 26 Oct. 1980, the source of the quotation.

37. Barker greatly underestimates the size of the EPM in 1966.

38. Notices regarding the spread of creationism overseas appeared frequently in Bible-Science Newsletter and Acts & Facts. On translations see "ICR Books Available in Many Languages" (1980, 2, 7).

References

Bailey, Kenneth K. 1950. "The enactment of Tennessee's anti-evolution law." *Journal of Southern History* 16:472-510.

_____. 1964. *Southern White Protestantism in the Twentieth Century.* New York: Harper & Row.

Bainbridge, William Sims and Rodney Stark. 1980. "Superstitions: Old and new." *Skeptical Inquirer* 4 (Summer).

Barker, Eileen. 1979. "In the beginning: The battle for creationist science against evolutionism." In *On the Margins of Science: The Social Construction of Rejected Knowledge*, ed. Roy Wallis, 197-200. Sociological Review Monograph, no. 27. Keele: Univ. of Keele.

Bates, Vernon Lee. 1976. "Christian Fundamentalism and the Theory of Evolution in Public School Education: A Study of the Creation Science Movement." Ph.D. diss., Univ. of California, Davis.

Bateson, William. 1922. "Evolutionary faith and modern doubts." *Science* 55:55-61.

Beale, Howard K. 1936. *Are American Teachers Free? An Analysis of Restraints upon the Freedom of Teaching in American Schools.* New York: Charles Scribner's Sons.

Betts, George Herbert. 1929. *The Beliefs of 700 Ministers and Their Meaning for Religious Education.* New York: Abingdon Press.

Bowler, Peter J. 1983. *The Eclipse of Darwinism: Anti-Darwinian Evolution Theories in the Decades around 1900.* Baltimore: Johns Hopkins Univ. Press.

B[oyer], F. J. 1939. "Harry Rimmer, DD" *Christian Faith and Life* 45.

Brand, Leonard R. 1974. "A philosophic rationale for a creation-flood model." *Origins* 1:73-83.

"British Scientists Form Creationist Organization." 1973. *Acts & Facts* 2 (Nov.-Dec.):3.

Bryan Papers. N.d. Library of Congress.

Bryan, William Jennings. 1922. *In His Image.* New York: Fleming H. Revel.

_____. 1923. Letter to the editor of *The Forum* 70:1852-53.

Carpenter, Joel A. 1980. "Fundamentalist institutions and the rise of evangelical protestantism, 1929-1942." *Church History* 49:62-75.

Cassel, J. Frank. 1959. "The evolution of evangelical thinking on evolution." *Journal of the American Scientific Affiliation* 11 (Dec.):26-27.

Chadwick, Owen. 1972. *The Victorian Church*, Part 2. 2d ed. London: Adam and Charles Black.

Christensen, Harold T. and Kenneth L. Cannon. 1978. "The fundamental emphasis at Brigham Young University: 1935-1973." *Journal for the Scientific Study of Religion* 17:53-57.

Clark, Edward Laser. 1952. "'The Southern Baptist Reaction to the Darwinian Theory of Evolution." Ph.D. diss., Southwestern Baptist Theological Seminary, Fort Worth.

Clark, Harold W. 1977. *The Battle over Genesis*. Washington: Review and Herald Publishing Association.

[Clark, Robert E. D.] 1972-73. "Evolution: Polarization of views." *Faith and Thought 100:227-29*.

_____. 1977. "American and English creationists." *Faith and Thought* 104:6-8.

Cole, Steward G. 1931. *The History of Fundamentalism*. New York: Richard R. Smith.

Coletta, Paolo E. 1969. *William Jennings Bryan. Vol. 3, Political Puritan, 1915-1925*. Lincoln: Univ. of Nebraska Press.

"Comment on the deluge geology paper of J. L. Kulp." 1950. *Journal of the American Scientific Affiliation*, 2 (June).

Couperus, Molleurus. 1980. "Tensions between religion and science." *Spectrum*, 10 (Mar.):74-78.

Creation Research Society Quarterly. 1964. 1 (July).

"Creationism in schools: The decision in MacLean versus the Arkansas Board of Education." 1982. *Science* 215:934-43.

"A critique of BSCS biology texts." 1966. *Bible-Science Newsletter* 4 (15 Mar.).

Culver, Robert D. 1955. "An evaluation of the Christian view of science and scripture by Bernard Ramm from the standpoint of Christian theology." *Journal of the American Scientific Affiliation* 7 (Dec.).

Dewar, Douglas. 1931. *The Difficulties of the Evolution Theory*. London: Edward Arnold and Co.

_____. 1932. "The limitations of organic evolution." *Journal of the Victoria Institute* 64.

Dillenberger, John and Claude Welch. 1954. *Protestant Christianity Interpreted Through Its Development*. New York: Charles Scribner's Sons.

Edmondson, William D. 1969. "Fundamentalist sects of Los Angeles, 1900-1930." Ph.D. diss., Claremont Graduate School, Claremont.

"EPM—40 years on; Evolution 114 years off." 1972. *Supplement to Creation I* (May).

Everest, Alton. 1951. "The American Scientific Affiliation—The first decade." *Journal of the American Scientific Affiliation* 3 (Sept.):31-38.

Evolution Protest Movement Pamphlet No. 125. 1965. April.

"Evolutionism in the pulpit." 1910-15. In *The Fundamentals*, vol. 8, 28-30. Chicago: Testimony.

"Fifteen years of creationism." 1979. *Five Minutes with the Bible and Science*. Supplement to *Bible-Science Newsletter* 17 (May):2.

"Fighting evolution at the fundamentals convention." 1925. *Christian Fundamentals in School and Church* 7 (July-Sept.).

"Finding: Let kids decide how we got here." 1980. *American School Board Journal* 167 (Mar.).

Foster, Frank Hugh. 1939. *The Modern Movement in American Theology: Sketches in the History of American Protestant Thought from the Civil War to the World War.* New York: Fleming H. Revell Co.

The Fundamentals. 1910-15. 12 vols. (Chicago: Testimony).

Furniss, Norman F. 1954. *The Fundamentalist Controversy, 1918-1931.* New Haven: Yale Univ. Press.

Gatewood, William B., Jr. 1966. *Preachers, Pedagogues and Politicians: The Evolution Controversy in North Carolina, 1920-1927.* Chapel Hill: Univ. of North Carolina Press.

_____. ed. 1969. *Controversy in the Twenties: Fundamentalism, Modernism, and Evolution.* Nashville: Vanderbilt Univ. Press.

Gish, Duane T. 1975. "A decade of creationist research." *Creation Research Society Quarterly* 12 (June):34-36.

Grabiner, Judith V. and Peter D. Miller. 1974. "Effects of the Scopes trial." *Science* 185:832-37.

"Grand Canyon presents problems for long ages." 1980. *Five Minutes with the Bible and Science.* Supplement to Bible-Science Newsletter 18 (June):1-2.

Gray, Asa. 1963. *Darwiniana: Essays and Reviews Pertaining to Darwinism.* Ed. A. Hunter Dupree. Cambridge, Mass.: Harvard Univ. Press.

Gray, Virginia. 1970. "Anti-evolution sentiment and behavior: The case of Arkansas." *Journal of American History* 57:352-66.

Halliburton, R., Jr. 1964. "The adoption of Arkansas' anti-evolution law." *Arkansas Historical Quarterly* 23.

Hastings, H. L. 1889. "Preface." In *The Errors of Evolution: An Examination of the Nebular Theory, Geological Evolution, the Origin of Life, and Darwinism,* by Robert Patterson. 3d ed.   Boston: Scriptural Tract Repository.

Hull, David L., Peter D. Tessner, and Arthur M. Diamond.   1978. "Planck's principle." *Science* 202.

"ICR books available in many languages." 1980. *Acts & Facts* 9 (Feb.).

"ICR schedules M.S. programs." 1981. *Acts & Facts* 10 (Feb.):1-2.

K[eyser], L. S. 1925. "No war against science-never!" *Bible Champion* 31.

Klotz, John W. 1955. *Genes, Genesis, and Evolution.* St. Louis: Concordia Publishing House.

Kulp, J. Laurence. 1949. "Some presuppositions of evolutionary thinking." *Journal of the American Scientific Affiliation* 1 (June).

_____. 1950. "Deluge geology." *Journal of the American Scientific Affiliation* 2 (Mar.):1-15.

Laba, Estelle R. and Eugene W. Gross. 1950. "Evolution slighted in high-school biology." *Clearing House* 24:396-99.

Lammerts, Walter E. 1964. "Introduction." *Annual.* Creation Research Society.

_____. 1974. "The creationist movement in the United States: A personal account." *Journal of Christian Reconstruction* (Summer):49-63.

Lang, Walter. 1977a. "A naturalistic cosmology vs. a biblical cosmology." *Bible-Science Newsletter* 15 (Jan.-Feb.).

_____. 1977b. "Editorial comments." *Bible-Science Newsletter* 15 (Mar.).

_____. 1978a. "Editorial comments." *Bible-Science Newsletter* 16 (June).

_____. 1978b. "Fifteen years of creationism." *Bible-Science Newsletter* 16 (Oct.).

Larson, Edward J. 1984. "Public science vs. popular opinion: The creation-evolution legal controversy." Ph.D. diss., Univ. of Wisconsin, Madison.

Leitch, Russel H. 1980. "Mistakes Creationists Make." *Bible-Science Newsletter* 18 (Mar.).

Levine, Lawrence W. 1965. *Defender of the Faith—William Jennings Bryan: The Last Decade, 1915-25.* New York: Oxford Univ. Press.

Lewis, William Bryant. 1963. "The Role of Harold Paul Sloan and his Methodist League for Faith and Life in the Fundamentalist-Modernist Controversy of the Methodist Episcopal Church." Ph.D. diss., Vanderbilt Univ., Nashville.

Loetscher, Lefferts A. 1954. *The Broadening Church: A Study of Theological Issues in the Presbyterian Church Since 1869.* Philadelphia: Univ. of Pennsylvania Press.

Lunn, Arnold, ed. 1947. *Is Evolution Proved? A Debate between Douglas Dewar and H. S. Shelton.* London: Hollis and Carter.

Marsden, George M. 1977. "Fundamentalism as an American phenomenon: A comparison with English evangelicalism." *Church History* 46:215-32.

_____. 1980. *Fundamentalism and American Culture: The Shaping of Twentieth Century Evangelicalism, 1870-1925.* New York: Oxford Univ. Press.

Martin, T. T. 1923. *Hell and the High School: Christ or Evolution, Which?* Kansas City: Western Baptist Publishing Co.

Mauro, Philip. 1910-15. "Modern philosophy." In *The Fundamentals*, vol. 2, 85-105. Chicago: Testimony.

McLoughlin, William G., Jr. 1959. *Modern Revivalism: Charles Grandison Finney to Billy Graham.* New York: Ronald Press.

"Meeting of the Religion and Science Association." 1936. *Christian Faith and Life* 42.

Moore, James R. 1979. *The Post-Darwinian Controversies: A Study of the Protestant Struggle to Come to Terms with Darwin in Great Britain and America, 1870-1900.* Cambridge: Cambridge Univ. Press.

Moore, John A. 1974. "Creationism in California." *Daedalus* 103:173-89.

Moore, John N. and Harold Schultz Slusher, eds. 1970. *Biology: A Search for Order in Complexity.* Grand Rapids, Mich.: Zondervan Publishing House.

Morris, Henry M. 1972. "Director's column." *Acts & Facts* I (June-July).

_____. 1974a. "Director's column." *Acts & Facts* 3 (Mar.).

_____. 1974b. "Director's column." *Acts & Facts* 3 (Sept.).

_____. ed. 1974c. *Scientific Creationism.* Gen. ed. San Diego: Creation-Life Publishers.

_____. 1974d. *The Troubled Waters of Evolution.* San Diego: Creation-Life Publishers.

_____. 1978. *That You Might Believe.* Rev. ed. San Diego: Creation-Life Publishers.

_____. 1981a. "Director's column." *Acts & Facts* I (June-July).

_____. 1981b. "Two decades of creation: Past and future." *Impact.* Supplement to Acts & Facts 10 (Jan.).

_____. 1984. *History of Modern Creationism.* San Diego: Master Book Publishers.

Morris, Henry M. and John C. Whitcomb, Jr. 1964. "Reply to reviews in the March 1964 issue." *Journal of the American Scientific Affiliation* 16 (June).

Morrison, John L. 1953. "American Catholics and the crusade against evolution." *Records of American Catholic Historical Society of Philadelphia* 64:59-7 1.

Nelkin, Dorothy. 1982. *The Creation Controversy: Science or Scriptures in the Schools.* New York: W. W. Norton.

Nelson, Roland T. 1964. "Fundamentalism and the Northern Baptist Convention." Ph.D. diss., Univ. of Chicago, Chicago.

Numbers, Ronald L. 1975. "Science falsely so-called: Evolution and the Adventists in the nineteenth-century." *Journal of the American Scientific Affiliation* 27 (Mar.).

_____. 1977. *Creation by Natural Law: Laplace's Nebular Hypothesis in American Thought.* Seattle: Univ. of Washington Press.

_____. 1979. "Sciences of Satanic origin: Adventist attitudes toward evolutionary biology and geology." *Spectrum* 9 (Jan.).

_____. 1984. "The dilemma of evangelical scientists." In *Evangelism and Modern America,* ed. George M. Marsden, 150-60. Grand Rapids, Mich.: William B. Eerdmans.

O'Brien, Charles F. 1971. *Sir William Dawson: A Life in Science and Religion.* Philadelphia: American Philosophical Society.

Orr, James. 1910-15. "Science and Christian faith." In *The Fundamentals,* vol.4, 91-104. Chicago: Testimony.

Osborn, Henry Fairfield. 1926. *Evolution and Religion in Education: Polemics of the Fundamentalist Controversy of 1922 to 1926.* New York: Charles Scribner's Sons.

Ouweneel, W. J. 1978. "Creationism in the Netherlands." *Impact.* Supplement to Acts & Facts 9 (Feb.): i-iv.

Patterson, Alexander. 1902. *The Other Side of Evolution: An Examination of Its Evidences.* Chicago: Winona Publishing Co.

Patterson, Robert. 1893. *The Errors of Evolution: An Examination of the Nebular Theory, Geological Evolution, the Origin of Life, and Darwinism.* 3d ed. Boston: Scriptural Tract Repository.

Paul, Harry W. 1979. *The Edge of Contingency: French Catholic Reaction to Scientific Change from Darwin to Duhem.* Gainesville, Fla.: Univ. Presses of Florida.

Pfeifer, Edward J.1974. "United States." In *The Comparative Reception of Darwinism,* ed. Thomas F. Glick. Austin: Univ. of Texas Press.

"Poll finds Americans split on creation idea." 1982. *New York Times,* Aug. 29.

Popper, Karl. 1980. Letter to the editor of *New Scientist* 87 (21 Aug.):61 1.

Price, George McCready. 1901. *Outlines of Modern Science and Modern Christianity.* Oakland, Calif: Pacific Press.

_____. 1906. *Illogical Geology: The Weakest Point in the Evolution Theory.* Los Angeles: Modern Heretic Co.

_____. 1913. *The Fundamentals of Geology and Their Bearings on the Doctrine of a Literal Creation.* Mountain View, Calif.: Pacific Press.

_____. 1923. *The New Geology.* Mountain View, Calif.: Pacific Press.

_____. 1935. "Guarding the sacred cow." *Christian Faith and Life* 41: 124-27.

_____. 1954. *The Story of the Fossils.* Mountain View, Calif.: Pacific Press.

Price Papers. N.d. Andrews Univ.

"Progress of anti-evolution." 1929. *Christian Fundamentalist* 2.

Ramm, Bernard. 1954. *The Christian View of Science and Scripture.* Grand Rapids, Mich.: William B. Eerdmans.

Reeve, J. J. 1910-15. "My personal experience with the higher criticism." In *The Fundamentals*, vol. 3, 98-118. Chicago: Testimony.

"The Religion and Science Association." 1936. *Christian Faith and Life* 42:159-60.

"Return to conservatism." 1973. *Bible-Science Newsletter* 11 (Aug.).

Rice, William North. 1904. *Christian Faith in an Age of Science*. 2d ed. New York: A. C. Armstrong and Son.

Riley, Marie Acomb. 1938. *The Dynamic of a Dream: The Life Story of Dr. William B. Riley*. Grand Rapids, Mich.: William B. Eerdmans.

[Riley, William B.] 1922. "The evolution controversy." *Christian Fundamentals in School and Church* 4 (Apr.-May).

_____. 1930. "The creative week." *Christian Fundamentalist* 4.

Riley, William B. and Harry Rimmer. N.d. *A Debate Resolved, That the Creative Days in Genesis Were Aeons, Not Solar Days*. Pamphlet.

Rimmer, Harry. 1945. *The Harmony of Science and Scripture*. 11th ed. Grand Rapids, Mich.: William B. Eerdmans.

Roberts, Frank H. 1964. "Review of The Genesis Flood by Henry M. Morris & John C. Whitcomb, Jr." *Journal of the American Scientific Affiliation* 16 (Mar.):28-29.

Roth, Ariel A. 1975. "The pervasiveness of the paradigm." *Origins* 2:55-57.

_____. 1977. "Does evolution qualify as a scientific principle?" *Origins* 4:4-10.

Rudnick, Milton L. 1966. *Fundamentalism and the Missouri Synod: A Historical Study of Their Interaction and Mutual Influence*. St. Louis: Concordia Publishing House.

Ruse, Michael. 1979. *The Darwinian Revolution: Science Red in Tooth and Claw*. Chicago: Univ. of Chicago Press.

Sandeen, Ernest R. 1971. *The Roots of Fundamentalism: British and American Millenarianism, 1800-1930*. Chicago: Univ. of Chicago Press.

Schuchert, Charles. 1924. "Review of The New Geology by George McCready Price." *Science* 59:486-87.

Science. 1926. 63:259.

Segraves, Nell J. 1977. *The Creation Report*. San Diego: Creation-Science Research Center.

Shipley, Maynard. 1927. *The War on Modern Science: A Short History of the Fundamentalist Attacks on Evolution and Modernism*. New York: Alfred A. Knopf.

_____. 1930. "Growth of the anti-evolution movement." *Current History* 32.

Skoog, Gerald. 1979. "Topic of evolution in secondary school biology textbooks: 1900-1977." *Science Education* 63:621-40.

Stonehouse, Ned B. 1954. *J. Gresham Machen: A Biographical Memoir.* Grand Rapids, Mich.: William B. Eerdmans.

Szasz, Ferenc Morton. 1969. "Three fundamentalist leaders: The roles of William Bell Riley, John Roach Straton, and William Jennings Bryan in the fundamentalist-modernist controversy." Ph.D. diss., Univ. of Rochester, Rochester.

_____. 1982. *The Divided Mind of Protestant America, 1889-1930.* University, Ala.: Univ. of Alabama Press.

Thompson, James J., Jr. 1975-76. "Southern Baptists and the anti-evolution controversy of the 1920's." *Mississippi Quarterly* 29:65-81.

"Two great Field Secretaries—Harry Rimmer and Dr. Arthur I. Brown."1926. *Christian Fundamentals in School and Church* 8 (July-Sept.)

Van de Fliert, J.R. 1969. "Fundamentalism and the fundamentals of geology." *Journal of the American Scientific Affiliation* 21 (Sept.):69-81.

Wade, Nicholas. 1972. "Creationists and evolutionists: Confrontations in California." *Science* 178:724-29.

Whalen, Robert D. 1972. "Millenarianism and Millennialism in America, 1790-1880." Ph.D. diss., State Univ. of New York at Stony Brook.

Wheeler, Gerald. 1975. *The Two-Taled Dinosaur: Why Science and Religion Conflict over the Origin of Life.* Nashville: Southern Publishing Association.

_____. 1976. "The third national creation science conference." *Origins* 3.

Whitcomb, John C., Jr., and Henry M. Morris. 1961. *The Genesis Flood: The Biblical Record and Its Scientific Implications.* Philadelphia: Presbyterian and Reformed Publishing Co.

Whitney, Dudley Joseph.1928. "What theory of Earth history shall we adopt?" *Bible Champion* 34.

Williams, Wayne C. 1936. William Jennings Bryan. New York: G. P. Putnam.

"World Religious Digest." 1939. *Christian Faith and Life* 45.

Wright, G. Frederick. 1898. "The first chapter of Genesis and modern science." *Homiletic Review* 35:392-999.

_____. 1902. "Introduction." In *The Other Side of Evolution: An Examination of Its Evidences,* by Alexander Patterson, xvii-xix. Chicago: Winona Publishing Co.

_____. 1910-15. "The passing of evolution." In *The Fundamentals,* vol. 7, 5-20. Chicago: Testimony.

_____. 1916. *Story of My Life and Work.* Oberlin, Ohio: Bibliotheca Sacra Co.

Young, Davis A. 1977. *Creation and the Flood: An Alternative to Flood Geology, and Theistic Evolution.* Grand Rapids, Mich.: Baker Book House.

Young, G. L. 1909. "Relation of evolution and Darwinism to the question of origins." *Bible Student and Teacher* 11 (July).

16

Nonoverlapping Magisteria

STEPHEN JAY GOULD

Incongruous places often inspire anomalous stories. In early 1984, I spent several nights at the Vatican housed in a hotel built for itinerant priests. While pondering over such puzzling issues as the intended function of the bidets in each bathroom, and hungering for something other than plum jam on my breakfast rolls (why did the basket only contain hundreds of identical plum packets and not a one of, say, strawberry?), I encountered yet another among the innumerable issues of contrasting cultures that can make life so interesting. Our crowd (present in Rome for a meeting on nuclear winter sponsored by the Pontifical Academy of Sciences) shared the hotel with a group of French and Italian Jesuit priests who were also professional scientists.

At lunch, the priests called me over to their table to pose a problem that had been troubling them. What, they wanted to know, was going on in America with all this talk about "scientific creationism"? One asked me: "Is evolution really in some kind of trouble; and if so, what could such trouble be? I have always been taught that no doctrinal conflict exists between evolution and Catholic faith, and the evidence for evolution seems both entirely satisfactory and utterly overwhelming. Have I missed something?"

A lively pastiche of French, Italian, and English conversation then ensued for half an hour or so, but the priests all seemed reassured by my general answer: Evolution has encountered no intellectual trouble; no new arguments have been offered. Creationism is a homegrown phenomenon of American socio-cultural history—a splinter movement (unfortunately rather more of a beam these days) of Protestant fundamentalists who believe that every word of the Bible must be literally true, whatever such a claim might mean. We all left satisfied, but I certainly felt bemused by the anomaly of my role as a Jewish agnostic, trying to reassure a group of Catholic priests that evolution remained both true and entirely consistent with religious belief.

Another story in the same mold: I am often asked whether I ever encounter creationism as a live issue among my Harvard undergraduate students.   I reply that only once, in nearly thirty years of teaching, did I experience such an incident.   A very sincere and serious freshman student came to my office hours with the following question that had clearly been troubling him deeply: "I am a devout Christian and have never had any reason to doubt evolution, an idea that seems both exciting and particularly well documented. But my roommate, a proselytizing Evangelical, has been insisting with enormous vigor that I cannot be both a real Christian and an evolutionist. So tell me, can a person believe both in God and evolution?" Again, I gulped hard, did my intellectual duty, and reassured him that evolution was both true and entirely compatible with Christian belief—a position I hold sincerely, but still an odd situation for a Jewish agnostic.

These two stories illustrate a cardinal point, frequently unrecognized but absolutely central to any understanding of the status and impact of the politically potent, fundamentalist doctrine known by its self-proclaimed oxymoron as "scientific creationism" —the claim that the Bible is literally true, that all organisms were created during six days of twenty-four hours, that the earth is only a few thousand years old, and that evolution must therefore be false. Creationism does not pit science against religion (as my opening stories indicate), for no such conflict exists. Creationism does not raise any unsettled intellectual issues about the nature of biology or the history of life. Creationism is a local and parochial movement, powerful only in the United States among Western nations, and prevalent only among the few sectors of American Protestantism that choose to read the Bible as an inerrant document, literally true in every jot and tittle.

I do not doubt that one could find an occasional nun who would prefer to teach creationism in her parochial school biology class, or an occasional orthodox rabbi who does the same in his yeshiva, but creationism based on biblical literalism makes little sense in either Catholicism or Judaism, for neither religion maintains any extensive tradition for reading the Bible as literal truth rather than illuminating literature, based partly on metaphor and allegory (essential components of all good writing) and demanding interpretation for proper understanding.   Most Protestant groups, of course, take the same position—the fundamentalist fringe notwithstanding.

The position that I have just outlined by personal stories and general statements represents the standard attitude of all major Western religions (and of Western science) today. (I cannot, through ignorance, speak of Eastern religions, although I suspect that the same position would prevail in most cases.) The lack of conflict between science and religion arises from a lack of overlap between their respective domains of professional expertise—science in the empirical constitution of the universe, and religion in the search for proper ethical values and the spiritual meaning of our lives. The attainment of wisdom in a full life requires extensive attention to both domains—for a great book tells us that the truth can make us free and that we will live in optimal harmony with our fellows when we learn to do justly, love mercy, and walk humbly.

In the context of this standard position, I was enormously puzzled by a statement issued by Pope John Paul II on October 22, 1996, to the Pontifical Academy of Sciences, the same body that had sponsored my earlier trip to the Vatican. In this document, entitled "Truth Cannot Contradict Truth," the Pope defended both the evidence for evolution and the consistency of the theory with Catholic religious doctrine. Newspapers throughout the world responded with front-page headlines, as in the *New York Times* for October 25: "Pope Bolsters Church's Support for Scientific View of Evolution."

Now I know about "slow news days," and I do admit that nothing else was strongly competing for headlines at that particular moment. (*The Times* could muster nothing more exciting for a lead story than Ross Perot's refusal to take Bob Dole's advice and quit the presidential race.) Still, I couldn't help feeling immensely puzzled by all the attention paid to the pope's statement (while being wryly pleased, of course, for we need all the good press we can get, especially from respected outside sources). The Catholic Church had never opposed evolution and had no reason to do so. Why had the pope issued such a statement at all? And why had the press responded with an orgy of worldwide, front-page coverage?

I could only conclude at first, and wrongly as I soon learned, that journalists throughout the world must deeply misunderstand the relationship between science and religion, and must therefore be elevating a minor papal comment to unwarranted notice. Perhaps most people really do think that a war exists between science and religion, and that (to cite a particularly newsworthy case) evolution must be intrinsically opposed to Christianity. In such a context, a papal admission of evolution's legitimate status might be regarded as major news indeed—a sort of modern equivalent for a story that never happened, but would have made the biggest journalistic splash of 1640: Pope Urban VIII releases his most famous prisoner from house arrest and humbly apologizes, "Sorry, Signor Galileo ... the sun, er, is central."

But I then discovered that the prominent coverage of papal satisfaction with evolution had not been an error of non-Catholic Anglophone journalists. The Vatican itself had issued the statement as a major news release. And Italian newspapers had featured, if anything, even bigger headlines and longer stories.

The conservative *Il Giornale*, for example, shouted from its masthead: "Pope Says We May Descend from Monkeys,"

Clearly, I was out to lunch. Something novel or surprising must lurk within the papal statement, but what could it be?—especially given the accuracy of my primary impression (as I later verified) that the Catholic Church values scientific study, views science as no threat to religion in general or Catholic doctrine in particular, and has long accepted both the legitimacy of evolution as a field of study and the potential harmony of evolutionary conclusions with Catholic faith.

As a former constituent of Tip O'Neill's, I certainly know that "all politics is local"—and that the Vatican undoubtedly has its own internal reasons, quite opaque to me, for announcing papal support of evolution in a major statement. Still, I knew that I was missing some important key, and I felt frustrated. I then remembered the primary rule of intellectual life: when puzzled, it never hurts to read the primary documents—a rather simple and self-evident principle that has, nonetheless, completely disappeared from large sectors of the American experience.

I knew that Pope Pius XII (not one of my favorite figures in twentieth-century history, to say the least) had made the primary statement in a 1950 encyclical entitled *Humani Generis*. I knew the main thrust of his message: Catholics could believe whatever science determined about the evolution of the human body, so long as they accepted that, at some time of his choosing, God had infused the soul into such a creature. I also knew that I had no problem with this statement, for whatever my private beliefs about souls, science cannot touch such a subject and therefore cannot be threatened by any theological position on such a legitimately and intrinsically religious issue. Pope Pius XII, in other words, had properly acknowledged and respected the separate domains of science and theology. Thus, I found myself in total agreement with *Humani Generis*—but I had never read the document in full (not much of an impediment to stating an opinion these days).

I quickly got the relevant writings from, of all places, the Internet. (The pope is prominently on-line, but a Luddite like me is not. So I got a computer literate associate to dredge up the documents. I do love the fracture of stereotypes implied by finding religion so hep and a scientist so square.) Having now read in full both Pope Pius's *Humani Generis* of 1950 and Pope John Paul's proclamation of October 1996, I finally understand why the recent statement seems so new, revealing, and worthy of all those headlines. And the message could not be more welcome for evolutionists and friends of both science and religion.

The text of *Humani Generis* focuses on the magisterium (or teaching authority) of the Church—a word derived not from any concept of majesty or awe but from the different notion of teaching, for magister is Latin for "teacher." We may, I think, adopt this word and concept to express the central point of this essay and the principled resolution of supposed "conflict" or "warfare" between science and religion. No such conflict should exist because each subject has a legitimate magisterium, or domain of teaching authority—and these magisteria do not overlap (the principle that I would like to designate as NOMA, or "nonoverlapping magisteria"). The net of science covers the empirical universe: what is it made of (fact) and why does it work this way (theory). The net of religion extends over questions of moral meaning and value. These two magisteria do not overlap, nor do they encompass all inquiry (consider, for starters, the magisterium of art and the meaning of beauty). To cite the arch clichés, we get the age of rocks, and religion retains the rock of ages; we study how the heavens go, and they determine how to go to heaven.

This resolution might remain all neat and clean if the nonoverlapping magisteria (NOMA) of science and religion were separated by an extensive no man's land. But, in fact, the two magisteria bump right up against each other, interdigitating in wondrously complex ways along their joint border. Many of our deepest questions call upon aspects of both for different parts of a full answer and the sorting of legitimate domains can become quite complex and difficult. To cite just two broad questions involving both evolutionary facts and moral arguments: Since evolution made us the only earthly creatures with advanced consciousness, what responsibilities are so entailed for our relations with other species? What do our genealogical ties with other organisms imply about the meaning of human life?

Pius XII's *Humani Generis* is a highly traditionalist document by a deeply conservative man forced to face all the "isms" and cynicisms that rode the wake of World War II and informed the struggle to rebuild human decency from the ashes of the Holocaust. The encyclical, subtitled "Concerning some false opinions which threaten to undermine the foundations of Catholic doctrine," begins with a statement of embattlement:

> Disagreement and error among men on moral and religious matters have always been a cause of profound sorrow to all good men, but above all to the true and loyal sons of the Church, especially today, when we see the principles of Christian culture being attacked on all sides.

Pius lashes out, in turn, at various external enemies of the Church: pantheism, existentialism, dialectical materialism, historicism, and of course and preeminently, communism. He then notes with sadness that some well-meaning folks within the Church have fallen into a dangerous relativism—"a theological pacifism and egalitarianism, in which all points of view become equally valid"—in order to include people of wavering faith who yearn for the embrace of Christian religion but do not wish to accept the particularly Catholic magisterium.

What is this world coming to when these noxious novelties can so discombobulate a revealed and established order? Speaking as a conservative's conservative, Pius laments:

> Novelties of this kind have already borne their deadly fruit in almost all branches of theology... Some question whether angels are personal beings, and whether matter and spirit differ essentially... Some even say that the doctrine of Transubstantiation, based on an antiquated philosophic notion of substance, should be so modified that the Real Presence of Christ in the Holy Eucharist be reduced to a kind of symbolism.

Pius first mentions evolution to decry a misuse by overextension often promulgated by zealous supporters of the anathematized "isms":

> Some imprudently and indiscreetly hold that evolution... explains the origin of all things.... Communists gladly subscribe to this opinion so that, when the souls of men have been deprived of every idea of a personal God, they may the more efficaciously defend and propagate their dialectical materialism.

Pius's major, statement on evolution occurs near the end of the encyclical in paragraphs 35 through 37. He accepts the standard model of NOMA and begins by acknowledging that evolution lies in a difficult area where the domains press hard against each other. "It remains for US now to speak about those questions which, although they pertain to the positive sciences, are nevertheless more or less connected with the truths of the Christian faith."[1]

Pius then writes the well-known words that permit Catholics to entertain the evolution of the human body (a factual issue under the magisterium of science), so long as they accept the divine Creation and infusion of the soul (a theological notion under the magisterium of religion).

> The Teaching Authority of the Church does not forbid that, in conformity with the present state of human sciences and sacred theology, research and discussions, on the part of men experienced in both fields, take place with regard to the doctrine of evolution, in as far as it inquires into the origin of the human body as coming from

preexistent and living matter—for the Catholic faith obliges us to hold that souls are immediately created by God.

I had, up to here, found nothing surprising in *Humani Generis*, and nothing to relieve my puzzlement about the novelty of Pope John Paul's recent statement. But I read further and realized that Pope Pius had said more about evolution, something I had never seen quoted, and that made John Paul's statement most interesting indeed. In short, Pius forcefully proclaimed that while evolution may be legitimate in principle, the theory, in fact, had not been proven and might well be entirely wrong. One gets the strong impression, moreover, that Pius was rooting pretty hard for a verdict of falsity.

Continuing directly from the last quotation, Pius advises us about the proper study of evolution:

> However, this must be done in such a way that the reasons for both opinions, that is, those favorable and those unfavorable to evolution, be weighed and judged with the necessary seriousness, moderation and measure.... Some, however, rashly transgress this liberty of discussion, when they act as if the origin of the human body from preexisting and living matter were already completely certain and proved by the facts which have been discovered up to now and by reasoning on those facts, and as if there were nothing in the sources of divine revelation which demands the greatest moderation and caution in this question.

To summarize, Pius generally accepts the NOMA principle of nonoverlapping magisteria in permitting Catholics to entertain the hypothesis of evolution for the human body so long as they accept the divine infusion of the soul. But he then offers some (holy) fatherly advice to scientists about the status of evolution as a scientific concept: the idea is not yet proven, and you all need to be especially cautious because evolution raises many troubling issues right on the border of my magisterium. One may read this second theme in two different ways: either as a gratuitous incursion into a different magisterium or as a helpful perspective from an intelligent and concerned outsider. As a man of good will, and in the interest of conciliation, I am happy to embrace the latter reading.

In any case, this rarely quoted second claim (that evolution remains both unproven and a bit dangerous)—and not the familiar first argument for the NOMA principle (that Catholics may accept the evolution of the body so long as they embrace the creation of the soul)—defines the novelty and the interest of John Paul's recent statement.

John Paul begins by summarizing Pius's older encyclical of 1950, and particularly by reaffirming the NOMA principle—nothing new here, and no cause for extended publicity:

> In his encyclical "Humani Generis" (1950), my predecessor Pius XII had already stated that there was no opposition between evolution and the doctrine of the faith about man and his vocation.

To emphasize the power of NOMA, John Paul poses a potential problem and a sound resolution: How can we reconcile science's claim for physical continuity in human evolution with Catholicism's insistence that the soul must enter at a moment of divine infusion:

> With man, then, we find ourselves in the presence of an ontological difference, an ontological leap, one could say. However, does not the posing of such ontological discontinuity run counter to that physical continuity which seems to be the main thread of research into evolution in the field of physics and chemistry? Consideration of the method used in the various branches of knowledge makes it possible to reconcile two points of view which would seem irreconcilable. The sciences of observation describe and measure the multiple manifestations of life with increasing precision and correlate them with the time line. The moment of transition to the spiritual cannot be the object of this kind of observation.

The novelty and news value of John Paul's statement lies, rather, in his profound revision of Pius's second and rarely quoted claim that evolution, while conceivable in principle and reconcilable with religion, can cite little persuasive evidence, and may well be false. John Paul states—and I can only say amen, and thanks for noticing—that the half century between Pius's surveying the ruins of World War II and his own pontificate heralding the dawn of a new millennium has witnessed such a growth of data, and such a refinement of theory, that evolution can no longer be doubted by people of good will:

> Pius XII added ... that this opinion [evolution] should not be adopted as though it were a certain, proven doctrine.... Today, almost half a century after the publication of the encyclical, new knowledge has led to the recognition of more than one hypothesis in the theory of evolution. It is indeed remarkable that this theory has been progressively accepted by researchers, following a series of discoveries in various fields of knowledge. The convergence, neither sought nor fabricated, of the results of work, that was conducted independently is in itself a significant argument in favor of the theory.

In conclusion, Pius had grudgingly admitted evolution as a legitimate hypothesis that he regarded as only tentatively supported and potentially (as I suspect he hoped) untrue. John Paul, nearly fifty years later, reaffirms the legitimacy of evolution under the NOMA principle—no news here—but then adds that additional data and theory have placed the factuality of evolution beyond reasonable doubt. Sincere Christians must now accept evolution not merely as a plausible possibility but also as an effectively proven fact. In other words, official Catholic opinion on evolution has moved from "say it ain't so, but we can deal with it if we have to" (Pius's grudging view of 1950) to John Paul's entirely welcoming "it has been proven true; we always celebrate nature's factuality, and we look forward to interesting discussions of theological implications." I happily endorse this turn of events as gospel—literally *good* news. I may represent the magisterium of science, but I welcome the support of a primary leader from the other major magisterium of our complex lives. And I recall the wisdom of King Solomon: "As cold waters to a thirsty soul, so is good news from a far country" (Prov. 25:25).

Just as religion must bear the cross of its hard-liners, I have some scientific colleagues, including a few prominent enough to wield influence by their writings, who view this rapprochement of the separate magisteria with dismay. To colleagues like me—agnostic scientists who welcome and celebrate the rapprochement, especially the pope's latest statement—they say: "C'mon, be honest; you know that religion is addlepated, superstitious, old-fashioned b.s.; you're only making those welcoming noises because religion is so powerful, and we need to be diplomatic in order to assure public support and funding for science." I do not think that this attitude is common among scientists, but such a position fills me with dismay—and I therefore end this essay with a personal statement about religion, as a testimony to what I regard as a virtual consensus among thoughtful scientists (who support the NOMA principle as firmly as the pope does).

I am not, personally, a believer or a religious man in any sense of institutional commitment or practice. But I have enormous respect for religion, and the subject has always fascinated me, beyond almost all others (with a few exceptions, like evolution, paleontology, and baseball). Much of this fascination lies in the historical paradox that throughout Western history organized religion has fostered both the most unspeakable horrors and the most heartrending examples of human goodness in the face of personal danger. (The evil, I believe, lies in the occasional confluence of religion with secular power. The Catholic Church has sponsored its share of horrors, from Inquisitions to liquidations—but only because this institution held such secular power during so much of Western history. When my folks held similar power more briefly in Old Testament times, they committed just as many atrocities with many of the same rationales.)

I believe, with all my heart, in a respectful, even loving concordat between our magisteria—the NOMA solution. NOMA represents a principled position on moral and intellectual grounds, not a mere diplomatic stance. NOMA also cuts both ways. If religion can no longer dictate the nature of factual conclusions properly under the magisterium of science, then scientists cannot claim higher insight into moral truth from any superior knowledge of the world's empirical constitution.   This mutual humility has important practical consequences in a world of such diverse passions.

Religion is too important to too many people for any dismissal or denigration of the comfort still sought by many folks from theology. I may, for example, privately suspect that papal insistence on divine infusion of the soul represents a sop to our fears, a device for maintaining a belief in human superiority within an evolutionary world offering no privileged position to any creature. But I also know that souls represent a subject outside the magisterium of science. My world cannot prove or disprove such a notion, and the concept of souls cannot threaten or impact my domain.   Moreover, while I cannot personally accept the Catholic view of souls, I surely honor the metaphorical value of such a concept both for grounding moral discussion and for expressing what we most value about human potentiality: our decency, care, and all the ethical and intellectual struggles that the evolution of consciousness imposed upon us.

As a moral position (and therefore not as a deduction from my knowledge of nature's factuality), I prefer the "cold bath" theory that nature can be truly "cruel" and "indifferent"—in the utterly inappropriate terms of our ethical discourse because nature was not constructed as our eventual abode, didn't know we were coming (we are, after all, interlopers of the latest geological microsecond), and doesn't give a damn about us (speaking metaphorically). I regard such a position as liberating, not depressing, because we then become free to conduct moral discourse—and nothing could be more important—in our own terms, spared from the delusion that we might read moral truth passively from nature's factuality.

But I recognize that such a position frightens many people, and that a more spiritual view of nature retains broad appeal (acknowledging the factuality of evolution and other phenomena, but still seeking some intrinsic meaning in human terms, and from the magisterium of religion).   I do appreciate, for example, the struggles of a man who wrote to the *New York Times* on November 3, 1996, to state both his pain and his endorsement of John Paul's statement:

> Pope John Paul II's acceptance of evolution touches the doubt in my heart. The problem of pain and suffering in a world created by a God who is all love and light is hard enough to bear, even if one is a creationist. But at least a creationist can say that the original creation, coming from the hand of God was good, harmonious, innocent and gentle. What can one say about evolution, even a spiritual theory of evolution? Pain and suffering, mindless cruelty and terror are its means

of creation. Evolution's engine is the grinding of predatory teeth upon the screaming, living flesh and bones of prey... If evolution be true, my faith has rougher seas to sail.

I don't agree with this man, but we could have a wonderful argument. I would push the "cold bath" theory; he would (presumably) advocate the theme of inherent spiritual meaning in nature, however opaque the signal. But we would both be enlightened and filled with better understanding of these deep and ultimately unanswerable issues. Here, I believe, lies the greatest strength and necessity of NOMA, the nonoverlapping magisteria of science and religion. NOMA permits—indeed enjoins—the prospect of respectful discourse, of constant input from both magisteria toward the common goal of wisdom. If human beings are anything special, we are the creatures that must ponder and talk. Pope John Paul II would surely point out to me that his magisterium has always recognized this distinction, for *in principio erat verbum* – "In the beginning was the Word."

Postscript

Carl Sagan organized and attended the Vatican meeting that introduces this essay; he also shared my concern for fruitful cooperation between the different but vital realms of science and religion. Carl was also one of my dearest friends. I learned of his untimely death on the same day that I read the proofs for this essay. I could only recall Nehru's observations on Gandhi's death—that the light had gone out, and darkness reigned everywhere. But I then contemplated what Carl had done in his short sixty-two years and remembered John Dryden's ode for Henry Purcell, a great musician who died even younger. "He long ere this had tuned the jarring spheres, and left no hell below."

The days I spent with Carl in Rome were the best of our friendship. We delighted in walking around the Eternal City, feasting on its history and architecture—and its food! Carl took special delight in the anonymity that he still enjoyed in a nation that had not yet aired *Cosmos*, the greatest media work, in popular science of all time.

I dedicate this essay to his memory. Carl also shared my personal suspicion about the nonexistence of souls—but I cannot think of a better reason for hoping we are wrong than the prospect of spending eternity roaming the cosmos in friendship and conversation with this wonderful soul.

Note

1. Interestingly, the main thrust of these paragraphs does not address evolution in general but lies in refuting a doctrine that Pius calls "polygenism" or the

notion of human ancestry from multiple parents—for he regards such an idea as incompatible with the doctrine of original sin, "which proceeds from a sin actually committed by an individual Adam and which, through generation, is passed on to all and is in everyone as his own." In this one instance, Pius may be transgressing the NOMA principle—but I cannot judge, for I do not understand the details of Catholic theology and therefore do not know how symbolically such a statement may be read. If Pius is arguing that we cannot entertain a theory about derivation of all modern humans from an ancestral population rather than through an ancestral individual (a potential fact) because such an idea would question the doctrine or original sin (a theological construct), then I would declare him out of line for letting the magisterium of religion dictate a conclusion within the magisterium of science.

Theological Perspectives

There are at least two religious approaches to science. One is to try and discern a religious meaning in the picture of the world drawn by science. The other is to explore the implications of scientific findings about nature for traditional theological ideas. The first article in the section by biologist Ursula Goodenough illustrates the first approach. She explores how a contemporary understanding of evolution might serve as a foundation for a "global religious myth."

The next three articles demonstrate the second approach. The first two address theological questions which arise for traditional religion in the light of evolutionary theory. John Haught asks, if natural selection can account for the apparent design of the world, does this "rule out God's existence?" He proposes that the acceptance of evolution does not require the abandonment of God. Similarly, Elizabeth Johnson considers the question of randomness and chance in the evolutionary process. Do these elements require that God "rolls dice?" She concludes that chance and divine providence are not mutually exclusive concepts.

Arthur Peacocke, a physical chemist and an Anglican theologian, explores the implications of evolutionary theory for traditional Christian theology generally. He interweaves a scientific account of the evolutionary process with a discussion of its theological significance and proposes that biological evolution is a "disguised friend" of theology.

One primary theological question concerns what it means to be human. An evolutionary account of the rise of the human species qualifies what can credibly be said theologically about humanity. Philip Hefner's article displays how this may be done as he discusses humans as "created co-creators." The concluding article by Stephen Pope continues the theological exploration of human nature with particular attention to the human virtue of "agape" (radical self-sacrifice) in the light of a neo-Darwinian understanding of evolution.

17

What Science Can and Cannot Offer to a Religious Narrative

URSULA GOODENOUGH

Scientists are trained to talk about what they understand. Most of us therefore avoid talking about religion. To move past this reluctance, I set about analyzing religious systems using the paradigm most familiar to me, the paradigm of biological evolution, asking how religions achieve reproductive success, what niches they fill, and so on. My goal was to develop a taxonomy of religious systems that would allow me to understand what they attempt to achieve. Only then, I reasoned, could I respond to the question of how science might or might not make a contribution. Out of this exercise has come a rather simple scheme, which I will set forth from the start.

The scheme makes use of the word *cult,* a word that connotes the mindless adulation of Elvis or Jim Jones. But in fact, the *Oxford English Dictionary* defines *cult* simply as "a particular form or system of religious worship, esp. in reference to its external rites and ceremonies." This emphasis on exteriors is useful in that it allows us to put into the same category a variety of traditions that may have different origins and precepts.

The simple scheme, then, sees three types of religious systems: ancestor-cults, sky-cults, and earth-cults.[1] We will consider each in turn.

Ancestor-cults

As nearly as I can tell, all religious systems are in part ancestor-cults. Reverence for ancestors takes specific expression, as in beliefs that the dead are actively engaged in bestowing benefits or harm, or it can be a very generalized concept, a concept of continuity, of preserving "the people of Israel," "the followers of Christ," and so on. An important spinoff of this orientation is the creation of religious community, of fellowship, the sense of shared tradition and purpose.

Ancestor-cults create linkage with the past through the use of compelling art and ritual: totems are carved, chants are sung, the stories are read from the holy texts, and these become the metaphors for the ancestors themselves: the images and the ceremonies endow the ancestors with a reality that yields a sense of continuity. The art and ritual become the myth; in evolutionary terms, one would say that a cult with a compelling myth is high in fitness.

Sky-cults

Sky-cult refers to a myth associated with questions of origins and destiny: Where did I come from? Where will I go when I die? The destiny promised by a sky-cult and an ancestor-cult may be one and the same: When I die, I will join my ancestors in some happy hunting ground, in some nonterrestrial existence devoid of the trials of this life. But ancestor-cults and sky-cults usually diverge on the question of origins. In sky-cult myths about the beginning, there are usually supernatural creators with supernatural powers. In certain New Guinea traditions this creator is a crocodile; Greek/Roman mythos features a panoply of gods; and Judeo-Christian and Islamic traditions worship God with a capital G.

A key distinction among the various sky-cults lies in the extent to which the creator is held to be actively involved in the daily affairs of the group. For Oceanic peoples, for example, the creator has negligible daily agency compared with the ancestors, who cause illness when behavior is inappropriate, and it is therefore the ancestors who are worshipped. In contrast, when the myth involves a god who not only creates but also watches and judges, ceremonial attention is focused primarily on this god and his agents (prophets, saints, messiahs, monarchs).

The major present-day religious institutions are sky-cults with myths that feature active, judging gods. The institutions serve to mediate access to these gods who are, by definition, otherwise remote and inaccessible. Since this mediation is performed by the likes of priests in the likes of ceremonial temples, institutional religions require financial support. The result has been a goods-for-services relationship which has had, in evolutionary terms, an important selective effect: the sky-cult institutions that have survived and now dominate the religious world are optimized for two traits, their compelling myths and their appealing rewards. I will return to the reward component later. Here we can ask, how do sky-cult myths become compelling? Several responses are particularly relevant.

First, sky-cult and ancestor-cult myths are often fused, generating stories of ancestral figures who have had direct interactions with the gods. When a person adopts such a religion, be it by birth or by conversion, these mythic ancestor/god relationships become the person's own story, and hence the sky becomes more immediate and accessible. If Moses or Jesus or Muhammad talked to God, then so might I.

Second, sky-cult myths are buttressed by some of the most wondrous art created by humankind. The mosques, the Kaddish, the saffron robes, the incense and candles, the hymns, the stained glass—not only do these reinforce the myth, but in many cases they serve to elicit transcendent states. Importantly, when these transcendent states are experienced, they are said to be the experience of God, of God within. Hence, there is continuous positive selection for myths that elicit transcendence since these experiences directly reinforce the validity of the myth.

The validity of the myth is, of course, the ultimate issue, and unquestionably the most important concept to be developed by sky-cults is the concept of faith. The *OED* defines *faith* as: "Belief in the truths of religion, in the authenticity of divine revelation; the spiritual apprehension of the realities beyond the reach of sensible experience or logical proof." Not only does faith in the myth render it, by definition, believable; the state of faith provides a state of grace, a transcendent state that is profoundly meaningful and soothing to persons who achieve it. The acquisition of faith, therefore, can be highly adaptive, and its achievement is highly dependent on compelling sky-cult myths and their attendant art and ritual.

Earth-cults

An earth-cult is most readily defined by the ceremonies it elicits: fertility rites, rain dances, celebrations of the harvest and the passage of the seasons. With closer scrutiny, however, many earth-cults prove to be sky-cults: to the extent that a rain dance is a petition to a supernatural god of the rains, then the ritual is in the service of a sky-cult myth. The dance becomes an earth-cult ritual when it is simply a celebration of the rains, for themselves, in and of themselves.

In the evolutionary lottery, earth-cults have fared poorly. Worship of earthly things, earthly pleasures, graven images, the sensate—these are activities that sky-cults have effectively pitted themselves against. The reason, I believe, is clear. If we now take up the question of reward, the reward offered by most sky-cults is some sort of afterlife, reincarnation, immortality of the soul—some liberation from earthly things and from earth's most formidable certainty, the certainty of death. And while it is true that the reward of rain would be a compelling reward for the rain-dancer, the problem, of course, is that very often it still doesn't rain after many days of dancing. In contrast, the reward of an afterlife is not amenable to experimental test. It is a matter of faith. Therefore, to the extent that a sky-cult can elicit faith states, it can offer reward.

A Cult for the Present Day

So where has this analysis taken us? It allows us to recognize that ancestor-cults and sky-cults are remarkably adaptive components of our culture. They provide to billions of people a sense of ethnic and historic continuity. They provide the means to achieve states of faith, grace, and transcendence, states that offer stability and enrichment. They provide the largest share of all art forms, probably the only art that most people experience. And they provide answers, based on faith, as to why one is here and where one is going. To my mind, the worldview provided by science cannot make any contribution to these orientations, nor should it attempt to do so.

The problem with leaving matters in the hands of ancestor-cults and sky-cults lies not in what they do, but in what it is that they fail to do and, indeed, have traditionally made no attempt to do. First, I agree with Loyal Rue (Rue 1994) that, by definition, these cults tell particular stories, not everyone's story. Any attempt to change this situation would be the equivalent of trying to transform one species into another. Each is highly selected for its particular niche, and the diversity of cults is to be deeply treasured. But particular cults with particular vocabularies don't get us very far in our search for a global myth.

Second, sky-cults and ancestor-cults leave global matters largely unaddressed. Morality, for example, is defined in terms of our behavior vis-a-vis one another, behavior ultimately dictated by the directives of the ancestors or the gods and their prophets. In contrast, our behavior vis-a-vis the earth itself is not part of the canon. Indeed, as we have noted, earthly matters are often regarded as negative testing grounds for the strengthening of one's faith.

If we look for examples of existing earth-cults, they can be found in a number of contexts. Local practices of Roman Catholicism, for example, have often come to include features of "pagan" traditions, although these are usually co-opted syncretistically rather than becoming part of the official canon, and they often retain a sky-cult focus on supernatural agency. During the past few decades, moreover, as the environmental movement has become more robust, observances such as Earth Day have come to include such rituals as parades and pageants as well as workshops on solar energy and recycling, even though these activities are not usually spoken of as religion (perhaps because scientists are not the only ones who have difficulty with the term).

Most relevant perhaps are present-day movements that celebrate the earth in revivals of Native American traditions, earth goddess traditions, and related approaches that can be collectively, if imprecisely, called New Age. While I have not begun to explore these movements exhaustively, those that I have encountered offer a mystical rather than a cognitive approach to the earth. The earth is evoked as power, energy, magic, fertility, a source of transformation. There is much symbolic use of fire, air, and water; and rituals focus on lunar and seasonal cycles. But none of this is oriented within the present-day scientific worldview. Indeed, if anything, these movements express either an overt hostility toward science or else an indifference to its understandings.

Mystical experience is intensely meaningful, whether evoked by drumming and dancing in the moonlight or by Gregorian chants in cathedrals or by group meditation in Buddhist temples. It can also be elicited by such stimuli as string quartets or romantic love. For me, a religion works only if it offers the opportunity for mystical experience, but it needs to be more than mystical experience. It also needs to be embedded in my cognitive reality, and the New Age earth-cults seem to be disinterested in this reality. Therefore, if we want an earth-cult grounded in a scientific cosmology, we're going to have to invent one.

For me, the easiest way to orient myself in such an earth-cult is to begin with the proposition, which may not be true but cannot as yet be disproved, that this planet is the only living planet, that there are no other life forms anywhere else in the universe, and that we humans are the only ones who understand the meaning of the word *meaning*. When I truly absorb this proposition, then I realize that I care about having life continue. Not my life, but life. I further realize that because of the way evolution has played itself out, humans are now the custodians of the planet. Were we to go extinct tomorrow, life would continue just fine without us. But we are here; we are, whether we like it or not, the dominant species; and we have unique capabilities to sustain life or destroy it. As I understand this, I realize that my participation in an earth-cult is not an option but an obligation. As soon as there is caring, and an obligation to care, then we have the foundation of a moral system. The moral fabric of an earth-cult is to care.

But what do we care about? How can we orient ourselves toward an earth that is so chaotic, so full of contradictions and tensions and impossibilities that we want to run back to the haven of our sky-cults and abandon the whole enterprise? This is, I believe, where science can help.

When the term *science-religion dialogue* is used, *science* usually refers to one or both of the great scientific insights of our time, namely, our understanding of the physical nature of matter and the universe and our understanding that life has evolved. The dialogue then proceeds to consider whether the god(s) in fact created matter and life via such seemingly unusual means as orchestrating the Big Bang or directing gene mutation, or whether things happened some other way. These, we can now say, are sky-cult issues. A recent version of the dialogue is to be found in the *Time* magazine cover story (29 December 1992) entitled, "What Does Science Tell Us about God?" The answer, of course, is that science tells us nothing about God. Indeed, any sky-cult can proclaim, and many have, that all of our understandings of the universe and of evolution have nothing to do with God: they are illusions, or they are irrelevant, or they somehow exist in addition to the Word. After hundreds of years of effort, in thousands of books written by thousands of theologians and physicists, the science/sky-cult dialogue remains a standoff, by definition. With faith as the wild card, nobody can define the rules.

In contrast, the sciences of the earth—biology, geology, anthropology, and psychology—have everything to say to an earth-cult. Scientific inquiry is telling us, in increasingly wondrous detail, how life works, how enzymes catalyze reactions, how nerves transmit impulses, how one cell divides into two, how continents drift about, how volcanoes erupt, what brains look like when they think. In the fields of biology that I study, there has occurred, during the past thirty years, such a breathtaking revolution in our understanding of how life works that those of us involved in the process of discovery are quite literally gasping with awe. In my experience, the awe feels the same as the awe I experience when I listen to a terrific performance of the St. Matthew Passion. Whether it is in fact the same brain state is beside the point. The point is that the beauty of molecular and cellular organization is a powerful complement to the beauty of rainfall and redwoods and owls. Life is beautiful all the way down. Unlike the physical universe, which for most people becomes increasingly bleak and terrifying the better it is known, the biological world yields an increasing sense of sacredness the better it is known. The more we know about life, the more we can care about it.

There is a subtle but important progression from *caring about* something to feeling *affection for* something. Affection requires direct knowledge, experience. A heterosexual may care about homosexual rights, but it is knowledge of, and affection for, particular homosexual friends that transforms the caring into morality. We can therefore say that the more we know about life, the deeper becomes our affection for it. Affection is that which binds together, and this is our definition of religion (Rue 1994).

The Search for a Global Myth

A second powerful resource for a global religious myth is our emerging picture of molecular evolution. Sky-cult interpretations of evolutionary theory have picked up on the concept of improvement, of simple life forms giving way to more complex life forms, presumably as the consequence of some divine plan. But as we clone and sequence genes, we find numerous cases where the very same genes are present in bacteria and yeast and ferns and humans. Moreover, these genes direct the same cellular processes: at a molecular level, yeast cells grow and divide and send signals to one another in much the same way that humans do. We have long understood that we are dependent on other organisms in the sense that photosynthesis provides our oxygen and the food chain provides our nutrition. But now we are saying that organisms are interconnected, that our interrelatedness goes all the way down. Evolutionary charts no longer depict trees that culminate in the crowning glory of humankind. Instead, they look like sunbursts, lines radiating out from central foci, with the lineage leading to humans being no more significant than the lineage leading to mushrooms.

Our genetic relatedness has pivotal relevance to the moral fabric of an earth-cult which, as we have developed it, is based on our capacity to care about life, to feel affection for it. Sociobiologists have given us the concept of kin selection as a calculus based on genetic relatedness: an organism is more likely to sacrifice its life for a sibling than for a cousin because it shares more genes with the former than with the latter. Our cognitive understanding of evolution now allows us to take this concept much further: to the extent that the genes are shared throughout all of life, this gives us a lot more to care about.

Our genetic relatedness also, of course, offers the potential for an ancestor-cult orientation within an earth-cult. It is not our particular human or ethnic ancestry that concerns us or unites us, but rather our collective relationship to the first forms of life, those foci at the center of the sunbursts. As research continues to probe the origins of life, it becomes increasingly clear how improbable those origins are, how dependent they would have to have been on the particular conditions of the planet as it cooled and condensed. It is a noble story, quite as compelling as *Genesis 1*, quite as capable of orienting our existence.

The earth is inhabited not just by its mountains and streams, its algae and antelopes. It is also inhabited by human history, by our memes, our ancestor-cults, and our sky-cults. These are the creations of our brains, themselves wondrous collections of cells and molecules. Therefore, an earth-cult celebrates not only geodiversity and biodiversity but also mythic diversity. To the extent that an earth-cult makes no claim, has no need to supplant other systems of faith or tradition, it has the unique potential to create a collective global myth and hence to serve as a global religion.

So, the biological scientific worldview could certainly enrich the mythos of an earth-cult. The real question, then, is whether the scientific worldview is in any way essential to an earth-cult. Certainly earth-cults have been forged in many cultures without an understanding of genes or molecules or plate tectonics. Does an earth-cult *need* the earth sciences?

My answer is a most emphatic yes. A global earth-cult is an appealing sort of concept in the abstract and can generate appealing notions that every species has an equal right to existence and that humans must return to their proper place in the ecosystem. But what *is* our proper place in the ecosystem? From an evolutionary perspective, what we are doing is precisely what we were selected for. We became the dominant species not by strength or speed or increased brood size but because we used our brains to exert control, to exploit the ecosystem to our maximum advantage. We are not the only organisms so selected: a bacterial cell, placed in a vial of nutrient medium, will divide and consume and pollute until the medium is putrid and most of the cells are dead. Bacteria are kept in balance by their predators; our brains have devised strategies to eliminate our predators. So how is balance achieved? Do we allow the human pox virus to reenter its habitat? Do we allow rattlesnakes and grizzly bears to roam our suburbs? Or do we use these same brains to devise strategies for global equilibrium which, by definition, are no longer shaped by Darwinian principles? If so, who makes the rules? On what basis? Who owns the oil? How is population stabilized? Which population?

These are political decisions, politics in the end being the alternative to Darwinism. Religions have always provided the moral basis, the justifications, for political systems, and a global earth-cult would aspire to no less. But it needs a text, a canon—the equivalent of the Bible or the Koran. The earth sciences could be such a text, a starting point for making such decisions, a basis preferable to the authority of custom. Such a canon would not dictate what choices are made—these would still have to be worked out by humans, on the basis of what is in the end deemed most fair and most feasible. But the scientific texts would help to identify what is fair and feasible, in a vocabulary that speaks of the entire biosphere and not just of a particular tradition. If scientists and nonscientists were to collectively take up the project of developing such a canon, it would be a most exciting enterprise indeed.

I close with a warning. While many *Zygon* readers may agree that the scientific worldview has much to offer a global religious myth, we are in a small minority. There is an antiscience orientation out there that can no longer be ignored. Science is seen to have created enormous problems and few solutions, and scientists are increasingly perceived as self-serving meddlers. While we can protest that this is a misunderstanding, that it is the application of science and not science itself that has created the problems, such protests miss the mark. What the scientists among us really need to be doing is to speak to nonscientists, at every opportunity, about the beauty of what we know, about the beauty of cells and molecules, indeed, about their mythic potential. When I first started doing this I felt completely ridiculous and not a little terrified: I had no data, no slides, no expertise. But it has become a part of my life. I guess it has become a part of my religion. To the extent that I've become an earth-cult evangelist, I feel like I'm earning my keep.

The Sengalese conservationist Baba Dioum can summarize: "In the end, we will conserve only what we love, we will love only what we understand, and we will understand only what we are taught."

Note

1.   Camille Paglia (1990) has developed this typology as well.

References

Paglia, Camille. 1990. *Sexual Personae.* New York: Vintage.

Rue, Loyal D. "Redefining myth and religion: Introduction to a conversation." *Zygon: Journal of Religion and Science* 29 (September): 315-19.

18

Does Evolution Rule Out God's Existence?

JOHN F. HAUGHT

In 1859 Charles Darwin published *On the Origin of Species*, his famous treatise on "evolution." It is one of the most important books of science ever written, and experts today still consider it to be largely accurate. Theologically speaking, it caused a fierce storm of controversy, and we are still wrestling with the question of what to make of it. Does Darwin's theory perhaps put the final nail in religion's coffin? Or can there be a fruitful encounter of religion with evolutionary thought?

For many scientists evolution means that the universe is fundamentally impersonal. In fact, the physicist Steven Weinberg asserts that evolution refutes the idea of an "interested" God much more decisively than physics does.[1] Only a brief look at Darwin's theory will show why it disturbs the traditional religious belief in a loving and powerful God.

Darwin observed that all living species produce more offspring than ever reach maturity. Nevertheless, the number of individuals in any given species remains fairly constant, which means that there must be a very high rate of mortality. To explain why some survive and others do not, Darwin noted that the individuals of any species are not all identical: some are better "adapted" to their environment than others. It appears that the most "fit" are the ones that survive to produce offspring. Most individuals and species lose out in the struggle for existence; but during the long journey of evolution there emerge the staggering diversity of life, millions of new species, and eventually the human race.

What, then, is so theologically disturbing about the theory? What is there about evolution that places in question even the very existence of God? It can be summarized in three propositions:

1. The variations that lead to differentiation of species are purely random, thus suggesting that the workings of nature are "accidental" and irrational. Today the source of these variations has been identified as genetic mutations. Most biologists today follow Darwin in attributing them to "chance."

2. The fact that individuals have to struggle for survival, and that most of them suffer and lose out in this contest, points to the basic cruelty of the universe, particularly toward the weak.

3. The mindless process of natural selection by which only the better adapted organisms survive suggests that the universe is essentially blind and indifferent to life and humanity.

These three ingredients—randomness, struggle, and blind natural selection—seem to confirm the strong impression of many scientific skeptics today that the universe is impersonal, utterly unrelated to any "interested" God. Darwin himself, reflecting on the "cruelty," randomness, and impersonality in evolution, could never again return to the benign theism of his ancestral Anglicanism. Though he did not casually forsake his religious faith, many of his scientific heirs have been much less hesitant to equate evolution with atheism.

From the middle of the last century up until today prominent thinkers have welcomed Darwinian ideas as the final victory of skepticism over religion. T. H. Huxley, Darwin's "bulldog" as he was known, thought evolution was antithetical to traditional theism. Ernst Haeckel, Karl Marx, Friedrich Nietzsche and Sigmund Freud all found Darwin's thought congenial to their atheism. And numerous others in our own time closely associate evolution with unbelief. Given this coalition of evolution and hostility to theism it is hardly surprising that the idea has encountered so much resistance from some religious groups.

Is the Darwinian—or now the "neo-Darwinian"—picture of evolution compatible with religion, and if it is, in what sense? Answers to this question fall into four distinct groups.

I. The "Conflict" Position

Both scientific skeptics and biblically literalist "creationists" maintain that Darwinian evolution inevitably conflicts with religion. Skeptics find in evolution a most compelling basis for rejecting theism in particular. The three features of chance, struggle, and blind natural selection seem so antithetical to any conceivable notion of divine providence or design that it is hard for them to understand how any scientifically educated person could still believe in God.

Richard Dawkins, the renowned British zoologist, presents this "conflict" position handily.[2] His thesis is that chance and natural selection, aided by immensely long periods of time, are enough to account for all the diverse species of life, including ourselves. Why would we need to invoke the idea of God if chance and natural selection alone can account for all of the creativity in the story of life? Before Darwin it may have been difficult to find definitive reasons for atheism. The order or patterning in nature seemed to beg for a supernatural explanation, and so the design argument for God's existence may have been plausible then. But this, Dawkins claims, is no longer the case. Evolutionary theory, brought up to date by the discoveries of molecular biology, has demolished the divine designer that most educated people believed in before the middle of the last century. Evolution has once and for all purged any remaining intellectual respectability from the idea of God.[3]

In his book *Natural Theology* which set forth the standard academic and theological wisdom of the early nineteenth century, William Paley had compared nature to a watch. If you chanced upon a watch lying alone on the ground, he wrote, and then examined its intricate structure, you could not help concluding that it had been made by an intelligent designer. It couldn't possibly be the product of mere chance. And yet, the natural world exhibits much more complex order than any watch. Thus, Paley concluded, there has to be an intelligent designer responsible for nature's fine arrangement. This designer, of course, would be none other than the Creator God of biblical religion.

But Dawkins argues that the divine designer is no longer needed:

> Paley's argument is made with passionate sincerity and is informed by the best biological scholarship of his day, but it is wrong, gloriously and utterly wrong. The analogy between ... watch and living organism, is false. All appearances to the contrary, the only watchmaker in nature is the blind forces of physics, albeit deployed in a very special way. A true watchmaker has foresight: he designs his cogs and springs, and plans their interconnections, with a future purpose in the mind's eye. Natural selection, the blind, unconscious, automatic process which Darwin discovered, and which we now know is the explanation for the existence and apparent purposeful form of all life, has no purpose in mind. It has no mind and no mind's eye. It does not plan for the future. It has no vision, no foresight, no sight at all. If it can be said to play the role of watchmaker in nature, it is the blind watchmaker.[4]

Even though David Hume and other philosophers had already severely battered the design argument for God's existence, Dawkins thinks that only Darwin's theory of natural selection provided a fully convincing refutation of natural theology. "Darwin made it possible to be an intellectually fulfilled atheist."[5]

The order and design in nature may seem on the surface to point to a divine "watchmaker" who devised its intricate parts. But evolution, the skeptic will insist, has allowed us to look beneath the deceptive surface of nature's orderly arrangements. The pattern and design that seem so wonderfully miraculous to the scientifically illiterate can now be fully accounted for by Darwin's impersonal theory of evolution. The theory rules out any proper appeal to the God-hypothesis. If there is a watchmaker at all, it is not divine intelligence but blind natural selection that has put the parts of nature so wonderfully together over the course of billions of years of trial and error. The aimless forces of evolution are sufficient to explain all the marvels of life and mind.

Clearly it is this reading of evolution that leads so many religious opponents of Darwin to adopt the "creationist" position. Creationists agree with skeptics that evolution is incompatible with the idea of a Creator. One version of creationism known as "scientific creationism" or "creation science," rejects evolutionary theory as scientifically unsound, and offers the Bible as an alternative "scientific" theory.[6] On the surface scientific creationists seem to embrace scientific method. And they argue on the basis of the paucity of intermediary forms in the fossil record that the biblical account provides a "scientific" hypothesis more suited to the actual data of geology, biology and paleontology than does Darwinian science.

Most scientists reply, however, that "creation science" is really not science at all. It does not seriously accept the self-revising method required by true science, nor does it acknowledge that the gaps in the fossil record might be compatible with other, revised versions of evolutionary theory, such as that of "punctuated equilibrium" proposed by Stephen Jay Gould and Niles Eldredge.[7] Creation science, they argue, would not even be worth discussing were it not for the fact that its devotees stir up so much public controversy in their attempts to keep evolutionary theory out of schools and textbooks.

II. The "Contrast" Response

A second response to the question of whether theology is possible after Darwin, argues that since science and religion are such disparate or "contrasting" ways of looking at the world that they cannot meaningfully compete with each other. This means that evolution, which may be quite accurate as a scientific theory, bears not the slightest threat toward religion. This position rejects both "scientific creationism" and scientific skepticism, both of which posit a conflict between evolution and religion. It would argue as follows.

So-called "scientific creationism" is objectionable in the first place because from the point of view of good science it refuses to look at the relevant data. The scientific evidence in favor of evolution is overwhelming. Although evolutionary theory is certainly not unrevisable, this does not mean that the world and life did not evolve, at least approximately along Darwinian lines. In the second place, scientific creationism is theologically embarrassing. It trivializes religion by artificially imposing scientific expectations on a mythic-symbolic text. It completely misses the Bible's religious point by placing the text of Genesis in the same arena with science, as an alternative "scientific" account. Creationism thus subverts the deeper meaning of the biblical account of creation, its covenantal motifs, its fundamental message that the universe is a gift and that the appropriate human response to this gift is gratitude and trust. Creationism turns a sacred text into a mundane treatise to be placed in competition with scientific attempts to explain things.

If our primary question to the Bible is one of scientific curiosity about cosmic beginnings or the origins of life, we will surely miss its real intentions. Since the text was composed in a prescientific age, its primary meaning cannot be unfolded in the idiom of twentieth century science. But that is exactly the demand put upon the Bible by scientific creationism. Needless to say, such an expectation ends up shriveling to prosaic dust a collection of deeply religious writings designed to open us to the ultimate mystery of the universe.

In the third place, scientific creationism is historically anachronistic. Creationists ironically situate the ancient biblical writings within the time-conditioned framework of modern science. They refuse to take into account the social, cultural and historical conditions in which the books of the Bible were fashioned over a period of two millennia. In doing so they close their eyes to modern historical awareness of the time-sensitive nature of all human consciousness, including that expressed in the sacred texts of religion. They are unable to discern the different types of literary genre—symbolic, mythic, devotional, poetic, legendary, historical, creedal, confessional etc.—that make up the Bible; and so they fail to read the scriptures in their proper context.

In spite of these problems, however, the contrast approach can entertain a certain empathy with the phenomenon of creationism. Creationism may be an unfortunate symptom of the much wider effort by traditionally religious people to cope with modernity. At heart creationists and other fundamentalists are sincerely and understandably troubled by the failings of the post-Enlightenment world. They deplore the breakdown of authority, the diminishment of "virtue," the absence of common purpose, the loss of a sense of absolute values, and the banishing of a sense of sacred mystery from our experience. For many creationists the notion of "evolution" sums up all the evils and emptiness of secularistic modernity. Creationism, in other words, is responding to something much more complex than the conflict between religion and science.

Moreover, according to our second approach, the phenomenon of creationism points to serious problems in the way science has been presented to the public by some of our most prominent scientific writers. These scientists also indulge in a conflation of science with belief: they unnecessarily fuse valuable scientific data with the ideology of "scientific materialism" which is antithetical to any religious perspective. Scientists of the stature of Carl Sagan, Stephen Jay Gould, E. O. Wilson, and Richard Dawkins, just to name a few, offer the theory of evolution already snugly wrapped up in the alternative "religion" of scientism and materialism. So, in a sense, creationism is an understandable, though ineffective, reaction to an alternative conflation of science and belief.

Scientific materialists, as the contrast position contends, generally write about evolution as though it were inherently anti-theistic. In doing so they uncritically accept the assumptions of secularistic ideology and culture. Stephen Jay Gould, for example, has stated that the reason so many people cannot accept Darwin's ideas is that, in his opinion, evolution is inseparable from a "philosophical" message, namely, materialism. He writes:

> ... I believe that the stumbling block to [the acceptance of Darwin's theory] does not lie in any scientific difficulty, but rather in the philosophical content of Darwin's message—in its challenge to a set of entrenched Western attitudes that we are not yet ready to abandon. First, Darwin argues that evolution has no purpose. Individuals struggle to increase the representation of their genes in future generations, and that is all.... Second, Darwin maintained that evolution has no direction; it does not lead inevitably to higher things. Organisms become better adapted to their local environments, and that is all. The "degeneracy" of a parasite is as perfect as the gait of a gazelle. Third, Darwin applied a consistent philosophy of materialism to his interpretation of nature. Matter is the ground of all existence; mind, spirit and God as well, are just words that express the wondrous results of neuronal complexity.[8]

If one is to accept evolution, Gould implies, one must first embrace materialism. Like many other scientists today, and in spite of serious disagreements with fellow Darwinians, he clearly approves of the alliance of materialist assumptions and evolutionary theory. But this merger seems no less illustrative of the conflation of science with a belief system than is scientific creationism. In both instances it is the (con)fusion of science with ideology that paves the way to conflict.

In order to avoid this kind of confusion the "contrast" approach consistently maintains a clear distinction between science and belief systems, whether the latter are religious or materialist. A contrast approach seeks to liberate science from all ideology. Consequently it insists that evolutionary thinking is not in a position to tell us anything about God, nor can religious experience shed any significant light on evolution. Theology, moreover, should stick to its task of opening us up to religious experience, and scientists should stick to science, steering clear of the kind of ideological propaganda that Gould exemplifies. Evolution is a purely scientific theory that need not be cast in materialist terms. It is not evolution itself, but the materialist spin some scientists put on evolution, that is incompatible with religion. When it is stripped of its materialist covering evolutionary theory in no way contradicts theism.

This is how the contrast position seeks to make room for theology after Darwin. But, one might ask, can evolution really be extricated from materialist dogma? What about those theologically troubling aspects of Darwinian theory: chance, the struggle for survival and impersonal natural selection? Do they not refute theism and require a materialist interpretation? Without getting bogged down in theological conjecture here, the contrast approach is content to show that none of these three items necessarily contradicts theism.

In the first place, the "chance" character of the variations which natural selection chooses for survival may just as easily be accounted for as the product of human ignorance. The apparent randomness of what we today call genetic mutations could be a mere illusion resulting from the limitedness of our perspective. Religions claim, after all, that any purely human angle of vision is always exceedingly narrow. Hence, what appears to be absurd chance from a purely scientific perspective could be quite rational and coherent from that of an infinite Wisdom.

Second, evolutionist complaints about the struggle, suffering, waste and cruelty of natural process add absolutely nothing new to the basic problem of evil of which religion has always been quite fully apprised. The Bible, for example, has surely heard of Job and the crucifixion of Jesus, and yet it proclaims the paradoxical possibility of faith and hope in God in spite of all evil and suffering. One might even argue that faith has no intensity or depth unless it is a leap into the unknown in the face of such absurdity. Faith, according to this contrast theology—which habitually appeals to thinkers like Soren Kierkegaard—is always faith "in spite of" all the objective difficulties that defy reason and science.

Finally, there is no more theological difficulty in the remorseless law of natural selection, which is said to be impersonal and blind, than in the laws of inertia, gravity or any other impersonal aspects of science. Gravity, like natural selection, has no regard for our inherent personal dignity either. It pulls toward earth the weak and powerful alike—at times in a deadly way. But very few thinkers have ever insisted that gravity is an argument against God's existence. Perhaps natural selection should be viewed in the same way.

Moreover, the contrast approach also rejects Paley's narrowly conceived "natural theology" since it seeks to know God independently of God's self-revelation. Nature itself provides evidence neither for nor against God's existence. Something so momentous as the reality of God can hardly be decided by a superficial scientific deciphering of the natural world. Hence religion should in no way be troubled by evolutionary theory.

III. The "Contact" Approach

A third repose to our question about the prospects for theology after Darwin is not content with the standoff endorsed by the contrast position just summarized. It allows that the contrast approach has the merit at least of shattering the facile fusion of faith and science that underlies most instances of apparent conflict. Its sharp portrayal of the ideological biases in both creationism and evolutionism is very helpful. Contrast may be an essential step in the process of thinking clearly and fruitfully about the relationship of evolution to religion.

But for many scientists and religious thinkers the contrast approach does not go nearly far enough. Evolution is more than just another innocuous scientific theory that theology can innocently ignore. Theologians need to do more than just show that evolution does not contradict theism. Evolution, according to what may be called the "contact" position, is a most appropriate framework in which to express the true meaning of theistic faith. The "contact" approach would go something like this:

Evolutionary science deepens not only our understanding of the cosmos but also of God. Unfortunately, many theologians have still not faced the fact that we live in a world after and not before Darwin, and that an evolving cosmos looks a lot different from the world-pictures in which most religious thought was born and nurtured. If it is to survive in the intellectual climate of today, therefore, our theology requires fresh expression in evolutionary terms. When we think about God in the post-Darwinian period we cannot have exactly the same thoughts that Augustine, Aquinas, or for that matter our grandparents and parents had. Today we need to recast all of theology in evolutionary terms.

In fact, evolution is an absolutely essential ingredient in our thinking about God today. As the Roman Catholic theologian Hans Küng puts it, evolutionary theory now makes possible: 1) a deeper understanding of God—

not above or outside the world but in the midst of evolution;   2) a deeper understanding of creation—not as contrary to but as making evolution possible; and 3) a deeper understanding of humans as organically related to the entire cosmos.[9]

Skeptics, of course, will immediately ask how theology can reconcile the idea of God with the role of chance in life's evolution. This is a crucial question, and the contrast position's casual conjecture that chance may not really exist is unsatisfactory. In fact, chance is quite real. It is a concrete fact in evolution, but it is not one that contradicts the idea of God. On the contrary, an aspect of indeterminacy is just what we should expect if, as religion maintains, God is love. For love never coerces. It allows the beloved—in this case the entire created cosmos—to be or to become itself. If, as theistic religious tradition has always insisted, God really cares for the well-being of the world, then the world has to be something other than God. It has to have a certain amount of "freedom" or autonomy. If it did not somehow exist on its own it would be nothing more than an extension of God's own being, and hence it would not be a world unto itself. So there has to be room for indeterminacy in the universe, and the randomness in evolution is one instance of it.

In other words, if the world is to be something distinct from God it must have scope for meandering about, for experimenting with different ways of existing. In their relative freedom from divine coercion, some of the world's evolutionary experiments may work and others may not. But divine love does not crudely interfere. It risks allowing the cosmos to exist in relative liberty. In the unfolding of life, the world's inherent quality of being uncompelled manifests itself in the form of "contingent" occurrences in natural history (as Stephen Gould insightfully emphasizes), or in the random variations or genetic mutations that comprise the raw material of evolution. Thus a certain amount of chance is not at all opposed to the idea of God.

A God of love influences the world in a persuasive rather than coercive way, and this is why chance and evolution occur. It is because God is involved with the world in a loving rather than domineering way that the world evolves.[10] If God were a magician or a dictator, then we might expect the universe to be finished all at once and remain eternally unchanged. If God controlled the world rigidly instead of willing its independence, we might not expect the weird organisms of the Cambrian explosion, the later dinosaurs and reptiles, or the many other wild creatures that seem so alien to us. We would want our divine magician to build the world along the lines of our own narrowly human sense of clean perfection. But what a pallid and impoverished world that would be. It would lack all the drama, diversity, adventure and intense beauty that evolution has produced. It might have a listless harmony to it, but it would have none of the novelty, contrast, danger, upheavals, and grandeur that evolution has in fact brought about over billions of years.

According to the contact position, God is not a magician but a creator.[11] And this God is much more interested in promoting freedom and adventure than in preserving the status quo. Since divine creative love has the character of letting things be, we should not be too surprised at evolution's strange and erratic pathways.   The long struggle of the universe to arrive at life, consciousness, and culture is consonant with faith's conviction that love never forces but always allows for the play of freedom, risk and adventure.

Love even gives the beloved a share in the creative process. Might it not be because God wants the world to partake of the divine joy of creating novelty, that it is left unfinished, and that it is invited to be, at least to some degree, self-creative? And if it is self-creative can we be too disconcerted that it has experimented with the many different, delightful, baffling and bizarre forms that we find in the fossil record and in the diversity of life that surrounds us now?

Ever since Darwin, scientists have found out things about the natural world that may not be consistent with an innocent notion of divine design such as the one proposed by Paley and lampooned by Dawkins. But the new discoveries of an evolving cosmic story correspond very well with the self-giving humility of the God of religious experience, a God who wishes to share the divine creative life with all creatures, and not just humans. Such a God renounces any will to control the process of creation and gives to creatures a significant role, indeed a partnership, in the ongoing evolution of the world. Such a gracious, self-giving love would be quite consistent with a world open to all the surprises that pertain to evolution.

In summary, the "hypothesis" of God, taken in consort with (and not as an alternative to) evolutionary theory, can help account for the complexity and consciousness that evolution has brought about. God may be thought of as the transcendent source not only of the order in the universe but also of the novelty and turbulence that evolution has brought with it. God creates by inviting (not forcing) the cosmos to express itself in increasingly more diverse ways. As novelty comes into the evolving world, the present order has to give way. And what we confusedly refer to as "chance" and "chaos" may be the result of the breakdown of present arrangements of order in the wake of novelty's coming into the world.

The ultimate origin of evolutionary novelty is God. God's will, in this version of the contact approach, is the maximization of novelty and diversity. And since the introduction of novelty and diversity is what turns the cosmos into a world of beauty, we may say that the God of evolution is a God who wants nothing less than the ongoing enhancement of cosmic beauty. Thus an evolutionary picture of the cosmos, with all of its craziness and serendipitous wanderings, corresponds quite well with the biblical understanding of an adventurous and loving God as the One "who makes all things new." [12]

However, God's role in evolution is not only that of being the stimulus that stirs the cosmos toward deeper novelty and beauty. Religious faith claims that the same God who creates also promises to save the world from suffering and death. This would mean that the whole history of cosmic evolution, in all its detail and incredible breadth, is permanently taken into God's loving memory. The suffering of the innocent and the weak, highlighted so clearly by evolutionary thought, becomes inseparable from the divine eternity. Theology cannot tolerate a deity who merely creates and then abandons the world. God is intimately involved in the evolutionary process and struggles along with all beings, participating in both their pain and enjoyment, ultimately redeeming the world so that nothing in its long evolution is ever completely forgotten or lost. [13]

This is only a brief sampling of how some contemporary theology is now being transformed by its encounter with evolutionary science. Many varieties of evolutionary theology exist today, and the "contact" position summarized in this section is just a small fragment of the rethinking going on in theology after Darwin. According to this third response, it is regrettable that so much contemporary religious thought goes the way of creationism or contrast. Although evolutionary theology is inevitably in need of constant revision—and prudence requires that theology avoid enshrining for all time any particular version of it—a number of theologians consider evolution to be at least provisionally the most appropriate and fruitful framework within which to think about God today.

IV. Confirmation

A fourth approach goes even further than the contact position in establishing the close connection between theism and evolution. It argues that biblical religion with its distinctive notion of God provides much of the soil in which Darwinian ideas have taken root in the first place. [14] In this sense, religion can be said to support or "confirm" the evolutionary picture of nature, not by providing any additional scientific information—which is not religion's function anyway—but by providing part of the general picture of reality which has made evolutionary science historically possible.

For example, evolutionary theory could hardly have originated and thrived outside of a cultural context shaped by the specifically biblical picture of the nature of time rooted ultimately in a very particular understanding of God. The Bible understands time in terms of God's bringing about a new and surprising future. When, through biblical faith, some people became aware of a promise offered by a God who appears out of the future, they began to experience time in a new way. As the promised new creation beckoned them, they no longer felt the compulsion to return to a golden age in the past. Time became directional and irreversible at a very deep level of their awareness. And even when the idea of God dropped out of the intellectual picture of the cosmos in the modern period, the feeling of time as directional and irreversible remained deeply lodged in western sensibilities, including that of secular scientists. But it was an originally biblical perception of temporality that made it possible for science to embrace an evolutionary picture of the universe.

In contrast to this linear-historical sensitivity, the argument continues, most non-biblical religions and cultures have understood time as a repeating circle. Time's destiny, in both primal and Eastern religious traditions, is not something radically new, but instead a return to the purity and simplicity of cosmic origins. The Bible's emphasis on God as the source of a radically new future, on the other hand, breaks open the ancient cycle of time. It calls the whole cosmos, through the mediation of human hope, to look forward in a more linear way for the coming of God's kingdom, either in the indefinite future or at the end of time.

According to our fourth approach, therefore, it is only on the template of this stretched out view of irreversible duration that evolutionary ideas could ever have taken shape. Even though evolution does not have to imply a vulgar notion of "progress," it still seems to have required an irreversible, future-oriented understanding of time as its matrix. This view of time, the confirmation position claims, originally came out of a religious experience of reality as promise.

However, there may be an even deeper way in which faith in God nourishes the idea of evolution. The central idea of theistic religion, as the Catholic theologian Karl Rahner (among others) has clarified, is that the Infinite pours itself out in love to the finite universe. This is the fundamental meaning of "revelation." But if we think carefully about this central religious teaching it should lead us to conclude that any universe related to the inexhaustible self-giving love of God must be an evolving one. For if God is infinite love giving itself to the cosmos, then the finite world cannot possibly receive this limitless abundance of graciousness in any single instant. In response to the outpouring of God's boundless love the universe would be invited to undergo a process of self-transformation. In order to "adapt" to the divine infinity the finite cosmos would likely have to intensify its own capacity to receive such an abounding love. In other words, it might endure what we now know scientifically as an arduous, tortuous and dramatic evolution.[15]

Viewed in this light, the evolution of the cosmos is more than just "compatible" with theism. Faith in a God of self-giving love, it would not be too much to say, actually anticipates an evolving universe. It may be very difficult to reconcile the religious teaching about God's infinite love with any other kind of cosmos.

Notes

1.   Steven Weinberg, *Dreams of a Final Theory:* (New York: Pantheon, 1992), 246-49.

2.   Richard Dawkins, *The Blind Watchmaker* (New York: W.W. Norton & Co., 1986); *River Out of Eden* and *Climbing Mount Improbable.*

3.   Ibid., 6.

4.   Ibid., 5.

5.   Ibid., 6.

6.   Duane Gish, *Evolution: The Challenge of the Fossil Record* (El Cajon: Creation-Life Publishers, 1985).

7.   See Niles Eldredge, *Time Frames: The Rethinking of Darwinian Evolution and the Theory of Punctuated Equilibria* (London: Heinemann, 1986).

8.   Stephen Jay Gould, *Ever Since Darwin* (New York: W.W. Norton, 1977), 12-13.

9.   Hans Küng, *Does God Exist,* trans. by Edward Quinn (New York: Doubleday, 1980), 347.

10.   For a discussion of this approach see John F. Haught, *The Promise of Nature* (New York: Paulist Press, 1993).

11.   See L. Charles Birch, *Nature and God* (Philadelphia: Westminster Press, 1965), 103.

12.   For a development of these ideas, many of which are suggested by Alfred North Whitehead, see John F. Haught, *The Cosmic Adventure* (New York: Paulist Press, 1984).

13.   These ideas are elucidated especially by what is called "process theology." See John B. Cobb, Jr. and David Ray Griffin, *Process Theology: An Introductory Exposition* (Philadelphia: Westminster Press, 1976).

14.   See, for example, Ernst Benz, *Evolution and Christian Hope* (Garden City, N.Y.: Doubleday, 1966).

15.   See Karl Rahner, S.J., *Hominization,* trans. W.J. O'Hara (New York: Herder & Herder, 1965).

19

Does God Play Dice? Divine Providence and Chance

ELIZABETH A. JOHNSON, C.S.J.

In every age theology interacts directly or indirectly with the view of the world prevalent in its culture, including knowledge of the world gained through observation or experimental means. Although certain encounters of theology with this "scientific" intelligence have been shot through with hostility, the history of theology may also be read to disclose how dialogue with technically learned insights about the World has enkindled new religious wisdom, inspired appealing metaphors, and provided a context for new interpretation of religious tradition.[1] In any event, theology's interaction with science is essential to make religious faith both credible and relevant within a particular generation's view of the world and how it works.

In the last two decades of the 20th century, dialogue between theology and science has entered into a newly flourishing state thanks to the emergence of a somewhat less dogmatic, more hermeneutical temper in each discipline, as well as the desire of certain key players to engage the questions of the other.[2] Significant for Catholic theology was the solid encouragement Pope John Paul II gave to this dialogue in a 1987 message:

> The scientific disciplines are endowing us with an understanding and appreciation of our universe as a whole and of the incredibly rich variety of intricately related processes and structures which constitute its animate and inanimate components.... The vitality and significance of theology for humanity will in a profound way be reflected in its ability to incorporate these findings.[3]

Continuing, the papal message presented an interesting list of possibilities:

> If the cosmologies of the ancient Near Eastern world could be purified and assimilated into the first chapters of Genesis, might contemporary

cosmology have something to offer to our reflections upon creation? Does an evolutionary perspective bring any light to bear upon theological anthropology, the meaning of the human person as the imago Dei, the problem of Christology—and even upon the development of doctrine itself? What, if any, are the eschatological implications of contemporary cosmology, specially in light of the vast future of our universe? Can theological method fruitfully appropriate insights from scientific methodology and the philosophy of science?[4]

Gently chiding theological research and teaching for being less than enthusiastic about pursuing these questions, the pope concluded by urging dialogue that can bring mutual benefit to both parties:

Science can purify religion from error and superstition; religion can purify science from idolatry and false absolutism. Each can draw the other into a wider world, a world in which both can flourish.[5]

In sum, theological reflection today should endeavor to speak about God's relation not to an ancient nor medieval nor Newtonian world, but to the dynamic, emergent, self-organizing universe that contemporary natural and biological sciences describe.

This is not an easy world to comprehend or to comprise within a religious perspective. One of the most challenging discoveries has to do with the natural occurrence of chance, seemingly more intrinsic to the evolutionary development of the world than ever before thought to be the case. Albert Einstein's famous remark denying that God plays dice with the universe is in fact an expression of his religiously based refusal to accept the uncertainty of events encountered at the heart of quantum reality. Subsequently, however, the indispensable role played by random events operating within a law-like framework has received greater appreciation. Now the theological search is on for language, models, and metaphors that will give expression to faith experience in ways coherent with this fundamental scientific insight.

In this article I will engage the particular question of how God's providential activity can be affirmed in a world where chance plays a more essential role than ever before imagined. The conclusion, that divine providence is compatible with genuine randomness and that this compatibility in turn can shed light on the incomprehensible, gracious mystery of God, will be arrived at in three steps. First I will describe the relevant scientific data essential for understanding the problem; next I will retrieve the Thomistic notion of dual agency; and finally I will explore the interface between the two. In no way does the analysis exhaust the topic nor does my proposal resolve the debate. Rather, it simply traces and attempts to contribute to the issue out of the heritage of the Thomistic tradition.

Science: The Interplay of Law and Chance

By almost any measure, twentieth-century science has brought to an end the mechanistic view of the world associated with Newtonian physics and has replaced it with a dynamic, open-ended view of the world in which some events are in principle unpredictable, although in retrospect they may make sense. This holds true for events at very small and very large magnitudes of space as well as for events through long reaches of time.

At the infinitesimal level of the atom and its subatomic particles, quantum mechanics uncovers a realm where time, space, and matter itself behave according to laws whose very functioning have uncertainty built into them. Statistical probability lends a measure of order to this realm, but precise subatomic events do not seem to occur according to any discernible regularity. For example, while it can be predicted that a certain mass of radioactive uranium will decompose within a given time, there is no way to predict which atom will decompose next, or why.[6] Furthermore, as the Heisenberg uncertainty principle asserts, a human observer cannot simultaneously plot both the position and velocity of a subatomic particle, for by charting one we disturb the other. Does this human inability to nail down and predict subatomic events point to the poor state of our equipment or rather an ontological indeterminacy in reality itself? Many philosophers of science argue for the latter. Judging from the realm of the infinitesimally small, the fundamental building blocks of the world are neither mechanically preprogrammed nor utterly chaotic, but spontaneous within an orderly system.

At the macro level of nonlinear, dynamical systems such as weather, chaos theory explores how very slight changes in initial conditions are ramified to produce massive effects.[7] A butterfly fluttering its wings in Beijing may set up an air current that amplifies upward through different levels of intensity to produce a major storm in New York a week later. While the ramifications of change through chaotic, nonlinear systems are regular enough to be traced in mathematical equations, the number of initial conditions that affect each system is so immense and their confluence so unique that human observation will never get a total handle on them. We will never have a completely accurate weather forecast earlier than a week ahead, and this is due not to the limitation of our instruments but to the nature of the weather system itself. Being intrinsically unpredictable in an epistemological sense, dynamical systems thus represent a form of "structured randomness" in the world.[8] Does this indicate an ontological indeterminacy in the dynamical systems themselves? Many philosophers of science think so.

The immensely long evolution of the cosmos from the Big Bang to the present and still-evolving clusters of galaxies, as well as the evolution of matter on earth from nonorganic to living states and from simple life to human consciousness is another story fraught with the subtle interplay between chance and law.[9] To stay with the example of life on earth, mutations in genes, caused by the sun's ultraviolet rays or exposure to chemicals, issue in variations on life forms. Natural selection then rewards the ones that adapt best to their environment and reproduce. On and on goes this process of a hundred thousand variables, dead ends, and breakthroughs. Roll back the clock to before the appearance of life on earth and then let it roll again: Would humanity appear as we are now? Scientists are virtually unanimous in saying "no," so multiple and diverse are the factors that combined to produce our species. Intelligent life would probably develop, for the matter of the universe has the potential to evolve into complex structures (brains) from which consciousness emerges. But it would be a group with a different genetic history, even a different physical appearance.

The emergence of human mind sheds light on a wondrous ability of matter, namely its capacity so to organize itself as to bring forth the truly new from within itself. Beginning with the featureless state right after the Big Bang, a rich diversity of physical systems and forms have emerged in a long, complex sequence of self-ordering processes even to the point where mind emerges from matter—and seeks to understand the process by which it came to be! This evolutionary interpretation of mind as emergent within the process of matter's self-organization leads to a holistic, nondualistic idea of the human person. Not a composite of the isolatable elements of material body and spiritual but somehow substantial mind, the human being is a single entity whose physical structure enables and supports the emergence of mind. As Paul Davies graphically puts it, mind is not some sort of extra ingredient glued onto brains at some stage of evolution; it did not require any factors external to the world itself.[10] Rather, consciousness is a power that emerges gradually in and through the increasing complexity of those intricately ramified and interlaced structures we call brains. We are the universe become conscious of itself. Material, physical reality is much richer in its possibilities than we are accustomed to think.

Taken together, scientific understandings of the indeterminism of physical systems at the quantum level, the unpredictability of chaotic systems at the macro level, and the random emergence of new forms through the evolutionary process itself undermine the idea that there is a detailed blueprint or unfolding plan according to which the world was designed and now operates.

Rather, the stuff of the world has an innate creativity in virtue of which the new continuously emerges through the interplay of chance and law: "there is no detailed blueprint, only a set of laws with an inbuilt facility for making interesting things happen."[11] The genuinely random intersects with deep-rooted regularities, issuing in a new situation which, when regularized, becomes in turn the basis for a new play of chance. The world develops, then, neither according to anarchy nor according to teleology, but purposively if unpredictably. Physical phenomena are constrained in an orderly way, but themselves give rise to novelty due to the intrinsic indeterminism and openness of physical processes.

In this construal of nature's constitutive dynamic, it becomes clear that the classical idea of the laws of nature also requires revision. These are now understood to be descriptive rather than prescriptive, that is, abstract descriptions read off from regularities in the universe that approximate what we observe, rather than rules that preexist platonically apart from the universe, operating to dictate or enforce behavior.[12] The laws of nature approximate the relationships in nature but do not comprehend them to their depths, which remain forever veiled. Nature itself is a mystery.

Furthermore, the laws of nature require the workings of chance if matter is to explore its full range of possibilities and emerge toward richness and complexity. Without chance, the potentialities of this universe would go unactualized. The movement of particles at the subatomic level, the initial conditions of nonlinear dynamic systems, the mutation of genes in evolutionary history, all are necessary for the universe's becoming, though none can be predicted or controlled. It seems that the full gamut of the potentialities of matter can be explored only through the agency of rapid and frequent randomization. This role of chance is what one would expect if the universe were constituted so as to be able to explore all the potential forms of the organization of matter, both living and nonliving, that it contains.

It can even be seen in retrospect that the emergence of human nature as we know it requires such an infrastructure. There is a deep compatibility between the autonomous ways physical, chemical, and biological systems operate though the interplay of law and chance on the one hand, and human consciousness and freedom on the other. These particular human qualities (consciousness and freedom) are intensely concentrated states of tendencies (purposiveness and chance) found throughout the universe in natural forms. The radical freedom of natural systems to explore and discover themselves is the condition for the possibility of the emergence of free and conscious human beings as part of the universe.

The capacity to form a world is there from the beginning in the fundamental constitution of matter. Chance's role is to enable matter to explore these potentialities. No chance, no evolution of the universe. If it were not such an impossible oxymoron, chance might even be called a law of nature itself. Chance, consequently, is not an alternative to law, but the very means whereby law is creative. The two are strongly interrelated and the universe evolves through their interplay.

On balance, the general character of the world as we know it from contemporary science calls for a more subtle notion of overall design, one that incorporates the occurrence of the genuinely novel and unpredictable in the context of laws that underdetermine what occurs. Great possibilities are left open.

God's Action in the World: Theological Options

This contemporary view of the world, which enjoys wide allegiance in the scientific community and is not contingent on particular, disputed points, provides a uniquely new context in which to understand God's creative and providential action. The traditional model of God as king and ruler, gifted with attributes of omniscience and omnipotence, who in creating and sustaining the world preprograms its development, who establishes its laws of nature but sets them aside to intervene miraculously when the occasion warrants—this monarchical model is less and less seriously imaginable. The potentiality of matter, the complexity of self-organizing systems, the potent unpredictability of evolution, the operation of chance within underdetermined laws, the presence of chaos and novelty, the interdependent processes of the world in becoming, all are putting pressure on the classical idea of God and divine action in the world.

Engaging this new question, recent theology has itself self-organized into a range of options. In his 1989-90 Gifford Lectures, Ian Barbour delineates eight different schools of thought on the issue, each of which has its strengths and shortcomings.   Classical theology understands God to be an omnipotent, omniscient, unchanging sovereign who relates to the world as ruler to kingdom. The Deist option sees God as designer of a law-abiding world to which God relates as clockmaker to clock.   Neo-Thomist theology predicates God as primary cause working through secondary causes, on the analogy of an artisan with tools.   The kenotic position perceives God as voluntarily self-limiting divine power in order to participate vulnerably in the life of the world, the way a parent enables a child to grow.   Since existentialist theology sees God acting only in personal life, it has no model of God's relation to the world.   Linguistic theology discerns God as the agent whose intention is carried out in the overall development of the cosmos, the whole then being interpreted as the one, all-encompassing action of God.   The option for the theme of embodiment sees the world as God's body to which God relates intimately as a person does to one's own body. Process theology sees God as a creative participant in the cosmic community, with a divine leadership role to play.[13]

In addition to these positions described by Barbour, there is also another, not uncommon view of God's relation to the world that springs from a more closely literal interpretation of the Bible, understanding God to act directly in the events of the world as an individual, personal player. In dialogue with contemporary science this position argues ingeniously that, thanks to the indeterminism of reality at the quantum level, God's direct intervention in any instance does not transgress the laws of nature. Rather, the natural system itself is "gappy" and open to outside influence without being violated.[14] Thus God can answer prayer, arranging, for example, that the sun shines on the church picnic as a result of God's setting certain initial conditions in the weather pattern a week ahead, and can do so without violating the laws of nature. The difficulty with this position, however, is that it confuses a gap, something missing in the ontological structure of natural systems, with indeterminacy, the openness of natural systems to a variety of outcomes. This openness of matter, however, is an intrinsic part of the working of nature and necessary for its creative development. In principle there are no gaps in the universe, which is complete on its own level.

Evaluating the current state of discussion in 1991, Owen Thomas, editor of a major volume on divine action, argues that while each position contributes some insight, only neo-Thomism and process theology are genuinely adequate as they alone give a philosophically satisfying and coherent account of how both divine and creaturely agents are fully active in one unified event.[15] How, in either case, can we conceive of the play of chance in the providential guidance of the world? Process theology would appear to have the advantage in this question with its understanding of how God continuously lures the world to its goal. In this ongoing process, God prehends every new event into the divine consequent nature and gives new initial aims to every ongoing experience on the basis of what has already transpired. Since God and the world are in process together, not only does chance not threaten divine control over the universe, as it does in the classical model, but chance positively enriches divine experience. At the same time it provides opportunity for God's ongoing providential guidance in the giving of new initial aims to actual occasions impacted by chance.

Neo-Thomism, with its roots in a medieval and thus scientifically static view of the world, would seem less able to account for the occurrence of genuinely random events. Assessing its strengths and weaknesses, Barbour notes as a problem its difficulty in moving away from divine determinism to allow for the genuinely random to occur.[16] My own wager at this point, however, is that

Aquinas's own thought is not all that closed to the possibility that chance may factor into divine creative and providential action. In fact, it seems to me that Aquinas's insight into how God acts in the world fairly resonates with potential to account for the play of chance.

Aquinas and the Integrity of Created Systems

At the heart of Aquinas's vision of the nature of created reality is the evocative idea of participation. In creating the world, God, whose essence is the very livingness of Being (*esse*), gives a share in that being to what is other than Godself:

> Whatever is of a certain kind through its essence is the proper cause of what is of such a kind by participation. Thus, fire is the cause of all things that are afire. Now, God alone is actual being through divine essence itself, while other beings are actual beings through participation.[17]

As to ignite is the proper effect of fire, so too is the sharing of being the proper effect of the Mystery of Being. Hence, all that exists participates in its own way in divine being through the very gift of creaturely existence. It is not as if God and creatures stood as uncreated and created instantiations of "being" which is held in common by both (a frequent misunderstanding). Rather, the mystery of God is the livingness of Being who freely shares being while creatures participate. Nor is the gift of being given only once in the instant when a creature begins to exist, but continuously in a ceaseless act of divine creation. To cite another fiery analogy, every creature stands in relation to God as the air to the light of the sun. For as the sun is light-giving by its very nature, while the air is illuminated only so long as the sun shines, so also God alone simply exists (divine essence is *esse*) while every creature exists insofar as it participates in being (creaturely essence is not *esse*).[18]

This notion of participation affects the understanding of both God and the world. Continuously creating and sustaining, the life-giving Spirit of God is in all things not as part of their essence but as the innermost source of their being, power, and action. There is, in other words, a constitutive presence of God at the heart of things. Conversely, in its own created being and doing, the world continuously participates in the livingness of the One who is sheer, exuberant aliveness. The universe, in other words, is a sacrament. Every excellence it exhibits is a participation in that quality which supereminently exists in the incomprehensible mystery of God. Take the key example of goodness. Since "it befits divine goodness that other things should be partakers therein,"[19] every created good is a good by participation in the One who is good by essence. It follows that "in the whole sphere of creation there is no good that is not a good participatively."[20] In having their own good, creatures share in a way coherent with their own finite reality in divine goodness which is infinite. Indeed for Aquinas, this is the basis for any speech about the transcendent mystery of God at all, for in knowing the excellence of the world we may speak analogically about the One in whose being it shares.

One of the strengths of Aquinas's vision is the autonomy he grants to created existence through its participation in divine being. He is so convinced of the transcendent mystery of God (*esse ipsum subsistens*) and so clear about the sui generis way God continuously creates the world into being that he sees no threat to divinity in allowing creatures the fullest measure of agency according to their own nature. In fact, it is a measure of the creative power of God to raise up creatures who participate in divine being to such a degree that they are also creative and sustaining in their own right. A view to the contrary would diminish not only creatures but also their Creator: "to detract from the perfection of creatures is to detract from the perfection of divine power."[21] This is a genuinely noncompetitive view of God and the world. According to its dynamism, nearness to God and genuine creaturely autonomy grow in direct rather than inverse proportion. That is, God is not glorified by the diminishment of the creature but by the creature's flourishing in the fullness of its powers. The nature of created participation in divine being is such that it grants creatures their own integrity, without reserve.[22]

This participatory relationship has strong implications for the question of agency. The power of creaturely forces and agents to act and cause change in the world is a created participation in the uncreated power of the One who is pure act. Conversely, God's generous goodness and wisdom are seen especially in the creation of a world with its own innate agency. As is the case with created things' participation in divine being and goodness, so too with agency. God's action is not part of the creature's essential action, which has its own creaturely integrity. Rather, God's act giving creatures their very nature is what makes creaturely act possible at all in its own created autonomy. Technically, God is primary cause of the world, the unfathomable Source of being who continuously creates and sustains it, while creatures are secondary causes, moved movers who receive from God their form and power to act with independence.[23]

These two causes are not two species of the same genus, not two different types of causes united by the commonality of causing. They operate on completely different levels (itself an inadequate analogy), one being the cause of all causes and the other participating in this power. In this system of thought it is incoherent to think of God as working in the world apart from secondary causes, or beside them, or in addition to them, or even in competition with them. God's act does not supply something that is missing from a creaturely act or rob it of its power so that it is only a sham cause. Rather, the mystery of God acts by divine essence, power, and presence in and through the acts of finite agents which have genuine causal efficacy in their own right. It is not the case that divine and finite agents are complementary, each contributing distinct elements to the one outcome. Instead, God acts wholly through and in the finite agents that also act wholly in the event. As a result, the one effect issues from both primary and secondary causes simultaneously, with each cause, however, standing in a fundamentally different relationship to the effect. God makes the world, in other words, in the process of things acting as themselves.

Working in this tradition, Karl Rahner argues that even in the creation of the human soul divine causality does not insert itself into the finite causal series but, through the power given to matter to evolve toward spirit, enables human parents to transcend themselves in the creation of a genuinely other person.[24] Rahner, among others, also appeals to the doctrine of the Incarnation, wherein the divine and human are united while remaining distinct, and to the doctrine of grace, wherein the Spirit brings wholeness to human beings without violating their freedom or responsibility, as paradigms for the Godworld relationship. It seems to me that it is so easy to forget this, slipping God into the web of interactions as though the divine were simply a bigger and better secondary cause. But the distinction between primary and secondary causality enables thought to hold firm to the mystery of the Godness of God and the integrity of creatures, seeing both acting in a unique *concursus*.

In Aquinas's discussion of divine governance of the world, this idea of double agency with respect to efficient causality is correlated with final causality to provide the grid for his understanding of providence. It would seem, he objects with a curiously modern ring, that the universe does not need to be governed by God, for the processes of the world seem to accomplish their purpose on their own and without any interference. However, he replies, this very self-direction is itself an imprint (*impressio*) from God, for in giving creatures their own being God gives them a natural inclination whereby through their own natural actions they tend toward the good. This dynamic tendency is genuinely part of their own nature but it also expresses God's purposes. While endowing creatures with their intrinsic nature and ways of acting, God leaves them free to follow the strivings of their natural inclination which aims them toward the good. Since all good is a participation in divine goodness, we can affirm that the universe as a whole tends toward the ultimate good which is God. While in scholastic categories this is summed up in the notion that God is immanent in the universe as final cause, Aquinas also finds this view resonating in the biblical depiction of Sophia or Holy Wisdom, who reaches from one end of the world to the other, ordering all things sweetly and mightily (Wisdom 8:1).[25]

Let us draw all of these threads together to see how they might deliver an interpretive view of how God acts providentially in the world. As Aquinas explains, the way God is governor of things matches the way God is their cause. As God is primary cause of the world as a whole and in every detail, endowing all created beings with their own participation in divine being (enabling them to exist), in divine agency (empowering them to act), and in divine goodness (drawing them toward their goal), so too God graciously guides the world toward its end in and through the natural workings of the processes found in creation as a whole. Immanent in these processes, divine providential purposes come to fruition by means of purposes inherent in creatures themselves.

Why is this fitting? Aquinas argues in a particularly insightful reply that those forms of governing are best that communicate a higher perfection to the governed. Now there is more excellence in a thing's being a cause in relation to others than in its not being a cause. Consequently, God governs in such a way as to empower creatures to be causes toward others. Indeed, "If God were to govern alone, the capacity to be causes would be missing from creatures,"[26] to the detriment of their flourishing and their Creator's glory. Looked at another way, if God did everything directly so that created causes did not really affect anything, this would be a less powerful God. For it shows more power to give others a causative capability than to do everything oneself.[27] Thus God is everywhere present and active, continuously interacting with the world to implement divine purpose while granting creatures and created systems a full measure of being and efficacy. This is a both/and sensibility that guarantees the integrity of the created causal nexus while affirming the gracious and intentional immanence of the transcendent God active within worldly purposiveness.

Divine purpose is accomplished in a *concursus*, or flowing together, of divine and creaturely act in which the latter mediates the former. This means that the world necessarily hides divine providential action from us. God's act is not a discrete object that can be isolated and known as a finite constituent of the world, for its very nature is transcendent mystery while its mode of operation transpires immanently in and through created causes. At the same time, faith affirms that the world, far from being merely a stage for divine action, is itself a sacrament of God's providential action, which is sweet and strong within every cause so that everything may truly contribute to the realization of the goal.

Providence and Chance

Bringing contemporary science's view of the creative role of chance within law-like structure into dialogue with Aquinas's understanding of the God-world relation yields interesting results. The latter's conviction of the integrity of natural causes, while formulated within a largely static worldview, accommodates evolutionary science with almost surprising ease. For the basic principle remains the same: God's providential guidance is accomplished in and through the free working of secondary causes. Indeed, for Aquinas the understanding that God's providential activity is exercised in and through secondary causes includes rather than excludes chance, contingency, and freedom of choice: "It is not the function of divine providence to impose necessity on things ruled by it."[28] Rather, random occurrences themselves are secondary causes with their own integrity. Science may describe these secondary causes in different ways today, but they still function theologically as the means by which God fulfills divine purpose.

As we have seen, the process of creation is described by the natural sciences as one in which new qualities and modes of existence continuously emerge out of simpler forms of matter by the operation of natural laws. These laws of nature are ingenious and felicitous in that they enable matter and energy to self-organize in unexpectedly remarkable ways from clouds of dust and gas to galaxies and solar systems, and from nonorganic matter to life to mind. Multilayered and underdetermined, these laws reflect the universe's potential to create richness and complexity spontaneously, from within, in a process whose inherent openness precludes detailed fixing in advance. As secondary causes, they realize God's purposes. In the words of astrophysicist and theologian William Stoeger, reflective of the Neo-Thomistic consensus, "God is always acting through the deterministic and indeterministic interrelationships and regularities of physical reality which our models and laws imperfectly describe."[29]

Today's science has discovered that chance is an essential element in the continuous working out of these laws of nature. "In the beginning" the Creator endows the material of this world with one set of potentialities rather than another. These are then unveiled by chance, exploring their gamut in an inevitable yet indeterminate evolutionary process. Indeed, in retrospect, this seems to be the only way in which all of matter's potentialities might eventually, given enough time and space, be actualized. Consequently, chance is not an alternative to law, but the very means whereby law is creative. The two are strongly interrelated and the universe evolves through their interplay. If *this* is the kind of universe created by the Holy Mystery who is God, then faith can affirm that God works not only through the deep regularities of the laws of nature but also through chance occurrence which has its own, genuinely random integrity. God uses chance, so to speak, to ensure variety, resilience, novelty, and freedom in the universe, right up to humanity itself. Absolute Holy Mystery dwells within, encompasses, empowers the evolutionary process, making the world through the process of things being themselves, thus making the world through chance and its genuinely irregular character. If God works through chance, then the natural creativity of chance itself can be thought of as a mode of divine creativity in which it participates. And the gracious mystery of God can be glimpsed as the Source not only of deep regularities in the universe, but also of novelty. The future remains genuinely open: God does not act like a bigger and better secondary cause to determine chance atomic events or initial conditions of chaotic systems. Randomness is real, for God respects the structure of creation while at the same time weaving events into providential patterns toward the realization of the whole. Divine sovereignty and creaturely freedom, of which chance is one instance, do not compete.

Risk-Taking God

How does this interpretation of providence working through chance in turn influence classical understanding of divine attributes? With this question we reach a frontier where scientific insight in dialogue with Christian faith is providing the occasion for new forays into the doctrine of God. In these explorations theology today seems to be making bolder use of its own particular wisdom of Christology and pneumatology than did early modern theologians caught on the cusp of scientific atheism's first attacks.[30] The appeal today is to God's gracious action expressed in Incarnation and the gift of grace as the basic paradigm of the God-world relationship.

The creating God is also the redeeming God whose self-emptying Incarnation into the vagaries of history reveals the depths of divine Love, and is also the sanctifying God whose self-gift in grace brings wholeness to the brokenness of sinful hearts and situations without violating human freedom. Could it not be the case that, rather than being uncharacteristic of the mystery of God, divine kenosis revealed in the human history of salvation is what is most typical of God's ways, and therefore also distinguishes God's working in the natural world? Could it not be that God's being edged out of the world and onto the cross, in Bonhoeffer's profound intuition, also refers to the cost of divine vulnerability in creation?[31] Could it not be that since the human world is on a continuum with the micro world, only mediated by more complex biological matter, the best way to understand God's action in the indeterminacy of the natural world is by analogy with how divine initiative relates to human freedom?

If so—and an eminently coherent case can be made for this position—then divine perfection is ultimately a perfection of relationality and love rather than of self-sufficiency and control. Consequently, omnipotence unfailingly manifests itself not as coercive "power over" but as sovereign love which empowers. Exercising this power, God's providential guidance eschews pre-ordaining or imposing exact sequences of events but rather makes itself known as the patient, subtle presence of a gracious Creator who achieves divine purpose through the free play of created processes. Indeed, it is quite likely that Love is able to work only in such a way, out of respect for the beloved. It should be noted that the basic difference between process theology and Thomism regarding God's self-limitation of omnipotence is that for process thought this is a metaphysical necessity while for Thomism it is a free and voluntary act of love.

Divine governance involves God in waiting upon the world, so to speak, patiently acting through its natural processes including unpredictable, uncontrollable random events to bring about the emergence of the new while consistently urging the whole toward fullness of life. Even more can be said. With the development of nerves and brains, suffering in both the natural and human world becomes a terrifying consequence of the free play of randomness. Indwelling the world with the power of providential love, the gracious mystery of God is involved in suffering with the beloved creation as new life is created through death. Not the monarch but the lover becomes the paradigm.[32]

In the course of thinking upon these things, theologians are finding it helpful to imagine new metaphors to capture the nuances of God's providential relation to the workings of chance. As might be suspected, these images are drawn more from artistic creativity and the relationship of love than from the classical model of an artisan working with inert tools. No one of these metaphors, of course, is adequate but each sheds a little light. They also point quite directly to the importance of responsible human action in cooperation with God's providential purpose. Among them: God is like a master theatrical improvisor in live performance, amplifying and embroidering each theme as it presents itself; like a choreographer composing steps in tandem with the creative insights of the whole dance troupe; like a composer of a fugue, starting with a simple line of melody and weaving a complex structure by endlessly folding it back upon itself; like a jazz player, inspired by the spirit of the audience and the night to improvise riffs upon a basic melody; like a designer who sets the rules of a game that includes wild cards and then lets it play. In every instance the image is arrived at through the logic set out in W. Norris Clarke's evocative passage:

> [W]hat must the "personality" or "character" be like of a Creator in whose image this astounding universe of ours is made, with its prodigal abundance of energy, its mind-boggling complexity, yet simplicity, its fecundity of creative spontaneity, its ever surprising fluid mixture of law and chance, etc. Must not the "personality" of such a Creator be one charged not only with unfathomable power and energy, but also with dazzling imaginative creativity? Such a creator must be a kind of daring Cosmic Gambler who loves to work with both law and chance, a synthesis of apparent opposites—of power and gentleness, a lover of both law and order and of challenge and spontaneity.[33]

Key biblical images for Creator Spirit, namely, dynamic wind, fire, and water, also express the moving, playing, unpredictable qualities of the God to whom chance is not a rival.

In dialogue with contemporary science, theology understands that the Creator God is neither a maker of clocks nor an instigator of anarchy, but the one ceaselessly at work bringing overall direction and order to the free play of the undetermined realms of matter and spirit, "an Improvisor of unsurpassed ingenuity."[34] In this evolutionary world, the essential role of genuine randomness does not contradict God's providential care but somehow illumines it. To use Christopher Mooney's lovely phrasing,

> Wave packets propagate and collapse, sparrows fall to the ground, humans freely decide for good or for ill; yet hairs of the head nevertheless get numbers, elusive quantum particles eventually statistically stabilize, and "where sin increased, grace abounded all the more."[35]

The world develops in an economy of divine superabundance, gifted with its own freedoms, in and through which God's gracious purpose is accomplished. "The Love that moves the sun and the stars,"[36] it now appears, is a self-emptying, self-offering, delighting, exploring, suffering, sovereign Love, transcendent wellspring of all possibilities who acts immanently through the matrix of the freely evolving universe.

Notes

1. For historical background of the theology-science exchange, see Ernan McMullin, "Natural Science and Belief in a Creator: Historical Notes," in Robert Russell, William Stoeger, and George Coyne, ed., *Physics, Philosophy, and Theology: A Common Quest for Understanding* (Vatican City: Vatican Observatory, 1988) 49-79; and Michael Buckley, "The Newtonian Settlement and the Origins of Aetheism," ibid. 81-102.

2. See results of dialogue in Ted Peters, ed., *Cosmos as Creation: Theology and Science in Consonance* (Nashville: Abingdon, 1989); David Burrell, ed., *God and Creation: An Ecumenical Symposium* (Notre Dame: University of Notre Dame, 1990); and Robert Russell, Nancey Murphy, and C. J. Isham, ed., *Quantum Cosmology and the Laws of Nature: Scientific Perspectives on Divine Action* (Vatican City: Vatican Observatory; and Berkeley: Center for Theology and the Natural Sciences, 1993). Ian Barbour's Gifford Lectures explore the theology-science encounter in illuminating detail: *Religion in an Age of Science*, 2 vols. (San Francisco: Harper and Row, 1990-91). Individuals who have scholarly credentials in both science and theology and whose work helpfully reflects this dialogue include John Polkinghorne (see, e.g., his *One World: The Interaction of Science and Theology* [Princeton: Princeton University, 1986]) and Arthur Peacocke (see, e.g.. his *Theology for a Scientific Age: Being and Becoming—Natural, Divine and Human* [Minneapolis: Fortress, 1993]).

3. Papal message reprinted in Robert Russell et al., ed., *John Paul II on Science and Religion: Reflections on the New View from Rome* (Vatican City: Vatican Observatory, 1990) M 1-M 14, at M 5.

4. Ibid., M 11.

5. Ibid., M 13.

6. For general background written for the non-specialist, see John Polkinghorne, *The Quantum World* (Princeton: Princeton University, 1984); and C.J. Isham, "Quantum Theories of the Creation of the Universe," in Russell et al., ed., *Quantum Cosmology*, 49-89.

7. For a general introduction, see James Gleick, *Chaos: Making a New Science* (New York: Penguin, 1987); a key refutation of the idea that chaos amounts to blind, purposeless chance is the volume of Ilya Prigogine and Isabelle Stengers, *Order Out of Chaos* (New York: Bantam, 1984).

8. Term used by John Polkinghorne, "The Laws of Nature and the Laws of Physics," in Russell et al., ed., *Quantum Cosmology* 437-48.

9. Helpful scientific introductions include Carl Sagan, *Cosmos* (New York: Ballantine,1980); Stephen Jay Gould, *Wonderful Life: The Burgess Shale and the Nature of History* (New York: Norton, 1989); and Edmund O. Wilson, *The Diversity of Life* (New York: Norton, 1992). For religious reflections on this data, see Robert Jastrow, *God and the Astronomers* (New York: Norton, 1978); Paul Davies, *God and the New Physics* (New York: Simon and Schuster, 1983); and Arthur Peacocke, *God and the New Biology* (San Francisco: Harper and Row, 1986).

10. Paul Davies, "The Intelligibility of Nature," in Russell et al., ed., *Quantum Cosmology* 145-61, at 152; see also George Ellis, "The Theology of the Anthropic Principle," ibid., 367-405.

11. Paul Davies, *The Cosmic Blueprint* (New York: Simon & Schuster, 1988) 202.

12. See William Stoeger, "Contemporary Physics and the Ontological Status of the Laws of Nature," in Russell et al., ed., *Quantum Cosmology* 209-34.

13. Ian Barbour, *Religion in an Age of Science* 1:243-70, with chart on 244. See also the organizing schema by Robert Russell, "Introduction," in Russell et al., ed., *Quantum Cosmology* 4-10.

14. Representative of this group is William Alston, "Divine Action, Human Freedom, and the Laws of Nature," in Russell et al., ed., *Quantum Cosmology* 185-207.

15. Owen Thomas, "Recent Thoughts on Divine Agency," in *Divine Action*, ed. Brian Hebblethwaite and Edward Henderson (Edinburgh: T. & T. Clark, 1991) 35-50. See Thomas's own edited volume, *God's Activity in the World: The Contemporary Problem* (Chico, Calif.: Scholars, 1983).

16. Ian Barbour, *Religion in an Age of Science* 1:249-50.

17. Thomas Aquinas, *Summa contra gentiles* 3, chap. 66.7 (hereafter cited as SCG; the edition used is translated by Vernon Bourke [Garden City, N.Y.: Doubleday, 1956]). Aquinas's extended discussion of divine governance can be found in *SCG* 3, especially chaps. 64-77, and his *Summa theologiae* 1, pp. 103-109 (hereafter cited as ST; the edition used is translated by the English Dominicans [New York: Benziger, 1956]).

18. *ST* 1, q. 104, a. 1.

19. *ST* 1, q. 19, a. 2.

20. *ST* 1, q. 103, a. 2.

21. *SCG* 3.69.15.

22. For further explanation of this position, see Piet Schoonenberg, "God or Man: A False Dilemma," in his *The Christ* (New York: Seabury, 1971) 13-49.

23. For explanation of this point, see Etienne Gilson, "The Corporeal World and the Efficacy of Secondary Causes," in Owen Thomas, ed., *God's Activity* 213-30. Gilson stresses how strong Aquinas is on the integrity of secondary causes, using Aristotle to combat the Platonism of Avicenna. See also David Burrell, *Aquinas: God and Action* (Notre Dame: University of Notre Dame, 1979).

24. Karl Rahner, *Hominization: The Evolutionary Origin of Man as a Theological Problem* (New York: Herder & Herder, 1965); see also his essays "Christology within an Evolutionary View of the World," in *Theological Investigations* 5 (New York: Seabury, 1975) 157-92; and "The Unity of Spirit and Matter in the Christian Understanding of Faith," in *Theological Investigations* 6 (New York: Crossroad, 1982) 153-77.

25. *ST* 1, q. 103, a. 8.

26. *ST* 1, q. 103, a. 6.

27. *ST* 1, q. 105, a. 5.

28. *SCG* 3.72.7; see also 3.73 and 74.

29. William Stoeger, "Contemporary Physics" 234.

30. See the magisterial study by Michael J. Buckley, *At the Origins of Modern Atheism* (New Haven: Yale University, 1987), who concludes: "It is not without some sense of wonder that one records that the theologians bracketed religion in order to defend religion" (345).

31. Dietrich Bonhoeffer, *Letters and Papers from Prison* (New York: Macmillan, 1953) 219 (letter of July 16, 1944). For development of the idea of divine kenosis in creation, see Jurgen Moltmann, *God in Creation* (San Francisco: Harper and Row, 1985); and John B. Cobb and Christopher Ives, ed., *The Emptying God* (Maryknoll, N.Y.: Orbis, 1990). In the latter collection, the pitfalls and strengths of this idea for subordinated groups are explored by Catherine Keller, "Scoop up the Water and the Moon is in Your Hands: On Feminist Theology and Dynamic Self-Emptying" 102-15.

32. Peter Hodgson, *God in History: Shapes of Freedom* (Nashville: Abingdon, 1989) develops this idea with depth and lucidity; Sallie McFague, *Models of God: Theology for an Ecological, Nuclear Age* (Philadelphia: Fortress, 1987), and *The Body of God: An Ecological Theology* (Minneapolis: Fortress, 1993) gives it imaginative depth. Cf. Elizabeth Johnson, *SHE WHO IS: The Mystery of God in Feminist Theological Discourse* (New York: Crossroad, 1992) 224-72.

33. Norris Clarke, "Is a Natural Theology Still Possible Today?" in Russell et al., ed., *Physics, Philosophy, and Theology* 103-23, at 121. The theme of improvisation is stressed by Peter Geach, *Providence and Evil* (Cambridge: Cambridge University, 1977). The model of a fugue is developed by Arthur Peacocke, *Theology for a Scientific Age* 173-77, and that of the game by Paul Davies, *God and the New Physics.* Jazz is my suggestion.

34. Arthur Peacocke, *Imitations of Reality* (Notre Dame: University of Notre Dame, 1984) 73.

35. Christopher Mooney, "Theology and the Heisenberg Uncertainty Principle," a paper delivered to the Catholic Theological Society of America in June 1992 and summarized in *Catholic Theological Society of America Proceedings* 47 (1992) 130-132; the citation is taken from p. 62 of the original unpublished paper, and the biblical reference is to Romans 5:21.

36. Dante, *The Divine Comedy: Paradise,* trans. Dorothy Sayers and Barbara Reynolds (Harmondsworth, England: Penguin, 1962) canto 33, line 145.

20

Welcoming the "Disguised Friend": A Positive Theological Appraisal of Biological Evolution

ARTHUR R. PEACOCKE

> Darwinism appeared, and, under the disguise of a foe, did the work of a friend. It has conferred upon philosophy and religion an inestimable benefit, by shewing us that we must choose betwen two alternatives. Either God is everywhere present in nature, or He is nowhere. (Aubrey Moore, in the 12th edition of Lux Mundi, 1891, p. 73).

1 Introduction

It would, no doubt, come as a surprise to many of the biologically-cultured "despisers of the Christian religion," to learn that, as increasingly thorough historical investigations are showing,[2] the nineteenth-century reaction to Darwin in theological and ecclesiastical circles was much more positive and welcoming than the legends propagated by both popular and academic biological publications are prepared to admit. Furthermore, the scientific reaction was also much more negative than usually depicted, those skeptical of Darwin's ideas including initially *inter alia* the leading comparative anatomist of his day, Richard Owen (a Cuverian), and the leading geologist, Charles Lyell. Many theologians deferred judgment, but the proponents of at least one strand in theology in nineteenth-century England chose to intertwine their insights closely with the Darwinian—that "catholic" revival in the Church of England of a stress on the doctrine of the Incarnation and its extension into the sacraments and so of a renewed sense of the sacramentality of nature and God's immanence in the world. I have summarized elsewhere[3] some of this history, not only in Britain but also in France, Germany, and America—suffice it to say that more of the nineteenth-century theological reaction to Darwin was constructive and reconciling in temper than practically any biological authors today will allow.

That is perhaps not surprising in view of the background to at least T. H. Huxley's aggressive propagation of Darwin's ideas and his attacks on Christianity, namely that of clerical restriction on, and opportunities for, biological scientists in England in the nineteenth century. His principal agenda was the establishment of science as a profession independent of ecclesiastical control—and in this we can sympathize. So it is entirely understandable that the present, twentieth-century *Zeitgeist* of the world of biological science is that of viewing "religion" as the opposition, if no longer in any way a threat. This tone saturates the writings of the biologists Richard Dawkins and Stephen Gould and many others—and even philosophers such as Daniel Dennett. Indeed, the strictures of Jacques Monod in his 1970 publication *Le hasard et la nÈcessitÈ*, especially in its English translation *Chance and Necessity*, could be said to be one of the strongest attacks in this century, in the name of science, on belief in God and in the universe having any attributable meaning and purpose. His remarks on this are well known and widely quoted.

Perhaps this has polarized the scene, but what I find even more surprising, and less understandable, is the way in which the "disguised friend" of Darwinism, and more generally of evolutionary ideas, has been admitted (if at all) only grudgingly, with many askance and sidelong looks, into the parlors of Christian theology. I believe it is vital for this churlishness to be rectified in this last decade of the twentieth century if the Christian religion (indeed any religion) is to be believable and have intellectual integrity enough to command even the attention, let alone the assent, of thoughtful people in the beginning of the next millennium. Hence the title of this contribution.

2 Biological Evolution and God's Relation to the Living World

We shall consider in this section various features and characteristics of biological evolution and any theological reflections to which they may give rise.

2.1 Continuity and Emergence*

A notable aspect of the scientific account of the natural world in general is the seamless character of the web that has been spun on the loom of time: the process appears as continuous from its cosmic "beginning," in the "hot big bang," to the present and at no point do modern natural scientists have to invoke any non-natural causes to explain their observations and inferences about the past. Their explanations are usually in terms of concepts, theories and mechanisms which they can confirm by, or infer from, present-day experiments, or reasonably infer by extrapolating from principles themselves confirmable by experiment. In particular, the processes of biological evolution also display a continuity which although at first a conjecture of Darwin (and, to be fair, of many of his predecessors), is now thoroughly validated by the established universality of the genetic code and by the study of past and present species of DNA nucleotide sequences and of amino acid sequences in certain widely-distributed proteins.

The process that has occurred can be characterized also as one of emergence, for new forms of matter, and a hierarchy of organization of these forms themselves, appear in the course of time. These new forms have new properties, behaviors and networks of relations that necessitate not only specific methods of investigation but also the development of new epistemologically irreducible concepts in order to describe and refer to them. To these new organizations of matter it is, very often, possible to ascribe new levels of what can only be called "reality": that is, the epistemology implies at least a putative ontology. In other words new kinds of reality may be said to "emerge" in time. Notably, on the surface of the Earth, new forms of living matter (that is, living organisms) have come into existence by this continuous process —that is what we mean by evolution.[4]

What the scientific perspective of the world, especially the living world, inexorably impresses upon us is a *dynamic* picture of entities and structures involved in continuous and incessant change and process without ceasing. Any static conception of the way in which God sustains and holds the cosmos in being is therefore precluded, for new entities, structures, and processes appear in the course of time, so that God's action as Creator is both past and present: it is continuous. The scientific perspective of a cosmos, and in particular that of the biological world, as being in development all the time must re-introduce into our understanding of God's creative relation to the world a dynamic element which

---

* General and theological reflections on biological evolution appear in this font, scientific accounts in this font. Some of the phrasing in this paper follows sections of *Theology for a Scientific Age* [henceforth *TSA*] (London: SCM Press. Minneapolis: Fortress Press, 2nd enlarged ed., 1993), and *Creation and the World of Science* [henceforth *CWS*] (Oxford: Clarendon Press, 1979).

was, even if obscured by the allocation of "creation" to an event in the past, always implicit in the Hebrew conception of a "living God," dynamic in action. Any notion of God as Creator must now take into account that God is continuously creating, continuously giving existence to, what is new; God is *semper Creator*, and the world is a *creatio continua*. The traditional notion of God *sustaining* the world in its general order and structure now has to be enriched by a dynamic and creative dimension—the model of God sustaining and giving continuous existence to a process which has a creativity built into it by God. God is creating at every moment of the world's existence in and through the perpetually-endowed creativity of the very stuff of the world. God indeed makes "things make themselves," as Charles Kingsley put it in The *Water Babies*, and aptly quoted by Charles Birch at the head of his paper in this volume.

Thus it is that the scientific perspective, and especially that of biological evolution, impels us to take more seriously and more concretely than hitherto the notion of the immanence of God-as-Creator—God is the Immanent Creator *creating in and through the processes of the natural order*. I would urge that all this has to be taken in a very strong sense. If one asks where do we see God-as-Creator during, say, the processes of biological evolution, one has to reply: "The processes themselves, as unveiled by the biological sciences, are God-acting-as-Creator, God *qua* Creator."[5] God gives existence in divinely-created time to a process that itself brings forth the new: thereby God is creating. This means we do not have to look for any extra supposed gaps in which, or mechanisms by which, God might be supposed to be acting as Creator in the living world.

The model of musical composition for God's activity in creation is, I would suggest, particularly helpful here. There is no doubt of the "transcendence" of the composer in relation to the music he or she creates—the composer gives it existence and without the composer it would not be at all. So the model properly reflects, as do all those of artistic creativity, that transcendence of God as Creator of all-that-is which, as the "listeners" to the music of creation, we wish to aver. Yet, when we are actually listening to a musical work, say, a Beethoven piano sonata, then there are times when we are so deeply absorbed in it that, for a moment we are thinking Beethoven's musical thoughts with him. In such moments the

> Music is heard so deeply
> That it is not heard at all, but you are the music
> While the music lasts[6]

Yet if anyone were to ask at that moment, "*Where* is Beethoven now?"—we could only reply that Beethoven-*qua*-composer was to be found only in the music itself. The music would in some sense be Beethoven's inner musical thought kindled in us and we would genuinely be encountering Beethoven-*qua*-composer. This very closely models, I am suggesting, God's immanence in creation and God's self-communication in and through the processes by means of which God is creating. The processes revealed by the sciences, especially evolutionary biology, are in themselves God-acting-as-Creator. There is no need to look for God as some kind of *additional* factor supplementing the processes of the world. God, to use language usually applied in sacramental theology, is "in, with, and under" all-that-is and all-that-goes-on.

2.2 The Mechanism of Biological Evolution

There appear to be no serious biologists who doubt that natural selection is a factor operative in biological evolution—and most would say it is by far the most significant one. At one end of the spectrum authors like Dawkins argue cogently for the all-sufficiency of natural selection in explaining the course of biological evolution. Certainly he has illustrated by his "biomorph" computer program how the counter-intuitive creativity of evolution could be generated by the interplay of chance events operating in a law-like framework—this is, in the case of biological evolution, the interplay between mutational events in the DNA of the genome with the environment of the phenotype to which it gives rise. This was well illustrated by Dawkins[7] with his program in which two-dimensional patterns of branching lines, "biomorphs," are generated by random changes in a defined number of features combined with a reproduction and selection procedure. It was striking how subtle, varied and complex were the "biomorph" patterns after surprisingly few "generations," that is, reiterations of the procedure. Such computer simulations go a long way toward making it clear how it is that the complexity and diversity of biological organisms could arise through the operation of the apparently simple principles of natural selection.

However, other biologists are convinced that even when the subtleties of natural selection are taken into account it is not the whole story; and some even go so far as to say that natural selection alone cannot account for speciation, the formation of distinctly new species.

What is significant about all these proposals[8] is that they are all operating entirely within a naturalistic framework—to use Dennett's graphic designation, they are all "cranes" and not "skyhooks"[9]—and, moreover, they assume a basically Darwinian process to be operating, even when they disagree about its speed and smoothness (e.g., the presence or absence of the sudden "saltations" proposed by Gould). That being so, it has to be recognized that the history of life on Earth involves chance in a way unthinkable before Darwin. There is a creative interplay of "chance" and law apparent in the evolution of living matter by natural selection. However what we mean by "chance" in this context first needs closer examination.

Events are unpredictable by us in basically two ways:

1. They can be unpredictable because we can never possess the necessary detailed knowledge with the requisite accuracy at this microlevel of description. In such cases talk of the role of "chance" can mean either: (A) we cannot determine accurately the microparameters of the initial conditions determining the macroevents (e.g., the forces on a tossed coin) while often knowing the overall constraints that must operate on the system as a whole (e.g., the symmetry constraints making for equal probabilities of heads and tails); or (B) the observed events are the outcome of the crossing of two independent causal chains, accurate knowledge of which is unattainable both with respect to the chains themselves and to their point of intersection.

2. At the subatomic level events can also be unpredictable because of the operation of the Heisenberg Uncertainty Principle and this unpredictability is inherent and ineradicable.

Events of type (1) and (2), unpredictable as they are, can produce effects at the macroscopic level which operate in a law-like framework which delimits the scope of the consequent events or provides them with new and unexpected outcomes. Both ways of viewing the matter are pertinent to biological evolution. Biological evolution depends on a process in which changes occur in the genetic-information carrying material (DNA) that are random with respect to the biological needs of the organisms possessing the DNA—in particular, random with respect to its need to produce progeny for the species to survive. What we call "chance" is involved both at the level of the mutational event in the DNA itself (1A and/or 2), and in the intersecting of two causally unrelated chains of events (1B)—the change in the DNA and the consequences of such change for survival in its particular biological niche. The biological niche in which the organism exists then filters out, by the processes of natural selection, those changes in the DNA that enable the organisms possessing them to produce more progeny in an entirely law-like fashion.

The interplay between "chance," at the molecular level of the DNA, and "law" or "necessity" at the statistical level of the population of organisms tempted Jacques Monod, in *Chance and Necessity*[10] to elevate "chance" to the level almost of a metaphysical principle whereby the universe might be interpreted. As is well known, he concluded that the "stupendous edifice of evolution" is, in this sense, rooted in "pure chance" and that *therefore* all inferences of direction or purpose in the development of the biological world, in particular, and of the universe, in general, must be false. As Monod saw it, it was the purest accident that any particular creature came into being, in particular *Homo sapiens*, and no direction or purpose or meaning could ever be expected to be discerned in biological evolution. A creator God, for all practical purposes, might just as well not exist, since everything in evolution went on in an entirely uncontrolled and fortuitous manner.

The responses to this thesis and attack on theism—mainly, it is interesting to note, from theologically informed scientists and some philosophers, rather than from theologians—have been well surveyed by D. J. Bartholomew,[11] and their relative strengths and weaknesses analyzed. I shall pursue here what I consider to be the most fruitful line of theological reflection on the processes that Monod so effectively brought to the attention of the twentieth century—a direction that I began to pursue[12] in response to Monod and which has been further developed by the statistically-informed treatment of Bartholomew.

There is no reason why the randomness of a molecular event in relation to biological consequence has to be given the significant metaphysical status that Monod attributed to it. The involvement of what we call "chance" at the level of mutation in the DNA does not, of itself, preclude these events from displaying regular trends and manifesting inbuilt propensities at the higher levels of organisms, populations and eco-systems. To call the mutation of the DNA a "chance" event serves simply to stress its randomness with respect to biological consequence. As I have earlier put it (in a response later supported and amplified by others):

> Instead of being daunted by the role of chance in genetic mutations as being the manifestation of irrationality in the universe, it would be more consistent with observation to assert that the full gamut of the potentialities of living matter could be explored only through the agency of the rapid and frequent randomization which is possible at the molecular level of the DNA.[13]

This role of "chance," or rather randomness (or "free experiment") at the microlevel is what one would expect if the universe were so constituted that all the potential forms of organization of matter (both living and non-living) which it contains might be thoroughly explored. Indeed, since Monod first published his book in 1970, there have been the developments in theoretical and molecular biology and physical biochemistry of the Brussels and Göttingen schools. They demonstrated that it is the interplay of chance and law that is in fact creative within time, for it is the combination of the two which allows new forms to emerge and evolve—so that natural selection appears to be opportunistic. As in many games, the consequences of the fall of the dice depend very much on the rules of the game.[14] It has become increasingly apparent that it is chance operating within a law-like framework that is the basis of the inherent creativity of the natural order, its ability to generate new forms, patterns and organizations of matter and energy. If all were governed by rigid law, a repetitive and uncreative order would prevail; if chance alone ruled, no forms, patterns or organizations would persist long enough for them to have any identity or real existence and the universe could never be a cosmos and susceptible to rational inquiry. It is the combination of the two which makes possible an ordered universe capable of developing within itself new modes of existence (cf., Dawkins' biomorphs). The "rules" are what they are because of the "givenness" of the properties of the physical environment and of the other already evolved living organisms with which the organism in question interacts.

This givenness, for a theist, can only be regarded as an aspect of the God-endowed features of the world. The way in which what we call "chance" operates within this "given" framework to produce new structures, entities and processes can then properly be seen as an eliciting of the potentialities that the physical cosmos possessed *ab initio*. Such potentialities a theist must regard as written into creation by the Creator's intention and purpose and must conceive as gradually being actualized by the operation of "chance" stimulating their coming into existence. One might say that the potential of the "being" of the world is made manifest in the "becoming" that the operation of chance makes actual. God is the ultimate ground and source of both law ("necessity") and "chance."[15]

For a theist, God must now be seen as acting to create in the world through what we call "chance" operating within the created order, each stage of which constitutes the launching pad for the next. The Creator, it now seems, is unfolding the divinely-endowed potentialities of the universe, in and through a process in which these creative possibilities and propensities (see next section), inherent by God's own intention within the fundamental entities of that universe and their inter-relations, become actualized within a created temporal development shaped and determined by those selfsame God-given potentialities.[16]

2.3 Trends in Evolution?

Are there any trends or discernable directions in evolution? This is a notoriously loaded question, which human beings are only too ready to answer on the basis of their own believed significance in the universe grounded on their own importance to themselves! Is there any objective, non-anthropocentrically biased evidence for directions or at least trends in biological evolution? Biologists have been especially cautious not to answer this question affirmatively, not least because they do not wish to give premature hostages to those seeking to gain a foothold for claiming some kind of "skyhook," such as divine action, intervention even, directing the course of evolution. Evolution is best depicted biologically not as a kind of Christmas tree, with *Homo sapiens* accorded an angelic position crowning the topmost frond, but rather as a bush—"Life is a copiously branching bush, continually pruned by the grim reaper of extinction, not a ladder of predictable progress."[17]

Nevertheless G.G. Simpson can affirm that "Within the framework of the evolutionary history of life there have been not one but many different kinds of progress."[18] While admitting that such lines of "progress" can be traced in the evolutionary "bush," other biologists would be more neutral.

The question of more general significance that is being addressed in relation to the biological evolutionary story is, it would seem, Are there any particular properties and functions attributable to living organisms which could be said to be in themselves helpful for evolution to occur because they are advantageous in natural selection (for survival of progeny) of organisms possessing them? Simpson's suggested list seems to fulfill this criterion and so it could be said that the evolutionary process manifests what Karl Popper[19] has called a "propensity" in nature for such properties to appear. He argued that a greater frequency of occurrence of a particular kind of event may be used as a test of whether or not there is inherent in a sequence of events (equivalent to throws of a die) a tendency or propensity to realize the event in question. He has pointed out that the *realization of possibilities*, which may be random, *depend on the total situation within which the possibilities are being actualized* so that "there exist weighted possibilities which are *more than mere possibilities*, but tendencies or propensities to become real"[20] and that these "propensities in physics are properties of *the whole situation* and sometimes even of the particular way in which a situation changes. And the same holds of the propensities in chemistry, in biochemistry, and in biology."[21] I suggest that there are propensities, in this Popperian sense, in evolution towards the possession of certain characteristics, propensities that are inherently built into an evolutionary process based on natural selection of the best procreators. Such properties naturally enhance survival for procreation in certain widely-occurring environments.

Among the plethora of such properties of living organisms which might in some circumstance or another be advantageous in natural selection, there are a number which characterize *Homo sapiens* and are pertinent to our wider concerns in this paper (and volume). They are as follows.

1. *Complexity*. The human brain is the most complex natural system in the universe known to us. Is there a propensity to complexity in *biological*[22] evolution? There certainly seems to be, and "increasing complexity" was included in Simpson's list (see n. 17) as characteristic of it. What significance is to be attributed to this? Is it simply that biological "evolution is a process of divergence and wandering rather than an inexorable progression towards increasing complexity" so that evolution "*permits* the emergence of new complexity, but does not in any particular case necessitate it"?[23]

The fact is that, taking biological evolution as a whole, there has been an emergence of increasingly complex organisms, even if in some evolutionary lines there has been a loss of complexity and so of organization. So, on Popper's criterion enunciated above, we would be correct in saying that there is a propensity towards increased complexity in the evolution of living organisms. Saunders and Ho[24] identify the basis of this tendency to be the process by which a self-organizing system optimizes its organization with respect to locally defined requirements for fitness. Even if it cannot be predicated as inevitable in any particular evolutionary line, there has been an overall trend towards and an increase in complexity along particular lines in biological evolution, so that it is right to speak of a propensity for this to occur.

The need for *organization* for survival was beautifully demonstrated by H. A. Simon[25] who showed that the simplest modular organization of, say, the structure of a watch, so that each module had a limited stability, led to an enormous increase in survivability during manufacture in the face of random destructive events. Hence the increases we observe during evolution in complexity and organization (subsumed under "complexity" from now on) in the biological world are entirely intelligible as contributing to success in natural selection and are not at all mysterious in the sense of requiring some non-naturalistic explanation.

2. *Information-processing* and *storage ability*. The more capable an organism is of receiving, recording, and analyzing signals and using the information to make predictions useful for survival about changes in its environment, the better chance it will have of surviving under the pressures of natural selection in a wide variety of habitats. In other words, there is a propensity towards the formation of systems having the functions we now recognize in nervous systems and brains. Such ability for information-processing and storage is indeed the necessary, if not sufficient, condition for the emergence of consciousness.

3. *Pain and suffering*. This sensitivity to, this sentience of, its surroundings inevitably involves an increase in its ability to experience pain, which constitutes the necessary biological warning signals of danger and disease, so that it is impossible readily to envisage an increase of information-processing ability without an increase in the sensitivity of the signal system of the organism to its environment. Hence an increase in "information-processing" capacity, with the advantages it confers in natural selection, cannot but have as its corollary an increase, not only in the level of consciousness, but also in the experience of pain. Insulation from the surrounding world in the biological equivalent of three-inch nickel steel would be a sure recipe for preventing the development of consciousness.

Each increase in sensitivity, and eventually of consciousness, as evolution proceeds inevitably, heightens and accentuates awareness both of the beneficent, life-enhancing, and of the inimical, life-diminishing, elements in the world in which the organism finds itself. The stakes for joy and pain are, as it were, continuously being raised, and the living organism learns to discriminate between them, so that pain and suffering, on the one hand, and consciousness of pleasure and well-being, on the other, are emergents in the world. Thus there can be said to be a propensity for them to occur. From a purely naturalistic viewpoint, the emergence of pain and its compounding as suffering as consciousness increases seem to be inevitable aspects of any conceivable developmental process that would be characterized by a continuous increase in ability to process and store information coming from the environment; for this entails an increase in sensitivity, hence in vulnerability, and consequently in suffering as consciousness (minimally the sum of the brain states reflecting it all) ramifies. In the context of natural selection, pain has an energizing effect and suffering is a goad to action: they both have survival value for creatures continually faced with new problematic situations challenging their survival.[26] In relation to any theological reflections, it must be emphasized that pain and suffering are present in biological evolution as a necessary condition for survival of the individual long before the appearance of human beings on the scene. So the presence of pain and suffering cannot be the result of any particular human failings, though undoubtedly human beings experience them with a heightened sensitivity and, more than any other creatures, inflict them on each other.

4. *Self-consciousness and language.* If an information-processing and storage system can also monitor its own state at any moment, then it has at least the basis for communicating what that state is to other similar systems. Hence, provided the physical apparatus for communicating has also evolved, the capacity for language becomes possible, and especially in the most highly developed of such systems. In other words, there is an inbuilt propensity for the acquisition of language and so for developing the necessary basis for self-consciousness. This would be an advantage in natural selection, for it is the basis of complex social cooperation in the creatures that possess it (apparently supremely *Homo sapiens*) with all the advantages this gives against predators and in gaining food.[27]

Given an immanentist understanding of God's presence "in, with, and under" the processes of biological evolution adopted up to this point, can God be said to be implementing any purpose in biological evolution? Or is the whole process so haphazard, such a matter of happenstance, such a matter of what Monod and Jacob called *bricolage* (tinkering), that no meaning, least of all a divinely intended one, can be discerned in the process?

I have given reasons above for postulating that there are propensities in evolution towards the possession of certain characteristics, propensities that are inherently built into an evolutionary process based on natural selection, for they naturally enhance survival for procreation in a wide range of environments. Thus it is that the evolutionary process is characterized by propensities towards increase in complexity, information-processing and storage, consciousness, sensitivity to pain, and even self-consciousness (a necessary prerequisite for social development and the cultural transmission of knowledge down the generations). Some successive forms, along some branch or "twig" (a la Gould), have a distinct probability of manifesting more and more of these characteristics. However, the actual physical form of the organisms in which these propensities are actualized and instantiated is contingent on the history of the confluence of disparate chains of events, including the survival of the mass extinctions that have occurred (96% of all species in the Permo-Triassic one).[28] So it is not surprising that recent re-interpretation of the fossils of very early (*circa* 530 million years ago) soft-bodied fauna found in the Burgess shale of Canada show that, had any larger proportion of these survived and prevailed, the actual forms of contemporary, evolved creatures would have been very much more disparate in anatomical *plans* than those now observed to exist—albeit with a very great diversity in the few surviving designs.[29] But even had these particular organisms, unique to the Burgess shale, been the progenitors of subsequent living organisms, the same propensities towards complexity, etc., would also have been manifest in their subsequent evolution, for these "propensities" simply reflect the advantages conferred in natural selection by these features. The same considerations apply to the arbitrariness and contingency of the mass extinctions, which Gould also strongly emphasizes. So that, providing there had been enough time, a complex organism with consciousness, self-consciousness, social and cultural organization (that is, the basis for the existence of "persons") would have been likely eventually to have evolved and appeared on the Earth (or on some other planet amenable to the emergence of living organisms), though no doubt with a physical form very different from *Homo sapiens*. There can, it seems to me (*pace* Stephen Gould[30]) be overall direction and implementation of divine purpose through the interplay of chance and law without a deterministic plan fixing all the details of the structure(s) of what emerges possessing personal qualities. Hence the emergence of self-conscious persons capable of relating personally to God can still be regarded as an intention of God continuously creating through the processes of that to which God has given an existence of this contingent kind and not some other. It certainly must have been possible since it actually happened—with us!

I see no need to postulate any *special* action of God—along the lines, say, of some divine manipulation of mutations at the quantum level (as proposed by others in this volume)—to ensure that persons emerge in the universe, and in particular on Earth. Not to coin a phrase, "I have no need of that hypothesis!"[31] If there are any such influences by God shaping the direction of evolutionary processes at specific points—for which I see no evidence (how could we know?) and no theological need—I myself could only envisage them as being through God's whole-part constraint on all-that-is affecting the confluence of what, to us, would be independent causal chains. Such specifically-directed constraints I would envisage as possible by being exerted upon the whole interconnected and interdependent system of the whole Earth in the whole cosmos which is in and present to God, who is therefore its ultimate boundary condition and therefore capable of shaping the occurrence of particular patterns of events, if God chooses to do so.

2.4 The Ubiquity of Pain, Suffering and Death.

The biological inevitability of the experience of pain in any creature that is going to be aware of—and can gain information from—its environment and thereby avoid dangers has already been emphasized. The pain associated with breakdown of health due to general organic causes also appears to be simply a concomitant of being a complex organized system containing internal as well as external sensors. When pain is experienced by a conscious organism, the attribution of "suffering" becomes appropriate and a fortiori, with self-consciousness the suffering of others also becomes a burden. The ubiquity of pain and suffering in the living world appears to be an inevitable consequence of creatures acquiring those information-processing and storage systems, so advantageous in natural selection, which we observe as nerves and brains in the later stages of evolution.

New patterns can only come into existence in a finite universe ("finite" in the sense of the conservation of matter-energy) if old patterns dissolve to make place for them. This is a condition of the creativity of the process—that is, of its ability to produce the new—which at the biological level we observe as new forms of life only through death of the old. For the death of individuals is essential for release of food resources for new arrivals, and species simply die out by being ousted from biological "niches" by new ones better adapted to survive and reproduce in them. Thus, biological death of the individual is the prerequisite of the creativity of the biological order, that creativity which eventually led to the emergence of human beings. At this biological level we discover the process to be one of "natural selection," but it is possible to discern cognate processes occurring also at other levels.

For complex living structures can only have a finite chance of coming into existence if they are not assembled de novo, as it were, from their basic subunits, but emerge through the accumulation of changes in simpler forms, as demonstrated by H. A. Simon in his classic paper.[32] Having come on to the scene, they can then survive, because of the finitude of their life spans, only by building pre-formed complex chemical structures into their fabric through imbibing the materials of other living organisms. For the chemist and biochemist there is the same kind of difficulty in conceiving how complex material structures, especially those of the intricacy of living organisms, could be assembled otherwise than from less complex units, as there is for the mathematician of conceiving of a universe in which the analytic laws of arithmetic were inapplicable. So there is a kind of structural logic about the inevitability of living organisms dying and preying on each other— for we cannot conceive, in a lawful, non-magical universe, of any way whereby the immense variety of developing, biological, structural complexity might appear, except by utilizing structures already existing, either by way of modification (as in biological evolution) or of incorporation (as in feeding).[33]   The statistical logic is inescapable: new forms of matter arise only through the dissolution of the old; new life only through death of the old. It would seem that the law of "new life through death of the old" (J. H. Fabre's "sublime law of sacrifice"[34]) is inevitable in a world composed of common "building blocks" (atoms, etc.).

But death not only of individuals but of whole species has also occurred on the Earth during the periods of mass extinction which are now widely attributed to chance extraterrestrial collisions of the planet with comet showers, asteroids or other bodies. These could be cataclysmic and global in their effects and have been far more frequent than previously imagined. This adds a further element of sheer contingency to the history of life on the Earth.

The theist cannot ignore these features of the created order. Any theodicy has to come to terms with the obliteration of far more species than now exist on the Earth. The spontaneity and fecundity of the biological world is gained at the enormous price of universal death and of pain and suffering during life.[35]   Yet individual living creatures scarcely ever commit suicide in any way that might be called intentional. Let us pay attention to this positive aspect first.

The natural world is immensely variegated in its hierarchies of levels of entities, structures, and processes, in its "being," and abundantly diversifies with a cornucopian fecundity in its "becoming" in time. From the unity in this diversity and the richness of the diversity itself, one may adduce,[36] respectively, both the essential oneness of its source of being, namely the one God the Creator, and the unfathomable richness of the unitive being of that Creator God. But now we must reckon more directly with the diversity itself. The forms even of non-living matter throughout the cosmos as it appears to us are even more diverse than what we can now observe immediately on the Earth. Furthermore the multiply-branching bush of terrestrial biological evolution appears to be primarily opportunist in the direction it follows and, in so doing, produces the enormous variety of biological life on this planet.[37]

We can only conclude that, if there is a Creator, least misleadingly described in terms of "personal" attributes, then that Creator intended this rich multiformity of entities, structures, and processes in the natural world and, if so, that such a Creator God takes what, in the personal world of human experience, could only be called "delight" in this multiformity of what he has created—and not only in what Darwin, called "the most exalted object which we are capable of conceiving, namely the production of the higher animals."[38] The existence of the *whole* tapestry of the created order, in its warp and woof, and in the very heterogeneity and multiplicity of its forms must be taken to be the Creator's intention. We can only make sense of that, utilizing our resources of personal language, if we say that God has something akin to "joy" and "delight" in creation. We have a hint of this in the satisfaction attributed to God as Creator in the first chapter of *Genesis*: "And God saw everything he had made, and behold, it was very good."[39] This naturally leads to the idea of the "play" of God in creation on which I have expanded elsewhere,[40] in relation to Hindu thought as well as to that of Judaism and Christianity.

But now for the darker side. The ubiquity of pain, suffering and death as the means of creation through biological evolution entails, for any concept of God which is morally acceptable and coherent, that if God is immanently present in and to natural processes, in particular those that generate conscious and self-conscious life, then we cannot but infer that God suffers in, with, and under the creative processes of the world with their costly unfolding in time.

Rejection of the notion of the impassibility of God has, in fact, been a feature of the Christian theology of recent decades. There has been an increasing assent to the idea that it is possible to speak consistently of *a God who suffers eminently and yet is still God, and a God who suffers universally and yet is still present uniquely and decisively in the sufferings of Christ.*[41]

As Paul Fiddes points out in his survey and analysis of this change in theological perspective, the factors that have promoted the view that God suffers are new assessments of "the meaning of love [especially, the love of God], the implications of the cross of Jesus, the problem of [human] suffering, and the structure of the world."[42] It is this last-mentioned—the "structure of the world"— on which the new perspectives of the biological sciences bear by revealing the world processes to be such, as described above, that involvement in them by the immanent Creator has to be regarded as involving suffering on the Creator's part. God, we find ourselves having to conjecture, suffers the "natural" evils of the world along with ourselves because—we can but tentatively suggest at this stage—God purposes *inter alia* to bring about a greater good thereby, namely, the kingdom of free-willing, loving persons in communion with God and with each other.[43]

Because sacrificial, self-limiting, self-giving action on behalf of the good of others is, in human life, the hallmark of love, those who believe in Jesus the Christ as the self-expression of God's own self have come to see his life as their ultimate warrant for asserting that God is essentially "Love," insofar as any one word can accurately refer to God's nature. Jesus' own teaching concerning God as "Abba," Father, and the conditions for entering the "Kingdom of God" pointed to this too, but it was the person of Jesus and what happened to him that finally, and early, established in the Christian community this perception of God as self-offering Love.

On their, and subsequent Christians', understanding Jesus the Christ is the definitive communication from God to humanity of the deep meaning of what God has been effecting in creation—and that is precisely what the Prologue to

John's Gospel says in terms of God the Word/*Logos* active in creation and as now manifest in the person of Jesus the Christ.

As we saw above, it may be inferred, however tentatively, from the character of the natural processes of creation that God has to be seen as suffering in, with, and under these selfsame processes with their costly unfolding in time. But if God was present in and one with Jesus the Christ, then we have to conclude that God also suffered in and with him in his passion and death. The God whom Jesus therefore obeyed and expressed in his life and death is indeed a "crucified God,"[44] and the cry of dereliction can be seen as an expression of the anguish also of God in and through creation.   If Jesus is indeed the self-expression of God in a human person, then the tragedy of his actual human life can be seen as a drawing back of the curtain to unveil a God suffering in and with the sufferings of created humanity and so, by a natural extension, with those of all creation, since humanity is an evolved part of it.   The suffering of God, which we could glimpse only tentatively in the processes of creation, is in Jesus the Christ concentrated into a point of intensity and transparency which reveals it to all who focus on him.

2.5 Human Evolution

1. *Homo sapiens a late arrival.* Remarkable and significant as is the emergence of self-conscious persons by natural processes from the original "hot big bang" from which the universe has expanded over the last ten to twenty billion years, this must not be allowed to obscure humanity's relatively recent arrival in the universe, even on a time-scale of the history of the Earth. How recent this is can be realized if one takes the age of the Earth as two days (forty-eight "hours"—one such "hour" equals 100 million years) then *Homo sapiens* appears only at the last stroke of midnight of the second day. Other living organisms had existed for some two billion or more years (which equals over twenty "hours" on the above scale) before our relatively late arrival.

2. *The emergence of humanity.* The biological-historical evidence is that human nature has emerged only gradually by a continuous process from other primates. No sudden breaks of any substantial kind in the sequences are noted by paleontologists and anthropologists. This is not to say that the history of human culture is simply a smooth rising curve. There must have been, for example, key turning points or periods in the development of speech and so of social cooperation and of rituals for burying the dead, with provision of food and implements, testifying to a belief in some form of life after death. These apparently occurred among the Neanderthals of the middle Paleolithic even before the emergence of *Homo sapiens* some 100,000 or so years ago, when further striking developments occurred.[45]   However there is no past period for which there is reason to affirm that human beings possessed moral perfection existing in a paradisal situation from

which there has been only a subsequent decline. All evidence points to a creature slowly emerging into awareness, with an increasing capacity for consciousness and sensitivity and the possibility of moral responsibility and, the religions would affirm, of response to God (especially after the "axial period" around 500 B.C.[46]). So there is no sense in which we can talk of a "Fall" from a past perfection. There was no golden age, no perfect past, no individuals, "Adam" or "Eve," from whom all human beings have now descended and declined and who were perfect in their relationships and behavior. We appear to be rising beasts[47] rather than fallen angels!

With regard to (1): the fact that human beings represent only an extremely small, and very recently-arrived, fraction of living organisms that have populated the Earth raises the question of God's purposes in creating such a labyrinth of life. To assume it was all there simply to lead to us clearly will not do. Hence the attribution to God of a sheer exuberance in creativity for its own sake, to which we have already referred. Since biological death was present on the Earth long before human beings arrived on the scene and was the pre-requisite of our coming into existence through the processes of biological evolution, when Saint Paul says that "sin pays a wage, and the wage is death"[48] that cannot possibly mean for us now *biological* death. It can only mean "death" in some other sense, such as the death of our relation to God consequent upon sin. I can see no sense in regarding biological death as the consequence of that very real alienation from God that is sin, because God had already used biological death as the means for creating new forms of life, including ourselves, long before we appeared on the Earth. This means those classical Christian formulations of the theology of the redemptive work of Christ that assume a causal connection between biological death and sin urgently need replacing.

With regard to (2): although there was no golden age, no perfect past, no original perfect, individual "Adam" from whom all human beings have now declined, what *is* true is that humanity manifests aspirations to a perfection not yet attained, a potentiality not yet actualized, but no "original righteousness." Sin as alienation from God, humanity, and nature is real and appears as the consequence of our very possession of that *self*-consciousness which always places us at the egotistical center of the "universe" of our consciousness. Sin is about a falling short from what God intends us to be and is part and parcel of our having evolved into self-consciousness, freedom and intellectual curiosity. The domination of Christian theologies of redemption by classical conceptions of the "Fall" urgently needs, it seems to me, to be rescinded and what we mean by redemption to be rethought if it is to make any sense to our contemporaries.

Now, we all have an awareness of the tragedy of our failure to fulfill our highest aspirations, to come to terms with finitude, death and suffering, to realize our potentialities, and to steer our path through life. Freedom allows us to make the wrong choices, so that sin and alienation from God, from our fellow human beings, and from nature, are real features of our existence. So the questions of not only "Who are we?" but even, "What should we be becoming— where should we be going?" remain acute for us. To be brief, I find the clue to the answers to these questions in the person of Jesus of Nazareth and what he manifested of God's perennial expression in creation (as the *Logos* of God incarnate). Hence I am impelled to consider specifically Christian affirmations in the light of the foregoing re-considerations of God's creating through an evolutionary process.

3   The significance of Jesus the Christ in a possible Christian evolutionary perspective

> Ö[I]n scientific language, the Incarnation may be said to have introduced a new species into the world—the Divine man transcending past humanity, as humanity transcended the rest of the animal creation, and communicating His vital energy by a spiritual process to subsequent generationsÖ (J. R. Illingworth, in the 12th edition of *Lux Mundi*, 1891, p. 132.)

Jesus' resurrection demonstrated to the disciples, notably to Paul, and now to us, that it is the union of *his* kind of life with God which is not broken by death and capable of being taken up into God. For he manifested the kind of human life which can become fully life with God, not only here and now, but eternally beyond the threshold of death. Hence his imperative "Follow me" now constitutes for us a call for the transformation of humanity into a new kind of human being and becoming. What happened to him, Jesus saw *could* happen to all.

In this perspective, Jesus the Christ, the whole Christ event, has shown us what is possible for humanity. The actualization of this potentiality can properly be regarded as the consummation of the purposes of God already incompletely manifested in evolving humanity. In Jesus there was a *divine* act of new creation because the initiative was *from God* within human history, within the responsive human will of Jesus inspired by that outreach of God into humanity designated as "God the Holy Spirit." Jesus the Christ is thereby seen, in the context of the whole complex of events in which he participated (the "Christ event"), as the paradigm of what God intends for all human beings, now revealed as having the potentiality of responding to, of being open to, of becoming united with, God.

But how can what happened in and to him, there and then, happen in us, here and now? Can what happened in and to him be effectual, some 2000 years later, in a way that might actually enable us to live in harmony with God, ourselves and our fellow human beings—that is, can we experience the fulfillment for which human nature yearns? I can here only sketchily outline how such questions might be answered in the affirmative.[49] Any answer to be credible today will have to be grounded on our sharing a common humanity with this Jesus. There are certain features in the evolutionary perspectives we have been delineating which now properly constrain this response, namely:

1. individual biological death, as the means of the evolutionary creation of new species by natural selection, cannot now be attributed to human "sin";

2. all evidence is against human beings ever in the past having been in some golden age of innocence and perfection from which they have "fallen."

The Nicene Creed simply affirms baldly that Christ "was crucified *for us* under Pontius Pilate. He suffered and was buried." This reticent "for us" encompasses a very wide range of interpretations. Although the church in its many branches has never officially endorsed any one particular theory of this claimed at-one-ment, yet a number have become widely disseminated doctrinally, liturgically and devotionally. Most (with the exception of the Abelardian) propose a change in God's relation and attitudes to humanity because of Jesus' death on the cross. These purportedly "objective" theories of the atonement also rely heavily on the two pre-suppositions I have just mentioned as no longer tenable in the light of well-founded science. Moreover they fail to incorporate our sense derived from the vista of evolution unfolded by the sciences of humanity as *emerging* into an individual and corporate consciousness and self-consciousness, an awareness of values, social cooperation, human culture, and a sense of and awareness of God. The classical theories of the atonement fail to express any dynamic sense of the process of human *becoming* as still going on. They also fail to make clear how the human response which is an essential part of the reconciliation between God and humanity is evoked.

So let us now put the question again as: How can what happened in and to Jesus the Christ actually evoke in us the response that is needed for our reconciliation to God and actually enable us to live in harmony with God and humanity *here and now*? This question may be answered most effectively, it seems to me, by seeing the life, suffering and death of Jesus the Christ as an act of love, an act of love *of God*, an act of love *by God*.

In the suffering and death of Jesus the Christ, we now also concomitantly perceive and experience the suffering, self-offering love of God in action, no more as abstract knowledge, but actually "in the flesh." For the openness and obedience of the human Jesus to God enabled him, as *the* God-informed human person, to be a manifest self-expression in history, in the confines of human personhood, of God as creative self-expressing Word/*Logos*/ "Son." Thereby is uniquely and definitively revealed the depths of the divine Love for humanity and the reality of God's gracious outreach to us as we are alienated from God, humanity, and ourselves, that is, as "sinners." As such this love of God *engages* us, where "to engage" means (*OED*): "to attract and hold fast; to involve; to lay under obligation; to urge, induce; to gain, win over." The cross is a proposal of God's love and *as such* engages our response. Once we have really come to know that it was God's love in action "for us" which was manifest in the self-offering love and obedience of Jesus the Christ, then we can never be the same again. God, in that outreach to humanity we denote as God the Holy Spirit, united the human Jesus with God's own self and can now kindle and generate in us, as we contemplate God in Christ on the cross, a love for God, for the humanity for whom Jesus died, and for the creation in which God was incarnated.

I am proposing here that this action of God as Holy Spirit in us engages our response and this itself effects our at-one-ment, is itself salvific, actually making us whole, making us "holier." *Such an understanding of the "work of Christ" coheres with our present evolutionary perceptions that the specifically human emerged and still emerges only gradually and fitfully in human history,* without a historic "Fall."

For since God took Jesus through death into his own life, it is implicit in this initiation and continuation of this process in us, that we too can thereby be taken up into the life of God, can be "resurrected" in some way akin to that of Jesus the Christ. Since Jesus was apprehended as having been taken through death with his personhood and identity intact and as having been "taken up" into the presence of God, it *could* happen to us and that is the ground of our hope for our individual future and that of humanity corporately.[50]

Furthermore the interpretation of the death and resurrection of Jesus as manifesting uniquely the quality of life which can be taken up by God into the fullness of God's own life implicitly involves an affirmation about what the basic potentiality of all humanity is. It shows us that, regardless of our particular human skills and creativities—indeed regardless of almost all that the social mores of our times applaud—it is through a radical openness to God, a thoroughgoing self-offering love for others and for God's creation, and obedience to God that we grow into such communion with the eternal God that *God* does not allow biological death to rupture that potentially timeless relation. Irenaeus, in accord with the Eastern Christian tradition, says it all:

The Word of God, our Lord Jesus Christ
Who of his boundless love
became what we are
to make us what even he himself is.[51]

Notes

1. For example, J.R. Moore, *The Post-Darwinian Controversies: A Study of the Protestant Struggle to Come to Terms with Darwin in Great Britain and America* (Cambridge: Cambridge University Press, 1979); J. R. Lucas, "Wilberforce and Huxley: A legendary encounter," *The Historical Journal* 22.2 (1979): 313-30; J. V. Jensen, "Return to Huxley-Wilberforce debate, *Brit. J. Hist. Sci.* 21 (1988): 161-79.

2. Arthur R. Peacocke, "Biological Evolution and Christian Theology—Yesterday and Today," in *Darwinism and Divinity*, ed. John Durant (Oxford: Blackwell, 1985), 101-30.

3. Even the "origin of life," that is the appearance of *living* matter on the surface of the Earth some four and a half billion years ago, can be subsumed within this seamless web of the operation of processes at least now intelligible to and entirely conformable with the sciences, if inevitably never entirely provable by repeatable experiments—the situation with all the *historical* natural sciences (cosmology, geology, evolutionary biology),. Studies on dissipative systems (the Brussels School) have shown how interlocking systems of reactions involving feedback can, entirely in accord with the second law of thermodynamics, undergo transitions to more organized and more complex forms, provided such systems are open, non-linear and far from equilibrium. All these conditions have been satisfied by many systems of chemical reactions present on the Earth during its first billion years of existence. Furthermore, with our increasing knowledge of how molecular patterns can be copied in present living systems, it is now possible to make plausible hypotheses concerning the way in which early forms of nucleic acids and/or proteins might have formed self-replicating molecular systems (*e.g.*, the "hypercycle" of the Göttingen school). Such systems can be shown to multiply at the expense of less efficient rival ones (*q.v.*, Peacocke, *The Physical Chemistry of Biological Organization* (Oxford: Clarendon Press, 1983), chap. 5). What these studies indicate is the inevitability of the appearance of more organized self-replicating systems, the properties of atoms and molecules being what they are; but what form of organization would be adopted is not strictly predictable (by us, at least) since it depends on fluctuations (M. Eigen, "The Self-Organization of Matter and the Evolution of Biological Macro-molecules," *Naturvissenschaften* 58 (1971): 465-523).

4. This is not pantheism for it is the *action* of God that is identified with the creative processes of nature, not God's own self.

5.   T. S. Elliot, "The Dry Salvages," *The Four Quartets*, 11 (London: Faber & Faber, 1944), 33.

6.   Richard Dawkins, *The Blind Watchmaker* (Harlow: Longmans, 1986).

7.   Some considerations other than natural selection which, it is claimed, are needed to be taken into account are thought to be:

1.   The "evolution of evolvability" (Daniel C. Dennett, *Darwin's Dangerous Idea* (London and New York: Allen Lane, Penguin, 1995), 222 and *n.* 20, for references.), in particular the constraints and selectivity effected by self-organizational principles which shape the possibilities of elaboration of structures and even direct its course (Stuart A. Kaufman, *The Origin of Order: Self-Organization and Selection in Evolution* (New York: Oxford Univ. Press, 1993); *idem. At Home in the Universe* (London: Penguin Books, 1995); B. C. Goodwin, *How the Leopard Changed Its Spots: The Evolution of Complexity* (New York: Scribner's Sons, 1994));

2.   The "genetic assimilation" of C. H. Waddington (*The Strategy of Genes: A Discussion of Some Aspects of Theoretical Biology* (London: Allen and Unwin, 1957);

3.   How an organism might evolve is a consequence of itself, its state at any given moment, historical accidents, as well as its genotype and environment (R. C. Lewontin, "Gene, Organism and Environment," in *Evolution from Molecules to Man*, D. S. Bendall, ed. (Cambridge: Cambridge University Press, 1983), 273-85);

4.   The innovative behavior of an individual living creature in a particular environment can be a major factor on its survival and selection and so in evolution (A. Hardy, *The Living Stream* (London: Collins, 1985), 161ff., 189ff.);

5.   "Top-down causation" operates in evolution (D. T. campbell, "Downward Causation," in *Studies in the Philosophy of Biology: Reduction and Related Problems*, F. J. Ayala and T. Dobzhansky, eds. (London: Macmillan, 1974), 179-86) and does so more by a flow of information between organism and environment and between different levels (q.v., *TSA*, 59) than by any obvious material or energetic causality;

6.   The "silent" substitutions in DNA are more frequent than non-silent ones (with an effect on the phenotype); in other words, the majority of molecular evolutionary change is immune to natural selection (M. Kimura, "The neutral theory of evolution," *Sci. Amer.* 241 (1979): 98-126);

7.   The recent re-introduction of *group* (alongside that of *individual*) selection in a unified theory of natural selection as operating at different levels in a nested hierarchy of units, groups or organisms being regarded as "vehicles" of selection (D. S. Wilson and E. Sober, "Reintroducing group selection to the human behavioral sciences," *Behavioral and Brain Sciences* 17 (1994): 585-654);

8.   Long-term changes in the genetic composition of a population resulting in "molecular drive," the process in which mutations are able to spread through a family and through a population as a consequence of a variety of mechanisms on non-reciprocal DNA transfer, thereby inducing the gain or loss of a variant gene in an individual's lifetime, leading to non-Mendelian segregation ratios (G. A. Dover, "Molecular drive in multigene families: How biological novelties arise, spread and are assimilated," *Trends in Genetics* 2 (1986): 159-65);

9.   An emphasis on the context of adaptive change (or, in many cases, non-change, *stasis*) in species regarded as existing in interlocking hierarchies of discrete biological entities (genes, populations, species, eco-systems, etc.) in a physical environment (N. Eldredge, *Reinventing Darwin: The Great Evolutionary Debate* (London: Wiedenfeld and Nicolson, 1996).

8.   A crane "is a sub-process or special feature of a design process that can be demonstrated to permit the local speeding up of the basic, slow process of natural selection, *and* that can be demonstrated to be itself the predictable (or retrospectively explicable) product of the process" (Daniel C. Dennett, *Darwin's Dangerous Idea* (London & New York: Allen Lane, Penguin, 2995), 76). Cranes include sex and the Baldwin Effect. Bennett means by a skyhook "a 'mind-first' force or power or process, an exception to the principle that all design, and apparent design, is ultimately the result of mindless, motiveless mechanicity" (*ibid.*).

9.   Jacques Monod, *Chance and Necessity* (London: Collins, 1972).

10.   David J. Bartholomew, *God of Chance* (London: SCM Press, 1984).

11.   Peacocke, "Chance, Potentiality and God," *The Modern Churchman*, 17 (New Series 1973): 13-23; *idem, Beyond Chance and Necessity*, ed. J. Lewis (London: Garnstone Press, 1974), 13-25; *idem*, "Chaos or Cosmos," *New Scientist*, 63 (1974): 386-89; and *CWS*, chap. 3.

12.   *CWS*, 94.

13.   R. Winkler and M. Eigen, *Laws of the Game* (New York: Knopf, 1981).

14.   D. J. Bartholomew in his *God of Chance* has urged that God and chance are not only logically compatible, as the foregoing has argued, but that there are "positive reasons for supposing that an element of pure chance would play a constructive role in creating a richer environment that would otherwise be possible." (p. 97) He argues (p. 97) that "chance offers the potential Creator many advantages which it is difficult to envisage being obtained in any other way." Since in many natural processes, often utilized by human beings, chance processes can in fact lead to determinate ends—for many of the laws of nature are statistical—"there is every reason to suppose that a Creator wishing to achieve certain ends might choose to reach them by introducing random processes whose macro-behavior would have a desired character." (p. 98) Thus the determinate ends to which chance processes could lead might well be "to produce intelligent beings capable of interaction with their Creator." (p. 98) For this it would be necessary, he suggests, to have an environment in which chance provides the stimulus and testing to promote intellectual and spiritual evolution.

15. Cf., *CWS*, 105-6.

16. S. J. Gould, *Wonderful Life: The Burgess Shale and the Nature of History* (London and New York: Penguin Books, 1989), 35.

17. G.G. Simpson, *The Meaning of Evolution* (New Haven: Bantam Books, Yale Univ. Press, 1971), 236. He instances the kinds of "progress" (prescinding from any normative connotation) as: the tendency for living organisms to expand to fill all available spaces in the livable environments; the successive invasion and development by organisms of new environmental and adaptive spheres; increasing specialization with its corollary of improvement and adaptability; increase in the general energy or maintained level of vital processes; protected reproduction-care of the young; individualization, increasing complexity, and so forth.

18. Karl Popper, *A World of Propensities* (Bristol: Thoemmes, 1990).

19. *Ibid.*, 12.

20. *Ibid.*, 17.

21. There certainly seems to be such a propensity in non-living matter, for in those parts of the universe where the temperature is low enough for molecules to exist in sufficient proximity to interact, there is a tendency for more and more complex molecular systems to come into existence and this process is actually driven, in the case of reactions that involve association of molecules to more complex forms, by the tendency to greater overall randomization, that is, as a manifestation of the Second Law (q.v., Peacocke, *The Physical Chemistry of Biological Organization* (Oxford: Clarendon Press, 1983), section 2.7). Such systems, if open and if they also exhibit feedback properties, can become "dissipative" and undergo sharp changes of regime with the appearance of new patterns in space and time. In other words, even in these non-living systems, there is an increase in complexity in the entities involved in certain kinds of natural process. This appears to be an example of "propensity" in Popper's sense.

22. W. McCoy, "Complexity in organic evolution," *J. Theor. Biol.*, 68 (1977): 457.

23. P. T. Saunders and M. W. Ho, "On the Increase in Complexity in Evolution" and C. Castrodeza, "Evolution, Complexity and Fitness," *J. Theor. Biol.*, 71 (1978): 469-71, for different views.

24. H. A. Simon, "The architecture of complexity," *Proc. Amer. Phil. Soc.*, 106 (1962): 467-82.

25. Holmes Rolston (*Science and Religion: A Critical Survey*, New York: Random House, 1987) has developed this characteristic of biological evolution in what he calls "cruciform naturalism." (pp. 289ff) Sentience, he argues, evolves with a capacity to separate the "helps" from the "hurts" of the world:

with sentience there appears caring (p. 287). With the appearance of life, organisms can not view events as "pro-" or "anti-life" and values and "dis-values" appear—the world becomes a "theater of meanings" and nature may be variously judged as "hostile," "indifferent," and "hospitable." (p. 244) "The step up that brings more drama brings more suffering." (p. 288) But "pain is an energizing force" so that "where pain fits into evolutionary theory, it must have, on statistical average, high survival value, with this selected for, and with a selecting against counterproductive pain." (p. 288) "Suffering moves us to action" and "all advances come in contexts of problem solving, with a central problem in sentient life the prospect of hurt. In the evolution of caring, the organism is quickened to its needs." (p. 288) "Suffering is a key to the whole, not intrinsically, not as an end in itself, but as a transformative principle, transvalued into its opposite." (p. 288)

26. It is interesting to note that Richard Dawkins, too, in his *River Out of Eden* (London: Weidenfeld and Nicolson, 1995) includes (p. 151ff) amongst the thresholds that will be crossed *naturally* in "a general chronology of a life explosion on any planet, anywhere in the universe thresholds that any planetary replication bomb can be expected to pass," e.g., those for high-speed information-processing (no. 5, achieved by possession of a nervous system), consciousness (no. 6, concurrent with brains), and language (no. 7). This list partly corresponds to the "propensities" referred to in the text.

27. Gould, *Wonderful Life*, 306, citing David M. Raup.

28. *Ibid.*, 49.

29. *Ibid.*, 51 and *passim*.

30. My basically theological and philosophical objections to the location of divine action in quantum events—in evolution, and elsewhere in the natural world (including that of the human brain) —may be summarized as follows.

1. This hypothesis assumes that if God does act to alter quantum events (e.g., in the present context, quantum events in DNA that constitute mutations), this would still be a "hands on" *intervention* by God in the very processes to which God has given existence, even if we never, in principal, could detect this divine action. It would imply that these processes without such intervention were inadequate to effect God's creative intentions if operating in the way God originally made and sustains them in existence.

2. Yet one of the principal reasons, certainly for a scientist and those influenced by the scientific perspective, for adducing from the nature of these processes the existence of a Creator God is their inherent rationality, consistence *and* creativity in themselves.

3. If one does not assume, with most physicists, that there are "hidden variables," that quantum events are indeed ontologically indeterminate within the restrictions of deterministic equations governing their probability—then God cannot know definitely the precise outcome of any quantum event because God can only know that which it is logically

possible to know (and God knows everything in this category—that is what constitutes God's omniscience). Ontological indeterminacy at the quantum level precludes such precise knowledge *for* God to have. Thus God could not know (logically could not know) the outcome of the interference by God in the quantum events which this hypothesis postulates and could not effect the divine purposes thereby.

4.   For the overall probabilistic relationships which govern statistically the ontologically indeterministic quantum events to be obeyed, if God were to alter one such event in a particular way, then many others would also have to be changed so that we, the observers, detected no abrogation of the overall statistics, as the hypothesis assumes. So it is certainly no tidy, neat way to solve the problem and one wonders where the chain of necessary alterations would end.

5.   Finally, in any case, the hypothesis is otiose if God is regarded as creating in evolution, as elsewhere, *through* the very processes, themselves creative, to which God gives existence and which God continuously sustains in existence.

This is why I think there is no need for this hypothesis in this evolutionary context—or indeed in that of any other (e.g., as a way God might affect human brain states and so thoughts).

31. H. A. Simon, "The architecture of complexity."

32. The depiction of this process as "nature, red in tooth and claw" (a phrase from Tennyson that actually pre-dates Darwin's proposal of evolution through natural selection) is a caricature, for, as many biologists have pointed out (e.g., G. G. Simpson in *The Meaning of Evolution* (New Haven: Bantam Books, Yale University Press, 1971 edition), 201), natural selection is not even in a figurative sense the outcome of struggle, as such. Natural selection involves many factors that include better integration with the ecological environment, more efficient utilization of available food, better care of the young, more cooperative social organization – and better capacity for surviving such "struggles" as do occur (remembering that it is in the interest of any predator that their prey survive as a species!).

33. Quoted by C. E. Raven, *Natural Religion and Christian Theology*, 1951 Gofford Lectures, Series 1, *Science and Religion* (Cambridge: Cambridge University Press, 1953), 15.

34. Cf., Dawkins' epithet, "DNA neither cares nor knows. DNA just is. And we dance to its music." (*River out of Eden*, 133).

35. *TSA*, chap. 8, section 1.

36. C. Darwin, *The Origin of Species* (London: Thinkers Library, Watts, 6th ed.), 408. As Charles Darwin himself put it in a famous passage: "It is interesting to contemplate a tangled bank, clothed with many plants of many kinds, with birds singing in the bushes, with various insects flitting about, and with worms crawling through the damp earth, and to reflect that these elaborately constructed forms, so different from each other, and dependent upon each other in so complex a manner, have all been produced by laws acting around us. There is grandeur in this view of life, with its several powers, having been originally breathed by the creator into a few forms or into one; and that, whilst this planet has gone cycling on according to the fixed law of gravity, from so simple a beginning endless forms most beautiful and most wonderful have been, and are being evolved."

37. *Ibid.*

38. *Genesis* 1:31.

39. *CWS*, 108-11.

40. Paul S. Fiddes, *The Creative Suffering of God* (Oxford: Clarendon Press, 1988), 3 (emphasis in the original).

41. *Ibid.*, 45 (see also all of chap. 2).

42. I hint here at my broad acceptance of John Hick's "Irenaean" theodicy in relation to "natural" evil (q.v., "An Irenaean theodicy," in *Encountering Evil*, ed. Stephen T. Davis (Edinburgh: T. & T. Clark, 1981), 39-52; and his earlier *Evil and the God of Love* (London: Macmillan, 1966), especially chapters 15 and 16); and the position outlined by Brian Hepplethwaite in chapter 5 ("Physical suffering and the nature of the physical world") of his *Evil, Suffering and Religion* (London: Sheldon Press, 1976).

43. The title of Jürgen Moltmann's profound book, *The Crucified God* (London: SCM Press, 1974).

44. See Karl J. Narr, "Cultural achievements of early man" in *The Human Creature*, ed. G. Altner (New York: Anchor Books, Doubleday, Garden City, 1974), 115-12. "a marked evolutionary expansion manifests itself after around 30,000 B.C., at the beginning of the upper Paleolithic. The new picture that emerges can be characterized by such terms as accumulation, differentiation and specialization. There is an increase and concentration of cultural goods, a more refined technology with greater variety in the forms of weapons and tools produced and corresponding specialization of their respective functions, more pronounced economic and general cultural differentiation of individual groups."

45. K. Jaspers, *The Origin and Goal of History* (London: Kegan Paul, 1953), chap. 13, section 2.

46. Rising from an a-moral (and in that sense) innocent state to the capability of moral, and immoral, action.

47. *Rom.* 6:23, REB.

48. For a fuller treatment, see *TSA*, 319ff. A more fully-argued exposition of this whole theological stance is given in *TSA*, part III, chaps. 14-16.

49. The virtue of being agnostic about the relation between the "empty tomb" and the risen Christ here becomes apparent. For, within a relatively short time after our own biological death, our bodies will lose their identity as their atomic and molecular components begin to disperse through the earth and its atmosphere, often becoming part of other human beings. (See the discussion in *TSA*, 279-88.)

50. Irenaeus, *Adv. Haer.*, v, praef. (author's translation).

21

The Evolution of the Created Co-Creator

PHILIP HEFNER

Is the cosmos essentially friend or foe? We ask this question from the human point of view, of course. Given the billions of geological aeons and light-years of astronomical distances that constitute the cosmos in which we wake up and find ourselves, do we find ourselves essentially at home or in a hostile environment? Are the elements out to destroy us or to edify us? The answer the Christian theologian gives is this; the cosmos is a creation, therefore, ultimately it is friend.

Our task in this chapter will be to examine the ways in which the theory of evolution is potentially important to Christian theology. In particular, we will focus on the Christian doctrine of anthropology within the wider *locus* of creation. Just how we should understand the human condition in light of evolutionary development and in light of the Christian belief that the cosmos is a creation will be the guiding question. Toward this end we will first cite the problem: the long evolutionary history of the nonhuman cosmos seems to swallow up any significance for the human race; therefore, it seems that the cosmos is not a creation. Yet we want to affirm divine purpose in the evolutionary processes. Following this formulation of the concern, we will identify three different approaches to relating evolutionary concepts to theology: the reforming, the historical, and the apologetic. We will then examine the apologetic approach and identify a number of issues to which Christian theologians should give attention. Turning finally to the reforming approach, we will define the human being as a "created co-creator" and draw out its implications within an evolutionary-conscious understanding of the doctrine of creation. All along we will work with the methodological assumption that theological theories should be commensurate—though not necessarily identical—with scientific theories about the world.

It will be my material contention that the evolving cosmos is an ongoing creation. The complex interaction in the co-evolution of genetic and cultural information, mediated by the human brain and selected by the system of forces that selects all things, can be said to be the means God has chosen to unfold the divine intention and to bring all of nature to a new stage of fulfillment. This entails a corollary understanding: the human being is God's created co-creator, whose purpose is the modifying and enabling of existing systems of nature so that they can participate in God's purposes in the mode of freedom.

Creation and the Theory of Evolution

The concept of evolution has been a difficult one for Christian theologians to handle. Since Charles Darwin formulated it in 1859, many church leaders have rejected it because it seems to leave out any divine role in the ongoing creative process. Numerous theologians have accepted the concept, but even these acceptors have done relatively little toward reformulating Christian doctrine to make it both commensurate with evolutionary theory yet faithful to the biblical tradition. The task of reformulating is one that needs to appear on the theological agenda in the near future.

One sub-item that must appear on this agenda is the enormous time scale needed for evolutionary development and the question regarding the significance of the human species which this raises. To put it in perspective, we note that the universe most likely came into existence with the Big Bang about 18 billion years ago; the earth's crust congealed about 4 billion years ago; dinosaurs flourished from 180 million to 63 million years ago; our important ancestor *homo erectus* flourished 600,000 to 350,000 years ago. If we were to plot this sequence of events on a calendar with one day equaling 14 million years and one hour equaling a half million years, our natural history would look like this: on January 1 the earth's crust congealed; dinosaurs appeared on December 21; Neanderthal man arrives only at 11:50 p.m. on New Year's Eve. Relative to the overall history of the natural cosmos, the role of the human species is staggering in its minuteness.

Yet we Christians think of ourselves as having been created in the image of God and of our history as the arena of divine providence. So we need to ask in light of evolutionary theory, Does this tiny portion of nature's history detract from the marvel that we attach to human existence? Or does it simply add a dimension of mystery and complexity without fundamentally changing our view? We need to ask further, Why was *homo sapiens* created in this manner? What is the significance of the aeons of nonhuman history? Why did God do it this way? In short, what does evolutionary theory do to Christian anthropology?

Evolutionary Interpretations of Christianity

The above list of questions aimed at reformulating our anthropology represents one way in which evolutionary theory may have an impact on Christian thinking. At the heart of this approach is the task of adapting doctrinal teachings to the evolutionary vision. We will call this the reforming approach, because it aims at a reform of Christian theology. Much of the work of Teilhard de Chardin[1] and, more recently, Arthur Peacocke[2] is of this type. This concern will draw our attention in the latter section of the present chapter.

A second and quite different approach, the *historical* approach, tries to show that the Christian faith itself has evolved in the context of its successive environments. This type of historical study has been extensive, and its significance is widely recognized. The great nineteenth-century theologians brought this approach to a high point, as the work of F. C. Baur, Albrecht Ritschl, Adolf von Harnack, and Ernst Troeltsch demonstrates. Revisionist accounts from many quarters today still carry on this effort. This will not be a concern of the present study.

The third approach shares much with the second; yet its main thrust is of another type. It seeks to identify just what significance Christian faith itself has for the evolutionary process. I call this the *apologetic* approach, because it aims at articulating a proposal that is of interest to Christians and non-Christians alike. Ralph W. Burhoe and especially Gerd Theissen follow the apologetic track.

The third or apologetic approach deserves our initial attention. This is the case not only because of its intrinsic interest, but also because decisions we make here will redound back upon the reforming approach and give direction to doctrinal reformulation. I therefore propose that we take a look at one example of the apologetic type, draw out some of the issues posed, and then return to our task of formulating a Christian anthropology in light of evolutionary theory.

The best example in the current discussion of the apologetic approach is Gerd Theissen's brilliant book of 1984, *Biblical Faith: An Evolutionary Approach*. There are six key arguments in this work. These arguments are not necessarily the ones Theissen himself gives most attention to, but they are the basic ideas that make the book possible.

Theissen's first argument is that the evolving world process (as a whole and in its parts) is caught up in a process of relating to a central reality that our religious traditions call "God." The second argument is that this process of relating to the central reality is today termed evolution, which is fundamentally a process of "finding increasingly more adequate structures for adapting" to this ultimate or central reality.[3]

Third, the process of evolution is both biological and cultural. We note that Theissen does not mention the pre-biological. He follows the now familiar insight that the phases of the process of evolution all take the course of producing a multitude of variations, of which one or a few are selected and integrated within systems that are adaptive to the environment. The most important environment for Theissen is the central reality, God.

Fourth, Theissen views the human being as a complex creature who is characterized most importantly as a biological animal that has become a cultural being, and whose most critical challenge is the ongoing task of properly integrating these two "natures," the biological and the cultural. A better way to put it is to say that the human being is a biologically evolved creature who is culturally ambient, and who must continually struggle, if it is to remain a genuinely human creature. This struggle consists in modulating its biological equipment and the rationale of that equipment in a way that is consistent with and appropriate to the possibilities of its present and future cultural ambiance. Or we could say that *the human being is always struggling to integrate its biological equipment into the cultural configuration that the human has become.* Teilhard painted this struggle vividly in his saying, "Pay attention to what is going on, because we are now leaving the stone age." He meant that we must attend carefully to the danger that exists because we bring stone-age biological drives into a contemporary technological milieu to which our biological equipment is but poorly adapted. Anthony Stevens points to this same issue when he subtitles one of his books, "a natural history of the self."[4] Victor Turner devoted his famed article, "Body, Brain, and Culture" to the same insight.[5] Theissen seems to understand the argument.

Fifth, the key to understanding biblical faith, says Theissen, is to perceive its significance as a phenomenon within the evolutionary process, specifically as it affects human persons in social or cultural evolution. We remember, of course, that these human persons have entered the evolutionary process as creatures who have also evolved biologically. This leads us to the sixth argument: the biblical faith contains a proposal for what is possible within cultural evolution by human creatures who are also biologically evolved. This proposal has both a scientific and a theological rendition:

SCIENTIFIC	THEOLOGICAL
1. Evolution of the cosmos is adapting to a central reality.	1. Evolution of the cosmos transpires within the hands of God and adapts to God.
2. Altruism beyond the kin group is a universal value for humanity.	2. The core of biblical faith is the revelation of the love-principle.
3. The premier possibility opened up for human cultural evolution is that we can diminish "selection." Such diminishment allows the biological components of the human being to be transcended, so that we can be the cultural creatures that we have it in us to be. Behaviors and social forms that inhibit us from becoming such cultural creatures are inadequate.	3. This love-principle is a significant option within human cultural evolution; it is the command of God. Behaviors and social forms that oppose or restrict the practice of universal love for neighbor are contrary to the will of God. God will enable us to practice it. This is the content of the "image of God.

These six arguments rest upon four assumptions, two theological and two scientific. The two theological assumptions are these: (1) the evolution of the cosmos transpires within the will of God and adapts to God, and (2) the central feature of God's will for this cosmic process is expressed in the love-principle. The scientific assumptions are these: (1) we cannot understand the human being unless we recognize that it is a culturally evolving form that entered the cultural evolutionary process as a creature that had already evolved biologically, and (2) the love-principle is significant for interpreting the process of cultural evolution, because of the impact that it has on the biological component of this biological-cultural human being.

Although interesting, none of these four assumptions is in itself startling or original. It is in the conjunction of the four that Theissen's thinking becomes exciting and provocative. Conjoined, the argument takes this useful shape: the evolving world process is actually a process of responding and adapting to God. God has created a process that is woven on the loom of adapting to its creator. This adapting is what constitutes the basic character of the world process.

The purpose of outlining Theissen's thought is to use it as a way of unearthing basic issues for the larger attempt to interpret Christian faith in evolutionary modes of thought. With this in mind, let me raise a number of issues and suggest possible directions for theological reflection if not reform.

Issue 1: Which aspects of evolution are to be considered?   Should we consider biological evolution and cultural evolution together?   In the past very few have attempted to deal seriously with the interface between biological and cultural evolution.   For some, it has been unacceptable even to bring culture within the evolutionary conceptuality; while for others, the interface has been dealt with only simplistically.   There is no question, however, in light of current research in the neurosciences, anthropology, psychiatry, experimental and developmental psychology, ethology, and related fields, that we have now reached the point where biogenetic and cultural processes must be examined in their interrelatedness if we are to understand cultural phenomena adequately. Perhaps no single text makes this point more clearly than the aforementioned article by Victor Turner, "Body, Brain, and Culture," even though dozens of other scholars have argued for this as well.

The imperative to interrelate cultural with biological evolution does not stem from any reductionistic impulse.   Rather, it is a response to the fact that culture has emerged within the realm of biological development.   Consequently, the meaning and coherence of the cultural dimension must be consistent and continuous with that of the biological dimension.   Just what this consistency and continuity are, precisely, is a matter of dispute—ranging from those sociobiologists who claim that culture is on a rather short genetic leash, to cultural anthropologists and humanities scholars who deny even a long leash between the two.   One thing is clear: any future attempts to interpret Christian faith in evolutionary perspective must take account of this relationship between biology and culture, and it must further attempt to sort out the results of the researchers in the field.   Among those thinkers, besides Turner, who have made attempts in this area are Ralph W. Burhoe, Donald Campbell, Solomon Katz, and Karl Peters.[6]

Although Theissen's work makes a contribution for its broad treatment of the concept of evolution, I believe it can still be faulted for not being broad enough.   What is missing is the cosmic and physical.   My point is not that Theissen should account for a greater quantity of data.   Rather, what he and we need to recognize is that the bio-cultural continuum is itself a development within the cosmic processes that were unleashed in the singularity that gave birth to the Big Bang.   Culture and biology are chapters in the physical story of the cosmos.

What is at issue is whether or not we will treat with consistency and continuity the cosmic-physical processes and the biological-cultural developments.   This issue is as intellectually demanding as any that a contemporary theologian might encounter.   The difficulty is not so much one of understanding how the animate and the cultural can emerge from the inanimate and impersonal—this question is being addressed by a large number of scientific researchers—but rather the challenge is to ask this question, How can we paint a picture of the meaningfulness of human developments when the canvas for interpretation is the unfolding of cosmic processes over an enormous 18-billion-year span?

Issue 2: The status of the Christian faith.   Nearly a century ago, the Yale natural historian Newman Smyth argued that theology could be done in the context of evolution on the grounds that scientific research into the nature of evolution would lead necessarily to the God of the Christian faith. Although that is still the conviction of many Christian adherents, virtually no one today would suggest that a presuppositionless study of evolutionary theory would lead to such a conclusion. The prevailing method today among theologians who take evolution seriously is to assume the actuality of Christian faith as a historical datum.   From this assumption we may then ask without apology (a) what difference evolutionary theory makes for Christian faith and (b) what significance might the Christian faith have for the evolution of the universe.

If the givenness of the Christian datum within the evolutionary continuum is our starting point, then the theologian ought not be inhibited from interpreting the Christian faith from the point of its most particular and distinctive identity, namely, Jesus Christ.   The evolutionary processes have engendered this distinctive particularity; no apology for this starting point is required. What is required, however, is the strenuous effort of articulating what the continuities are between the evolutionary processes and Jesus Christ, and what the significance of Christ within those processes is.

Issue 3: Evolutionary processes within God's action. Since the time of Charles Darwin there has existed a tradition of theological interpretation that has asserted that "evolution is God's way of doing things." This basic assertion has taken on different meanings depending on the intention of the theologian. One thread of interpretation is the simplistic assertion of Newman Smyth and Asa Gray that evolutionary process is the way God brings spirit to life from matter. Another interpretation is that of Social Darwinism, which adds quite a different nuance to the way God's action is understood.   In our own time Arthur Peacocke's image of God as the composer of fugues, the creator of an infinite set of complexities from simple foundations, is yet another variation on this theme.[7] Along with Gerd Theissen, Ralph W. Burhoe adds the emphasis that evolutionary processes are themselves responses to God, and through the processes of selection, divine purposes are achieved.[8]

Now not all thinkers who see evolution as God's tool focus on selection as part of that tool. Still fewer understand adaptation in the selection process as itself a response to God. Evolutionary interpretations that are silent on the role of selection are less credible, in my judgment, because the concept of selection is so significant to evolutionary theory.

Be that as it may, to focus on selection within God's activity is to face directly the issue of theodicy. Why? Because the selection processes go hand-in-hand with the failure and death of living forms, human persons, social institutions, and ideas. There is perhaps no more difficult issue for the theologian than the interpretation of why there is selection and what divine purpose it might serve. Few theologians even attempt to deal with this challenge. The issue of selection raises the same questions as those that are part of the reflection on why God should have created an evolutionary process that responds to God as the selecting environment.

In the context of thinking about theodicy, John Hick rightly raises the question of freedom in relation to the selection process. For freedom to be genuine, he argues, the creation could not be fashioned initially in a fully free state; rather, it must become free. In order to become free, the initial conditions of any individual must be at an epistemic distance from the goal that is to be attained.[9] Furthermore, the goal must be worthwhile, not on extrinsic or utilitarian grounds, but rather it must have intrinsic worth, with no sure extrinsic profit. The evolutionary process makes freedom possible, provided that evil and misfortune fall haphazardly and randomly upon the world, so that no free behavior can be certain to avoid evil. The free choice must, on the contrary, be chosen for its intrinsic worth alone.

This kind of fundamental reflection is required by today's theologians if an evolutionary interpretation of the Christian faith is to be pursued adequately. The question of freedom is of particular significance, because I believe a good case ought to be made for interpreting the entire physical and biological nonhuman prehistory as the instrumentality employed by God to introduce freedom into the cosmos and set up the introduction of the human being as the created co-creator.

Issue 4: The human being as a two-natured creature. Can we through culture transcend our biological foundation without eroding it? This is a double challenge. On the one hand, will the biological dimension allow itself to participate in the sort of transcendence that the cultural dimension represents? On the other hand, can culture fashion a lifeway that can actualize the possibilities that culture can attain while at the same time doing so in a way that represents the genuine destiny of the biological processes? Or, to put it another way, Can culture open up genuine possibilities that are appropriate to both the biological and the cultural dimensions without either destroying the biological or betraying the cultural?

It is in the cultural sphere we know as ethics and morality where the issue arises. H. Kummer, working with the definition of morality as the "absence of selfish opportunism," argues that there is no analog to morality among animals, even at the higher primate level.[10] Selfish opportunism reigns in the nonhuman animal kingdom. Kummer believes it is the evolution of human cognitive abilities—especially self-consciousness and decision-making —which makes morality both possible and necessary. The purpose of morality is to enhance cooperation, thereby reducing the dangers of species self-annihilation through competition. If Kummer is correct, then two things become significant. First, the cultural configurations of the human race make it possible to destroy itself. Second, the cultural phenomenon of morality may itself be an adaptive process belonging to the long history of evolutionary selection. In either case, the cultural production of altruistic moral codes represents a going beyond our biological determinants.

The transcending of the biological has been a topic in several discussions in recent years. The issue is altruism: Is the love-principle anti-evolutionary because, as self-sacrificing, it tends toward self-elimination rather than self-selection?[11] Richard Dawkins, in his book *The Selfish Gene*, argues that culture must oppose the "selfishness" of the genes if love and other basic human values are to succeed; because the genes act in no other way than to work for their own literal survival.[12] In a similar fashion Theissen speaks of cultural evolution—and particularly the Christian faith within culture—as "anti-selection." Now this position has been criticized in part. Yet a truth remains: if altruism in culture really does oppose the genes, it will be signing culture's death warrant, since genetic evolution is the host in this symbiosis. Without the biological host, culture cannot enjoy the party.

Despite the possible inadequacy of "anti-selection" rhetoric, the intention of Dawkins and Theissen is clear and significant. They are asking us to face the fact that culture enables the biological host to surmount or even alter patterns of behavior which might otherwise seem inevitable. Genetic evolution, for example, limits the range of altruism to the kin-group; whereas Christian faith enables the human creature to extend the principle of altruism beyond the kin-group. The biological component of a human being faces the developmental challenge to sculpt itself in ways that surmount some of the basic drives or behaviors that are wholly undesirable in a human community.[13] It is no mean developmental task for culture to enable such surmounting without destroying the biological ladder by which it has climbed to this position.

Once again, freedom enters into the discussion. Human agency becomes a factor in evolution proper. The human agent, though certainly conditioned by its genetic and environmental host, enjoys a certain measure of freedom. This freedom is concomitant with the self-consciousness and decision-making capacities endemic to cultural life.

The appearance of ethics and morality reminds us of our biological dependence and our cultural freedom. Although we cannot go to the party unless invited by the host, once we are there, we have sufficient freedom to alter the menu, determine which games are played, make it joyful or boring, and even to leave early. What theologians need to do, I think, is negotiate the complexities of the genes-culture interface and relate that interface to the physical cosmos as well.

Issue 5: How should we understand divine revelation? On the basis of the above, we should be able to say that our creator God has mandated that we should come to know life in a two-natured way: biological and cultural. Therefore, it seems to me that we should also be able to say the following: the task of properly integrating the two natures is God's way of sculpting the means by which we attain and exercise our humanity and also the path by which we enter into relationship with God. The divinely intended fulfillment of human destiny will include the proper integration of our biological and cultural natures.

If this is the set of conditions in which God has created us, then it should not surprise us that the good God bestows gifts that are relevant to the task that is ours by virtue of our creation. God's revelation, consequently, cannot but be a cultural evolutionary possibility for the carrying out of our humanity in ways appropriate to the two-natured creatures that we are. If the heart of our Christian revelation is that of unqualified love for all creatures as the nature and will of God, then that love-principle must be seen as a cultural evolutionary proposal for the well-being of the creation in general and for us humans in particular. It belongs to our process of becoming fully human. It is not helpful to think of the revelation as some initially abstract and unrelated reality that only secondarily is a possibility of cultural evolution. That could be true only if we were created initially in the abstract and only secondarily as the two-natured creatures that we have described. We were created in no other way than as such bio-cultural creatures, and God's revelation has neither reality nor force apart from its significance as a possibility for creatures such as we are.

Issue 6: The significance of Christian faith. I contend that the Christian faith, if it is to be interpreted adequately in an evolutionary framework must be related to the sorts of issues that have figured in the discussion to this point. It must be related to all the phases of evolution and to the processes of selection.

We need to ask just what is it that the historic Christian faith contributes to the cultural evolutionary process.

More than simply placing the Christian faith in the evolutionary context is called for. We need to speak theologically to the question of God's will for the destiny of the processes themselves. The majority of interpreters who have tackled this issue in recent decades have focused on something to do with the love-principle, with altruism, with the freedom to cross boundaries and identify with outsiders. We need to show that such things as the love-principle are not essentially anti-evolutionary but rather intrinsic to the broader evolutionary purpose. To do so means, among other things, bringing the Christian doctrine of eschatology to bear, since we cannot speak of the destiny of the world without speaking about its future and its eventual culmination.

Teilhard de Chardin, among preciously few others, understood the cultural evolutionary significance of Christianity to be the embodiment of the love for the world that can motivate acts that would actualize human solidarity in tandem with enhanced individualization. This individualization-within-solidarity is what he termed "building the earth," and he considered it to be the current imperative required by the trajectory of evolution in which we exist.[14]

Ralph Burhoe interprets Christianity (and by extension he would apply this interpretation to other religions as well) as a body of well-winnowed wisdom (Donald Campbell's term) which has emerged within the evolutionary process precisely because it has been selected. Hence, it has served the survival value of the process in which it has appeared.[15] This large packet of cultural information cannot be identified with only a single message, since its mores and rituals pertain to many aspects of life. However, Burhoe gives special attention to the love-principle, which he is inclined to speak of as "trans-kin altruism." This altruism has not only been instrumental in enabling the higher primates to become human beings, but it has also played a key role in subsequent developments. Today the love-principle is, in Burhoe's opinion, the chief imperative for the human community if it is to avoid destroying itself.

Gerd Theissen also emphasizes the love-principle as the force that enables human beings to transcend and yet fulfill the biological dimension of existence. The biological dimension manifests itself as *sarkic* (fleshly) behavior, which seems to be explicitly biological; but it also manifests itself as deadening "law" in the cultural sphere, as rigid "tradition" at the level of cognitive systems. Christ's love-principle enables persons to dare to transcend flesh, law, and tradition. At this point, Theissen brings to bear his concept of evolution as variability, selection, and adaptation. All the variable attempts that arise in the process are essential for satisfactory adaptation, since a large number of variants is desirable so that the best options can be winnowed by the selection process.   Even the abortive variations are therefore integral to the process. Further, each of the variable attempts is equidistant from the center of the process and whatever intentionality it has.   Theologically, this train of thinking is equivalent to a concept of justification and grace.   God requires no set pattern of successful adaptation.   Rather God requires an earnest and responsible life of attempting to adapt to the divine reality and will, from which attempts the most adequate can be selected.   All such attempts are equidistant from the center of God's will and grace.

The Created Co-Creator

What we have been looking at is the broad range of issues that we must confront if we are to follow the apologetic approach, the approach that seeks to identify the significance the Christian faith has for the evolutionary process. Now let us turn back to the Christian doctrine of anthropology, thinking it through with an eye to the reforming approach and what we have learned from evolutionary concepts.   Granting a degree of consonance between evolutionary science and constructive theology, what can we say about the human condition?

I recommend that we think of the human being as the *created co-creator*. This term does a number of things.   Because we are *created*, we are reminded that we are dependent creatures.   We depend for our very existence on our cosmic and biological prehistory; we depend on the creative grace of God.   Yet, we are also *creators*, using our cultural freedom and power to alter the course of historical events and perhaps even evolutionary events.   We participate with God in the ongoing creative process.   In addition, the term "created co-creator" connotes the fact that we have a destiny.   We have a future toward which we are being drawn by God's will.   Only when we understand what this destiny is will we be able to measure and evaluate the direction we take in our creative activity. To unearth the significance of this understanding of the human condition, let us look at the idea of the created co-creator in light of five classical Christian doctrines.

Doctrine 1: Creation Out of Nothing

Fundamental to both the Jewish and Christian view of the world is the doctrine of creation out of nothing, *creatio ex nihilo*.   This affirms that God is the source of all that is.   The nub of *creatio ex nihilo* is this: the only relationship between the world and God that is consistent with what Christians and Jews believe about God is one in which the universe and our planet within it are totally dependent upon God for its origin and perseverance.

The doctrine of *creatio ex nihilo* is not so much a material concept as it is a methodological strategy. The point of *ex nihilo* is not specifically aimed at identifying the lack of preexisting materials from which he constructed the world. It does not assert that God created all things out of the prior reality called "nothing," "nonbeing," what the Greeks dubbed ουκ ον. The doctrine has less to do with origins than it does with dependence. Rather, as a methodological strategy, it insists that everything that is depends for its being on God the creator.

On the basis of this assertion of the total dependence of all things on the creator God, I raise as an additional axiom that there is a correlation between the nature of the world and the nature of the God who created the world.[16] As a negative correlation it affirms that if God is the creator out of nothing, then this world is totally and completely a creature. When Christian witnesses take this axiom seriously, its proclamation demands attention. What it says makes a difference. It affirms, among other things, that our cosmos is a creation.

We human beings, then, are first and foremost creatures. We are caused. We are created. We are not self-generating. This is obvious whether one reads Genesis 2-3 to see that we have sprung from God and dust, or when one looks through evolutionary glasses and reviews the long prehistory about the emergence of life in planet Earth's primordial soup. We have come from a source well beyond ourselves.

We humans, then, can claim no arrogant credit for being co-creators. We have been created as co-creators. Put in scientific terms, we did not evolve ourselves to this point; rather, the evolutionary process—under God's rule, I am arguing—evolved us as co-creators. We could not even choose to be created as non-creators. God chose. That we exist as created co-creators is God's decision, not ours.

Doctrine 2: Continuing Creation

Creation for Christian theology is by no means limited to protology. It is not limited by what happened at the beginning when time was first created. Creation also refers to God's ongoing sustaining of the world. Every moment of the world's existence depends on the ongoing grace of God.

This assertion of continuing creation, when coupled with the creation-out-of-nothing concept, makes a powerful statement about the nonhuman creation as a trustworthy environment for the human. It asserts that the world about us is not antithetical to our human destiny and God's will; but rather it is a fundamentally friendly home for us. The ecosystem is benevolent and reliable.

It cannot be otherwise if it has proceeded originally from God's creative intention and continues to be sustained by the will of God.[17]

If we invoke our correlation axiom at this point, we get a positive correlation: God creates and so do we. We are active participants in the ongoing divine work. We make decisions and take actions that determine in part the course of events. Events bring new things. The human race is daily inventing new things that hitherto never existed. It is a dependent co-creation, to be sure; yet there is a genuine advance due to the contributions of human ingenuity and energy.

And, if evolutionary advance is influenced by our adaptation to God, then altruism may eventually lead to a qualitatively new reality. As co-creators with God, the dramatic possibility is opening up that the love-principle might actually introduce into bio-cultural evolution a new selection principle, a principle that goes beyond the previous gene selfishness.

Doctrine 3: The Imago Dei

A third and important component in theology's understanding of the world's status is the teaching concerning the *imago dei*, the image of God in the human race. Although the term has a long history and is almost universally attested in the theological tradition, there is only modest agreement regarding its exact meaning. At least two distinct traditions of interpretation can be identified: the common characteristic tradition and the relationship tradition. The first tries to identify specific human characteristics that are Godlike: love, uprightness, the capacity for dominion over the animals, and so forth. The second, the relationship perspective, suggests that the *imago dei* refers to the basic structure of the human being that enables communication between humans and God. Augustine gave voice to this second strand with his oft-quoted prayer: "O God, Thou hast created me for Thyself, and my heart is restless until it find its rest in Thee."[18] Of these two traditions, my inclination is to side with those who hold that the *imago dei* refers to our relationship with God.

I suggest that we identify our co-creatorhood with the image of God. We humans have certain characteristics that constitute the *imago dei* in us—we are able to make self-conscious and self-critical decisions, we are able to act on those decisions, and we are able to take responsibility for them. The human race can be dubbed *homo faber*, as our great technological achievements testify. We have altered the face of the earth and even dented the facade of outer space. In addition, we have moral capacity. We can look at what we have done and evaluate it. We can ask about its purpose and decide to redirect our decision-making and action-taking. God creates. So do we.

Now it may appear that I am identifying with the common characteristics tradition. But the relational perspective is what I really have in mind. It is the *co* in *co-creator* that I wish to emphasize. It is because we are grounded in a prior relationship with God who is bearing us along according to his will for the destiny of the cosmos that we find our creative characteristics significant. We are participants in a much larger ongoing creative process. Without such grounding, these characteristic abilities would mean little.

Doctrine 4: Christology

Through adaptive and creative work in culture, the human being represents a proposal for the further evolution of the created world. We humans have the potential to actualize a new phase of evolution. This is one of the implications of the doctrine of the image of God in us. But something else needs to be added here, namely, that in the New Testament the phrase "image of God" refers to Jesus Christ. Jesus Christ is the New Adam, the prototype of the true humanum. We fulfill the image of God insofar as we participate in Christ's new nature.

In Jesus Christ we find the power that enables us to participate in the purposes of God. Jesus, the second Adam, embodies anticipatorily what the first Adam can become. Jesus is that for which the creation of the first Adam was intended. Whereas the first Adam is a symbol of the essential humanity that belongs to every member of the species, the second Adam speaks of what humanity may yet become.

Jesus Christ becomes the central event for understanding what it means for humans to be God's proposal for the future of the evolutionary process. In freedom—a freedom that has been bequeathed to our race from the aeons of previous physical and biological and cultural development freedom—we have the option to live now according to what has been set forth by Jesus as God's ultimate purpose: the renewal and perfection of all creation.

We can think of the Christ-event as an act of God to which we should adapt and of our adaptation itself as having an impact on the future of evolution. Gerd Theissen said that we encounter "the central reality," God, on all levels of evolution.[19] In his life, death, and teachings, Jesus offers us the possibilities for raising human living to a higher plane, one which will reveal new ways of adapting to the reality system of nature and of God. Jesus' proposal for the love-principle—a universal love that crosses boundaries, including the boundaries of kinship—is a new way of life that stretches and bends the requirements of adaptation in novel ways. This proposal for trans-kin altruism is scandalous to many, because it appears to be a formula for maladaptation if not extinction. Yet, theologically, we want to say that the cross and resurrection represent the divinely willed direction for future cultural evolution.

Doctrine 5: The Eschatological Destiny of the Creation

The question of ultimate destiny is central to the assessment of the world and of the human place in it, because destiny suggests that there is a basic purpose or meaning inherent in existence as creation. If this is so, then the condition of the world at any moment can be judged by comparing its trajectory with its destiny.

What is the intention of God toward the world? I believe Christian theology is clear on this point: God intends to perfect or fulfill the creation. This is based upon two elements within the revelation, God's promises and God's faithfulness. God is faithful. God is not a deceiver. And, furthermore, God makes promises. Therefore, we can expect God to keep the promises he has made. Time and again this has been asserted in the Jewish and Christian interpretation of historical events. It is equally applicable to the history of nature, to cosmic history. Indeed, with our knowledge that humans are a part of the ecosystem and its evolution and not separate from it, if God is faithful in any portion of the world, such as human affairs, then God must be faithful in the whole, since the world is a seamless robe.

What this means for cosmic evolution seems to be this: the material order carries out its career from origin to end as God's creative process. This speaks to our earlier question as to the relationship between the 18-billion-year prehistory and the place the present human race has in this larger scheme. All must be conceived as somehow belonging together as part of God's grand program for the created world.

What this means for us humans seems to be this: our created status is thoroughly eschatological; that is, it is an unleashing, not a full-blown given that has simply to be reiterated and replicated throughout time. Human nature was not defined and fixed at some point of origin in the past. Whatever we were in the primordial past, we are not that now. Nor will we be the same in the future. Our essence is yet to be determined. Our nature is dynamic. And the dynamism comes from the eschatological future. The essential humanum that is emerging is being continually called by its destiny, and our ability to participate as an ordained co-creator is the result of the creative thrust of God. That thrust consists of sharing as a free, self-conscious creature in shaping the passage forward toward God's own *telos* or purpose which will appear in its fullness at the consummation, at the final perfection of the whole cosmic history of the creation.

Conclusion

Is nature friend or foe? Friend, we can say theologically. Nature in its entirety—from its original singularity 18 billion years ago, through the Big Bang, through the formation of planet earth, through the appearance of primordial soup and the flourishing of animate life, through the long genetic history of biological development, through the appearance of human culture, through the history of the Hebrew and Christian religions, and through chapters in our future story that have yet to be written—is being guided by the eschatological purpose of the one God who is the creator of all things. And this purpose is to perfect all that constitutes the creation, human beings included. More than that, we humans created in the image of God are participants and co-creators in the ongoing work of God's creative activity. We are being drawn toward a shared destiny that will ultimately determine what it means to be a true human being.

Notes

1. Pierre Teilhard de Chardin, *The Phenomenon of Man* (New York: Harper & Row, 1959).

2. Arthur Peacocke, *Creation and the World of Science* (Oxford: Clarendon Press, 1979) and *God and the New Biology* (New York: Harper & Row, 1986).

3. Gerd Theissen, *Biblical Faith: An Evolutionary Approach* (Philadelphia: Fortress, 1985), pp. 23, 25.

4. Anthony Stevens, *Archetypes: A Natural History of the Self* (New York: Morrow, 1982).

5. Victor Turner, "Body, Brain, and Culture," *Zygon* 18:3 (September1983), pp. 221-45.

6. See "Religion's Role in the Context of Genetic and Cultural Evolution: Campbell's Hypotheses and Some Evaluative Responses," ed. Ralph W. Burhoe in *Zygon* 11:3 (September 1976), pp. 115-303.

7. Peacocke, Creation and the World of Science, pp. 105-6; and "Theology and Science Today," in *Cosmos as Creation*, ed. Ted Peters (Nashville: Abingdon, 1989), pp. 28-43.

8. Ralph W. Burhoe, *Toward a Scientific Theology* (Belfast, Dublin, and Ottawa: Christian Journals, 1981).

9. John Hick, *Evil and the God of Love* (New York: Harper & Row, rev. ed., 1978), pp. 280 ff; and "An Irenaean Theodicy" in *Encountering Evil*, ed. Stephen Davis (Atlanta: John Knox Press, 1981), pp. 69-100.

10. H. Kummer, "Analogs of Morality Among Nonhuman Creatures," in *Morality as a Biological Phenomenon*, ed. Gunter Stent (Berkeley: University of California Press, 1980), pp. 33-42.

11. E. O. Wilson has said altruism is the "central theoretical problem of sociobiology." *Sociobiology: The New Synthesis* (Cambridge, Mass.: Harvard University Press, 1975), p. 46. John Maynard Smith poses the issue by defining altruism as "a trait which, in some cases, lowers the fitness of the individual displaying it, but increases the fitness of some other members of the same species." "The Evolution of Science Behavior – A Classification of Models," in *Current Problems in Sociobiology*, ed. King's College Sociobiology Group (Cambridge: Cambridge University Press, 1982), p. 43.

12. Richard Dawkins, *The Selfish Gene* (Oxford: Oxford University Press, 1976).

13. See my discussion in "Sociobiology, Ethics, and Theology," *Zygon* 19:2 (June 1984), pp. 185-207; and "Survival as a Human Value," *Zygon* 15:2 (June 1980), pp. 203-12.

14. Teilhard de Chardin, *The Phenomenon of Man*.

15. Burhoe, *Toward a Scientific Theology*.

16. See my "Fourth Locus: The Creation," in *Christian Dogmatics*, 2vols., Carl E. Braaten and Robert E. Jenson, eds. (Philadelphia: Fortress Press, 1984), I:298, 310.

17. Cf. Hefner, "Sociobiology, Ethics and Theology," p. 191; cf. Also "Creation Viewed by Science, Affirmed by Faith," in *Cry of the Environment*, ed. Philip N. Joranson and Ken Butigan (Sante Fe: Bear & Co,, 1984), pp. 199ff.

18. Augustine, *Confessions*, 1:1.

19. Theissen, *Biblical Faith*, p. 114.

22

Agape and Human Nature: Contributions from Neo-Darwinism

STEPHEN J. POPE

How is the central Christian virtue of "agape" related to "human nature" as depicted by evolutionary theorists? How are what E.O. Wilson (1978, 89) calls our "genetically influenced behavioral predispositions"[1] related to the high ideals of Christian love and charity? Several relations are suggested in the current literature. One account, probably the most popular, argues that they are fundamentally opposed. Agape consists of turning the other cheek, walking the second mile, not returning evil for evil, loving one's enemy, in short, radical self-sacrifice. Human nature, in sharp contrast, is said to have evolved in a radically egoistic way, to consist of predominantly and perhaps exclusively self-referential motives. As Ghiselin (1974, 247) puts it, "No hint of genuine charity ameliorates our vision of society, once sentimentalism has been laid aside. What passes for cooperation turns out to be a mixture of opportunism and exploitation... Scratch an 'altruist,' and watch a 'hypocrite' bleed."

On this view, genuinely loving another person for his or her own sake is impossible. At best, belief in other-regarding agape is a helpful illusion that facilitates social cooperation; at worst, it is a mechanism of social control that represses all possibility of genuine human flourishing and produces neurotic guilt in its place.[2] Agape is an ethics for "suckers," welcomed by the "cheaters" who exploit them, and rejected by the hardheaded and realistic "grudgers."[3] Agape in this position might be described as a weapon of "moralistic aggression" (Trivers 1971, 35-57) par excellence and as a central element in a self-serving system of "indirect reciprocity" that attempts to induce others to sacrifice their interests to the net gain of the self and his or her relatives.[4]

Though at odds on many fundamental issues, those who oppose agape and human nature are united in their depiction of the latter as egoistic and of the former as radically self-sacrificial. This paper rejects this dichotomy between agape and human nature and, in fact, attempts to suggest several ways in which contemporary human sociobiology might be critically appropriated within Christian ethics. The paper tries to establish three points. First, it attempts to indicate the dubious status of this dualism by distinguishing between two approaches to human nature within the sociobiological literature, egoistic and non-egoistic, and by arguing that the latter provides an anthropological basis for agape. Second, the paper distinguishes three contending interpretations of agape in order to indicate that at least one major position within Christianity does not argue for a completely indiscriminate altruism. Third, it argues that the natural preferences analyzed in kin selection theory can play a positive role within a Christian ethics of love—a claim that runs contrary both to those outside Christianity who believe that evolutionary theory debunks Christian ethics and to those Christian theologians who view sociobiology, as the antithesis of morality.

Sociobiologists on sociality

I would first like to argue that while they differ among themselves, human sociobiologists provide grounds for a non-egoistic view of human nature, i.e., a view of human nature that accounts for genuinely altruistic as well as egoistic motivations. Sociobiologists provide accounts of various forms of helping, cooperative and prosocial behavior, but their discussions of sociality have of course focused primarily on "altruism." The distinction between moral altruism as such (as usually understood in ordinary discourse) and "genetic altruism" is important to maintain in spite of its awkwardness. Behavior that is described as "altruistic" is always motivated by concern for another person for his or her own good; as such, it contrasts with behavior that is primarily self-concerned.[5] "Egoism," on the other hand, is the doctrine that human actions are primarily motivated by self-interest. "Genetic altruism," on the other hand, prescinds from motives and concerns only behavior that somehow contributes to the benefit of another at some expense to the agent's inclusive fitness (Wilson 1975, 3).[6]

Sociobiologists are divided over the nature of altruism. First, the egoistic position argues that altruism is an illusion and that we are motivated ultimately (at times unconsciously) only by self-concern (Dawkins 1976, 3-4; Wilson 1978, 154;[7] Alexander 1987;[8] Campbell 1975; Mackie 1978).[9] In this view altruism is a desirable character trait that allows one to appear to be trustworthy and attractive and thereby to advance both the agent's self-interest and inclusive fitness, but in reality individuals always seek a "net gain" in their interactions with others (at least over the long haul). Some of the authors who endorse this position seem to project the egoism of classical liberalism onto nature.[10] Even acts of "indiscriminate beneficence" (such as charitable donations) are said to contribute to the interests of benefactors by contributing to their reputation, building up social unity and tacitly encouraging others to act in a self-sacrificing manner (Alexander 1987, 101-2).[11]   The experience of genuinely altruistic motives is one of evolution's' masterpieces: self-deception regarding our own deepest (i.e., egoistic) motives best advances our own inclusive fitness. It is conceded that we might occasionally run across a genuinely altruistic person but with the qualification that they are exceedingly rare (Alexander 1987, 191).[12] This position attempts to debunk altruism (see Kiteher 1985, 396-406).

When discussing human action it is helpful to distinguish (1) stated reasons for actions, (2) conscious intentions, desires and motives, (3) unconscious desires and motivations, and (4) biologically based instinctual proclivities, inclinations and drives. Descriptions of human behavior as "altruistic" in ordinary discourse normally refer to level (2), i.e., action reflecting an agent's conscious desire to help another person. Sociobiological analyses of "altruism" refer primarily to consequences of acts that benefit the recipient at some expense to the agent's inclusive fitness. Evolution has shaped human nature at levels (3), our unconscious desires, and (4), the level of our instinctual drives, so that, as individual organisms, we are not spontaneously drawn to actions which would be self-destructive or systematically reduce our inclusive fitness.

Many sociobiological accounts of altruism fail to provide an adequate account of the links between these four levels of human being and do not sufficiently distinguish our unconscious desires from conscious intentions. The effort to debunk altruism relies on the belief that other-regarding reasons for action (level 1) and conscious motives (level 2) reflect the deeper working of unconscious egoistic desires (level 3). However, the primarily self-regarding character of our unconscious motivations (level 3)—granted here for the sake of the argument—by no means entails that the conscious experience of other-regard is illusory or self-deceptive. Those who make the latter claim seem to be conflating levels which should be distinguished.

These distinctions allow one to claim that an act might be both morally altruistic and "genetically egoistic," that is, motivated by genuine concern for another person (level 2) yet yielding consequences (the object of level 4) that contribute to the agent's inclusive fitness (e.g., the altruism of a parent who spends the night caring for a sick child). Acts of "kin favoritism" (acts which promote inclusive fitness) can be either egoistic or altruistic, depending on the quality of the agent's conscious motivation (the mixed motives of real life complicate the matter but do not invalidate the point).

A second position, clearly in the minority but worth considering, maintains that, alongside self-regard, genuinely altruistic motivations do exist, if only because they offer the best overall strategy for securing reproductive advantage (see Ruse 1986, 237; Hoffmann;[13] Chandler 1991; Masters 1978; Maxwell 1984).[14] Ruse (1985, 180) writes, for example, that "In the case of humans, biology achieves its ends by making us altruistic in the literal sense." Mary Maxwell (1984, 154) argues that kin selection theory does not claim that, "each parent calculates his or her advantage.... And it doesn't mean that love and genuine care in fact are not involved. It means that emotions such as love and genuine care in fact evolved because of underlying causes: principally, the biological need to maximize the probability that Homo sapiens will survive."[15]

Complexity, mixed motives, deep-seated ambivalence—rather than pure egoism—characterize human nature: some tendencies inclining us to service, empathy, and communion, others to aggression, indifference and isolation. What is significant is the claim that human nature has evolved in such a way as to include not only egoistic inclinations but also capacities for genuine altruism and related affective capacities like empathy, sympathy and compassion. As Ruse (1985, 180) puts it, "As part of our biology, we have feelings of sympathy and caring for others. We do desire the well-being—the happiness—of others, as well as of ourselves, and judge that this desire is a good thing. That is one of the key conclusions of modern evolutionary biology."

It needs to be said, however, that a number of the authors cited under the first category actually speak at times as if they were in the second. Wilson is a case in point. He claims that acts of kin favoritism are not conducted with expectation of return but that in acts of "soft core" altruism we expect reciprocation from society for ourselves or our closest relatives. Wilson (1978, 158-9) thus seems to be claiming that all acts outside kin favoritism are motivated by self-concern. Sociobiologists seem to be persistingly confused on this distinction, at least to the non-sociobiologist reader. They are either ambiguous or waver incoherently between these two, sometimes claiming that sociobiology accounts for the ultimate human motives underlying all external acts and at other times suggesting a more distant relation between genetic fitness and human motivation.

I maintain that the second approach to altruism is the most plausible on three grounds. First, it best accounts for the genuine altruism that is experienced by most normally emotionally developed people at least some of the time. We are not simply indifferent to the suffering of others who are non-kin and non-reciprocators. Not unlike the work of the great "masters of suspicion," Nietzsche, Marx and Freud, the "unmasking" potential of sociobiology which discovers the self-serving nature of some of our ostensibly other-regarding actions provides lines for interpreting some human behavior but not *all*.

Second, sociobiological attempts to provide credible explanations of every kind of well-known altruism have not been successful. R.M. Titmuss's (1971) famous study of blood donors is employed effectively by Peter Singer (1981, 134) to make the point that "Genuine non-reciprocal altruism directed toward strangers does occur." Alexander's claim that each and every one of Titmuss's blood donors were motivated (consciously or unconsciously) by the desire for social reputation is not convincing (Alexander 1987, 158).[16] In many theological and philosophical circles, sociobiology is dismissed because, among other reasons, it is perceived as attempting, against the evidence of ordinary moral experience, to force human motives into a Procrustean bed of egoism. Ordinary moral experience is more complex than egoistic reductionism recognizes.

Third, some version of "genetic selfishness" examined by sociobiologists may be compatible with moral altruism as long as the distinction between "self" and "genes" is carefully maintained. A loving parent caring for a child is acting from altruistic motives and contributing to his or her inclusive fitness. When this distinction collapses, as it often seems to do in popular sociobiology, the self is identified with its genes and with copies of its genes, and every act that remotely positively affects the self, relatives, or friends is described as "selfish." As philosopher John Chandler (1991, 181) points out, when we scrupulously retain this distinction, "it becomes clear that the attribution of 'selfishness' to genes in the sociobiological sense of the term is perfectly compatible with genuine altruism on the part of the individual."[17] This is simply to say that conscious motives and desires (level 2 above) cannot be simplistically identified with unconscious desires (level 3), let alone biological inclinations (level 4).

It seems plausible to argue that what was at one time an adaptive emotional proclivity to engage in altruism within small groups (e.g., in Pleistocene hunter-gatherer tribes) now is able to take on a life of its own and transcend its original limits, e.g., regarding care for strangers or the handicapped. Just as our eyes and intelligence are capable of beholding much more than is necessary for (or even remotely related to) our survival and repro-duction, so our altruistic capacities are able to transcend the confines of the behavioral repertoire of our early human ancestors.[18] Affirming a degree of transcendence, of course, by no means implies that human nature does not impose limits on the range of human love, e.g., we are simply incapable of establishing close affective bonds with every human being we encounter. Thus evolutionary accounts of human nature add an important element of realism to religious accounts of love or agape.

For these reasons, sociobiology ought to be taken not to support a relentless egoism (a la Ghiselin) but rather a more complex view of human nature that accounts for its altruistic capacities and inclinations. Yet even this approach to human nature might be dismissed as diametrically opposed to agape, if the latter is taken to entail the elimination of all reference to the self or to special bonds of affection and loyalty. We must thus next consider the meaning of agape as such before attempting to relate it to human nature as conceived by evolutionary theory.

Theologians on agape

Agape is a highly contested concept in contemporary Christian theology and, without going into great detail here, it should be said that theologians are clearly divided over the fundamental quality that marks agape. First, the most dramatic and distinctive position is that mentioned above, namely, that agape is radically self-sacrificial, admits of no trace of self-love, and is in no way to be identified with any form of friendship (which is ultimately always "selfish") (Nygren 1982). The "purist" allows no distinction between what Rousseau called *amour de soi*, self-love, and *amour propre*, self-conceit or egocentrism (Rousseau 1987, 53 and 106, note 15).[19] This view of agape is maintained not only by many devout Christians but also by sociobiologists (if only to discredit agape as naive and unworkable). Thus Ruse (1985, 178) summarizes the Christian ethics as demanding "that you give without reservation or limit to others, without discrimination to relative, friend, foe, or stranger, and continue, no matter what harm befalls you."

A second position claims that agape should not be seen as self-sacrifice but rather as respect for persons. Unlike self-sacrifice, equal regard is neither required nor allowed to issue a "blank check" to the neighbour (see Outka 1972).[20] Yet equal regard shares with self-sacrifice an abiding mistrust of particular attachments, natural desires and sentiments, special loyalties— especially the kind of kinship ties and reciprocal loyalties discussed by sociobiology. All of these attachments reflect individual preferences, which detract from or threaten to undermine impartiality and respect.

The fundamental affinity of "equal regard" with Kantian impartiality is clear. According to the *Grundlegung*, the moral law is "completely a priori, free from everything empirical, and found exclusively in rational concepts," i.e., independent of "empirical anthropology" (Kant 1959, 27, para. 410). Kant argued that the goal of establishing a "completely isolated metaphysics of morals, mixed with no anthropology" provides not only the prerequisite for a theoretical knowledge of moral duties but is also "a desideratum of the highest importance to the actual fulfillment of its precepts" (27, para. 110). Why?

> For the pure conception of duty and of the moral law generally, with no admixture of empirical inducements, has an influence on the human heart so much more powerful than all other incentives which may be derived from the empirical field that reason, in the consciousness of its dignity, despises them and gradually becomes master over them (Kant 1959, 27, paras 110-11).

"Empirical inducements" and other motives not rooted exclusively in what Kant calls "rational concepts" cannot consistently lead the agent to act rightly. Moral laws, properly understood, hold for every rational being as such and are derived by pure reason from "the universal concept of a rational being generally" (Kant 1959, p28, para. 142). Ethics thus applies to "rational beings as such" and not to the contingent nature of existing human beings.

Agape thus acts not from "inclination," which reflects the unstable emotions and self-preference of human nature, but from duty. Non-teleological "respect" thus replaces the teleological notion of love. Whereas the latter responds to the goodness of an apprehended object, the former, Kant says, is a feeling that is "not received through any [outer] influence but is self-wrought by a rational concept" (Kant 1959, 17, para. 400). Respect for a rational being generated by a "good will" cannot be confused with love motivated by natural inclinations. Human nature is too frail, corrupt and subject to the distortions of egocentrism and the temptations of conceit to adhere to the moral law by inclination and natural desires. Only duty based upon moral law will consistently produce right actions and consistently resist the "radical evil in human nature" (see Kant 1960, Book I: 15-39). We are to transcend nature completely—the purposes and desires of the phenomenal world—and establish our identity as moral beings in the will.

Christians who identify agape with Kantian' respect argue that we love the other qua human being. As Gene Outka expresses this succinctly: "Agape is a regard for the neighbor which in crucial respects is independent and unalterable. To these features there is a corollary: the regard is for every person qua human existent, to be distinguished from those special traits, actions, etc., which distinguish particular personalities from each other" (Outka 1972). I am not to act out of agape because I am fond of this particular person but rather, as Kant put it, "on grounds which are valid for every rational being as such" (Kant 1959, 30, para. 414).

An abstract ethic thus replaces particular ties by respect for every rational being as an end in itself. This exclusive respect for reason leads proponents of equal regard to disregard many of the essential characteristics of the human person—our mores, affections, sentiments, historical bonds, traditional attachments as well as the particular familial, social, religious and political ties that sustain and nourish our humanity. Kant's fundamental belief that reason must replace nature as the guiding force of human life strips ethics of its human foundation, because the human is not only rational (let alone Kant's version of the rational). The hope that human reason will transform human society into a harmonious community of free and rational beings in effect abstracts rational community from human love, friendship and sociality.

A third interpretation of agape rejects the primacy of both self-sacrifice and equal regard and instead understands agape as most fundamentally a form of mutuality and friendship. Mutuality includes reciprocity, though not the instrumentalism implied in "I'll scratch your back, you scratch mine." Self-sacrifice is instrumental either to the deeper bonds of communion or expressive of a more "thin" if still necessary virtue of benevolence. Equal regard for its part is a feature of justice that acts to protect human relationships; it is a necessary condition of agape but by no means its highest achievement or most profound expression. Though the warrants cannot be provided in the space allotted, this third view of agape is the one endorsed here.[21]

Each of these views has its own advocates, who appeal to a characteristic set of Biblical and theological warrants. One central issue concerns the proposed relation between human nature and God's grace. It is obviously no accident that those who assume a radical opposition between these often claim that there is an unbridgeable abyss between agape and human nature. As a result, Christian ethics tends to be conducted with little or no attention to the human sciences. An alternative view maintains that "fallen" or "corrupt" human nature can be "healed" by God's grace and that the attempt to divorce grace from nature altogether is an insult to the Creator. For this reason the complete opposition of agape from natural love has been resisted by many of the major figures within Christian theological tradition (that is, before the powerful influence of Kant on modern theology, particularly Protestant).

The classical position on agape and human nature offered by thirteenth-century theologian Thomas Aquinas reflects the fundamental axiom that grace perfects rather than destroys human nature. This view underlies the further claim that agape is the grace-inspired transformation of ordinary human love, not its replacement or obliteration. According to Aquinas, "Grace and virtue imitate the order of nature, which is established by Divine wisdom" (Aquinas *Summa Theologiae*, 2: 1322). The proper justification, details, and full explication of this position cannot be provided here, but two implications are fundamental. First, if this view is correct, natural self-love is legitimate and proper, not an aberration or distortion of true virtue. "Selfishness" needs to be corrected and replaced with proper self-love but the self should not and cannot be eradicated.

Second, the Christian moral life involves a retention and perfection (rather than rejection or complete transcendence) of the various objects of love that characterize ordinary social life (e.g., ties rooted in marriage and family, social roles, local community), though not with the typical distortions by which these are often accompanied (moral bias, nepotism, parochialism, xenophobia, etc.). Aquinas followed an ancient and venerable tradition of distinguishing among objects of agape according to the "order of love" (an *ordo amoris*) established by God and implanted in our nature as human beings. According to the Thomistic order of love, we are to love God above all else, then the self, then the neighbor. Various neighbors are to be loved in a way that respects the moral priorities that suit human nature, properly conceived (see Augustine, *On Christian Doctrine*, I; and Aquinas, *Summa Theologiae*, II-II, 26). According to Aquinas, "[T]he order of nature is such that every natural agent pours forth its activity first and most of all on the things which are nearest it" (*Summa Theologiae*, II-II, 31, 3, 2: 1322). Since "Grace and virtue imitate the order of nature, which is established by Divine wisdom (*Summa Theologiae*, II-II, 31, 3, 2: 1322), Aquinas infers that the moral priorities of agape imitate the order of natural love whereby moral priority is given to special connections. Ties of blood are the most important of all special connections because they are "prior to and more stable than all other unions" (*Summa Theologiae*, II-II, 26, 8, 2: 1300).

Agape interpreted in light of the medieval doctrine of the "order of love" thus respects the axiom coined much later that "ought imples can" and moreover—in contrast to Kantian interpretations of agape—it allows for the incorporation of natural priorities into the Christian moral life, though not in such a way as to compromise or domesticate the Christian ethic. Regarding the arena of the necessities of life, first priority is given to one's children, spouse and parents. Contrary to the view of those deeply suspicious of "special relations," according to Aquinas, giving proper care to one's own children before others' is neither a scandal to nor a betrayal of agape, but in fact one of its fundamental moral requirements (pace Ruse 1985, 179). One who follows the injunction to sell all and give alms to the poor commits a sin when doing so harms one's dependents. Almsgiving is meritorious when it observes the order of love which requires that, "other things being equal, we should, in preference, help those who are more closely connected with us" (*Summa Theologiae*, II-II, 31, 9, 2: 1332). Of course, the criterion of urgent need can outweigh special connection in some cases, and thus Aquinas argues that failure to meet the urgent needs of another person, including a stranger, when one is able to do so constitutes a mortal sin (*Summa Theologiae*, II-II, 32, 5, 2: 1328). Yet special bonds are given the highest prima facie priority.

Interestingly, despite opposition on other fundamental theological issues, the great sixteenth-century Protestant theologian John Calvin agreed with Aquinas on the ordering of love. "I do not deny," the Reformer wrote in the *Institutes of the Christian Religion* (Calvin 1960, 1:418), "that the more closely a man is linked to us, the more intimate obligation we have to assist him. It is the common habit of mankind that the more closely men are bound together by the ties of kinship or acquaintanceship, or of neighborhood, the more responsibilities for one another they share. This does not offend God, for his providence, as it were, leads to it." Like Aquinas, Calvin held that God works through human nature, its habits and conventions. Again, according to Calvin (1960 1:418), Christianity insists that every human being is neighbor: "The term 'neighbor' includes even the most remote person; we are not expected to limit the precept of love to those in close relationships." At the same time, the order of love builds upon human nature and custom rather than replaces them; grace and nature complement one another at this level.

What we owe to others and do for them out of love depends not only upon their rational nature as such but also, more concretely, upon one's place in the community. Thus in his exposition of the eighth commandment, "Thou shaft not steal" (Ex. 20: 15), Calvin (1960 1:411) comments, "let each man consider what, in his rank and station, he owes to his neighbors, and pay what he owes." Calvin, like Aquinas, represents the general acceptance of the order of love within the Christian tradition up to the modern period, when a more rigorous ethic, based upon the severence of reason and nature, proposed that agape ignore special attachments and natural priorities.

Kin selection and the "order of love"

As mentioned earlier, some Christian theologians completely reject the moral centrality of natural priorities and instead claim that genuine agape abandons merely human preferences and requires instead a completely indiscriminate concern for others. Theologians who maintain that natural priorities can and ought to be incorporated into the Christian moral life are better able to heed the sociobiological claim that "promiscuous altruism"—i.e., altruism practiced "without discrimination of kinship, acquaintanceship, shared values, or propinquity in time or space" (Hardin 1982, 172)—as a practice is not possible and that some form of priority system is necessary if human caregiving is to persist over time. The claim of this paper is that the latter view of agape can incorporate kin preference as *one important feature* of such a priority system.

The evolutionary basis of kin preference is hardly controversial. The elemental desire to form and maintain deep bonds of attachment, occurring predominantly between parents and newborns, provides an obvious selective advantage to members of the species by supporting the extended parental caregiving needed during the infant's prolonged process of physical, cognitive and psychological maturation. Kin selection helps us understand why, for example, we give special degrees of care to closest kin and why "expectations of reciprocity vary inversely with closeness of kinship" (Essock-Vitale and McGuire 1980, 237).[22] Kin selection theory explains why "the greater (more costly) the help, the more likely the help is coming from kin" (McGuire 1980, 236; see also, among others, Hames 1988). Despite many exceptions, ties of blood seem to be the strongest and most durable of bonds, and it does seem to be the case that "altruism appears to be substantially hard-core when directed at closest relatives" (Wilson 1978, 158).[23]

Kin preference may be one of the most intuitively compelling tenets of sociobiology. It is obvious to even the "purist" that mature, interpersonal love depends upon affective and social capacities developed first in some form of family life and that relatively secure bonds of love within the family create the emotional basis for a later extension of love to persons outside the family (see Hoffman 1975; Kagan 1984; Konner 1982; Ricks 1985; and Rutter 1978).

Those who interpret love as mutuality are able to see intra- familial love and friendship as central loci of the ethics of love rather than as merely peripheral because of their preferential nature. Kin preference, if properly balanced with concern for non-kin, is of course valuable for families, but it is also valuable for their communities, their societies and the human species as a whole. It is good, in other words, that we feel strongly about our families, take care of family members (especially the young) teach our children to love and care for theirs when the time is right, and try to work for a society in which families thrive and children are loved and respected.

Conclusion: Human nature and agape

This paper has attempted to delineate the contributions of sociobiology to our understanding of the relation of agape to human nature by drawing some significant distinctions within both Christian views of agape and within sociobiological accounts of altruism. Agape in several dominant perspectives (self-sacrifice and equal regard) stands in stark opposition to *all* sociobiological accounts of altruism because the latter are said to accommodate self-love and/or special preferences. On the other hand, the more traditional view of agape held by Aquinas stands in opposition to *some* views of sociobiology—i.e., those which posit exclusively or ultimately egoistic views—but *not* to *all* others—i.e., those which recognize the fact that human nature is marked by *altruistic* as well as egoistic motives. In the latter case, sociobiology provides insights valuable for those theologians who are interested in understanding the natural roots of the order of love.

In a Christian context, agape stands as a check on some of the excesses of sociobiological accounts of altruism. First, agape corrects the narrow and exclusive use of sociobiological interpretations of the range of human concern and love. Kin selection theory cannot be taken to provide a comprehensive explanation of familial love, nor does it intend to do so. Moreover, interpersonal reciprocity must not be confused with sociobiological notions of reciprocity, both in the descriptive sense of expressing affective capacities not reducible to biological forces and in the moral sense of invoking genuine other-regard and self-donation.[24] A crude egoism that calculates the costs and benefits of actions in quid pro quo terms stands in diametrical opposition to the duty to treat persons in need as did the good Samaritan, regardless of whether it is "profitable"—genetically or otherwise.

Agape leads us to transcend the narrow circle prescribed by considerations of reciprocity and kinship. It rejects all forms of narrow exclusivity toward those who lie on the margins or altogether outside of our various communities. Indeed, some of the better writings of sociobiologists proclaim our need to move beyond tribalism and moral parochialism for the sake of our survival as a species.

According to Wilson (1978, 155-9), for the good of the human race we must work against "pure, hard-core altruism based upon kin selection" and build social harmony through the extension of "soft-core" reciprocity. The Christian ethic, on the other hand, extends at least a degree of "hard-core" as well as "soft-core" altruism to non-kin and non-reciprocators—including those who are, in a general sense, socially and economically "unproductive" (e.g., the elderly, the mentally and physically handicapped, etc.).

In this sense, Christians are enjoined to work against biological "nature" (as sociobiologists depict it) in light of higher values (Wilson 1978, 208), a suggestion that is by no means foreign to sociobiology. Sociobiologists themselves propose that we work against those aspects of our nature that threaten our present social and even biological existence. They are not Spencerians or social Darwinians who claim that what has evolved is ipso facto morally good. One of the tasks of culture, in fact, is to correct the anti-social tendencies that evolved over the course of our primate and especially hunter-gatherer past. Wilson (1978, 208), for example, hopes that "New patterns of sociality could be installed in bits and pieces" into human nature, despite the fact that it rests on a "jerrybuilt foundation of partly obsolete Ice-Age adaptations." Alexander (1987, 9-10) writes, similarly, that "The value of an evolutionary approach to human sociality is thus not to determine the limits of our actions so that we can abide by them. Rather, it is to examine our life strategies so that we can change them when we wish, as a result of understanding them." The point of sociobiological attention to tendencies   that subvert altruism and social cooperation seems to help us to appreciate   the difficulty of adjusting the social order to better serve human survival and, if possible, human flourishing.

Sociobiology contributes to contemporary theological discussions of agape and human nature in several ways. First, it helps us to understand that natural processes and patterns of caregiving and cooperation need to be recognized, properly appreciated and supported within the ethics of love, contrary to illusions of radical independence that underlie some of the rhetoric of total self-sacrifice or equal regard.

Second, it helps us retrieve an insight common to the history of Christianity but lost in the modern period: that to a partial degree at least, we are affectively ordered by our biologically based emotional constitution. As one source of knowledge about human nature, sociobiology provides insight into the "is" upon which the "ought" of agape is built. We are not, Mary Midgley (1978, 71) notes, "disembodied intelligences, tentatively considering possible incarnations" but concrete, embodied human beings with "highly particular, sharply limited needs and possibilities." We are human beings whose love—and this includes agape—is shaped in particular ways by our evolved natures and not in others. The variation of human affection is extensive but it is not infinite. Regarding the ethics of love, we are not free to love and care for all people in the same way, or to love all people with the mutuality encouraged in some accounts of agape—a realization that is resisted by one-sided emphases on self-sacrifice or impartiality.

Third, sociobiological accounts of kin preference point to a natural basis for understanding the ordering of love. Natural priorities should be retained in the Christian ethics of love, though without the myopia and exclusivity that mark disordered special loyalties. While partiality is frequently based on primarily personal rather than biological grounds, at times personal grounds may overlap with and even express biological ordering and fulfill natural desires. Thus there are, for example, both personally and biologically based reasons for giving family members greater care than other persons. The human person may be oriented by his/her emotional constitution to love "the nearest and the dearest", but the concrete shape that love takes in each person's life is the result of the exercise of human freedom rather than a mechanical execution of blind, fitness-maximizing biological imperatives.

Fourth, evolutionary theorists from Darwin to this day have argued that kin preference provides a natural basis for expanding the range of human altruism. The theme of extending human concern for others through an expansion of natural social capacities is anticipated in David Hume and developed by Darwin in *The Descent of Man*, especially Books IV and V. Darwin writes, for example: "The moral nature of man has reached its present standard, partly through the advancement of his reasoning powers and consequently of a just public opinion, but especially from his sympathies having been rendered more tender and widely diffused through the effects of habit, example, instruction, and reflection" (Appleton 1970, 201). Authentic interpersonal love results in part from the directing and maturing of innate affective and social capacities; it is, as Midgley (1978, 260) notes, "part of our animal nature, not a colonial imposition." At least in some interpretations of human nature discussed earlier, altruism is seen as going *with* rather than always *against* the grain of essential aspects of human nature. Rather than being simply transcended, suspended, or eliminated, then, natural human social capacities can be developed, unfolded and amplified in a Christian ethic of love.

Finally, it can be suggested that sociobiological attentiveness to our common descent and species membership provides grounds for seeing each person primarily as a fellow human being rather than as only a member of another income level, profession, race, nation, ethnic group, tribe, etc. A greater realization of our common humanity can check the parochial tendencies in which "each individual [is] devalued in proportion as [he or she] is more distantly related" (Barash 1982, 74). In this way neo-Darwinian accounts of human nature can assist in balancing the ethics of agape in a way that accounts for obligations of both a particular and a universal nature.

Notes

1.   As Wilson (1978, 50) puts it. "We are a single species. not two or more, one great breeding system through which genes flow and mix in each generation. Because of that flux, mankind viewed over many generations shares a single human nature within which relatively minor hereditary influences recycle through ever changing patterns, between the sexes and across families and entire populations." "Human nature" is also taken to refer to what philosopher Mary Midgley (1978, 58) calls "a certain range of powers and tendencies, a repertoire, inherited and forming a fairly firm characteristic pattern." The term "human nature" should thus be taken to refer to the general characters shared by most members of the human species; it does imply a static "essentialism" or some kind of naive Biblical creationism that ignores evolution.

2. This argument was advanced by Sigmund Freud (1961, especially Ch. 5), and of course preceded the emergence of sociobiology. A synthesis of Freud and neo-Darwinism is attempted in Badcock (1986).

3. This language is used by Richard Dawkins in *The Selfish Gene* (Oxford: Oxford University Press, 1976), e.g., 198.

4. On self-sacrificial morality as self-serving "indirect reciprocity," see Alexander (1987, 96, 177). According to Richard D. Alexander, love of enemy and "universal benevolence" suited early Christianity under the dominance of Rome ("turning the other cheek" is the best "strategy" for subject peoples) but became irrelevant with the emergence of Christendom (see Alexander 1987, 175-6).

5. Other-regarding motivation is central to the standard notion of altruism and is found in a variety of sources, e.g., Bernard Williams (1973, 250-65) and Dennis L. Krebs (1970, 258-302).

6. For a helpful analysis, see Brian C.R. Bertram (1982, 252-67). It should be noted that "love" is not to be equated with either sense of altruism.

7. The evolutionary theory of human altruism is greatly complicated by the ultimately self-serving quality of most forms of that altruism. No sustained form of human altruism is explicitly and totally self-annihilating. Regarding "soft-core" altruism, Wilson argues that, "The 'altruist' expects reciprocation from society for himself or his closest relatives. His good behavior is calculating, often in a wholly conscious way, and his maneuvers are orchestrated by the excruciatingly intricate sanctions and demands of society" (Wilson 1978, 155-6).

8. "I suspect that nearly all humans believe it is a normal part of the functioning of every human individual now and then to assist someone else in the realization of that person's interests to the actual net expense of those of the altruist. What [evolutionary theory] tells us is that, despite our intuitions, there is not a shred of evidence to support this view of beneficence, and a great deal of convincing theory suggests that any such view will eventually be judged false" (Alexander 1987, 3). Alexander's view of morality also exudes egoist assumptions: "My view of moral systems in the real world, however, is that they are systems in which costs and benefits of specific actions are manipulated so as to produce reasonably harmonious associations in which everyone nevertheless pursues his own (in evolutionary terms) self-interest" (p. 191). Alexander argues that motives of self-interest need not be conscious, and suggests, indeed, that they are often not conscious to the agent (p. 40). In this case, egoism seems to function more as an a priori postulate rather than as an empirically verifiable claim.

9. In response to Mackie, see Midgley (1979).

10. E.g., Alexander (1987, 3) argues that "ethics, morality, human conduct, and the human psyche are to be understood *only* if societies are seen as collections of individuals seeking their own self-interests" (emphasis added). Alexander's focus on "conflicts of interest" (Ch. 2 and throughout) reflects this socially atomistic view. Yet he adds this caveat: "I would not contend that we always carry out cost-benefit analyses deliberately or consciously. I do, however, contend that such analyses occur, sometimes consciously, sometimes not, and that we are evolved to be exceedingly accurate and quick at making them" (p. 97). Again, Alexander is vague. Of course, cost-benefit calculations occur, but how often and how dominant is this kind of deliberation?

11. Alexander refers to "indiscriminate beneficence" as "indiscriminate social investment," which he defines as "willingness to risk relatively small expenses in certain kinds of social donations to whomever may be needy—partly because of the prevalence of interested audiences and keenness of their observation and the use of beneficent acts by others to identify individuals appropriate for later reciprocal interactions" (Alexander 1987, 100). As St. Paul and St. Thomas knew, acts of indiscriminate beneficence can be self-interested; but need they always be so? The latter has not been demonstrated.

12. "I do not doubt that occasional individuals lead lives that are truly altruistic and self-sacrificing. However admirable and desirable such behavior may be from others' points of view, it represents an evolutionary mistake for the individual showing it. This only means that I do not suppose it likely that such behavior can easily be induced generally. I think there have been fewer such truly self-sacrificing individuals than might be supposed, and most cases that might be brought forward are likely instead to be illustrations of the complexity and indirectness of reciprocity, especially the social value of appearing more altruistic than one is" (Alexander 1987, 191).

13. The position that human nature has evolved to possess genuinely altruistic as well as egoistic emotional predispositions, is found in Hoffman (1981). See also, from a psychological perspective, Batson (1990). On a concern related to this paper, but drawing on social psychology rather than sociobiology, see Rigby and O'Grady (1990).

14. Alexander (1987, 88) describes genetic altruism as a "mistake." It should also be noted that a third term is sometimes employed by sociobiologists: Acts which are detrimental to one's own self or body are called "phenotypically altruistic" by Alexander (pp. 41-2, 84). Phenotypically altruistic acts can result from altruism or egoism and can issue in either genetic altruism or genetic egoism. Use of the term here threatens to confuse more than clarify.

15. Alexander is not always clear in this regard. E.g., he criticizes moral philosophers for not treating "the beneficence of humans as a part, somehow, of their selfishness.... [T]he normally expressed beneficence, or altruism, of parenthood—and nepotism and the temporary altruism (or social investment) of reciprocity are expected to result in greater (genetic) returns than their alternatives" (Alexander 1987, 86). Read literally, Alexander seems to claim that we are motivated to care for our children and other relatives because at some (perhaps unconscious) level we recognize this as the genetically most beneficial strategy. To call this "selfish" seems to identify fallaciously the self with copies of its genes, a problem throughout Alexander's text. The concept of an act being "genetically selfish" (Alexander 1987, 93, also 164) reflects this confusion and is an oxymoron (see Kiteher 1985, 404; Midgley 1978, 129). To avoid this confusion it would be helpful to distinguish kin preference from self preference. As van den Berghe notes, my "interests" are definitely not the "interests" of my genes (even if such a concept is allowed): "We have been programmed to love ourselves, directly, and indirectly in our children and relatives, because that is how our constituent genes were selected in the first place. Genes that had this effect in their carriers were selected for. But human consciousness now turns that self-love against the genes. We use the proximate mechanisms of genetic selection, including sexual behavior, not only as means to the end of gene reproduction, but as ends in themselves. We proclaim, in effect, that we love the entire assemblage of genes we call 'me' better than our genes taken separately, and that therefore we are going, in some circumstances, to gratify that 'me,' even at the expense of reproducing our genes" (van den Berghe 1979, 181-3).

16. Other classic illustrations of sociobiological speculations that completely fail to persuade are found in Barash's (1979, 167-8) account of the selfishness of kamikaze pilots and Wilson's (1978, 165) speculations on Mother Teresa's ultimately egoistic motives.

17. A similar point is made by Barash (1982, 105) "Behavior may thus be phenotypically altruistic yet still genotypically selfish if the benefit derived by the recipient, multiplied by the probability that relevant genes occur within the recipient, exceeds the cost incurred by the altruist."

18. What are now taken to be undesirable traits, such as conformism, suggestibility, nepotism, ethnocentrism, self-deception, racism, excessive competitiveness and "moralistic aggression," are various expressions of a more general tendency to form "in-groups" and "out-groups" that at one time provided adaptive advantages to members of the species, e.g., in defense against external aggression. On "clique selfishness," see Campbell (both 1975 and 1979). See also Wilson (1978, 149-67) and Levine and Campbell (1972).

19. See also the distinction between "selfishness" and "rational self-love" in Kant, *Critique of Practical Reason* (1956, Pt. 1, Ch. 3, 76).

20. Outka's account of impartiality is informed by Kant and Kierkegaard, and should be distinguished from the utilitarian form of impartiality employed in Singer (1981). The best discussion of the limits of impartiality as an ethical ideal is found in Blum (1980).

21. It seems to me that "mutuality" is the closest of the three positions to Thomas Aquinas' notion of *caritas*. A defense of this position would proceed through a careful examination and retrieval of Thomas' position as discussed in the *Summa Theologiae* II-II, 26 and in *De Caritate*.

22. This is not to deny the obvious fact that individuals feel differently about family attachments, within and across cultures. For a sociobiological account of kinship variations, see, among others, van den Berghe (1979).

23. Recall that in "hard-core" altruism the "bestower expresses no desire for equal return and performs no unconscious actions leading to the same end" (Wilson 1978, 149-67). "Hard-core" altruism, according to Wilson, is directed exclusively toward close kin. This is not to overlook the unfortunate but common direction of "hard-core" violence and destruction at close kin.

24. By "transcends" I mean that interpersonal reciprocity involves attitudes and affections that cannot be fully understood or completely generated by biological features of human nature, without remainder. The capacity for mutuality must of course lie within and to some extent depend upon our biological natures, otherwise we would be "disembodied spirits."

References

Alexander, R. D. (1987) *The Biology of Moral Systems*. New York: Aldine/de Gruyter.

Appleton, P., ed. (1970) *Darwin: A Norton Critical Edition*, 2d ed. New York: W. W. Norton.

Aquinas, Thomas. (1947) *Summa Theologiae*, 3 vols., trans. Fathers of the English Dominican Province. New York: Benziger.

_____. *On Charity [De Caritate]*, trans. L. H. Kendzierski. Milwaukee, WI: Marquette University Press.

Augustine *On Christian Doctrine I.*

Badcock, C.R. (1986) *The Problem Of Altruism: Freudian-Darwinian Solutions*. New York: Basil Blackwell.

Barash, D. (1979) *The Whispering Within*. New York: Penguin.

_____. (1982) *Sociobiology and Behavior*, 2d ed. Toronto: Hodder and Stoughton.

Batson, C.D. (1990) "How social an animal? The human capacity for caring." *American Psychologist* 45: 336-46.

Bertram, B.C.R. (1982) "Problems with altruism," in King's College Sociobiology Group *Current Problems in Sociobiology*. Cambridge: Cambridge University Press.

Blum, L. (1980) *Friendship, Altruism and Morality*. London: Routledge and Kegan Paul.

Calvin, J. (1960) *Institutes of the Christian Religion*, 2 vols., trans. F. L. Battles. Philadelphia, PA: Westminster.

Campbell, D.T. (1975) "On the conflicts between biological and social evolution and between psychology and moral tradition." *American Psychologist* 30:1102-26.

_____. (1979) "Comments on the sociobiology of ethics and moralizing." *Behavioral Science* 24: 37-45.

Dawkins, R. (1976) *The Selfish Gene*. Oxford: Oxford University Press.

Essock-Vitale, S. and McGuire, M. T. (1980) "Predictions derived from the theories of kin selection and reciprocation assessed by anthropological data." *Ethology and Sociobiology* 1: 233-43.

Freud, S. (1961) *Civilization and its Discontents*, trans. J. Strachey. New York: W. W. Norton.

Ghiselin, M. T. (1974) *The Economy of Nature and the Evolution of Sex*. Berkeley, CA: University of California Press.

Hames, R.B. (1988) "The allocation of parental care among the Ye'Kwana." in L. Betzig, M. Borgerhoff Mulder and Turke, eds. *Human Reproductive Behavior: A Darwinian Perspective*. New York: Cambridge University Press, 237-51.

Hardin, G. (1982) "Discriminating altruisms." *Zygon* 17 (June): 163-86.

Hoffman, M.L. (1975) "Altruistic behavior and the parent-child relationship." *Journal of Personality and Social Psychology* 31: 937-43.

_____. (1981) "Is altruism part of human nature?" *Journal of Personality and Social Psychology* 40: 121-37.

Kagan, J. (1984) *The Nature of the Child*. New York: Basic Books.

Kant, I. (1956) *Critique of Practical Reason*, trans. L. White Beck. Indianapolis, IN: Bobbs-Merrill.

_____. (1959) *Foundations of the Metaphysics of Morals*, trans. L. White Beck. Indianapolis, IN: Bobbs-Merrill.

_____. (1960) *Religion within the Limits of Reason Alone*, trans. T. M. Greene and H.H. Hudson. New York: Harper.

Kitcher, (1985) *Vaulting Ambition: Sociobiology and the Quest for Human Nature*. Cambridge, MA: MIT Press.

Konner, M.J. (1982) "Biological aspects of the mother-child bond." in R. Emde and R. Harmon, eds. *Development of Attachment and Affiliation Processes*. New York: Plenum.

Krebs, D. L. (1970) "Altruism - An examination of the concept and a review of the literature." *Psychological Bulletin* 73: 258-302.

Levine, R. A. and Campbell, D. T. (eds) (1972) *Ethnocentrism: Theories of Conflict: Ethnic Attitudes and Group Behavior*. New York: Wiley.

Mackie, J. (1978) "The law of the jungle." *Philosophy* 53: 553-73.

Masters, Roger D. (1978) "Of marmots and men: Animal behavior and human altruism," in L. Wispe, ed. *Altruism, Sympathy, and Helping: Psychological and Sociological Principles*. New York: Academic Press.

Maxwell, M., ed. (1984) *Human Evolution: Philosophical Anthropology*. New York: Columbia University Press.

Midgley, M. (1978) *Beast and Man: The Biological Roots of Human Nature*. Ithaca, NY: Cornell University Press.

_____. (1979) "Gene-juggling." *Philosophy* 54: 439-58.

Nygren, A. (1982) *Agape and Eros*, trans. S. Watson. Chicago, IL: University of Chicago Press.

Outka, G. (1972) *Agape: An Ethical Analysis*. New Haven, CT: Yale University Press.

Ricks, M.H. (1985) "The social transmission of parental behavior: Attachment across generations," in I. Bretherton and E. Waters, eds. "Growing Points Attachment and Research," *Monographs of the Society for Research on Development* 50 (1-2): 211-27.

Rigby, and O' Grady, (1990) "Agape and altruism: Debates in theology and social psychology." *Journal of the American Academy of Religion*, 719-37.

Rousseau, J.J. (1987) "Discourse on the origin of inequality," in *Rousseau, The Basic Political Writings*, trans. D. A. Cress. Indianapolis, IN: Hackett.

Ruse, M. (1985) "The morality of the gene." *The Monist* 67: 167-99.

_____. (1986) *Taking Darwin Seriously*. Oxford: Basil Blackwell.

Rutter, M. (1978) "Early sources of security and competence." in J.S. Bruner and A. Garton, eds. *Human Growth and Development*. Oxford: Clarendon.

Singer, (1981) *The Expanding Circle, Ethics and Sociobiology*. New York: New American Library.

Titmuss, R.M. (1971) *The Gift Relationship*. New York: Pantheon.

Trivers, R.L. (1971) "The evolution of reciprocal altruism." *Quarterly Review of Biology* 46: 35-57.

Van den Berghe, (1979) *Human Family Systems: An Evolutionary View*, New York: Elsevier North Holland.

Williams, B. (1973) *Problems of the Self: Philosophical Papers 1956-72*. Cambridge: Cambridge University Press.

Wilson, E.O. (1975) *Sociobiology: The New Synthesis*. Cambridge, MA: Harvard University Press.

_____. (1978) *On Human Nature*, Cambridge, MA: Harvard University Press.

Evolution and Design

In 1802 William Paley argued in his *Natural Theology: or, Evidences of the Existence and Attributes of the Deity, Collected from the Appearances of Nature* that the fittedness of organs in a body and of organisms in their environment bespoke the action of a transcendent designer just as the mechanism of a watch would bespeak a watchmaker. The logic of this argument for God from design was challenged with the advent of Darwin's theory of evolution, which offered an explanation for this fittedness in the fully naturalistic terms of variation among offspring and natural selection. Today, however, there is a movement to reintroduce the idea of design in nature that involves scientists and philosophers, called the Intelligent Design movement. The papers in this section provide an introduction to that movement as well as critical assessments of it from the standpoint of biological science and philosophy.

The opening paper by William Dembski provides a history of this movement from one who is at its forefront. Dembski identifies both the people and the writings that lie at the foundation of the movement. The second article in this section is by biochemist Michael Behe, whose idea of "irreducible complexity" is one of the primary conceptual foundations of the movement. The following article by molecular biologist Kenneth Miller, although not a direct response to Behe, offers an account of how complex biochemical processes and structures can result from the ordinary processes of nature.

William Dembski's article on the "design inference" is an argument for the ability to infer design in nature based on information theory and statistical analysis. The article by Branden Fitelson, Christopher Stevens and Elliott Sober is a philosophical critique of Dembski's position.

The concluding paper is by Raymond Grizzle who is both a marine biologist and an evangelical Christian. It raises broader issues concerning the appropriateness of the contemporary "intelligent design" argument both in relation to the nature of science and in relation to the Christian theological tradition.

23

The Intelligent Design Movement

WILLIAM A. DEMBSKI

According to Darwinism, undirected natural causes are solely responsible for the origin and development of life. In particular, Darwinism rules out the possibility of God or any guiding intelligence playing a substantive role in life's origin and development. Within western culture Darwinism's ascent has been truly meteoric. And yet throughout its ascent there have always been dissenters who regarded as inadequate the Darwinian vision that undirected natural causes could produce the full diversity and complexity of life.

Until the mid 1980s this dissent was sporadic, focused largely at the grass roots, and seeking mainly to influence public opinion through the courts (and not very effectively at that). With the Intelligent Design movement this dissent has now become focused, promising to overturn the cultural dominance of Darwinism much as the freedom movements in eastern Europe overturned the political dominance of Marxism at the end of the 1980s.

The Intelligent Design movement begins with the work of Charles Thaxton, Walter Bradley, Michael Denton, Dean Kenyon, and Phillip Johnson. Without employing the Bible as a scientific text, these scholars critiqued Darwinism on scientific and philosophical grounds. On scientific grounds they found Darwinism an inadequate framework for biology. On philosophical grounds they found Darwinism hopelessly entangled with naturalism, the view that nature is self-sufficient and thus without need of God or any guiding intelligence. More recently, scholars like Michael Behe, Stephen Meyer, Paul Nelson, Jonathan Wells, and myself have taken the next step, proposing a positive research program wherein intelligent causes become the key for understanding the diversity and complexity of life.

Through this two-pronged approach of critiquing Darwinism on the one hand and providing a positive alternative on the other, the Intelligent Design movement has rapidly gained adherents among the best and brightest in the academy.   Already it is responsible for Darwinism losing its corner on the intellectual market. If fully successful, Intelligent Design will unseat not just Darwinism but also Darwinism's cultural legacy. And since no aspect of western culture has escaped Darwinism's influence, so no aspect of western culture will escape reevaluation in the light of Intelligent Design.

What then is Intelligent Design? Intelligent Design begins with the observation that intelligent causes can do things which undirected natural causes cannot. Undirected natural causes can place scrabble pieces on a board, but cannot arrange the pieces as meaningful words or sentences. To obtain a meaningful arrangement requires an intelligent cause. This intuition, that there is a fundamental distinction between undirected natural causes on the one hand and intelligent causes on the other, has underlain the design arguments of past centuries.

Throughout the centuries theologians have argued that nature exhibits features which nature itself cannot explain,   but which instead require an intelligence over and above nature. From Church fathers like Minucius Felix and Basil the Great (3rd and 4th centuries) to medieval scholastics like Moses Maimonides and Thomas Aquinas (12th and 13th centuries) to reformed thinkers like Thomas Reid and Charles Hodge (18th and 19th centuries), we find theologians making design arguments, arguing from the data of nature to an intelligence operating over and above nature.

Design arguments are old hat. Indeed, design arguments continue to be a staple of philosophy and religion courses. The most famous of the design arguments is William Paley's watchmaker argument (as in Paley's *Natural Theology*, published 1802). According to Paley, if we find a watch in a field, the watch's adaptation of means to ends (that is, the adaptation of its parts to telling time) ensure that it is the product of an intelligence, and not simply the output of undirected natural processes. So too, the marvelous adaptations of means to ends in organisms, whether at the level of whole organisms, or at the level of various subsystems (Paley focused especially on the mammalian eye), ensure that organisms are the product of an intelligence.

Though intuitively appealing, Paley's argument had until recently fallen into disuse. This is now changing. In the last five years design has witnessed an explosive resurgence. Scientists are beginning to realize that design can be rigorously formulated as a scientific theory. What has kept design outside the scientific mainstream these last hundred and thirty years is the absence of precise methods for distinguishing intelligently caused objects from unintelligently caused ones. For design to be a fruitful scientific concept, scientists have to be sure they can reliably determine whether something is designed.

Johannes Kepler thought the craters on the moon were intelligently designed by moon dwellers. We now know that the craters were formed naturally. It's this fear of falsely attributing something to design only to have it overturned later that has prevented design from entering science proper. With precise methods for discriminating intelligently from unintelligently caused objects, scientists are now able to avoid Kepler's mistake.

What has emerged is a new program for scientific research known as Intelligent Design. Within biology, Intelligent Design is a theory of biological origins and development. Its fundamental claim is that intelligent causes are necessary to explain the complex, information-rich structures of biology, and that these causes are empirically detectable.

To say intelligent causes are empirically detectable is to say there exist well-defined methods that, on the basis of observational features of the world, are capable of reliably distinguishing intelligent causes from undirected natural causes. Many special sciences have already developed such methods for drawing this distinction-notably forensic science, cryptography, archeology, and the search for extraterrestrial intelligence (as in the movie *Contact*).

Whenever these methods detect intelligent causation, the underlying entity they uncover is information. Intelligent Design properly formulated is a theory of information. Within such a theory, information becomes a reliable indicator of intelligent causation as well as a proper object for scientific investigation. Intelligent Design thereby becomes a theory for detecting and measuring information, explaining its origin, and tracing its flow. Intelligent Design is therefore not the study of intelligent causes per se, but of informational pathways induced by intelligent causes.

As a result, Intelligent Design presupposes neither a creator nor miracles. Intelligent Design is theologically minimalist. It detects intelligence without speculating about the nature of the intelligence. Biochemist Michael Behe's "irreducible complexity," physicist David Bohm's "active information," mathematician Marcel Schützenberger's "functional complexity," and my own "complex specified information" are alternate routes to the same reality.

It is the empirical detectability of intelligent causes that renders Intelligent Design a fully scientific theory, and distinguishes it from the design arguments of philosophers, or what has traditionally been called "natural theology." The world contains events, objects, and structures which exhaust the explanatory resources of undirected natural causes, and which can be adequately explained only by recourse to intelligent causes. Scientists are now in a position to demonstrate this rigorously. Thus what has been a long-standing philosophical intuition is now being cashed out as a scientific research program.

Intelligent Design entails that naturalism in all forms be rejected. Metaphysical naturalism, the view that undirected natural causes wholly govern the world, is to be rejected because it is false. Methodological naturalism, the view that for the sake of science, scientific explanation ought never exceed undirected natural causes, is to be rejected because it stifles inquiry. Nothing is gained by pretending science can get along without intelligent causes. Rather, because intelligent causes are empirically detectable, science must ever remain open to evidence of their activity.

Where does this leave special creation and theistic evolution? Logically speaking, Intelligent Design is compatible with everything from the starkest creationism (i.e., God intervening at every point to create new species) to the most subtle and far-ranging evolution (i.e., God seamlessly melding all organisms together in a great tree of life). For Intelligent Design the first question is not how organisms came to be (though this is a research question that needs to be addressed), but whether they demonstrate clear, empirically detectable marks of being intelligently caused. In principle, an evolutionary process can exhibit such "marks of intelligence" as much as any act of special creation.

If you're a Christian, what is the theological payoff of Intelligent Design? It is important to realize that Intelligent Design is not an apologetic ploy to cajole people into God's Kingdom. Intelligent Design is a scientific research program.

That said, Intelligent Design does have implications for theology. The most severe challenge to theology over the last two hundred years has been naturalism. Within western culture, naturalism has become the default position for all serious inquiry. From biblical studies to law to education to art to science to the media, inquiry is expected to proceed only under the supposition of naturalism.

C. S. Lewis put it this way: "Naturalistic assumptions ... meet you on every side.... It comes partly from what we may call a "hangover." We all have Naturalism in our bones and even conversion does not at once work the infection out of our system. Its assumptions rush back upon the mind the moment vigilance is relaxed." (quoted from *Miracles*)

By making the design in nature evident, Intelligent Design promises to cure western culture of this unfortunate Enlightenment hangover. Indeed, Intelligent Design provides the clearest refutation of naturalism to date. Naturalism looks to science to justify its rejection of purpose in nature. Intelligent Design shows that naturalism fails on its own terms. To be sure, there are good philosophical reasons for rejecting naturalism—the very existence of the world and the intelligibility of the world raise questions which science cannot answer, and which point beyond the world. Intelligent Design shows there are also good scientific reasons for rejecting naturalism.

For Further Study:

The Intelligent Design movement begins with the publication of *The Mystery of Life's Origin* by Charles Thaxton, Walter Bradley, and Roger Olson (Philosophical Library, 1984) and *Evolution: A Theory in Crisis* by Michael Denton (Alder & Adler, 1986). These two books presented a powerful scientific critique of evolutionary theory. Moreover, they set the tone for subsequent publications by refusing to mix the scientific evidence for design with theological views about creation.

The next key text in the movement was Phillip Johnson's *Darwin on Trial* (InterVarsity, 1991). Johnson not only reviewed the scientific evidence against evolutionary theory, but also showed how evolutionary theory was hopelessly compromised with naturalism. Johnson continued his analysis in *Reason in the Balance* (InterVarsity, 1995) and *Defeating Darwinism by Opening Minds* (InterVarsity, 1997).

Dean Kenyon and Percival Davis's *Of Pandas and People* (Haughton, 1993) and J. P. Moreland's *Creation Hypothesis* (InterVarsity, 1994) proved transitional texts. Whereas previous texts criticized evolutionary theory without offering a positive alternative, these texts began examining what a design-theoretic alternative to evolutionary theory would look like.

With the publication of Michael Behe's Darwin's *Black Box* (Free Press, 1996) the dam burst. Here for the first time were the outlines of a full-fledged scientific research program for design in biology. Behe's book was reviewed everywhere from *Science* and *Nature* to the *New York Times* and the *Wall Street Journal*. It was voted *Christianity Today's* "Book of the Year." Its impact has been phenomenal.

My own books started to appear fall of 1998. Key researchers with books in preparation include Stephen Meyer, Paul Nelson, Del Ratzsch, John Mark Reynolds, and John Wells. The movement has a professional journal entitled Origins & Design (www.arn.org). The Discovery Institute's Center for the Renewal of Science and Culture coordinates many of its efforts (www.discovery.org). Baylor University's Michael Polanyi Center* focuses on turning intelligent design into a fruitful research program for the natural sciences (www.baylor.edu/~polanyi).

---

* **Editor's Note:** In 2000 the name of Michael Polanyi was removed from this Center, its focus was broadened and it became more directly a program if the Baylor Institute on Faith and Learning. Its URL is inactive.

24

Evidence for Intelligent Design from Biochemistry

MICHAEL J. BEHE

A Series of Eyes

How do we see? In the 19th century the anatomy of the eye was known in great detail, and its sophisticated features astounded everyone who was familiar with them. Scientists of the time correctly observed that if a person were so unfortunate as to be missing one of the eye's many integrated features, such as the lens, or iris, or ocular muscles, the inevitable result would be a severe loss of vision or outright blindness. So it was concluded that the eye could only function if it were nearly intact.

Charles Darwin knew about the eye too. In the *Origin of Species*, Darwin dealt with many objections to his theory of evolution by natural selection. He discussed the problem of the eye in a section of the book appropriately entitled "Organs of extreme perfection and complication." Somehow, for evolution to be believable, Darwin had to convince the public that complex organs could be formed gradually, in a step-by-step process.

He succeeded brilliantly. Cleverly, Darwin didn't try to discover a real pathway that evolution might have used to make the eye. Instead, he pointed to modern animals with different kinds of eyes, ranging from the simple to the complex, and suggested that the evolution of the human eye might have involved similar organs as intermediates.

Here is a paraphrase of Darwin's argument. Although humans have complex camera-type eyes, many animals get by with less. Some tiny creatures have just a simple group of pigmented cells, or not much more than a light sensitive spot. That simple arrangement can hardly be said to confer vision, but it can sense light and dark, and so it meets the creature's needs. The light-sensing organ of some starfishes is somewhat more sophisticated. Their eye is located in a depressed region. This allows the animal to sense which direction the light is coming from, since the curvature of the depression blocks off light from some directions. If the curvature becomes more pronounced, the directional sense of the eye improves. But more curvature lessens the amount of light that enters the eye, decreasing its sensitivity. The sensitivity can be increased by placement of gelatinous material in the cavity to act as a lens. Some modern animals have eyes with such crude lenses. Gradual improvements in the lens could then provide an image of increasing sharpness, as the requirements of the animal's environment dictated.

Using reasoning like this, Darwin convinced many of his readers that an evolutionary pathway leads from the simplest light sensitive spot to the sophisticated camera-eye of man. But the question remains, how did vision begin? Darwin persuaded much of the world that a modern eye evolved gradually from a simpler structure, but he did not even try to explain where his starting point for the simple light sensitive spot came from. On the contrary, Darwin dismissed the question of the eye's ultimate origin.

How a nerve comes to be sensitive to light hardly concerns us more than how life itself originated. He had an excellent reason for declining the question: it was completely beyond nineteenth century science. How the eye works; that is, what happens when a photon of light first hits the retina simply could not be answered at that time. As a matter of fact, no question about the underlying mechanisms of life could be answered. How did animal muscles cause movement? How did photosynthesis work? How was energy extracted from food? How did the body fight infection? No one knew.

To Darwin vision was a black box, but today, after the hard, cumulative work of many biochemists, we are approaching answers to the question of sight. Here is a brief overview of the biochemistry of vision. When light first strikes the retina, a photon interacts with a molecule called 11-cis-retinal, which rearranges within picoseconds to trans-retinal. The change in the shape of retinal forces a change in the shape of the protein, rhodopsin, to which the retinal is tightly bound. The protein's metamorphosis alters its behavior, making it stick to another protein called transducin. Before bumping into activated rhodopsin, transducin had tightly bound a small molecule called GDP. But when transducin interacts with activated rhodopsin, the GDP falls off and a molecule called GTP binds to transducin. (GTP is closely related to, but critically different from, GDP.)

GTP-transducin-activated rhodopsin now binds to a protein called phosphodiesterase, located in the inner membrane of the cell. When attached to activated rhodopsin and its entourage, the phosphodiesterase acquires the ability to chemically cut a molecule called cGMP (a chemical relative of both GDP and GTP). Initially there are a lot of cGMP molecules in the cell, but the phosphodiesterase lowers its concentration, like a pulled plug lowers the water level in a bathtub.

Another membrane protein that binds cGMP is called an ion channel. It acts as a gateway that regulates the number of sodium ions in the cell. Normally the ion channel allows sodium ions to flow into the cell, while a separate protein actively pumps them out again. The dual action of the ion channel and pump keeps the level of sodium ions in the cell within a narrow range. When the amount of cGMP is reduced because of cleavage by the phosphodiesterase, the ion channel closes, causing the cellular concentration of positively charged sodium ions to be reduced. This causes an imbalance of charge across the cell membrane which, finally, causes a current to be transmitted down the optic nerve to the brain. The result, when interpreted by the brain, is vision.

My explanation is just a sketchy overview of the biochemistry of vision. Ultimately, though, this is what it means to "explain" vision. This is the level of explanation for which biological science must aim. In order to truly understand a function, one must understand in detail every relevant step in the process. The relevant steps in biological processes occur ultimately at the molecular level, so a satisfactory explanation of a biological phenomenon such as vision, or digestion, or immunity must include its molecular explanation.

Now that the black box of vision has been opened it is no longer enough for an "evolutionary explanation" of that power to consider only the anatomical structures of whole eyes, as Darwin did in the nineteenth century, and as popularizers of evolution continue to do today. Each of the anatomical steps and structures that Darwin thought were so simple actually involves staggeringly complicated biochemical processes that cannot be papered over with rhetoric. Darwin's simple steps are now revealed to be huge leaps between carefully tailored machines. Thus biochemistry offers a Lilliputian challenge to Darwin. Now the black box of the cell has been opened and a Lilliputian world of staggering complexity stands revealed. It must be explained.

Irreducible Complexity

How can we decide if Darwin's theory can account for the complexity of molecular life? It turns out that Darwin himself set the standard. He acknowledged that:

> If it could be demonstrated that any complex organ existed which could not possibly have been formed by numerous, successive, slight modifications, my theory would absolutely break down. But what type

of biological system could not be formed by "numerous, successive, slight modifications"?

Well, for starters, a system that is irreducibly complex. Irreducible complexity is just a fancy phrase I use to mean a single system which is composed of several interacting parts, and where the removal of any one of the parts causes the system to cease functioning.

Let's consider an everyday example of irreducible complexity: the humble mousetrap. The mousetraps that my family uses consist of a number of parts. There are: 1) a flat wooden platform to act as a base; 2) a metal hammer, which does the actual job of crushing the little mouse; 3) a spring with extended ends to press against the platform and the hammer when the trap is charged; 4) a sensitive catch which releases when slight pressure is applied, and 5) a metal bar which connects to the catch and holds the hammer back when the trap is charged. Now you can't catch a few mice with just a platform, add a spring and catch a few more mice, add a holding bar and catch a few more. All the pieces of the mousetrap have to be in place before you catch any mice. Therefore the mousetrap is irreducibly complex.

An irreducibly complex system cannot be produced directly by numerous, successive, slight modifications of a precursor system, because any precursor to an irreducibly complex system that is missing a part is by definition nonfunctional. An irreducibly complex biological system, if there is such a thing, would be a powerful challenge to Darwinian evolution. Since natural selection can only choose systems that are already working, then if a biological system cannot be produced gradually it would have to arise as an integrated unit, in one fell swoop, for natural selection to have anything to act on.

Demonstration that a system is irreducibly complex is not a proof that there is absolutely no gradual route to its production. Although an irreducibly complex system can't be produced directly, one can't definitively rule out the possibility of an indirect, circuitous route. However, as the complexity of an interacting system increases, the likelihood of such an indirect route drops precipitously. And as the number of unexplained, irreducibly complex biological systems increases, our confidence that Darwin's criterion of failure has been met skyrockets toward the maximum that science allows.

The Cilium

Now, are any biochemical systems irreducibly complex? Yes, it turns out that many are. A good example is the cilium. Cilia are hairlike structures on the surfaces of many animal and lower plant cells that can move fluid over the cell's surface or "row" single cells through a fluid. Inhumans, for example, cells lining the respiratory tract each have about 200 cilia that beat in synchrony to sweep mucus towards the throat for elimination. What is the structure of a cilium? A cilium consists of bundle of fibers called an axoneme. An axoneme contains a ring of 9 double "microtubules" surrounding two central single microtubules. Each outer doublet consists of a ring of 13 filaments (subfiber A) fused to an assembly of 10 filaments (subfiber B). The filaments of the microtubules are composedof two proteins called alpha and beta tubulin. The 11 microtubules forming an axoneme are held together by three types of connectors: subfibers A are joined to the central microtubules by radial spokes; adjacent outer doublets are joined by linkers of a highly elastic protein called nexin; and the central microtubules are joined by a connecting bridge. Finally, every subfiber A bears two arms, an inner arm and an outer arm, both containing a protein called dynein.

But how does a cilium work? Experiments have shown that ciliary motion results from the chemically-powered "walking" of the dynein arms on one microtubule up a second microtubule so that the two microtubules slide past each other. The protein cross-links between microtubules in a cilium prevent neighboring microtubules from sliding past each other by more than a short distance. These cross-links, therefore, convert the dynein-induced sliding motion to a bending motion of the entire axoneme.

Now, let us consider what this implies. What components are needed for a cilium to work? Ciliary motion certainly requires microtubules; otherwise, there would be no strands to slide. Additionally we require a motor, or else the microtubules of the cilium would lie stiff and motionless. Furthermore, we require linkers to tug on neighboring strands, converting the sliding motion into a bending motion, and preventing the structure from falling apart. All of these parts are required to perform one function: ciliary motion. Just as a mousetrap does not work unless all of its constituent parts are present, ciliary motion simply does not exist in the absence of microtubules, connectors, and motors. Therefore, we can conclude that the cilium is irreducibly complex; an enormous monkey wrench thrown into its presumed gradual, Darwinian evolution.

Blood Clotting

Now let's talk about a different biochemical system of blood clotting. Amusingly, the way in which the blood clotting system works is reminiscent of a Rube Goldberg machine.

The name of Rube Goldberg; the great cartoonist who entertained America with his silly machines, lives on in our culture, but the man himself has pretty much faded from view. Here's a typical example of his humor. In this cartoon Goldberg imagined a system where water from a drain-pipe fills a flask, causing a cork with attached needle to rise and puncture a paper cup containing beer, which sprinkles on a bird.   The intoxicated bird falls onto a spring, bounces up to a platform, and pulls a string thinking it's a worm. The string triggers a cannon which frightens a dog. The dog flips over, and his rapid breathing raises and lowers a scratcher over a mosquito bite, causing no embarrassment while talking to a lady.

When you think about it for a moment you realize that the Rube Goldberg machine is irreducibly complex. It is a single system which is composed of several interacting parts, and where the removal of any one of the parts causes the system to break down. If the dog is missing the machine doesn't work; if the needle hasn't been put on the cork, the whole system is useless.

It turns out that we all have Rube Goldberg in our blood. Here's a picture of a cell trapped in a clot. The meshwork is formed from a protein called fibrin. But what controls blood clotting? Why does blood clot when you cut yourself, but not at other times when a clot would cause a stroke or heart attack? Here's a diagram of what's called the blood clotting cascade. Let's go through just some of the reactions of clotting.

When an animal is cut a protein called Hageman factor sticks to the surface of cells near the wound. Bound Hageman factor is then cleaved by a protein called HMK to yield activated Hageman factor.   Immediately the activated Hageman factor converts another protein, called prekallikrein, to its active form, kallikrein. Kallikrein helps HMK speed up the conversion of more Hageman factor to its active form. Activated Hageman factor and HMK then together transform another protein, called PTA, to its active form. Activated PTA in turn, together with the activated form of another protein (discussed below) called convertin, switch a protein called Christmas factor to its active form. Activated Christmas factor, together with antihemophilic factor (which is itself activated by thrombin in a manner similar to that of proaccelerin) changes Stuart factor to its active form. Stuart factor,working with accelerin, converts prothrombin to thrombin. Finally thrombin cuts fibrinogen to give fibrin, which aggregates with other fibrin molecules to form the meshwork clot you saw in the last picture.

Blood clotting requires extreme precision. When a pressurized blood circulation system is punctured, a clot must form quickly or the animal will bleed to death. On the other hand, if blood congeals at the wrong time or place, then the clot may block circulation as it does in heart attacks and strokes. Furthermore, a clot has to stop bleeding all along the length of the cut, sealing it completely. Yet blood clotting must be confined to the cut or the entire blood system of the animal might solidify, killing it. Consequently, clotting requires this enormously complex system so that the clot forms only when and only where it is required. Blood clotting is the ultimate Rube Goldberg machine.

The Professional Literature

Other examples of irreducible complexity abound in the cell, including aspects of protein transport, the bacterial flagellum, electron transport, telomeres, photosynthesis, transcription regulation, and much more. Examples of irreducible complexity can be found on virtually every page of a biochemistry textbook. But if these things cannot be explained by Darwinian evolution, how has the scientific community regarded these phenomena of the past forty years? A good place to look for an answer to that question is in the *Journal of Molecular Evolution*. JME is a journal that was begun specifically to deal with the topic of how evolution occurs on the molecular level. It has high scientific standards, and is edited by prominent figures in the field. In a recent issue of JME there were published eleven articles; of these, all eleven were concerned simply with the comparison of protein or DNA sequences. A sequence comparison is an amino acid-by-amino acid comparison of two different proteins, or a nucleotide-by-nucleotide comparison of two different pieces of DNA, noting the positions at which they are identical or similar, and the places where they are not. Although useful for determining possible lines of descent, which is an interesting question in its own right, comparing sequences cannot show how a complex biochemical system achieved its function; the question that most concerns us here. By way of analogy, the instruction manuals for two different models of computer putout by the same company might have many identical words, sentences, and even paragraphs, suggesting a common ancestry (perhaps the same author wrote both manuals), but comparing the sequences of letters in the instruction manuals will never tell us if a computer can be produced step by step starting from a typewriter.

None of the papers discussed detailed models for intermediates in the development of complex biomolecular structures. In the past ten years JME has published over a thousand papers. Of these, about one hundred discussed the chemical synthesis of molecules thought to be necessary for the origin of life, about 50 proposed mathematical models to improve sequence analysis, and about 800 were analyses of sequences. There were ZERO papers discussing detailed models for intermediates in the development of complex biomolecular structures. This is not a peculiarity of JME. No papers are to be found that discuss detailed models for intermediates in the development of complex biomolecular structures in the *Proceedings of the National Academy of Science*,

Nature, *Science*, the *Journal of Molecular Biology* or, to my knowledge, any science journal whatsoever.

"Publish or perish" is a proverb that academicians take seriously. If you do not publish your work for the rest of the community to evaluate, then you have no business in academia and, if you don't already have tenure, you will be banished. But the saying can be applied to theories as well. If a theory claims to be able to explain some phenomenon but does not generate even an attempt at an explanation, then it should be banished. Despite comparing sequences, molecular evolution has never addressed the question of how complex structures came to be. In effect, the theory of Darwinian molecular evolution has not published, and so it should perish.

Detection of Design

What's going on? Imagine a room in which a body lies crushed, flat as a pancake. A dozen detectives crawl around, examining the floor with magnifying glasses for any clue to the identity of the perpetrator. In the middle of the room next to the body stands a large, gray elephant. The detectives carefully avoid bumping into the pachyderm's legs as they crawl, and never even glance at it. Over time the detectives get frustrated with their lack of progress but resolutely press on, looking even more closely at the floor. You see, textbooks say detectives must "get their man," so they never consider elephants.

There is an elephant in the roomful of scientists who are trying to explain the development of life. The elephant is labeled "intelligent design." To a person who does not feel obliged to restrict his search to unintelligent causes, the straightforward conclusion is that many biochemical systems were designed. They were designed not by the laws of nature, not by chance and necessity. Rather, they were planned. The designer knew what the systems would look like when they were completed; the designer took steps to bring the systems about. Life on earth at its most fundamental level, in its most critical components, is the product of intelligent activity.

The conclusion of intelligent design flows naturally from the data itself, not from sacred books or sectarian beliefs. Inferring that biochemical systems were designed by an intelligent agent is a humdrum process that requires no new principles of logic or science. It comes simply from the hard work that biochemistry has done over the past forty years, combined with consideration of the way in which we reach conclusions of design every day.

What is "design"? Design is simply the purposeful arrangement of parts. The scientific question is how we detect design. This can be done in various ways, but design can most easily be inferred for mechanical objects. While walking through a junkyard you might observe separated bolts and screws and bits of plastic and glass, most scattered, some piled on top of each other, some wedged together. Suppose you saw a pile that seemed particularly compact, and when you picked up a bar sticking out of the pile, the whole pile came along with it. When you pushed on the bar it slid smoothly to one side of the pile and pulled an attached chain along with it. The chain in turn yanked a gear which turned three other gears which turned a red-and-white striped rod, spinning it like a barber pole. You quickly conclude that the pile was not a chance accumulation of junk, but was designed, was put together in that order by an intelligent agent, because you see that the components of the system interact with great specificity to do something.

It is not only artificial mechanical systems for which design can easily be concluded. Systems made entirely from natural components can also evince design. For example, suppose you are walking with a friend in the woods. All of a sudden your friend is pulled high in the air and left dangling by his foot from a vine attached to a tree branch. After cutting him down you reconstruct the trap. You see that the vine was wrapped around the tree branch, and the end pulled tightly down to the ground. It was securely anchored to the ground by a forked branch. The branch was attached to another vine, hidden by leaves so that, when the trigger-vine was disturbed, it would pull down the forked stick, releasing the spring-vine. The end of the vine formed a loop with a slipknot to grab an appendage and snap it up into the air. Even though the trap was made completely of natural materials you would quickly conclude that it was the product of intelligent design.

A Complicated World

A word of caution; intelligent design theory has to be seen in context: it does not try to explain everything. We live in a complex world where lots of different things can happen. When deciding how various rocks came to be shaped the way they are a geologist might consider a whole range of factors: rain, wind, the movement of glaciers, the activity of moss and lichens, volcanic action, nuclear explosions, asteroid impact, or the hand of a sculptor. The shape of one rock might have been determined primarily by one mechanism, the shape of another rock by another mechanism. The possibility of a meteor's impact does not mean that volcanos can be ignored; the existence of sculptors does not mean that many rocks are not shaped by weather. Similarly, evolutionary biologists have recognized that a number of factors might have affected the development of life: common descent, natural selection, migration, population size, founder effects (effects that may be due to the limited number of organisms that begin a new species), genetic drift (spread of neutral, nonselective mutations), gene flow (the incorporation of genes into a population from a separate population), linkage (occurrence of two genes on the same chromosome), meiotic drive (the preferential selection during sex cell production of one of the two copies of a gene inherited from an organism's parents), transposition (the transfer of a gene between widely separated species by non-sexual means), and much more. The fact that some biochemical systems were designed by an intelligent agent does not mean that any of the other factors are not operative, common, or important.

Curiouser and Curiouser

So as this talk concludes we are left with what many people feel to be a strange conclusion: that life was designed by an intelligent agent. In a way, though, all of the progress of science over the last several hundred years has been a steady march toward the strange. People up until the middle ages lived in a natural world. The stable earth was at the center of things; the sun, moon, and stars circled endlessly to give light by day and night; the same plants and animals had been known since antiquity. Surprises were few.

Then it was proposed, absurdly, that the earth itself moved, spinning while it circled the sun. No one could feel the earth spinning; no one could see it. But spin it did. From our modern vantage it's hard to realize what an assault on the senses was perpetrated by Copernicus and Galileo; they said in effect that people could no longer rely on even the evidence of their eyes.

Things got steadily worse over the years. With the discovery of fossils it became apparent that the familiar animals of field and forest had not always been on earth; the world had once been inhabited by huge, alien creatures who were now gone. Sometime later Darwin shook the world by arguing that the familiar biota was derived from the bizarre, vanished life over lengths of time incomprehensible to human minds. Einstein told us that space is curved and time is relative. Modern physics says that solid objects are mostly space, that sub atomic particles have no definite position, that the universe had a beginning.

Now it's the turn of the fundamental science of life, modern biochemistry, to disturb. The simplicity that was once expected to be the foundation of life has proven to be a phantom. Instead, systems of horrendous, irreducible complexity inhabit the cell. The resulting realization that life was designed by an intelligence is a shock to us in the twentieth century who have gotten used to thinking of life as the result of simple natural laws. But other centuries have had their shocks and there is no reason to suppose that we should escape them. Humanity has endured as the center of the heavens moved from the earth to beyond the sun, as the history of life expanded to encompass long-dead reptiles, as the eternal universe proved mortal. We will endure the opening of Darwin's black box.

25

Life's Grand Design

KENNETH R. MILLER

Though some insist that life as we know it sprang from a Grand Designer's Original blueprints, biology offers new evidence that organisms were cobbled together layer upon layer by a timeless tinkerer called evolution.

"The relief prayed for is granted." With those words, on January 5, 1982, Federal Judge William K. Overton struck down a state law that would have mandated the teaching of creation-science in the public schools of Arkansas. Overton's decision followed an extraordinary public trial in which a series of scientific heavyweights, including Harvard's Steven J. Gould, persuasively argued in court that "creation-science" was a religious idea that did not meet the generally-accepted tests for scientific theory. As such, the Arkansas creation-science law had the primary effect of advancing a religion in the public schools, and was invalidated under the First Amendment's clause prohibiting establishment of religion. A similar law in Louisiana was invalidated shortly thereafter. Case closed? Not at all.

There is a new movement to counter the teaching of evolution in the schools, and it claims to be based on a non-religious critique of evolution. In many respects, the anti-evolution crusades of the '80s may have failed because they were aimed too high at State Boards of Education and Legislatures. The public pressure was obvious, easily recognized, and quickly invalidated by court orders and scientific counterattacks. This time the opponents of evolution have targeted a campaign at the grassroots at local school boards and it looks like they are having some success.

In September of 1993, an anti-evolution majority of newly elected board of education members in Vista, California voted to implement a "creation-science" component as part of their biology curriculum. The science teachers of the district were critical of the decision, and their textbook selection committee flatly rejected a book put forward to support anti-evolution teachings. Backing down only slightly, the elected local board has now instructed the schools to include "discussions of divine creation " at "appropriate times" in the social science and language arts curricula.   Similar actions have been urged upon scores of school boards around the country, and in some places, challenges to evolution are already part of the standard curriculum. Since 1986, for example, the school board of Louisville, Ohio, has directed its teachers to teach "alternate theories to evolution" The centerpiece of these challenges to evolution is something that has become known as "intelligent design theory."

Intelligent design has been embraced by critics of evolution around the country who are eager to find an seemingly non-religious alternative to the teaching of evolution. Intelligent design is the modern synthesis of a classic argument that an engineer would love. Quite simply, it states that living organisms are the product of careful and conscious design. A close examination of living organisms, so the argument goes, reveals details of structure and physiology that cannot be accounted for by the workings of evolution. Therefore, these organisms must be the products of design.

The Argument from Design

If you were walking through the woods, and saw two objects lying on the ground, a stone and a pocket watch, what would your first thoughts be? Suppose a companion asked you where the stone and the pocket watch had come from? You might well have laughed as you answered that for all you knew, the stone had been there forever. It's safe to say, however, that you would not have given that answer concerning the watch. It could not have been there forever, for the very simple reason that it was produced by a watch-maker, and watch-makers have not existed forever. Every gear, spring, and screw in a watch is evidence of the fact that watches are not natural objects that have existed forever. Rather, they have been produced by the conscious design and handiwork of watch-makers.

In 1802, Rev. William Paley of Carlisle made that argument in his book *Natural Theology*. As you might suspect, watches and stones were not the real objects of his interest, for Paley was concerned with a timeless question that still rivets our attention nearly two centuries later. With all of its astonishing variety, complexity, and diversity, did life itself have a designer? To Paley, the answer was clear.

> ... There cannot be design without a designer; contrivance without a
> contriver ... The marks of design are too strong to be got over. Design

must have had a designer. That designer must have been a person. That person is GOD.

Paley's writings form one of the most lucid examples of a train of reasoning known as the "Argument from Design." In various forms, it has served for centuries as a classic argument for the existence of God, and more recently, as a counter-argument for a very different explanation of the diversity of living species. That alternative explanation was advanced more than 50 years after Paley by his countryman, Charles Darwin. Darwin's "abstract" of his work, *On the Origin of Species*, was an instant scientific and popular sensation. The theory of evolution, as Darwin's ideas have come to be known, accounts for the origin of living species in ways that could not be more different from those of William Paley. In Darwin's world, living things did not have a conscious, intelligent designer. Instead of being designed, their exquisite adaptations and specializations were the products of natural selection, acting on the raw materials of variation and genetic change.

Paley's argument for conscious design was well known to Darwin, and he answered it effectively, showing that natural selection could account for many of the classic examples of structures and organs that were thought to demand conscious design. But Darwin did not put the argument from design to rest. Far from it. The modern advocates of this argument now clamor for a place in the science classroom under the banner of "intelligent design theory." In fact, a modern restatement of the argument is found in the book *Of Pandas and People* by Percival Davis & Dean Kenyon. This well-illustrated 170 page text is the very book rejected by Vista's science teachers in 1993. Despite this recent setback, *Of Pandas and People* is often put forward as an example of how intelligent design might be placed in the biology classroom.

The book argues that "In creating a new organism, as in building a new house, the blueprint comes first. We cannot build a palace by tinkering with a tool shed and adding bits of marble piecemeal here and there. We have to begin by devising a plan for the palace that coordinates all the parts into an integrated whole. Darwinian evolution locates the origin of new organisms in material causes, the accumulation of individual traits. That is akin to saying the origin of a palace is in the bits of marble added to the tool shed. Intelligent design, by contrast, locates the origin of new organisms in an immaterial cause: in a blueprint, a plan, a pattern, devised by an intelligent agent."

Of all the arguments that have been advanced against evolution, intelligent design is the most appealing, most common, and in my view, the most effective. The reasons should be obvious. First, the argument is easy to make and easy to understand. Second, the argument appeals to the emotional sense that we, and other living things, are what we are and where we are as the conscious result of intelligent design. Third, and most telling, the argument seems strengthened by each advance in our understanding of the complexity of life. The grander the palace, the greater the leap of imagination that is required to imagine that it could have been constructed by "tinkering with a tool shed."

I would not argue, even for a minute, that living organisms are not complex or intricate. In fact, I'd claim that even William Paley underestimated the complexity of living organisms by several orders of magnitude. One case in point is a structure often cited as a perfect example of intelligent design: the human eye. Indeed, the eye is often compared to a camera, but such comparisons are unfair. The eye is better than any camera.

Like a top-of-the-line modern camera, the eye contains a self-adjusting aperture, and an automatic focus system. Like a camera, its inner surfaces are surrounded by dark pigment to minimize the scattering of stray light. However, the sensitivity range of the eye, which gives us excellent vision in bright sunlight as well as in the dimmest moonlight, far surpasses that of any film. The neural circuitry of the eye produces automatic contrast enhancement and sensitivity to motion. Its color analysis system enables it to quickly adjust to lighting conditions (incandescent, fluorescent, and sunlight) that would require a photographer to change film or add filters.

Finally, the eye-brain combination produces depth perception that is still beyond the range of an camera or video system. Just ask your local photo or video engineer to design a system that will calculate, from a snapshot, the exact force required to sink a basket, on the run, from 25 feet away. Charles Barkley and his NBA colleagues perform such calculations with astonishing regularity, all based on the information that their eyes acquire in a split second glance at the basket.

The argument from design asserts that the combination of nerves, sensory cells, muscles, and lens tissue in the eye could only have been "designed" from scratch. It would be too much, the argument goes, to ask evolution, acting on one gene at a time, to assemble so many interdependent parts. After all, how could evolution start with a sightless organism and produce a retina, which would itself be useless without a lens, or a lens, which would be useless without a retina? As Paley himself wrote: "Is it possible to believe that the eye was formed without any regard to vision; that it was the animal itself which found out, that, although formed with no such intention, it would serve to see with?"

Complex physiological systems are not the only cases to which the argument from design can be applied. One might well ask whether the careful and precise movements of cells and tissues during human embryonic development do not argue for the role of intelligent design, rather than evolution, in the formation of the structures of a new human life. The intricacies of the human genome, with its 6 billion base pairs of DNA encoding an estimated 100,000 genes, can also be taken as an argument for intelligent design. Proponents of intelligent design often compare the DNA sequence of the genome to a computer program, powerful and flexible and carefully designed. Surely the chance forces of evolution could not assemble so much purposeful complexity, and surely the very sequences of human DNA argue for intelligent design.

Evolution as a Creative Force

Intelligent-Design advocates content that evolution could not have produced such complex structures and processes because its instrument, natural selection, simply isn't up to the test. Such advocates agree that natural selection does a splendid job of working on the variation that exists within a species. Given a range of sizes, shapes, and colors, those individuals whose characteristics give them the best chance to reproduce will pass on traits that will increase in frequency in the next generation. The real issue, therefore, is whether or not the "input" into genetic variation, which is often said to be the result of random mutation, can provide the beneficial novelty that would be required to produce new structures, new systems, and even new species. Could the marvelous structures of the eye have been produced "just by chance"?

The simple answer to that question is "no." The extraordinary number of physiological and structural changes that would have to appear at once to make a working, functioning eye is simply too much to leave to chance. The eye could not have evolved in a single event. That, however, is not the end of the story. The real test is whether or not the long-term combination of genetic variation and natural selection could indeed produce a structure as complex and well-adapted as the eye, and the answer to that question is a resounding "yes."

The pathway by which evolution can produce such structures has been explained many times, most recently in Richard Dawkins' extraordinary book, *The Blind Watchmaker*. The essence of Dawkins' explanation is simple. Given time (thousands of years) and material (millions of individuals in a species), many genetic changes will occur that result in slight improvements in a structure or system. However slight that improvement, so long as it is a genuine improvement, natural selection will favor its spread throughout the species over several generations.

Little by little, one improvement at a time, the system becomes more and more complex, eventually resulting in the fully-functioning, well-adapted organ that we call the eye. The retina and the lens did not have to evolve separately, because they evolved together. As Dawkins is careful to point out, this does not mean that evolution can account for any imaginable structure, which may be why living organisms do not have biological wheels, X-ray vision, or microwave transmitters.

But evolution can be used as an explanation for complex structures, if we can imagine a series of small, intermediate steps leading from the simplex to the complex. Further, because natural selection will act on every one of those intermediates, these intermediate steps cannot be justified on the basis of where they are going (the final structure). Each step must stand on its own as an improvement that confers an advantage on the organism that possesses it.

Evolution of the eye: A complex eye could easily have evolved from a simple eyespot through a series of minor and reasonable variations. When a change conferred even a slight advantage, it would have spread throughout the population over several generations.

This step-by-step process is the real reason why it is unfair to characterize evolution as "mere chance," even though chance plays a role in it. The continuing power of natural selection fine-tunes each stage of the process in a way that is not determined by chance. Can we apply this step-by-step criterion to a complex organ like the eye? Yes, we can, quite easily in fact. We can begin with the simplest possible case, a small animal with a single light-sensitive cell. We can then ask, at each stage, whether natural selection would favor the incremental changes that are shown, knowing that it if would not, the final structure could not have evolved, no matter how beneficial.

Starting with the simplest light-sensing device, a single photoreceptor cell, it is easy to draw a series of incremental changes that would lead, step-by-step, directly to lens-and-retina eye. None of the intermediate stages requires anything more than an incremental change in structure: an increase in cell number, a change in surface curvature, a slight increase in transparency. Therefore, all the changes are reasonable.

The critic might ask what good that first tiny step, perhaps only 5% of an eye, might be. As the saying goes, in the land of the blind, the one-eyed man is king. In a population with limited ability to sense light, every slight improvement is favored, even if it represents only 5% of an eye. If each individual, incremental change would be favored by natural selection, the whole sequence is would be favored as well. Since none of the steps involves an unreasonable genetic change, the contention that evolution cannot explain the evolution of a complex eye is refuted.

One might rightly claim, of course, that if this were really true, then evolution should have driven the independent development of light-sensing abilities in scores of organisms. Has it? In their 1992 review of the evolution of vision, Michael F. Land and Russell D. Fernald cite evidence that primitive eye-spot light-sensing systems have evolved independently as many as 65 times, and that more complex image-forming systems have evolved many times, employing roughly 10 optically distinct image-formation mechanisms. In the mollusks alone, distinct light-sensing systems exist that bear an uncanny resemblance to each of the stages in our hypothetical scheme. Obviously, each of these intermediates has to be considered reasonable if an organism living today possesses it.

Flawed Designs

If we can account for the evolution of complex structures by incremental advances, this might seem to leave us with no way to distinguish design from evolution. Evolution, then, might have produced such structures. But did it? In fact, there is a way to tell. Evolution, unlike design, works by the modification of pre-existing structures. Intelligent design, by definition, works fresh, on a clean sheet of paper, and should produce organisms that have been explicitly (and perfectly) designed for the tasks they perform.

Evolution, on the other hand, does not produce perfection. The fact that every intermediate stage in the development of an organ must confer a selective advantage means that the simplest and most elegant design for an organ cannot always be produced by evolution. In fact, the hallmark of evolution is the modification of pre-existing structures. An evolved organism, in short, should show the tell-tale signs of this modification. A designed organism should not. Which is it?

The eye, that supposed paragon of intelligent design, is a perfect place to start. We have already sung the virtues of this organ, and described some of its extraordinary capabilities. But one thing that we have not considered is the neural wiring of its light-sensing units, the photoreceptor cells in the retina. These cells pass impulses to a series of interconnecting cells that eventually pass information to the cells of the optic nerve, which leads to the brain. Given the basics of this wiring, how would you orient the retina with respect to the direction of light? Quite naturally, you (and any other designer) would choose the orientation that produces the highest degree of visual quality. No one, for example, would suggest that the neural wiring connections should be placed on the side that faces the light, rather than on the side away from it. Incredibly, this is exactly how the human retina is constructed.

What are the consequences of wiring the retina backwards? First, there is a degradation of visual quality due to the scattering of light as it passes through layers of cellular wiring. To be sure, this scattering has been minimized because the nerve cells are nearly transparent, but it cannot be eliminated, because of the basic flaw in design. This design flaw is compounded by the fact that the nerve cells require a rich blood supply, so that a network of blood vessels also sits directly in front of the light-sensitive layer, another feature that no engineer would stand for. Second, the nerve impulses produced by photoreceptor cells must be carried to the brain, and this means that at some point the neural wiring must pass directly through the wall of the retina. The result? A "blind spot" in the retina, a region where thousands of impulse-carrying cells have pushed the sensory cells aside, and consequently nothing can be seen. Each human retina has a blind spot roughly 1 mm in diameter, a blind spot that would not exist if only the eye were designed with its sensory wiring behind the photoreceptors instead of in front of them.

Do these design problems exist because it is impossible to construct an eye that is wired properly, so that the light-sensitive cells face the incoming image? Not at all. Many organisms have eyes in which the neural wiring is neatly tucked away below the photoreceptor layer. The squid and the octopus, for example, have a lens-and-retina eye quite similar to the vertebrate one, but these mollusk eyes are wired right-side-out, with no light-scattering nerve cells or blood vessels above the photoreceptors and no blind spot.

None of this should be taken to suggest that the eye functions poorly. Quite the contrary, it is a superb visual instrument that serves us exceedingly well. To support the view that the eye was produced by evolution, one does not have to argue that the eye is defective or shoddy. Natural selection, after all, has been fine-tuning every organ in the body, including the vertebrate eye, for millions of years. The key to the argument from design is not whether or not an organ or system works well, but whether its basic structural plan is the obvious product of design. The structural plan of the eye is not.

Evolution, which works by repeatedly modifying preexisting structures, can explain the inside-out nature of the vertebrate eye quite simply. The verterbate retina evolved as a modification of the outer layer of the brain. Over time, evolution progressively modified this part of the brain for light-sensitivity. Although the layer of light-sensitive cells gradually assumed a retina-like shape, it retained its original orientation, including a series of nerve connections on its surface. Evolution, unlike an intelligent designer, cannot start over from scratch to achieve the optimal design.

Tinkering with Success: the Mark of Evolution

The living world is filled with examples of organs and structures that clearly have their roots in the opportunistic modification of a preexisting structure rather than the clean elegance of design. Steven Jay Gould, in his famous essay "The Panda's Thumb," makes exactly this point. The giant panda has a distinct and dexterous "thumb" which, like our own thumb, is opposable. These animals nimbly strip the leaves off bamboo shots by pulling the shoots between thumb and their five other fingers. Five? No, the panda doesn't have six fingers, because it's thumb isn't a true digit at all. In fact, it grips the shoot of bamboo between its palm and a bone in the wrist which, in giant pandas, has been enlarged to form a stubby protuberance.

A true designer would have been capable of remodeling a complete digit, like the thumb of a primate, to hold the panda's food. Evolution, on the other hand, settled for much less: a bamboo-gripping pseudo-digit that conferred just enough of an advantage to be favored by natural selection. As Gould himself notes, a single mutation increasing the rate of growth of this wristbone could explain the formation of the Panda's "thumb." Natural selection itself explains how this simple modification was advantageous. It is a clear case of the way in which evolution produces organisms that are well-adapted, but not necessarily well-designed.

A true designer could begin with a clean sheet of paper, and produce a design that did not depend, as evolution must, on re-using old mechanisms, old parts, and even old patterns of development. The use of old developmental patterns is particularly striking in human embryonic development. The early embryos of reptiles and birds, which produce eggs containing massive amounts of yolk, follow a particularly specialized pattern of development. This pattern enables them to produce the three vertebrate body layers in a disc of cells that sits astride a hugh sphere of nutritive yolk. They eventually surround that yolk with a "yolk sac," a layer of cells that supplies the embryo with nutrition from the stored yolk.

Placental mammals produce tiny eggs, so there would be no need to follow a developmental pattern that surrounds the non-existent mass of yolk. Nevertheless, as Scott F. Gilbert, the author of an influential book on developmental biology notes:

> What is surprising is that the gastrulation movements of reptilian and avian embryos, which evolved as an adaptation to yolky eggs, are retained even in the absence of large amounts of yolk in the mammalian embryo. The inner cell mass can be envisioned as sitting atop an imaginary ball of yolk, following instructions that seem more appropriate to its ancestors.

Indeed, human embryos even go so far as to form an empty yolk sac, surrounding that non-existent stored food. The human yolk sac develops from the same tissues as the yolk sacs of reptiles and birds, performs many of the same functions (except, of course, for using the non-existent yolk), and gives rise to the same adult tissues. That it why it has been known as a "yolk sac" for more than a century. The cells of the sac channel nutrients to the embryo (much as they do in birds and reptiles), and play a role in the formation of the circulatory, reproductive, and digestive systems. These functions do not explain, however, why the cells that perform them should take the form of a sac.

There is no reason, from the standpoint of intelligent design, for the human embryo to produce an empty yolk sac. Evolution, of course, can supply the answer. If placental mammals are descended from egg-laying animals, like reptiles, then the empty yolk sac can be understood as a evolutionary remnant. The yolk sac is produced by a process of development that could not be re-designed simply because mammalian eggs had lost their yolk. It suggests that mammals evolved from animals that once had eggs with large amounts of yolk. Does the historic fossil record support that contention? Absolutely. The very first recognizable mammals in the fossil history of life on Earth are known by a telling name: they are the "reptile-like mammals."

Hints of the Past

The concept of intelligent design is particularly clear on one point: organisms have been designed to meet the distinct needs of their lifestyles and environments, not to reflect an evolutionary history. Is this distinction between evolution and design testable? I think it is, and the test is a simple one. Intelligent design dictates that the genetic system of a living organism should be constructed to suit its present needs, and should not contain superfluous genes or gene sequences that obviously correspond to structures or substances for which the organism has no need. In short, the master genetic plan should correspond precisely to the organism for which it codes.

No living bird has teeth, and that fact, of course, is behind the old saying that a rare object is "as scarce as hen's teeth." Why don't birds have teeth? A proponent of intelligent design must answer that they have not been designed to have teeth, quite probably because the designer equipped them with alternatives (hard beaks and food-grinding gizzards) that are superior for lightweight flying organisms.

Is this in fact the case? In 1980 Edward Kollar and his colleague C. Fisher decided to test whether or not chicken cells still have the capacity to become teeth. Intelligent design would predict that they cannot, because teeth were never designed into the organism.

Kollar & Fisher's experiment was simple. They took mouse tissue that normally lies just beneath the epithelial cells that develop into teeth, and put it in contact with chick epithelial cells. What happened? The chick cells, apparently influenced by the mouse tissue, dutifully began to develop into teeth. The produced impact-resistant enamel on their surfaces, and developed into clear, recognizable teeth (Figure 5). The experimenters took great care to exclude the possibility that mouse tissue had produced the teeth, first by making sure that no mouse epithelium was included in the experiments, and second by confirming that the cells in the tooth-producing tissue were indeed chick cells. Their experiments have since been confirmed by two independent groups of investigators.

No plan of intelligent design can account for the presence of tooth-producing genes in chicken cells. Indeed, it would be remarkably un-intelligent to endow birds with such useless capabilities. Evolution, on the other hand, has a perfectly good explanation for these capabilities. Birds are descended from organisms that once had teeth, and therefore they may retain these genes, even if other genetic changes normally turn their expression off. In short, birds have a genetic mark of their own history that no designed organism should ever possess. Designed organisms, after all, do not have evolutionary histories.

The Story in DNA

In today's world, it is possible to test evolution and intelligent design as never before. Rather than depending upon the indirect evidence of structure and physiology, we can go right to the source to the genetic code itself. If the human organism is, indeed, the product of careful, intelligent design, a detailed analysis of human DNA should reveal that design. Remember the quotation from *Of Pandas and People*: "We cannot build a palace by tinkering with a tool shed and adding bits of marble piecemeal here and there. We have to begin by devising a plan for the palace that coordinates all the parts into an integrated whole." We can test intelligent design simply by examining the genome to see if it matches the prediction of a coordinated, integrated plan.

If, on the other hand, the human genome is the product of an evolutionary history, that DNA should be a patchwork riddled with duplicated and discarded genes, and loaded with hints and traces of our evolutionary past. This, too, can be tested by directly examining the coded sequences of human DNA.

Although a complete sequence for all human DNA is at least a decade away, we already know more than enough of that sequence to begin to address the question of design. Let's take, as a representative example, a piece of chromosome # 11 known as the b-globin cluster. About 60,000 DNA "bases" are in the cluster, each base effectively representing 1 letter of a code that contains the instructions for assembling part of a protein. b-globin is an important part of hemoglobin, the oxygen-carrying protein that gives blood its red color. There are 5 different kinds of b-globin, and the cluster contains a gene for each one.

Why are there so many different forms of the b-globin gene? Here both evolution and intelligent design could supply an answer. Two of the genes are expressed in adults, and the other three are expressed during embryonic and fetal development. Evolution maintains that the multiple copies have arisen by gene duplication, a random process in which mistakes of DNA replication resulted in extra copies of a single ancestral gene. Once the original b-globin gene had been duplicated a number of times, so the explanation goes, slight variations within each sequence could produce the 5 different forms of the globin gene.

Why would different forms of b-globin be useful? The embryo, which is engaged in a tug-of-war for oxygen with its mother, must have hemoglobin that binds oxygen more tightly than the mother's adult hemoglobin. The 3 versions of the gene that are expressed during embryonic development enable hemoglobin to do exactly that. These slight variations enable embryonic blood to draw oxygen out of the maternal circulation across the placenta into it own circulation. Hence, gene duplication provided a chance for special forms of the b-globin gene to evolve that are expressed in fetal development.

Intelligent design proposes much the same mechanism, except that the production of extra copies and their modification to suit the embryo were a matter of intentional design, not chance and natural selection. Intelligent design maintains that the DNA sequences of each of the 5 genes of the cluster are matters of engineering, not random gene duplications fine-tuned by natural selection. So which is it? Are the 5 genes of this complex the elegant products of design, or a series of mistakes of which evolution took advantage?

The cluster itself, or more specifically a sixth b-globin gene, provides the answer. This gene is easy to recognize as part of the globin family because it has a DNA sequence nearly identical to that of the other five genes. Oddly, however, this gene is never expressed, it never produces a protein, and it plays no role in producing hemoglobin. Biologists call such regions "pseudogenes," reflecting the fact that however much they may resemble working genes, in fact they are not.

How can we be sure the sixth gene really is a pseudogene? Molecular biologists know that the expression of a gene like b-globin is a two-step process. First, the DNA sequence has to be copied into an intermediate known as RNA. That RNA sequence is then used to direct the assembly of a polypeptide, in this case, a b-globin. There is no evidence that the first step ever takes place for the pseudogene. No RNA matching its sequence has ever been found. Why? Because it lacks the DNA control sequences that precede the other 5 genes and signal the cell where to start producing RNA This means that the pseudogene is "silent." Furthermore, even if it were comehow copied into RNA, it still could not direct the assembly of a polypeptide. The pseudogene contains 6 distinct defects, any one of which would prevent it from producing a functional polypeptide. In short, this sixth gene is a mess, a nonfunctional stretch of useless DNA.

From a design point of view, pseudogenes are indeed mistakes. So why are they there? Intelligent design cannot explain the presence of a nonfunctional pseudogene, unless it is willing to allow that the designer made serious errors, wasting millions of bases of DNA on a blueprint full of junk and scribbles. Evolution, however, can explain them easily. Pseudogenes are nothing more than chance experiments in gene duplication that have failed, and they persist in the genome as evolutionary remnants of the past history of the b-globin genes.

The b-globin story is not an isolated one. Hundreds of pseudogenes have been discovered in the 1 or 2% of human DNA that has been explored to date, and more are added every month. In fact, the human genome is littered with pseudogenes, gene fragments, "orphaned" genes, "junk" DNA, and so many repeated copies of pointless DNA sequences that it cannot be attributed to anything that resembles intelligent design.

If the DNA of a human being or any other organism resembled a carefully constructed computer program, with neatly arranged and logically structured modules each written to fulfill a specific function, the evidence of intelligent design would be overwhelming. In fact, the genome resembles nothing so much as a hodgepodge of borrowed, copied, mutated, and discarded sequences and commands that has been cobbled together by millions of years of trial and error against the relentless test of survival. It works, and it works brilliantly; not because of intelligent design, but because of the great blind power of natural selection to innovate, to test, and to discard what fails in favor of what succeeds. The organisms that remain alive today, ourselves included, are evolution's great successes.

A Process Set in Motion

It is crucial to recognize the stakes of this debate. "Intelligent design theory" requires that we pretend to know less than we do about living organisms and that we pretend to know less than we do about design, engineering, and information theory. It demands that we set aside evolution's simple and logical explanations for the design flaws of living organisms in favor of a nebulous theory that pretends to account for everything by stating "well, that's the way the designer made it." In short, it requires a retreat back into an unknowledge of biology that is unworthy of the scientific spirit of this century.

It is particularly unfortunate that the advocates of intelligent design theory seem to see it as a way of countering what they view as evolution's inherent incompatibility with religion. In reality, evolution is not at all inconsistent with a belief in God, a fact recognized by Darwin himself in the concluding passage of *Origin of Species*:

> There is grandeur in this view of life, with its several powers, having been originally breathed by the Creator into a few forms or into one; and that. whilst this planet has gone cycling on according to the fixed law of gravity, from so simple a beginning endless forms most beautiful and most wonderful have been and are being evolved.

William Paley once hoped that the study of life could tell us something about the personality of the creator. Although Paley was wrong about the argument from design, he may have been right about the issue of personality. It seems to me that the scope and scale of evolution can only magnify our admiration for a creator who could set such a process in motion. To the deeply religious, evolution may not be seen as a challenge, but rather as proof of the power and subtletly of the creator's ways. The great Architect of the universe might not have written down each DNA base of the human genome, but He would still be a very clever fellow indeed.

26

Intelligent Design as a Theory of Information

WILLIAM A. DEMBSKI

Information

In *Steps Towards Life* Manfred Eigen (1992, p. 12) identifies what he regards as the central problem facing origins-of-life research: "Our task is to find an algorithm, a natural law that leads to the origin of information." Eigen is only half right. To determine how life began, it is indeed necessary to understand the origin of information. Even so, neither algorithms nor natural laws are capable of producing information. The great myth of modern evolutionary biology is that information can be gotten on the cheap without recourse to intelligence. It is this myth I seek to dispel, but to do so I shall need to give an account of information. No one disputes that there is such a thing as information. As Keith Devlin (1991, p. 1) remarks, "Our very lives depend upon it, upon its gathering, storage, manipulation, transmission, security, and so on. Huge amounts of money change hands in exchange for information. People talk about it all the time. Lives are lost in its pursuit. Vast commercial empires are created in order to manufacture equipment to handle it." But what exactly is information? The burden of this paper is to answer this question, presenting an account of information that is relevant to biology.

What then is information? The fundamental intuition underlying information is not, as is sometimes thought, the transmission of signals across a communication channel, but rather, the actualization of one possibility to the exclusion of others. As Fred Dretske (1981, p. 4) puts it, "Information theory identifies the amount of information associated with, or generated by, the occurrence of an event (or the realization of a state of affairs) with the reduction in uncertainty, the elimination of possibilities, represented by that event or state of affairs." To be sure, whenever signals are transmitted across a communication channel, one possibility is actualized to the exclusion of others, namely, the signal that was transmitted to the exclusion of those that weren't. But this is only a special case. Information in the first instance presupposes not some medium of communication, but contingency. Robert Stalnaker (1984, p. 85) makes this point clearly: "Content requires contingency. To learn something, to acquire information, is to rule out possibilities. To understand the information conveyed in a communication is to know what possibilities would be excluded by its truth." For there to be information, there must be a multiplicity of distinct possibilities any one of which might happen. When one of these possibilities does happen and the others are ruled out, information becomes actualized. Indeed, information in its most general sense can be defined as the actualization of one possibility to the exclusion of others (observe that this definition encompasses both syntactic and semantic information).

This way of defining information may seem counterintuitive since we often speak of the information inherent in possibilities that are never actualized. Thus we may speak of the information inherent in flipping one-hundred heads in a row with a fair coin even if this event never happens. There is no difficulty here. In counterfactual situations the definition of information needs to be applied counterfactually. Thus to consider the information inherent in flipping one-hundred heads in a row with a fair coin, we treat this event/possibility as though it were actualized. Information needs to referenced not just to the actual world, but also cross-referenced with all possible worlds.

Complex Information

How does our definition of information apply to biology, and to science more generally? To render information a useful concept for science we need to do two things: first, show how to measure information; second, introduce a crucial distinction--the distinction between specified and unspecified information. First, let us show how to measure information. In measuring information it is not enough to count the number of possibilities that were excluded, and offer this number as the relevant measure of information. The problem is that a simple enumeration of excluded possibilities tells us nothing about how those possibilities were individuated in the first place. Consider, for instance, the following individuation of poker hands:

(i) A royal flush.

(ii) Everything else.

To learn that something other than a royal flush was dealt (i.e., possibility (ii)) is clearly to acquire less information than to learn that a royal flush was dealt (i.e., possibility (i)). Yet if our measure of information is simply an enumeration of excluded possibilities, the same numerical value must be assigned in both instances since in both instances a single possibility is excluded.

It follows, therefore, that how we measure information needs to be independent of whatever procedure we use to individuate the possibilities under consideration. And the way to do this is not simply to count possibilities, but to assign probabilities to these possibilities. For a thoroughly shuffled deck of cards, the probability of being dealt a royal flush (i.e., possibility (i)) is approximately .000002 whereas the probability of being dealt anything other than a royal flush (i.e., possibility (ii)) is approximately .999998. Probabilities by themselves, however, are not information measures. Although probabilities properly distinguish possibilities according to the information they contain, nonetheless probabilities remain an inconvenient way of measuring information. There are two reasons for this. First, the scaling and directionality of the numbers assigned by probabilities needs to be recalibrated. We are clearly acquiring more information when we learn someone was dealt a royal flush than when we learn someone wasn't dealt a royal flush. And yet the probability of being dealt a royal flush (i.e., .000002) is minuscule compared to the probability of being dealt something other than a royal flush (i.e., .999998). Smaller probabilities signify more information, not less.

The second reason probabilities are inconvenient for measuring information is that they are multiplicative rather than additive. If I learn that Alice was dealt a royal flush playing poker at Caesar's Palace and that Bob was dealt a royal flush playing poker at the Mirage, the probability that both Alice and Bob were dealt royal flushes is the product of the individual probabilities. Nonetheless, it is convenient for information to be measured additively so that the measure of information assigned to Alice and Bob jointly being dealt royal flushes equals the measure of information assigned to Alice being dealt a royal flush plus the measure of information assigned to Bob being dealt a royal flush.

Now there is an obvious way to transform probabilities which circumvents both these difficulties, and that is to apply a negative logarithm to the probabilities. Applying a negative logarithm assigns the more information to the less probability and, because the logarithm of a product is the sum of the logarithms, transforms multiplicative probability measures into additive information measures. What's more, in deference to communication theorists, it is customary to use the logarithm to the base 2. The rationale for this choice of logarithmic base is as follows. The most convenient way for communication theorists to measure information is in bits. Any message sent across a communication channel can be viewed as a string of 0's and 1's. For instance, the ASCII code uses strings of eight 0's and 1's to represent the characters on a typewriter, with whole words and sentences in turn represented as strings of such character strings. In like manner all communication may be reduced to the transmission of sequences of 0's and 1's. Given this reduction, the obvious way for communication theorists to measure information is in number of bits transmitted across a communication channel. And since the negative logarithm to the base 2 of a probability corresponds to the average number of bits needed to identify an event of that probability, the logarithm to the base 2 is the canonical logarithm for communication theorists. Thus we define the measure of information in an event of probability p as $-\log_2 p$ (see Shannon and Weaver, 1949, p. 32; Hamming, 1986; or indeed any mathematical introduction to information theory).

What about the additivity of this information measure? Recall the example of Alice being dealt a royal flush playing poker at Caesar's Palace and that Bob being dealt a royal flush playing poker at the Mirage. Let's call the first event A and the second B. Since randomly dealt poker hands are probabilistically independent, the probability of A and B taken jointly equals the product of the probabilities of A and B taken individually. Symbolically, $P(A\&B) = P(A) \times P(B)$. Given our logarithmic definition of information we therefore define the amount of information in an event E as $I(E) =_{def} -\log_2 P(E)$. It then follows that $P(A\&B) = P(A) \times P(B)$ if and only if $I(A\&B) = I(A)+I(B)$. Since in the example of Alice and Bob $P(A) = P(B)$ .000002, $I(A) = I(B) = 19$, and $I(A\&B) = I(A)+I(B) = 19 + 19 = 38$. Thus the amount of information inherent in Alice and Bob jointly obtaining royal flushes is 38 bits.

Since lots of events are probabilistically independent, information measures exhibit lots of additivity. But since lots of events are also correlated, information measures exhibit lots of non-additivity as well. In the case of Alice and Bob, Alice being dealt a royal flush is probabilistically independent of Bob being dealt a royal flush, and so the amount of information in Alice and Bob both being dealt royal flushes equals the sum of the individual amounts of information. But consider now a different example. Alice and Bob together toss a coin five times. Alice observes the first four tosses but is distracted, and so misses the fifth toss. On the other hand, Bob misses the first toss, but observes the last four tosses. Let's say the actual sequence of tosses is 11001 (1 = heads, 0 = tails). Thus Alice observes 1100* and Bob observes *1001. Let A denote the first observation, B the second. It follows that the amount of information in A&B is the amount of information in the completed sequence 11001, namely, 5 bits. On the other hand, the amount of information in A alone is the amount of information in the incomplete sequence 1100*, namely 4 bits. Similarly, the amount of information in B alone is the amount of information in the incomplete sequence *1001, also 4 bits. This time information doesn't add up: $5 = I(A\&B)$ _ $I(A)+I(B) = 4+4 = 8$.

Here A and B are correlated. Alice knows all but the last bit of information in the completed sequence 11001. Thus when Bob gives her the incomplete sequence *1001, all Alice really learns is the last bit in this sequence. Similarly, Bob knows all but the first bit of information in the completed sequence 11001. Thus when Alice gives him the incomplete sequence 1100*, all Bob really learns is the first bit in this sequence. What appears to be four bits of information actually ends up being only one bit of information once Alice and Bob factor in the prior information they possess about the completed sequence 11001. If we introduce the idea of conditional information, this is just to say that $5 = I(A\&B) = I(A)+I(B|A) = 4+1$. $I(B|A)$, the conditional information of B given A, is the amount of information in Bob's observation once Alice's observation is taken into account. And this, as we just saw, is 1 bit.

$I(B|A)$, like $I(A\&B)$, $I(A)$, and $I(B)$, can be represented as the negative logarithm to the base two of a probability, only this time the probability under the logarithm is a conditional as opposed to an unconditional probability. By definition $I(B|A) =$def $-\log2 P(B|A)$, where $P(B|A)$ is the conditional probability of B given A. But since $P(B|A) =$def $P(A\&B)/P(A)$, and since the logarithm of a quotient is the difference of the logarithms, $\log2 P(B|A) = \log2 P(A\&B) - \log2 P(A)$, and so $-\log2 P(B|A) = -\log2 P(A\&B) + \log2 P(A)$, which is just $I(B|A) = I(A\&B) - I(A)$. This last equation is equivalent to

$$(*)\ I(A\&B) = I(A)+I(B|A)$$

Formula (*) holds with full generality, reducing to $I(A\&B) = I(A)+I(B)$ when A and B are probabilistically independent (in which case $P(B|A) = P(B)$ and thus $I(B|A) = I(B)$).

Formula (*) asserts that the information in both A and B jointly is the information in A plus the information in B that is not in A. Its point, therefore, is to spell out how much additional information B contributes to A. As such, this formula places tight constraints on the generation of new information. Does, for instance, a computer program, call it A, by outputting some data, call the data B, generate new information? Computer programs are fully deterministic, and so B is fully determined by A. It follows that $P(B|A) = 1$, and thus $I(B|A) = 0$ (the logarithm of 1 is always 0). From Formula (*) it therefore follows that $I(A\&B) = I(A)$, and therefore that the amount of information in A and B jointly is no more than the amount of information in A by itself.

For an example in the same spirit consider that there is no more information in two copies of Shakespeare's *Hamlet* than in a single copy. This is of course patently obvious, and any formal account of information had better agree. To see that our formal account does indeed agree, let A denote the printing of the first copy of *Hamlet*, and B the printing of the second copy. Once A is given, B is entirely determined. Indeed, the correlation between A and B is perfect. Probabilistically this is expressed by saying the conditional probability of B given A is 1, namely, P(B|A) = 1. In information-theoretic terms this is to say that I(B|A) = 0. As a result I(B|A) drops out of Formula (*), and so I(A&B) = I(A). Our information-theoretic formalism therefore agrees with our intuition that two copies of Hamlet contain no more information than a single copy.

Information is a complexity-theoretic notion. Indeed, as a purely formal object, the information measure described here is a complexity measure (cf. Dembski, 1998, ch. 4). Complexity measures arise whenever we assign numbers to degrees of complication. A set of possibilities will often admit varying degrees of complication, ranging from extremely simple to extremely complicated. Complexity measures assign non-negative numbers to these possibilities so that 0 corresponds to the most simple and to the most complicated. For instance, computational complexity is always measured in terms of either time (i.e., number of computational steps) or space (i.e., size of memory, usually measured in bits or bytes) or some combination of the two. The more difficult a computational problem, the more time and space are required to run the algorithm that solves the problem. For information measures, degree of complication is measured in bits. Given an event A of probability P(A), I(A) = -log2P(A) measures the number of bits associated with the probability P(A). We therefore speak of the "complexity of information" and say that the complexity of information increases as I(A) increases (or, correspondingly, as P(A) decreases). We also speak of "simple" and "complex" information according to whether I(A) signifies few or many bits of information. This notion of complexity is important to biology since not just the origin of information stands in question, but the origin of complex information.

Complex Specified Information

Given a means of measuring information and determining its complexity, we turn now to the distinction between specified and unspecified information. This is a vast topic whose full elucidation is beyond the scope of this paper (the details can be found in my monograph The Design Inference). Nonetheless, in what follows I shall try to make this distinction intelligible, and offer some hints on how to make it rigorous. For an intuitive grasp of the difference between specified and unspecified information, consider the following example. Suppose an archer stands 50 meters from a large blank wall with bow and arrow in hand. The wall, let us say, is sufficiently large that the archer cannot help but hit it. Consider now two alternative scenarios. In the first scenario the archer simply shoots at the wall. In the second scenario the archer first paints a target on the wall, and then shoots at the wall, squarely hitting the target's bull's-eye. Let us suppose that in both scenarios where the arrow lands is identical. In both scenarios the arrow might have landed anywhere on the wall. What's more, any place where it might land is highly improbable. It follows that in both scenarios highly complex information is actualized. Yet the conclusions we draw from these scenarios are very different. In the first scenario we can conclude absolutely nothing about the archer's ability as an archer, whereas in the second scenario we have evidence of the archer's skill.

The obvious difference between the two scenarios is of course that in the first the information follows no pattern whereas in the second it does. Now the information that tends to interest us as rational inquirers generally, and scientists in particular, is not the actualization of arbitrary possibilities which correspond to no patterns, but rather the actualization of circumscribed possibilities which do correspond to patterns. There's more. Patterned information, though a step in the right direction, still doesn't quite get us specified information. The problem is that patterns can be concocted after the fact so that instead of helping elucidate information, the patterns are merely read off already actualized information.

To see this, consider a third scenario in which an archer shoots at a wall. As before, we suppose the archer stands 50 meters from a large blank wall with bow and arrow in hand, the wall being so large that the archer cannot help but hit it. And as in the first scenario, the archer shoots at the wall while it is still blank. But this time suppose that after having shot the arrow, and finding the arrow stuck in the wall, the archer paints a target around the arrow so that the arrow sticks squarely in the bull's-eye. Let us suppose further that the precise place where the arrow lands in this scenario is identical with where it landed in the first two scenarios. Since any place where the arrow might land is highly improbable, in this as in the other scenarios highly complex information has been actualized. What's more, since the information corresponds to a pattern, we can even say that in this third scenario highly complex patterned information has been actualized. Nevertheless, it would be wrong to say that highly complex specified information has been actualized. Of the three scenarios, only the information in the second scenario is specified. In that scenario, by first painting the target and then shooting the arrow, the pattern is given independently of the information. On the other hand, in this, the third scenario, by first shooting the arrow and then painting the target around it, the pattern is merely read off the information.

Specified information is always patterned information, but patterned information is not always specified information. For specified information not just any pattern will do. We therefore distinguish between the "good" patterns and the "bad" patterns. The "good" patterns will henceforth be called specifications. Specifications are the independently given patterns that are not simply read off information. By contrast, the "bad" patterns will be called fabrications. Fabrications are the post hoc patterns that are simply read off already existing information.

Unlike specifications, fabrications are wholly unenlightening. We are no better off with a fabrication than without one. This is clear from comparing the first and third scenarios. Whether an arrow lands on a blank wall and the wall stays blank (as in the first scenario), or an arrow lands on a blank wall and a target is then painted around the arrow (as in the third scenario), any conclusions we draw about the arrow's flight remain the same. In either case chance is as good an explanation as any for the arrow's flight. The fact that the target in the third scenario constitutes a pattern makes no difference since the pattern is constructed entirely in response to where the arrow lands. Only when the pattern is given independently of the arrow's flight does a hypothesis other than chance come into play. Thus only in the second scenario does it make sense to ask whether we are dealing with a skilled archer. Only in the second scenario does the pattern constitute a specification. In the third scenario the pattern constitutes a mere fabrication.

The distinction between specified and unspecified information may now be defined as follows: the actualization of a possibility (i.e., information) is specified if independently of the possibility's actualization, the possibility is identifiable by means of a pattern. If not, then the information is unspecified. Note that this definition implies an asymmetry between specified and unspecified information: specified information cannot become unspecified information, though unspecified information may become specified information. Unspecified information need not remain unspecified, but can become specified as our background knowledge increases. For instance, a cryptographic transmission whose cryptosystem we have yet to break will constitute unspecified information. Yet as soon as we break the cryptosystem, the cryptographic transmission becomes specified information.

What is it for a possibility to be identifiable by means of an independently given pattern? A full exposition of specification requires a detailed answer to this question. Unfortunately, such an exposition is beyond the scope of this paper. The key conceptual difficulty here is to characterize the independence condition between patterns and information. This independence condition breaks into two subsidiary conditions: (1) a condition to stochastic conditional independence between the information in question and certain relevant background knowledge; and (2) a tractability condition whereby the pattern in question can be constructed from the aforementioned background knowledge. Although these conditions make good intuitive sense, they are not easily formalized. For the details refer to my monograph The Design Inference.

If formalizing what it means for a pattern to be given independently of a possibility is difficult, determining in practice whether a pattern is given independently of a possibility is much easier. If the pattern is given prior to the possibility being actualized—as in the second scenario above where the target was painted before the arrow was shot—then the pattern is automatically independent of the possibility, and we are dealing with specified information. Patterns given prior to the actualization of a possibility are just the rejection regions of statistics. There is a well-established statistical theory that describes such patterns and their use in probabilistic reasoning. These are clearly specifications since having been given prior to the actualization of some possibility, they have already been identified, and thus are identifiable independently of the possibility being actualized (cf. Hacking, 1965).

Many of the interesting cases of specified information, however, are those in which the pattern is given after a possibility has been actualized. This is certainly the case with the origin of life: life originates first and only afterwards do pattern-forming rational agents (like ourselves) enter the scene. It remains the case, however, that a pattern corresponding to a possibility, though formulated after the possibility has been actualized, can constitute a specification. Certainly this was not the case in the third scenario above where the target was painted around the arrow only after it hit the wall. But consider the following example. Alice and Bob are celebrating their fiftieth wedding anniversary. Their six children all show up bearing gifts. Each gift is part of a matching set of china. There is no duplication of gifts, and together the gifts constitute a complete set of china. Suppose Alice and Bob were satisfied with their old set of china, and had no inkling prior to opening their gifts that they might expect a new set of china. Alice and Bob are therefore without a relevant pattern whither to refer their gifts prior to actually receiving the gifts from their children. Nevertheless, the pattern they explicitly formulate only after receiving the gifts could be formed independently of receiving the gifts—indeed, we all know about matching sets of china and how to distinguish them from unmatched sets. This pattern therefore constitutes a specification. What's more, there is an obvious inference connected with this specification: Alice and Bob's children were in collusion, and did not present their gifts as random acts of kindness.

But what about the origin of life? Is life specified? If so, to what patterns does life correspond, and how are these patterns given independently of life's origin? Obviously, pattern-forming rational agents like ourselves don't enter the scene till after life originates. Nonetheless, there are functional patterns to which life corresponds, and which are given independently of the actual living systems. An organism is a functional system comprising many functional subsystems. The functionality of organisms can be cashed out in any number of ways. Arno Wouters (1995) cashes it out globally in terms of viability of whole organisms. Michael Behe (1996) cashes it out in terms of the irreducible complexity and minimal function of biochemical systems. Even the staunch Darwinist Richard Dawkins will admit that life is specified functionally, cashing out the functionality of organisms in terms of reproduction of genes. Thus Dawkins (1987, p. 9) will write: "Complicated things have some quality, specifiable in advance, that is highly unlikely to have been acquired by random chance alone. In the case of living things, the quality that is specified in advance is . . . the ability to propagate genes in reproduction."

Information can be specified. Information can be complex. Information can be both complex and specified. Information that is both complex and specified I call "complex specified information," or CSI for short. CSI is what all the fuss over information has been about in recent years, not just in biology, but in science generally. It is CSI that for Manfred Eigen constitutes the great mystery of biology, and one he hopes eventually to unravel in terms of algorithms and natural laws. It is CSI that for cosmologists underlies the fine-tuning of the universe, and which the various anthropic principles attempt to understand (cf. Barrow and Tipler, 1986). It is CSI that David Bohm's quantum potentials are extracting when they scour the microworld for what Bohm calls "active information" (cf. Bohm, 1993, pp. 35-38). It is CSI that enables Maxwell's demon to outsmart a thermodynamic system tending towards thermal equilibrium (cf. Landauer, 1991, p. 26). It is CSI on which David Chalmers hopes to base a comprehensive theory of human consciousness (cf. Chalmers, 1996, ch. 8). It is CSI that within the Kolmogorov-Chaitin theory of algorithmic information takes the form of highly compressible, non-random strings of digits (cf. Kolmogorov, 1965; Chaitin, 1966).

Nor is CSI confined to science. CSI is indispensable in our everyday lives. The 16-digit number on your VISA card is an example of CSI. The complexity of this number ensures that a would-be thief cannot randomly pick a number and have it turn out to be a valid VISA card number. What's more, the specification of this number ensures that it is your number, and not anyone else's. Even your phone number constitutes CSI. As with the VISA card number, the complexity ensures that this number won't be dialed randomly (at least not too often), and the specification ensures that this number is yours and yours only. All the numbers on our bills, credit slips, and purchase orders represent CSI. CSI makes the world go round. It follows that CSI is a rife field for criminality. CSI is what motivated the greedy Michael Douglas character in the movie *Wall Street* to lie, cheat, and steal. CSI's total and absolute control was the objective of the monomaniacal Ben Kingsley character in the movie *Sneakers*. CSI is the artifact of interest in most techno-thrillers. Ours is an information age, and the information that captivates us is CSI.

Intelligent Design

Whence the origin of complex specified information? In this section I shall argue that intelligent causation, or equivalently design, accounts for the origin of complex specified information. My argument focuses on the nature of intelligent causation, and specifically, on what it is about intelligent causes that makes them detectable. To see why CSI is a reliable indicator of design, we need to examine the nature of intelligent causation. The principal characteristic of intelligent causation is directed contingency, or what we call choice. Whenever an intelligent cause acts, it chooses from a range of competing possibilities. This is true not just of humans, but of animals as well as extra-terrestrial intelligences. A rat navigating a maze must choose whether to go right or left at various points in the maze. When SETI (Search for Extra-Terrestrial Intelligence) researchers attempt to discover intelligence in the extra-terrestrial radio transmissions they are monitoring, they assume an extra-terrestrial intelligence could have chosen any number of possible radio transmissions, and then attempt to match the transmissions they observe with certain patterns as opposed to others (patterns that presumably are markers of intelligence). Whenever a human being utters meaningful speech, a choice is made from a range of possible sound-combinations that might have been uttered. Intelligent causation always entails discrimination, choosing certain things, ruling out others.

Given this characterization of intelligent causes, the crucial question is how to recognize their operation. Intelligent causes act by making a choice. How then do we recognize that an intelligent cause has made a choice? A bottle of ink spills accidentally onto a sheet of paper; someone takes a fountain pen and writes a message on a sheet of paper. In both instances ink is applied to paper. In both instances one among an almost infinite set of possibilities is realized. In both instances a contingency is actualized and others are ruled out. Yet in one instance we infer design, in the other chance. What is the relevant difference? Not only do we need to observe that a contingency was actualized, but we ourselves need also to be able to specify that contingency. The contingency must conform to an independently given pattern, and we must be able independently to formulate that pattern. A random ink blot is unspecifiable; a message written with ink on paper is specifiable. Wittgenstein (1980, p. 1e) made the same point as follows: "We tend to take the speech of a Chinese for inarticulate gurgling. Someone who understands Chinese will recognize language in what he hears. Similarly I often cannot discern the humanity in man."

In hearing a Chinese utterance, someone who understands Chinese not only recognizes that one from a range of all possible utterances was actualized, but is also able to specify the utterance as coherent Chinese speech. Contrast this with someone who does not understand Chinese. In hearing a Chinese utterance, someone who does not understand Chinese also recognizes that one from a range of possible utterances was actualized, but this time, because lacking the ability to understand Chinese, is unable to specify the utterance as coherent speech. To someone who does not understand Chinese, the utterance will appear gibberish. Gibberish—the utterance of nonsense syllables uninterpretable within any natural language—always actualizes one utterance from the range of possible utterances. Nevertheless, gibberish, by corresponding to nothing we can understand in any language, also cannot be specified. As a result, gibberish is never taken for intelligent communication, but always for what Wittgenstein calls "inarticulate gurgling."

The actualization of one among several competing possibilities, the exclusion of the rest, and the specification of the possibility that was actualized encapsulates how we recognize intelligent causes, or equivalently, how we detect design. Actualization-Exclusion-Specification, this triad constitutes a general criterion for detecting intelligence, be it animal, human, or extra-terrestrial. Actualization establishes that the possibility in question is the one that actually occurred. Exclusion establishes that there was genuine contingency (i.e., that there were other live possibilities, and that these were ruled out). Specification establishes that the actualized possibility conforms to a pattern given independently of its actualization.

Now where does choice, which we've cited as the principal characteristic of intelligent causation, figure into this criterion? The problem is that we never witness choice directly. Instead, we witness actualizations of contingency which might be the result of choice (i.e., directed contingency), but which also might be the result of chance (i.e., blind contingency). Now there is only one way to tell the difference—specification. Specification is the only means available to us for distinguishing choice from chance, directed contingency from blind contingency. Actualization and exclusion together guarantee we are dealing with contingency. Specification guarantees we are dealing with a directed contingency. The Actualization-Exclusion-Specification triad is therefore precisely what we need to identify choice and therewith intelligent causation.

Psychologists who study animal learning and behavior have known of the Actualization-Exclusion-Specification triad all along, albeit implicitly. For these psychologists—known as learning theorists--learning is discrimination (cf. Mazur, 1990; Schwartz, 1984). To learn a task an animal must acquire the ability to actualize behaviors suitable for the task as well as the ability to exclude behaviors unsuitable for the task. Moreover, for a psychologist to recognize that an animal has learned a task, it is necessary not only to observe the animal making the appropriate behavior, but also to specify this behavior. Thus to recognize whether a rat has successfully learned how to traverse a maze, a psychologist must first specify the sequence of right and left turns that conducts the rat out of the maze. No doubt, a rat randomly wandering a maze also discriminates a sequence of right and left turns. But by randomly wandering the maze, the rat gives no indication that it can discriminate the appropriate sequence of right and left turns for exiting the maze. Consequently, the psychologist studying the rat will have no reason to think the rat has learned how to traverse the maze. Only if the rat executes the sequence of right and left turns specified by the psychologist will the psychologist recognize that the rat has learned how to traverse the maze. Now it is precisely the learned behaviors we regard as intelligent in animals. Hence it is no surprise that the same scheme for recognizing animal learning recurs for recognizing intelligent causes generally, to wit, actualization, exclusion, and specification.

Now this general scheme for recognizing intelligent causes coincides precisely with how we recognize complex specified information: First, the basic precondition for information to exist must hold, namely, contingency. Thus one must establish that any one of a multiplicity of distinct possibilities might obtain. Next, one must establish that the possibility which was actualized after the others were excluded was also specified. So far the match between this general scheme for recognizing intelligent causation and how we recognize complex specified information is exact. Only one loose end remains-- complexity. Although complexity is essential to CSI (corresponding to the first letter of the acronym), its role in this general scheme for recognizing intelligent causation is not immediately evident. In this scheme one among several competing possibilities is actualized, the rest are excluded, and the possibility which was actualized is specified. Where in this scheme does complexity figure in?

The answer is that it is there implicitly. To see this, consider again a rat traversing a maze, but now take a very simple maze in which two right turns conduct the rat out of the maze. How will a psychologist studying the rat determine whether it has learned to exit the maze. Just putting the rat in the maze will not be enough. Because the maze is so simple, the rat could by chance just happen to take two right turns, and thereby exit the maze. The psychologist will therefore be uncertain whether the rat actually learned to exit this maze, or whether the rat just got lucky. But contrast this now with a complicated maze in which a rat must take just the right sequence of left and right turns to exit the maze. Suppose the rat must take one hundred appropriate right and left turns, and that any mistake will prevent the rat from exiting the maze. A psychologist who sees the rat take no erroneous turns and in short order exit the maze will be convinced that the rat has indeed learned how to exit the maze, and that this was not dumb luck. With the simple maze there is a substantial probability that the rat will exit the maze by chance; with the complicated maze this is exceedingly improbable. The role of complexity in detecting design is now clear since improbability is precisely what we mean by complexity (cf. section 2).

This argument for showing that CSI is a reliable indicator of design may now be summarized as follows: CSI is a reliable indicator of design because its recognition coincides with how we recognize intelligent causation generally. In general, to recognize intelligent causation we must establish that one from a range of competing possibilities was actualized, determine which possibilities were excluded, and then specify the possibility that was actualized. What's more, the competing possibilities that were excluded must be live possibilities, sufficiently numerous so that specifying the possibility that was actualized cannot be attributed to chance. In terms of probability, this means that the possibility that was specified is highly improbable. In terms of complexity, this means that the possibility that was specified is highly complex. All the elements in the general scheme for recognizing intelligent causation (i.e., Actualization- Exclusion -Specification) find their counterpart in complex specified information--CSI. CSI pinpoints what we need to be looking for when we detect design.

As a postscript, I call the reader's attention to the etymology of the word "intelligent." The word "intelligent" derives from two Latin words, the preposition *inter*, meaning between, and the verb *lego*, meaning to choose or select. Thus according to its etymology, intelligence consists in choosing between. It follows that the etymology of the word "intelligent" parallels the formal analysis of intelligent causation just given. "Intelligent design" is therefore a thoroughly apt phrase, signifying that design is inferred precisely because an intelligent cause has done what only an intelligent cause can do, make a choice.

The Law of Conservation of Information

Evolutionary biology has steadfastly resisted attributing CSI to intelligent causation. Although Manfred Eigen recognizes that the central problem of evolutionary biology is the origin of CSI, he has no thought of attributing CSI to intelligent causation. According to Eigen natural causes are adequate to explain the origin of CSI. The only question for Eigen is which natural causes explain the origin of CSI. The logically prior question of whether natural causes are even, in principle, capable of explaining the origin of CSI he ignores. And yet it is a question that undermines Eigen's entire project. Natural causes are in-principle incapable of explaining the origin of CSI. To be sure, natural causes can explain the flow of CSI, being ideally suited for transmitting already existing CSI. What natural causes cannot do, however, is originate CSI. This strong proscriptive claim, that natural causes can only transmit CSI but never originate it, I call the Law of Conservation of Information. It is this law that gives definite scientific content to the claim that CSI is intelligently caused. The aim of this last section is briefly to sketch the Law of Conservation of Information (a full treatment will be given in *Uncommon Descent*, a book I am jointly authoring with Stephen Meyer and Paul Nelson).

To see that natural causes cannot account for CSI is straightforward. Natural causes comprise chance and necessity (cf. Jacques Monod's book by that title). Because information presupposes contingency, necessity is by definition incapable of producing information, much less complex specified information. For there to be information there must be a multiplicity of live possibilities, one of which is actualized, and the rest of which are excluded. This is contingency. But if some outcome B is necessary given antecedent conditions A, then the probability of B given A is one, and the information in B given A is zero. If B is necessary given A, Formula (*) reduces to $I(A\&B) = I(A)$, which is to say that B contributes no new information to A. It follows that necessity is incapable of generating new information. Observe that what Eigen calls "algorithms" and "natural laws" fall under necessity.

Since information presupposes contingency, let us take a closer look at contingency. Contingency can assume only one of two forms. Either the contingency is a blind, purposeless contingency—which is chance; or it is a guided, purposeful contingency—which is intelligent causation. Since we already know that intelligent causation is capable of generating CSI (cf. section 4), let us next consider whether chance might also be capable of generating CSI. First notice that pure chance, entirely unsupplemented and left to its own devices, is incapable of generating CSI. Chance can generate complex unspecified information, and chance can generate non-complex specified information. What chance cannot generate is information that is jointly complex and specified.

Biologists by and large do not dispute this claim. Most agree that pure chance—what Hume called the Epicurean hypothesis—does not adequately explain CSI. Jacques Monod (1972) is one of the few exceptions, arguing that the origin of life, though vastly improbable, can nonetheless be attributed to chance because of a selection effect. Just as the winner of a lottery is shocked at winning, so we are shocked to have evolved. But the lottery was bound to have a winner, and so too something was bound to have evolved. Something vastly improbable was bound to happen, and so, the fact that it happened to us (i.e., that we were selected--hence the name selection effect) does not preclude chance. This is Monod's argument and it is fallacious. It fails utterly to come to grips with specification. Moreover, it confuses a necessary condition for life's existence with its explanation. Monod's argument has been refuted by the philosophers John Leslie (1989), John Earman (1987), and Richard Swinburne (1979). It has also been refuted by the biologists Francis Crick (1981, ch. 7), Bernd-Olaf Küppers (1990, ch. 6), and Hubert Yockey (1992, ch. 9). Selection effects do nothing to render chance an adequate explanation of CSI.

Most biologists therefore reject pure chance as an adequate explanation of CSI. The problem here is not simply one of faulty statistical reasoning. Pure chance is also scientifically unsatisfying as an explanation of CSI. To explain CSI in terms of pure chance is no more instructive than pleading ignorance or proclaiming CSI a mystery. It is one thing to explain the occurrence of heads on a single coin toss by appealing to chance. It is quite another, as Küppers (1990, p. 59) points out, to follow Monod and take the view that "the specific sequence of the nucleotides in the DNA molecule of the first organism came about by a purely random process in the early history of the earth." CSI cries out for explanation, and pure chance won't do. As Richard Dawkins (1987, p. 139) correctly notes, "We can accept a certain amount of luck in our [scientific] explanations, but not too much." If chance and necessity left to themselves cannot generate CSI, is it possible that chance and necessity working together might generate CSI? The answer is No. Whenever chance and necessity work together, the respective contributions of chance and necessity can be arranged sequentially. But by arranging the respective contributions of chance and necessity sequentially, it becomes clear that at no point in the sequence is CSI generated. Consider the case of trial-and-error (trial corresponds to necessity and error to chance). Once considered a crude method of problem solving, trial-and-error has so risen in the estimation of scientists that it is now regarded as the ultimate source of wisdom and creativity in nature. The probabilistic algorithms of computer science (e.g., genetic algorithms--see Forrest, 1993) all depend on trial-and-error. So, too, the Darwinian mechanism of mutation and natural selection is a trial-and-error combination in which mutation supplies the error and selection the trial. An error is committed after which a trial is made. But at no point is CSI generated.

Natural causes are therefore incapable of generating CSI. This broad conclusion I call the Law of Conservation of Information, or LCI for short. LCI has profound implications for science. Among its corollaries are the following: (1) The CSI in a closed system of natural causes remains constant or decreases. (2) CSI cannot be generated spontaneously, originate endogenously, or organize itself (as these terms are used in origins-of-life research). (3) The CSI in a closed system of natural causes either has been in the system eternally or was at some point added exogenously (implying that the system though now closed was not always closed). (4) In particular, any closed system of natural causes that is also of finite duration received whatever CSI it contains before it became a closed system.

This last corollary is especially pertinent to the nature of science for it shows that scientific explanation is not coextensive with reductive explanation. Richard Dawkins, Daniel Dennett, and many scientists are convinced that proper scientific explanations must be reductive, moving from the complex to the simple. Thus Dawkins (1987, p. 316) will write, "The one thing that makes evolution such a neat theory is that it explains how organized complexity can arise out of primeval simplicity." Thus Dennett (1995, p. 153) will view any scientific explanation that moves from simple to complex as "question-begging." Thus Dawkins (1987, p. 13) will explicitly equate proper scientific explanation with what he calls "hierarchical reductionism," according to which "a complex entity at any particular level in the hierarchy of organization" must properly be explained "in terms of entities only one level down the hierarchy." While no one will deny that reductive explanation is extremely effective within science, it is hardly the only type of explanation available to science. The divide-and-conquer mode of analysis behind reductive explanation has strictly limited applicability within science. In particular, this mode of analysis is utterly incapable of making headway with CSI. CSI demands an intelligent cause. Natural causes will not do.

References

Barrow, John D. and Frank J. Tipler. 1986. *The Anthropic Cosmological Principle*. Oxford: Oxford University Press.

Behe, Michael. 1996. *Darwin's Black Box: The Biochemical Challenge to Evolution*. New York: The Free Press.

Bohm, David. 1993. *The Undivided Universe: An Ontological Interpretation of Quantum Theory*. London: Routledge.

Chaitin, Gregory J. 1966. "On the Length of Programs for Computing Finite Binary Sequences." *Journal of the ACM*, 13:547-569.

Chalmers, David J. 1996. *The Conscious Mind: In Search of a Fundamental Theory*. New York : Oxford University Press.

Crick, Francis. 1981. *Life Itself: Its Origin and Nature*. New York: Simon and Schuster.

Dawkins, Richard. 1987. *The Blind Watchmaker*. New York: Norton.

Dembski, William A. 1998. *The Design Inference: Eliminating Chance through Small Probabilities*. Cambridge University Press.

Dennett, Daniel C. 1995. *Darwin's Dangerous Idea: Evolution and the Meanings of Life*. New York: Simon & Schuster.

Devlin, Keith J. 1991. *Logic and Information*. New York: Cambridge University Press.

Dretske, Fred I. 1981. *Knowledge and the Flow of Information*. Cambridge, Mass.: MIT Press.

Earman, John. 1987. "The Sap Also Rises: A Critical Examination of the Anthropic Principle." *American Philosophical Quarterly*, 24(4): 307-317.

Eigen, Manfred. 1992. *Steps Towards Life: A Perspective on Evolution*, translated by Paul Woolley. Oxford: Oxford University Press.

Forrest, Stephanie. 1993. "Genetic Algorithms: Principles of Natural Selection Applied to Computation." *Science*, 261:872-878.

Hacking, Ian. 1965. *Logic of Statistical Inference*. Cambridge: Cambridge University Press.

Hamming, R. W. 1986. *Coding and Information Theory*, 2nd edition. Englewood Cliffs, N. J.: Prentice-Hall.

Kolmogorov, Andrei N. 1965. "Three Approaches to the Quantitative Definition of Information." *Problemy Peredachi Informatsii* (in translation), 1(1): 3-11.

Küppers, Bernd-Olaf. 1990. *Information and the Origin of Life*. Cambridge, Mass.: MIT Press.

Landauer, Rolf. 1991. "Information is Physical." *Physics Today*, May: 23-29.

Leslie, John. 1989. *Universes*. London: Routledge.

Mazur, James. E. 1990. *Learning and Behavior*, 2nd edition. Englewood Cliffs, N.J.: Prentice Hall.

Monod, Jacques. 1972. *Chance and Necessity*. New York: Vintage.

Schwartz, Barry. 1984. *Psychology of Learning and Behavior*, 2nd edition. New York: Norton.

Shannon, Claude E. and W. Weaver. 1949. *The Mathematical Theory of Communication*. Urbana, Ill.: University of Illinois Press.

Stalnaker, Robert. 1984. *Inquiry*. Cambridge, Mass.: MIT Press.

Swinburne, Richard. 1979. *The Existence of God*. Oxford: Oxford University Press.

Wittgenstein, Ludwig. 1980. *Culture and Value*, edited by G. H. von Wright, translated by P. Winch. Chicago: University of Chicago Press.

Wouters, Arno. 1995. "Viability Explanation." *Biology and Philosophy*, 10:435-457.

Yockey, Hubert P. 1992. *Information Theory and Molecular Biology*. Cambridge: Cambridge University Press.

27

How Not to Detect Design

BRANDEN FITELSON, CHRISTOPHER STEPHENS, ELLIOTT SOBER[1]

As every philosopher knows, "the design argument" concludes that God exists from premises that cite the adaptive complexity of organisms or the lawfulness and orderliness of the whole universe. Since 1859, it has formed the intellectual heart of creationist opposition to the Darwinian hypothesis that organisms evolved their adaptive features by the mindless process of natural selection. Although the design argument developed as a defense of theism, the logic of the argument in fact encompasses a larger set of issues. William Paley saw clearly that we sometimes have an excellent reason to postulate the existence of an intelligent designer. If we find a watch on the heath, we reasonably infer that it was produced by an intelligent watchmaker. *This* design argument makes perfect sense. Why is it any different to claim that the eye was produced by an intelligent designer? Both critics and defenders of the design argument need to understand what the ground rules are for inferring that an intelligent designer is the unseen cause of an observed effect.

Dembski's book is an attempt to clarify these ground rules. He proposes a procedure for detecting design and discusses how it applies to a number of mundane and nontheological examples, which more or less resemble Paley's watch. Although the book takes no stand on whether creationism is more or less plausible than evolutionary theory, Dembski's epistemology can be evaluated without knowing how he thinks it bears on this highly charged topic. In what follows, we will show that Dembski's account of design inference is deeply flawed. Sometimes he is too hard on hypotheses of intelligent design; at other times he is too lenient. Neither creationists nor evolutionists nor people who are trying to detect design in nontheological contexts should adopt Dembski's framework.

The Explanatory Filter

Dembski's book provides a series of representations of how design inference works. The exposition starts simple and grows increasingly complex. However, the basic pattern of analysis can be summarized as follows. Dembski proposes an "explanatory filter" (37), which is a procedure for deciding how best to explain an observation E:

(1) There are three possible explanations of E -- Regularity, Chance, and Design. They are mutually exclusive and collectively exhaustive. The problem is to decide which of these explanations to accept.

(2) The Regularity hypothesis is more parsimonious than Chance, and Chance is more parsimonious than Design. To evaluate these alternatives, begin with the most parsimonious possibility and move down the list until you reach an explanation you can accept.

(3) If E has a high probability, you should accept Regularity; otherwise, reject Regularity and move down the list.

(4) If the Chance hypothesis assigns E a sufficiently low probability and E is "specified," then reject Chance and move down the list; otherwise, accept Chance.

(5) If you have rejected Regularity and Chance, then you should accept Design as the explanation of E.

The entire book is an elaboration of the ideas that comprise the Explanatory Filter.[2] Notice   that the filter is *eliminativist*, with the Design hypothesis occupying a special position.

We have interpreted the Filter as sometimes recommending that you should accept Regularity or Chance. This is supported, for example, by Dembski's remark (38) that "if E happens to be an HP [a high probability] event, we stop and attribute E to a regularity."   However, some of the circumlocutions that Dembski uses suggest that he doesn't think you should ever "accept" Regularity or Chance.[3] The most you should do is "not reject" them. Under this alternative interpretation, Dembski is saying that if you fail to reject Regularity, you can believe any of the three hypotheses, or remain agnostic about all three. And if you reject Regularity, but fail to reject Chance, you can believe either Chance or Design, or remain agnostic about them both. Only if you have rejected Regularity and Chance must you accept one of the three, namely Design. Construed in this way, a person who believes that every event is the result of Design has nothing to fear from the Explanatory Filter—no evidence can ever dislodge that opinion. This *may* be Dembski's view, but for the sake of charity, we have described the Filter in terms of rejection *and* acceptance.

The Caputo Example

Before discussing the filter in detail, we want to describe Dembski's treatment of one of the main examples that he uses to motivate his analysis (9-19,162-166). This is the case of Nicholas Caputo, who was a member of the Democratic party in New Jersey. Caputo's job was to determine whether Democrats or Republicans would be listed first on the ballot. The party listed first in an election has an edge, and this was common knowledge in Caputo's day. Caputo had this job for 41 years and he was supposed to do it fairly. Yet, in 40 out of 41 elections, he listed the Democrats first. Caputo claimed that each year he determined the order by drawing from an urn that gave Democrats and Republicans the same chance of winning. In spite of his protestations, Caputo was brought up on charges and the judges found against him. They rejected his claim that the outcome was due to chance, and were persuaded that he had rigged the results. The ordering of names on the ballots was due to Caputo's intelligent design.

In this story, the hypotheses of Chance and Intelligent Design are prominent. But what of the first alternative, that of Regularity? Dembski (11) says that this can be rejected because our background knowledge tells us that Caputo probably didn't innocently use a biased process. For example, we can rule out the possibility that Caputo, with the most honest of intentions, spun a roulette wheel in which 00 was labeled "Republican" and all the other numbers were labeled "Democrat." Apparently, we know before we examine Caputo's 41 decisions that there are just two possibilities—he did the equivalent of tossing a fair coin (Chance) or he intentionally gave the edge to his own party (Design).

There is a straightforward reason for thinking that the observed outcomes favor Design over Chance. If Caputo had allowed his political allegiance to guide his arrangement of ballots, you'd expect Democrats to be listed first on all or almost all of the ballots. However, if Caputo did the equivalent of tossing a fair coin, the outcome he obtained would be very surprising. This simple analysis also can be used to represent Paley's argument about the watch (Sober 1993). The key concept is *likelihood*. The likelihood of a hypothesis is the probability it confers on the observations; it is not the probability that the observations confer on the hypothesis. The likelihood of H relative to E is $Pr(E*H)$, not $Pr(H*E)$. Chance and Design can be evaluated by comparing their likelihoods, relative to the same set of observations. We do not claim that likelihood is the whole story, but surely it is relevant.

The reader will notice that the Filter does not use this simple likelihood analysis to help decide between Chance and Design. The likelihood of Chance is considered, but the likelihood of Design never is. Instead, the Chance hypothesis is evaluated for properties additional to its likelihood. Dembski thinks it is possible to reject Chance and accept Design without asking what Design predicts. Whether the Filter succeeds in showing that this possible is something we'll have to determine.

The Three Alternative Explanations

Dembski defines the Regularity hypothesis in different ways. Sometimes it is said to assert that the evidence E is noncontingent and is reducible to law (39, 53); at other times it is taken to claim that E is a deterministic consequence of earlier conditions (65, 146n5); and at still other times, it is supposed to say that E was highly probable, given some earlier state of the world (38). The Chance Hypothesis is taken to assign to E a lower probability than the Regularity Hypothesis assigns (40). The Design Hypothesis is said to be the complement of the first two alternatives. As a matter of stipulation, the three hypotheses are mutually exclusive and collectively exhaustive (36).

Dembski emphasizes that design need not involve intelligent agency (8-9, 36, 60, 228- 229). He regards design as a mark of intelligent agency; intelligent agency can produce design, but he seems to think that there could be other causes as well. On the other hand, Dembski says that "the explanatory filter pinpoints how we recognize intelligent agency" (66) and his section 2.4 is devoted to showing that design is reliably correlated with intelligent agency. Dembski needs to supply an account of what he means by design and how it can be caused by something other than intelligent agency.[4] His vague remark (228- 229) that design is equivalent to "information" is not enough. Dembski quotes Dretske (1981) with approval, as deploying the concept of information that the design hypothesis uses. However, Dretske's notion of information is, as Dembski points out, the Shannon-Weaver account, which describes a probabilistic dependency between two events labeled source and receiver. Hypotheses of mindless chance can be stated in terms of the Shannon-Weaver concept. Dembski (39) also says that the design hypothesis isn't "characterized by probability."

Understanding what "regularity," "chance," and "design" mean in Dembski's framework is made more difficult by some of his examples. Dembski discusses a teacher who finds that the essays submitted by two students are nearly identical (46). One hypothesis is that the students produced their work independently; a second hypothesis asserts that there was plagiarism. Dembski treats the hypothesis of independent origination as a Chance hypothesis and the plagiarism hypothesis as an instance of Design. Yet, both describe the matching papers as issuing from intelligent agency, as Dembski points out (47). Dembski says that context influences how a hypothesis gets classified (46). How context induces the classification that Dembski suggests remains a mystery.

The same sort of interpretive problem attaches to Dembski's discussion of the Caputo example. We think that all of the following hypotheses appeal to intelligent agency: (i) Caputo decided to spin a roulette wheel on which 00 was labeled "Republican" and the other numbers were labeled "Democrat"; (ii) Caputo decided to toss a fair coin; (iii) Caputo decided to favor his own party. Since all three hypotheses describe the ballot ordering as issuing from intelligent agency, all, apparently, are instances of Design in Dembski's sense. However, Dembski says that they are examples, respectively, of Regularity, Chance, and Design.

The Parsimony Ordering

Dembski says that Regularity is a more parsimonious hypothesis than Chance, and that Chance is more parsimonious than Design (38-39). He defends this ordering as follows:

> Note that explanations that appeal to regularity are indeed simplest, for they admit no contingency, claiming things always happen that way. Explanations that appeal to chance add a level of complication, for they admit contingency, but one characterized by probability. Most complicated are those explanations that appeal to design, for they admit contingency, but not one characterized by probability (39).

Here Dembski seems to interpret Regularity to mean that E is nomologically necessary or that E is a deterministic consequence of initial conditions. Still, why does this show that Regularity is simpler than Chance? And why is Chance simpler than Design? Even if design hypotheses were "not characterized by probability," why would that count as a reason? But, in fact, design hypotheses *do* in many instances confer probabilities on the observations. The ordering of Democrats and Republicans on the ballots is highly probable, given the hypothesis that Caputo rigged the ballots to favor his own party. Dembski supplements this general argument for his parsimony ordering with two examples (39). Even if these examples were convincing,[5] they would not establish the general point about the parsimony ordering.

It may be possible to replace Dembski's faulty argument for his parsimony ordering with a different argument that comes close to delivering what he wants. Perhaps determinism can be shown to be more parsimonious than indeterminism (Sober 1999a) and perhaps explanations that appeal to mindless processes can be shown to be simpler than explanations that appeal to intelligent agency (Sober 1998). But even if this can be done, it is important to understand what this parsimony ordering means. When scientists choose between competing curves, the simplicity of the competitors matters, but so does their fit-to-data. You don't reject a simple curve and adopt a complex curve just by seeing how the simple curve fits the data and without asking how well the complex curve does so. You need to ask how well *both* hypotheses fit the data. Fit-to-data is important in curve-fitting because it is a measure of *likelihood*; curves that are closer to the data confer on the data a higher probability than curves that are more distant. Dembski's parsimony ordering, even if correct, makes it puzzling why the Filter treats the likelihood of the Chance hypothesis as relevant, but ignores the likelihoods of Regularity and Design.

Why Regularity is Rejected

As just noted, the Explanatory Filter evaluates Regularity and Chance in different ways. The Chance hypothesis is evaluated in part by asking how probable it says the observations are. However, Regularity is not evaluated by asking how probable it says the observations are. The filter starts with the question, "Is E a high probability event?" (38) This doesn't mean "is E a high probability event according to the Regularity hypothesis?" Rather, you evaluate the probability of E on its own. Presumably, if you observe that events like E occur frequently, you should say that E has a high probability and so should conclude that E is due to Regularity. If events like E rarely occur, you should reject Regularity and move down the list.[6] However, since a given event can be described in many ways, any event can be made to appear common, and any can be made to appear rare.

Dembski's procedure for evaluating Regularity hypotheses would make no sense if it were intended to apply to *specific* hypotheses of that kind. After all, specific Regularity hypotheses (e.g., Newtonian mechanics) are often confirmed by events that happen rarely—the return of a comet, for example. And specific Regularity hypotheses are often *dis*confirmed by events that happen frequently. This suggests that what gets evaluated under the heading of "Regularity" are not *specific* hypotheses of that kind, but the *general* claim that E is due to some regularity or other. Understood in this way, it makes more sense why the likelihood of the Regularity hypothesis plays no role in the

Explanatory Filter. The claim that E is due to some regularity or other, *by definition*, says that E was highly probable, given antecedent conditions.

It is important to recognize that the Explanatory Filter is enormously ambitious. You don't just reject a given Regularity hypothesis; you reject all possible Regularity explanations (53). And the same goes for Chance—you reject the whole category; the Filter "sweeps the field clear" of *all* specific Chance hypotheses (41, 52-53). We doubt that there is any general inferential procedure that can do what Dembski thinks the Filter accomplishes. Of course, you presumably can accept "E is due to some regularity or other" if you accept a specific regularity hypothesis. But suppose you have tested and rejected the various specific regularity hypotheses that your background beliefs suggest. Are you obliged to reject the claim that *there exists* a regularity hypothesis that explains E? Surely it is clear that this does not follow.

The fact that the Filter allows you to accept or reject Regularity without attending to what specific Regularity hypotheses predict has some peculiar consequences. Suppose you have in mind just one specific regularity hypothesis that is a candidate for explaining E; you think that if E has a regularity-style explanation, this has got to be it. If E is a rare type of event, the Filter says to conclude that E is not due to Regularity. This can happen even if the specific hypothesis, when conjoined with initial condition statements, predicts E with perfect precision. Symmetrically, if E is a common kind of event, the Filter says not to reject Regularity, even if your lone specific Regularity hypothesis deductively entails that E is false. The Filter is too hard on Regularity, and too lenient.

The Specification Condition

To reject Chance, the evidence E must be "specified." This involves four conditions -- CINDE, TRACT, DELIM, and the description D* that you use to delimit E must have a low probability on the Chance hypothesis. We consider these in turn.

CINDE

Dembski says several times that you can't reject a Chance hypothesis just because it says that what you observe was improbable. If Jones wins a lottery, you can't automatically conclude that there is something wrong with the hypothesis that the lottery was fair and that Jones bought just one of the 10,000 tickets sold. To reject Chance, further conditions must be satisfied. CINDE is one of them.

CINDE means conditional independence. This is the requirement that Pr(E* H & I) = Pr(E * H), where H is the Chance hypothesis, E is the observations, and I is your background knowledge. H must render E conditionally independent of I. CINDE requires that H capture everything that your background beliefs say is probabilistically relevant to the occurrence of E.

CINDE is too lenient on Chance hypotheses—it says that their violating CINDE suffices for them to be accepted (or not rejected). Suppose you want to explain why Smith has lung cancer (E). It is part of your background knowledge (I) that he smoked cigarettes for thirty years, but you are considering the hypothesis (H) that Smith read the works of Ayn Rand and that this helped bring about his illness. To investigate this question, you do a statistical study and discover that smokers who read Rand have the same chance of lung cancer as smokers who do not. This study allows you to draw a conclusion about Smith— that Pr(E * H&I) = Pr(E * not-H&I). Surely this equality is evidence *against* the claim that E is due to H. However, the filter says that you can't reject the causal claim, because CINDE is false—Pr(E * H&I) ≠ Pr(E * H).[7]

TRACT and DELIM

The ideas examined so far in the Filter are probabilistic. The TRACT condition introduces concepts from a different branch of mathematics – the theory of computational complexity.   TRACT means tractability – to reject the Chance hypothesis, it must be possible for you to use your background information to formulate a description D* of features of the observations E. To construct this description, you needn't have any reason to think that it might be true. For example, you could satisfy TRACT by obtaining the description of E by "brute force" – that is, by producing descriptions of *all* the possible outcomes, one of which happens to cover E (150- 151).

Whether you can produce a description depends on the language and computational framework used. For example, the evidence in the Caputo example can be thought of as a specific sequence of 40 Ds and 1 R. TRACT would be satisfied if you have the ability to generate all of the following descriptions: "0 Rs and 41 Ds," "1 R and 40 Ds," "2 Rs and 39 Ds," ... "41 Rs and 0 Ds." Whether you can produce these descriptions depends on the character of the language you use (does it contain those symbols or others with the same meaning?) and on the computational procedures you use to generate descriptions (does generating those descriptions require a small number of steps, or too many for you to perform in your lifetime?). Because tractability depends on your choice of language and computational procedures, we think that TRACT has no evidential significance at all. Caputo's 41 decisions count against the hypothesis that he used a fair coin, and in favor of the hypothesis that he cheated, for reasons that have nothing to do with TRACT. The relevant point is simply that Pr(E*Chance) << Pr(E*Design).   This fact is not relative to the choice of language or computational framework.

The DELIM condition, as far as we can see, adds nothing to TRACT. A description D*, generated by one's background information, "delimits" the evidence E just in case E entails D*. In the Caputo case, TRACT and DELIM would be satisfied if you were able to write down all possible sequences of D's and R's that are 41 letters long. They also would be satisfied by generating a series of weaker descriptions, like the one just mentioned. In fact, just writing down a tautology satisfies TRACT and DELIM (165). On the assumption that human beings are able to write down tautologies, we conclude that these two conditions are always satisfied and so play no substantive role in the Filter.

Do CINDE, TRACT, and DELIM "Call the Chance Hypothesis into Question"?

Dembski argues that CINDE, TRACT and DELIM, if true, "call the chance hypothesis H into question." We quote his argument in its entirety:

> The interrelation between CINDE and TRACT is important. Because I is conditionally independent of E given H, any knowledge S has about I ought to give S no knowledge about E so long as --- and this is the crucial assumption --- E occurred according to the chance hypothesis H. Hence, any pattern formulated on the basis of I ought not give S any knowledge about E either. Yet the fact that it does in case D delimits E means that I is after all giving S knowledge about E. The assumption that E occurred according to the chance hypothesis H, though not quite refuted, is therefore called into question (147).

Dembski then adds:

> To actually refute this assumption, and thereby eliminate chance, S will have to do one more thing, namely, show that the probability P(D* | H), that is, the probability of the event described by the pattern D, is small enough (147).

We'll address this claim about the impact of low probability later.

To reconstruct Dembski's argument, we need to clarify how he understands the conjunction TRACT & DELIM. Dembski says that when TRACT and DELIM are satisfied, your background beliefs I provide you with "knowledge" or "information" about E (143, 147). In fact, TRACT and DELIM have nothing to do with informational relevance understood as an evidential concept. When I provides information about E, it is natural to think that Pr(E | I) – Pr(E); I provides information because taking it into account changes the probability you assign to E. It is easy to see how TRACT & DELIM can both be satisfied by brute force without this evidential condition's being satisfied. Suppose you have no idea how Caputo might have obtained his sequence of D's and R's; still, you are able to generate the sequence of descriptions we mentioned before. The fact that you can generate a description which delimits (or even matches) E does not ensure that your background knowledge provides evidence as to whether E will occur. As noted, generating a tautology satisfies both TRACT and DELIM, but tautologies don't provide information about E.

Even though the conjunction TRACT & DELIM should not be understood evidentially (i.e., as asserting that $Pr[E \mid I] - Pr[E]$), we think this *is* how Dembski understands TRACT & DELIM in the argument quoted. This suggests the following reconstruction of Dembski's argument:

(1) CINDE, TRACT, and DELIM are true of the chance hypothesis H and the agent S.

(2) If CINDE is true and S is warranted in accepting H (i.e., that E is due to chance), then S should assign $Pr(E \mid I) = Pr(E)$.

(3) If TRACT and DELIM are true, then S should not assign $Pr(E \mid I) = Pr(E)$.

----

(4) Therefore, S is not warranted in accepting H.

Thus reconstructed, Dembski's argument is valid. We grant premise (1) for the sake of argument. We've already explained why (3) is false. So is premise (2); it seems to rely on something like the following principle:

(*)   If S should assign $Pr(E|H\&I) = p$ and S is warranted in accepting H, then S should assign $Pr(E|I) = p$.

If (*) were true, (2) would be true. However, (*) is false. For (*) entails

If S should assign $Pr(H|H) = 1.0$ and S is warranted in accepting H, then S should assign $Pr(H) = 1.0$.

Justifiably accepting H does not justify assigning H a probability of unity. Bayesians warn against assigning probabilities of 1 and 0 to any proposition that you might want to consider revising later. Dembski emphasizes that the Chance hypothesis is always subject to revision.

It is worth noting that a weaker version of (2) is true:

(2*)   If CINDE is true and S should assign $Pr(H)=1$, then S should assign $Pr(E \mid I) = Pr(E)$.

One then can reasonably conclude that

(4*)   S should not assign Pr(H) = 1.

However, a fancy argument isn't needed to show that (4*) is true. Moreover, the fact that (4*) is true does nothing to undermine S's confidence that the Chance hypothesis H is the true explanation of E, provided that S has not stumbled into the brash conclusion that H is entirely certain. We conclude that Dembski's argument fails to "call H into question."

It may be objected that our criticism of Dembski's argument depends on our taking the conjunction TRACT & DELIM to have probabilistic consequences. We reply that this is a *charitable* reading of his argument. If the conjunction does not have probabilistic consequences, then the argument is a nonstarter. How can purely non-probabilistic conditions come into conflict with a purely probabilistic condition like CINDE? Moreover, since TRACT and DELIM, *sensu strictu*, are always true (if the agent's side information allows him/her to generate a tautology), how could these trivially satisfied conditions, when coupled with CINDE, possibly show that H is questionable?

The Improbability Threshold

The Filter says that Pr(E * Chance) must be sufficiently low if Chance is to be rejected. How low is low enough? Dembski's answer is that Pr(E(n) * Chance) < ½ , where n is the number of times in the history of the universe that an event of kind E actually occurs (209, 214-217). As mentioned earlier, if Jones wins a lottery, it does not follow that we should reject the hypothesis that the lottery was fair and that he bought just one of the 10,000 tickets sold. Dembski thinks the reason this is so is that lots of *other* lotteries have occurred. If p is the probability of Jones' winning the lottery if it is fair and he bought one of the 10,0000 tickets sold, and if there are n such lotteries that ever occur, then the relevant probability to consider is Pr(E(n) * Chance) = 1 - (1-p)^n . If n is large enough this quantity can be greater than ½, even though p is very small. As long as the probability exceeds ½ that Smith wins lottery L2, or Quackdoodle wins lottery L3, or ... or Snerdley wins lottery Ln, given the hypothesis that each of these lotteries was fair and the individuals named each bought one of the 10,000 tickets sold, we shouldn't reject the Chance hypothesis about Jones.

Why is ½ the relevant threshold? Dembski thinks this follows from the Likelihood Principle (190-198). As noted earlier, that principle states that if two hypotheses confer different probabilities on the same observations, the one that entails the higher probability is the one that is better supported by those observations. Dembski thinks this principle solves the following prediction problem. If the Chance hypothesis predicts that either F or not-F will be true, but says that the latter is more probable, then, if you believe the Chance hypothesis and must predict whether F or not-F will be true, you should predict not-F. We agree that if a gun were put to your head, that you should predict the option that the Chance hypothesis says is more probable if you believe the Chance hypothesis and this exhausts what you know that is relevant. However, this doesn't follow from the likelihood principle. The likelihood principle tells you how to evaluate different hypotheses by seeing what probabilities they confer on the observations. Dembski's prediction principle describes how you should choose between two predictions, not on the basis of observations, but on the basis of a theory you already accept; the theory says that one prediction is more *probable*, not that it is more *likely*.

Even though Dembski's prediction principle is right, it does not entail that you should reject Chance if Pr(E(n) * Chance) < ½ and the other specification conditions are satisfied. Dembski thinks that you face a "probabilistic inconsistency" (196) if you believe the Chance hypothesis and the Chance hypothesis leads you to predict not-F rather than F, but you then discover that E is true and that E is an instance of F. However, there is no inconsistency here of any kind. Perfectly sensible hypotheses sometimes entail that not-F is more probable than F; they can remain perfectly sensible even if F has the audacity to occur.

An additional reason to think that there is no "probabilistic inconsistency" here is that H and not-H can *both* confer an (arbitrarily) low probability on E. In such cases, Dembski must say that you are caught in a "probabilistic inconsistency" *no matter what you accept.* Suppose you know that an urn contains either 10% green balls or 1% green balls; perhaps you saw the urn being filled from one of two buckets (you don't know which), whose contents you examined. Suppose you draw 10 balls from the urn and find that 7 are green. From a likelihood point of view, the evidence favors the 10% hypothesis. However, Dembski would point out that the 10% hypothesis predicted that most of the balls in your sample would fail to be green. Your observation contradicts this prediction. Are you therefore forced to reject the 10% hypothesis? If so, you are forced to reject the 1% hypothesis on the same grounds. But you know that one or the other hypothesis is true. Dembski's talk of a "probabilistic inconsistency" suggests that he thinks that improbable events can't really occur—a true theory would *never* lead you to make probabilistic predictions that fail to come true.

Dembski's criterion is simultaneously too hard on the Chance hypothesis, and too lenient. Suppose there is just one lottery in the whole history of the universe. Then the Filter says you should reject the hypothesis that Jones bought one of 10,000 tickets in a fair lottery, just on the basis of observing that Jones won (assuming that CINDE and the other conditions are satisfied). But surely this is too strong a conclusion. Shouldn't your acceptance or rejection of the Chance hypothesis depend on what alternative hypotheses you have available? Why can't you continue to think that the lottery was fair when Jones wins it? The fact that there is just one lottery in the history of the universe hardly seems relevant. Dembski is too hard on Chance in this case. To see that he also is too lenient, let's assume that there have been many lotteries, so that Pr(E(n) * Chance) > ½. The Filter now requires that you not reject Chance, even if you have reason to consider seriously the Design hypothesis that the lottery was rigged by Jones' cousin, Nicholas Caputo. We think you should embrace Design in this case, but the Filter disagrees. The flaw in the Filter's handling of both these examples traces to the same source. Dembski evaluates the Chance hypothesis without considering the likelihood of Design.

We have another objection to Dembski's answer to the question of how low Pr(E(n) * Chance) must be to reject Chance. How is one to decide which actual events count as "the same" with respect to what the Chance hypothesis asserts about E? Consider again the case of Jones and his lottery. Must the other events that are relevant to calculating E(n) be lotteries? Must exactly 10,000 tickets have been sold? Must the winners of the other lotteries have bought just one ticket? Must they have the name "Jones?" Dembski's E(n) has no determinate meaning.

Dembski supplements his threshold of Pr(E(n)*Chance) < ½ with a separate calculation (209). He provides generous estimates of the number of particles in the universe (10^{80}), of the duration of the universe (10^{25} seconds), and of the number of changes per second that a particle can experience (10^{45}). From these he computes that there is a maximum of 10^{150} specified events in the whole history of the universe. The reason is that there can't be more agents than particles, and there can't be more acts of specifying than changes in particle state.[8] Dembski thinks it follows that if the Chance hypothesis assigns to any event that occurs a probability lower than $1/[(2)10^{150}]$, that you should reject the Chance hypothesis (if CINDE and the other conditions are satisfied). This is a fallacious inference. The fact that there are no more than 10^{150} acts of specifying in the whole history of the universe tells you nothing about what the probabilities of those specified events are or should be thought to be. Even if sentient creatures manage to write down only N inscriptions, why can't those creatures develop a well confirmed theory that says that some actual events have probabilities that are less than $1/(2N)$?

Conjunctive, Disjunctive, and Mixed Explananda

Suppose the Filter says to reject Regularity and that TRACT, CINDE and the other conditions are satisfied, so that accepting or rejecting the Chance hypothesis is said to depend on whether $Pr(E(n) * Chance) < \frac{1}{2}$. Now suppose that the evidence E is the conjunction E1&E2&...& Em. It is possible for the conjunction to be sufficiently improbable on the Chance hypothesis that the Filter says to reject Chance, but that each conjunct is sufficiently probable according to the Chance hypothesis that the Filter says that Chance should be accepted. In this case, the Filter concludes that Design explains the conjunction while Chance explains each conjunct. For a second example, suppose that E is the disjunction E1v E2 v ... v Em. Suppose that the disjunction is sufficiently probable, according to the Chance hypothesis, so that the Filter says not to reject Chance, but that each disjunct is sufficiently improbable that the Filter says to reject Chance. The upshot is that the Filter says that each disjunct is due to Design though the disjunction is due to Chance. For a third example, suppose the Filter says that E1 is due to Chance and that E2 is due to Design. What will the Filter conclude about the conjunction E1&E2? The Filter makes no room for "mixed explanations" –it cannot say that the explanation of E1&E2 is simply the conjunction of the explanations of E1 and E2.

Rejecting Chance as a Category Requires A Kind of Omniscience

Although specific chance hypotheses may confer definite probabilities on the observations E, this is not true of the generic hypothesis that E is due to some chance hypothesis or other. Yet, when Dembski talks of "rejecting Chance" he means rejecting the whole category, not just the specific chance hypotheses one happens to formulate. The Filter's treatment of Chance therefore applies only to agents who believe they have a complete list of the chance processes that might explain E. As Dembski (41) says, "... before we even begin to send E through the Explanatory Filter, we need to know what probability distribution(s), if any, were operating to produce the event." *Dembski's epistemology never tells you to reject Chance if you do not believe you have considered all possible chance explanations.*

Here Dembski is *much* too hard on Design. Paley reasonably concluded that the watch he found is better explained by postulating a watchmaker than by the hypothesis of random physical processes. This conclusion makes sense even if Paley admits his lack of omniscience about possible Chance hypotheses, but it does not make sense according to the Filter. What Paley did was compare a *specific* chance hypothesis and a *specific* design hypothesis without pretending that he thereby surveyed all possible chance hypotheses. For this reason as well as for others we have mentioned, friends of Design should shun the Filter, not embrace it.

Concluding Comments

We mentioned at the outset that Dembski does not say in his book how he thinks his epistemology resolves the debate between evolutionary theory and creationism.[9] Still, it is abundantly clear that the overall shape of his epistemology reflects the main pattern of argument used in "the intelligent design movement." Accordingly, it is no surprise that a leading member of this movement has praised Dembski's epistemology for clarifying the logic of design inference (Behe 1996, pp. 285-286). Creationists frequently think they can establish the plausibility of what they believe merely by criticizing the alternatives (Behe 1996; Plantinga 1993, 1994; Phillip Johnson, as quoted in Stafford 1997, p. 22). This would make sense if two conditions were satisfied. If those alternative theories had deductive consequences about what we observe, one could demonstrate that those theories are false by showing that the predictions they entail are false. If, in addition, the hypothesis of intelligent design were the only alternative to the theories thus refuted, one could conclude that the design hypothesis is correct. However, neither condition obtains. Darwinian theory makes probabilistic, not deductive, predictions. And there is no reason to think that the only alternative to Darwinian theory is intelligent design.

When prediction is probabilistic, a theory cannot be accepted or rejected just by seeing what it predicts (Royall 1997, ch. 3). The best you can do is compare theories with each other. To test evolutionary theory against the hypothesis of intelligent design, you must know what *both* hypotheses predict about observables (Fitelson and Sober 1998, Sober 1999b). The searchlight therefore must be focused on the design hypothesis itself. What does *it* predict? If defenders of the design hypothesis want their theory to be scientific, they need to do the scientific work of formulating and testing the predictions that creationism makes (Kitcher 1984, Pennock 1999). Dembski's Explanatory Filter encourages creationists to think that this responsibility can be evaded. However, the fact of the matter is that the responsibility must be faced.

References

Behe, M. (1996) *Darwin's Black Box*. New York: Free Press.

Dembski, W. (1998), "Intelligent Design as a Theory of Information," unpublished manuscript. Reprinted electronically at the following web site: http://www.arn.org/docs/dembski/.

Dretske, F. (1981): *Knowledge and the Flow of Information*. Cambridge, MA: MIT Press.

Fitelson, B. and Sober, E. (1998): "Plantinga's Probability Arguments Against Evolutionary Naturalism." *Pacific Philosophical Quarterly* 79: 115-129.

Kitcher, P. (1984): *Abusing Science—the Case Against Creationism*. Cambridge, MA: MIT Press.

Pennock, R. (1999): *Tower of Babel*. Cambridge, MA: MIT Press.

Plantinga, A. (1993): *Warrant and Proper Function*. Oxford: Oxford University Press.

_____. (1994): "Naturalism Defeated." unpublished manuscript.

Royall, R. (1997): *Statistical Evidence—a Likelihood Paradigm*. London: Chapman and Hall.

Sober, E. (1993): *Philosophy of Biology*. Boulder, CO: Westview Press.

_____. (1998): "Morgan's Canon." In C. Allen and D. Cummins (eds.), *The Evolution of Mind*, Oxford University Press, pp. 224-242.

_____. (1999a): "Physicalism from a Probabilistic Point of View." *Philosophical Studies,* forthcoming.

_____. (1999b): "Testability." *Proceedings and Addresses of the American Philosophical Association*, forthcoming.

Stafford, T. (1997): "The Making of a Revolution." *Christianity Today*. December 8, pp. 16-22.

Notes

1. We thank William Dembski and Philip Kitcher for comments on an earlier draft.

2. Dembski (48) provides a deductively valid argument form in which "E is due to design" is the conclusion. However, Dembski's final formulation of "the design inference" (221-3) deploys an epistemic version of the argument, whose conclusion is "S is warranted in inferring that E is due to design." One of the premisses of this latter argument contains two layers of epistemic operators; it says that if certain (epistemic) assumptions are true, then S is warranted in asserting that "S is not warranted in inferring that E did not occur according to the chance hypothesis." Dembski claims (223) that this convoluted epistemic argument is valid, and defends this claim by referring the reader back to the quite different, nonepistemic, argument presented on p. 48. This establishes nothing as to the validity of the (official) epistemic rendition of "the design inference."

3. For example, he says that "to retain chance a subject S must simply lack warrant for inferring that E did not occur according to the chance hypothesis H (220)."

4. Dembski (1998) apparently abandons the claim that design can occur without intelligent agency; here he says that after regularity and chance are eliminated, what remains is the hypothesis of an intelligent cause.

5. In the first example, Dembski (39) says that Newton's hypothesis that the stability of the solar system is due to God's intervention into natural regularities is less parsimonious than Laplace's hypothesis that the stability is due solely to regularity. In the second, he compares the hypothesis that a pair of dice is fair with the hypothesis that each is heavily weighted towards coming up 1. He claims that the latter provides the more parsimonious explanation of why snake-eyes occurred on a single roll. We agree with Dembski's simplicity ordering in the first example; the example illustrates the idea that a hypothesis that postulates two causes R and G is less parsimonious than a hypothesis that postulates R alone. However, this is not an example of Regularity versus Design, but an example of Regularity&Design versus Regularity alone; in fact, it is an example of two causes versus one, and the parsimony ordering has nothing to do with the fact that one of those causes involves design. In Dembski's second example, the hypotheses differ in likelihood, relative to the data cited; however, if parsimony is supposed to be a different consideration from fit-to-data, it is questionable whether these hypotheses differ in parsimony.

6. Dembski incorrectly applies his own procedure to the Caputo example when he says (11) that the regularity hypothesis should be rejected on the grounds that background knowledge makes it improbable that Caputo in all honesty used a biased device. Here Dembski is describing the probability of Regularity, not the probability of E.

7. Strictly speaking, CINDE requires that $Pr(E * H\&J) = Pr(E * J)$, for all J such that J can be "generated" by the side information I (145). Without going into details about what Dembski means by "generating," we note that this formulation of CINDE is logically stronger than the one discussed above. This entails that it is even harder to reject chance hypotheses than we suggest in our cancer example.

8. Note the *materialistic* character of Dembski's assumption here.

9. Dembski has been more forthcoming about his views in other manuscripts. The interested reader should consult the following web site:

http://www.arn.org/docs/dembski/.

28

A Few Suggestions for the Proponents of Intelligent Design

RAYMOND E. GRIZZLE

Several recent publications, including papers in *Perspectives on Science and Christian Faith*[1] have dealt with the concepts of intelligent design (ID)[2], methodological naturalism (MN)[3] and related topics. Arguments (for God's existence) from design, especially in the Judeo-Christian tradition, have a long history. Many psalms, remind us that the wonder of creation point to their Creator. The apostle Paul argues that "... God's invisible qualities - his eternal power and divine nature - have been, clearly seen, being understood from what has been made..." Romans 1:20). Natural theology, which was built on the pretense that nature revealed much about its Creator, occupied a prominent position in academic circles for centuries. Recent work by scientists has also pointed in the direction of a Creator.[4] All of us in the American Scientific Affiliation must be proponents of design, at least in so far as we see the evidence of God in the world we study. However, compared to traditional arguments from design, there is one crucial difference for me in the current push for ID—the attempt to make design a part of science. In contrast, I view traditional arguments from design as pointing beyond science to our Creator. This difference is at the core of why I remain unconvinced of the overall merits of the movement.

Arguments for ID are typically lengthy, philosophically heavy, and deal with a variety of topics. So far, the ID literature contains much with which I agree. However, I remain skeptical because the vast majority of ID arguments seem to be only, peripherally related to my major objections. By this communication, I hope to distill these objections to three major areas, and I will discuss them in the context of some suggestions.

A personal testimony

The primary suggestion I offer to proponents of ID is to disconnect explicitly and emphatically your argument from arguments for eliminating MN as a restriction on science. Stop arguing for a "theistic science."[5] If this is done, you will then stand more directly in line with what I believe is a powerful and still influential tradition of using the characteristics of creation to point beyond science and toward the Creator. I see design in nearly everything I study as a scientist, but I see this design as coming from a realm beyond science. For me, MN has been a kind of guidepost that has allowed me to sort through the plethora of writings on creation, evolution, and related topics, and arrive at a position where I have begun to work on a satisfying integration of faith and science. Let me explain.

When I began to explore the relationship between science (particularly biology, which is my major area of study) and theology, I quickly encountered the writings of "young-earth creationists" who insisted there were only two options for interpreting the biotic world: (their brand of) creationism and evolutionism. These creationists and some atheistic scientists further insisted that the two positions were mutually exclusive, thus requiring a conflict approach to science/theology interactions. As a biologist, this meant I needed to find problems with evolution that were serious enough to warrant its abandonment. Fortunately, this really only meant I would have to read, analyze, and learn all the objections to evolution being raised by several individuals, who had apparently dedicated their lives to attacking it. The job seemed easy. Even if difficult times came along, I could always fall back on the notion that creationism would undoubtedly win in the end because it was clearly God's position. Several things happened along the way, however, to upset my plan.

The most important thing was that I encountered some alternative viewpoints on the relationship between science and theology that made a lot of sense, some of which are at least touched upon in Bernard Ramm's (1954) well-known book, *The Christian View of Science and Scripture*. Ramm's book is a bit dated now, but it is still useful as a survey of much of the early literature on science/theology interactions and as a concise statement of one very influential view of what science is and how it can be related to theology.

Both science and theology deal with the same universe. The goal of science is to understand what is included in the concept of nature, and the goal of theology is to understand what is included under the concept of God. The emphasis in science is on the visible universe, and in theology the emphasis is on the invisible universe, *but it is one universe*. If it is one universe then the visible and the invisible interpenetrate epistemologically and metaphysically (p.28).

Ramm's view of science and theology suggests some general domains for each, indicating that science mainly deals with the natural world and theology mainly deals with God. Perhaps more importantly, however, it asserts that the boundaries between the domains of science and theology will not be neat, suggesting that there may be problems with determining explicit boundaries. Later, Ramm makes the important point that God is the ultimate cause of the Universe and all other causes discovered by humans are secondary (p. 192). Ramm's view provides the basis for a dualistic view of nature with respect to explanatory causes. It also supports the development of concepts like complementarity and levels of explanation. It is just such a view that led me out of what I now consider the quagmire of "creation science." I saw that evolutionary theory was a theory of science and it need not be set against belief in a Creator. It provided Science against one interpretation of the early chapters of Genesis but it did not provide any evidence against the existence of God. I felt as if my science—and my theology—had been freed so that both could be explored in a satisfying and effective way.

My message in all this is that I continue to cling to MN because it has been so useful. So far, the ID literature with which I am familiar has offered the same confusion I found in the creation-science literature, except it is packaged in some new terminology.[6] Because arguments to eliminate MN from science are really what concern me the most, I will turn to two related areas in the ID literature where I find the arguments particularly unconvincing. I do this to further elaborate how MN has been helpful to me, and because I doubt anybody in the ID movement will heed my first suggestion—to disconnect his or her argument from arguments for eliminating MN as a restriction on science. At this point, most ID proponents have far too much invested in what I feel are revisionist arguments for modern science which center on eliminating MN.

Some history of MN

My second suggestion to proponents of ID is to stop stating or implying that MN is just an "arbitrary" restriction on modern science. It is not an "arbitrary restriction in any sense of ordinary usage of the word. Methodological naturalism is, in fact, a central part of the practice of science that has completely emerged against all disciplines in the last 100 or so years. It has been a major force within the scientific community generally for centuries.[7] The history of MN is complex and intertwined with a variety of philosophical and social issues. It has been developing at least since the 1500s, when Francis Bacon and

Galileo Galilei were struggling with a science that was deeply intertwined with theology. It persists as perhaps the distinguishing characteristic of what many consider to be a general definition of science. For example, in his introduction to the philosophy of science, Del Ratzsch.[8] discusses this restriction as one way science is usually defined today. Paul de Vries has provided an insightful assessment of MN as a central component of modern science from a theological perspectives.[9] Several recent papers in *PSCF* have dealt with MN as a core concept of modern science.[10] And in all my training in science, there was never any mention of even the possibility that anything other than natural causes should be included in scientific explanations. Therefore, I was more than a little surprised to read the following statement by J. P. Moreland:

> Theistic science has been recognized as science by philosophers and scientists throughout much of the history of science. Thus the burden of proof is on anyone who would revise this tradition...[11]

I agree that theistic science has been recognized as science throughout much of the history of science, but this recognition for approximately the last 100 years has only come from fringe groups. I suggest to Moreland that he needs to do more work on the modern history of science, including research on how science is taught today in undergraduate and graduate programs. If he still thinks theistic science has any standing at all in modern science, he should simply read a few science textbooks looking for God as a casual explanation. Moreland is among the revisionists, not the other way around.

MN and Demarcation Arguments

The final suggestion I make to proponents of ID is simply to admit that science and religion are different in at least some respects, then decide how they are different. One disturbing aspect of the ID literature is page after page of discussion indicating there is really no difference between science and other disciplines: the articles by Moreland and Meyer in the March 1994 issue of *PSCF* are examples (see note 1). I do not question the contention by both Meyer and Moreland that many philosophers long ago abandoned attempts at distinguishing science from non-science. However, I maintain that it would be difficult indeed to find anyone (other than some philosophers?) who thinks science and religion are the same thing. I begin with quotes from Moreland and Meyer to further explain my objections.

Moreland argues in favor of a view he says is prevalent among philosophers: "there is no adequate line of demarcation between science and non-science/pseudoscience, no set of necessary and sufficient conditions for something to count as scientific"(p.4). He continues later: "The plain fact is that historians and philosophers are almost universally agreed that there is no adequate definition of science...no line of demarcation between science and non-science or pseudo-science..."(p.23). Meyer concurs: "Philosophers of science have generally lost patience with attempts to discredit theories as 'nonscientific' by using philosophical or methodological litmus tests. Such so-called 'demarcation criteria' - criteria that purport to distinguish true science from pseudo-science, metaphysics and religion - have inevitably fallen prey to death by a thousand counter examples."(p.14).

If these statements are taken in a straightforward manner, then all modern dictionaries need to be revised. If, however, they refer mainly to assessment of the relative merits or certainty of some scientific theories to another form of knowledge, then I could accept them in part. I talked with Steve Meyer, and he assures me that there are differences between science and religion and in the quote here he was mainly referring to attempts at determining where the two overlap (personal communication, 12 May, 1994). In other works, he feels the problem is largely one of determining boundary conditions, I concur. This is the problem Ramm (1954, p.28) was referring to in the above quote. It will always be difficult to define in detail the relationship between science and religion, particularly their boundaries, but surely, we can agree the two are different. I suggest that proponents of ID begin with this assumption and turn to determining what makes science and religion different rather than continuing to wring their hands over how similar they are. I further suggest that if they do this, they will find MN at the core of the [scientific] disciplines.

Closing Remarks

I have primarily argued here against one major component of the ID movement: the re-introduction of God as a causal explanation into science. My position is based on a high respect for both science and theology in their present forms. I just do not see the problems with a naturalistic science that so many proponents of ID bemoan. In contrast, I think a careful look at the history of science/religion interactions will show that MN is the most important concept to be developed thus far. It has allowed both to flourish without undue control by the other. I believe that if the ID movement successfully resulted in the theistic science some envision, we would be well on our way backwards in time to the old confrontational, either/or debates fought by Galileo and others. The overall result would be no different from that of some kinds of creationism (e.g. "young-earth creationism") where one is forced to accept either a naturalistic explanation or God. I much prefer a dualistic approach where the natural mechanisms described by science are at lease potentially accepted along with

514 Raymond E. Grizzle

the supernatural descriptions of theology. I see the most productive work ahead of us to be determining how the two disciplines in their present forms should interact. There may be some "ultimate theory" developed someday that incorporates all disciplines. The road that leads to such a theory is not clear to me but I do not think most proponents of ID are even moving in the right direction. If I am mistaken, I sincerely hope they will (again) take some tie to try to help me see the errors in my ways.

Acknowledgments

Chuck Austerberrv, Wilbur Bullock, Paul Rothrock and Andy Whipple reviewed an earlier version of the manuscript. In some areas we differ in our views, but in all cases I am most appreciative of their comments.

Notes

1. Hasker, W., 1992, "Evolution and Alvin Plantinga," *Perspectives on Science and Christian Faith (PSCF),*44 (3):150-162; Murphey, N., 1993, "Phillip Johnson on Trial: A Critique of His Critique of Darwin," *PSCF,*45(1) 26-36; Moreland, J.P.,1994a, "Conceptual Problems and the Scientific Status of Creation Science," *PSCF*, 46(1) 2-13; Moreland, J.P., 1994b "Response to Meyer and Bube," *PSCF.*

2. ID refers to a movement that is partially defined by the title of a recent book edited by J. P. Moreland(1994) *The Creation Hypothesis: Scientific Evidence for an Intelligent Designer*, University Press. According to the back cover, this book aims to "...offer the foundation for a new paradigm of scientific thinking." ID was first popularized in a volume entitled, *Of Pandas and People* by P. Davis and D. H. Kenyon,, published in 1989 by Haughton Publishing Company, Dallas, Texas. Most ID proponents specifically aim, to construct a Theistic Science, whereby God (but see note 5) can be invoked as a casual explanation in science.

3. I define MN as the restriction of scientific explanations to natural causes. I explicitly do not use the term to give legitimacy to Scientism and related views, whereby science is declared to be the only valid explanation of something. Nor do I define it as the restriction of science to information provided by nature. In other words, I do not eliminate theology or the Bible as possible sources of information to be used in carrying out scientific investigations, but any scientific explanations that result from such investigations must not include - or imply - supernatural causes.

4. E.g. Templeton, J. M. and. R. L. Herrmann, 1989, *The God Who Would be Known: Revelations of the Divine in Contemporary Science.* Harper & Row;

Van Till, H. ... et al. 1990. *Portraits of Creation: Biblical and Scientific Perspectives on the World's Formation*, Eerdmans.

5. I am aware that some ID proponents emphatically deny they necessarily refer to God by their arguments but I think they are only deceiving themselves if they think those outside the ID movement feel the same way. For example, see *The Wall Street Journal*, Monday, November 14, 1994 for an article on the ID movement and subtitled "Who did the Designing. It Doesn't Say: Critics See Disguised Creationism, 'Agent' Who Hath No Name."

6. E.g Meyer, S.C. 1994. *"The Methodological Equivalence of Design & Descent: Can There Be a Scientific Theory of Creation."* pp. 67-112 in: Moreland, J.P. 1994 (ed.) (note 2), p. 70.

7. Barbour, Ian G., 1966, *Issues in Science and Religion,* Harper & Row; Klaarer,, Eugene M., 1977, *Religious Origins of Modern Science,* Eerdmans Hummel, Charles E., 1986, *The Galileo Connection,* InterVarsity Press; Barbour, Ian G. 1990. *Religion in an Age of Science,* Harper & Row.

8. Ratzsch, Del, 1986, *Philosophy of Science: The Natural Sciences in Christian Perspective,* InterVarsity Press, p.14.

9. de Vries, Paul, 1986, "Naturalism in the Natural Sciences: A Christian Perspective." *Christian Scholar's Review* 15(4):399-396.

10. See papers in note 1 by Bube, Hasker, and Murphy.

11. Moreland, J.P. 1994. "Theistic Science and Methodoligical Naturalism" in Moreland, J.P.1994 (ed.) (note 2), p.51.

Contributors

Francisco J. Ayala, Donald Bren Professor of Biological Sciences, Department of Ecology and Evolution, University of California - Irvine

Michael J. Behe, Professor, Department of Biological Sciences, Lehigh University

William A. Dembski, Research Associate Professor, Baylor University

John R. Durant, Assistant Director, National Museum of Science and Industry, England

Freeman J. Dyson, Faculty, Institute for Advanced Study, Princeton

Niles Eldredge, Curator, Department of Invertebrates, American Museum of Natural History, New York

Ursula Goodenough, Professor, Department of Biology, Washington University

Douglas J. Futuyma, Professor, Department of , State University of New York – Stony Brook

Stephen Jay Gould, Alexander Agassiz Professor of Zoology and Curator of Invertebrate Paleontology in the Museum of Comparative Zoology, Harvard University

Raymond Grizzle, Research Scientist, Jackson Estuarine Laboratory, University of New Hampshire

John F. Haught, Professor, Department of Theology, Georgetown University

Philip Hefner, Director, Zygon Center for Religion and Science

Elizabeth A. Johnson, C.S.J., Department of Theology, Fordham University

Charles R. Marshall, Professor of Molecular Paleobiology, Department of Earth and Space Science, University of California – Los Angeles

Ernst Mayr, Alexander Agassiz Professor of Zoology, Emeritus, Harvard University

James B. Miller, Senior Program Associate, American Association for the Advancement of Science Program of Dialogue on Science, Ethics and Religion

Kenneth R. Miller, Professor of Biology, Department of Molecular Biology, Cell Biology, and Biochemistry, Brown University

Ronald L. Numbers, Hilldale and William Coleman Professor of the History of Science and Medicine, Department of the History of Medicine, University of Wisconsin-Madison

Arthur R. Peacocke, Warden Emeritus of the Society of Ordained Scientists and Honorary Canon at Christ Church Cathedral in Oxford

Stephen J. Pope, Associate Professor and Chair, Department of Theology,
    Boston College
Mark Ridley, Department of Zoology, Oxford University
*G. Ledyard Stebbins**, Emeritus Professor, University of California - Davis
Ian Tattersall, Curator, Department of Anthropology, American Museum of
    Natural History, New York
David Sloan Wilson, Professor, Department of Biological Sciences, State
    University of New York – Binghamton

*Deceased.

Bibliography

General Science and Religion

Barbour, Ian G. *Science and Religion: Historical and Contemporary Issues.* Harper San Francisco, 1997.

Brooke, John H. *Science and Religion: Some Historical Perspectives.* Cambridge University Press, 1991.

Haught, John. *Science and Religion: From Conflict to Conversation.* Paulist Press, 1998.

Lindberg, David C. and Ronald L. Numbers, eds. *God and Nature: Historical Essays on the Encounter Between Christianity and Science.* University of California Press, 1986.

Richardson, W. Mark and Wesley J. Wildman. *Religion and Science: History, Method, Dialogue.* Routledge, 1996) .

The Theory of Evolution

Darwin, Charles. *The Origin of Species.* Grammercy, 1998.

Dobzhansky, Theodosius, Francisco J. Ayala, G. Ledyard Stebbins and James W. Valentine, eds. *Evolution.* Freeman, 1977.

Eldredge, Niles. *Reinventing Darwin: The Great Debate at the High Table of Evolutionary Theory* John Wiley & Sons, 1995.

Futuyma, Douglas J. *Evolutionary Biology, 3rd ed.* Sinauer Assoc., 1997.

_____. *Science on Trial: The Case for Evolution.* Sinauer Assoc., 1995.

Marshall, Charles and J. William Schopf, eds. *Evolution and the Molecular Revolution.* Jones and Bartlett Publishers, 1996.

Mayr, Ernst. *One Long Argument: Charles Darwin and the Genesis of Modern Evolutionary Thought.* Harvard University Press, 1993.

Ridley, Mark. *Evolution.* Blackwell Science, Inc., 1996.

Ross, Robert M., Warren D. Allmon and Stephen Jay Gould. *Causes of Evolution : A Paleontological Perspective.* University of Chicago Press, 1991.

Smith, John Maynard and Richard Dawkins. *The Theory of Evolution.* Cambridge University Press, 1993.

Williams, George C. *Adaptation and Natural Selection: A Critique of Some Current Evolutionary Thought.* Princeton University Press, 1996.

The History of Life

Ayala, Francisco J. *Origin of Species.* Carolina Biological Supply Co., 1992.

Dawkins, Richard. Lalla Ward Illustrator. *Climbing Mount Improbable.* W.W. Norton & Company, 1997.

_____. *River Out of Eden: A Darwinian View of Life.* Basic Books, 1996.

de Duve, Christian. *Blueprint for a Cell: The Nature and Origin of Life.* Carolina Biological Supply Co., 1991.

Dobzhansky, Theodosius. *Human Culture: A Moment in Evolution.* Columbia University Press, 1986.

Dyson, Freeman J. *Origins of Life.* Cambridge University Press, 1986.

Eldredge, Niles. Murray Alcosser Photographer. *Fossils: The Evolution and Extinction of Species.* Princeton University Press, 1997.

Fitch, Walter M. and Francisco J. Ayala, eds. *Tempo and Mode in Evolution: Genetics and Paleontology 50 Years After Simpson.* National Academy Press, 1995.

Gould, Stephen Jay. *Wonderful Life: The Burgess Shale and the Nature of History.* W.W. Norton & Company, 1990.

Life in the Universe: Scientific American - A Special Issue. W. H. Freeman & Co., April 1995.

Margulis, Lynn and Rene Fester, eds. *Symbiosis As a Source of Evolutionary Innovation: Speciation and Morphogenesis.* MIT Press, 1991.

Margulis, Lynn, Dorion Sagan and Lewis Thomas. *Microcosmos: Four Billion Years of Evolution from Our Microbial Ancestors.* University of California Press, 1997.

Tattersall, Ian. *The Fossil Trail: How We Know What We Think We Know About Human Evolution.* Oxford University Press, 1995.

_____. *The Last Neanderthal: The Rise, Success, and Mysterious Extinction of Our Closest Human Relatives.* Macmillan General Reference, 1996.

Tattersall, Ian and Donald C. Johanson. *The Human Odyssey: Four Million Years of Human Evolution* Macmillan General Reference, 1993.

Walker, Alan and Pat Shipman. *The Wisdom of the Bones: In Search on Human Origins.* Alfred A. Knopf, 1996.

Historical and Philosophical

de Duve, Christian. *Vital Dust: Life As a Cosmic Imperative.* Basic Books, 1996.

Durant, John, ed. *Darwinism and Divinity: Essays on Evolution and Religious Belief.* Blackwell, 1985.

Griffin, David Ray. *Religion and Scientific Naturalism: Overcoming the Conflicts.* State University of New York Press, 2000.

Hull, David L. and Michael Ruse, eds. *The Philosophy of Biology.* Oxford University Press, 1998.

Larson, Edward J. *Summer for the Gods: The Scopes Trial and America's Continuing Debate over Science and Religion.* Basic Books, 1997.

Livingstone, David N. *Darwin's Forgotten Defenders: The Encounter Between Evangelical Theology and Evolutionary Thought.* Scottish Academic Press, 1987.

Mayr, Ernst. *The Growth of Biological Thought.* Belknap Press, 1982.

Numbers, Ronald. *The Creationists.* University of California Press, 1993.

Ruse, Michael, ed. *Philosophy of Biology.* Prometheus Books, 1998.

Sober, Elliott, ed. *Conceptual Issues in Evolutionary Biology.* Bradford Books, 1993.

_____. *The Nature of Selection: Evolutionary Theory in Philosophical Focus.* University of Chicago Press, 1993.

Religious Interpretations

Birch, Charles and John B. Cobb, Jr. *The Liberation of Life.* Cambridge University Press, 1984.

Gilkey, Langdon. *Nature, Reality, and the Sacred: The Nexus of Science and Religion.* Fortress Press, 1993.

Goodenough, Ursula. *The Sacred Depths of Nature.* Oxford University Press, 1998.

Hefner, Philip. *The Human Factor: Evolution, Culture, and Religion.* Fortress Press, 1993.

Peacocke, Arthur. *Theology for a Scientific Age.* Fortress Press, 1993.

Russell, Robert J., William R. Stoeger and Francisco J. Ayala, eds. *Evolution and Molecular Biology: Scientific Perspectives on Divine Action.* Center for Theology and the Natural Sciences and the Vatican Observatory, 1998.

Ruse, Michael. *Can a Darwinian Be a Christian?: The Relationship Between Science and Religion.* Cambridge University Press, 2000.

Schmitz-Moormann, Karl and James F. Salmon. *Theology of Creation in an Evolutionary World.* Pilgrim Press, 1997.

Evolution and Design

Behe, Michael. *Darwin's Black Box: The Biochemical Challenge to Evolution.* Touchstone Books, 1998.

Behe, Michael and William Dembski. *Intelligent Design: The Bridge Between Science and Theology.* InterVarsity Press, 1999.

Dembski, William. *The Design Inference: Eliminating Chance Through Small Probabilities.* Cambridge University Press, 1998.

Haught, John. *God After Darwin: A Theology of Evolution.* Westview Press, 1999.

Miller, Kenneth. *Finding Darwin's God: A Scientist's Search for Common Ground Between God and Evolution.* Cliff Street Books, 1999.

Pennock, Robert. *Tower of Babel: The Evidence Against the New Creationism.* MIT Press, 2000 (Reprint Edition).

Indexes

Persons

A

Agassiz, Louis, 267
Anaximander, 11
Aquinas, Thomas, 11, 254, 346, 360-363, 365, 424, 425, 426, 428, 440
Aristotle, 98, 219, 254-258, 267, 268, 276
Augustine, 11, 346, 412, 425

B

Barbour, Ian, 358, 359
Bartholomew, D.J., 377
Bateson, William, 15, 287
Behe, Michael, 437, 439, 441, 443, 480
Birch, Charles, 374
Bryan, William Jennings 2, 282-286, 289, 291, 292
Burhoe, Ralph Wendel, 401, 404, 405, 409

C

Cairns-Smith, A.G., 62
Campbell, Donald, 404, 409
Carlisle, Bishop of, 56, 57
Cobb, John B. , Jr., 371
Crick, Francis, 7, 16, 486
Cuvier, Georges, 85, 267

D

Darrow, Clarence, 2, 291
Darwin, Charles, 9, 10, 12, 53, 139, 149, 181, 228, 233, 263, 265, 266, 269, 272, 277, 279, 339, 400, 405, 445, 459
Darwin, Erasmus, 12
Davies, Paul, 356, 371
Davis, Percival, 443, 459
Dawson, John William, 279
Dawkins, Richard, 58, 150, 263, 341, 344, 351, 372, 407, 431, 461, 480, 486

de Chardin, Pierre Teilhard, 254, 275, 409, 415
Dembski, William, 437, 439, 471, 476, 488, 491-497, 499-507
de Vries, Hugo, 15
Dennett, Daniel, 372
Dewar, Douglas, 296
Dobzhansky, Theodosius, 4, 9, 16, 181, 275

E

Eigen, Manfred, 141, 142, 471, 480, 485
Eldredge, Niles, 191, 342
Empedocles, 11

F

Fisher, C., 467
Fisher, R.A. , 16, 31
Freud, Sigmund, 165, 166, 340, 421

G

Ghiselin, M.T., 96, 226, 228, 422
Gish, Duane T., 302, 306
Goethe, Johann Wolfgang von, 267
Gould, Stephen Jay, 139, 191, 211, 342, 344
Gray, Asa, 271-273, 405
Guyot, Arnold, 279

H

Haldane, J.B.S., 16, 70, 103
Hefner, Philip, 5, 327
Hick, John, 406
Hodge, Charles, 19, 280, 440
Hume, David, 341, 430
Huxley, Thomas Henry, 2, 14, 263, 256

Subjects

A

adaptation, 13, 15, 31, 32, 34, 38, 39, 53- 62, 68, 113, 119, 124, 139, 164, 170, 171, 197, 199, 233, 234, 237, 241, 244, 253, 254, 270, 405, 409, 412, 413, 440, 465
agnosticism, 271
altruism, 37, 403
anagenetic, 41, 42, 97, 118-120, 167, 171, 172, 176, 192
atheism, 264, 280, 340, 341, 365

B

biogeography, 17, 24: allopatric, 101, 107, 109, 110, 113- 115, 120; parapatric, 100, 104, 109, 110, 116, 117, 121, 225; sympatric, 100, 101, 109-111, 113-115, 120, 121, 215, 216, 222
Biological Species Concept (BSC), 80, 99, 100, 101, 217- 224, 227, 228

C

Cambrian explosion, 157, 161, 162, 347
Catholicism, (Roman), 316, 322, 332
chance, 13, 33, 35, 55, 58-61, 65, 68, 75, 76, 79, 111, 112, 130, 145, 181-183, 189, 190, 195, 197, 217, 218, 231, 233, 234, 238, 242, 296, 327, 340, 341, 345, 347, 348, 354, 356-360, 364-366, 375-378, 380, 382-384, 452, 453, 461, 462, 468, 469, 478, 480-482, 484, 485, 486, 493-495, 498, 499, 500, 504
chance and necessity, 486
Christianity, 11, 18, 268, 271, 272, 275, 276, 281, 283, 292, 293, 317, 372, 385, 401, 409, 418, 426, 429, 443
cladogenesis, 41, 97, 192
co-creator, 399, 400, 406, 410, 413, 414

colonization, 25, 26, 33, 110
comparative anatomy, 16, 20, 24, 28, 42, 47
complex specified information, 480, 481, 483- 486
consciousness, 157, 161, 165, 319, 324, 343, 348, 356, 357, 380, 381, 383, 387, 389, 407, 408, 423, 480
conservation biology, 82
cooperation, 132, 139, 325, 366, 381, 386, 389, 407, 417, 429
creatio continua, 374
creatio ex nihilo, 410, 411
creation science, 264, 298, 342, 511
creationism, 2, 263, 269, 279, 280, 282, 288, 290, 293-303, 315, 316, 342-344, 346, 349, 442, 491, 510, 513
creationists, 22, 182, 211, 264, 265, 270, 272, 276, 279, 280, 281, 284, 286, 287, 291, 292, 293, 294, 295, 296, 297, 298, 299, 300, 301, 302, 303, 340, 342, 343, 491, 510; progressive creationist, 290; special creationists, 270, 272, 276, 279, 282; young-earth creationists, 211, 510
creatuionist organizations: Biblical Creation Society, 264; Creation-Deluge Society, 297; Creation-Science Research Center, 299; Creation Research Society, 264, 297-299; Deluge Geology Society, 292; Institute for Creation Research, 299, 300, 301
Creator, 13, 19, 231, 233, 243, 256, 271, 282, 341, 342, 361, 363, 364, 366, 367, 373-375, 378, 384, 385, 399, 410, 424, 470, 509-511
cytology, 42

D

Darwinian theory of evolution, 265
Darwinism, 7, 14, 58, 61, 65, 53, 77, 167, 170, 181, 182, 195, 263, 264,